THE
PORTABLE MBA
IN FINANCE
AND ACCOUNTING

The Portable MBA Series

The Portable MBA, Eliza G.C. Collins and Mary Anne Devanna
The Portable MBA in Marketing, Alexander Hiam and Charles D. Schewe
The Portable MBA in Finance and Accounting, John Leslie Livingstone

Forthcoming Titles

The Portable MBA Desk Reference, Donna Carpenter
The Portable MBA in Management, Allan R. Cohen

THE
PORTABLE MBA
IN FINANCE
AND ACCOUNTING

John Leslie Livingstone

John Wiley & Sons, Inc.

New York • Chichester • Brisbane • Toronto • Singapore

Copyright © 1992 by John Wiley & Sons, Inc.
Chapter 7 copyright by Jeffry A. Timmons

Library of Congress Cataloging-in-Publication Data

The portable MBA in finance and accounting / John Leslie
   Livingstone.
      p.   cm.
   Includes index.
   ISBN 0-471-53226-6 (cloth) 0-471-11983-0 (paper)
   1. Business enterprises—Finance.   2. Accounting.
   I. Livingstone, John Leslie.
   HG4026.P665   1992
   658.15—dc20   91–42243

Printed in the United States of America.

10 9 8 7

ACKNOWLEDGMENTS

A book like this can only result from the contributions of many people. First, I want to thank the authors of the chapters that make up this book for their fine work and their excellent professional explanations of the powerful methods of finance and accounting. Next, I am grateful to John Mahaney, Senior Editor, John Wiley & Sons, Inc. John has been the guiding spirit and facilitator who kept shepherding this book over, around, and through many obstacles as it progressed phase by phase, from the beginning idea to final fruition. His unfailing good humor, optimism, common sense, and perseverance has added to the pleasure of working with him. Saving the best until the last, my deepest appreciation goes to my wife, Trudy, and our son, Robert, who gave me the time, the encouragement, and the inspiration to undertake my role in this exciting project.

John Leslie Livingstone
Palm Beach, Florida
January 1992

Preface

Do you know how to accomplish these vital managerial tasks?

- Do a breakeven analysis
- Prepare a budget
- Interpret financial statements
- Figure out return on investment
- Compute the blended cost of capital
- Use a computer spreadsheet for financial analysis
- Put together a business plan
- Legitimately minimize your firm's income taxes
- Decide whether to incorporate your business
- Manage exposure to foreign currency
- Take your company public
- Evaluate an acquisition target
- Select the most profitable long term investments
- Collect on a loan to a firm in Chapter 11 bankruptcy
- Measure productivity

These are some of the important topics explained in this book. It will enable you to pick up the basics in finance and accounting without having to incur the considerable time and expense of a formal MBA program.

This book consists of practical and valuable "how to do it" information, applicable to an entire range of businesses, from very small firms and start-ups to the largest companies, including long-established "Fortune 500" corporations. The text tells you "what the numbers mean" as well as discussing the more qualitative and intuitive aspects of financial planning and control.

The various chapters have been written by an outstanding team of leading professors from well-known business schools across the United States, as well as seasoned practitioners in the fields of finance, accounting, and law. The authors are experts who have obtained national recognition. They have been drawn from all over the United States, literally from coast to coast: from Boston to San Diego and Miami to Seattle. The authors include Harvard Business School professors, a partner in one of the "Big 6" international accounting firms, a lawyer who specializes in an entrepreneur clientele, a much sought-after mergers and acquisitions adviser, and several top business consultants. In each case, they are masters of their subjects.

The book offers a comprehensive array of key topics in finance and accounting. It can be read and reread with a good deal of profit. Keep it handy on a nearby shelf as a reference tool to answer financial and accounting questions. This book will help you deal with finance and accounting experts on their own turf and in their own jargon. You will know what questions to ask, and you will understand the replies without being intimidated or confused.

Who can benefit from this book?

- Managers who want to sharpen their business skills
- Professionals in any field—e.g., architects, engineers, editors, marketers, etc.—who want to develop their knowledge of finance and accounting concepts or prepare to take on increased managerial responsibilities
- MBA alumni who majored in marketing, human resources, manufacturing, or general management, and who now need specialized knowledge in finance and accounting
- MBA alumni who graduated several years ago and could use an update

Whether you belong in one or more of the above categories or have other motivations to increase your financial and accounting knowledge, you will find that this book has much of value to offer you.

Contents

PART ONE   UNDERSTANDING THE NUMBERS   1

1. Understanding and Analyzing Financial Statements   3

Learn how to unlock the powerful and useful information contained in
financial statements. Learn to read a financial statement like a skilled
doctor reading an X-ray.

2. Cost-Profit-Volume Analysis   28

Learn how powerful techniques like contribution analysis and breakeven
analysis can help you make winning business decisions. Understand
which costs are fixed and which vary as volume increases.

3. Activity-Based Costing   59

Key strategic decisions may depend on your cost assumptions. How to
obtain reliable information on the costs of different products, operations,
or activities in order to make sound decisions on pricing, plant expansion
or closing, and entering or exiting certain markets.

4. Using the Computer in Finance and Accounting   84

The computer is an essential and powerful tool in every area of finance
and accounting. This chapter shows how to use the power of the
computer for financial analysis in general, and for financial modeling
and spreadsheets (such as Lotus 1-2-3) in particular.

5. Budgetary Control Analysis: Techniques
for Measuring Productivity   105

Learn how to measure productivity in order to improve or maintain
a company's competitive position. Learn how to use the techniques of
standard costs, variance analysis, and flexible budgeting.

PART TWO   PLANNING AND FORECASTING   127

6. Choosing a Business Form: To Incorporate
    or Not to Incorporate   129

Should a business be organized as a sole proprietorship, partnership, corporation, or in some other legal form? Learn the pluses and minuses of each form: how they affect the exposure of the owners to personal liability and their impact on income taxes paid.

7. The Business Plan: A Step-By-Step Guide   166

Learn how to create, use, and update a sound business plan. New and rapidly developing firms need a sound business plan in order to attract that necessary financing. Learn the key points that venture capitalists look for in a business plan.

8. Forecasts and Budgets   230

The best way to be prepared in business is to budget for the future. Budgets are the financial expressions of business plans and are an important ingredient in effective management. They help ensure that all parts of the enterprise are on track. Learn the methods of budgeting in this chapter.

9. Managing Long-Term Investments: Financial Structure,
    Cost of Capital, and Capital Budgeting   254

Learn how to pick the winners: finding, selecting, funding, and managing profitable long-term capital investment projects. The long-run success of a business demands use of key strategic skills to search for optimal major investment projects. The manager must ensure that the profits earned will be sufficient to cover the costs of the funds used to finance these projects and must manage the related risks.

10. Taxes and Business Decisions   289

Why it's important to take tax factors into consideration before entering into business commitments and how to do so. There are often legitimate ways to accomplish desired goals at lower tax expense, thereby saving considerable sums. This chapter illustrates some of these legitimate tax avoidance strategies.

11. The Impact of Globalization on Management
    and Financial Reporting   335

Learn how to deal with foreign currencies and exchange rates. Learn how to control exposure to foreign exchange risks and cope with hyperinflation. Also, learn how a firm dealing in foreign currencies, even with volatile rates of exchange and runaway inflation, can translate those currencies into one common denominator in order to measure the success of each foreign operation and the performance of the firm as a whole.

PART THREE   MAKING KEY STRATEGIC DECISIONS   379

12. Going Public   381

Learn the pluses and minuses of going public and the factors involved in making an initial public offering (IPO) of stock. Regulatory agencies and financial markets: who are the major government regulators, what are their requirements, and what restrictions are imposed by the financial markets?

13. Mergers and Acquisitions: Strategies for Growth   409

The financial strategy involved in mergers, acquisitions, and divestitures is discussed. Learn how to evaluate potential merger partners for the features that add value to target companies and how to avoid the pitfalls.

14. Corporate Governance: The Board of Directors   433

Once a company raises funds from the public, it also takes on some very important responsibilities to its investors. These responsibilities rest with the company's board of directors. Examine the role of the board in developing and setting financial policy and strategy.

15. Bankruptcy   462

Analyze emerging and submerging businesses: while some businesses soar to success, others may enter bankruptcy and be liquidated, or be reorganized and emerge in a restructured form. Learn about the famous Chapter 11, as well as cram-downs, preferences, priorities, and payouts of "x" number of cents on the dollar.

Chapter Notes   505

About the Authors   511

Index   517

THE
PORTABLE MBA
IN FINANCE
AND ACCOUNTING

PART ONE

UNDERSTANDING THE NUMBERS

UNDERSTANDING AND ANALYZING FINANCIAL STATEMENTS

1

Michael L. Fetters

Linda Weber's expertise as a gardener was a source of wonder to all who knew her. Each year she had increased the amount of land tilled until she had overwhelmed her friends with vegetables, and her freezer could hold no more. She decided to build a farmer's stand and sell her produce. Compulsively, she kept her receipts in a box for the lumber, tools, wiring, and so on.

Business at the farmer's stand went extremely well. In fact, one might describe the scene as frenetic. Unsure about pricing, Linda decided to set her prices at one half of the prices at local supermarkets. Low prices would be an excellent incentive for people to drive to her stand. Linda succeeded beyond her wildest expectations and had to hire high school kids to help run her stand.

At the end of the growing season, Linda had dreams of a pile of cash for her efforts. Although she did not begin the enterprise for the money, she had worked hard and expected to have surplus cash in her safe. She wanted to take this cash and rent more land as well as a truck in order to haul her vegetables to farmers's markets around the city. In this way, she could sell more, build a more diverse base of customers, and develop a demand that might eventually help her own a store rather than a stand.

As she counted her cash, she became painfully aware that there wasn't as much as she had hoped. When compared to a salary offer she had received at the beginning of the growing season, she was way behind. What had happened? Where was the cash? What would she have to change in order to meet her goals for the next growing season?

STATEMENT OF CASH FLOWS

Linda contacted her friend Joyce, a business manager, who suggested she go back through her records. She pulled out the shoebox where she had kept records of her cash outflows for the stand, employees, and utilities and collected her daily cash register tapes. With this data, she would try to trace her business's cash flow.

Joyce helped Linda establish categories to classify her costs; these included the farmer's stand, seed, organic fertilizer, wages, supplies, utilities, tools, and "other." Soon columns were set up and cash outflows were grouped under the appropriate categories. The checkbook and reconciled bank statements were examined to identify the sources of cash. Although cash came primarily from customer sales, Linda had also invested some personal savings and taken out a bank loan for the growing season. This loan, plus interest, had been repaid. The information collected is presented in Exhibit 1.1.

After Linda had collected the information, Joyce rearranged the cash flow by activity. This format is presented in Exhibit 1.2.

The ease with which she understood the logic of the cash flow statement surprised Linda (she had thought accounting was difficult). She needed cash to get her business going and this information was collected in the financing section. Her start-up investment in tools, tractors, and stand were included under investment activities and the cash generated by operations was at the

EXHIBIT 1.1.   Linda's Farm Stand, Cash flows: First growing season.

Outflows	
Seed	$ 1,000
Fertilizer from stables	1,500
Wages	20,000
Farmer's stand	5,000
Tools including small tractor	10,000
Supplies (bags)	1,000
Utilities	2,000
Other (includes loan interest)	2,000
Loan repaid	10,000
Total outflows	52,500
Inflows	
Personal savings	5,000
Loan received	10,000
Cash from sales	40,000
Total inflows	55,000
Net cash inflow	$ 2,500

EXHIBIT 1.2.   Linda's Farm Stand, Statement of cash flows by activity: First growing season.

Cash activities: Operations		
Inflow from sales		$40,000
Outflows		
Seed	$ 1,000	
Fertilizer	1,500	
Wages	20,000	
Supplies	1,000	
Utilities	2,000	
Other (includes loan interest)	2,000	27,500
Net inflow from operations		12,500
Cash activities: Investment		
Outflows		
Farmer's stand	5,000	
Tools/tractor	10,000	(15,000)
Cash Activities: Financing		
Inflows		
From personal savings	5,000	
Bank loan received	10,000	
Outflows		
Repayment of bank loan	(10,000)	5,000
Net cash inflow		$ 2,500

top of the form. But she was not sure what should go in the "cash activities: operations" section. For instance, it seemed to her that the tractor was used in operations so shouldn't it be shown in operations? Joyce explained that the cash flow for the tractor and tools would benefit many seasons of operations, not just a few. It was a major investment of $10,000 in the operating assets of the business. The core of the operating section focused on the normal cash inflows and outflows caused by the day-to-day operation of the farm stand. Cash inflows were from customers and cash outflows were for typical daily business expenditures, such as seed, fertilizer, and wages.

Although Linda still had some nagging questions, overall she felt pretty comfortable with the format. The reason she did not have as much money as expected was not because of a poor cash flow from operations but because she had purchased major equipment. She reasoned that if she continued the operations at the same level next year, she could expect to have a larger net cash inflow. In order to be sure, she decided to make some projections using the cash statement format from the first growing season. These projections, also known as pro forma statements, are shown in Exhibit 1.3. (Quite simply,

**EXHIBIT 1.3. PRO FORMA—Linda's Farm
Stand, Projected cash flows:
Second growing season
(operations stay the same).**

Operations		
Cash inflow		$40,000
Cash sales outflow		
Seed	$ 1,000	
Fertilizer*	5,000	
Wages	20,000	
Supplies	1,000	
Utilities	2,000	
Other	2,000	31,000
Net inflow from operations		9,000
Cash activities: Investment tools[†]		(500)
Cash activities: Financing		–0–
Expected net cash inflow		$ 8,500

* Includes $2,500 she owes from first growing season plus
$2,500 expense expected for the second growing season.
[†] Additional tools purchased.

pro formas are the financial representation of management predictions. They present the expected financial state of the company after the forecast period.)

Now Linda's cash flow looked much better. The pro forma model even allowed her to play "what if" games. If she raised her prices to 62 percent of the supermarket prices, cash inflow from customers would increase from $40,000 to $50,000, assuming demand was unaffected by this price increase. Net cash flow from operations would climb to $19,000 and expected net cash inflow would be $18,500.

Linda looked at a second scenario. If she did not haul the fertilizer herself, but subcontracted this work, the cash outflow for fertilizer would be $6,000 and then her net flow would be $7,500. Perhaps, she could get by with less labor.

Linda still had some doubts about her cash flows. For instance, she still owed $2,500 for the fertilizer she had used during her first growing season. Using the cash flow statement format, the $2,500 expense would not be acknowledged until the second growing season. Linda also wondered about the tractor, tools, and farm stand. How would they show up in her operating results? Her cash flow statement was a valuable document, but it didn't seem to capture the whole picture.

INCOME STATEMENT AND
BALANCE SHEET DEVELOPMENT

From Exhibit 1.2, Linda understood that while her operations had generated a decent cash flow, her investment activities had significantly reduced her net cash position. She wondered how this would affect her expansion plans, and how she could use this information to plan the next season's operations.

Again, Joyce offered some advice: She suggested that Linda create an income statement and a balance sheet. Joyce explained that the income statement differs from cash flow: Income statements try to match effort and accomplishment within one period (in this case a growing season); cash flow matches cash inflows and outflows. Joyce noted that while cash flow from operations did not include any expense for Linda's tractor or tools during the first season, these items were an important part of the effort to produce crops. Furthermore, during that season, Linda owed $2,500 for fertilizer to the manager of the stables and $1,000 to an organic farmer from Maine. The organic farmer had flown down to advise Linda on organic farming and expansion of her operations. Although integral to operations, these items were not a part of the cash flow statement for the first season.

Exhibit 1.4 represents Linda's income statement for the first growing season. Linda saw the logic of the accounting information: It showed sales

**EXHIBIT 1.4.　Linda's Farm Stand, Income statement:
First growing season.**

Sales		$40,000
Expenses		
Seed	$ 1,000	
Fertilizer*	4,000	
Wages	20,000	
Supplies	1,000	
Utilities	2,000	
Other	2,000	
Consultant*	1,000	
Depreciation*		
Equipment	1,000	
Farmer's stand	1,250	33,250
Net income		$ 6,750

* These items differ from the Statement of Cash Flows. Fertilizer expense is the sum of the $1,500 which had been used and paid for and the $2,500 which had been used but not as yet paid for. The consultant's advice helped this growing season but the bill for these services had not been paid. Finally, depreciation is the allocation of the cost of major assets to the operating periods they benefit. The $1,000 for equipment depreciation is one-tenth of the $10,000 cost of the tractor and tools, which are expected to last ten years. The $1,250 depreciation for the stand represents one year's use of the stand, which has an expected service life of four years.

to customers and the costs which produced those sales. Linda liked the idea that expenses and revenues were not tied solely to cash flow. If she did something to effect the operations in the first growing season, it would be captured on the income statement for that season. For instance, she had used $4,000 worth of fertilizer and that is what she saw on the income statement.

Expenses associated with the use of the farm stand, tools, and tractor were also included in the income statement. Linda had determined that the farm stand would benefit her operations for four years and the tractor and tools would yield ten years of benefits. The costs associated with these benefits should be shown within these time frames. Joyce had explained that this association is represented by depreciation. As these assets were used up, the original investments in these assets should be allocated to the periods of wear and tear. Depreciation was $1,250 for the farm stand and $1,000 for the tractor and tools. Although they were not cash outflows, Linda liked the idea that income calculations included a cost associated with the wear and tear on her major assets.

Linda also thought an income statement would be helpful in reviewing her choice of price, which she had set significantly below the supermarket price. After all, if her sales did not cover all her costs, in the long run, she would not survive.

Now for the balance sheet. She needed to know what she had to start with for the second growing season. As she understood the balance sheet, it contained a listing of her assets, liabilities, and investments at a particular date. Assets were the resources owned or controlled by her business. They were good things to have because she could use them to help make a future profit. Liabilities were commitments to pay out assets (typically cash) or to render services to creditors. Liabilities seemed to be necessary in order to help fund the business's assets.

The final category on the balance sheet was owner's equity. This represented the owner's investment in the company and took two forms: Direct investment by the owner or a positive income flow. Linda understood direct investment. She had invested $5,000 of her own cash to get the farm stand going: This was owner's equity. However, she was a little fuzzy about the positive income flow notion. Joyce explained that revenues bring assets into the business and expenses are outflows of assets to help generate revenues. If revenues were greater than expenses, assets would increase, benefiting the owner. The increase in the owner's assets means that the owner's equity has increased. If revenues were less than expenses, the owner's equity would decrease. Increases of owner's equity caused by profitable operations (when revenues exceed expenses) are called retained earnings: These earnings are reinvested in order to fund the growth of the business.

Linda now felt that she had mastered the owner's equity concept, and she hoped that actually creating a balance sheet would solidify her understanding of this statement. First, she listed her assets. Cash, farmer's stand, and tractor and tools were the only assets of her farm stand business. She thought about listing the land she farmed but that was really her family's land, and she was just using it in her business. Maybe someday her growing operations would include land, but not now. She also had a file for bills. At the end of the growing season, she owed $2,500 to the stables for fertilizer used during the first growing season and $1,000 payable to the organic farming consultant. Linda listed her assets and liabilities. She still was not sure what to do with owner's equity, but she knew it had to help balance her balance sheet. After all, something called a balance sheet should balance!

Joyce looked at Linda's balance sheet and explained that assets are listed at their purchase cost, minus depreciation where appropriate. She stressed

EXHIBIT 1.5. Linda's Farm Stand, Balance sheet:
End of the first growing season.

Assets			
Current assets			
Cash			$ 2,500
Long-term assets			
Farm stand at cost	$5,000		
Less: Accumulated depreciation*	(1,250)	$3,750	
Tractor/Tools at cost	10,000		
Less: Accumulated depreciation*	(1,000)	9,000	12,750
Total assets			$15,250
Liabilities			
Current liabilities			
Payable to stables manager	$2,500		
Payable to organic farming consultant	1,000		
Total liabilities			3,500
Owner's Equity			
Original investment	$5,000		
Retained earnings	6,750		
Total owner's equity			11,750
Total liabilities and owner's equity			$15,250

* Accumulated depreciation is simply the sum of the yearly depreciation expensed to date. At the end of the second growing season, accumulated depreciation for the farm stand would be $2,500 (2 seasons at $1,250 per season). The balance sheet at the end of the third year would list $3,750 as accumulated depreciation for the farm stand.

that assets are not shown at today's estimated value but at the price paid for them. Thus, the farm stand is shown at $3,750: The original cost of $5,000, less $1,250 of depreciation during the first growing season. Joyce also noted that both assets and liabilities are separated into current items (used or paid within one year) and long-term items (used or paid after one year). Linda felt comfortable with the concept of asset and liabilities and the form of her balance sheet (Exhibit 1.5 on page 9). However, Linda was surprised that the owner's equity equaled just the amount needed to balance her balance sheet. She asked Joyce why this had occurred.

Joyce reviewed the concept of owner's equity with Linda, explaining that owner's equity consists of two items: The owner's original investment plus any profitable operations. The original investment by Linda was $5,000, and operations had generated $6,750 of profit (Exhibit 1.2). The $5,000 is original investment or contributed capital and the $6,750 is retained earnings. Together, they total $11,750 of owner's equity.

In summary, the balance sheet lists assets at cost and shows how these assets are financed: Either by creditors (liabilities) or owner's investment. For Linda's operations, most of the financing was done by owner's investment. Of the total assets, 77 percent ($11,750) were financed by contributed capital or profitable operations. Linda was proud of this, but she did see a problem highlighted by the balance sheet. She had $2,500 of cash and $3,500 worth of liabilities. Where would the extra $1,000 cash come from? Next year's operations would have to take that into account. Since those bills were due soon, she better start her planning process immediately.

PLANS: PRO FORMA FINANCIAL STATEMENTS

Cash flows are critical to remaining in business, but do not necessarily measure operating results. Income statements match effort and accomplishment that result from the operations of a business. Balance sheets are a list, at a point in time, of an entity's assets and how they are funded (liabilities and owner's equity). These financial statements made sense to Linda and she knew they would be useful in organizing her analysis and evaluation of her business. Further, she could use these three financial statements to help her plan for the next growing season.

Her pro forma cash flow statement would help her evaluate her cash flow activities after the first growing season. She realized she could use pro forma income statements and balance sheets, as well as cash flow statements, to estimate what her farm stand's financial position would be after implementation of her expansion. These pro formas would help her organize her plan and present the expected results in a logical manner.

First, she listed all her projected changes in operations.

1. Prices would increase to 90 percent of local supermarket prices.
2. She would purchase and resell organically grown produce from farmers who lived further from the metropolitan location than her.
3. She would truck her vegetables to farmers's markets located within the city, in order to expand her customer base.

These three changes would generate many effects on her business. For instance, if she was going to sell more, she might have to increase her stand size, her employee hours, and the size of her crop. Two of her projected changes would require a truck. Linda saw that her stated changes would have a ripple effect and decided that she might want to do variations on these changes. She had been experimenting with a new computer spreadsheet: This forecasting would be a perfect application for the spreadsheet.

Linda made projections for each of her proposed changes: She showed their effect on cash flow, income from operations, and the balance sheet, at the end of the second growing season. She found it useful to organize all of her projected changes into one list, which showed the dollar amount of each change and the reason for the change.

Sales: $130,000

In her second year of operation, Linda expected a substantial increase in her sales. For that reason, she planned to plant more, purchase produce from other organic farmers for resale, and raise her prices to 90% of supermarket prices. She reasoned she could do this because she was better known than last year; if she trucked her vegetables to market, the price incentive would not have to be as great; and she was buying produce for resale, so she would need higher prices to make a profit.

Seed: $3,000

Prices and amounts would be higher because of her planned expansion.

Fertilizer: $8,000

The amount doubled because she was going to pay the stable to deliver the organic fertilizer. She would no longer clean the stables and haul the fertilizer.

Wages: $30,000

Included a truck driver and increased help.

Utilities: $2,200

Minimal change because the stand was big enough to support the additional sales.

Other: $4,000

Doubled because of gas and insurance for the truck.

Depreciation: $7,000

This was much higher because of the truck depreciation.

Farmer's stand: $1,250

It would not have to be expanded to do the additional business. Same amount depreciated as last year.

Using these projections and following her previous reporting format, Linda developed the following financial statements (Exhibits 1.6, 1.7, and 1.8).

As the numbers flashed upon her computer screen, Linda gulped. She had expanded her operations, yet ended up with a negative cash bal-

EXHIBIT 1.6. Linda's Farm, Projected financial statements: Second growing season.

Statement of Cash Flows

Cash inflows		$130,000
Cash outflows—harvest		
Seed	$ 3,000	
Produce	50,000	
Fertilizer*	10,500	
Wages	30,000	
Supplies	1,500	
Utilities	2,200	
Other	4,000	
Consultant[†]	1,000	102,200
Cash from operations		27,800
Cash outflows—investments		
Truck	40,000	(40,000)
Net outflow		(12,200)
Beginning cash		2,500
Projected negative ending cash balance		$ (9,700)

* Includes $2,500 owed from last growing season.
† From last growing season's commitment.

EXHIBIT 1.7. Linda's Farm, Projected financial statements: Second growing season.

Income Statement

Sales		$130,000
Expenses		
Seed	$ 3,000	
Produce	50,000	
Fertilizer	8,000	
Wages	30,000	
Supplies	1,500	
Utilities	2,200	
Other	4,000	
Depreciation		
Truck	6,000	
Farmer's stand	1,250	
Other	1,000	106,950
Net income		$ 23,050

EXHIBIT 1.8. Linda's Farm, Projected financial statements: End of second growing season.

Balance Sheet

Assets
  Current
    Cash—negative $ (9,700)

Long term: at cost less depreciation		
Farm stand	$ 2,500	
Tractor/tools	8,000	
Truck	34,000	44,500
Total assets		$34,800

Liabilities		–0–
Owner's equity		
Beginning owner's equity	11,750	
Retained earnings (provided by operations—second growing season)	23,050	
Ending owner's equity—projected		$34,800

ance. Why did this happen? She quickly realized that her investment in a major asset would use up all her cash and she would have to finance the asset. However, she had expected that tripling her sales would increase her cash by far more than it had. She decided to go back and look at each of her business strategies: Raising prices, selling other farmers's materials, and trucking produce to farmers's markets.

First, she looked at the price changes. By her calculations, her prices were, on average, about 65 percent of supermarket prices. If nothing changed but her pricing policy (and the unavoidable increases in fixed expenses), the projected income statement and cash flow for the second growing season would be quite good (Exhibit 1.9). By raising her prices and keeping her costs essentially level, she could have an excellent summer.

Therefore, she reasoned, her projected cash flow problems must have developed by purchasing and reselling other farmers's produce and/or her trucking operations. Although she thought these were separate business strategies, they were closely related. If she was going to inspect the produce she was buying, she might as well pick it up in a truck. If she was going to buy enough to be a worthwhile customer of the other farmers, she would not only have to sell more at her farm stand but also sell produce at the farmers's markets.

Exhibit 1.10 represents Linda's next iteration of her cash projections from operations, incorporating her two additional management strategies. She presents columns for projected price increase only, projected full plan (all three changes), and an incremental column to highlight the difference

EXHIBIT 1.9. **Linda's Farm Stand, Projected income and cash flow statements: Second growing season pricing policy change.**

| | Income Statement | | Cash Flow | |
	Previous Year	Projected	Previous Year	Projected
Sales	$40,000	$ 56,000	$ 40,000	$ 56,000
Seed	(1,000)	(1,100)	(1,000)	(1,100)
Fertilizer	(4,000)	(6,000)	(1,500)	(8,500)
Wages	(20,000)	(21,000)	(20,000)	(21,000)
Supplies	(1,000)	(1,000)	(1,000)	(1,000)
Utilities	(2,000)	(2,200)	(2,000)	(2,200)
Other	(2,000)	(2,500)	(2,000)	(2,500)
Depreciation	(1,000)	(1,000)	—	—
Consultant	(1,000)	—	—	(1,000)
Farmer's stand	(1,250)	(1,250)		
Total expenses/ outflows	(33,250)	(36,050)	(27,500)	(37,300)
Net from operations	$6,750	$19,950	$12,500	$18,700

EXHIBIT 1.10. **Linda's Farm Stand, Projected statement of cash flows—operations: Second growing season.**

	Projected Prices Only	Projected Full Plan	Increment
Inflow			
Sales	$56,000	$130,000	$74,000
Outflows			
Seed	(1,100)	(3,000)	(1,900)
Fertilizer	(8,500)	(10,500)	(2,000)
Produce	–0–	(50,000)	(50,000)
Wages	(21,000)	(30,000)	(9,000)
Supplies	(1,000)	(1,500)	(500)
Utilities	(2,200)	(2,200)	–0–
Other	(2,500)	(4,000)	(1,500)
Consultant	(1,000)	(1,000)	–0–
Total outflows	(37,300)	(102,200)	(64,900)
Net increase in cash	$18,700	$ 27,800	$ 9,100

in results between the two projections. The full plan increased Linda's cash by $9,100, which did not seem like a lot for the addition of $40,000 in assets and the hard work necessary to triple sales. Although she tripled sales, her cash from operations only increased by approximately 50 percent. Maybe her income would look better, but she doubted it. After all, depreciation was included in the income statement.

Exhibit 1.11 shows Linda's projected income statement. From these projections, Linda began to see some additional considerations—possibly problems. The monetary rewards reaped in the second growing season from her proposed operations would not compensate sufficiently for her increased effort and risk. She projected only a $3,100 increase in profits. Linda had not expected such a low return for the risk of expanding her business. Her incremental investment would be $40,000 and her incremental income would be $3,100; only a 7.7 percent return ($3,100/$40,000). She suddenly began to understand the short-run management versus long-run management issues. If managing for the short run, she would keep operations about the same, raise prices, and things would probably go smoothly. If managing for the long run, she would need to look at market penetration, product recognition, and potential for long-run growth in profits and cash flow. If she moved now with her organic produce, she would be the first significant presence in her area. This would be bound to have some favorable long-run consequences, even if the short-run rewards were meager.

Before she made her final decision, Linda would have to go back over her projections and make sure she was comfortable with her assumptions. She would change some of them to see how sensitive her income statement and statement of cash flows were to her assumptions. And, she would expand her analysis from a one year time span to a 5-year time horizon. Whatever she decided, she now knew the scope of her cash needs and the impact of her strategies on her financial statements.

EXHIBIT 1.11.   Linda's Farm Stand, Projected income statement: Second growing season.

	Projected Prices Only	Projected Full Plan	Increment
Sales	$56,000	$130,000	$74,000
Expenses			
Seed	(1,100)	(3,000)	(1,900)
Fertilizer	(6,000)	(8,000)	(2,000)
Produce	–0–	(50,000)	(50,000)
Wages	(21,000)	(30,000)	(9,000)
Supplies	(1,000)	(1,500)	(500)
Utilities	(2,200)	(2,200)	–0–
Other	(2,500)	(4,000)	(1,500)
Depreciation	(1,000)	(7,000)	(6,000)
Farm stand	(1,250)	(1,250)	–0–
	(36,050)	(106,950)	(70,900)
Net from operations	$19,950	$ 23,050	$ 3,100

A CHECKLIST FOR FINANCIAL STATEMENTS

Linda developed a memory helper (MH) that she placed next to her computer. Listed on this MH were things she wanted to remember about financial statements. Her list is as follows.

Cash Flow Statements

- A format to make order out of checkbook chaos—deposits are inflows, checks are outflows
- Cover a period of time
- Divide into three sections: Operations, investing, and financing
- Are not net income measurements

Income Statements

- Income equals revenues minus expenses
- Efforts are matched to accomplishments
- Cash sales and credit sales are considered revenues
- Expenses occur when cash is paid, when major assets are used (depreciation), or when material is used that was bought on credit (e.g., organic fertilizer)
- Income statements are for a period of time
- You can have income and still be short of cash
- Income should be a major source of owner's equity

Balance Sheets

- Assets equal liabilities plus owner's equity
- Liabilities and owner's equity are two ways to finance assets
- Assets are shown at original costs, not their current value
- Current assets will be used or turned into cash within one year
- Current liabilities will be paid within one year
- Retained earnings is not a pool of cash but accumulated income amounts that have been reinvested in assets

EMERGING BUSINESS AND INDUSTRY DATA

Fifteen years after Linda had started her farm stand, she was on the verge of taking her local business regional. In the 1970s, she had gambled and expanded her organic farming operations in spite of her initial projections of small profits. The gamble paid off: She had gone from one farm stand to four grocery stores, which featured organically grown produce from all over the world. Her stores were expensive, but her food was perceived as "healthy." People did not have to worry about chemicals in or on her products.

Business was excellent and she had just been approached to open up new stores in four neighboring states. Although she had borrowed some money from a local bank, she had developed her business largely through her own operations and savings. If she was going to expand again, moving quickly to penetrate the market, she would need a major infusion of capital. She was not quite sure how the capital markets would evaluate her efforts to date, or how they would evaluate her future plans. She called Joyce who told her to grab her most recent set of financial statements and come down to her office. This was an important decision—partly because Linda now wanted Joyce to join the business.

Linda's most recent financial statements represented a typical year for her business. Sales had grown about 10 percent annually from 1985 to 1988. Then, in 1989, sales had jumped 25 percent as people became more concerned about the food they ate. As Linda laid her statements on the desk (Exhibits 1.12 and 1.13), Joyce put a collection of percentages and other numbers on the desk (Exhibit 1.14). These were numbers that Joyce had calculated from two major supermarket chains in the United States. The Arden Group was a high-end grocery store. Expensive food was sold, and high quality service and shopping area were provided. Food Lion was a low cost, bargain-oriented supermarket chain. Joyce proposed that she and Linda go through each of the ratios and numbers from the benchmark companies and calculate the same numbers for Linda's past operations. Joyce would then explain how the numbers might be put together by an outside creditor or potential investor.

CASH ASSESSMENT

Joyce explained that the analysis of a company's cash position had many different components: These are divided into a company's ability to meet its short-term cash needs (solvency), a company's financial flexibility (capital structure), and a company's annual cash flow (statement of cash flows).

In the short term, the availability of cash to pay bills is essential to a company's survival. Insufficient cash resources means bankruptcy. There are many ways to measure a company's ability to meet short-term cash needs. Joyce explained that analysts would look at many financial indicators and then make an overall evaluation of a company's solvency position. Joyce began by describing the current account indicators on the balance sheet: Working capital (current assets − current liabilities) and the current ratio (current assets/current liabilities) are indications of short-term cash position. Assuming

EXHIBIT 1.12. Linda's Organic Markets.

INCOME STATEMENT
Periods Ending 31 August

	1988	1989
Sales	$30,000,000	$40,000,000
Cost of goods sold	19,500,000	25,600,000
Gross profit	10,500,000	14,400,000
Operating expenses	9,000,000	12,300,000
Operating income	1,500,000	2,100,000
Interest expense	100,000	120,000
Income before taxes	1,400,000	1,980,000
Taxes	420,000	594,000
Net income	$ 980,000	$ 1,386,000

BALANCE SHEET
As of 31 August

	1988	1989
Assets		
Current		
Cash/short-term investments	$ 500,000	$ 900,000
Receivables	360,000	580,000
Inventories	2,600,000	3,900,000
Prepaid expenses	40,000	60,000
Total current assets	3,500,000	5,440,000
Property, plant & equipment	3,000,000	3,800,000
Total assets	$6,500,000	$9,240,000
Liabilities		
Current		
Accounts payable	$1,817,000	$2,420,000
Short-term credit	200,000	200,000
Misc. payables	200,000	137,000
Total current liabilities	2,217,000	2,757,000
Long-term debt	200,000	200,000
Owner's equity	4,083,000	6,283,000
Total assets and owner's equity	$6,500,000	$9,240,000

that current liabilities will be paid by current assets, the excess of current assets over current liabilities is an indicator of a company's short-term safety position. It indicates a company's ability to meet short-term commitments.

Linda and Joyce now compared the financial analysis completed on Linda's organic market to the benchmark firms (Exhibits 1.14 and 1.15).

EXHIBIT 1.13. Linda's Organic Markets, Statement of cash flow: Periods ending 31 August.

	1988	1989
Cash from operations	$350,000	$686,000
Investing activities		
Property, plant, & equip.	(300,000)	(900,000)
Financing activities		
Issue common stock	100,000	814,000
Increase in cash during the year	$150,000	$400,000

EXHIBIT 1.14. Financial data from Benchmark Companies, 1989.

	High-End Store ARDEN GROUP*	Low-End Store FOOD LION*
Cash assessment		
Working capital	$42,100,000	$160,400,000
Current ratio	1.96	1.31
Quick ratio	.96	.17
Accounts receivable turnover	10.0	82.75
Inventory turnover	6.0	6.87
Payables turnover	13.4	17.0
Long-term debt/Owner's Equity	99%	43%
Times interest earned	5.4	8.67
Cash operations	$25,800,000	$94,900,000
Cash operations/cash investments	2.25	1.06
Profitability assessment		
Return on Owner's Equity (ROE)	14%	28.8%
Return on Assets (ROA)	8.5%	11.8%
Profit margin	3.5%	2.95%
Asset turnover	2.45	3.98
Total Assets/Owner's Equity	2.86	2.38
EPS	7.22%	1.63%
Price/Earnings ratio	8%	15%
Gross profit margin	49%	20%
Operating income margin	6%	5.5%
Income before tax margin	5.9%	4.8%

* Information calculated from company's SEC 10-K report.

Clearly her working capital was not as big as Arden Group's or Food Lion's, but they were much larger companies. Linda's working capital was positive and growing. Linda decided that it would be more useful to compare her current ratio with those of the two benchmark companies. When she did so, her figures were in the same range as the supermarkets's. She was close to Arden Group's number for 1989 and there had been improvement in her

EXHIBIT 1.15. Linda's Organic Market, Financial data.

	1988	1989
Cash assessment		
Working capital	$1,283,000	$2,483,000
Current ratio	1.58	1.84
Quick ratio	0.41	0.52
Accounts receivable		
turnover	83.3	69
Inventory turnover	7.5	6.56
Payables turnover	10.7	10.58
Long-term debt/Owner's Equity	4.9%	3.2%
Times interest earned	15	17.5
Cash operations	$350,000	$686,000
Cash operations/		
Cash investments	1.17	0.76
Probability assessment		
Return on Owner's Equity	24%	27.2%
Return on Assets	15.1%	15%
Profit margin	3.27%	3.46%
Asset turnover	4.6	4.33
Total Assets/		
Owner's Equity	1.59	1.47
EPS		
Gross profit margin	35%	36%
Operating income margin	5%	5.3%
Income before tax margin	4.67%	4.95%

numbers. Food Lion could probably afford a lower short-term safety margin because of its high volume and high turnover of food.

Next, prospective creditors and investors would examine a more conservative short-term ratio: The quick ratio. Cash, marketable investments (those easy to sell), and accounts receivable are summed and divided by current liabilities to obtain the quick ratio. This ratio excludes inventory, because inventory frequently takes a long time to be converted into cash. Analysts want to look at the safety margin in a worst-case scenario: That is, a situation where nobody wants the current inventory. Along with these static measures (the current and quick ratios are calculated using only balance sheet items), analysts may also look at activities that measure the length of time it takes to sell inventory, collect accounts receivable, and receive payment for inventory purchases. These three ratios are "activity" ratios and are labeled inventory turnover, accounts receivable turnover, and accounts payable turnover, respectively. They are calculated by combining information from the income statement (a dynamic flow statement) and the static balance sheet.

Evaluation must consider the interconnections among the ratios. For instance, if a company has a low current ratio, but very rapid inventory and account receivable turnovers, it might be in better liquidity position than a company with a high current ratio but very low (slow) turnovers. If a company has a rapid inventory turnover, then the quick ratio may be too conservative an estimate of liquidity: The worst-case scenario in which inventory cannot be sold is inappropriate. Inventory may be converted into cash quickly enough to cover current liabilities.

For example, say a small company has the following current position:

Current Assets		Current Liabilities	
Cash	$10,000	Accounts payable	$120,000
Accounts receivable	60,000		
Inventory	80,000		

If accounts receivable and inventory turnovers are slow, then clearly this company is in a difficult short-term position. Its quick ratio of 0.583 highlights the firm's possible jeopardy. However, if accounts receivable and inventory turnovers are quite rapid (accounts receivable within 30 days and inventory within 30 days), then this company could quite easily meet its short-term commitments. In this case, the current ratio of 1.25 is more indicative of the company's ability to meet its current obligations. This example shows why investors look at many indicators to assess cash and liquidity positions.

Linda compared her accounts receivable and inventory turnovers to the benchmark companies and fared fairly well. As expected, her turnovers were not quite as good as Food Lion, but they were better than Arden Group. However, there was some cause for concern. Her inventory turnover dropped substantially from 1988 to 1989. Further, she might have to follow Arden Group's policy of extending more credit to maintain her status as a high quality, high price store. If she had to implement such a credit strategy, her receivables would increase and turnover would slow. The future cash from credit sales would not be realized as quickly. Although she would have to explore these possibilities and develop some answers for her inventory turnover slowdown, overall, her current cash position was pretty solid.

Looking at her payables turnover, she saw she was a bit slow compared to the benchmark companies. Payables turnover (cost of goods sold/payable to inventory suppliers) is a measure of how long a company takes to pay its accounts payable. However, her suppliers were pleased with her payment record and she wanted to continue financing some of her current cash needs with supplier credit. She preferred supplier credit to a bank loan because the former carried no interest cost.

As discussed earlier, a company can fund growth in its operations through money borrowed from creditors, additional owner investments, or cash generated by operations. A company's financial flexibility may be measured by several ratios, but Joyce recommended that they keep it simple and focus on only two: Long-term debt/owner's equity and times interest earned. Long-term debt/owner's equity measures how much of other people's money management is using to earn money for the owners. The higher this ratio, the more debt being used to finance the business: The more debt used to finance assets, the less the owner has to finance. As long as management can earn a higher return than the interest it pays on the debt, the owner's profit will increase.

However, risk of business failure increases with higher levels of debt financing. If operations decline, there may not be sufficient cash flows to meet the required interest and principle payments associated with the debt instruments (e.g., notes and mortgage payables). In such situations, debt instruments have to be renegotiated. The creditors have a measure of control over the company and can force bankruptcy proceedings.

The company's ability to meet existing or projected fixed payments is measured by times interest earned (income before taxes plus interest expense/interest expense). It represents a safety margin—it gauges how much earnings could decrease and still cover the required interest payments. The higher the leverage, the higher the interest expense, and this cuts into a company's pretax earnings. Too much leverage will be highlighted by a low times interest earned ratio.

Linda and Joyce noted that Linda's company had used far less debt to finance its expansion than her comparison companies had. Her times interest earned was two to three times higher than the benchmark companies, and her long-term debt/owner's equity ratio was negligible. Clearly, she had tremendous financial flexibility with respect to long-term cash needs. The numbers indicated that she could expand her operations with substantial long-term debt and still have a reasonable level of debt/owner's equity.

A firm's cash position can be evaluated by judging if cash generated from operations is sufficient to cover the cost of operations. A potential investor would determine if cash from operations is positive or negative. If negative, a company needs to have other means of generating cash to meet current obligations because operations are a drain on cash. If a company throws off a lot of cash from its operations, then it is generating a regular cash flow that could be used to meet short-term obligations and help expand the business.

Here again Linda's numbers look fine. Her cash from operations was positive and essentially covered her expansion. From a cash assessment perspective, Linda had felt that she was doing well and this analysis supported her instincts. With the exception of the decline in inventory turnover, she felt that external investors and creditors would probably view her short-term cash position and long-term funds position as quite strong. Now she needed to look at her company's profitability assessment.

PROFITABILITY ASSESSMENT

The second major area of analysis is operations. Is the company profitable? How is management using assets? What affect does the financing strategy have on operations? These are all questions to which analysts seek answers. Joyce found that the best way to do this analysis was to begin with something called the Du Pont chart. The chart begins with return on owner's equity (ROE); a measure of management's success with the owner's investment. This can be split into components that allow focus on various aspects of ROE. Linda suggested they keep it simple and Joyce obliged with the following chart (Exhibit 1.16).

ROE is dichotomized into return on assets (ROA) (NI/TA) and financial leverage (TA/OE). These ratios are used to explore management's handling of the firm's accumulated assets and the effects of its financing methods on ROE.

At first, Linda thought ROA was a pretty simple concept. A company had a certain dollar amount invested in assets and it earned net income with these assets. NI/TA measured the return on management's investment, while ROE measured the return on the owner's investment. However, the concept of financial leverage (TA/OE) gave her some difficulty. Joyce explained that assets can be funded either through loans from creditors (liabilities) or investment from owners (owner's equity). On the balance sheet, Assets equal Liabilities plus Owner's Equity. TA/OE is a way to measure how assets are financed. The smaller the owner's equity, the higher the amount of liabilities that were used to finance assets. Management has used other people's money to produce earnings for the owners. This is termed financial leverage and the greater the leverage, the higher TA/OE will be. Joyce pointed out that this ratio is multiplied by ROA to calculate the owner's return. Thus, TA/OE acts as a financing multiplier to raise the owner's return (ROE).

EXHIBIT 1.16.   Du Pont chart.

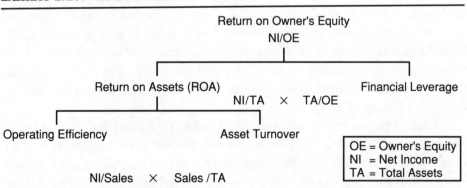

To illustrate the effects of financial leverage, Joyce set up the following example.

	Company A	Company B
Total assets	$1,000,000	$1,000,000
Net income	200,000	200,000
Liabilities	500,000	250,000
Owner's equity	500,000	750,000

ROAs for Companies A and B are equal at 20 percent ($200,000/$1,000,000). However, the financial leverage measures (TA/OE) are quite different. Company A has a TA/OE of 2 ($1,000,000/$500,000); Company B has a TA/OE of 1.3 ($1,000,000/$750,000). When Joyce multiplied the ROAs and TA/OEs to calculate the ROE, Linda could see the impact of financial leverage. Company A's ROE is 40 percent (20 percent × 2); Company B's ROE is 26 percent (20 percent × 1.3).

Next, Linda and Joyce looked at operating efficiency (NI/Sales) and asset turnover (Sales/TA). These components allow a more in-depth study of how management generates return on assets. NI/Sales looks at how much profit was generated out of each sales dollar, while Sales/TA is a measure of asset utilization.

The benchmark companies can be used to further explore the relationships highlighted in the Du Pont chart. Food Lion has a much higher ROE (28.8 percent) than does Arden Group (14 percent). The first dichotomy shows that Food Lion is more conservatively financed than Arden Group (2.38 TA/OE versus 2.86 TA/OE, respectively). Food Lion must generate a far better ROA in order to have a high ROE. Food Lion's ROA (11.8 percent) is substantially higher than Arden's (8.5 percent), providing evidence of the success of Food Lion's operations.

Why were Food Lion's operations so successful? Was it operating efficiency, total asset turnover, or a combination of both? Arden Group has a better profit margin (3.5 percent versus 2.96 percent), which Linda had expected. After all, Arden Group is a high-end grocer, whereas Food Lion's strategy is to attract people through low costs. But look at the asset turnover! Food Lion's sales/total asset was near 4 but Arden Group's was only 2.45. Food Lion had made better use of its assets. Linda was anxious to see how her company would compare to these two companies. She expected to be closer to Arden Group's numbers because her operating strategy resembled the Arden Group strategy.

Linda first put her information into the Du Pont chart format that Joyce had outlined (Exhibit 1.17). Linda's organic market stores did quite well in terms of ROE and ROA; in fact, they were outstanding! The site selections for her stores and her early entry into the market had really paid off. Her

EXHIBIT 1.17.   Linda's Du Pont chart: 1989.

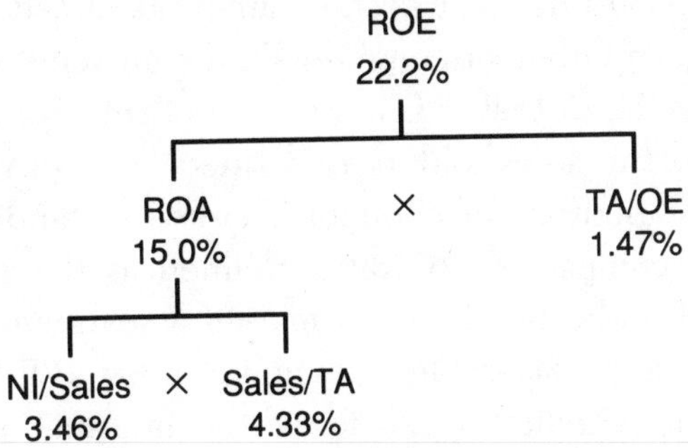

```
                              ROE
                             22.2%
              ┌─────────────────┬─────────────────┐
            ROA                 ×              TA/OE
           15.0%                               1.47%
        ┌──────────┬──────────┐
   NI/Sales   ×   Sales/TA
     3.46%         4.33%
```

only problem was the small decline in her ROE and asset turnover. However, she did have an increase in her profit margin, and she could see that if her TA/OE stayed at the 1988 level, her ROE would stay at. roughly the 24 percent level.

This chart really helped Linda make the connection between her financial numbers and her management decisions. She could see the value of electronic spreadsheets, for now she could play with the components of ROE, equate these manipulations to operating policies, and evaluate strategies. At the same time, she would get a sense of how potential creditors would view her operations, to date, as well as her plans for the future.

Joyce then suggested a more in-depth look at operations. She proposed that Linda compare various profit calculations to sales, and then compare these new margins to her benchmark companies. Linda compared her gross profit, operating profit, and income before tax margins to Arden Group and Food Lion. The comparisons between Arden Group and Food Lion were striking. Consistent with its high quality, high price profile, Arden Group's gross profit margin was just about double that of Food Lion. However, the difference dwindled to 0.5 percent when operating margins were examined. Operating expenses from the quality chain must have been quite a bit higher (gross profit − operating expenses = operating income) than those for the low cost, low price Food Lion chain.

Linda felt her business strategy was closer to the Arden Group's than that of Food Lion. Her company was a high quality, relatively high price grocery store, specializing in organically grown food. However, she was closer to Food Lion's margins than those of the Arden Group. Although her ROE was respectable, she needed to take a closer look at operations and be able to explain why her percentages differed from a chain with a similar business strategy. A large part of her explanation would be the outstanding total asset turnover that her organic grocery stores enjoyed. However, she still wanted to take a closer look at operations.

Joyce thought Linda should also be cognizant of earnings per share (EPS) and the price/earnings (P/E) ratio. Linda calculated her EPS for 1989 (net income/average number of common shares outstanding): It was $1.39. EPS is similar to ROE, in that it is a measure of return to the owners. Net income available to the stockholders is divided by a surrogate for owner's investment (average number of common shares outstanding for the year). Joyce noted that a company's P/E ratio, defined as the market price of a common share/EPS, indicates the stock market assessment of that company. A high P/E ratio means a favorable assessment; a low P/E ratio shows a less favorable assessment. Although Linda found this information interesting, she did not feel it was pertinent to her because she and her family were the sole investors in her company. Thus, there was no stock market assessment of Linda's company. Linda knew, however, that this knowledge would be useful in the future, if she continued to expand her company.

Linda's session with Joyce had not only helped Linda understand prospective investors' and creditors' viewpoints, but also had helped her to understand her own company. She could now follow the effects of her operating strategies on financial statements and conduct ratio analysis. She could perform sensitivity analysis on her operations to determine the outcome of critical management actions. Her accounting knowledge had helped her systematically review her performance and plan her operations. She realized that accounting was a powerful tool: It had helped her with past business decisions and would be critical in her current decision process.

GLOSSARY OF TERMS

Assets: Resources, owned or controlled by a company, that have future benefits. These benefits must be quantifiable in monetary terms.

Balance Sheet: A list of a company's assets, liabilities, and owner's equity at a particular point in time.

Cash Flow Statement: A presentation of the cash inflows and outflows for a particular period of time. These flows are grouped into the major categories of cash from operations, cash-investing activities, and cash-financing activities.

Expenses: Outflows of resources to generate revenues.

Financial Flexibility: The ability of a company to raise funds (cash) to expand operations, pay off debt, or reduce stockholder's equity.

Income Statement: A matching of a company's accomplishments (i.e., sales) with effort (expenses of operations) during a particular period of time. (Revenues − Expenses = Net Income.)

Liabilities: Commitments to pay out assets (typically cash) to or render services for creditors.

Owner's Equity: Represents the owner's investment in a business either by direct investment or profitable operations.

Pro Forma Statement: A financial statement detailing management's predictions.

Revenues: Inflows of resources (assets) into a business generated through operations.

Solvency: The ability of a company to meet its short-term cash needs.

GLOSSARY OF RATIOS

Accounts Payable Turnover: Cost of goods sold/Accounts payable.

Accounts Receivable Turnover: Sales/Accounts receivable.

Asset Turnover: Sales/Total assets.

Current Ratio: Current assets/Current liabilities.

Financial Leverage: Total assets/Owner's equity.

Inventory Turnover: Cost of goods sold/Inventory.

Operating Efficiency: Net income/Sales.

Quick Ratio: (Current assets − inventory)/Current liabilities.

Return on Assets (ROA): Net income/Owner's equity.

Return on Owner's Equity (ROE): Net income/Total assets.

Times Interest Earned: (Income before taxes + interest expense)/Interest expense.

FOR FURTHER READING

Anthony, Robert N. and James S. Reece, *Accounting Text and Cases*, 8th ed. (Homewood, IL: Irwin, 1989).

Fraser, Lyn M., *Understanding Financial Statements*, 2nd ed. (Englewood Cliffs, NJ: Prentice Hall, 1988).

Helfert, Erick A., *Techniques of Financial Analysis*, 7th ed. (Homewood, IL: Irwin, 1991).

Higgins, Robert C., *Analysis for Financial Management*, 2nd ed. (Homewood, IL: Irwin, 1989).

Horngren, C. T. and Gary L. Sundem, *Introduction to Financial Accounting*, 4th ed. (Englewood Cliffs, NJ: Prentice Hall, 1990.)

Horngren, C. T. and Gary L. Sundem, *Introduction to Management Accounting*, 7th ed. (Englewood Cliffs, NJ: Prentice Hall, 1987).

Solomon, L. M., R. J. Vargo, and L. M. Walther, *Financial Accounting*, 2nd ed. (New York: John Wiley & Sons, 1989).

2 COST-PROFIT-VOLUME ANALYSIS

John Leslie Livingstone

Eileen opened her restaurant a year ago, and was successful right from the start. Her "healthburgers" satisfied consumers' desire for food that was healthy as well as fast. Healthburgers were made from soybeans and contained no meat, fat, chemical additives, or cholesterol. Eileen served the patties broiled (not fried), on wholewheat buns with lettuce and tomato slices, free of preservatives, fat, and sugar. For food that was so wholesome, healthburgers were surprisingly delicious. As a result, business was brisk, and satisfied customers packed the seating section, or ordered healthburgers to go at the drive-through window.

Healthburgers sold for $1.95, and the ingredients cost Eileen 75 cents per burger, including the paper wrapping. The difference between the selling price and the cost of ingredients is $1.20: This is called the "contribution" because it is the amount from the sale of each healthburger that is contributed toward paying the business's monthly costs. These monthly costs were as follows:

Employee wages	$12,000
Rent	3,600
Utilities	2,400
Depreciation of equipment	1,200
Advertising	2,000
Repairs and maintenance	1,300
Insurance, dues, and subscriptions	700
Miscellaneous expenses	800
Total	$24,000

Sales averaged 1,000 healthburgers per day (30,000 per month). Monthly profit was as follows:

Sales: 30,000 healthburgers @ $1.95	$58,500
Less cost of ingredients @ $0.75	22,500
Contribution: 30,000 @ $1.20	36,000
Less monthly costs of doing business	24,000
Monthly profit before income taxes	$12,000

Note that we could have shortened the profit calculation by going directly to the contribution approach, as follows:

Contribution: 30,000 @ $1.20	$36,000
Less monthly costs of doing business	24,000
Monthly profit before income taxes	$12,000

The "contribution analysis" method is very useful for several purposes, as we shall soon see.

Eileen's business situation had been very comfortable. But recently, two new fast food restaurants had opened nearby: They had attractive menus and low prices. The vigorous competition had driven healthburger sales down to 800 per day (24,000 per month). Monthly profit was cut as follows:

Contribution: 24,000 @ $1.20	$28,800
Less monthly costs of doing business	24,000
Profit before income taxes	$ 4,800

Monthly profit fell from $12,000 to $4,800, a drop of $7,200. The $7,200 represents a monthly sales decline of 6,000 healthburgers (30,000 − 24,000) multiplied by the contribution of $1.20 per unit. We can quickly compute the result of each further drop of 1,000 units per month in healthburger sales: 1,000 times $1.20, or $1,200. If sales fell by another 4,000 units, the further decrease in profit would be $4,800 (4,000 × $1.20); this would wipe out the entire monthly profit of $4,800.

In every competitive business, it is essential to understand the response of costs and profits to changes in unit volume. Exhibit 2.1 displays this information for Eileen's business. Using a computer spreadsheet, all monthly unit volumes are displayed from 0 to 40,000 units. Also shown are dollar sales, ingredient costs, contribution, and the resulting monthly profit or loss. Although the computer prepared these figures very quickly and easily, the exhibit contains a wealth of vital information, that is well worth the time required to study it in depth.

COST BEHAVIOR

It is important to understand how costs respond to changes in unit volume. Exhibit 2.2 displays this information, derived from the spreadsheet in

EXHIBIT 2.1. Healthburger cost-profit-volume speadsheet.

A	B	C	D	E	F	G	H
	A × $1.95	A × $0.75	(B−C)		(D−E)	(C+E)/A	(F/A)
Units Sold	Dollar Sales	Ingre- dient Costs	Contri- bution	Monthly Costs	Pretax Profit	Total Cost per Unit	Pretax Profit per Unit
0	$ 0	$ 0	$ 0	$24,000	$(24,000)	$ n/a	$ n/a
1,000	1,950	750	1,200	24,000	(22,800)	24.75	(22.80)
2,000	3,900	1,500	2,400	24,000	(21,600)	12.75	(10.80)
3,000	5,850	2,250	3,600	24,000	(20,400)	8.75	(6.80)
4,000	7,800	3,000	4,800	24,000	(19,200)	6.75	(4.80)
5,000	9,750	3,750	6,000	24,000	(18,000)	5.55	(3.60)
6,000	11,700	4,500	7,200	24,000	(16,800)	4.75	(2.80)
7,000	13,650	5,250	8,400	24,000	(15,600)	4.18	(2.23)
8,000	15,600	6,000	9,600	24,000	(14,400)	3.75	(1.80)
9,000	17,550	6,750	10,800	24,000	(13,200)	3.42	(1.47)
10,000	19,500	7,500	12,000	24,000	(12,000)	3.15	(1.20)
11,000	21,450	8,250	13,200	24,000	(10,800)	2.93	(0.98)
12,000	23,400	9,000	14,400	24,000	(9,600)	2.75	(0.80)
13,000	25,350	9,750	15,600	24,000	(8,400)	2.60	(0.65)
14,000	27,300	10,500	16,800	24,000	(7,200)	2.46	(0.51)
15,000	29,250	11,250	18,000	24,000	(6,000)	2.35	(0.40)
16,000	31,200	12,000	19,200	24,000	(4,800)	2.25	(0.30)
17,000	33,150	12,750	20,400	24,000	(3,600)	2.16	(0.21)
18,000	35,100	13,500	21,600	24,000	(2,400)	2.08	(0.13)
19,000	37,050	14,250	22,800	24,000	(1,200)	2.01	(0.06)
20,000	39,000	15,000	24,000	24,000	0	1.95	0.00
21,000	40,950	15,750	25,200	24,000	1,200	1.89	0.06
22,000	42,900	16,500	26,400	24,000	2,400	1.84	0.11
23,000	44,850	17,250	27,600	24,000	3,600	1.79	0.16
24,000	46,800	18,000	28,800	24,000	4,800	1.75	0.20
25,000	48,750	18,750	30,000	24,000	6,000	1.71	0.24
26,000	50,700	19,500	31,200	24,000	7,200	1.67	0.28
27,000	52,650	20,250	32,400	24,000	8,400	1.64	0.31
28,000	54,600	21,000	33,600	24,000	9,600	1.61	0.34
29,000	56,550	21,750	34,800	24,000	10,800	1.58	0.37
30,000	58,500	22,500	36,000	24,000	12,000	1.55	0.40
31,000	60,450	23,250	37,200	24,000	13,200	1.52	0.43
32,000	62,400	24,000	38,400	24,000	14,400	1.50	0.45
33,000	64,350	24,750	39,600	24,000	15,600	1.48	0.47
34,000	66,300	25,500	40,800	24,000	16,800	1.46	0.49
35,000	68,250	26,250	42,000	24,000	18,000	1.44	0.51
36,000	70,200	27,000	43,200	24,000	19,200	1.42	0.53
37,000	72,150	27,750	44,400	24,000	20,400	1.40	0.55
38,000	74,100	28,500	45,600	24,000	21,600	1.38	0.57
39,000	76,050	29,250	46,800	24,000	22,800	1.37	0.58
40,000	78,000	30,000	48,000	24,000	24,000	1.35	0.60

EXHIBIT 2.2. Healthburger, Cost chart.

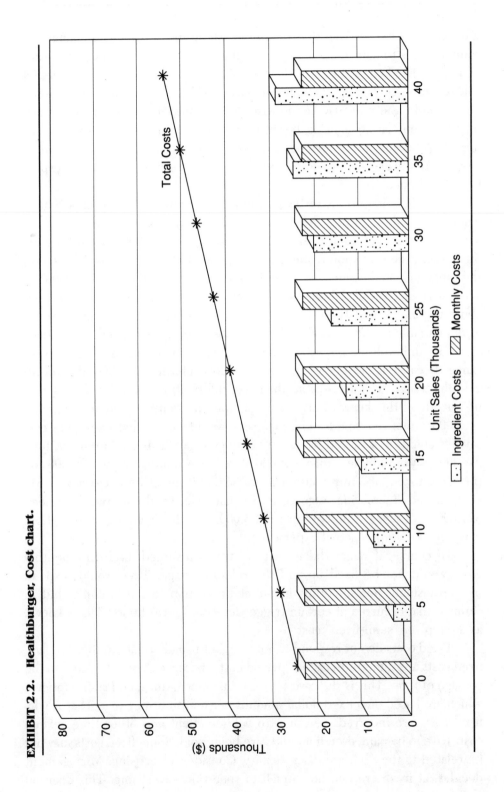

Exhibit 2.1. First, we see that monthly costs do not respond to changes in volume. They remain at $24,000 per month for all levels of volume. These are known as "fixed costs" because they remain fixed with respect to volume. Of course, these costs may fluctuate for reasons other than changes in volume. For example, the rent may be increased by the property owner, more money may be spent on advertising because of fiercer competition, or wage costs may drop because an experienced worker leaves and is replaced by an inexperienced, lower-paid employee. So fixed costs are fixed only with respect to unit volume.

Also, it is important to bear in mind the limits of recent experience. Eileen has only operated the restaurant for one year. It was an immediate success, and unit volume in the very first month was 16,000 healthburgers. Since then, the unit volume increased to 30,000 but never higher. Therefore, the range of actual experience is limited to unit volumes of 16,000 to 30,000. The chart in Exhibit 2.2 shows cost estimates for unit volumes below and above this range, but these costs are only theoretical estimates and are not as dependable as the costs that have actually been experienced in practice.

The unit volume between 16,000 and 30,000 is known as the "relevant range" because it has been experienced. Cost information derived from inside this range is more reliable than cost information for unit volumes that lie outside of this known range. For example, if monthly volume was as low as 5,000 units, perhaps fewer employees would be needed and some cost savings could be achieved by cutting employee hours. If this occurred, total fixed costs would be less than $24,000 at or below a unit volume of 5,000. By the same token, at a unit volume above 35,000 it might be necessary to add staff, thereby increasing wage costs. In that case, fixed costs would exceed $24,000 at or above a unit volume of 35,000. But this is only an assumption; it is not based upon actual experience.

Of course, if wages did in fact behave as assumed, then the monthly costs would not be fixed beyond the relevant range. They would respond in step fashion, not smoothly, in direct proportion to unit volume, but in "lumps" that occurred at certain trigger levels of unit volume. This is known as a "step" or "semi-fixed" cost.

Fixed costs do not respond to volume, but usually relate to time. In fact, fixed costs are sometimes called "period costs" because they are related to the passage of time. This is the case for rent, insurance, dues, and subscriptions, which are based on a fixed dollar amount per month or per year. That is why fixed costs are incurred even at zero volume: Rent and other time related costs have to be paid, even if no units are being sold. Some fixed costs may not be related to time but are discretionary. Consider advertising. Management decides, at its discretion, how much to spend on advertising. This decision may take several factors into account, but in the last analysis, the amount to be spent is set at management's discretion.

In addition to fixed costs, Exhibit 2.2 also shows the cost of ingredients, which vary in direct proportion to unit volume. The ingredients for each healthburger sold cost $0.75. The cost of ingredients increases (or decreases) in direct proportion to unit volume. Costs that respond in direct proportion to changes in unit volume are known as "variable costs," because they vary directly with volume. Again, the concept of "relevant range" applies: We can place reliance upon actual experience, but we must be cautious when speculating outside the range of experience.

Caution is also in order because variable costs may change for reasons other than a change in volume. For instance, the cost of healthburger ingredients may rise because a drought has pushed up tomato costs. Or, the company may switch to a recycled paper wrapping for environmental reasons: This would probably change the cost of its wrapping paper.

In order to ascertain total costs, we must combine the fixed and variable costs. Exhibit 2.2 displays total costs in a line, representing the sum of monthly and ingredient costs. This total-cost line increases with volume because the variable costs are included, but it does not increase in direct proportion to volume because of the fixed-cost component.

COST-PROFIT-VOLUME ANALYSIS

The total cost charted in Exhibit 2.2 can be compared with sales revenue in order to arrive at a profit for each level of unit volume (Exhibit 2.3).

In Exhibit 2.3, the total-cost line starts at $24,000 (for zero volume) and rises as volume grows. The sales-revenue line begins at zero (when unit sales are zero, sales revenues are likewise zero). But total costs grow more slowly than sales, and thus the sales revenue line catches up with and overtakes total costs. As long as total costs are greater than sales revenue, losses are incurred. But once sales revenue exceeds total costs, profits are earned.

At the point where sales revenue just catches up with total costs, there is neither profit nor loss. This is known as the break-even point. As shown by the spreadsheet in Exhibit 2.1 and also the chart in Exhibit 2.3, the break-even point occurs at a unit volume of 20,000 per month. At this volume, sales revenue is $39,000, ingredient costs are $15,000 (making the total contribution $24,000), and fixed costs are $24,000. The total costs are $39,000, and the resulting profit is zero. At all unit volumes less than the break-even point, losses are incurred; profits are earned at all unit volumes above the break-even point.

EXHIBIT 2.3. Healthburger, Cost-profit-volume chart.

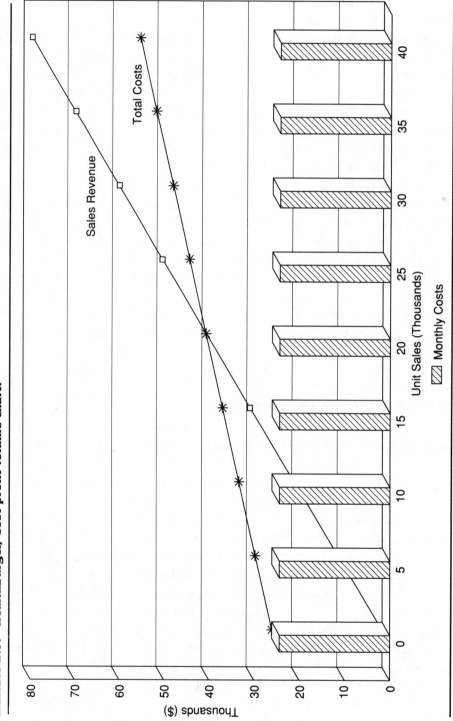

The break-even point may be computed (Exhibit 2.1), plotted (Exhibit 2.3), or calculated by formula as follows:

$$\text{Profit} = \text{Revenues} - \text{Variable Costs} - \text{Fixed Costs}$$
$$\text{Profit} = \text{Contribution} - \text{Fixed Costs}$$

Setting profit equal to zero to establish the break-even point:

$$\text{Zero} = \text{Contribution} - \text{Fixed Costs}$$
$$\text{Contribution} = \text{Fixed Costs}$$
$$\text{Contribution per unit} = \text{Fixed Costs}/\# \text{ units to break even}$$
$$\# \text{ units needed to break even} = \text{Fixed Costs}/\text{Contribution per Unit}$$
$$= \$24{,}000/(\$1.95 - \$0.75)$$
$$= \$24{,}000/\$1.20$$
$$= 20{,}000 \text{ units}$$

This formula makes it easy to answer relevant questions: for example, what would be the break-even point if fixed costs increase to a level of $27,000 per month? The new break-even point is 22,500 units ($27,000/$1.20). Or, how many units must be sold to earn a profit of $6,000 per month? Adding the fixed costs of $24,000 and the desired profit of $6,000, the new total contribution required is $30,000. Then $30,000 divided by the unit contribution of $1.20 is 25,000 units.

Break-even analysis is a most practical and useful technique. For instance, Eileen's volume has fallen from 30,000 per month to 24,000. It would be helpful for her to know at what volume she will break even, or at what volume she will lose $3,000 a month. Break-even analysis shows that she will lose $3,000 if she sells 17,500 units: ($24,000 − $3,000)/$1.20.

It is especially helpful for people considering opening a new business to use cost-profit-volume (CPV) analysis. If, for example, you are exploring the purchase of a franchise, you will soon find that the franchisors are reluctant to give you any profit projections: They are afraid of being sued if the business fails to produce the projected profits. While they do not want to give out this information, you really do need to know what kind of profits you can reasonably earn. How do you overcome this obstacle?

Usually you can get information from the franchisor and other franchisees about unit prices, and about fixed and variable costs. With this information, you can calculate break-even volume and the unit volumes required to earn various levels of monthly or yearly profits. Next, you can estimate how realistic and how difficult it may be to reach these unit-volume targets. Franchisors and other franchisees are usually quite willing to discuss unit volumes, although they are extremely reluctant to reveal profit information. With an understanding of break-even and CPV analysis, you can easily compute the necessary profit information from the available facts on costs and selling prices.

To summarize, break-even volume, in units, is determined by the following formula:

$$\frac{\text{Fixed Costs} + \text{Target Amount of Profit}}{\text{Unit Contribution}}$$

Break-even analysis is a widely used and helpful technique, but, like all techniques, it can be misused. Note that it is only as good as the information that goes into it. Accurate results depend on obtaining current and accurate information on selling price, variable costs, and fixed costs. If any of these elements changes, the break-even analysis will have to be revised.

CONTRIBUTION ANALYSIS

We have seen that the essence of break-even and CPV analysis is the notion of contribution toward fixed costs and profit. This valuable notion allows us to simplify the break-even chart (Exhibit 2.3), by creating a contribution-profit chart (Exhibit 2.4).

In Exhibit 2.4, the striped bars represent the monthly fixed costs, and the sloping line depicts the contribution at each level of volume. The unstriped bars are the monthly profits. As the contribution increases with volume, it covers a larger portion of the fixed costs: this reduces the losses incurred at all levels of volume below breakeven. At the point of break-even volume, the contribution is just sufficient to compensate for the monthly fixed costs. Therefore, there is neither a profit nor a loss. Above the break-even point, the contribution exceeds the fixed costs by a growing amount as volume increases. This means profit increases as volume increases.

A Special Order

The contribution approach can be useful in many practical business situations. One example is when a special order is received. The president of a local bank stopped by to see Eileen. He asked if she would like to supply 1,000 healthburgers for the annual company picnic next month. "Of course," he added "with such a huge order, we will certainly expect to pay a lot less than your regular price of $1.95 per burger. In fact, Burger Queen has already offered us a price of $1.25. Can you match that price?"

Eileen knew that she could not make all of the 1,000 extra burgers during the restaurant's regular business hours of 11 A.M. to 11 P.M. She would need to schedule overtime hours for some of the work. She estimated that she would need two people for four hours, which would cost $60 in wages.

EXHIBIT 2.4. Healthburger, Contribution-profit chart.

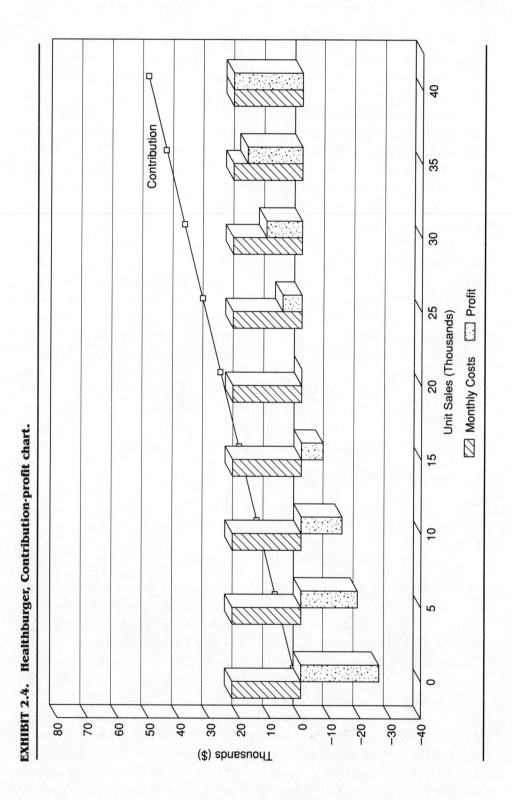

It seemed wise to think through this offer very carefully, so she said, "Thank you for giving me an opportunity to make a bid. Could I get back to you in about an hour with a final answer?" "Of course, Eileen. Call me at the bank," replied the president.

What should Eileen do? Contribution analysis will provide the information she needs to make a sound decision. At the special price of $1.25, minus the ingredient costs of $0.75, the contribution per burger will be $0.50. For 1,000 burgers this adds up to a $500 contribution. Subtract the extra wage costs of $60, and the remaining contribution toward fixed costs and profit is $440. Eileen would be well advised to accept the offer from the bank, which will give her a profit of $440.

If necessary, just how low a price could Eileen charge on this special order? Note that the order increases fixed costs by $60. Therefore, it must have a contribution of at least $60 to be a break-even proposition. A contribution of $60 on 1,000 burgers translates into 6 cents per burger as the required contribution per unit. Variable (ingredient) cost per burger is $0.75, so a 6-cent required contribution per burger would necessitate a price of $0.81 to break-even. The calculation, using the break-even formula, is as follows:

$$\text{Break-even Volume} = \text{Fixed Costs}/\text{Unit Contribution}$$
$$1,000 \text{ units} = \$60/\text{Unit Contribution}$$
$$\text{Unit Contribution} = \$60/1,000$$
$$= 6 \text{ cents}$$

For the total order, the result would be:

Sales revenue: 1,000 times $0.81	$810
Less ingredients: 1,000 times $0.75	750
Less extra wage costs	60
Remaining profit	$ 0

Eileen needs to consider two other important factors before making her decision. First, she should be very sure that the special order does not involve any other extra costs. If it does, she will have to redo her break-even analysis. It is all too easy to overlook extra costs in a new situation, especially if a company really needs the new business. In Eileen's case, she does face a possible extra cost: Who will transport the 1,000 burgers to the picnic, what cost will that entail, and who is responsible for paying that cost?

Second, Eileen must consider whether her decision will have any indirect consequences. We have assumed that the special order is separate, independent, and a "one shot" event, which will have no impact on regular business. If this is not true, then any indirect effects must be considered. For example, say that Eileen has been supplying 200 burgers per week to the cafeteria at the nearby high school at the regular price. The high school principal learns that the bank paid only $1.25 rather than $1.95 per burger and demands that the school price also be cut to $1.25. If Eileen has to agree to that request, her sales revenue will be reduced by $4,200 a year (200 burgers × 30 weeks per school year × the price reduction of $0.70 per burger). The profit of $440 on the bank annual picnic does not even come close to compensating for this lost $4,200.

It is plain that consequences can be serious, and they may be unintended or even unforeseen. Contribution analysis should therefore be used with care, and with diligent attention to qualitative as well as quantitative factors.

Short and Long Run

Note that contribution analysis is a short run approach. Consider, once more, the bank's special order for the 1,000 healthburgers. The special order at $1.25 per burger minus the ingredient cost of $0.75 leaves a contribution of $0.50 per burger. But monthly fixed costs are $24,000 and at this time, average monthly unit volume is running at 24,000 healthburgers. This means that average fixed cost per burger is $1 ($24,000/24,000), and the 50-cent contribution will not cover this $1 fixed cost per burger.

Does this mean that Eileen was wrong to accept the order? No, our contribution analysis was valid and led to the right decision in the short run. But, in the long run, all costs (fixed as well as variable) must be covered in order to make profits and remain in business. Therefore, on an occasional basis, it is fine to accept special orders, based on contribution analysis. But it should not become a regular way of life. This would lead to disaster.

Price Discrimination

With respect to granting price cuts to some customers, but not to others, there is a need to avoid price discrimination. Like several other forms of discrimination, discrimination on the basis of price may be illegal under state laws and under the federal Robinson-Patman Act. However, it is legitimate to practice price discrimination under certain mitigating conditions; for instance, if the lower price can be justified by a lower manufacturing cost, a lower sales cost, or a lower delivery cost.

Over the long run, a business must sell its products at a price sufficient to pay back all costs (fixed as well as variable) and provide a reasonable profit. Therefore, a useful rule of thumb is that contribution analysis is fine for occasional short-run decisions, but in the long run, fixed costs cannot be left out of consideration.

MULTIPLE PRODUCTS

Up until now, we have considered only a single-product situation. But break-even analysis can also be applied to multiple products. Assume that the typical order at Eileen's restaurant consists of the following items.

	Selling Price	Variable Cost	Contribution
Healthburger	$1.95	$0.75	$1.20
Onion Rings	1.20	0.40	0.80
Beverage	1.00	0.30	0.70
Combined	$4.15	$1.45	$2.70

The contribution per order is now $2.70: The break-even volume becomes 8,889 units ($24,000/$2.70). Or, if the target profit is $6,000, the required volume will be 11,111 units ([$24,000 + $6,000]/$2.70).

This is valid as long as the typical order remains unchanged. But if there is a change in the mix (say customers lose their taste for onion rings) or a change in the price or variable cost of any of the items, then the contribution per order is altered. When the contribution changes, there is a corresponding change in the break-even volume. In other words, there is a break-even volume for any given product mix, and a different mix will result in a different break-even.

ECONOMIES OF SCALE

Consider what happens to the cost per burger as volume grows. The ingredient cost of $0.75 must be incurred on each burger, regardless of whether the monthly volume is 5,000 units or 40,000 units. But the fixed cost of $24,000 per month can be spread over more and more burgers as volume increases. If 6,000 burgers are sold this month, then the fixed cost per burger is $4 ($24,000/6,000). If 12,000 burgers are sold this month, then the fixed cost per burger is $2 ($24,000/12,000): If 24,000 burgers are sold, then the fixed cost per burger is $1 ($24,000/24,000).

This can seem confusing. The total fixed cost does not respond to changes in volume. However, the fixed cost per unit decreases as volume grows because there are more units to share the total fixed costs. The total variable cost changes in direct proportion to fluctuations in volume; this is why it is known as variable. However, the variable cost per unit tends to stay the same as volume changes. In the case of healthburgers, the variable cost of $0.75 for ingredients is incurred for each burger; whether it is the first one sold or the 40,000th one. The key to understanding costs is to be clear what cost is being considered: total cost or cost per unit.

As more and more burgers are sold, their average fixed cost per unit declines. Of course, the variable cost per unit for ingredients remains at

$0.75: the total variable cost for all units increases as volume expands. In some cases, the variable cost per unit may decrease with a major increase in volume. For example, the healthburger ingredients costing 75 cents may cost only 60 cents if bought in much larger quantities.

The total cost per unit falls as volume grows because the fixed cost per unit decreases, while the variable cost per unit remains unchanged or decreases. This volume-cost relationship is an economy of scale. When unit cost is falling, but unit selling price is steady, profit per unit increases with volume. Therefore, economies of scale tend to be linked to increasing profit per unit as volume grows.

The term "economies of scale" is mostly used by economists: Accountants normally refer to the volume-cost relationship as "cost leverage." Which of these two terms is used may indicate whether the user is an economist or an accountant. Both terms continue to exist, which suggests that economists and accountants still live in separate worlds.

Exhibit 2.5 shows the healthburger cost and profit per unit in chart form, based on the numbers from the last two columns of Exhibit 2.1. Note the rapid decline in unit cost between 1,000 and 15,000 units per month. At 1,000 units, the fixed cost per burger is a lofty $24 ($24,000/1,000)! But at 15,000 units, the fixed cost per burger is only $1.60 ($24,000/15,000).

Economies of scale occur when unit costs decrease as volume increases. These economies are usually due to the existence of fixed costs. Recall that variable costs per unit do not change as volume increases; therefore, they do not give rise to economies of scale. But fixed costs per unit do drop as volume increases, and this results in economies of scale.

The extent of economies of scale can have a major impact on the size of businesses in a given industry. If there are significant economies of scale, then, the larger the firm, the more profit it can earn per unit of output. The very largest firms will be the lowest-cost producers. Taken to the extreme, one giant firm could be the lowest-cost producer in its industry: It could drive out all of its less efficient competitors by undercutting their prices.

Would this be beneficial? Eliminating all but the single most efficient, lowest-cost firm represents survival of the fittest competitor: Its customers would now be paying the lowest possible price. On the other hand, the surviving firm would become a monopoly, with the power to raise its prices (and profits) due to the absence of competition. The benefits of economies of scale might still be reaped by the firm, but would no longer be passed on to its customers. In this case, the public would be the losers.

Use of economies of scale raises important issues of public policy that are dealt with in our antitrust laws and various other areas of government regulation: One of these areas is known as predatory pricing.

EXHIBIT 2.5. Healthburger, Per unit cost-profit chart.

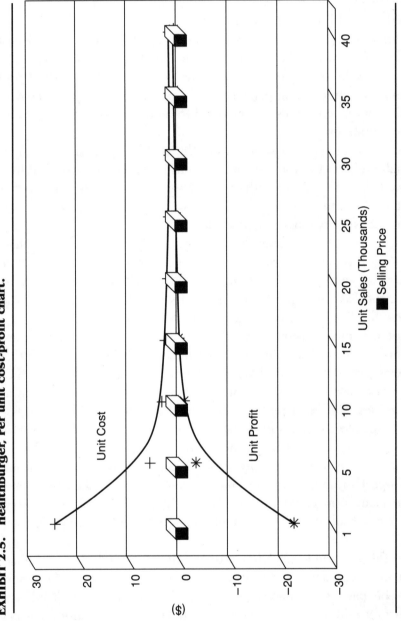

42

PREDATORY PRICING

In recent years a legal battle has been raging between two of the nation's largest tobacco companies. The Brooke Group, Inc. (previously known as Liggett Group, Inc.), accused Brown & Williamson Tobacco Corporation of predatory pricing in the wholesale cigarette market. At the trial in federal court, the jury decided that Brown & Williamson had indeed engaged in predatory pricing against Brooke. The jury awarded damages of $150 million to be paid to Brooke by Brown & Williamson. However, the presiding judge threw out this verdict. Since then, Brooke has filed an appeal, and the case continues.

Predatory pricing cases are not unusual, and damage awards as large as $150 million are not uncommon. Predatory pricing, as the name implies, is a tactic whereby the predator company slashes prices in order to force its competitors to follow suit. The purpose is to wage a price war and inflict such severe losses upon competitors that they will be driven out of business. After destroying the competition, the predator company will be free to raise prices, thus recovering the losses it sustained in the price war. Without competition, the predatory firm can rake in profits that greatly exceed its normal earnings. Predatory pricing is harmful to competition: therefore, it has been made unlawful.

In order to determine whether a firm has engaged in predatory pricing, the courts have devised a number of tests. One of the usual tests is whether or not there is a sustained pattern of pricing below the average variable cost. If the answer is yes, this indicates predatory pricing. Let us examine the logic underlying this widely used test.

First, recall that contribution is the margin between selling price and variable cost. Contribution is used to pay fixed costs and provide a profit. Now, if price is less than variable cost, contribution is negative. In that case, the firm cannot fully cover its fixed costs and will certainly suffer losses. Therefore, it makes no sense for the firm to charge a price that is below variable cost: unless the firm is engaging in predatory pricing—trying to destroy competing firms. That is why pricing below variable cost is considered to be evidence of predatory pricing.

We should bear in mind that the variable cost used in the test is that of the alleged predator, not that of the alleged victim. This is because the alleged predator may be an efficient low cost producer, while the alleged victim may be an inefficient high cost producer. Therefore, a price below the alleged victim's variable cost may be above that of the alleged predator. In which case it could be a legitimate price; simply a reflection of the superior efficiency of the alleged predator. The antitrust laws are designed to protect competition, but not competitors (especially those competitors who are inefficient).

Of course, this is only one indicator of predatory pricing, and all of the relevant evidence must be considered. There should be a pattern of sustained pricing below variable cost. Prices that are only slashed sporadically or occasionally are probably legitimate business tactics. This includes "loss leader" pricing to attract customers or clearance sales to clear out obsolete goods.

Predatory pricing is an important topic, and has been the subject of major lawsuits in a wide variety of industries. Because variable cost is a common test for predatory pricing, it is an important topic that should be understood by everyone involved with business.

Predatory pricing is usually thought of in a regional sense, and, sometimes, on a national scale: But it can also occur on an international basis. When this happens, it is known as "dumping."

Dumping

If a foreign company is the predator, there is no inherent difference in the tactics or goal of predatory pricing. Pricing below variable cost would still be a valid indicator. However, our law imposes a stricter test on foreigners than on domestic companies. The legal test for dumping does not involve variable cost. Rather, it focuses on whether or not the foreign company is selling its product here, at a price less than the price in its home market.

Dumping is simply predatory pricing by a foreign company. Although variable cost could be used as a test for predatory pricing, the test actually used is domestic selling price (usually higher than variable cost). This test makes it easier to prove dumping than to prove predatory pricing. It favors the domestic firms over the foreign company. This is a matter of politics as well as one of economics.

Perhaps the best known cases of dumping have involved the textile industry and the steel industry. Other recent cases of dumping involve Japanese automobile companies, accused by U.S. competitors of dumping minivans in the U.S., and Japanese makers of flat screens for laptop computers (active matrix liquid crystal displays). The latter were lately found to have sold their products in the U.S. at prices below their home market prices.

It is not always easy to ascertain the home market selling price. Even if there are list prices or catalog prices in the home market, there may be discounts or rebates that are difficult to detect. Therefore, instead of using the home market selling price as the test, the production cost may be used instead. This is reasonable because it is almost certain that the production cost is below the home market selling price. If this is true, a dumping price below production cost is virtually certain to be below the home market selling price. But bear in mind that "production cost" includes both fixed and variable costs, and is, therefore, above variable cost. It is debatable which elements should be included in production cost: some consider it logical to include interest expense on money borrowed to purchase manufacturing material inventories. Others believe that interest is not part of production cost.

If it is determined that dumping has indeed taken place, the U.S. International Trade Commission (ITC) will impose an import duty on the foreign product involved. This duty will be sufficiently high to boost the U.S. selling price to the same level as the home market price.

THE SHUT-DOWN POINT

We now return to Eileen and the healthburger restaurant. The competition has intensified, and unit volume has dropped to 15,000 healthburgers. At this volume, Exhibit 2.1 indicates that a loss of $6,000 is incurred. Eileen has become discouraged, and wonders whether she should close temporarily.

If the restaurant is closed for several weeks, or even months, most of the monthly costs will still be incurred (as long as there is an intent to reopen). It will be necessary to keep paying the rent, to continue insurance coverage, and to keep the equipment repaired and maintained. Some employees may be laid off, but it is probably wise to keep at least a core group on the payroll. Eileen carefully examines all of her costs, and finds that she can cut the monthly fixed cost of $24,000 down to $18,000 if the restaurant is temporarily shut down.

Now the decision is clearer. Staying open at a monthly volume of 15,000 units incurs a loss of $6,000 per month. But if the restaurant is shut down, the monthly cost (i.e., loss, because there is no revenue) is $18,000. It is definitely better to stay open. However, Eileen must keep a close watch on her available cash. Whether she stays open (at a cost of $6,000 per month) or shuts down (at a cost of $18,000 per month), there is a question of how long she can incur losses and still survive? The answer depends on how much cash is available. When the cash runs out, the end will come quickly.

Returning to the shut-down decision, at what volume will Eileen be better off closing the restaurant? Exhibit 2.1 shows that at a monthly volume of 5,000 units, the loss amounts to $18,000, which is the same amount as the monthly cost of a temporary shut-down. This is the shut-down point, where Eileen will break-even whether she is open or closed: either way, the loss is $18,000.

Fortunately, the shut-down decision did not materialize for Eileen, as business picked up again and continued to improve. Therefore, we leave Eileen to live long and prosper. We now turn our attention to a different company in a different industry.

EXHIBIT 2.6.   Banana Computer Corporation.

	Sales ($ Million)	Unit Sales (Thousands)	Operating Costs ($ Million)
1981	335	92	260
1982	583	163	464
1983	983	301	830
1984	1,516	509	1,387
1985	1,918	681	1,728
1986	1,902	699	1,577
1987	2,661	1,008	2,219
1988	4,071	1,619	3,375
1989	5,284	2,198	4,523
1990	5,558	2,503	4,641
1991	6,600	3,138	5,544
1992	7,500	3,654	6,302

BANANA COMPUTER CORPORATION

Banana Computers was started in a home garage by two highly innovative engineers with excellent business intuition. The firm grew fast and became a seven-billion-dollar corporation after only ten years of existence. Its product is a personal computer system, and Exhibit 2.6 shows the sales (in dollars and units) and operating costs.

Thinking back to Eileen's restaurant, how did we know that the cost of ingredients was $0.75 or that monthly fixed costs were $24,000? Someone must have figured that out and kindly given us that useful information. But in real life, we need to understand how to do this for ourselves. Banana Computer Corporation will provide this opportunity.

The numbers in Exhibit 2.6 do not give us information about fixed costs per period or variable costs per unit. But they do provide a basis for determining these costs. This may be done as follows.

COST ESTIMATION

It is usually helpful to chart this type of information, as has been done in Exhibit 2.7. Each square on the chart is one year of unit sales and operating cost information taken from Exhibit 2.6. For example, the 1991 unit sales of 3,138 are paired with the 1991 operating cost of 5,544 to form the dot second furthest from the right.

After plotting all 12 of these dots (for the years 1981-92), we study the relationship between the operating costs and the unit volume. In Exhibit 2.7, the dots are roughly in a straight line, which implies that there is a consistent relationship between cost and volume. The next task will be to plot this line because this will tell us the fixed and variable costs.

If the dots did not approximate a line (straight or curved), but were more widely scattered, then it would be likely that:

1. Other factors instead of (or in addition to) volume were the cost drivers, or

2. Production operations were in a volatile state, and must be allowed to settle down before any stable cost-volume relationship can be found, or

3. There were serious errors in the cost or unit volume data that we used, and the data should be thoroughly checked.

EXHIBIT 2.7. Banana Computer Corporation, Cost-volume chart.

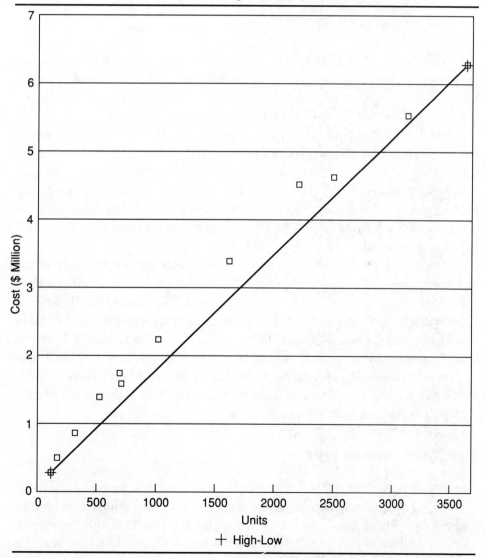

In these cases, further study is required. Fortunately, the dots in Exhibit 2.7 fall within a normal pattern, so we may proceed to estimate the fixed and variable costs. There are three different methods to do this.

The High-Low Method

First is the "high-low" approach in which a straight line is drawn, connecting the highest and lowest dots (Exhibit 2.7). This line is used, in conjunction with the information in Exhibit 2.6, to estimate the fixed and variable costs.

	Unit Volume (thousands)	Operating Costs ($ million)
High	3,654	6,302
Low	92	260
High minus Low	3,562	6,042

The volume increased by 3,562 thousand units, while the costs went up by $6,042 million. For each increase of 1,000 units, costs increased by about $1.7 million ($6,042 million/3,562 thousand). Therefore, the variable costs are $1.7 million per 1,000 units, which is $1,700 per unit.

For the high volume of 3,654 thousand units, the variable costs would total $6,212 million (3,654 thousand × $1,700). Now, as shown above, the actual total cost of the 3,654 thousand units was $6,302 million. Total cost minus variable cost leaves fixed cost, so fixed costs are $90 million ($6,302 million minus $6,212 million). To recap: using the high-low line, we have estimated fixed costs to be $90 million per year and variable costs to be $1.7 million per thousand units ($1,700 per unit).

The high-low approach has the virtue of simplicity, but it is very crude and imprecise. Although there were 12 years of information, this method only used two years: the highest and the lowest. The remaining 10 years of information were totally neglected, resulting in a crude estimate. Information is valuable, and there is no excuse for throwing it away. In Exhibit 2.7, we see that quite a few of the squares do not lie on the high-low line: this illustrates the inexact nature of this approach. It should be used only when there is absolutely no other way to proceed (for example, if only two years' of data can be obtained). A better method is the "eyeball" technique.

The Eyeball Technique

The eyeball technique also fits a line to the dots, but it is done by judgment. Usually, a transparent ruler is placed over the dots and adjusted by eye to find the best fitting line. Exhibit 2.8 illustrates the results of this technique. The eyeball line is clearly more representative of all the dots than was the

EXHIBIT 2.8.   Banana Computer Corporation, Cost-volume chart.

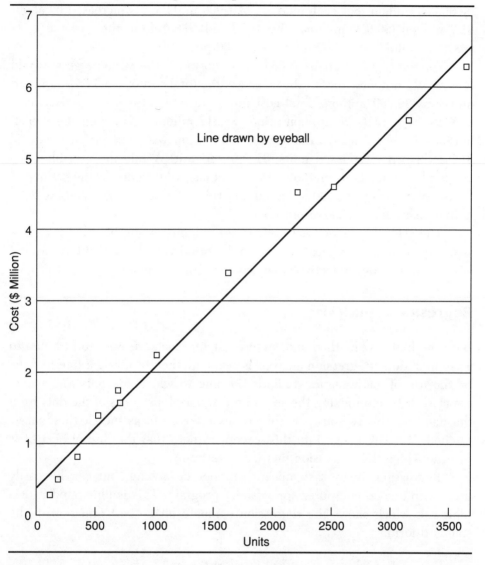

Line drawn by eyeball

high-low line. More of the dots now lie on or near the line; thus, it is more accurate than the high-low line.

From the eyeball line, the fixed and variable costs can be estimated in exactly the same way as was done with the high-low line, by reading the relevant numbers off the chart. This is shown below.

	Estimated Unit Volume (thousands)	Estimated Operating Costs ($ million)
High	3,654	6,650
Low	92	600
High minus Low	3,562	6,050

The volume increased by 3,562 thousand units, while the costs went up by $6,050 million. For each increase of 1,000 units, costs increased by about $1.7 million ($6,050 million/3,562 thousand). Therefore, the variable costs are $1.7 million per 1,000 units, or $1,700 per unit.

For the high volume of 3,654 thousand units, the variable costs would total $6,212 million. Now, as shown above, the total cost of the 3,654 thousand units was $6,650 million. Total cost minus variable cost leaves a fixed cost of $438 million ($6,650 million minus $6,212 million). To recap: the eyeball line has estimated fixed costs of $438 million per year, and variable costs of $1.7 million per thousand units ($1,700 per unit). While the variable costs are similar under both methods, there is a large difference in the estimated fixed costs which were $90 million under the high-low method, and are $438 million using the eyeball approach.

The eyeball approach is superior to the high-low method, but it can be arbitrary or subjective because it depends on individual judgment. A method which can be more objective is known as regression analysis.

Regression Analysis

Both the high-low method and the eyeball approach are ways to fit a line to a group of dots. Regression analysis is also a method of fitting a line to dots, by the use of mathematics. It finds the line to which the dots as a whole are closest, by minimizing the sum of the squared distances of the dots from the line. For this reason, it is sometimes referred to as the "least squares" method. We will not go into this, except to note that the line of best fit is the one which the regression method determines.

Regression involves significant number crunching, but can be easily done with a good computer spreadsheet program. This is illustrated in Exhibit 2.9, which shows the regression estimate of the cost equation in the standard form:

$$Y \text{ (total cost)} = \text{constant (fixed cost)} + \text{unit variable cost}$$
$$\text{times } X \text{ (number of units)}$$

In Exhibit 2.9, these results are: $Y = 408.95 + 1.69X$. Therefore the regression line has found that fixed costs are $408.95 million and variable costs are $1.69 million per one thousand units (or $1,690 per unit).

The regression output shown in Exhibit 2.9 also contains some further information. Some of this is highly technical, and we will not go into it in depth. But, we will briefly discuss a few of the main features. First, let us look at the chart showing the regression line, which is displayed in Exhibit 2.10 on page 52.

EXHIBIT 2.9. Banana Computer Corporation.

	Sales ($ Million)	Unit Sales (Thousand)	Operating Costs ($ Million)	Average Selling Price per Unit ($)	Average Cost per Unit ($)	Average Profit per Unit ($)	Average Profit Percent per Unit	Regression Estimate of Operating Costs ($ Million)	Regression Error (Actual Less Est. Cost) ($ Million)	Percent Error
1981	335	92	260	3,639	2,828	812	22.30	564	(304)	−116.97
1982	583	163	464	3,577	2,848	730	20.40	684	(220)	−47.46
1983	983	301	830	3,265	2,759	506	15.50	918	(87)	−10.50
1984	1,516	509	1,387	2,978	2,725	253	8.50	1,269	118	8.50
1985	1,918	681	1,728	2,817	2,538	279	9.90	1,560	169	9.75
1986	1,902	699	1,577	2,721	2,256	465	17.10	1,590	(14)	−0.86
1987	2,661	1,008	2,219	2,640	2,202	438	16.60	2,112	107	4.82
1988	4,071	1,619	3,375	2,515	2,085	430	17.10	3,145	230	6.82
1989	5,284	2,198	4,523	2,404	2,058	346	14.40	4,124	400	8.83
1990	5,558	2,503	4,641	2,221	1,854	366	16.50	4,639	2	0.05
1991	6,600	3,138	5,544	2,103	1,767	337	16.00	5,712	(168)	−3.03
1992	7,500	3,654	6,302	2,053	1,725	328	15.97	6,584	(282)	−4.48

Regression of Operating Costs (Y) on Unit Sales (X)

Constant	408.95
Std. Error of Y Est.	228.64
R Squared	0.99
No. of Observations	12.00
Degrees of Freedom	10.00
X Coefficient(s)	1.69
Std. Error of Coef.	0.06

Cost equation: $Y = 408.95 + 1.69X$

EXHIBIT 2.10.   Banana Computer Corporation, Cost-volume chart.

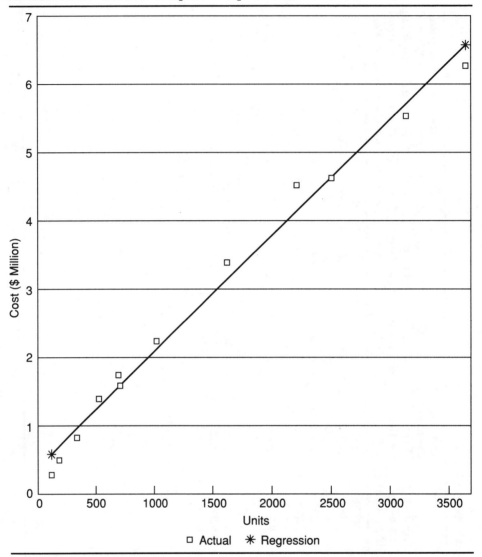

Interpreting the Regression Output

In Exhibit 2.10, note that the regression line seems to fit the dots very closely, and is quite similar to the eyeball line: this will not always be the case. While the fit of the regression line is good, it is not perfect, and there is some variation between the dots and the line itself. So, if we use the line to make a cost estimate at any given level of volume, there is likely to be some difference between this regression estimate and the actual cost at that volume. For instance, at a volume of 2,198 units, the actual operating costs were $4,523 million (see Exhibit 2.9). But the regression line estimate is lower: It appears to be just over $4,100 from (Exhibit 2.10). This is an error of about $400 million. Of course, at other volumes, the error seems lower.

To provide a measure of the average error, the regression output tells us the standard error of estimated cost (Y) is $228.64 million (Exhibit 2.9). This means that the difference between the regression estimate and the actual cost will be less than $228.64 (the estimate may be under or over the cost) about two thirds of the time. This cautions us to take the cost estimated from the regression with a grain of salt.

The other use of a standard error is in the estimate of X, the unit variable cost. The regression output shows that the unit variable cost of $1.69 is subject to an error (over or under) of less than $0.06, two thirds of the time. This is a very small error (less than 4%) and indicates a high level of precision in the estimate of unit variable cost. Therefore, this unit variable cost number may be taken with a very small grain of salt.

There is a helpful statistical indicator of how well the regression line fits the dots, that is, how well the line explains the variation (scatter) in the dots. This indicator is known as "R Squared" on the regression output: in Exhibit 2.9, it is 0.99, indicating that the line accounts for 99% of the variation. Clearly this is an excellent fit. It is rare and almost suspiciously fortunate to encounter such an extremely high R Square. Experienced practitioners would probably double-check their work if this were to occur.

In order to display the size of the regression errors, they are shown in the last two columns of Exhibit 2.9. The second to last column shows the errors in total dollar cost; the last column shows the errors as percentages. The errors in percentage terms are quite large in the first two years. They fall to 10% or less for the remaining ten years, which is a relatively small error.

These regression results appear to be excellent, and the cost estimates based on the regression would seem to be extremely precise. This raises a very important question: Is this regression the last word, or are there further issues in this cost estimation study that we should examine?

Beyond the Regression

When a regression is excellent, it is tempting to consider our work complete. But there is more information that should be taken into account. Exhibit 2.9 shows average cost per unit, and this continuously decreases as volume grows. This is evidence of economies of scale and should come as no surprise because we have already noted that fixed costs give rise to economies of scale. Average selling prices also exhibit a steady decline, indicating that the economies of scale are not being retained by Banana Computer: they are being passed on to customers (probably because of competition and its downward pressure on prices).

This is consistent with the average profit per unit, which has remained steady in percentage terms at about 16% since 1986. Hence, the competition was sufficient to induce the pass-through of cost savings (from economies of scale) to customers, but was not so fierce as to cause erosion of profit margins.

The cost numbers are plotted in Exhibit 2.11, which shows the regression line and a new line fitted to the dots. The new line is curved, not straight. It reveals some useful information: at unit volumes between 1,000 and 2,500, the regression systematically tends to undershoot actual costs. But at volumes above 2,500, the regression line systematically tends to over-

EXHIBIT 2.11.   Banana Computer Corporation, Cost-volume chart.

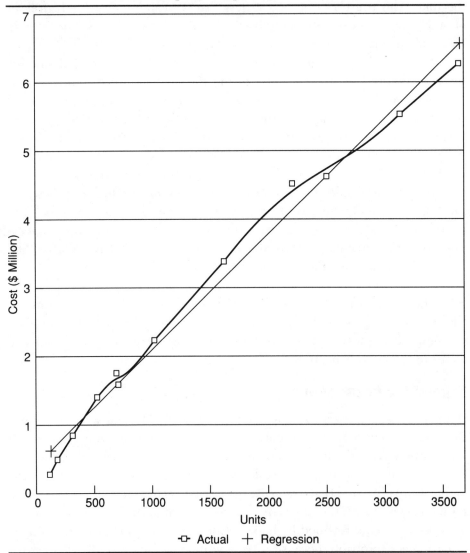

estimate the costs. This information is valuable because it makes us aware that the regression, as excellent as it is, does not tell the whole story. Regression does not show that actual costs follow a curved line, not a straight line. In other words, the unit variable cost is not constant at $1,690 per computer: it falls as volume increases. Thus, economies of scale are due to variable costs as well as fixed costs.

There has been considerable technological change in personal computers through the 1980s and into the 1990s. This change has certainly had favorable effects on costs: but the pattern still shows a falling rather than a constant variable cost. This fact can be of great strategic importance in marketing, pricing policies, plant expansion plans, and product design, as well as in other important areas of management.

Exhibit 2.12 displays the average variable cost per unit, derived by subtracting estimated fixed costs ($408.95 million) from operating costs (to obtain total variable costs); then dividing by unit volume. The resulting unit variable costs are not meaningful for 1981–1983, probably because of some instability in the fixed cost estimates for those early years. But from 1985 through 1992, there is a definite downward trend in unit variable cost: from above $1,900 down to about $1,600. This important trend was masked by the regression, which estimated variable cost at a constant $1,690 per unit. We therefore conclude that regression is a most valuable technique, but it can never be the last word in analysis. Nothing can substitute for common sense, close observation, and good judgment.

EXHIBIT 2.12. Banana Computer Corporation.

	Sales ($ Million)	Unit Sales (Thousands)	Operating Costs ($ Million)	Total Variable Costs* ($ Million)	Average Variable Cost per Unit ($)
1981	335	92	260	(149)	(1,618)
1982	583	163	464	55	339
1983	983	301	830	422	1,400
1984	1,516	509	1,387	978	1,922
1985	1,918	681	1,728	1,319	1,938
1986	1,902	699	1,577	1,168	1,671
1987	2,661	1,008	2,219	1,810	1,796
1988	4,071	1,619	3,375	2,966	1,832
1989	5,284	2,198	4,523	4,114	1,872
1990	5,558	2,503	4,641	4,232	1,691
1991	6,600	3,138	5,544	5,135	1,636
1992(E)	7,500	3,654	6,302	5,893	1,613

* Operating costs less estimated fixed costs of $408.95 million.

SUMMARY OF COST ESTIMATES

The three approaches used to estimate costs have produced the following results:

Method	Fixed Costs ($ million)	Unit Variable Cost
High – Low	$ 91	$1,700
Eyeball	438	1,700
Regression	409	1,690

Unit variable cost is virtually identical under all three of the methods. Fixed costs are in the same ballpark for the eyeball and the regression approaches, but are very different for the high-low method. This indicates how deceptive and unreliable the high-low method can be.

The disadvantages of using unreliable information are major: For example, consider the break-even calculation for the three methods:

	High-Low	Eyeball	Regression
Average 1992 unit selling price	$2,053	$2,053	$2,053
Unit variable cost	1,613	1,613	1,613
Contribution	440	440	440
Fixed costs ($ million)	91	438	409
Break-even point	91/440	438/440	409/440
Break-even volume	206,818	995,455	929,545

There is an enormous difference between the breakeven point under the high-low method and under the other two methods. Clearly it would be unfortunate to have made any important business decisions based on a break-even point of 206,818 units, when the actual break-even is more than four times higher. These results underscore the necessity of using reliable information when making business decisions.

CONCLUSION

This chapter has explored some powerful and practical methods that can be used in business analysis. These methods use the contribution approach and include CPV analysis and break-even analysis. In order to put the contribution approach into effect, there must be reliable information on fixed and variable costs. The cost information may be found using the high-low method (this should only be used when there is no better alternative), the eyeball technique, or regression analysis. The steps necessary to obtain valid business information are summarized in Exhibit 2.13.

EXHIBIT 2.13. Business decisions: Obtaining valid information.

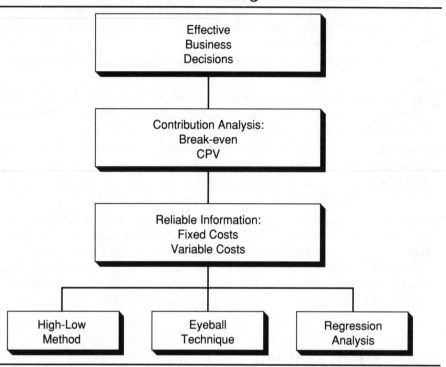

No matter which method is used, careful judgment is always needed. Not even the most scientific analytical methods can take the place of skilled human judgment. Neither can human intuition substitute for rigorous analytical techniques. But when the most powerful analytical methods are used in tandem with good judgment, the blending of objective scientific analysis and subjective human intuition becomes an unbeatable combination.

GLOSSARY

Break-even: The unit volume where total revenue equals total cost; there is neither profit nor loss.

Contribution: Total revenue less total variable costs.

CPV (Cost-Profit-Volume) Analysis: Technique for estimating the contribution and profit at various levels of volume, or determining the unit volume for given levels of profit.

Dumping: Selling in a given country by a foreign producer at a price below the price in the home market.

Economies of Scale: The decline of the total cost per unit as volume increases, often due to the existence of fixed costs.

Fixed Costs: Those costs that are not responsive to changes in volume over the relevant range, but which may respond to factors other than volume. Fixed costs are sometimes known as "period costs" when they depend on time (for example, rent, depreciation, insurance).

Predatory Pricing: Slashing selling prices below variable cost in order to drive out competitors.

Regression Analysis: A mathematical technique for finding the line that best fits points on a chart. The result is a line that minimizes the sum of the squared distances of the points from the line, and is also known as the "least squares" line.

Relevant Range: The range of unit volume which lies within recent experience, and which can therefore provide reasonably reliable cost information.

Semi-Fixed Costs: Costs which remain fixed over a certain range of volume, but then increase in a step fashion, at one or more trigger points.

Variable Costs: Those costs that are directly responsive to changes in volume over the relevant range. Variable costs may increase in direct proportion to volume, or may increase at a slower rate due to bulk discounts or other savings that relate to volume. While variable costs are responsive to volume, they can also respond to other factors, including changes in wage rates or prices of raw materials used in the production process.

FOR FURTHER READING

Anthony, Robert N. and James S. Reece, *Accounting: Text and Cases*, 8th ed. (Homewood, IL: Dow Jones-Irwin, Inc., 1989).

Atkinson, Anthony and Robert S. Kaplan, *Advanced Management Accounting*, 2nd ed. (Englewood Cliffs, NJ: Prentice-Hall, Inc., 1989).

Collins, Eliza G. C. and Mary Anne Devanna, eds., *The Portable MBA* (New York: John Wiley & Sons, Inc., 1990).

Ferris, Kenneth R. and John Leslie Livingstone, eds., *Management Planning and Control* (Columbus, OH: Publishing Horizons, Inc., 1987).

Foster, George and Charles T. Horngren, *Cost Accounting: A Managerial Emphasis*, 6th ed. (Englewood Cliffs, NJ: Prentice-Hall, Inc., 1987).

Helfert, Erich A., *Techniques of Financial Analysis*, 6th ed. (Homewood, IL: Dow Jones Irwin, Inc., 1987).

Rotch, William, Brandt Allen, and C. Ray Smith, *The Executive Guide to Management Accounting*, 4th ed. (Houston, TX: Dame Publishing Company, Inc., 1991).

3 ACTIVITY-BASED COSTING

William C. Lawler

Dan ("Doc") Webster sat staring out the window. Not even coffee-break time yet, and already three major battles had been waged. Wednesday was the worst day of the week—the most chaotic of all. It was the day when the promises made at the end of last week come home to roost and the idyllic promises of this week would be made. To make matters worse, Doc's accountant had informed him that the record was intact: For the seventh consecutive quarter, revenues had increased while profits had fallen.

The day started with a 7:15 A.M. call from the marketing manager, Jane Conole. She informed Doc that, once again, customer orders were backlogged because of production inefficiencies. These orders were for the new Turtles that they had "guaranteed for delivery" no later than last Friday. She also informed him that she was through dealing with Jim Thompson, the production manager. Thompson reported directly to Doc, so Doc could handle him.

A subsequent call to Thompson revealed that production was not to blame; procurement had not purchased the correct subcomponents. The line had been tooled and setup, but the misspecified subcomponents had jammed the hoppers (automatic feeders). Thompson's workers had tried valiantly to retool, but the components were just not compatible with the process. The better part of two days had been wasted on this order.

By 8:00 A.M. Doc was on the phone to Mike Green, head of procurement. After hearing Green's tone, Doc was amazed that the phone had not melted. Green, in very few words, made his position quite clear. He said that Conole was in the habit of selling products that were not yet part of the production line. Because Thompson's production line was very inflexible, Green had to ensure that any new product was sourced so that the subcomponents were compatible with the existing production technology. This meant that the product engineer working with Green had to draw up the specifications on the promised product (spec out the order), source it, and test it, before any suppliers could be qualified. Often, this process was relatively easy: Most new products were similar to existing products, and there was no need to qualify a new supplier. Usually, this process took less than two weeks. For the Turtle line, however, a new supplier had to be qualified, and problems were to be expected. The product had not been misspecified; the supplier had misconstrued the specifications. Green assured Doc that the mix-up had been corrected and the order would soon be running.

As Doc reached for the Bushmill's to fortify his coffee, he could not help but remember that the bottle had been a gift commemorating the one-million-dollar mark in sales. He wondered how a business that once was so promising could have gone so sour so quickly.

THE EARLY YEARS

The founding of the Smiling Feline, Ltd. had been pure serendipity. In the summer of 1985, while driving to a golf outing, Doc and three friends had an inane discussion on what could possibly motivate people to stick yellow bouncing plastic signs in the windows of their cars. One friend argued that the signs were quite practical, offering the sign Baby on Board as an example. He noted that this was similar to the red stickers that local fire departments give out to residents, to designate rooms in a house where children are located. This argument held sway until another car went by with an equally popular yellow bouncing sign: Mother-in-Law in the Trunk.

At the golf course, one of Doc's friends paid $20 for an animal headcover to put on his driver. When Doc asked him why on earth he would pay that amount for one novelty headcover when he could have bought a complete set of regular headcovers for the same amount, the friend answered: "For the same reason a person would buy a Mother-in-Law-in-the-Trunk sign and stick it in a rear window."

The idea for The Smiling Feline was born. If people would stick yellow signs in their car windows by the millions, surely they would stick crazy animals in their windows by the thousands, at least.

Doc was a design engineer for a medical instruments company and had worked on a few systems that had ancillary parts that could be attached to standard systems with suction cups. Through contacts, he soon had an obsolete injection molding machine in his basement for which he had paid only scrap value plus transportation. Within two weeks, he had fashioned a crude mold that would attach four suction cups to a variety of stuffed toys that his daughter had outgrown. A number of novelty stores in local malls were interested in the concept but wanted an item with more sales appeal.

By the winter of 1985, just in time for the Christmas season, four machines crammed into Doc's basement were turning out stick-on cats similar to a popular cartoon character. He had negotiated a rather exorbitant (in his mind) royalty agreement of 2.5 percent of the targeted retail price ($19.95) for the cat likeness, giving him a royalty of approximately 50 cents per animal. He had sourced the animal body at a price of $2.50 per unit, dependent on a minimum order of 5,000. He paid his four children a piece-work rate of $1 per good unit to attach the four suction cups, and each child managed to turn out four good units per hour—while also ruining approximately two per hour, because of the primitive equipment and conditions in the basement.

Initially, Doc spent most of his time convincing retailers that they should buy his product for $8 because they could undoubtedly resell it for $19.95. Within a month, he was spending most of his time trying to manage the many retailers who were clamoring for his product. By the time the first Christmas season ended, he believed that he had a viable economic venture: He had made $10,000 on sales of 12,000 units (Exhibit 3.1).

The next year was spent turning a potentially viable economic venture into a solid business enterprise. Many wrong turns were made, but, by the

Exhibit 3.1a. The Smiling Feline, Ltd., Comparative income statements.

	Qtr. 4, 1985	FY 1986	FY 1987	FY 1988	FY 1989
Sales (units)	12,000	60,000	150,000	300,000	550,000
Sales ($)	$96,000	$480,000	$1,050,000	$2,100,000	$3,850,000
Cost of goods sold:					
Rubber	3,000	15,000	37,500	75,000	137,500
Bodies	36,000	150,000	337,500	675,000	1,375,000
Labor	12,000	90,000	75,000	150,000	311,500
Overhead	34,000	146,000	447,000	895,500	1,646,000
Subtotal	$85,000	$401,000	$897,000	$1,795,500	$3,470,000
Gross Profit	$11,000	$79,000	$153,000	$304,500	$380,000
Operating expenses:					
Freight-out	1,000	7,000	20,000	30,000	58,500
Professional fees		5,000	5,000	8,000	10,000
Conole (sales rep.)			27,000	45,000	65,000
Other costs				29,000	30,000
Subtotal	$1,000	$12,000	$52,000	$112,000	$163,500
Pretax profit	$10,000	$67,000	$101,000	$192,500	$216,500
Cost of goods sold/unit	$7.08	$6.68	$5.98	$5.99	$6.31
Operating cost/unit	0.08	0.20	0.35	0.37	0.30
Total cost/unit	$7.16	$6.88	$6.33	$6.36	$6.61

Exhibit 3.1b.   The Smiling Feline, Ltd., Overhead detail.

	Qtr. 4, 1985	FY 1986	FY 1987	FY 1988	FY 1989
Depreciation:					
Mold	$ 6,000	$15,000	$ 37,500	$ 75,000	$137,500
Machinery	6,000	30,000	187,500	375,000	687,500
Royalty	6,000	30,000	75,000	112,500	100,000
Utilities	4,000	12,000	21,000	36,000	66,000
Scrap	12,000	30,000	40,000	78,000	185,000
Lease		29,000	36,000	75,000	100,000
Thompson			50,000	55,000	70,000
Green & assistant				35,000	95,000
Other production:					
Set-up				24,000	108,000
Warehouse				20,000	30,000
Material handling				1,500	9,000
EDP system/software				5,500	40,000
Quality control				3,000	18,000
Total overhead	$34,000	$146,000	$447,000	$895,500	$1,646,000
Overhead/unit	$2.83	$2.43	$2.98	$2.99	$2.99

end of the year, The Smiling Feline, Ltd., occupied 6,000 square feet in an old textile mill at a leased cost of $35,000 per year. Sales continued to be strong across all four quarters of 1986 and reached 60,000 units, yielding $480,000 in revenues. After lecturing Doc on the importance of record keeping, the CPA brought in to prepare the financial statements and tax return revealed that the pretax profit was $67,000. Doc quit his job to devote all his time to his new venture.

Vast changes were made in the business in 1987. Jim Thompson, hired as head of production, immediately upgraded the injection molding machines. Hoppers and other enhancements were added, thereby cutting the labor cost by two thirds and the cost of scrap plastic generated during production by an estimated 50 percent. Although the machinery was bought secondhand, it was not cheap; still, the net result was a decrease in unit cost of approximately 50 cents (Exhibit 3.2). Thompson's first decision not only paid for his annual salary but also assured Doc that his greatest headache, production, was now in able hands.

EXHIBIT 3.2.   Automation cost savings.

	Unit Cost Prior to Enhancements	Unit Cost after Enhancements	Savings
Labor	$1.50	$ .50	$1.00
Scrap	.50	.27	.23
Machine depreciation	.50	1.25	(.75)
Total	$2.50	$2.02	$ .48

Next, recognizing that if sales were to continue to grow he needed to expand his markets, Doc hired a sales representative, Jane Conole. Her job was to expand the company's market beyond the local area. By the end of the year, she had earned the title of sales manager, by negotiating a national sales contract with one of the biggest novelty store chains.

During the year, competition had pushed the wholesale price down to $7 on average, but sales again more than doubled and the pretax profit exceeded $100,000. Workers had presented Doc with the Bushmill's when the Christmas season pushed the total sales figure over the million-dollar mark. Doc was confident that he had made the correct decision on expansion.

The cracks began to show in 1988. Conole had managed to negotiate two additional national contracts, but competitive pressures had forced the wholesale price down to $6.75 and, by the second quarter, sales of The Smiling Feline, the company's only product, had leveled.

To spur sales, Conole drafted a memo suggesting that the product line be expanded. A number of midwest universities had approached her. Each home football game brought close to 100,000 fans to the home campus, and a reasonable portion of these fans probably would be willing to drive home with the team mascot firmly stuck to their windows. On a test basis, two such schools were each willing to sign contracts for 25,000 units at a price of $7.75 and to waive the school's customary royalty ($.50), which made The Smiling Feline price comparable to each school's current standard product price of $8.25. A novelty chain also suggested reindeer for the Christmas season—another item that would have no royalty cost. After the three special orders were accepted, The Smiling Feline was deluged with additional orders, from Cupids for the Valentine season to a mascot called the Fighting Sandcrab, which was rejected outright because it had more than four limbs.

Thompson put his foot down. He did not have enough time to spec out each order and still run the production operation. Soon after, Mike Green, a retired purchasing curmudgeon, was hired part-time to work with Thompson in drawing up the specifications, sourcing prototypes for a test run, and qualifying a supplier if the order was accepted. Green quickly found himself working 40-hour weeks.

Utter chaos marked 1989. Rising production costs, together with increased competition, threatened the profitability of the company's main product, the Smiling Feline. In fact, the accounting numbers for the year revealed that it cost approximately $6.61 per unit to produce and ship the main product to the customer (Exhibit 3.1). The competition had pushed the wholesale price of this product down to only $6.60. Because rising costs could not be passed on to the consumer for this product line, more and more of the higher-revenue specialty product orders were accepted and run. Thompson and Webster seemed to be constantly nose-to-nose over the rising production costs or "inefficiencies," as the accountant called them. Webster had faith in Thompson, yet the accounting numbers showed that the costs per unit were increasing.

Conole also was unhappy. To get this specialty business, she had promised service, and Thompson was not delivering. Late shipments was the quickest way to lose a customer, and this had happened all too often. To make matters worse, Green, having proved himself more than capable, was reminding everyone that he was supposed to be working part time. A 60-hour week was not his idea of a part time job; an additional engineer had to be hired. The quarreling and infighting escalated throughout 1989, leading to the miserable day Doc Webster was having at the end of the first quarter in 1990.

THE FIRST RETREAT

At his wit's end, Doc suggested a three-day top-management meeting—a corporate retreat, so to speak. Although Thompson, Conole, Green, and the outside accountant expressed varying degrees of reluctance to attend the meeting, they all agreed that operations could not continue the way they were going. The retreat was set for the beginning of June.

The first morning at the retreat began with each accusing the other (as usual) of being the root cause of the problem. Conole repeated, once again, that potential customers were beating down the doors trying to order specialty products. She seemed to have the specialty market to herself and, in fact, was spending the majority of her time placating customers whose orders had been backlogged. She assured all present that sales and income would have increased if Thompson had delivered.

Thompson and Green again emphasized that the lead time necessary to bring a new product to market was expensive. Many activities had to take place before a product could be produced. They also reiterated their commitment to quality, stressing their refusal to rush a product only to ruin the reputation of the company. Conole responded that the company probably had little reputation left to ruin, because a key facet of quality is meeting delivery deadlines.

The Light at the End of the Tunnel

The one positive aspect of the morning session was that the outside accountant, Jack Hughes, was present to explain the financial numbers. Toward the end of the morning, when the combatants had exhausted themselves, he managed to gain the floor. Hughes made a startling statement: "It seems that the services I have been providing are not what you need." He went on to note that, to date, he had only "recorded history." His focus had been on the collation of past transactions for IRS tax reports and not on the preparation of information for management decision making. "For example," he stated, "it seems that marketing and production have different views of the business. Jane is pushing the heck out of the specialty side because of its higher revenue potential, while Jim and Mike are suffering from the confusing effects of this specialty business in their respective areas. There may be a cost to this confusion that is not being recognized."

He now had their attention. Hughes continued, explaining that the production costs per unit of $5.98, $5.99, and $6.34, reported for the past three years, were average costs. The conversation he was hearing indicated that the product lines were not homogeneous, that is, there were few "average" products. Thus, calculating average costs might not be appropriate. It was clear that everyone felt the specialty business was more chaotic and, therefore, probably more costly.

Hughes summarized by stating that the products did not cause costs to be incurred; rather, it was the activities undertaken to bring the product from a raw state through production to the satisfied customer that incurred the costs. If The Smiling Feline wanted to properly judge the profitability of its individual products—or, at a minimum, its two business segments, standard and specialty items—it needed to look at the underlying activities that supported the segments and assign a cost to each segment based on that segment's activities.

The group unanimously agreed with what they had just heard and asked Hughes to prepare cost allocation based on these "activities." Hughes smiled and shook his head.

"You people still don't understand. I don't know the activities that cause your costs to be incurred. Only you know these cost drivers. I suggest that you envision the flow of a product through your business. Map out in your minds what happens when a customer approaches you with a valid proposal and what happens when that valid proposal is converted to a production order and goes through your factory. Finally, map out what happens when you have completed production of that order and it has to be delivered and supported. Once you do that, we, as a group, should be able to attribute costs to the activities and get a reasonable idea of your costs for each of your business segments."

At the end of the session, everyone agreed that the last 45 minutes of discussion had probably been management's most promising discussion in the past two years. For the afternoon, the group decided that the idea of process mapping should be discussed among The Smiling Feline staff, and that Hughes should gather as much financial data as possible. They would reconvene in the morning.

The Light Grows Brighter

The second morning began with an air of anticipation and confusion. The group now had a somewhat different view of their business. What they were not sure of was how this tied in to Hughes's numbers or how they were going to generate more useful information for decision making. Hughes had managed to find all the income statements and some supporting detail for The Smiling Feline, Ltd. He told them to be patient and to take things one step at a time.

The discussion began with Conole and Green mapping the steps from a customer inquiry to a production order (Exhibit 3.3). Conole stated that she routed all reasonable inquiries to Green. Green then talked with the potential customer, to ascertain all of the product specifications. Next, he brought these specifications to their mini-design shop where a prototype was constructed. The prototype had to meet both customer specifications and Thompson's ability to manufacture, given the somewhat inflexible manufacturing process. Green and Conole next brought the model to the customer for approval. If acceptable, Conole would work out a price and quantity.

Once a contract was signed, Green would source the body by bringing the prototype to the supplier(s) most apt to take the order and negotiating a price. Green had instituted a dominant source strategy where he dealt with a limited number of suppliers. However, on occasion, usually because of a unique product design, he would have to qualify a new supplier. Concurrently, Thompson would double-check the prototype to ensure its feasibility and would schedule a production run.

Green then noted: "It's now obvious that I was hired as a direct result of the specialty line. In 1988, I did spend some time organizing the procurement process for the standard line, which was in a bit of disarray. Since then, almost all of my time, and that of my assistant, has been spent on specialty orders. My log book for 1989 shows that Conole brought in 45 potential customers, and, of those, 18 signed contracts. We only needed new suppliers for 6 of the 18 contracts. It looks like it takes about one week to develop the prototype and gain customer acceptance, one week to talk to suppliers and negotiate the supply contract, and two additional weeks to qualify a new supplier."

Green passed around a chart showing the time allocated to various components of his job during the 75 weeks that he and his assistant logged in 1989 (Exhibit 3.4). Conole asked him whether the Turtle order had cost more to bring to market because he had needed to qualify a new supplier. Green said that he wasn't sure; after a supplier had been qualified, that supplier could be used again. Because the additional two weeks spent qualifying the supplier would benefit other orders (not just the Turtle order), Green was not comfortable attributing this activity and its cost solely to the Turtle order.

EXHIBIT 3.3. Steps of a production order.

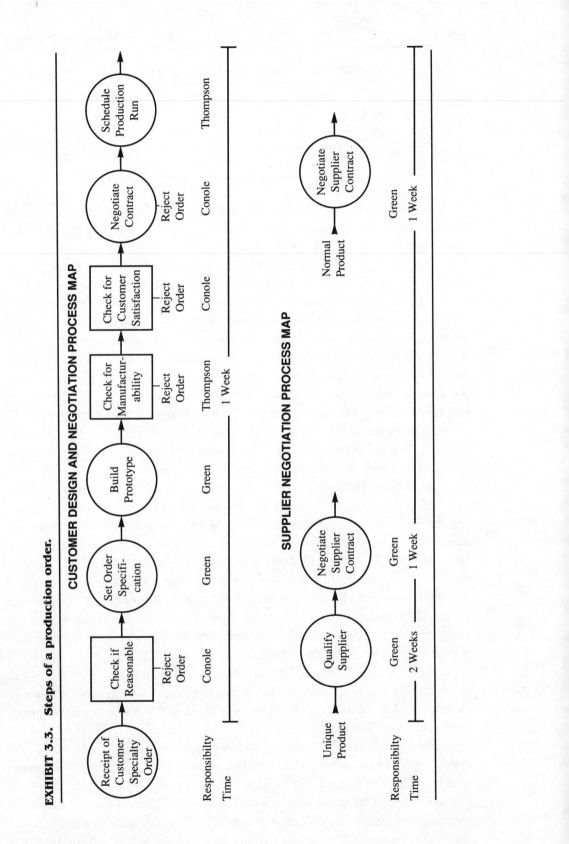

CUSTOMER DESIGN AND NEGOTIATION PROCESS MAP

Receipt of Customer Specialty Order	Check if Reasonable	Set Order Specification	Build Prototype	Check for Manufacturability	Check for Customer Satisfaction	Negotiate Contract	Schedule Production Run
	Reject Order			Reject Order	Reject Order	Reject Order	

Responsibility: Conole, Green, Green, Thompson, Conole, Conole, Thompson

Time: 1 Week

SUPPLIER NEGOTIATION PROCESS MAP

Unique Product	Qualify Supplier	Negotiate Supplier Contract

Responsibility: Green, Green

Time: 2 Weeks, 1 Week

Normal Product → Negotiate Supplier Contract

Green

1 Week

EXHIBIT 3.4. Procurement activity

Activity	Time (Weeks of Work)
45 Design orders	45
18 Supplier negotiations	18
6 Supplier qualifications	12
	75

He was sure, though, that it was chargeable to the specialty line. In fact, the costs of his area, procurement, were not chargeable at all to the standard line because his area had spent virtually no time on it.

Hughes, smiling at Green's final comment, said, "Mike, let me repeat what you just said, but in accounting terminology. Your process-map analysis revealed that the activity in your functional area, which we will call product design and procurement, is dependent on the uniqueness of the potential product. A unique product takes one week to design, and one week to negotiate a supplier contract. An extra-unique product takes one week to design, and three weeks to qualify and negotiate a supplier contract. You could create a crude initial cost model by taking the total costs of your function—let's call this the cost pool for design and negotiation—and dividing it by the 75 weeks you logged. This rate could then be used to directly charge your costs to the individual products. A unique product would be charged two weeks' worth of cost and an extra-unique product, four weeks'.

"Design and supplier negotiation are vastly different activities, so we may want to design the accounting system to recognize these two activities separately. Thus, we probably should separate cost pools for the design costs and the supplier negotiation costs, thereby developing rates for each activity. Because only 18 of the 45 designs resulted in orders, you would have to figure how to handle this factor when computing the design rate. You will find that, as you study your operations, the real activities or cost drivers will eventually reveal themselves. At this stage, it is sufficient to know that the costs of your function should be directly charged to the specialty line and not allocated over all units produced."

Next, the group turned to the production process. It had been studied in detail during the latter part of 1988, when the proposal to double production capacity had been investigated and accepted, so Thompson was relatively confident of his information (Exhibit 3.5).

"First," he stated, "each production order requires molds, to 'shoot' the heated rubber onto the limbs of the animal, and grates for the hoppers, which automatically feed the molding machines. For instance, the reindeer run of the 1988 Christmas season was 20,000 units. Each of the five machines running that year was producing at a rate of 30 good units per hour. To fill the order, we needed to run all five machines for close to a month, from the

EXHIBIT 3.5. Production process map.

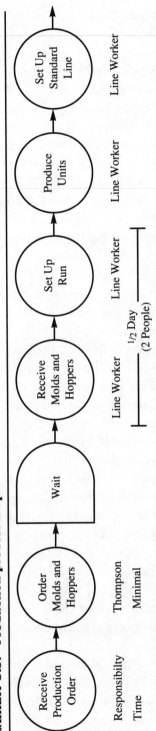

Receive Production Order	Order Molds and Hoppers	Wait	Receive Molds and Hoppers	Set Up Run	Produce Units	Set Up Standard Line
Responsibility	Thompson		Line Worker	Line Worker	Line Worker	Line Worker
Time	Minimal		½ Day (2 People)			

69

second week of October through the first week of November (5 machines ×
8 hours per day × 30 units/hour × 17 working days is approximately 20,000
units).

"Five molds, each of which would hold the four legs of the reindeer,
were ordered from a local casting shop at a cost of $1,000 per mold. A mold
only lasts about 4,000 shots (injections), 5,000 if we are very lucky, so there
was little waste for this order. Historically, given the size of our orders, we
can usually avoid only partially utilizing a mold. On this job, an approximate
cost for the mold activity was 25 cents per good unit ($1,000/4,000 units).

"Likewise, the hoppers and injection molding machines are really nothing more than a bundle of potential units of output. A standard versus a
specialty item makes no difference in the cost of using these machines. After
calculating the total price we paid for the injection molding machines plus
enhancements, I estimate that the depreciation cost is $1.25 per good unit
of output.

"The grates for the hoppers are somewhat different. They cost approximately $1,400 per grate per machine and would last for many more than
4,000 or 5,000 units. However, each animal body is relatively unique, and
we have a policy of throwing the grates out after the production run. Saving
them in hopes of a similar body in the future would result in a shop piled
to the ceiling with grates. This cost can be easily traced to an order, but
it might not make sense to trace it to the individual units produced in the
order, because the order quantities vary to a wide degree."

Thompson went on to say that to set up a production run took two
people about a half day and cost about $100. Likewise, a material handling
cost was incurred. These, again, were order costs, not really per-unit costs.
The group reminded Thompson that, after each specialty run, the production
line would have to be set up once again, to return to the standard line. They
all agreed that the specialty run was the cause of this second set-up and,
thus, the cost of the set-up activity was doubled to $200 per machine.

Thompson also noted that the warehouse and electronic data processing
(EDP) system costs should be analyzed with respect to what activities drove
these costs. With limited knowledge of these functional areas, he had no
ability to map their activities, but was fairly certain that they were a direct
result of the specialty items.

The costs that had given him the most trouble were the lease, the
utilities, and his own salary. He stated that these costs represented running
the total production facility and could not be traced in any direct manner
to a unit-produced activity, an order-run activity, or even a product line-
supported activity.

Hughes was pleased with Thompson's presentation. "It is always easier
to understand the concept of an activity-based cost system when dealing

with the tangible production of units than when dealing with intangibles, such as design and procurement. Let's summarize what Jim just said. First, the molds and the injection molding machinery can be viewed as nothing more than a bundle of potential units of output, and you, as a group have agreed to trace these costs to the products on a units-of-production method. As long as there is little risk of obsolescence, your method of tracing these costs to the units make sense. Fine.

"Next, the set-up and the grates caused Jim some discomfort, because the cost per unit of an order would depend on the run size. A $1,400 grate for a 20,000-unit order results in a cost of 7 cents per unit; for a 10,000-unit order, it would double. None of you offered any advice to Jim on this problem." Hughes then turned to Conole and asked: "Jane, do you really need the cost per unit to negotiate with your potential customers?"

Jane thought for a few minutes and then lit up. "Of course not. In fact, I'm usually asked to quote a price for the order rather than a price per unit. If Jim can tell me the cost of the order, this would be fine."

"Exactly," said Hughes. "You are now beginning to realize that the purpose of a costing system is not to push all costs down to the unit level. Costs can only be driven to certain levels and to push them any further, using somewhat arbitrary methods, may not make any sense. The key is to design your cost information system so that you can trace costs, by activity, to the level necessary for managerial decision making. The set-up and grate costs are a perfect example of this; there is no need to trace these costs to the unit level. With further work, Jim can probably trace a good portion of the warehouse and EDP costs to the order level. Jane will have the information she needs to effectively negotiate prices with her customers.

"Sadly, I have to say that I do not have all the answers. The facility costs that Jim mentioned—the lease, utilities, and his salary—cannot be traced to a unit, an order, or even a product-line activity level. As Jim stated, they have to do with running the total production process. For now, let's arbitrarily allocate them on a units-of-production basis. Simply total these costs and divide them by the total units of output to arrive at a cost per unit."

The group was not satisfied with this. Hughes seemed happy with this reaction and threw down the gauntlet. "Okay, by now you realize that activities are the key to an effective cost information system. I challenge you to rip these facility costs apart and in six months report back to me what degree of traceability makes sense regarding these facility costs. After all, you are the ones performing the activities!"

The next person to speak was Conole. Her discussion focused on outbound product logistics. After the units were produced, they went to a distribution area. The standard products went to an established customer base and were shipped in reusable containers. Because the production workers were familiar with the process, they did their own quality inspection and the units went directly from the shop floor to a shipping container and to the carrier. The cost per container resulted in a shipping cost of only 9 cents per unit. However, most of the specialty orders had to go through an inspection station. In addition, they often were shipped in odd lots and used various styles of containers. Thus, their costs were substantially greater. Although data to trace these costs were not available, Conole did vow to track these on an order basis in the future. She was, however, comfortable in charging these costs to the product-line level. All shipping costs in excess of the 9 cents per unit times the standard volume, and all quality costs, were charged to the specialty line. Likewise, although data were not available, the "other" costs in the operating expense area were most assuredly chargeable to the unique requirements of specialty orders.

The cost that caused the most controversy was Conole's salary. Her job description indicated that the majority of her time should be spent on finding new business with only a small part spent on managing existing customers. At first, the group thought that they should charge her salary ratably to the cost of units sold, as they did Thompson's. Conole was not so sure. She noted that in 1989 she had spent the majority of her time on speciality orders. "Then charge her salary to the specialty line," the group exclaimed. However, Conole argued that, based on what she had heard over the past two days, she felt she should have been spending more time on the standard units. After the discussion had cycled through many ways to charge her salary, the group finally agreed that if the method of charging her salary was that arbitrary, then maybe they should not charge it at all. A similar conclusion was reached for the cost of professional fees.

By then, it was close to the end of the second day and the group was exhausted but anxious to apply their newfound understanding of their cost structure to the income statements. They agreed that they were at a good stopping point and should save the income statements for the third day.

The Light Dawns

The next day, Hughes entered the room with a laptop computer under his arm. Using a spreadsheet software package and the company's general ledger, he had input the company's total costs for the past two years. He challenged the group to use the operational information they had developed yesterday to trace the total costs down to the level of the two product lines, in as objective a manner as possible.

Throughout the morning, the discussion of the prior day was rehashed but, this time, cost dollars were included. By the lunch break, Hughes's spreadsheet revealed a group consensus on allocation of the overhead costs for the prior two years. There was so much discussion that the group agreed to include an additional column, traceability, which would indicate to what degree these costs could be traced (Exhibits 3.6 and 3.7).

Given the previous day's discussion, the results did not surprise anyone. In fact, most of the group expected what they found—that it was much more expensive to produce a specialty item than originally thought. Of the $1.65 million in the overhead account, which had all been charged to products on a volume basis in 1989, only 56% ([$137,500 + $687,500 + $100,000]/$1,646,000 = 56%) could be directly attributed to the unit-of-output measure. More important, almost 30% of the cost was activity related (the total of the line and order costs divided by $1.65 million) rather than volume related. Twenty-nine percent of overhead costs, or approximately $500,000, had been incorrectly allocated.

At lunch, Thompson stated that this allocation of costs made much more sense than the pure averaging they had been using. Hughes was quick to point out that what they just had done was not technically "allocation." In accounting, one only allocates costs if a direct method of attaching the cost

EXHIBIT 3.6. The Smiling Feline, Ltd., Cost detail by segment—1988.

	Total	Feline Line	Specialty Line	Traceability
Overhead:				
Mold dep.	$ 75,000	$ 56,250	$ 18,750	Unit
Machinery dep.	375,000	281,250	93,750	Unit
Royalty	112,500	112,500	0	Unit
Utilities	36,000	27,000	9,000	Facility
Scrap	78,000	35,000	43,000	Line
Lease	75,000	56,250	18,750	Facility
Thompson	55,000	41,250	13,750	Facility
Green & assistant	35,000		35,000	Line
Other production:				
Set-up	24,000		24,000	Order
Warehouse	20,000	5,000	15,000	Line
Material handling	1,500		1,500	Order
EDP system/software	5,500		5,500	Line
Quality control	3,000		3,000	Order
Total overhead	$895,500	$614,500	$281,000	
Overhead/unit		$2.73	$3.75	
Operating expenses:				
Freight-out	$ 30,000	$ 20,250	$ 9,750	Order
Professional fees	8,000	n/a	n/a	
Conole	45,000	n/a	n/a	
Other costs	29,000		29,000	Order
Total operating	$112,000	$ 20,250	$ 38,750	
Operating/unit		$0.09	$0.52	
Traceable cost/unit		$2.82	$4.27	

EXHIBIT 3.7.   The Smiling Feline, Ltd., Cost detail by segment—1989.

	Total	Feline Line	Specialty Line	Traceability
Overhead:				
Mold dep.	$ 137,500	$ 50,000	$ 87,500	Unit
Machinery dep.	687,500	250,000	437,500	Unit
Royalty	100,000	100,000	0	Unit
Utilities	66,000	24,000	42,000	Facility
Scrap	185,000	30,000	155,000	Line
Lease	100,000	37,000	63,000	Facility
Thompson	70,000	25,000	45,000	Facility
Green & assistant	95,000		95,000	Line
Other production:				
Set-up	108,000		108,000	Order
Warehouse	30,000	5,000	25,000	Line
Material handling	9,000		9,000	Order
EDP system/software	40,000		40,000	Line
Quality control	18,000		18,000	Order
Total overhead	$1,646,000	$521,000	$1,125,000	
Overhead/unit		$2.61	$3.21	
Operating expenses:				
Freight-out	$58,500	$18,000	$40,500	Order
Professional fees	10,000	n/a	n/a	
Conole	65,000	n/a	n/a	
Other costs	30,000		30,000	Order
Total operating	$163,500	$18,000	$70,500	
Operating/unit		$0.09	$0.20	
Traceable cost/unit		$2.70	$3.41	

is not available. What they had done was to use the process flows to trace costs directly to the product lines. The only costs that were allocated were the facility costs, which could not be directly attributed to either line.

Conole then stated that she was interested in tracing some of those "other" costs down to the customer order level, to see how profitable the specialty orders were when all the costs were taken into account. She now feared that some specialty lines might be unprofitable, in which case, the more sales she made, the more money she would lose. Hughes reiterated that they should refine this crude costing system at a future meeting. "Good cost information systems evolve over time; they are not born overnight."

Now that the group was somewhat comfortable with tracing costs, the afternoon was spent developing profitability by line. Revenues were broken out by product line, and material and labor costs were reviewed. This analysis immediately brought two new pieces of information to light. First, the specialty bodies were actually more expensive than the standard ones, and, second, the specialty labor cost was also higher in 1989. Neither Green nor

Thompson had explanations for this, but both agreed that it did make some sense because of the small lots sizes they dealt with at times.

After the analysis from the morning session was added to the spread-sheet (Exhibits 3.8 and 3.9), a quiet fell over the group. For 1989, specialty items were only one quarter as profitable as the standard line, and The Smiling Feline, Ltd. had done everything in its power to move away from the standard line in the past year.

Conole was the first to speak. "I now know why my customers were virtually beating down the door. I obviously had this specialty segment of the market to myself because I was underpricing the product. My God, I'm barely pricing them above cost."

Green and Thompson came quickly to her defense. They said that they were the ones who should have known something was amiss. After all, it was their operations that caused the inequity in costs. They should have challenged the accounting numbers.

They then turned to Hughes. He just shrugged and noted that Doc Webster had hired him to do the taxes, no more. "Doc should have known that you can't run a business in today's world without a top-notch management

EXHIBIT 3.8. The Smiling Feline, Ltd., Segmented income statement for year ended 12/31/88.

| | Feline Line | | Specialty Line | | |
	Entire Line	Per Unit	Entire Line	Per Unit	Total
Sales (units)	225,000		75,000		300,000
Sales ($)	$1,518,750	$6.75	$581,250	$7.75	$2,100,000
Cost of goods sold:					
Rubber	$ 56,250	$0.25	$ 18,750	$0.25	$ 75,000
Bodies	483,750	2.15	191,250	2.55	675,000
Labor	112,500	0.50	37,500	0.50	150,000
Overhead	614,500	2.73	281,000	3.75	895,500
Subtotal	$1,267,000	$5.63	$528,500	$7.05	$1,795,500
Gross profit	$ 251,750	$1.12	$ 52,750	$0.70	$ 304,500
Operating expenses:					
Freight-out	$ 20,250		$ 9,750		$ 30,000
Other costs			29,000		29,000
Subtotal	$ 20,250	$0.09	$ 38,750	$0.52	$ 59,000
Traceable profit					
Margin	$ 231,500	$1.03	$ 14,000	$0.18	$ 245,500
Nontraceable costs:					
Conole					$ 45,000
Professional fees					8,000
Pretax profit					$ 192,500

EXHIBIT 3.9.   The Smiling Feline, Ltd., Segmented income statement for year ended 12/31/89.

	Feline Line		Specialty Line		
	Entire Line	Per Unit	Entire Line	Per Unit	Total
Sales (Units)	200,000		350,000		550,000
Sales ($)	$1,320,000	$6.60	$2,530,000	$7.23	$3,850,000
Cost of Goods Sold:					
Rubber	50,000	0.25	87,500	0.25	137,500
Bodies	430,000	2.15	945,000	2.70	1,375,000
Labor	100,000	0.50	211,500	0.60	311,500
Overhead	521,000	2.61	1,125,000	3.21	1,646,000
Subtotal	$1,101,000	$5.51	$2,369,000	$6.76	$3,470,000
Gross Profit	$ 219,000	$1.09	$ 161,000	$0.47	$ 380,000
Operating Expenses:					
Freight-out	$ 18,000		$ 40,500		$ 58,500
Other Costs			30,000		30,000
Subtotal	$ 18,000	$0.09	$ 70,500	$0.20	$ 88,500
Traceable Profit					
Margin	$ 201,000	$1.00	$ 90,500	$0.27	$ 291,500
Nontraceable Costs:					
Conole					65,000
Professional Fees					10,000
Pretax Profit					$ 216,500

accounting information system. Global competition has made management accounting information a strategic weapon. Without it, you are outgunned."

Doc was a bit embarrassed but quite happy. In three short days, his management team had traveled a great distance. They were now tripping over themselves trying to take the blame for something that was probably his fault. He knew that his main task now was to hire Hughes, but the negotiations were going to be difficult. Hughes knew what he was worth.

At the end of the next week, Jack Hughes was hired as chief financial officer and chief information officer. The only stipulation in his contract was that he allocate less that 10 percent of his time to tax matters.

THE SECOND RETREAT

Doc could not believe the difference. Six months before, when the first retreat convened, this group was at each other's throats. They attended with only one common purpose, to blame each other for their problems. Today, they were actually smiling and congratulating each other!

Jim Thompson began the meeting by reading a "regrets" letter from Mike Green. Green was now actually working only 20-hour weeks and he had scheduled a round of golf for this day. He could only be with them in spirit.

The meeting quickly turned serious. Thompson began. "The 1989 Cost Detail by Segment Report that we produced six months ago really opened my eyes (Exhibit 3.7). By simply going down the columns of numbers, it was obvious that certain activities were killing our profitability, namely, the $155,000 of scrap, the $108,000 of set-up, and the $95,000 cost of Mike's operation. These were all traceable to the speciality line and were caused by the uniqueness of the specialty products that we were running. The set-up costs have been fairly easy to fix. I simply dedicated half of our ten machines to specialty items. This has cut the set-up costs in half because we avoid having to reset the line for the Smiling Feline. We now go from one specialty item to another on these five machines.

"This quickly led to a more focused design for our factory. We are moving toward a mini-factory within our facility, totally dedicated to the standard line. Demand is relatively consistent over the years, so we are now trying to bring inbound bodies straight to the production area. These units are immediately run, containerized, and shipped. We plan to eliminate all warehousing for this product line and are in the advanced stages of implementing this plan. These changes should now make it easier to trace the lease and utility costs directly, using the square footage occupied by each of the two product lines as a cost measure.

"We have also made great strides in attacking the costs of the specialty line. Unique products were killing us. Jane, Mike, and I sat down and went through the scrap and procurement costs on a line-item basis. It became obvious that only the "very" unique products were really hurting us. So, we have moved to a "standard" specialty line. Jane now has a sample case of ten specialty items that we are prepared to run, and she has found that this satisfies the majority of our potential customers. Rather than letting them totally design their own products, we start them with a basic body type—for example, fat body, thin body, long legs, short legs—and let them pick their options.

"Under this new system, I now reuse grates, my scrap is down almost 50 percent, and Mike is playing golf rather than running around qualifying suppliers for one-of-a-kind body styles. We are all satisfied with this new strategy for the specialty line, and it seems to be working. The three items I mentioned should be reduced by 60 percent by the end of the year. It seems so obvious now, but I just never realized this before we started thinking about activities driving costs."

The meeting lasted only a half day rather than the three days of the previous retreat. It focused on how easy and rewarding it was to manage the operations, once the activities revealed the "real" sources of resource consumption.

ACTIVITY-BASED COST SYSTEMS

In the early 1950s, the United States produced close to 80 percent of the world's gross national product (GNP). Faulty information systems did little damage because competition was not intense. In the last two decades, this has certainly changed.

To sustain a competitive advantage in the global marketplace of the 1990s, firms must follow one of two strategies. If they find themselves in a commodity marketplace, they must push themselves to be the low-cost producer. If they decide to differentiate their products, they must make sure that the price the consumer is willing to pay will cover the extra costs they have incurred to differentiate their products. Good cost information is a crucial part of either of these strategies. Firms that spread their overhead costs evenly across their product lines simply cannot compete. Global competition has brought a need for state-of-the-art management accounting information systems. As stated above, information has become a strategic weapon.

In today's world, The Smiling Feline, Ltd., could easily be competing with an Asian or a European Community firm. Imagine that you had been Conole, looking at that 1987 income statement. The cost to produce and deliver your major product was $6.33, and the competition coming into your market was forcing the price down (i.e., the product was becoming a commodity). What would you have done? Add a few more pieces of information to the scenario: A number of customers were clamoring for specialty units and were willing to pay a premium. By 1988, competition had pushed the price down even further and specialty items were obviously almost $2 more profitable (the premium price plus the avoidance of the royalty) than the standard line—at least this is what the accounting information system said. By 1989, the cost per unit on the accounting statement showed that the standard item was now "losing money"; it cost $6.61 to produce but sold for only $6.60. If you were Conole, would you have handed over the standard line, a market that you essentially developed yourself, to your Asian or European competition?

Recent research has shown that many American firms have abandoned lucrative markets because of poor accounting information rather than an inability to compete. Like the experience of the management of The Smiling Feline, intense competition has forced American firms to look not only at their production and distribution systems, but also at their costing system.

Cost accounting systems were initially developed in this country in the early 1800s, during the rise of the textile industry. Because the product was relatively homogeneous, costs were charged to production on a unit-of-output basis. As production processes became more complicated, costs were attached to products based on the factor that caused them to be incurred: labor. Envision the many pictures you have seen of early American industry. Invariably, the pictures show a multitude of workers tending machines. The overhead costs were incurred to support this labor input, and accountants, rightfully allocated this pool of support costs on a labor usage basis. Overhead costs would be accumulated in a pool and divided by the labor hours to arrive at an overhead cost per hour, often only a small percentage of the labor cost.

Now envision a manufacturing environment in today's world. Rather than a multitude of workers, you would probably see only machinery. Lights-out factories (automated factories, with no workers) are a reality. Manufacturing processes have changed dramatically. The majority of American firms today produce a multitude of products using technology as the main production input. Cost accounting systems, however, have changed little over these same 175 years.

It has been estimated that three quarters of American companies still allocate their overhead costs using direct labor as a basis. On average, direct labor in these firms now amounts to less than 10 percent of the product cost! Overhead rates greater than 1,000 percent of direct labor costs are not uncommon.

The system that was developed for The Smiling Feline, Ltd., could be termed a crude activity-based cost system (ABCS). The better managed firms of today are recognizing that the costs they incur are the direct result of the activities they undertake to design, produce, and support their products. If they can identify those activities through process-flow mapping, they can better understand and better manage their resource consumption.

Early ABCS implementations have yielded consistent results. Under a volume-based cost system, high-volume items subsidize low-volume business. High-volume items generate more labor hours and are, thus, burdened with more of the overhead pool. Only after the overhead pool is broken down by activity, and traced accordingly, do the "real" costs begin to be approximated. Again and again, volume has proven to be a poor basis on which to charge overhead costs.

One additional benefit of an ABCS is that it "makes sense." In many firms, manufacturing people pay little heed to the accounting numbers because they do not "make sense." Accounting is a "black box"; costs are fed in and magically allocated to end-units. The box does not capture what is truly happening on the shop floor or in the distribution center. The result is that line management often ignores the cost information or else develops its own "guerilla" cost system, which is considered better matched to the shop-floor situation. Activity-based systems rely on the knowledge of the shop-floor management. Grouping costs by activities is both intuitive and logical, and management has much more confidence in the new accounting systems. In fact, at least two companies have moved their management accounting staff to the shop floor, to better communicate with line managers.

Although first developed as "cost accounting systems," ABCSs are quickly becoming decision support systems. For instance, once Jim Thompson, in the above narrative, had calculated the activity costs, he quickly dedicated a number of machines to the specialty line; he knew, and the accounting system now concurred, that there was a double set-up cost. In addition, this freed the standard-line machines to run continually, thereby pushing the cost of this commodity item as low as possible. Jane Conole could now negotiate price on the specialty orders according to any special accommodations the customer requested. When the accounting system gives managers better information on the cost ramifications of their decisions, they will be better able to manage these decisions. Doc Webster's management team should now run a much more competitive business.

Steps in the Design of an ABCS

1. Establish that your firm's cost accounting problems stem from lack of an ABCS, not from other factors. Initial feedback usually comes from your marketing function: "We cannot compete given our high costs." This can be caused by three factors: your technology is substandard, your operations are inefficient, or your cost accounting information system is obsolete. Ensure that neither of the first two factors is the culprit.

2. Envision your operation as a continuum, from design stage to customer support. Develop process-flow maps for each stage: design, production, distribution, support, etc. Identify activities that are the cause of resource consumption.

3. Trace the functional costs, as reported in the general ledger, to the activities identified by the process maps. Do not be surprised if an activity draws from many different functional areas. For example, an activity such as "support of a product in the product line" may draw costs from both the industrial engineering function and the logistics function. Or, "set-up" may draw from material handling, indirect labor, and tooling. Think of a grid. You are used to thinking of costs in a functional format (column totals); think of them in an activity format (row totals).

Activities	Functions...........................				Activity Totals
·	xxx	xxx	xxx	xxx	XXX
·	xxx	xxx	xxx	xxx	XXX
·	xxx	xxx	xxx	xxx	XXX
·	xxx	xxx	xxx	xxx	XXX
Function Totals	XXX	XXX	XXX	XXX	XXX

4. Develop a costing rate by dividing the total cost for each activity by an appropriate measure of that activity. An appropriate measure is defined as a measure that is constant over the activity. For instance, if all set-ups were relatively the same, the appropriate measure would be simply the number of set-ups. If they vary, however—say, due to complexity—one might use a measure of time (cost per minute of set-up) or of complexity (simple, average, or difficult).

5. Using these costing rates, trace the costs of your operation to the appropriate level: unit, batch/order, product line, facility, or customer. Note, as The Smiling Feline management team discovered, not all costs can be traced to the unit level. But also remember that it is not always necessary to trace the costs to this level. The Smiling Feline found the order level was sufficient for decision making.

6. Facility costs will undoubtedly cause the most problems. Some accountants feel that a cost-versus-price (CVP) model is sufficient. They argue that one can price the products such that the margin (price less direct costs) covers the facility costs plus the desired profit. If you feel that total costs must be calculated, then allocate the facility cost to the units. But do this carefully. For instance, what if the financial accounting system depreciates equipment using a declining-balance method for tax reasons, but the operational flow indicates that a units-of-production method would be more appropriate? The inflated depreciation charge may prove to be a major disadvantage when developing cost information for competitive pricing. You may want to adjust this cost using the units-of-production depreciation method. Likewise, you may want to give thought to using future replacement estimates rather than past historical costs, to value the asset being depreciated.

Above all, remember that you are making a major change in the way your organization processes information. Do not attempt to institute too major a change. Be happy to start the ball rolling. Experience to date has indicated that activity-based systems are well received. Operations people readily accept the concepts integral to this information system. Unlike the black box accounting system, this new system is logical, almost to the extent of being instinctive. Operations people understand that activities consume resources; they see this effect every working day. Once you start the ball rolling, it will gain its own momentum. Most companies have found that, once the initial system is implemented, refinements and extensions naturally flow upward from the people performing the activities that cause the costs to be incurred.

GLOSSARY

Activity-Based Cost System: Accounting cost information system that focuses on the underlying activities that are necessary to produce the product and, in turn, consume the resources.

Allocation: Process by which costs are charged to products. Traditionally, allocation processes are volume-based (e.g., direct labor hours, machine hours, or material dollars); this is only appropriate for process-type production systems.

Cost Driver: Vehicle used to trace (or "drive") cost-pool dollars to cost objects. For instance, a set-up cost pool might be used to cost a production run on a simple driver basis (set-up cost is $30) or on a more detailed basis (complex set-up is $45, typical set-up is $15).

Cost Hierarchy: Various levels within an organization to which one can directly trace a cost. As one moves up the hierarchy from the organization as a whole, to a division, product line, and ultimately a product or customer, it becomes more and more difficult to trace the cost directly. Often, decisions do not require that all costs be directly traced to the top of the hierarchy.

Cost Object: Level within the hierarchy for which a separate determination of cost is desired; may be a customer, an individual product, a distribution channel, a product line, or an organizational unit. For all decisions, one should start by identifying the relevant cost object.

Cost Pool: An aggregation of costs. Traditionally, costs are aggregated along a functional orientation consistent with general ledger accounts (e.g., indirect labor, repairs and maintenance, material handling). Activity-based cost systems pool costs by activity across functional lines (e.g., set-up, order process, machining process). This orientation demands a horizontal view of a company (costs grouped through integration of activities across functions) rather than a vertical one (costs grouped by isolated functions).

Process Maps: Visual depiction of the manufacturing processes, which allows one to "see" activities that cause costs and, thus, to develop cost pools. Process maps should be developed for all aspects of the manufacturing process, from design through customer service.

Traceability: The ability to directly associate a cost with a cost object, as opposed to allocation, which often involves an arbitrary association. The foundation of activity-based costs systems is traceability.

Volume-Based Cost System: Traditional cost system in which costs are allocated to products using functionally aggregated cost pools and volume drivers. For instance, material dollars are often used to drive a material-related cost pool to the unit level; machine hours, to drive a machine-related cost pool; and labor hours, to drive a labor-related cost pool. The more diverse the production process, the more likely it is that this system will distort individual product costs.

FOR FURTHER READING

Cooper, Robin, "Implementing an Activity-Based Cost System," *Cost Management* (Spring 1990).

_____, "You Need a New Cost System When..." *Harvard Business Review* (January–February 1989).

Cooper, Robin, and Robert S. Kaplan, "How Cost Accounting Distorts Product Costs," *Management Accounting* (April 1988).

_____, "Profit Priorities from Activity-Based Costing," *Harvard Business Review* (May–June 1991).

_____, *The Design of Cost Management Systems* (Englewood Cliffs, NJ: Prentice-Hall, 1991).

Ferrara, William L., "More Questions Than Answers," *Management Accounting* (October 1990).

Howell, Robert A., and Stephen R. Soucy, "Customer Profitability," *Management Accounting* (October 1990).

Jones, Lou, "Competitor Cost Analysis at Caterpillar," *Management Accounting* (October 1988).

Shank, John and V. J. Govindarajan, *Strategic Cost Analysis* (Homewood, IL: Dow Jones-Irwin, 1989).

Turk, William T., "Management Accounting Revitalized: The Harley-Davidson Experience," *Cost Management* (Winter 1990).

USING THE COMPUTER IN FINANCE AND ACCOUNTING

4

Brian Forst

Computer hardware and software are essential aspects of contemporary finance and accounting. The data of finance and accounting in the 1990s are, after all, computerized data, and the information that is produced by the company's finance and accounting systems is the product of electronic data processing systems. The success or failure of even the smallest of today's firms frequently revolves around management's understanding of the basics of computerized finance and accounting systems.

Companies rely on computerized financial accounting systems to ensure the reliable recording of transactions and for generation of the basic financial reports: the income statement, balance sheet, and statement of cash flows. Firms use accounting systems to generate invoices, checks, and payroll statements. They rely on computers to process and submit tax information and for planning and control: Creating operating budgets to manage operations by profit and cost centers, creating cash budgets to determine the firm's short-term needs for working capital, and creating capital budgets to support decision making about the firm's mix of fixed assets.

A critical aspect of the firm's business plan is its pro formas, statements of financial expectations that are usually developed using electronic spreadsheets or accounting software. Managers use computers to track the ratios that measure short- and long-term solvency and financial performance.

In this chapter we will examine the foundations of the following essential aspects of financial management: Hardware and software basics, accounting systems in large and small environments, electronic spreadsheets for financial analysis, and advanced computer applications that are transforming financial operations.

84

HARDWARE, SOFTWARE, AND INFORMATION SYSTEMS

Computer systems consist of tangible components, known as hardware, and intangible components, known as software. Computer hardware and software components are integrated under a variety of designs to create information systems. Let's see what each of these is about.

Hardware

The computer itself is the most basic type of hardware. The "brain" of the computer is its central processing unit, or CPU. The CPU manages the input and output of both programs and data between the computer's internal or "main" memory (consisting of hundreds of thousands of addressable cells on silicon chips) and the peripheral storage devices that serve as data warehouses. Each cell contains a "bit" of information, which is represented as 0 or 1. Eight successive bits equals a "byte" of information and permits 256 different permutations of 0s and 1s. This allows a computerized coding of all of the characters on the standard keyboard and several symbols not on the standard keyboard. The CPU also performs the calculations and logical comparisons that are the heart and soul of computing.

Other essential components of the computer are the monitor (or cathode ray tube), which displays information for the user, much like a television screen, and the computer keyboard, similar to a typewriter keyboard, which gives the user direct control over the computer. Personal computers, or PCs, typically come with both floppy disk drives, to permit the loading and storing of programs and data from floppy disks, and hard disks that are installed in the computer chassis (although, technically they are peripheral to the internal functioning of the computer).

Computers are classified by size, speed, data storage capacity, and cost. Mainframe computers are the largest, fastest, most expensive computers that process finance and accounting data. Mainframes typically consist of a large roomful of equipment costing over $1 million. Minicomputers, usually costing tens of thousands of dollars, take up much less space than mainframes: They also process data more slowly and have less internal memory capacity. Microcomputers, typified by the PC, are the desktop or laptop variety of computers that have proliferated throughout the workplace and home. Microcomputers cost anywhere from a few hundred to several thousand dollars; they vary widely in computing speed and capacity, but are generally smaller and slower than minicomputers.

Peripheral equipment that is linked to the computer is also computer hardware. This includes external memory devices (floppy disks, CDs, tape drives, disk packs, data drums); printers (laser printers for fast, high-quality output and dot-matrix printers for low-cost draft copies); modems, for long-distance inter-computer data transfer through telephone lines; cables, which serve as data conduits between the computer and peripheral equipment; and mice, for data entry in graphical applications.

An important development that took hold in the late 1980s and early 1990s is the institution of computer networks. Large-scale computer systems have been largely replaced by computer networks that are faster, more capable, and less expensive than their clunky mainframe predecessors. These networks link smaller computers in a variety of alternative configurations. The basic network configuration consists of a file server or "host" machine that is linked to a number of PC work stations which access data and programs from the host.

Software

Software is the magnetic-coded set of instructions that run the computer. It consists of system software, for computer professionals (e.g., operating systems, programming tools, and utility programs) and application software for end users. Software for finance and accounting is an example of application software; system software is needed to create and manage application software.

The earliest software was written in machine language, computer code consisting entirely of 0s and 1s. In the 1950s and 1960s, computers became accessible to a wider audience with the development of procedural languages such as FORTRAN, COBOL, and BASIC. These programming languages allowed users to control computers with algebraic-like instructions that were translated into the 0s and 1s of machine language, through compilers or translators (important types of system software).

Computer usage mushroomed in the 1980s with the development of user-friendly application software. Word-processing and electronic spreadsheet software led this explosion; these applications permitted PC users to perform a wide range of tasks without any knowledge of computer programming languages. Accounting software, which was fairly cumbersome in the early days of mainframe and minicomputers, became much easier to use with the explosion of PCs in the 1980s.

Information Systems

Hardware and software are configured to perform data processing functions needed by the user. Effective configurations are ones that permit the orderly accumulation, aggregation, and reporting of data so that detailed data can become transformed into useful information. Systems that transform detailed data into useful information are called information systems.

Information systems perform different functions. Some, known as transaction processing information systems (TPIS), are designed to permit the orderly recording of transactions into a data base. Common examples of TPIS include the information systems that retrieve and process the data keyed into the computer on a passenger's arrival at an airport check-in counter, or at a supermarket checkout counter. Another example, one that is the foundation for most finance and accounting systems, is the transactions module of general ledger software. Transactions are recorded in TPIS in one of two modes. The on line or "real time" mode means recording the transaction at the time it occurs, so that the data will always be up to date. In batch mode, transactions are recorded after a series of them have occurred, so that they can be printed and checked for errors prior to entry.

Regardless of whether TPIS data entry is on-line or batch, frequent data back-up procedures are needed to prevent valuable data from being lost to power failures or personnel who inadvertently exit the system before saving data. Backed-up data are usually stored off-site, periodically, to protect against fire, flood, and other hazards.

A second type of information system is the management information system (MIS). Management information systems are ones that produce standardized, periodic reports, typically from the data that are produced by a TPIS. Standard outputs of general ledger software, such as trial balances, income statements, balance sheets, statements of cash flows, statements of retained earnings, and monthly operating budget updates, are the sorts of reports produced by management information systems. So are the monthly customer statements and receivables aging reports that are produced by the accounts receivable module of an accounting system, as well as the periodic reports produced by the accounts payable, payroll, inventory, and fixed-asset modules.

A third type of information system provides more flexible reports in response to one-of-a-kind or other infrequent types of inquiries for information within a data base. This system, aimed specifically at those making management decisions, is called the decision support system (DSS). Created in the 1970s using mainframe and minicomputer technology,[1] decision support systems became widely accessible to mid-level managers and executives in the 1980s, with the advent of electronic spreadsheets in PC environments. Decision support systems permit relatively quick and inexpensive answers to "what-if" questions; questions that can be answered by simulating the effect of a change in one parameter value (e.g., cost of a resource) on other values (e.g., revenues, profits).

Here are some common examples of the sorts of questions that DSS addresses:

- *Marketing.* How will our bottom line be affected if we add three experienced salespersons to our staff, under alternative incentive and salary base assumptions?

- *Capital Budgeting.* How will our needs for external financing change if we expand our operations by 10,000 square feet at $40 per square foot, given our cost of capital, our marginal tax rate, and current cash projections, under three alternative estimates of the effect of the expansion on revenues over a 5-year horizon: optimistic (20% likely), realistic (60% likely), and pessimistic (20% likely)?

- *Aggregate Production Planning.* What should our full-time capacity level be next year, given our starting inventory, our best estimates of monthly demand, and the respective unit production costs of full-time staff, overtime pay, and subcontracting?

Each of these questions can be addressed by extracting data from a large data base, either from MIS reports or from data-base inquiries, and combining these data with estimates of or assumptions about other factors that influence the future. Later in the chapter, we will see how electronic spreadsheets are used to coherently integrate such facts, estimates, and assumptions.

The fourth major type of information system, the executive information system (EIS), aims to provide top management with immediate answers to specific inquiries about organizational detail. The EIS evolved in the late 1980s, after the emergence of user-friendly graphics, seamless system interfaces (software that links disparate systems so that the user is unaware of movement from one system to another), and touch-screen technology (a combination of hardware and software that allows the user to select options displayed on a monitor, simply by touching a point on the screen). The EIS permits the executive to see the latest information on the performance or condition of the organization and to engage in a series of successively more detailed inquiries to obtain deeper insights. A typical EIS dialogue between the executive and the computer is depicted in the following box.

A CONVERSATION WITH AN EXECUTIVE INFORMATION SYSTEM

Computer: Please indicate what you want.

Executive: (Touches "Inquiry" on the screen menu.)

C: Do you wish to inquire about Operations, Finance, Marketing, or something Else?

E: (Touches "Finance.")

Computer:	Would you rather examine financial Performance or financial Condition?
Executive:	(Touches "Performance.")
C:	For what period: a Month, Quarter, or Year?
E:	(Touches "Month.")
C:	Which month?
E:	(Touches "June," the month ending yesterday.)
C:	Profit for June was $1.7 million, up 10 percent from May, and down 3 percent from June last year. Do you want more details?
E:	(Touches "Yes.")
C:	Profits were up from May, due primarily to sales, which are generally 20 percent higher in June than in May. They are down from a year ago primarily because of a 30 percent loss in our Northeast Operations and secondarily because of a 12 percent loss in our Maintenance Services segment. The strongest increases in profits were in the Central region (18 percent over the same month last year) and in the Software Sales segment (15 percent over the same month last year). If you want more details, please point to the item you want more detail about; otherwise touch Graph, Previous Screen, or Main Menu of options.
E:	(Touches "Northeast Operations.")
C:	Profits were down in the Northeast region primarily because of a 15 percent decline in revenues and a one-time writeoff of $15,000 in inventory losses. If you want more details, please point to the item you want more detail about; otherwise touch Graph, Previous Screen, or Main Menu of options.
E:	(Touches "Revenues.")
C:	Revenues were down by 15 percent primarily because of a 23 percent decline in the Boston area and secondarily because of a 21 percent decline in Maintenance Services. If you want more details, please point to the item you want more detail about; otherwise touch Graph, Previous Screen, or Main Menu of options.
E:	(Touches "Main Menu.")
C:	Please indicate what you want.
E:	(Touches "Memo.")
C:	To whom?
E:	(Touches "Director of Northeast Operations" on menu.)
C:	Please enter your message.
E:	"Don, I've just seen your latest revenue numbers for last month, and they're not terrific for either the Boston area or for Maintenance Services in your region. Could you please give me some qualitative information behind the numbers and advise me as to how I can help and as to any action you're taking? Thanks, Amy."
C:	Do you want this memo sent now?
E:	(Touches "Yes.")

Computer:	Memo has been sent. Please indicate what else you want.
Executive:	(Touches "Memo.")
C:	To whom?
E:	(Touches "Director of Central Operations" on menu.)
C:	Please enter your message.
E:	"John, I've just seen your latest revenue numbers for last month. You're #1. Way to go! Amy."
C:	Do your want this memo sent now?
E:	(Touches "Yes.")
C:	Memo has been sent. Please indicate what else you want.
E:	(Touches "Exit system.")

ACCOUNTING SYSTEMS IN LARGE AND SMALL ENVIRONMENTS

Accounting was strictly a manual operation until recently: Transactions were recorded in journals by a person wearing the proverbial green eye shade, and the entries were recorded in ink on buff-colored sheets of paper in a bound book to inhibit alterations. Journal entries were periodically posted to ledgers. Ledger accounts were balanced and closed at the end of each period. The closing amounts of each T-account in the general ledger were used to create a trial balance. If the numbers all checked out, the trial balance amounts were used to manually create the four primary financial statements—the income statement, balance sheet, statement of cash flows, and statement of retained earnings—all in accordance with generally accepted accounting principles (GAAP).

Today, the basic elements of this accounting structure have been maintained, with transactions recorded in journals, posted to ledgers, and aggregated in financial reports. However, the formerly all-manual process has given way to extensive computerization. Consider the modern supermarket as an extreme example. Transactions are recorded automatically at the point of sale as the customer goes through the checkout counter, with the use of a bar-code reader, which scans each product sold. The information about each sale is immediately converted to (1) a receipt for the customer, (2) a transaction record in the individual store's sales journal, which is posted to the general ledger, and (3) the record of inventory reduction in the inventory module, with restocking orders generated for individual items when inventories decline to predetermined levels.

Regardless of the extent of computerization or the size of the organization, accounting systems must accomplish a variety of critical tasks. They must perform the basic functions of general accounting: recording, classifying, and summarizing financial transactions and events according to GAAP, so that the information can be interpreted both for internal management and for external financial reporting purposes. They must have clear audit trails to permit a tracking of the flow of data through the system from the transaction to the financial report. Audit trails provide dates and unique system-generated numbers for tracing transactions in a general ledger report, both forward and backward, from the source document and individual who recorded the transaction, to the financial statement. These systems must also support budgeting, tax reporting, and financial analysis.

Accounting System Modules

From the smallest to the largest of organizations, contemporary accounting systems typically consist of an integration of separate modules. The central module is the general ledger, a data base organized around the organization's chart of accounts. The chart of accounts provides details about six basic categories of general ledger accounts: assets, liabilities, equity, revenues, cost of goods sold (or cost of sales, in service organizations), and operating expenses. The general ledger takes transactions in double-entry format (debits and credits) either directly or through another module, posts information about each transaction in the appropriate general ledger accounts, and generates the four primary periodic financial reports—income statement, balance sheet, statement of retained earnings, and cash flow statement.

Other modules are linked to the general ledger. The accounts receivable module is organized around the customer. It generates sales orders, whenever customers place orders with the company; billing statements, either periodically or soon after the sale; and customer status reports either periodically or as needed. It also generates aging reports that show how many accounts (and their dollar amounts) are less than 30 days old, how many are between 31 and 60 days old, how many are between 61 and 90 days old, and how many are more than 90 days old—information that is critical for the effective management and collection of receivables.

The accounts payable module, organized around vendors, is the flip side of the accounts receivable module. It generates purchase orders to vendors; checks to vendors at time of payment; discrepancy reports, to show differences between the items and amounts on purchase orders sent to vendors and the invoices received from them; aging reports to support the management of payables; and cash requirement forecasts by due date, to minimize interest costs without jeopardizing vendor relations.

The payroll module processes employee time sheets and generates payroll checks and statements to employees and taxing authorities. The amounts shown on these statements are based on each employee's pay rate, overtime provisions, authorized deductions (for health insurance, voluntary pension contributions, and so on), income tax information (federal, state, and local), and current social security tax rates and ceilings.

The inventory module, critical in manufacturing and merchandising settings, provides information needed both for financial reporting and for management purposes. It calculates the cost of goods sold for the firm's income statement and the inventory level reported on the firm's balance sheet. In manufacturing operations, the inventory module processes data on raw materials, work in process, and finished goods. As a management tool, the inventory module generates inventory status reports: These provide detailed periodic reckoning of inventory items, to support the management of both purchasing and production. It also calculates the economic order quantity (the order size that minimizes the sum of holding costs and ordering costs); generates periodic usage reports, which provide important information about how much material has been used in each production center, to provide a basis for minimizing waste; and produces inventory reconciliation reports for firms that use perpetual inventory systems.

Other frequently used accounting system modules include fixed assets, to account for the depreciation of existing capital assets and the purchase of new ones, and job costing, to keep track of costs (labor, material, equipment, subcontracting, and overhead) and profitability on a job-by-job basis.

These modules are typically purchased from and installed by a vendor. The selection of the vendor can be as important as the selection of the software. It is generally best to use vendors with experience in installing the software in settings similar to your firm's, and to protect the firm with a contract that stipulates that the system will work as promised by the vendor and that the vendor will provide support as needed.

The similarities between the finance and accounting systems of large and small corporations end at this point. Next, we will examine some fundamental differences between accounting systems in large and small organizations.

The Large Corporation

Finance and accounting systems are as different from one large corporation to another as are the organizations themselves. Corporations differ as to the nature of the business, the nature of the transactions between parent and subsidiary entities within the corporation, sophistication of computing equipment and data bases, linkages between financial and nonfinancial data bases, top management interest in and support of the accounting and management information functions, and the somewhat random way in which accounting and nonaccounting systems tend to evolve in organizations. The corporation's stand on each of these dimensions can have a profound impact on the shape, complexity, comprehensiveness, and effectiveness of its finance and accounting systems.

Certain basic characteristics of automated systems that support the finance and accounting function in large corporations can nonetheless be identified. One is the scale of operations and sheer magnitude of transactions, which typically requires a mainframe or minicomputer-based accounting system. As capable as microcomputer systems have become in the past several years, the need for substantial computing power is still very much a reality in the large corporation.

Another essential characteristic of finance and accounting systems in large corporations is the need to integrate these systems with automated systems for the management of operations: These are systems that are needed to plan production schedules by product and stage of production and to determine orders for raw materials. Material requirements planning (MRP) software, or a more sophisticated alternative, the manufacturing resource planning (MRP II) system, is often integrated with just-in-time inventory systems to create complex hybrid systems. Sophisticated MRP II systems are usually capable of automatically ordering inventory, recording transactions in accounting systems, and generating associated paperwork. These hybrid systems are frequently linked to the marketing, strategic planning, and accounting systems. Such integrated systems are complex and expensive to construct and maintain: They are generally far more elaborate than those needed by small companies.

An important aspect of this complexity is a greater extent of unique, home-grown software in large organizations. Most corporations have a staff of programmers to develop and maintain software in house. These programmers adapt the software as the need for integration with new corporate hardware and software arises, debug it as errors become evident, enhance it as opportunities present themselves, and document it so that others can understand how to maintain it. Large corporations rarely get by on commercially available, packaged software.

The scale and complexity of the hardware and software in large corporations, and the need to integrate finance and accounting systems with other systems, combine to induce a need for greater coordination among individuals responsible for the effective performance of these systems. In a small organization, one or two people may have primary responsibility for a finance and accounting system; in a large organization, a change in the system can significantly affect the operations of the controller, the director of data processing, the director of operations, the director of planning, and a host of other corporate executives.

Large corporations deal with this complexity by structuring their analysis of computer systems under a process known as system analysis. System analysis is needed periodically, as the organization's needs and available technology changes. It is also needed whenever the organization's executives wish to consider a system change, or whenever one organization merges with, or is acquired by, another organization using a different accounting system.

System analysis consists of the orderly assessment of three essential factors:

1. The organization's information requirements
2. Its existing hardware and software configurations
3. The cost, availability, and characteristics of superior technology not currently in use in the organization.

Knowledge of the organization's information requirements, usually delineated by each report that is needed, and its existing hardware and software, is obtained through interviews with the primary users of the information, together with observations of how the information is produced and used. Questionnaires can also be useful for obtaining comprehensive and systematic information about the perceived strengths and weaknesses of existing reports and information processes.

The system analysis process typically rates each alternative configuration under consideration by scoring the option across a variety of characteristics: functional capabilities, speed, ease of use, capacity, flexibility, cost, compatibility with existing hardware and software, quality of support, documentation, and training. Each of these characteristics can be assigned a weight so that options can be assessed in terms of both the score and importance of each attribute.

A system analysis must include more than the organization's requirements for information alone. It must also consider the organization's needs for security of data and software. Data must be protected against modification by unauthorized personnel. It must also be kept confidential, to protect both the privacy of individuals and the proprietary nature of corporate information in a competitive environment. Corporate data and the software must also be protected against sabotage, either by disgruntled employees or by outsiders.

Proper system security consists of the use of passwords that give the user access only to information that is needed by that user. Password codes are designed to be difficult for unauthorized users to discover. They do not appear on the screen as the user keys them in; they are changed from time to time, especially whenever there is reason to suspect that an unauthorized user has gained access; and the terminal shuts down when two successive invalid access codes are keyed in.

In addition to system security, system analysis associated with any significant conversion must also consider the needs for training personnel in the use of new systems. Systems in widespread use are sometimes accompanied by on-line, self-study programs. While some formal training is generally essential, automated training tends to be less expensive, and is often more effective than training programs that rely exclusively on human trainers.

Once a system is selected, the installation is managed using standard project management tools, such as the Program Evaluation and Review Technique (PERT) and the Critical Path Method (CPM). Such tools are useful for determining how to allocate resources to each installation task, when to begin each task, and how long it will take to complete the installation. Installation problems are especially common when different vendors are involved in system installation or conversion. Such problems can be reduced by ensuring accountability: This is accomplished by requiring that all vendor agreements be confirmed in writing.

The new system, once it is installed, is typically run in parallel with the old system for several months, to ensure that the new system is producing accurate results. While switching systems without parallel operations may shorten conversion time, the risk that the new system will produce fatal errors is too great: this "cold turkey" approach to system conversion should not be used.

The Small Organization

Small organizations, like large ones, must have their basic finance and accounting needs served. The relative simplicity and standard nature of these needs in small organizations, generally means that all of the organization's finance and accounting needs can be served by purchasing microcomputers, sometimes connected in local area networks, and by relying on packaged software from vendors. Unlike large accounting systems that run on minicomputers or mainframes, most commercially available accounting software for microcomputers has been well tested, with users numbering in the thousands. These systems tend also to be much easier to use than their large system counterparts: They come with good documentation and context-sensitive help screens.

Standardization applies not only to basic hardware and software configuration options, but to such details as the chart of accounts as well. Basic systems have been designed for each major type of business setting, from dental offices and law firms to auto repair shops and beauty salons. These systems are quite flexible, permitting the user to adapt a standard chart of accounts and standard report formats to the particular needs of the user.

Some vendors sell a niche market item, such as a particular brand of accounting software; others offer completely integrated hardware and software systems. The latter systems, known as "turnkey" systems (basic idea: you buy the system, plug it in, and turn it on), are typically more expensive than systems in which the individual components are purchased separately; but they can save the purchaser the time and aggravation associated with system design. Turnkey systems have generally been well tested, so errors and malfunctions are rare. In the event that something does go wrong with the system, the purchaser needs to deal with only one vendor.

Other characteristics of small organizations influence their needs for financial computing systems. They often lack in-house accounting specialists, and thus need simple, easy-to-master system designs, sometimes at the expense of flexibility and comprehensiveness. Small firms are often closely held; run by owners who are familiar with the detailed operations of the organizations. This tends to limit the need for details in the automated financial system. The firms generally have limited budgets: Budgets that call for simple, no-frills computer hardware and software.

ELECTRONIC SPREADSHEETS
FOR FINANCIAL PLANNING AND ANALYSIS

Financial planning has long required the use of spreadsheets to test the impact of prospective organizational decisions and policies on bottom-line measures of performance and condition. Clearly, it is better to do such testing using a model before committing the firm's scarce capital to a prospect that may turn out, under careful scrutiny, to be inferior.

The use of spreadsheets was vastly facilitated in the 1980s with the development of PC-based programs such as VisiCalc®, Lotus 1-2-3®, Excel®, and Quattro®. These software packages have become much more widely used than the procedural language programs of the 1960s and 1970s. They are extremely popular largely because they have removed the need for the programming middleman. They give the user the ability to perform all of the basic computer functions—data input and output, data organization and reduction, graphing, and labeling—without the need to master a cryptic coded language, such as COBOL or PASCAL. These spreadsheets have shortened the distance between corporate data and the executive and have induced managers to "download" data from mainframe and minicomputer environments into microcomputers, where the data can be more readily used for planning and analysis.

The spreadsheet is built around a grid of multiple rows and columns. Each cell in the grid can contain a number, a label, a formula that refers to other cells in the spreadsheet, or a "macro" (i.e., a command that allows the user to perform any particular sequence of keystrokes to be used repeatedly). For example, the contents of a cell in a row labeled "Gross Profit" for an accounting period would be a formula; one that subtracts whatever number is in the cell that represents "Cost of Goods Sold" for the period from whatever number is in the cell that represents "Revenues."

The power of the electronic spreadsheet is largely that it eliminates the need for an eraser. Since spreadsheet formulas refer to the contents of cell locations rather than to the numbers themselves, the formulas do not have to be altered when the numbers in the cells referred to change. It is this feature of spreadsheets that makes them so well-suited to perform "what-if" analysis. Electronic spreadsheets are used in a variety of other applications, including the development of pro forma income statements and balance sheets and the determination of cash requirements.

An illustration of a simple spreadsheet to produce pro forma income statements and balance sheets is shown in Exhibit 4.1. Pro forma reports are

EXHIBIT 4.1. Pro forma income statements and balance sheets created on an electronic spreadsheet.

	A	B	C	D	E	F	G
1	Assumptions:						
2	a. Annual revenue growth				20%		
3	b. COGS as a % of revenue				65%		
4	c. Operating expenses as a % of revenue				15%		
5	d. Federal tax as a % of pretax profit				30%		
6	e. New equity per year				$ 0		
7	f. Annual asset growth				25%		
8	g. Annual dividends				$ 0		
9	– –						
10							
11							
12	INCOME STATEMENTS: CURRENT YEAR & 5-YEAR PROJECTION						
13	($ '000)						
14		Current	Year	Year	Year	Year	Year
15		Year	1	2	3	4	5
16	Sales	220.0	264.0	316.8	380.2	456.2	547.4
17	Cost of goods sold	140.0	171.6	205.9	247.1	296.5	355.8
18	Gross profit	80.0	92.4	110.9	133.1	159.7	191.6
19	Operating expenses	35.0	39.6	47.5	57.0	68.4	82.1
20	Pretax profit	45.0	52.8	63.4	76.0	91.3	109.5
21	Federal tax	20.0	15.8	19.0	22.8	27.4	32.9
22	Net profit	25.0	37.0	44.4	53.2	63.9	76.6
23							
24							
25	BALANCE SHEETS: CURRENT YEAR & 5-YEAR PROJECTION						
26	($ '000)						
27		Current	Year	Year	Year	Year	Year
28		Year	1	2	3	4	5
29	Assets	130.0	162.5	203.1	253.9	317.4	396.7
30	Liabilities	51.0	46.5	42.8	40.4	40.0	42.7
31	Stock	10.0	10.0	10.0	10.0	10.0	10.0
32	Retained earnings	69.0	106.0	150.3	203.5	267.4	344.0

projected financial reports, commonly prepared by businesses and given to banks, to assist the banks in determining whether to advance a credit line, as well as the terms and amount of credit. Note that the assumptions underlying the projections are listed conspicuously at the top of the spreadsheet, so that the user can quickly see the effect of altering any assumption on the numbers of primary interest.

The spreadsheet shown in Exhibit 4.1 makes a variety of assumptions in order to determine how much corporate debt will be required each year to support a 25 percent annual growth in corporate assets. Under the assumptions shown in the assumption box, the spreadsheet indicates that no new corporate debt will be needed. Indeed, if all goes as assumed, liabilities will decline from a current level of $51,000 to $42,700 in five years.

EXHIBIT 4.2. Pro forma income statements and balance sheets with spreadsheet formulas for two years.

	A	B	C	D	E
1	Assumptions:				
2	a. Annual revenue growth				20% |
3	b. COGS as a % of revenue				65% |
4	c. Operating expenses as a % of revenue				15% |
5	d. Federal tax as a % of pretax profit				30% |
6	e. New equity per year				$ 0 |
7	f. Annual asset growth				25% |
8	g. Annual dividends				$ 0 |
9	− −				
10					
11					
12	INCOME STATEMENTS: CURRENT YEAR & 1-YEAR PROJECTION				
13	($ '000)				
14			Current		Year
15			Year		1
16	Sales		220.0	+B16+($E$2*B16)	
17	Cost of goods sold		140.0	+$E$3*C16	
18	Gross profit		+B16−B17	+C16−C17	
19	Operating expenses		35.0	+$E$4*C16	
20	Pretax profit		+B18−B19	+C18−C19	
21	Federal tax		20.0	+$E$5*C20	
22	Net profit		+B20−B21	+C20−C21	
23					
24					
25	BALANCE SHEETS: CURRENT YEAR & 1-YEAR PROJECTION				
26	($ '000)				
27			Current		Year
28			Year		1
29	Assets		$130.0	+B29+($E$7*B29)	
30	Liabilities		51.0	+C29−C31−C32	
31	Stock		10.0	+B31+$E$6	
32	Retained earnings		69.0	+B32+C22−$E$8	

If you recreate this spreadsheet on a computer, you will discover you can instantly examine the effect of a given change in any assumption. For example, a 5 percentage-point change in revenue growth does not have the same effect as a 5 percentage-point change in cost of goods sold, operating expenses as a percent of revenues, or the rate of asset growth. An annual revenue growth of only 15 percent would cause liabilities to be $78,900 in Year 5, 85 percent higher than if revenue growth were 20%. If annual revenue growth were only 10 percent, liabilities would be $110,900 in Year 5: under that scenario, $59,900 of additional debt would be required. If the annual cost of goods sold was 70 percent instead of 65 percent, or if annual operating expenses were 20 percent instead of 15 percent, debt would be $111,450 in Year 5. If the rate of asset growth was 30 percent instead of 25 percent, liabilities would be $147,950 in Year 5. Thus, the user can instantly see precisely what any change in the assumptions will do to the bottom line. The spreadsheet formulas that produce these results for the current year and for the first year of the projection are shown in Exhibit 4.2.[2]

Another common use of electronic spreadsheets is to analyze capital budgeting alternatives. Suppose, for example, a manager must decide whether to purchase or lease an asset, such as a truck. The truck can be

EXHIBIT 4.3. Should the firm purchase or lease a truck?

	A	B	C	D	E	F
1			PURCHASE OPTION			
2						
3		Loan			Tax	After-
4		Cost	Depre-	Pretax	Benefit	Tax
5	Year	(10%)	ciation	Cost	(34%)	Cost
6	1	$9,000	$20,000	$29,000	$9,860	$19,140
7	2	7,000	20,000	27,000	9,180	17,820
8	3	5,000	20,000	25,000	8,500	16,500
9	4	3,000	20,000	23,000	7,820	15,180
10	5	1,000	20,000	21,000	7,140	13,860
11						
12					@NPV(.12,F6..F10) = $60,592	
13						
14						
15			LEASE OPTION			
16						
17		Loan			Tax	After-
18		Cost	Lease	Pretax	Benefit	Tax
19	Year	(10%)	Cost	Cost	(34%)	Cost
20	1	$1,000	$25,000	$26,000	$8,840	$17,160
21	2	1,000	25,000	26,000	8,840	17,160
22	3	1,000	25,000	26,000	8,840	17,160
23	4	1,000	25,000	26,000	8,840	17,160
24	5	1,000	25,000	26,000	8,840	17,160
25						
26					@NPV(.12,F20..F24) = $61,858	

purchased for $100,000, with a 5-year note, in monthly payments totaling $20,000 annually, in repayment of principal plus 10 percent interest on the unpaid balance. Or it can be leased for $25,000 per year, with the company financing each year's lease expense with a 10 percent (on unpaid balance) loan, paid in monthly installments. If the truck has a zero salvage value at the end of 5 years and is depreciated on a straight-line basis, and if the firm is in the 34 percent tax bracket and uses a 12 percent hurdle rate to discount future amounts, what should the manager do? The answer: run the numbers through an electronic spreadsheet, using the net present value criterion (see Chapter 9. The analysis, shown in Exhibit 4.3 on page 99, reveals that the firm minimizes the net present value of costs by purchasing the truck, rather than leasing it.

ADVANCED COMPUTER APPLICATIONS IN FINANCE AND ACCOUNTING

The notion that computers might be able to emulate human thinking—artificial intelligence—has captured the imagination of science fiction writers and their readers for decades. Artificial intelligence software has become nonfictional on a fairly large scale in the 1990s, and much of this technology has entered the domain of finance and accounting. Artificial intelligence systems known as "expert systems," because they encode the rules used by the experts who handle factual information, have become the most widely used type of artificial intelligence systems.

Expert systems are more useful as finance and accounting advisors than conventional computing software because they offer solutions to a broad range of problems in a variety of general domains. Because they are designed for use by nonexperts in those domains, they are more widely accessible than conventional software. Thus, they make the knowledge of a few available to many; knowledge that can be put to use quickly, easily, and in the absence of a human expert.

Expert systems are used by the largest accounting firms:

- Coopers and Lybrand in tax auditing
- KPMG in assisting banking clients to assess their loan portfolios and detect probable losses
- Ernst & Young in audit planning and in the interpretation of the rules for value added tax collection in international operations
- Arthur Andersen and Company to analyze mortgage loans and financial statements[3]

Expert systems are used to give advice in a variety of financial applications. They are used by Chase Manhattan Bank to help reduce losses in corporate loans,[4] by American Express to give advice in credit authorization decisions, by the Securities and Exchange Commission to analyze financial statements, by the Bank of America to assist in validating letters of credit, and by Texas Instruments to analyze capital expense proposals.[5] They are used also to assist in the management of cash flow, in the determination of allowance for bad debts, in the control of inventory, in the evaluation of a firm's internal controls, in estate planning,[6] in portfolio management, in investment planning, and in auditing.[7]

How do expert systems work? They are not like conventional computing software, which is based on algorithms—mathematical formulas or step-by-step procedures for solving a particular type of problem. Expert systems capture and represent expertise heuristically in a "knowledge base," and arrive at recommendations by applying that body of knowledge to the facts of a particular case, using an "inference engine" to control the logic. The expertise is obtained by interviewing one or more experts in a particular "knowledge domain," such as inventory management or assessment of credit worthiness. The facts are keyed into the expert system for each new case under consultation; the inference engine causes the system to ask only those questions that are relevant in light of the responses to previous questions. The system offers advice when sufficient information has been provided. Well-designed expert systems also provide reasons for the advice given, at the request of the user—just as any competent consultant would.

CONCLUSION

As the end of the twentieth century approaches, a single generation of humankind has witnessed several generations of computer hardware and software. Computing speeds and capacities have taken great leaps forward, while the costs of computers have plummeted. Software has become infinitely more effective and user-friendly. This unprecedented revolution in information processing has transformed the worlds of finance and accounting. Technologies such as optical scanning, fiber optics, and touch screens have allowed accounting and finance processes to become fully automated, subject to human intervention. This intervention is needed to control errors and fraud and to process exceptions to the rule.

Have these developments reduced the need for humans? By most accounts, they have increased the need for labor, not decreased it. Extensive human energy is required, both to ensure proper internal controls, so that the occurrence of undetected errors and irregularities—deliberate misstatements of accounting figures to conceal wrongdoing—is minimized, and to maintain the software, so that it functions properly at all times and is efficiently adapted to changes in hardware and other software in the system.

Although the nature of the work is totally different from the world of accounting just two decades ago, these functions are every bit as labor-intensive as the accounting function of the past.

The speed and accuracy with which finance and accounting data are processed today easily justify the costs associated with the hardware, software, and labor of computerized finance and accounting information. These benefits have been accompanied by some sensational problems—sophisticated computer crimes, viruses created by high-tech vandals, and bugs that have disabled financial processing and threatened to bring down entire companies. Even these problems, however, are fairly small when measured against the overwhelming benefits that have accompanied the computerization of finance and accounting. Rapid change in information technology is sure to continue, presenting additional opportunities and challenges for everyone with financial responsibilities.

GLOSSARY

Application Software: Software for end users, as distinct from system software; examples include accounting software, spreadsheet software, and word processing software.

Arithmetic and Logic Unit: The component of the central processing unit that performs calculations and logical comparisons among data entities.

Audit Trail: The existence of procedures that permit a transaction to be traced through all stages of information processing, from its appearance on a source document through its transformation into information on a final report.

Auxiliary Memory: Memory that is peripheral to the computer's main memory; auxiliary memory includes hard disks, floppy disks, compact disks (CD ROM), data tapes, and data drums.

Bit: The smallest element of data, represented as a 0 or 1 in computer memory.

Byte: A series of eight consecutive bits, permitting the representation of a character (letter, number, or symbol).

Capital Budgeting: Analysis of the organization's options to expand or economize operations—options that affect the organization's fixed assets—usually conducted on an electronic spreadsheet. Examples include decisions to diversify operations, purchase a supplier, buy or lease space, or replace aging equipment.

Central Processing Unit (CPU): The "brain" of the computer, including its internal or main memory, the controller, the arithmetic/logic unit, and a "bus" that moves data within the CPU.

Computer Network: Integrated computer systems, workstations, and communication links.

Controller: The component of the central processing unit that regulates traffic, moving data in and out of the computer.

Decision Support System (DSS): An information system that provides flexible reports in response to one-of-a-kind or other infrequently requested inquiries for information, aimed specifically to support planning, analysis, and decision making.

Electronic Spreadsheet: A type of computer software useful for planning; the electronic spreadsheet allows the user to enter, calculate, organize, and analyze data in a rows-and-columns format.

Executive Information System (EIS): An information system that aims to provide top management with immediate answers to specific inquiries on organizational detail, typically using user-friendly graphics, touch screens, and software that links disparate systems, so that the user is unaware of movement from one system to another.

Expert Systems: Computer-based systems that codify human knowledge and emulate human inference processes to derive conclusions in a variety of decision-making settings, including the review of credit applications, auditing, and financial analysis.

General Ledger: A computerized data base (or book) containing detailed information about an organization's assets, liabilities, equity, revenues, and costs.

Hardware: Physical aspects of the computer, including the computer itself, monitor ("screen" or cathode ray tube), keyboard, modem, disks, tapes, printers, and cables.

Information Systems: Configurations of hardware and software to perform specific data processing functions needed by the user; includes transaction processing information systems, management information systems, decision support systems, and executive information systems.

Local Area Network (LAN): A computer system consisting of hardware, software, and communication links, connecting devices within an office.

Machine Language: Computer code consisting entirely of 0s and 1s; first generation computer software, which can be read directly by the computer.

Main Memory: A primary component of the central processing unit, consisting typically of hundreds of thousands of addressable cells on silicon chips.

Mainframe Computers: Large, fast computers, typically costing over $1 million.

Management Information System (MIS): A computer system that produces standardized, periodic reports, extracted and organized from a database.

Manufacturing Resource Planning (MRP II) Software: Software that supports the planning of production schedules, usually capable of automatically ordering inventory, and linked to the firm's accounting, marketing, and strategic planning systems; an advanced version of material requirements planning software.

Material Requirements Planning (MRP) Software: Software that supports the planning of production schedules and the ordering of raw material inventory.

Microcomputers: Small (desktop or laptop), relatively slow computers, typically costing between $1,000 and $10,000; also known as personal computers PCs).

Minicomputers: Mid-sized, fairly fast computers, costing tens (occasionally hundreds) of thousands of dollars.

Modem: A device for long-distance data transfer between computers through telephone lines; "modem" is short for "modulator-demodulator," which refers to the conversion of data from computer-readable signals to signals suitable for data transmission over the telephone.

Procedural Languages: Programming languages such as FORTRAN, COBOL, and BASIC, which consist of algebraic-like instructions that are translated into the 0s and 1s of machine language through compilers or translators (important types of system software).

Software: A set of magnetically coded instructions that are carried out by computers to perform a specific function or task.

Spreadsheet: A worksheet consisting of rows and columns.

System Analysis: Analysis of the organization's information processing needs and options for satisfying them.

System Software: Software designed for computer professionals; examples include operating systems, programming tools, and utility programs. System software is needed to create and manage application software.

Transaction Processing Information System (TPIS): An information system that permits the orderly recording of transactions in a data base; examples include point-of-sale processing systems and airline passenger check-in systems.

FURTHER READING

Blissmer, Robert H. *Introducing Computers: Concepts, Systems, and Applications* (New York: John Wiley & Sons, 1991).

Gelinas, Jr., Ulric J., Allan E. Oram, and William P. Wiggins, *Accounting Information Systems* (Boston: PWS-KENT, 1990).

Long, Larry, *Introduction to Computers and Information Processing*, 3rd ed. (Englewood Cliffs, NJ: Prentice-Hall, 1991).

Moscove, Stephen A., Mark G. Simkin, and Nancy A. Bagranoff, *Accounting Information Systems: Concepts and Practice for Effective Decision Making*, 4th ed. (New York: John Wiley & Sons, 1990).

Acknowledgment: The author gratefully acknowledges the thoughtful comments of Professor Frank Segel on a draft of this chapter.

BUDGETARY CONTROL ANALYSIS: TECHNIQUES FOR MEASURING PRODUCTIVITY

5

Michael F. van Breda

"Control is what we need. Cost control. And urgently." said owner-manager Ernest Wylie with great emphasis to his management team. "Just a glance at these reports tells me that our costs are going up faster than our revenues. We won't survive much longer on that basis."

"Well, we could try using cheaper inks and lower quality paper," said Ken Hutchison, production manager of Wylie Printing.

"That's not the answer," exclaimed marketing manager Roy Goslett. "We're having a hard enough time selling as it is in this depressed market. If we start to produce an inferior product, our sales will tumble even further. Nobody is going to pay our prices and take cheaper quality."

"Roy's right," said Ernest. "Our aim should not be to reduce costs so much as to control them. Remember that we have a goal to meet in this organization—to produce the best quality products that we can. If we don't keep our eye on that goal we won't be effective as an organization.

"What I am really after is efficiency. I want to see us produce quality products as cheaply as possible, but I don't want us to produce cheap products. We must improve productivity.

"To get the ball rolling, I want Ken to draw up a set of standards for production. Then we'll have an idea whether the production staff is working efficiently or not. If we have those standards in hand, then we can check how much our product should be costing us. And we'll be able to compare that with what the product actually cost. Checking the difference between actual and standard will tell us where our big variances are. With that information in hand, we should be able to make some significant inroads into getting our costs under control and improving our productivity."

"Agreed," responded Roy. "People will pay for a quality product provided it is competitively priced. We've just got to make sure that we're working as efficiently as our competition and we'll be fine. That means, when we draw up a price quote, we need to be able to come in at or below their quote."

"That's all very well for you to say," said Ken, feeling a little aggrieved. "You're not the one who has to draw up these productivity standards. I've tried doing this before and it's not easy. For starters, everyone seems to want perfection."

With that, the meeting broke up. Ken went back to his office, realizing that he was not quite sure where to begin. For one thing, he hadn't shared the fact that he had not succeeded in his last attempt to install a standard cost system. What chance did he have this time? He decided to call a friend of his, Jenny Ryan, who had just completed her MBA.

"Jenny, I need your help badly. My boss is after a set of production standards, and I don't know what to do or where to begin!"

BUDGETARY CONTROL

Defining Standards

That evening Ken went over to Jenny's home where she produced her cost accounting text. "Tell me everything you think I need to know about standard costs."

"OK! First, Ken, let's get straight what we mean by a standard, and why we're calculating it. A standard is a basis of comparison, it's a norm if you will, or a yardstick. Some like to compare it to a gauge, which measures efficiency.

"But a standard is more than that really because it is also the basis for control. Standards enable management to keep score. The difference between standards and actuals directs management's attention to areas requiring its efforts. In that sense, standards are attention getters. They form the heart of what is known as management by exception. That's the concept that one does not watch everything all the time: instead, one focuses ones attention on the exceptions, the events that are unexpected."

Ken smiled knowingly. "I've experienced this and it's terrible. My boss at my last job never noticed the good job that I did every day. But, when something went wrong, he was down like a shot to bawl me out!"

"That is one of the traps of managing by exception," said Jenny. "But you're smart enough as a manager to know that people need to be rewarded for their regular jobs. You also know that the exceptions are highlighted so that you can help them remedy things—not shout at them."

Types of Standards

"Then you have to realize," Jenny went on, "that there are different kinds of standards. First, you have your basic standards. These are the ones that are unchanging over long periods of time. Many of these are captured in policy statements and may reflect things like the percentage of waste that is permitted, or the amount of time one might be away from a work station. Basic standards are not much use in forming costs, though, because the work environment tends to change too much.

"At the other extreme, there are theoretical or ideal standards. These get set by engineers and are the ideals for which one is expected to strive. These are the standards that I think you feel are unrealistic."

"Hear! Hear!" broke in Ken, "My guys would never take that—that's the perfection mentality I was telling you about."

"But," asked Jenny, "aren't the Japanese always striving toward ideal standards?"

"True, but the difference between them and us is that their system of lifetime employment provides a more supportive atmosphere in which they can strive for perfection and not feel they are going to get fired if they don't quite make it this time around. It's not enough to look at standards in isolation. One must view them in the context of total management."

"Right!" said Jenny approvingly. "And that means that your best norms to develop are probably those called currently attainable standards. These are standards that can be met, but still represent a challenging goal. Let me read you a quote.

> Such standards provide definite goals which employees can usually be expected to reach and they also appear to be fair bases from which to measure deviations for which the employees are held responsible. A standard set at a level which is high yet still attainable with reasonably diligent effort and attention to the correct methods of doing the job may also be effective for stimulating efficiency.[1]

I think that's the kind of standard you are after."

"You're right. And, I tell you there are real advantages to standards set at this level. My guys find them very motivating. Also, when it comes time to costing jobs out for pricing purposes, we have a reasonable shot at making those standards. Of course, that wouldn't stop us from trying for perfection. It's just that we wouldn't have management breathing down our necks when we didn't make it."

Budgets

"Tell me one more thing though. Why do we have to go to all this bother to develop standards. Why can't top management just use last year's numbers? That will give them a base for comparison."

"True," said Jenny. "But you've got to remember that last year's actuals reflect last year's circumstances. Things may have changed this year so much that last year is not a fair comparison. How would you like it if they didn't adjust your materials budget for inflation, but expected you to produce as much this year as you did last year?"

"OK, you've made your point. But, why can't they just get our controller to draw up a budget at the start of the year? Why do I have to get involved?"

"Two reasons. One is that the controller can't draw up a budget without standards. Standard costs are the unit costs that go into a budget. The budget contains your standards multiplied by the expected volume of sales provided by the marketing department."

"The other reason you need to get involved is that the budget needs to be adjusted for volume. You want them to evaluate you on the basis of a flexible budget, as opposed to a static budget. The only way to be fair to people is to use a flexible budget. Look at these numbers, for instance." She jotted down the numbers appearing in Exhibit 5.1.

"Notice how the budget is drawn up in the first column: you estimate the volume for the year and multiply it by the estimated unit selling price or the estimated unit cost , the standard cost. Fixed costs are fixed, of course, and are just inserted into the budget. The last column shows the actual revenues and costs: to get them, you multiply the actual selling price or the actual unit cost by the actual volume. The middle column shows the estimated selling price and the estimated unit costs multiplied by the actual volume.

EXHIBIT 5.1. Static versus flexible budgets.

	Budget (Static)	Budget (Flexible)	Actual
Volume in units	1,000	1,200	1,200
Revenues	$10,000 @$10/unit	$12,000 @$10/unit	$11,400 @$9.50/unit
Variable costs	5,000 @$5.00/unit	6,000 @$5.00/unit	5,400 @$4.50/unit
Fixed costs	4,000	4,000	4,680
Net income	$1,000	$2,000	$1,320

"Note that the only difference between the flexible budget in Column 2 and the static budget in Column 1 lies in the volume being used. The static budget uses the expected volume, while the flexible budget uses the actual volume. In other words, the difference between flexible and static may be attributed to changing activity levels. It is, therefore, dubbed an activity variance.

"The unit price and cost terms for the actual revenues and costs in Column 3 differ from the corresponding price and cost terms for the flexible budget in Column 2; however, the activity level is the same: both use the actual level of sales. In other words, the difference between actual and flexible may be attributed to changes in prices and costs. These differences are dubbed price variances. Let's summarize the definitions of these terms."

Activity variance = static budget – flexible budget
Price variance = actual results – flexible budget
Activity index = static budget/flexible budget
Price index = actual results/flexible budget

"Now look what happens if all you have is the budget from the beginning of the year. The variable costs, for which you are responsible, are $400 above budget. You could reasonably expect to have your boss down here chewing you out for not controlling your costs. But, if you know your unit costs, you can adjust the budget for volume, and give him the number in the second column. That shows that you actually got your costs down by $600. Let me show you what I mean in more depth."

With that, Jenny started to prepare Exhibit 5.2. First she compared the actual results with the original budget, the static budget. She derived the percentage change by dividing the actual by the budget, subtracting one from the result, and multiplying the remainder by 100. For instance, in the case of revenue:

Step 1. 11,400/10,000 = 1.14
Step 2. 1.14 − 1 = 0.14
Step 3. .14 ×100 = 14 percent

Negative percentages accompany indices that are less than 1.

Price Indices

"If you examine Panel A of Exhibit 5.2," Jenny said, "you will see that the reason for the sharp 40 percent increase in profit lies in the relatively sharp revenue increase of 14 percent. This happened despite the increase in variable and fixed costs. The increase in profits might be interpreted as showing the superior ability of the sales staff.

EXHIBIT 5.2.   Comparing the budgets.

Panel A
Actual versus Static Budget

	Static Budget	Actual	Indices	Percentage Change
Revenue	$10,000	$11,400	1.14	14
Variable costs	5,000	5,400	1.08	8
Contribution	$ 5,000	$ 6,000	1.20	20
Fixed costs	$ 4,000	$ 4,680	1.17	17
Net income	$ 1,000	$ 1,320	1.32	32

Panel B
Actual versus Flexible Budget

	Flexible Budget	Actual	Indices	Percentage Change
Revenue	$12,000	$11,400	0.95	(5)
Variable costs	6,000	5,400	0.90	(10)
Contribution	$ 6,000	$ 6,000	1.00	0
Fixed costs	$ 4,000	$ 4,680	1.17	17
Net income	$ 2,000	$ 1,320	0.66	(34)

Panel C
Static versus Flexible Budget

	Static Budget	Flexible Budget	Indices	Percentage Change
Revenue	$10,000	$12,000	1.20	20
Variable costs	5,000	6,000	1.20	20
Contribution	$ 5,000	$ 6,000	1.20	20
Fixed costs	$ 4,000	$ 4,000	1.00	0
Net income	$ 1,000	$ 2,000	2.00	100

"The fallacy of this interpretation is apparent when you look at Panel B, which compares the flexible budget with the actual results. Now you can see that, after adjusting for sales activity, variable costs actually showed a steep decline rather than the increase shown in Panel A. In other words, with a volume of 1,200 units, as opposed to 1,000, you should budget more for variable costs than at first expected. The $6,000 is the more appropriate budget figure. But when you compare the actual cost of $5,400 against the flexible budget, you find a decrease of 10 percent. With the activity effect eliminated, all of this rise must be must be attributed to a rise in variable costs. More precisely, budgeted unit variable costs equal $5.00 and actual unit variable costs equal $4.50. Dividing the actual cost of $4.50 by the budgeted variable cost of $5.00 yields an index of 0.90, or a percentage decrease of 10 percent.

"The apparent rise in revenues shown in Panel A melts away in Panel B; the apparent rise in variable costs shown in Panel A also melts away in Panel B. The result is a whole new story. Volume rose, perhaps due to the efforts of the sales staff, but probably due to the fall in the selling price. Fortunately," she said, with a broad grin on her face, "this was offset by the heroic efforts of the production staff in lowering their unit costs by 10 percent."

"I like that heroic part," said Ken, approvingly.

Activity Indices

"Now look at Panel C. This compares the static budget with the flexible budget. Now the only factor to change is sales activity, so the percentages measure the change in the number of units sold. As there is only one measure of activity, it is not surprising that all the activity-based indices show an increase of 20 percent, i.e., 200 units in 1,000. Fixed costs, though, are independent of activity levels. Net income, which is a combination of activity-related and activity-independent numbers, shows a decline that reflects its mixed nature."

Market Effects

"The rise in volume may, or may not, be attributable to good management. One possibility is that it was driven by an increase in the total market. For instance, one can imagine that the larger market expected 8,000 units in sales. The company was expecting to get 12.5 percent of the market. If one now assumes that the market grew to 12,000 units, then the company's sales of 1,200 units actually represents a decrease in market share. Writing this out more formally:

$$\text{Sales activity index} = 1,200/1,000$$
$$= (10\% \times 12,000)/(12.5\% \times 8,000)$$
$$= 0.80 \times 1.50$$

In other words, given this scenario, the sales staff should be queried on why they had a decrease of 20 percent in their market share, in a market that increased 50 percent."

Summary

"Finally, let's try to summarize what we have learnt to this point. First, note that Panel B confirms that the price index in any variance computation can be derived by dividing the actual figure by the static budget figure. Panel C demonstrates that the usage index can be derived by dividing the static figure by the flexible figure. In short, the relationship between the overall index of the change from budget to actual is given by:

$$\begin{aligned} \text{Overall index} &= \text{actual/static} \\ &= (\text{actual/flexible}) \times (\text{flexible/static}) \\ &= \text{price index} \times \text{activity index} \end{aligned}$$

To summarize, then, in the example shown in Exhibits 5.1 and 5.2, one has the following relationships:

$$\begin{aligned} \text{Overall index} &= \text{Price index} \times \text{Activity index} \\ \text{Revenue:} \quad 1.14 &= 0.95 \times 1.20 \\ \text{Variable cost:} \quad 1.08 &= 0.90 \times 1.20 \\ \text{Fixed cost:} \quad 1.17 &= 1.17 \times 1.000 \end{aligned}$$

So, as you can see, the pieces fit together quite logically. The points underlying these pieces can be summarized quite briefly."

1. First, we saw the need to distinguish between basic, ideal, and currently attainable standards.
2. Second, we saw the wisdom of distinguishing flexible from static budgets.
3. Third, we noted that our standards are the foundation stones on which these budgets are based.
4. We noted that all cost variances follow one simple formula: Actual cost − Budgeted cost = Standard cost variance.
5. Activity variances = static budget − flexible budget

   Price variances = actual results − flexible budget.

   Activity indices = static budget/flexible budget

   Price indices = actual results/flexible budget.
6. Flexible budgets adjust variable costs and their variances for volume.
7. Volume has no effect on fixed costs or the variances derived from fixed costs.

VARIABLE COSTS BUDGETS

"That's fine, but what am I going to do with these variances?" Ken asked a little impatiently. "Everything that I've seen so far may help top management, but it's not much help to me."

"Good point, Ken. That's why we need to examine productivity, which is the relationship between inputs and outputs. We'll enhance your productivity and your control over costs, if we can focus on the elements that go into making up your costs."

Jenny began to explain how in a typical cost accounting system, the variable cost of a product or service is a function of:

1. The hours of labor (both direct and indirect) that go into it
2. The units of material that are used
3. The other components of overhead
4. The unit cost of each of these items

"Let's call the amount of input that goes into one unit of output the productivity rate. For instance, one might need 500 sheets of paper and 16 minutes of labor to produce a ream of letterhead. The material productivity rate is 500 sheets per ream; the labor productivity rate is 16 minutes per ream. When the expected cost of the inputs are attached to the expected productivity rates, a standard cost results. The productivity rates themselves are also known as standards. They are typically established by engineers."

As before, Jenny began sketching a numerical illustration of the points that she was making. Her sketches appear in Exhibit 5.3. "These are the standards," she said, "that determine the variable portion of the budget for production. Note the assumption here that variable overhead is a function of direct labor hours. Other assumptions are possible but we will stick with this one in our example.

EXHIBIT 5.3.   Standards for letterhead paper.

Material:	
Budgeted productivity rate	= 500 sheets/ream
Budgeted cost per unit of input	= $0.04/sheet
Actual productivity rate	= 500 sheets/ream
Actual cost per unit of input	= $0.035/sheet
Labor:	
Budgeted productivity rate	= 0.30 hr/ream
Budgeted wage per hour	= $5.00/hr
Actual productivity rate	= 0.25 hr/ream
Actual wage per hour	= $6.00/hr
Variable overhead:	
Budgeted productivity rate	= 0.30 hr/ream
Budgeted cost per unit of input	= $5.00/hr
Actual productivity rate	= 0.25 hr/ream
Actual cost per unit of input	= $5.00/hr
Fixed overhead:	
Budgeted fixed cost	= $4.00/ream
Actual fixed cost	= $3.90/ream

"Fixed overhead is a little different because it does not really have a productivity rate. Let's just put down the unit fixed overhead on a budgeted and an actual basis, and we can come back and discuss the details later." With that, she inserted $4.00 per ream for the budget figure, based on $4,000 divided by 1,000 units and $3.90 for the actual figure, based on $4,680 divided by 1,200 units.

From these standards she began to derive the standard and actual costs of the product.

$$\begin{aligned}
\text{Standard cost} &= \text{Material cost} + \text{labor cost} + \text{variable overhead cost} \\
&\quad + \text{fixed overhead cost} \\
&= (1{,}000 \times \$0.02) + (0.30 \times \$5.00) + (0.30 \times \$5.00) + \$4.00 \\
&= \$2.00 + \$1.50 + \$1.50 + \$4.00 \\
&= \$9.00
\end{aligned}$$

$$\begin{aligned}
\text{Actual cost} &= \text{Material cost} + \text{labor cost} + \text{variable overhead cost} \\
&\quad + \text{fixed overhead cost} \\
&= (1{,}000 \times \$0.175) + (0.25 \times \$6.00) + (0.25 \times \$5.00) + \$3.90 \\
&= \$1.75 + \$1.50 + \$1.25 + \$3.90 \\
&= \$8.40
\end{aligned}$$

She then used these numbers to show how the budgeted and actual variable costs in Exhibit 5.1 were derived.

For the static budget:

$$\begin{aligned}
\text{Material costs} &= \$2.00 \times 1{,}000 = \$2{,}000 \\
\text{Labor costs} &= \$1.50 \times 1{,}000 = \$1{,}500 \\
\text{Variable O/H} &= \$1.50 \times 1{,}000 = \$1{,}500 \\
\text{Total variable costs} &= \$5{,}000
\end{aligned}$$

For the flexible budget:

$$\begin{aligned}
\text{Material costs} &= \$2.00 \times 1{,}200 = \$2{,}400 \\
\text{Labor costs} &= \$1.50 \times 1{,}200 = \$1{,}800 \\
\text{Variable O/H} &= \$1.50 \times 1{,}200 = \$1{,}800 \\
\text{Total variable costs} &= \$6{,}000
\end{aligned}$$

For the actual costs:

$$\begin{aligned}
\text{Material costs} &= \$1.75 \times 1{,}200 = \$2{,}100 \\
\text{Labor costs} &= \$1.50 \times 1{,}200 = \$1{,}800 \\
\text{Variable O/H} &= \$1.25 \times 1{,}200 = \$1{,}500 \\
\text{Total variable costs} &= \$5{,}400
\end{aligned}$$

Material Indices

Jenny also used the standards in Exhibit 5.3 to show Ken how indices for each of the variable components could be determined. First, they considered the material costs.

$$
\begin{aligned}
\text{Material index} &= \text{Actual costs/flexible budget} \\
&= \$2,100/\$2,400 \\
&= (\$0.0175 \times 1,000 \times 1,200)/(\$0.02 \times 1,000 \times 1,200) \\
&= (0.0175/0.02) \times (1,000/1,000) \\
&= 0.875 \times 1.00 \\
&= 0.875
\end{aligned}
$$

$$
\begin{aligned}
\text{Usage index} &= \text{Actual productivity rate/budgeted productivity rate} \\
&= 1,000/1,000 \\
&= 1.0000
\end{aligned}
$$

$$
\begin{aligned}
\text{Cost index} &= \text{Actual unit cost/budgeted cost} \\
&= \$0.0175/0.02 \\
&= 0.875
\end{aligned}
$$

The material portion of the variable cost dropped \$2.00 per unit to \$1.75 because of a decline in the unit cost of paper, i.e., there was a 12.5 percent reduction in the cost of paper. No efficiencies were gained or lost in the use of the paper.

Labor Indices

Jenny performed an identical analysis for labor costs.

$$
\begin{aligned}
\text{Labor index} &= \text{Actual costs/flexible budget} \\
&= \$1,800/\$1,800 \\
&= (\$6.00 \times 0.25 \times 1,200)/(\$5.00 \times 0.30 \times 1,200) \\
&= (6.00/\$5.00) \times (0.25/0.30) \\
&= 1.20 \times 0.833 \\
&= 1.00
\end{aligned}
$$

$$
\begin{aligned}
\text{Efficiency index} &= \text{Actual productivity rate/budgeted productivity rate} \\
&= 0.25/0.30 \\
&= 0.8333
\end{aligned}
$$

$$
\begin{aligned}
\text{Wage index} &= \text{Actual unit cost/budgeted cost} \\
&= \$6.00/\$5.00 \\
&= \$1.20
\end{aligned}
$$

The labor portion of the variable cost remained static at $1.50 because of a 16.67 percent increase in efficiency in the use of labor, offset by a 20 percent increase in hourly wages.

"You'll realize that what we have here," said Jenny, "is a great way to measure increases in productivity. The president keeps on talking about how our productivity is falling. One way to counteract that is to check how efficiently people are working. Before you measure physical productivity, though, you have to eliminate the wage effect, which is just what we have done here."

Variable Overhead Indices

Finally, Jenny repeated the analysis for variable overhead costs, showing that:

$$\text{Variable OH index} = \text{Actual costs/flexible budget}$$
$$= \$1{,}500/\$1{,}800$$
$$= (\$5.00 \times 0.25 \times 1{,}200)/(\$5.00 \times 0.30 \times 1{,}200)$$
$$= (\$5.00/\$5.00) \times (0.25/0.30)$$
$$= 1.00 \times 0.833$$
$$= 0.833$$

$$\text{Efficiency index} = \text{Actual productivity rate/budgeted productivity rate}$$
$$= 0.25/0.30$$
$$= 0.8333$$

$$\text{Rate index} = \text{Actual unit cost/budgeted cost}$$
$$= \$5.00/\$5.00$$
$$= \$1.00$$

The overhead portion of the variable cost fell from $1.50 to $1.25 because of the 16.67 percent increase in labor efficiency. Unlike direct labor, this was not offset or assisted by a change in the variable overhead rate.

Review

By now it was apparent that Ken was beginning to tire, so Jenny suggested that they do a quick review and then take a break.

"One last question, Jenny—where do these variable overhead rates come from?"

"That's another subject," said Jenny. "Do you want a cup of coffee? I'm bushed. But before we break, let's summarize what we've learnt."

1. The cost of a product consists of material, labor, plus overhead.
2. Each of these components is made up of a productivity rate multiplied by a unit cost for that component.

3. Standard costs equals standard productivity rates times standard unit costs.
4. Actual costs equal actual productivity rates times actual unit costs.
5. The price indices equal actual unit costs divided by standard unit costs.
6. The activity indices equal actual productivity rate divided by standard productivity rate.

COLLECTING STANDARDS

After their coffee break, Jenny and Ken discussed how to develop these standard costs. Jenny reminded Ken that standard costs are made up of two parts: A standard cost per unit and a standard usage or quantity of units of input; these are multiplied together. She pointed out that it was his responsibility to define the amount of material and labor that should go into the product. It was the responsibility of the purchasing department to determine the amount that should be paid for materials, and it was up to the personnel department to determine wages. She explained that there are several ways to determine the appropriate usage.

Engineering Studies

"First, you can do an engineering study. In other words, you can look at the specifications of the product. Many products that are designed by engineers have quite detailed and explicit instructions on what materials should go into them. These standards often include an allowance for waste, although this is not necessary. When they do not include such an allowance, they border on the ideal.

"To take an obvious example, most automobiles have one battery and an engineering statement would state this. A perfection standard would call for one battery per automobile. On the other hand, when it comes to actual production, it would not be unusual for one or more batteries to be damaged during installation. On average, then, it might appear as if automobiles actually had 1.1 batteries. One might, therefore, want to set as one's standard a currently attainable goal of 1.05 batteries; thus providing a 5 percent allowance for waste.

Time and Motion Studies

"Time and motion studies are the usual way in which engineering standards are set for the labor component. An engineer watches over the employees as they work and determines how much time it should take for each part of the production process. When doing this, it is vital that one gain the employees' cooperation. If it is not obtained, disastrous results can occur. I love the following quotation."

> ...You got to use your noodle while you're working and think your work out ahead as you go along! You got to add in movements you know you ain't going to make when you're running the job! Remember, if you don't screw them, they're going to screw you! ...Every moment counts!

> ...When the time-study man came around, I set the speed at 180. I knew damn well he would ask me to push it up, so I started low enough. He finally pushed me up to 445, and I ran the job later at 610. If I'd started out at 445, they'd have timed it at 610. Then I got him on the reaming, too. I ran the reamer for him at 130 speed and .025 feed. He asked me if I couldn't run the reamer any faster than that, and I told him I had to run the reamer slow to keep the hole size. I showed him two pieces with oversize holes that the day man ran. I picked them out for the occasion! But later on I ran the reamer at 610 speed and .018 feed, same as the drill. So I didn't have to change gears.[2]

Ken smiled appreciatively at the story. As an old floor hand, he understood the sentiments completely.

Motivation

"This raises a broader question, you know," said Ken. "Should we invite people to participate in setting the standards? Will it make them more motivated? I've pondered this from a variety of different angles. What's so interesting about it is that participation doesn't always work.

"What I have discovered from my reading on the topic is that many people prefer to be told what to do. This seems to be particularly true for people who find their jobs boring and for those with a more authoritarian personality. So one has to be really careful when inviting people to participate."

"You know more about this than I do," responded Jenny. "How do you handle feedback then? That's a sort of after-the-fact participation isn't it?"

"Well, everything that I have read—and my own experience for that matter—indicates that timely feedback is essential and a good motivator. People really need to know and to know as soon as possible how they have done. That's especially true when they have done a good job, because it really builds their self-esteem. And in some cases, it makes them want to participate more before the fact.

"Of course, I must not lead you to think that a little participation and a lot of feedback is all one needs. These are what the psychologists call intrinsic motivators. People need these, but they also need extrinsic motivators like better pay for doing a better job.

"The other problem that one encounters is that the more you focus people's attention on one goal, the more they tend to ignore other goals. It's only human nature: Ask sales people to increase their turnover and they will sell goods at a loss.

"That's one of the reasons I have had misgivings about calling in a bunch of engineers to set standards. It is much easier to time how long a job should take and reward people for quantity than to measure and to reward quality. I really rely upon the innate good sense of my staff to provide quality products. Too much emphasis on measurement can make my task of maintaining quality much more difficult."

Past Data

"In that case," Jenny said, "an easier way to get the data you need for your business is to go back over your past records to see how much time various jobs have taken and how much material was used in the past. Some of that will have to be adjusted for changes in machines, changes in personnel, different kinds of material, and so on. But you know all that better than I do.

"But enough for now. Come on over tomorrow night, and we can talk some more. We do need to discuss fixed overheads."

FIXED COST BUDGETS

"Fixed costs," Jenny said, after they had gathered together again, "are both easier and more difficult to control than variable costs. They are easier because there are no components into which to break them. Their variance is simply: Actual fixed costs minus budgeted fixed costs. Their index is simply: Actual fixed costs divided by budgeted fixed costs. In our case, the budgeted fixed costs were $4,000 and the actual fixed costs were $4,680. The variance was simply $680, which means a percentage increase of 17 percent. Fixed costs are more difficult to control than variable costs because one cannot create an illusion of control through the elaborate computation of price, mix, and usage variances or indices."

"How then does one control fixed costs?" asked Ken.

"First, one must recognize that if costs are truly fixed, there is no reason to control them. Consider depreciation costs as an example. Once one has purchased an item, the total depreciation costs are set—unless one disposes of the machinery, in which case a disposal cost will substitute for the depreciation cost. No control is possible here. The control in this case has to be exerted when the machinery is purchased. Thereafter, it is a sunk cost which cannot be controlled. In other words, controlling fixed costs is a matter of timing.

"It is also a matter of scale. Consider the machine again. Assume it has a capacity of 1,000 boxes of greeting cards per day. Its cost is certainly fixed within this range. However, if the analysis is being done in terms of tens of thousands of boxes, and if the corporation has a hundred of these machines, then it is possible to think of this as a variable cost. One can ask, in other words, what the cost would be to produce an additional "unit" of 1,000 boxes.

"This last example highlights the fact that most fixed costs are only fixed within the context of a particular analysis. Consider, for instance, the ink you use in production. Assume its price is reset by a cartel every three months. Assume also that its planned usage is reset at the same time. A budgetary control system that computed variances every month and set the budgeted price and quantity to that of the latest quarter might show a variance of zero each month. This might lead everyone to believe that they were dealing with a fixed cost. However, were the same analysis to be done on an annual basis, with prices and quantities set at the start of the year, a substantial variance would arise. The example points up the old truism that all costs are variable in the long run.

"The example also points up the need to set your net large enough to catch the fish you want to catch. Many fixed costs cannot be controlled by a monthly or even an annual budget system because they change too slowly. One needs a coarser net, i.e., an annual, or triennial, or an even longer budgetary system, to capture their change. The reverse is also true. A net that is too fine can capture a great deal of random noise. Consider, for instance, a product whose price fluctuates randomly around a fixed mean. If all you want is to see the true exceptions then you should set the net to capture only those fluctuations that are greater than a certain number of standard deviations away from the mean.

"In short, fixed costs are best controlled in the long run and at a more aggregate level. In other words, it is important in the budgetary control of fixed costs to establish appropriate time and space horizons for one's analysis."

"Most of that's pretty obvious," said Ken. "What you haven't yet told me is where the $4 overhead rate that you put in Exhibit 5.3 fits into the whole picture."

"Well, it does and it doesn't," responded Jenny. "The rate itself comes from knowing the total fixed overhead and dividing it by the volume, i.e., $4,000 divided by 1,000 units. In that sense, fixed overhead rates are residuals—unlike variable overhead rates which are primary: Variable overhead is computed by multiplying the variable overhead rate by the volume.

"Variable overhead rates are used in computing variances and indices. Fixed overhead rates are completely ignored in this context. Their main purpose is to give you an estimate of the total product cost. So they fit in when calculating unit costs; they don't fit into budgetary control systems. But let's talk about standard cost systems and all this may become clearer."

STANDARD COST ACCOUNTING SYSTEMS

"Companies rarely enter their budgets into their ledgers," Jenny said. "Usually budgetary control takes place outside of the company books. In other words, the budget is typically drawn up using spreadsheets outside of the general ledger system. At the end of the period under investigation, the actual results are drawn out of the ledger and transferred to the spreadsheet where the comparisons are done. Two exceptions to this general rule occur."

Government Accounting

"The first does not affect private companies, but does affect state and local governments. It is common practice, in their accounting systems, to enter budgeted numbers into the ledgers in reverse order to an actual number. For instance, city governments will enter budgeted revenues as follows.

    dr Revenue (with budgeted sales)
        cr Accounts Receivable (with budgeted sales)

As sales are made, they are entered into the books in their usual order.

    dr Accounts Receivable (with actual sales)
        cr Revenue (with actual sales)

The effect is that at the end of the year, only variances are left in accounts. For instance, sales greater than expected would leave a credit variance."

Standard Variable Costs

"The second exception involves so-called standard cost systems. In a typical implementation, the standard cost of a product is entered into the work-in-process account, although an actual cost is incurred. The difference between the two creates a variance. For example, in the case of variable production costs, the journal entry for a single unit of product would read:

    dr WIP $5.00
        cr Sundry asset and liability accounts $4.50
            Variance   0.50

The existence of a credit variance indicates that the budgeted unit cost exceeds the actual unit cost, i.e., there is a favorable variance. Were the variance a debit, one would have an unfavorable variance.

"Over the course of a year, the entry to work-in-process would be:

```
dr WIP              $6,000
    cr Sundry asset and liability accounts   $5,400
        Variance                              600
```

Note that the entry to work in process is the flexible budget amount. The difference between the charge to work in process and the actual cost credited to sundry asset and liability accounts is the same $600 we saw in Exhibit 5.1. These variable costs may be traced back to material, labor, and variable overhead effects. In fact, the journal entries would probably have read:

```
dr WIP              $2,100
    Material variance     300
    cr Direct material    $2,400

dr WIP              $1,800
    cr Direct labor     $1,800

dr WIP              $1,800
    cr Overhead      $1,500
        O/H variance    300
```

Each of these variances is identical to the variances computed above; each can be stated in percentage terms to indicate its relative size: e.g., material costs are down 12.5 percent, labor costs are even, and variable overhead costs are up 16.67 percent. The key point is that variances generated by a standard cost system are identical to those generated by a budgetary control system, once one removes the volume effect."

Standard Fixed Costs

"Unfortunately, the parallels between standard cost systems and those of budgetary control systems do not extend to fixed costs," Jenny continued. "The reason for this lies in the way in which fixed costs are applied to products. In a standard cost system, a predetermined fixed overhead rate is established at the start of a period, by dividing the budgeted fixed overhead by the budgeted volume. In our case, the predetermined fixed overhead rate was $4,000 divided by 1,000 units, which gave the $4.00 per unit found in Exhibit 5.3. Given that each product takes an estimated 0.30 hours, one can write this as $13.33 per hour.

"Fixed overhead is then applied to goods as they are produced, by multiplying the predetermined overhead rate per hour by the number of standard hours in each product. In our example, one simply charges $4.00 of fixed overhead to each product. The total amount of fixed overhead charged this way can be computed by multiplying the predetermined overhead rate on a per product basis by the actual number of products produced. In our case, the result is $4,800. This is known as the applied overhead. The journal entry would be:

```
dr WIP            $4,800
   cr Overhead       $4,680
      O/H variance      120
```

The net overhead variance in the ledger is:

$$\text{Actual overhead} - \text{applied overhead} = \$4,680 - \$4,800$$

But the only variance one is interested in is:

$$\text{Actual overhead} - \text{budgeted overhead} = \$4,680 - \$4,000$$

The difference between the variance produced by a standard cost system and the variance we want for budgetary control purposes is:

$$\text{Budgeted overhead} - \text{Applied overhead} = \$4,000 - \$4,800$$
$$= (\$4 \times 1,000) - (\$4 \times 1,200)$$

In short, the error in the fixed overhead variance appearing in a standard cost system is due to volume changing from 1,000 units to 1,200 units. Stated otherwise, the standard cost system should have used an overhead rate of $3.33 ($4,000/1,200). It did not, and the result is a variance in the standard cost system that is useless for control purposes.

"The budgeted overhead will only be equal to the applied overhead when the actual volume equals the budgeted volume. Since this rarely happens, the fixed cost variance found in the ledger is of little interest for budgetary control. Instead, one should compute the spending variance directly and simply ignore the net overhead variance written in the books."

"Now, I see why you ignored the fixed overhead when doing the variances originally," said Ken. "Let's hope that my management understands this as well as you do."

BUDGETARY CONTROL REVISITED

Budgetary control, as we noted at the outset, consists of comparing actual results with budget estimates.. When doing this, one is advised to distinguish between revenues and costs that vary with volume, and those that are fixed with respect to volume changes. A revised budget, adjusted for the actual volumes rather than the predicted volumes, yields a flexible budget as opposed to the original or static budget.

Since the static and the flexible budgets for fixed costs are identical, the fixed cost spending variance is simply the difference between the actual and the original budget. The fixed cost spending index is their quotient.

In the case of variable costs and revenues, a few simple rules emerge. The ratio between the flexible and the static budgets indicates the difference in the quantities expected and the quantities actually experienced. The ratio between the actual results and the flexible budget indicates the change in costs or revenues that can be attributed to changes in unit cost or selling price.

In the case of multiple outputs or multiple inputs, the quantity indices can be further refined. They break into at least two indices. The first reveals the effect of changing mixes of either outputs or inputs. The second reveals the effect of changing the overall volume. The mix variance may be computed directly or simply by dividing the quantity index by the volume index. In the case of variable costs, it is usually possible to draw out another index, indicating the total yield, i.e., the amount of input required to produce a given amount of output.

All these indices can be computed using an accounting system that collects only actual costs and comparing these in a spreadsheet with the budgeted costs. Alternatively, they may be derived by keeping a standard cost system. The variances that emerge as one enters standard costs into work in process and credits the corresponding asset or liability account at actual are identical to those derived from a flexible budgeting control system. The one exception to this is fixed costs, but the difference here is easily reconciled.

In short, budgetary control analysis provides one with a vehicle for controlling one's business. The budget represents, ideally, one's strategies and objectives. As actual results emerge, they are compared with the budget to see to what extent the enterprise has met its goals and productivity targets. Any differences encountered can be broken down into components to determine whether it was due to a change in usage or a change in price. Where inputs or outputs are substitutable, one can also examine the changing mix for further insight into how one achieved one's goals.

In each case, the index derived is neither good nor bad. It simply indicates a change. As noted earlier, the same rise in sales may be a matter for congratulation, when markets are declining, and a matter for concern, when markets are expanding faster than one's sales. All that the index does is to highlight areas where more information needs to be gathered.

GLOSSARY

Budgets: Projected financial statements reflecting the plans of the organization. If they adjust for volume they are called flexible; otherwise they are static.

Effectiveness: The degree to which a goal is met; efficiency measures the inputs needed to produce a given level of output in pursuit of a goal.

Labor Variances: Measure the change in the cost of labor, analyzed according to wage changes and changes in labor productivity.

Material Variances: Measure the change in cost of materials used, analyzed according to price changes and changes in material efficiency.

Overhead Variances: Measure the change in the cost of overhead items, analyzed according to price and salary changes and changes in labor productivity.

Productivity: Output divided by input. Productivity rates measure the input required for a unit of output.

Standards: Predetermined, expected levels of efficiency. A standard cost is the predetermined cost of an input per unit of output. Standards may be unchanging (basic), perfect (ideal), or currently attainable.

Variances: Measure the difference between actual costs and standard costs. They are favorable if costs are less than expected and unfavorable otherwise. Variances may be analyzed by looking at the effect of changing prices (price variances) or changing usage (quantity or usage variances).

FOR FURTHER READING

Anthony, Robert N. and James S. Reece, *Accounting: Text and Cases*, 8th ed. (Homewood, IL: Richard D. Irwin, 1989).

Davidson, Sidney and Roman L. Weil, *Handbook of Cost Accounting* (New York: McGraw-Hill Book Co., 1978).

Ferris, Kenneth R. and J. Leslie Livingstone, eds., *Management Planning and Control: The Behavioral Foundations* (Columbus, OH: Century VII Publishing Company, 1989).

Horngren, Charles T. and Gary L. Sundem, *Introduction to Management Accounting*, 8th ed. (Englewood Cliffs, NJ: Prentice-Hall, 1990).

Kaplan, Robert S., *Advanced Management Accounting* (Englewood Cliffs, NJ: Prentice-Hall, 1982).

Maher, Michael W., Clyde Stickney, Roman L. Weil, and Sidney Davidson, *Management Accounting* (San Diego, CA: Harcourt Brace Jovanovich, 1991).

Shank, J. K. and N. C. Churchill, "Variance Analysis: A Management-Oriented Approach," *The Accounting Review* (October 1977).

Welsch, Glenn A., Ronald W. Hilton, and Paul N. Gordon, *Budgeting: Profit Planning and Control*, 5th ed. (Englewood Cliffs, NJ: Prentice-Hall, 1989).

PART TWO

PLANNING AND FORECASTING

CHOOSING A BUSINESS FORM: TO INCORPORATE OR NOT TO INCORPORATE

6

Richard P. Mandell

The Consulting Firm

Jennifer, Jean, and George had earned their graduate business degrees to-gether and had paid their dues in middle management positions in various large corporations. Despite their different employers, the three had main-tained their friendship and were now ready to realize their dream of starting a consulting practice. Their projections showed modest consulting revenue in the short term, offset by expenditures for supplies, a secretary, a small library, personal computers, and similar necessities. Although each expected to clear no more than perhaps $25,000 for his/her efforts in their first year in business, they shared high hopes for future growth and success. Besides, it would be a great pleasure to run their own company and have sole charge of their respective fates.

The Software Entrepreneur

At approximately the same time that Jennifer, Jean, and George were hatch-ing their plans for entrepreneurial independence, Phil was cashing a seven figure check for his share of the proceeds from the sale of the computer software firm he had founded seven years ago with four of his friends. Rather than rest on his laurels, however, Phil saw this as an opportunity to capital-ize on a complex piece of software he had developed in college. Although Phil was convinced that there would be an extensive market for his software, there was much work to be done before it could be brought to market. The software had to be converted from a mainframe operating system to the various popular microcomputer systems. In addition, there was much marketing to be done prior to its release. Phil anticipated that he would probably spend over $300,000 on programmers and salespeople before the first dollar of royalties would appear. But he was prepared to make that investment himself, in anticipation of retaining all the eventual profit.

The Hotel Venture

Bruce and Erika were not nearly as interested in high technology. Directly following their graduation from business school, they were planning to construct and operate a resort hotel near a popular ski area. They had chosen as their location a beautiful parcel of land in Colorado, owned by their third partner, Michael. Rich with ideas and enthusiasm, the three were lacking in funds. They were certain, however, that they could attract investors to their enterprise. The location, they were sure, would virtually sell itself.

The Purpose of This Chapter

Each of these three groups of entrepreneurs would soon be faced with what might well be the most important decision of the initial years of their businesses: which of the various legal business forms to choose for the operation of their enterprises. It is the purpose of this chapter to describe, compare, and contrast the most popular of these forms, in the hope that the reader then be able to make such choices intelligently and effectively. After discussing the various business forms, we will revisit our entrepreneurs and analyze their choices.

BUSINESS FORMS

Two of the most popular business forms could be described as the default forms because the law will deem a business to be operating under one of these forms unless it takes affirmative action otherwise. The first of these forms is the sole proprietorship. Unless he or she has actively chosen another form, the individual operating his own business is considered to be a sole proprietor. Two or more persons operating a business together are considered a partnership (or general partnership), unless they have actively elected otherwise. Both of these forms share the characteristic that, for all intents and purposes, they are not entities separate from their owners. Every act taken or obligation assumed as a sole proprietorship or partnership is an act taken or obligation assumed by the business owners as individuals.

Many of the rules applicable to the operation of partnerships are set forth in the Uniform Partnership Act, which has been adopted in one form or another by 49 states. That Act defines a partnership as "an association of two or more persons to carry on as co-owners a business for profit." Notice that the definition does not require that the individuals agree to be partners. Although most partnerships can point to an agreement between the partners (whether written or oral), the Act applies the rules of partnership to any group of two or more persons whose actions fulfill the above definition. Thus, the U. S. Circuit Court of Appeals for the District of Columbia, in a rather extreme case, held, over the defendant's strenuous objections, that she was a partner in her husband's burglary "business" (for which she kept the books and upon whose proceeds she lived), even though she denied knowing what her husband was doing at nights. As a result of this status, she was held personally liable for damages to the wife of a burglary victim her husband had murdered during a botched theft.

In contrast, a corporation is a legal entity separate from the legal identities of its owners, the shareholders. In the words used by James Thurber to describe a unicorn, the corporation "is a mythical beast," created by the state at the request of one or more business promoters, upon the filing of a form and the payment of the requisite modest fee. Thereupon, in the eyes of the law, the corporation becomes for most purposes, a living breathing "person" with its own federal identification number! Of course, one cannot see, hear, or touch a corporation, so it must interact with the rest of the world through its agents, the corporation's officers and employees.

Corporations come in different varieties. The so-called professional corporation is available in most states for persons conducting professional practices, such as doctors, lawyers, architects, psychiatric social workers, and the like. A subchapter S corporation is a corporation that is the same as a regular business corporation in all respects other than taxation. These variations will be discussed later.

A fourth common form of business organization is the limited partnership, which may be best described as a hybrid of the corporation and the general partnership. The limited partnership consists of one or more general partners, who manage the business, much in the same way as do the partners in a general partnership, and one or more limited partners, who are essentially silent investors. Like the general partnership, limited partnerships are governed in part by a statute, the Uniform Limited Partnership Act (or its successor, the Revised Uniform Limited Partnership Act), which have also been adopted in one form or another by 49 states.

COMPARISON FACTORS

The usefulness of the above four basic business forms could be compared on a myriad number of measures, but the most effective comparisons will most likely result from employing the following eight:

1. *Complexity and Cost of Formation.* What steps must be taken before your business can exist in each of these forms?
2. *Barriers to Operation Across State Lines.* What steps must be taken to move your business out of state? What additional cost may be involved?
3. *Recognition as a Legal Entity.* Who does the law recognize as the operative entity? Who owns the business's assets? Who can sue and be sued?
4. *Continuity of Life.* Does the legal entity outlive the owner? This may be especially important if the business wishes to attract investors, or if the goal is an eventual sale of the business.
5. *Transferability of Interest.* How does one go about selling or otherwise transferring one's ownership of the business?
6. *Control.* Who makes the decisions regarding the operation, financing, and eventual disposition of the business?
7. *Liability.* Who is responsible for the business's debts? If the company cannot pay its creditors, must the owners satisfy these debts from their personal assets?
8. *Taxation.* How does the choice of business form determine the tax payable on the profits of the business and the income of its owners?

FORMATION

Sole Proprietorships

Reflecting its status as the default form for the individual entrepreneur, the sole proprietorship requires no affirmative act for its formation. One operates a sole proprietorship because one has not chosen to operate in any of the other forms. The only exception to this rule arises in certain states, when the owner chooses to use a name other than his own as the name of his business. In such event, he may be required to file a so-called D/B/A certificate with the local authorities, stating that he is "doing business as" someone other than himself. This allows creditors and those otherwise injured by the operation of the business to determine who is legally responsible for the business's acts.

Partnerships

Similarly, a general partnership requires no special act for its formation other than a D/B/A certificate, if a name other than that of the partners will be used. If two or more people act in a way which fits the definition set forth in the Uniform Act, they will find themselves involved in a partnership. However, it is strongly recommended that prospective partners consciously enter an agreement (preferably in writing) setting forth their understandings on the many issues which will arise in such an arrangement. Principal among these are the investments each will make in the business, the allocation and distribution of profits (and losses), the method of decision making (majority or unanimous vote), any obligations to perform services for the business, the relative compensation of the partners, and so on. Regardless of the agreements that may exist among the partners, the partnership will be bound by the actions and agreements of each partner: as long as these actions are reasonably related to the partnership business, and even if they were not properly authorized by the other partners pursuant to the agreement. After all, third parties have no idea what the partners's internal agreement says, and are in no way bound by it.

Corporations

On the other hand, in order to form a corporation, one must pay the appropriate fee and must complete and file with the state and corporate charter (otherwise known as a Certificate of Incorporation, Articles of Incorporation or similar name in the various states). The fee is payable both at the outset and annually thereafter (often approximately $200). A promoter may form a corporation under the laws of whichever state he wishes; one is not required to form the corporation under the laws of the state in which one intends to conduct most of one's business. This partially explains the popularity of the Delaware corporation. Delaware has spent most of the last century competing with other states for corporation filing fees, by repeatedly amending its corporate law to make it increasingly favorable to management. By now, the Delaware corporation has taken on an aura of sophistication, so that many promoters form their companies in Delaware just to appear to know what they are doing! However, the statutory advantages of Delaware apply mostly to corporations with many stockholders (such as those which are publicly traded) and will rarely be significant to a small business, such as those described at the beginning of this chapter. Also, formation in Delaware (or any state other than the site of the corporation's principal place of business) will subject the corporation to additional, unnecessary expense. It is, thus, usually advisable to incorporate in the company's home state.

The charter sets forth the corporation's name (which cannot be confusingly similar to the name of any other corporation operating in the state) as well as its principal address. The names of the initial directors and officers of the corporation are often listed. Most states also require a statement of corporate purpose. Years ago this purpose defined the permitted scope of the corporation's activities. A corporation which ventured beyond its purposes risked operating "ultra vires," resulting in liability of its directors and officers to its stockholders and creditors. Today, virtually all states allow a corporation to define its purposes extremely broadly (e.g., "any activities which may be lawfully undertaken by a corporation in this state"), so that operation ultra vires is generally impossible. Still directors are occasionally plagued by lawsuits brought by stockholders asserting that the diversion of corporate profits to charitable or community activities runs afoul of the dominant corporate purpose, which is to generate profits for its stockholders. The debate over the responsibility of directors to so-called corporate "stakeholders" (employees, suppliers, customers, neighbors, etc.) currently rages in many forms, but is normally not a concern of the beginning entrepreneur.

Corporate charters also normally set forth the number and classes of equity securities that the corporation is authorized to issue. Here an analysis of a bit of jargon may be appropriate. The number of shares set forth in the charter is the number of shares "authorized," i.e., the number of shares that the directors may issue to stockholders at the directors's discretion. The number of shares "issued" is the number that the directors have, in fact, issued and is obviously either the same or smaller than the number authorized. In some cases, a corporation may have repurchased some of the shares previously issued by the directors. In that case, only the shares which remain in the hands of shareholders are "outstanding" (a number obviously either the same or lower than the number issued). Only the shares outstanding have voting rights, rights to receive dividends, and rights to receive distributions upon full or partial liquidation of the corporation. Normally, we would expect an entrepreneur to authorize the maximum number of shares allowable under the state's minimum incorporation fee (e.g., 200,000 shares for $200 in Massachusetts). He would then issue only 10,000 or so, leaving the rest "on the shelf" for future financings, employee benefits, etc.

The charter also sets forth the "par value" of the authorized shares, another antiquated concept, of interest, mainly to accountants. The law requires only that the corporation not issue shares for less than the par value, but it can, and usually does, issue the shares for more. Thus, typical par values are $0.01 per share or even "no par value." Shares issued for less than par are "watered stock," subjecting both the directors and holders of such stock to liability to other stockholders and creditors of the corporation.

Corporations also adopt bylaws which are not filed with the state, but are available for inspection by stockholders. These are usually fairly standard documents, describing the internal governance of the corporation and setting forth such items as the officers's powers and notice periods for stockholders's meetings.

Limited Partnerships

As you might expect, given the limited partnership's hybrid nature, the law requires both a written agreement among the various general and limited partners and a Certificate of Limited Partnership to be filed with the state, along with the appropriate initial and annual fees. The agreement sets forth the partners's understanding of the items discussed earlier, in the context of a general partnership. The certificate sets forth the name and address of the partnership, its purposes, and the names and addresses of its general partners. In states where recent amendments to the Revised Uniform Limited Partnership Act have been adopted, it is no longer necessary to reveal the names of the limited partners, just as the names of corporate stockholders do not appear on the company's incorporation documents.

OPERATION OUT OF STATE

Sole Proprietorships and Partnerships

Partly as a result of both the Commerce and Privileges and Immunities clauses of the United States Constitution, states may not place limits or restrictions on the operations of out-of-state sole proprietors or general partnerships that are different than those placed on domestic businesses. Thus, a state cannot force registration of a general partnership simply because its principal office is located elsewhere, but it can require an out-of-state doctor to undergo the same licensing procedures it requires of its own residents.

Corporations and Limited Partnerships

Things are different, however, with corporations and limited partnerships. As creations of the individual states, they are not automatically entitled to recognition elsewhere. All states require (and routinely grant) qualification as a foreign corporation or limited partnership to nondomestic entities doing business within their borders. This procedure normally requires the completion of a form very similar to a corporate charter or limited partnership certificate, and the payment of an initial and annual fee, similar in amount to the fees paid by domestic entities. This, incidentally, is one reason not to form a corporation in Delaware, if it will operate principally in New York or elsewhere. Much litigation has occurred over what constitutes "doing business" within a state for the purpose of requiring qualification. Similar issues arise over the obligation to pay income tax, collect sales tax, or accept personal jurisdiction in the courts of a state. Generally these cases turn on the individualized facts of the particular situation, but courts generally look for offices or warehouses, corporate employees, widespread advertising, or negotiation and execution of contracts within the state.

Perhaps more interesting may be the penalty for failure to qualify. Most states will impose liability for back fees, taxes, interest, and penalties. More important, many states will bar a nonqualified foreign entity from access to its courts and, thus, from the ability to enforce obligations against its residents. In most of these cases, the entity can regain access to the courts merely by paying the state the back fees and penalties it owes, but in a few states, access will then be granted only to enforce obligations incurred after qualification was achieved, leaving all prior obligations unenforceable.

RECOGNITION AS A LEGAL ENTITY

Sole Proprietorships

By now it probably goes without saying that the law does not recognize a sole proprietorship as a legal entity, separate from its owner. If Phil, our computer entrepreneur, were to choose this form, he would own all the company's assets: He would be the plaintiff in any suits it brought, and the defendant in any suits brought against it. There would be no difference between Phil, the individual, and Phil, the business.

Partnerships

A general partnership raises somewhat more difficult issues. Although most states allow partnerships to bring suit, be sued, and own property in the partnership name, this does not mean that the partnership exists, for most purposes, separately from its partners. As will be seen, especially in the areas of liability and taxation, partnerships are very much collections of individuals, not separate entities.

Ownership of partnership property is a particularly problematic area. All partners own an interest in the partnership, which entitles them to distributions of profit, much like stock in a corporation. This interest is the separate property of each partner, and is attachable by the individual creditors of a partner, in the form of a so-called "charging order." However, each partner also owns the assets of the partnership jointly with his other partners. This form of ownership (similar to joint ownership of a family home by two spouses) is called "tenancy in partnership." Each partner may use partnership assets only for the benefit of the partnership's business, and such assets are exempt from attachment by the creditors of an individual partner, although not from the creditors of the partnership. Tenancy in partnership also implies that, in most cases of dissolution of a partnership, the ownership of partnership assets devolves to the remaining partners, to the exclusion of the partner who dies or leaves—in violation of the partnership agreement. The former partner is left only with the right to a dissolution distribution, with respect to his partnership interest.

Corporations

The corporation is our first full-fledged separate legal entity. Ownership of the corporation's assets is vested solely in the corporation, as a separate legal entity. The corporation itself is plaintiff and defendant in suits and is the legally contracting party in all its transactions. Stockholders own only their stock and have no direct ownership rights in the corporation's assets.

Limited Partnerships

The limited partnership, continuing in its role as a hybrid, is a little of both. The general partners own the partnership's property as tenants in partnership, operating in the same manner as partners in a general partnership. The limited partners, however, have only their partnership interests and no direct ownership of the partnership's property. This is logically consistent with their roles as silent investors. If they directly owned partnership property, they would have to be consulted with regard to its use.

CONTINUITY OF LIFE

Sole Proprietorships

The issue of continuity of life is one which should concern most entrepreneurs because it can affect their ability to sell the business as a unit, when it comes time to cash in on their efforts as founders and promoters. The survival of the business as a whole, in the form of a separate entity, must be distinguished from the survival of the business's individual assets and liabilities. Although a sole proprietorship does not survive the death of its owner, its individual assets and liabilities do. In Phil's case, for example, to the extent that these assets consist of the computer program, filing cabinets, and the like, they would all be inherited by Phil's heirs, who could then choose to continue the business or liquidate the assets as they pleased. Should they decide to continue the business, they would then have the same choices of business form which confront any entrepreneur. However, if Phil's major asset were a government license, qualification as an approved government supplier, or a contract with a software publisher, the ability of the heirs to carry on the business might be entirely dependent upon the assignability of these items. If the publishing contract is not assignable, Phil's death may terminate the business's major asset. If the business had operated as a corporation, Phil's death would likely have been irrelevant: The corporation, not Phil, would have been party to the contract.

Partnerships

Consistent with the general partnership's status as a collection of individuals, not an entity separate from its owners, a partnership is deemed dissolved upon the death, incapacity, bankruptcy, resignation, or expulsion of a partner. This is true even if a partner's resignation violates the express terms of the partnership agreement. Those assets of the partnership that may be assigned devolve to those partners who are entitled to ownership, pursuant to the rules of tenancy in partnership. These rules favor the remaining partners if the ex-partner has died, become incapacitated or bankrupt, been expelled, or resigned in violation of the partnership agreement. If the ex-partner resigned without violating the underlying agreement, he retains ownership rights under tenancy in partnership. Those who thus retain ownership may continue the business as a new partnership or corporation with the same or new partners and investors or may liquidate the assets at their discretion. The sole right of any partner who has forfeited direct ownership rights is to be paid a dissolution distribution, after the partnership's liabilities have been paid.

Corporations

Corporations, on the other hand, normally enjoy perpetual life. Unless the charter contains a stated dissolution date (extremely rare), and as long as the corporation pays its annual fees to the state, it will go on until and unless it is voted out of existence by its stockholders. The death, incapacity, bankruptcy, resignation, or expulsion of any stockholder is entirely irrelevant to the corporation's existence. Such a stockholder's stock continues to be held by the stockholder, is inherited by his heirs, or is auctioned by creditors as the circumstances demand, with no direct effect on the corporation.

Limited Partnerships

As you may have guessed, the hybrid nature of the limited partnership dictates that the death, incapacity, bankruptcy, resignation, or expulsion of a limited partner will have no effect on the existence of the limited partnership. The limited partner's partnership interest is passed in the same way as that of a stockholder's. However, the death, incapacity, bankruptcy, resignation, or expulsion of a general partner does automatically dissolve the partnership, in the same way as it would in the case of a general partnership. This can be extremely inconvenient if the limited partnership is conducting a far-flung enterprise with many limited partners. Thus, in most cases, the partners agree in their limited partnership agreement, that upon such a dissolution, the limited partnership will continue under the management of a substitute general partner, chosen by those general partners who remain. In such a case, the entity continues until it is voted out of existence by its partners, in accordance with their agreement, or until the arrival of a termination date, specified in its certificate.

TRANSFERABILITY OF INTEREST

Sole Proprietorships

To a large extent, transferability of an owner's interest in the business is similar to the continuity of life issue. A sole proprietor has no interest to transfer because he and the business are one and the same. He must be content to transfer each of the assets of the business individually, an administrative nightmare at best and possibly impractical in the case of nonassignable contracts, licenses, and government approvals.

Partnerships

To discuss transferability in the context of a general partnership, it is necessary to keep in mind the difference between ownership of partnership assets as tenants in partnership, and ownership of an individual partnership interest. A partner has no right to transfer partnership assets, except as may be authorized by vote, in accordance with the partnership agreement and in furtherance of the partnership business. However, he may transfer his partnership interest, and it may be attached by his individual creditors pursuant to a charging order. This does not make the transferee a partner in the business because partnerships can only be created by agreement of all parties. Rather, it sets up the rather awkward situation in which the original partner remains, but his economic interest is, at least temporarily, in the hands of another. In such cases, the Uniform Partnership Act gives the remaining partners the right to dissolve the partnership by expelling the transferor partner.

Corporations

No such complications attend the transfer of one's interest in a corporation. Stockholders simply sell or transfer their shares. Since stockholders have no day-to-day involvement in the operation of the business, the transferee becomes a full-fledged stockholder upon the transfer. This means that if Bruce, Erika, and Michael decide to operate as a corporation, each risks waking up one day to find that he or she has a new "partner" if one of the three has sold his or her shares. To protect themselves against this eventuality, most closely held corporations include restrictions on stock transfer in their charter, their bylaws, or in stockholder agreements. The restriction sets forth some variation of a right of first refusal, either for the corporation or the other stockholders, whenever a transfer is proposed. In addition, corporate stock, as well as most partnership interests (general and most especially limited), are securities under the federal and state securities laws, and because the securities of these entitles will not initially be registered under any of these laws, their transfer is closely restricted.

Limited Partnerships

Just as with general partnerships, the partners of limited partnerships may transfer their partnership interests. The rules regarding the transfer of the interests of the general partners are similar to those governing general partnerships described above. Limited partners may usually transfer their interests (subject to securities laws restrictions) without fear of dissolution, but transferees normally do not become substituted limited partners without the consent of the general partners.

CONTROL

Sole Proprietorships

Simply put, control in the context of a business entity means the power to make decisions regarding all aspects of its operations. But the implications of control extend to many levels. These include control of the "equity" or value of the business, control over distribution of profits, control over day-to-day and long-term policy making, and control over distribution of cash flow. Each of these is different from the others, and control over each can be allocated differently among the owners and other principals of the entity. This can be seen either as complexity or flexibility, depending upon one's perspective, but no such debate exists over the sole proprietorship. In that business form, control over all these factors belongs exclusively to the sole proprietor. Nothing could be simpler or more straightforward.

Partnerships

Things are not so simple in the context of general partnerships. It is essential to appreciate the difference between the partners's relationships with each other (internal relationships) and the partnership's relations with third parties (external relationships).

Internally, the partnership agreement governs the decision-making process and sets forth the agreed division of equity, profits, and cash flows. Decisions made in the ordinary course of business are normally made by a majority vote of the partners, while major decisions, such as changing the character of the partnership's business may require a unanimous vote. Some partnerships may weight the voting in proportion to each partner's partnership interest, while others delegate much of the decision-making power to an executive committee or a managing partner. In the absence of an agreement, the Uniform Partnership Act prescribes a vote of the majority of partners for most issues and unanimity for certain major decisions.

External relationships are largely governed by the law of agency; that is, each partner is treated as an agent of the partnership and derivatively, of the other partners. Any action that a partner appears to have authority to take will be binding upon the partnership and the other partners, regardless of whether such action has been internally authorized (Exhibit 6.1).

Thus, if Jennifer purchases a subscription to the Harvard Business Review for the partnership, and such an action is perceived to be within the ordinary course of the partnership's business, that obligation can be enforced against the partnership, even if Jean and George had voted against it.

EXHIBIT 6.1. Principal and agent.

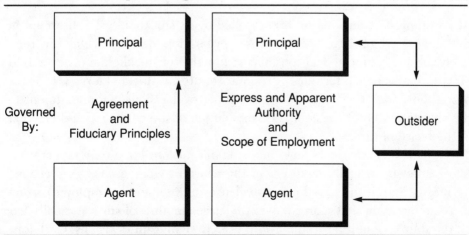

Such would not be the case, however, if Jennifer had signed a purchase and sale agreement for an office building in the name of the partnership, because reasonable third parties would be expected to know that such a purchase was not in the ordinary course of business.

These rules extend to tort liability, as well. If Jean were to wrongfully induce a potential client to breach its consulting contract with a competitor, the partnership would be liable for interference with contractual relations, even if the other two partners were not aware of Jean's actions. Such would not be the case, however, if Jean decided to dynamite the competition's offices because such an act would be judged to be outside the normal scope of her duties as a partner.

These obligations to third parties can even extend past the dissolution of the partnership, if an individual partner has not given adequate notice that he or she is no longer associated with the others. Thus, an ex-partner can be held liable for legal fees incurred by his former partners, if he has not notified the partnership's counsel that he has left the firm.

It should also be noted that agency law reaches into the internal relationships of partners. The law imposes upon partners the same obligations of fiduciary loyalty, noncompetition, and accountability as it does upon agents with respect to their principals.

Corporations

Although there can be much flexibility in the allocation of control in the partnership form, it is in the corporate form that the opportunities for flexibility and complexity probably reach their height. Many aspects of the corporate form have been designed specifically for the purpose of splitting off individual aspects of control and allocating them differently.

Stockholders

At its simplest, a corporation is controlled by its stockholders. Yet, except in those states which have specific close corporation statutes (which are relatively rarely used), the decision-making function of stockholders is exercised only derivatively. Under most corporate statutes, a stockholders's vote is required only with respect to four basic types of decisions: an amendment to the charter; a sale of the company; dissolution of the company; and election of the board of directors.

Charter amendments may sound significant, until one remembers what information is normally included in the charter. A name change, a change in purpose (given the broad purpose clauses now generally employed), or an increase in authorized shares (given the large amounts of stock normally left on the shelf) are neither frequent nor usually significant decisions. Certainly, a sale of the company is significant, but it normally can occur only after the recommendation of the board and will only happen once, if at all. The same can be said of the decision to dissolve. It is the board of directors which makes all the long-term policy decisions for the corporation. Thus the right to elect the board is significant, but indirectly so. Day-to-day operation of the corporation's business is accomplished by its officers who are normally elected by the board, not the stockholders.

Even given the relative unimportance of voting power for stockholders, the corporation provides many opportunities to differentiate voting power from other aspects of control and allocate it differently. Assume Bruce and Erika (our hotel developers) were willing to give Michael a larger piece of the equity of their operation, to reflect his contribution of the land, but wished to divide their voting rights equally. They could authorize a class of nonvoting common stock and issue, for example, 1,000 shares of voting stock to each of themselves and an additional 1,000 shares of nonvoting stock to Michael. As a result, each would have one third of the voting control, but Michael would have one half of the equity interest.

Alternatively, Michael could be issued a block of preferred stock representing the value of the land. This would guarantee him a fair return on his investment, before any dividends could be declared to the three of them as holders of the common stock. As a holder of preferred stock, Michael would also receive a liquidation preference upon dissolution or sale of the business, in the amount of the value of his investment, but any additional value created by the efforts of the group would be reflected in the increasing value of the common shares.

The above illustrates how one can separate and allocate decision-making control differently from that of the equity in the business, as well as from the distribution of profits. Distribution of cash flow can, of course, be accomplished totally separately from the ownership of securities, through salaries based upon the relative efforts of the parties, rent payments for assets leased to the entity by the principals, or interest on loans to the corporation.

Stockholders exercise what voting power they have at meetings of the stockholders, held at least annually, but more frequently if necessary. Each stockholder of record, on a future date, chosen by the party calling the meeting, is given a notice of the meeting containing the date, time, and purpose of the meeting. Such notice must be sent at least seven to ten days prior to the date of the meeting depending upon the individual state's corporate law; although, the Securities and Exchange Commission requires 30 days notice for publicly traded corporations. No action may be taken at a meeting unless a majority of voting shares is represented (known as a quorum). This results in the aggressive solicitation of proxy votes in most corporations with widespread stock ownership. Unless otherwise provided (as with the two-thirds vote of all shares, required in most states for a sale or dissolution of the company), a resolution is carried by a majority vote of those shares represented at the meeting.

The above rules require the conclusion that the board of directors will be elected by the holders of a majority of the voting shares. Thus, in the above scenario, even though Bruce and Erika may have given Michael one third of the voting shares of common stock, as long as they continue to vote together, Bruce and Erika will be able to elect the entire board. To prevent this result, prior to investing, Michael could insist upon a cumulative voting provision in the charter (under those states's corporate laws which allow it). Under this system, each share of stock is entitled to a number of votes equal to the number of directors to be elected. By using all one's votes to support a single candidate, individuals with a significant minority interest can guarantee themselves representation on the board (e.g., ownership of more than one fifth if the board consists of five or more directors, more than one fourth if it consists of four or more, more than one third if it consists of three or more, etc.).

More directly, (and in states which do not allow cumulative voting), Michael could insist upon two different classes of voting stock, differing only in voting rights. Bruce and Erika would each own 1,000 shares of Class A and elect two directors. Michael, the sole owner of the 1,000 outstanding shares of Class B stock, would elect a third director. Of course, the board also acts by majority, so Bruce and Erika's directors could dominate board decisions in any case, but at least Michael would have access to the deliberations.

In the absence of a meeting, stockholders may vote by unanimous written consent, where each stockholder indicates his approval of a written resolution by signing it. This eliminates the need for a meeting and is very effective in corporations with only a few stockholders (such as our hotel operation). Unlike the rules governing stockholders's meetings, however, in most states, unaminity is required to adopt resolutions by written consent. This apparently reflects the belief that a minority stockholder is owed an opportunity to sway the majority with his arguments. A few states, notably Delaware, permit written consents of a majority, apparently reacting to the dominance of proxy voting at most meetings of large corporations, where the most eloquent of minority arguments would fall upon deaf ears (or proxy cards).

Directors

At the directors's level, absent a special provision in the corporation's certificate, all decisions are made by majority vote. Typically, directors concentrate on long-term and significant decisions, leaving day-to-day management to the officers of the corporation. Decisions are made at regularly scheduled directors meetings; or at a special meeting, if there is need to react to a specific situation. Under most corporate laws, no notice need be given for regular meetings, and only very short notice need be given for special meetings (24–48 hours). The notice must be sent to all directors and must contain the date, time, and place of the meeting, but, unlike stockholders's notices, need not contain the purpose of the meeting. It is assumed that directors are much more involved in the business of the corporation and do not need to be warned about possible agenda items or given long notice periods.

At the meeting itself, no business can be conducted in the absence of a quorum, which, unless increased by a charter or bylaw provision, is a majority of the directors then in office. Reflecting recent advances in technology, many corporate statutes allow directors to attend meetings by conference call or teleconference, as long as all directors are able to hear and speak to each other at all times during the meeting. Individual telephone calls to each director will not suffice. Unlike stockholders, directors cannot vote by proxy, because each director owes to the corporation his individual judgment on items coming before the board. The board of directors can also act by written consent, but, even in Delaware, such consent must be unanimous, in recognition that the board is fundamentally a deliberative body.

Boards of directors, especially in publicly held corporations with larger boards, frequently delegate some of their powers to executive committees, or other committees formed for defined purposes. However, most corporate statutes prohibit boards form delegating certain fundamental powers, such as the declaration of dividends, the recommendation of charter amendments, or sale of the company. The executive committee can, however, be a powerful organizational tool to streamline board operations and increase efficiency and responsiveness.

Although directors are not agents of the corporation, in that they cannot bind the corporation to contract or tort liability through their individual actions, they are subject to many of the obligations of agents discussed in the context of partnerships, such as fiduciary loyalty. Directors are bound by the so called "corporate opportunity doctrine," which prohibits them from taking personal advantage of any business opportunity that may come their way, if the opportunity is such as would reasonably be expected to interest the corporation. In such an event, the director must disclose the opportunity to the corporation, which normally must consider it and vote not to take advantage before the director may act on his own behalf.

Unlike stockholders who, under most circumstances, can vote their shares totally in their own self-interest, directors must use their best business judgment and act in the corporation's best interest when making decisions for the corporation. At the very least, the director must keep himself informed regarding the corporation's operations, although he may in most circumstances rely on the input of experts hired by the corporation, such as its attorneys and accountants. Thus, when the widow of a corporation's founder accepted a seat on the board as a symbolic gesture of respect to her late husband, she found herself liable to minority stockholders for the misbehavior of her fellow board members. Nonparticipation in the misdeeds was not enough to exempt her from liability: She had failed to keep herself informed and exercise independent judgment.

Directors may also find themselves sued personally by minority stockholders or creditors of the corporation, for declaration of dividends or other distributions to stockholders, which render the corporation insolvent, or for other decisions of the board that have injured the corporation. Notwithstanding such lawsuits, however, directors are not guarantors of the success of the corporation's endeavors; they are required only to have used their best independent "business judgment" in making their decisions. When individual directors cannot be totally disinterested (such as the corporate opportunity issue or when the corporation is being asked to contract with a director or an entity in which a director has an interest), the interested director is required to disclose his interest and is disqualified from voting. In many states, his presence will not even count for the maintenance of a quorum.

Apart from the question of the interested director, much of the modern debate on the role of the corporate director has focused around which constituencies a director may take into account when exercising his best "business judgment." The traditional view has been that the director's only concern is to maximize return on the investment of the stockholders. More recently, especially in the context of hostile takeovers, directors have been allowed to take into account the effect of their decision on other constituencies, such as suppliers, neighboring communities, customers, and employees.

In an early case on this subject, the board of directors of the corporation which owned Wrigley Field and the Chicago Cubs baseball team was judged to have appropriately considered the effect on its neighbors and on the game of baseball, in voting to forgo the extra revenue that it would probably have earned if it had installed lights for night games.

When the stockholders believe the directors have not been exercising their best independent business judgment in a particular instance, the normal procedure is to make a demand on the directors to correct the decision, either by reversing it or by reimbursing the corporation from their personal funds. Should the board refuse (as it most likely will), the stockholders then bring a derivative suit against the board on behalf of the corporation. They are, in effect, taking over the board's authority to decide whether such a suit should be brought in the corporation's name. The board's vote not to institute the suit is not likely to be upheld on the basis of the business judgment rule, since the board members are clearly "interested" in the outcome of the vote. As a result, the well-informed board will delegate the power to make such a decision to an independent "litigation committee," usually composed of directors who were not involved in the original decision. The decision of such a committee is much more likely to be upheld in a court of law; although the decision is not immune from judicial review.

Officers

The third level of decision making in the normal corporation is that of the officers, who take on the day-to-day operational responsibilities. Officers are elected by the board and consist, at a minimum, of a president, a treasurer, and a secretary or clerk (keeper of the corporate records). Many corporations elect additional officers such as vice presidents, assistant treasurers, CEOs, and the like.

Thus, the decision making control of the corporation is exercised on three very different levels: Where each decision properly belongs may not be entirely obvious in every situation. Thus, the decision to go into a new line of business would normally be thought of as a board decision. Yet, if by some chance, the decision requires an amendment of the corporate charter, a vote of stockholders may be necessary. On the contrary, if the decision is merely to add a twelfth variety of relish to the corporation's already varied line of condiments, the decision may be properly left to a vice-president of marketing.

Often persons who have been exposed to the above analysis of the corporate control function conclude that the corporate form is too complex for any but the largest and most complicated publicly held companies. This is a gross overreaction. For example, if Phil, our software entrepreneur, should decide that the corporate form is appropriate for his business, it is very likely that he will be the corporation's 100% stockholder. As such, he will elect himself the sole director and his board will then elect him as the president, treasurer, and secretary of the corporation. Joint meetings of the stockholders and directors of the corporation may be held in the shower on alternate Monday mornings.

Limited Partnerships

As you might expect, the allocation of control in a limited partnership is reflective of its origin as a hybrid of the general partnership and the corporation. Simply put, virtually all management authority is vested in the general partners. The limited partners normally have little or no authority, analogous to outside stockholders in a corporation. Third parties cannot rely on any apparent authority of a limited partner because a limited partner's name will not appear, as a general partner's name will, on the limited partnership's certificate on the public record.

General partners exercise their authority in the same way as they do in a general partnership. Voting control is allocated internally as set forth in the partnership agreement, but each general partner has the apparent authority to bind the partnership to unauthorized contracts and torts to the same extent as the partners in a general partnership.

Limited partners will normally have voting power over a very small list of fundamental business events, such as amending the partnership agreement and certificate, admitting new general partners, changes in the basic business purposes of the partnership, or dissolution. These are similar to the decisions that must be put to a stockholders' vote in a corporation. A recent amendment to the Revised Uniform Limited Partnership Act, now accepted by many states, has widened the range of decisions in which a limited partner may participate, without losing his status as a limited partner. However, this range is still determined by the language of the agreement and certificate for each individual partnership.

LIABILITY

Possibly, the factor that most concerns the entrepreneur is personal liability. If the company encounters catastrophic tort liability, finds itself in breach of a significant contract, or just plain can't pay its bills, must the owner reach into his own personal assets to pay the remaining liability, after the company's assets have been exhausted? If so, potential entrepreneurs may well believe that the risk of losing everything is not worth the possibility of success, resulting in diminished innovation throughout society. On the other hand, most entrepreneurs are willing to take significant risk, if the amount of that risk can be limited ot the amount they have chosen to invest in the venture.

Sole Proprietorships

With the sole proprietorship, the owner has essentially traded off limitation of risk in favor of simplicity of operation. Since there is no difference between the entity and its owner, all the liabilities and obligations of the business are also liabilities and obligations of its owner. Thus, all the owner's personal assets are at risk. Failure of the business may well mean personal bankruptcy for the owner.

Partnerships

If possible, the result may be even worse within a general partnership. There, each owner is personally liable not only for his own mistakes, but also for those of his partners. Each partner is jointly and severally liable for the debts of the partnership remaining, after the partnership's assets have been exhausted. This means that a creditor may choose to sue any individual partner for 100 percent of any liability. The partner may have a right to sue the other partners for their share of the debt, as set forth in the partnership agreement, but that is of no concern to a third party. If the other partners are bankrupt or have fled the jurisdiction, the partner left may end up holding the entire bag.

If our three consultants operate as a partnership, Jennifer is not only 100 percent personally liable for any contracts she may enter into, but she is also 100 percent personally liable for any contracts entered into by either Jean or George. What's more, she is liable for those contracts, even if they were entered into in violation of the partnership agreement, because, as was earlier demonstrated, each partner has the apparent authority to bind the partnership to contracts in the ordinary course of the partnership's business, regardless of the partners's internal agreement. Worse, Jennifer is also 100 percent individually liable for any torts committed by either of her partners, as long as they were committed within the scope of the partnership's business. The only good news in all this is that neither the partnership nor Jennifer is liable for any debts or obligations of Jean or George incurred in their personal affairs. If George has incurred heavy gambling debts in Las Vegas, his creditors can affect the partnership only by obtaining a charging order against George's partnership interest.

Corporations

Thus we have the historical reason for the invention of the corporation. Unlike sole proprietorship and partnership, the corporation is recognized as a legal entity, separate from its owners. Its owners are thus not personally liable for its debts; they are granted liability. If the corporation's debts exhaust its assets, the stockholders have lost their investment, but they are not responsible for any further amounts. In practice, this may not be as attractive as it sounds, because sophisticated creditors such as the corporation's bank, will likely demand personal guarantees from major stockholders. But the stockholders will normally escape personal liability for trade debt and, most important, for torts.

This major benefit of incorporation does not come without some cost. Creditors may, on occasion, be able to "pierce the corporate veil" and assert personal liability against stockholders, using any one of three major arguments. First, to claim limited liability behind the corporate shield, stockholders must have adequately capitalized the corporation at or near its inception. There is no magic formula with which to calculate the amount necessary to achieve adequate capitalization, but the stockholders normally will be expected to invest enough money or property and obtain enough liability insurance to offset the kinds and amounts of liabilities normally encountered by a business in their industry. Thus, the owner of a fleet of taxicabs did not escape liability by cancelling his liability insurance and forming a separate corporation for each of his cabs. The court deemed each such corporation inadequately capitalized, and, in a novel decision, pierced the corporate veil laterally, by combining all the corporations into one for purposes of liability.

It is necessary to capitalize only for those liabilities normally encountered by corporations in the industry. The word "normally" is key because it is obviously not necessary to have resources adequate to handle any circumstance, no matter how unforeseeable. And adequate capitalization is necessary only at the outset. A corporation does not expose its stockholders to personal liability by incurring substantial losses and ultimately dissipating its initial capitalization.

A second argument used by creditors to reach stockholders for personal liability is failure to respect the corporate form. This may occure in many ways. The stockholders may fail to indicate that they are doing business in the corporate form, by leaving the words "Inc." or "Corp." off their business cards and stationery, thus giving the impression that they are operating as a partnership. They may mingle the corporate assets in personal bank accounts, or routinely use corporate assets for personal business. They may fail to respect corporate niceties, such as holding annual meetings and filing the annual reports required by the state. After all, if the stockholders don't take the corporate form seriously, why should its creditors? They are entitled to adequate notice that they may not rely on the personal assets of the stockholders. Even Phil, the software entrepreneur, would be well advised to record the minutes of his damp stockholder's and director's meetings in a corporate record book.

A third argument arises from a common mistake made by entrepreneurs. Fearful of the expense involved in forming a corporation, they wait until they are sure that the business will get off the ground before they spring for the attorneys and filing fees. In the meantime, they may enter into contracts on behalf of the corporation and perhaps even commit a tort or two. Once the corporation is formed, they may even remember to have it expressly accept all liabilities incurred by the promoters on its behalf. However, under simple agency law, one cannot act as an agent of a nonexistent principal. And a later assignment of one's liabilities to a newly formed corporation does not act to release the original obligor without the consent of the obligee. The best advice here is to form the corporation before incurring any liability on its behalf. Most entrepreneurs are surprised at how little it actually costs to get started.

Limited Partnerships

In the tradition of its hybrid nature, a limited partnership borrows some of its aspects from the corporation and some from the general partnership. In summary, each general partner has unlimited, joint and several, liability for the debts and obligations of the limited partnership after exhaustion of the partnership's assets. In this respect, the rules are identical to those governing the partners in a general partnership. Limited partners are treated as stockholders in a corporation. They have risked their investment, but their personal assets are exempt from the creditors of the partnership.

However, as you might expect, things aren't quite as simple as they may initially appear. It is rather common, in limited partnerships, for limited partners to make their investments in the form of a cash down payment and a promissory note for the rest. This occurs partially for reasons of cash flow and partially for purposes of tax planning. This arrangement is much less common in corporations because many corporate statutes do not permit it, and because the tax advantages associated with this arrangement are generally not available in the corporate form. Should the limited partnership's business fail, limited partners will be expected to honor their commitments to make future contributions to capital, despite limited liability.

In addition, it is fundamental to the status of limited partners that they have acquired limited liability in exchange for foregoing virtually all management authority over the business. The corollary to that rule is that a limited partner who excessively involves himself in management may forfeit his limited liability and be treated, for the purposes of creditors, as a general partner, with unlimited personal liability. In mitigation of this somewhat harsh rule, the Revised Uniform Limited Partnership Act was recently amended to increase the categories of activities in which a limited partner may participate without crossing the line. Furthermore, and perhaps more fundamentally, in states that have adopted this amendment, the transgressing limited partner is now only personally liable to those creditors who were aware of the limited partner's activities and detrimentally relied upon his apparent status as a general partner.

TAXATION

It is remarkable how many significant business decisions are made without first taking into account the tax consequences of the various options. Tax consequences should almost never be allowed to force an entrepreneur to take actions she otherwise would not have considered. But often tax considerations lead one to do what one wants in a different manner and to reap substantial savings as a consequence. Such is often the case in the organization of a business. The discussion that follows will be confined to the federal income tax, the tax with the largest and most direct effect upon organizational issues. Each entrepreneur would be well advised to consult her tax adviser regarding this tax as well as state income, estate, payroll, and other taxes and find out how they might impact upon her specific business.

Sole Proprietorships

Not surprisingly, given the factors already discussed, a sole proprietorship is not a separate taxable entity for federal income tax purposes. The taxable income and deductible expenses of the business are set forth on Schedule C of the entrepreneur's Form 1040 and the net profit (loss) is carried back to page one, where it is added to (or subtracted from) all the taxpayer's other income. The net effect of this is that the sole proprietor will pay tax on the income from this business at his highest marginal rate, normally either 28 percent or 31 percent, depending upon the amount of income received from this and other sources (Exhibit 6.2).

EXHIBIT 6.2.   Individual federal income tax rates.

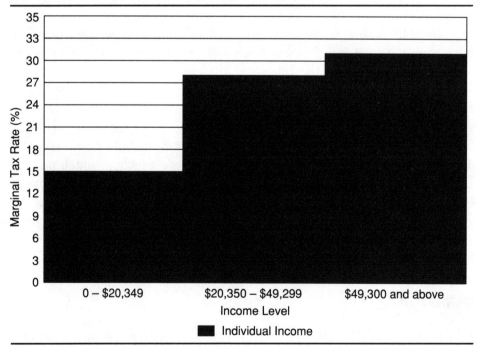

In Phil's case, for example, if his software business netted $100,000 in a particular year, that amount would be added to the substantial interest and dividend income his other investments, so that he would likely owe the Internal Revenue Service (IRS) $31,000 on this income. One might see this as a positive result because the highest individual income tax rate is still lower than the highest marginal corporate tax rate of 39 percent. However, this argument is based upon an inaccurate comparison. If Phil's business was run as a separate taxable entity, the income generated from it would be taxed at the lowest levels of the tax rate structure, because it would not be added to any other income. If it were a corporation, for example, the first $50,000 of income would be taxed at only 15 percent and the next $25,000 at only 25 percent (Exhibit 6.3).

This argument is turned on its head, however, if a business anticipates losses in the short term. Using Phil as an example, if his business operated at a $100,000 loss and as a separate taxable entity, the business would pay no tax in its first year and would only be able to net its early losses against profits in future years and only if it ever realized such profits. At best, the value of this tax benefit is reduced by the time value of money, and, at worst, the loss may never yield a tax benefit, if the business never turns itself around. On the other hand, if Phil operated the business as a sole proprietorship, the loss calculated on his Schedule C would be netted against the dividend

EXHIBIT 6.3. Corporate federal income tax rates.

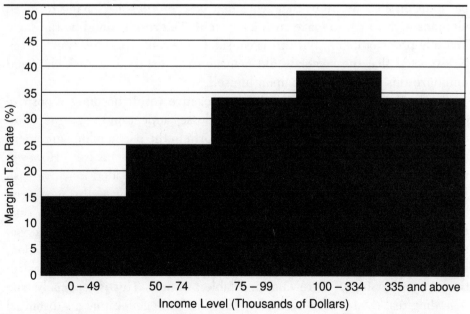

and interest income generated by his investments, thus effectively rendering $100,000 of that income tax free. Thus, one can strongly argue that the form in which one should operate one's business is dictated, in part, by the likelihood of its short-term success and the presence or absence of other income flowing to its owner.

Partnerships

Partnerships are also not separate taxable entities for the purposes of the federal income tax, although, in most cases, they are required to file informational tax returns with the IRS. Any profits generated by a partnership appear on the federal income tax returns of the partners, generally in proportions indicated by the underlying partnership agreement. Thus, as with sole proprietorships, this profit is taxed at the individual partner's highest marginal tax rate and the lower rates for the initial income of a separate taxable entity are forgone. In addition, each partner is taxed upon his proportion of the income of the partnership, regardless of whether that income was actually distributed to him.

As an example, if Bruce and Erika, our hotel magnates, were to take $25,000 of a year's profits to purchase a courtesy van for the business, this expenditure would not lower the business's profits by that amount. As a capital expense it may only be deducted over time in the form of depreciation. Thus, assuming they were equal partners, even if Michael had objected to this expenditure, each of the three, including Michael, would be forced to pay a tax on $8,333 (minus that year's depreciation) despite having received no funds with which to make such a payment. The result would be the same in a sole proprietorship, but this is considered less of a problem since it can be expected that the owner would manage cash flow in a way which would minimize this negative effect upon himself.

As with a sole proprietorship, this negative result becomes a positive one if the partnership is losing money. The losses appear on the partners's individual tax returns in the proportions set forth in the partnership agreement and render an equal amount of otherwise taxable income tax free. However, not all losses suffered by businesses result from the dreaded negative cash flow. As illustrated earlier in the case of the courtesy van, the next year, the hotel business might well break even or show a small profit on a cash flow basis, but the depreciation generated by the earlier purchase of the van might well result in a loss for tax purposes. Thus, with enough depreciation, a partner might have the double benefit of a tax sheltering loss on his tax return and ownership of a growing, profitable business. This is especially true regarding real estate, such as the hotel itself. While generating a substantial depreciation loss each year, the value of the building may well be increasing, yielding the partners a current tax-sheltering loss while at the same time generating a long-term capital gain for a few years hence.

Corporations

Corporations are treated as separate entities for federal income tax purposes, consistent with their treatment as separate entities for most other purposes. They have their own set of progressive tax rates, moving from 15 percent for the first $50,000 of income, through 25 percent for the next $25,000 and 34 percent for amounts above that. There is also a 5 percent additional tax at higher levels of income, to compensate for the lower rates on the first $50,000 of profit made by the more profitable corporations. Although these rates exceed the personal income tax rates at the highest levels, it is important for the small-business person to remember that they are usually lower than comparable personal rates at the lower end of the spectrum. In addition, so-called "professional service corporations" have only a flat 34 percent rate at all levels of income. Also, losses generated by a corporation may be carried back as many as three years to generate a tax refund or carried forward as many as 15 years to shelter future income.

Although corporate rates may be attractive at lower levels of income, the common fear of using the corporate form is the potential for "double taxation." Simply put, the corporation pays tax upon its profits and then distributes the remaining profit to its stockholders as nondeductible dividends. The stockholders then pay tax on the receipt of the dividends, thus amounting to two taxes on the same money. For a corporation in the 34 percent bracket with stockholders in the 28 percent bracket, the net effect is a combined tax rate of approximately 52.5 percent. Yet double taxation is rarely a concern for the small business. Such businesses generally manage compensation to their employees, who are usually their shareholders, in such a way that there is rarely much, if any, corporate profit remaining at the end of the year. Since compensation (as opposed to dividends) is deductible, the only level of taxation incurred by such businesses is at the stockholder level. Other opportunities for legitimate deductible payments to stockholders, which have the effect of eliminating corporate profit, include rental payments on assets leased by a stockholder to the corporation and interest on that portion of a stockholder's investment made in the form of debt.

Thus, the existence of the separate corporate entity with its own set of tax rates presents more of an opportunity for tax planning than a threat of double taxation. If the corporation intends to distribute all of its excess cash to its owners, it should manage compensation and other payments so as to show little profit and incur taxation only upon the stockholder level. If the corporation intends to retain some of its earnings in the form of capital acquisitions (thus resulting in an unavoidable profit for tax purposes), it can take advantage of the lower corporate rates without subjecting its stockholders to taxation at their level. Contrast this to a partnership where the partners would be required to pay tax at their highest marginal rates upon profits that they never received.

There are limits to the usefulness of these strategies. To begin with, one cannot pay salaries and bonuses to nonemployee stockholders who are not performing services for the corporation. In their cases, dividends may be the only way to give them a return on their investment. In addition, the Internal Revenue Service will not allow deductions for what it considers to be unreasonable compensation (measured by compensation paid to comparable employees in the same industry). Thus, a highly profitable corporation might find some of its excessive salaries to employee-stockholders recharacterized as nondeductible dividends.

However, for most start-up businesses, this corporate tax planning strategy will be useful, at least in the short term. In addition, entrepreneurs will find certain employee benefits are better offered in the corporate form because they are deductible to employers, but excluded from income only for employees. Since a sole proprietor or partner is not considered an employee, the value of benefits such as group medical insurance, group life insurance, and disability insurance policies would be taxable income to them, but tax free to the officers of a corporation.

Professional Corporations

There are two common variations of the corporate form. The first of these is the "professional corporation." Taxation played a major part in its invention. Originally, limitations on the amounts of money that could be deducted as a contribution to a qualified retirement plan varied greatly, depending upon whether the business maintaining the plan was a corporation, a partnership or a sole proprietorship. The rules greatly favored the corporation. Partnerships and sole proprietorships were required to adopt Keogh or HR-10 plans with their substantially lower limits on deductibility. However, doctors, lawyers, architects, and other professionals who often could afford large contributions to retirement plans, were not allowed to incorporate under applicable state laws. The states were offended by the notion that such professionals could be granted limited liability for the harms caused by their businesses.

Eventually, a compromise was struck and the so-called "professional corporation" was formed. Using that form, professionals could incorporate their businesses, thus qualifying for the higher retirement plan deductions, but they gave up any claim to limited liability. As time went by, however, the Internal Revenue Code was amended to eliminate most of the differences between the deductions available to Keogh plans and those available to corporate pension and profit-sharing plans. Today, professional corporations are subject to virtually all the same rules as other corporations, with the exception that most are classified as "professional service corporations" and therefore taxed at a flat 34 percent rate.

As the tax incentive for forming professional corporations has decreased, many states, perhaps with an eye toward maintaining the flow of fees from these corporations, have greatly liberalized the availability of limited liability for these corporations. Today, in many states, professional corporations now afford their stockholders protection from normal trade credit as well as tort liability arising from the actions of their employees or other stockholders. Even under the normal business corporation form, a stockholder is personally liable for torts arising from his own actions.

Subchapter S Corporations

The second common variation is the subchapter S corporation, named for the sections of the Internal Revenue Code that govern it. Although indistinguishable from the normal (or subchapter C) corporation in all other ways, including limited liability for its stockholders, the subchapter S corporation has affirmatively elected to be taxed as if it were a partnership. Thus, like the partnership, it is not a separate taxable entity and files only an informational return. Profits appear on the tax returns of its stockholders in proportion to shares of stock owned, regardless of whether those profits were distributed to the stockholders or retained for operations. Losses appear on the returns of the stockholders and may potentially be used to shelter other income.

Although the subchapter S corporation is often referred to as a "small business corporation," the size of the business has no bearing on whether this election is available. Any corporation that meets the following tests may, but need not, elect to be taxed as a subchapter S corporation.

1. It must have 35 or fewer stockholders.
2. It may have only one class of stock (although variations in voting rights are acceptable).
3. All stockholders must be individuals (or certain pass-through trusts).
4. No stockholder may be a nonresident alien.
5. It may not be a member of an affiliated group (no subsidiaries).

The subchapter S corporation is particularly suited to resolving the problems presented by certain discrete situations. For example, if a corporation is concerned that its profits are likely to be too high to eliminate double taxation through compensation to its stockholders, the subchapter S election eliminates the worry over unreasonable compensation. Since there is no tax at the corporate level, it is not necessary to establish the right to a compensation deduction. Similarly, if a corporation has nonemployee stockholders who insist upon current distributions of profit, the subchapter S election would allow declaration of dividends without the worry of double taxation. This would undoubtedly be attractive to most publicly traded corporations were it not for the 35-stockholders limitation mentioned earlier.

Since the Tax Reform Act of 1986, many entrepreneurs have turned to the subchapter S election in order to eliminate the two layers of tax, otherwise payable upon sale or dissolution of a corporation. The corporate tax, otherwise payable upon the gain realized on the sale of corporate assets, is eliminated by the use of the subchapter S election, as long as the election has been in effect for 10 years or, if less, since the corporation's inception. Finally, many entrepreneurs elect subchapter S status for their corporations if they expect to show losses in the short term. These losses can then be passed through to their individual tax returns to act as a shelter for other income. When the corporation begins to show a profit, the election can be reversed.

Limited Partnerships

The tax treatment of limited partnerships is much the same as general partnerships and subchapter S corporations. The profits and losses of the business are passed through to the partners in the proportions set forth in the partnership agreement. It must be emphasized that these profits and losses are passed through to all partners, including limited partners, even though one could argue that those profits and losses are derived entirely from the efforts of the general partners. It is this aspect of the limited partnership which made it the form of choice for tax-sheltered investments. The loss incurred by the business (much of which was created on paper through depreciation and the like), could be passed through to the limited partners who, typically, had a considerable amount of other investment and compensation income to be sheltered.

The IRS, in its quest to eliminate perceived abuses of these tax shelters, has taken the position that it is not bound by the taxpayer's characterization of the form of an entity. Thus, the IRS has often recharacterized an entity, formed under the limited partnership law of a state, as an association taxable as a corporation, thus trapping its losses at the corporate level. The IRS looks at four factors common to corporations to determine whether a limited partnership is a candidate for recharacterization.

1. *Centralized Management.* Corporations with numerous stockholders are nonetheless operated by a relatively small board of directors. Part-

nerships with many limited partners may be run by one or two general partners.

2. *Perpetual Life.* Corporations last forever, barring dissolution. A limited partnership which has provided in its agreement that the partners will accept a substitute general partner if an original general dies or otherwise withdraws, may also last forever.

3. *Free Transferability of Interests.* Stockholders can sell their shares relatively easily. Unless otherwise provided in the agreement, limited partners may similarly transfer their partnership interests.

4. *Limited Liability.* In a corporation, no individual is personally liable for its losses. If a limited partnership is established with a corporate general partner, the same result may be achieved.

The IRS will recharacterize the partnership if it finds three of the above four factors present. Although one cannot do much about centralized management, one could establish an outside date when the partnership will automatically dissolve in order to avoid perpetual life. One might also require all transfers of limited partnership interests to be approved, at the discretion of the general partners, to avoid free transferability. And, if one insists upon a corporate general partner, be sure it is well capitalized, in accordance with IRS regulations, so that it has something substantial at risk (Exhibit 6.4).

Although the tax treatments of limited partnerships and subchapter S corporations are essentially the same, there are some differences, which drive the operators of tax shelters to use partnerships over the corporate form, even at the risk of some unlimited liability. For one, although profits and losses must be allocated according to stock ownership in the subchapter S corporation, they are allocated by agreement in the limited partnership. Thus, in order to give the investors the high proportion of losses they demand, promoters did not necessarily have to give them an identically high proportion of the equity. The IRS has been attacking economically unrealistic allocations in recent years, but some of these opportunities may still exist. In addition, while the amount of loss the investor can use to shelter other income is limited to his tax basis, in both types of entities, the tax basis in subchapter S stock is essentially limited to direct investment in the corporation, while in a limited partnership, it is augmented by certain types of debt incurred by the entity itself.

Both types of entities have recently been afflicted by the operation of the passive loss rules, added by the Tax Reform Act of 1986, in the hope of eliminating the tax shelter. Thus, unless one materially participates in the operations of the entity (virtually impossible, by definition, for a limited partner), losses generated by those operations can normally be applied only

EXHIBIT 6.4. Association taxable as a corporation.

PROBLEM	SOLUTION
Centralized Management	_____
Perpetual Life	Include Dissolution Date in Agreement
Transferable Interests	Require Consent of General Partners
Limited Liability of Corporate General Partner	Adequate Capitalization

against so-called passive income and not against active (salaries and bonuses) or portfolio (interest and dividend) income.

CHOICE OF ENTITY

The sole proprietorship, partnership, corporation (including the professional corporation and subchapter S corporation), and the limited partnership are the most commonly used business forms. Other forms exist, such as the so-called Massachusetts business trust, in which the business is operated by trustees for the benefit of beneficiaries who hold transferable shares. But these are generally used for limited, specialized purposes. Armed with this knowledge and the comparative factors discussed above, how should our budding entrepreneurs operate their businesses?

Consulting Firm

It will be obvious to Jennifer, Jean, and George that they can immediately eliminate the sole proprietorship and limited partnership as choices for their consulting business. The sole proprietorship, by definition, allows for only one owner and there does not seem to be any need for the passive, silent investors who would serve as limited partners. Certainly, no one of the three would be willing to sacrifice the control and participation necessary to achieve limited partnership status.

The corporation gives the consultants the benefit of limited liability, not for their own mistakes, but for the mistakes of each other and their employees. It also protects them from personal liability for trade debt. This protection, however, comes at the cost of additional complexity and cost, such as additional tax returns, annual reports to the state, and annual fees. Ease of transferability and enhanced continuity do not appear to be deciding factors because a small consulting firm is often intensely personal and not likely to be transferable apart from its principals. Also, fear of double taxation does not appear to be a legitimate concern, since it is likely that the stockholders will be able to distribute any corporate profit to themselves in the form of compensation. In fact, to the extent that they may need to make some capital expenditures for word processing equipment and office furniture, the corporate form would afford them access to the lower corporate tax brackets for small amounts of income (unless the fell victim to characterization as a personal service corporation). Furthermore, if the consultants earn enough money to purchase various employee benefits, such as group medical insurance and group life and disability, they will qualify as employees of the corporation and can exclude the value of such benefits from their taxable income, while the corporation deducts these amounts.

These positive aspects of choosing the corporate form argue strongly against making the subchapter S election. That election would eliminate the benefit of the low-end corporate tax bracket and put our consultants in the position of paying individual income tax on the capital purchases made. The election would also eliminate the opportunity to exclude the value of employee benefits from their personal income tax.

The other possibility would be the general partnership. In essence, by choosing the partnership, the consultants would be trading away limited liability for less complexity. The partnership would not be a separate taxable entity and would not be required to file annual reports and pay annual fees. From a tax point, the partnership presents the same disadvantages as the subchapter S corporation.

In summary, it appears that our consultants will be choosing between the so-called C corporation and the partnership. The corporation adds complexity, but grants limited liability. And it certainly is not necessary for a business to be large in order to be incorporated. One might question, however, how much liability exposure a consulting firm is likely to face. In addition, although the corporation affords them the tax benefits associated with employee benefits and capital expenditures, it is not likely that our consultants will be able to afford much in the way of employee benefits and capital expenditures in the short term. Further, it is not likely that these consultants will have personal incomes placing them in tax brackets considerably higher than the corporation's. A strong case can be made for either the C corporation or the partnership in this situation. One can always incorporate the partnership in the future if the business grows to the point that some of the tax benefits become important.

It may also be interesting to speculate on the choice that would be made if our three consultants were lawyers or doctors. Then, the choice would be between the partnership and the professional corporation. The comparisons would be the same with the exception that, as a personal service corporation, the professional corporation does not have the benefit of the low-end corporate tax brackets.

Software Entrepreneur

In Phil's case, he can easily eliminate the partnership and the limited partnership. Phil is clearly the sole owner of his enterprise and will not brook any other controlling persons. In addition, his plan to finance the enterprise with earnings from his last business eliminates the need for limited partner investors. Almost as easily, Phil can eliminate the sole proprietorship, since it would seem highly undesirable to assume personal liability for whatever damage may be done by a product manufactured and distributed to thousands of potential plaintiffs. The corporation, therefore, appears to be Phil's obvious choice. It gives the benefit of limited liability, as well as the transferability and continuity essential to a business that seems likely to be an acquisition candidate in the future. Again, the lack of size is not a factor in this choice. Phil will likely act as sole director, president, treasurer, and secretary.

There remains, however, the choice between subchapters C and S. As may well be obvious by now, Phil's corporation fits the most common profile of the subchapter S candidate. For the first year or more, the corporation will suffer serious losses as Phil pays programmers and marketers to develop and presell his product. Subchapter S allows Phil to show these losses on his personal tax return, where they will shelter his considerable investment income. The passive loss limitations will not affect Phil's use of these losses, since he is clearly a material participant in his venture.

Hotel Venture

The hotel venture contemplated by Bruce, Erika, and Michael presents the opportunity for some creative planning. One problem they may encounter in making their decision is the inherent conflict presented by Michael's insistence upon recognition and reasonable return for his contribution of the land. Also, Bruce and Erika fear being unduly diluted by Michael's share, in the face of their more than equal contribution to the ongoing work.

One might break this logjam by looking to one of the ways of separating cash flow from equity. Michael need not contribute the real estate to the business entity at all. Instead, the business could lease the land from Michael on a long-term (99-year) basis. This would give Michael his return, in the form of rent, without distorting the equity split among the three entrepreneurs. From a tax point, this plan also changes a nondepreciable asset (land) into deductible rent payments for the business. As their next move, the three may decide to form an entity to construct and own the hotel building, separate from the entity that manages the ongoing hotel business.

This plan would convert a rather confusing real estate/operating venture into a pure real estate investment opportunity for potential investors. The real estate entity would receive enough revenue from the management entity to cover its cash flow and would generate tax losses through depreciation, interest, and real estate taxes. These short-term losses will eventually yield long-term capital gains when the hotel is sold, so this entity will attract investors looking for short-term losses and long-term capital appreciation. For the short-term losses to be attractive, however, they must be usable by the investors on their personal returns and not trapped at the business entity level.

All these factors point inevitably to the use of either the limited partnership or the subchapter S corporation for the hotel building entity. Both entities allow the tax losses to pass through to the owners, for use on their personal returns. Between these two choices, the limited partnership allows more flexibility in allocating losses to the investors, and away from Bruce, Erika, and Michael (who most likely do not need them), and it provides higher limits on the amounts of losses each investor may use.

The subchapter S corporation would give limited liability to all parties, while the limited partnership would require one, two, or all of our entrepreneurs to accept unlimited risk. Nonetheless, the likely choice for this real estate entity will be the limited partnership, since the principals will have to entice investors with losses and will not wish to sacrifice a disproportionate amount of future appreciation in order to allocate short-term losses to them. The general partners will have to be comforted by the knowledge that the most likely liability exposures in this type of venture are likely to be insurable. However, the passive loss limitations will impact upon the usefulness of the losses for the limited partners who do not have significant passive income, making this project (as is the case with most real estate investments in today's climate) more difficult to sell.

This leaves the entity which will operate the hotel business itself. The presence of our three principals immediately eliminates the sole proprietorship as a possibility. Because all the investment capital has already been raised for the real estate entity, there does not seem to be a need for further investors, thus eliminating the limited partnership as a possibility. The partnership seems inapplicable, since it is unlikely that any of the principals would wish to expose himself or herself to unlimited liability in such a consumer-oriented business.

Thus, the corporation, with its limited liability, continuity, and transferability, seems to be the obvious choice for this potentially growing and successful business. As with Phil, it becomes necessary to decide whether to make the subchapter S election. This decision will be made on the basis of the parties's projections. Are there likely to be serious losses in the short-term, which might be usable on their personal tax returns? Will there be a need for significant capital expenditures, thus indicating a need for the low-end corporate tax rates? Will the company offer a variety of employee benefits, which our principals would wish to exclude from their taxable income? Is the company likely to generate more profit than can be distributed in the form of "reasonable" compensation, thus calling for the elimination of the corporate tax entity through the S election?

CONCLUSION

These and the many other factors described in this chapter deserve careful consideration by the thousands of entrepreneurs forming businesses every month. After the basic decision to start a new business itself, the choice of the appropriate form for the business may well be the most significant decision facing the entrepreneur in the short run.

GLOSSARY

Account, Duty to: The obligation of an agent or employee to keep accurate records of and turn over to his/her principal or employer any property received on behalf of said principal employer.

Apparent Authority: The power of an agent to bind his/her principal to contracts with third parties based, not upon express authority granted by the principal, but upon an appearance of authority created by the principal's acts or omissions.

Assignability: The ability to transfer the benefits and/or obligations under a contract to a third party without the consent of the other party to the contract.

Basis, Tax: The taxpayer's cost for an asset, adjusted for any further improvements or additions to such asset and for any previous cost recoveries, such as depreciation or non-taxable distributions with respect to stock.

Charging Order: The right of a partner's creditors to have all distributions from the partnership which would otherwise be payable to that partner paid to the creditors.

Close Corporation: A corporation, all of the stock of which is owned by a small group of individuals who are usually directly involved with the operation of its business.

Derivative Suit: A lawsuit brought by a stockholder of a corporation on the corporation's behalf in order to pursue alleged rights of the corporation which its directors have refused to pursue. Usually these rights are asserted against the directors themselves.

Joint and Several Liability: Each potentially responsible party is responsible for the entire amount of the liability, not just his/her proportionate share.

Material Participation: The level of activity necessary by an equity owner to escape characterization of the enterprise as a passive activity. Absent special circumstances, such activity must exceed 1000 hours in the tax year.

Passive Income and Loss: Income and loss generated by a passive activity. As a general rule, an individual taxpayer will not be able to use passive loss to offset any of his or her income other than passive income.

Personal Service Corporation: A corporation, virtually all of whose revenues are derived from the personal services of its shareholders.

Promoter: An individual who intends to form a corporation for the conduct of his/her business.

Proxy: The grant by a stockholder to another party of the right to vote the stockholder's shares of stock.

Torts: Any of a series of civil wrongs committed by one party against another. Examples include: assault, battery, libel, slander, interference with contractual relations, unfair competition, negligence, etc.

Ultra Vires: Actions by a corporation which violate or go beyond the purposes expressed in its corporate charter.

FOR FURTHER READING

Burstiner, Irving, *The Small Business Handbook: A Comprehensive Guide to Starting and Running Your Own Business* (New York: Prentice-Hall Press, 1989).

Harper, Stephen C., *The McGraw-Hill Guide to Starting Your Own Business* (New York: McGraw-Hill, 1991).

Pollan, Stephen M. and Mark Levine, *The Field Guide to Starting a Business* (New York: Simon & Schuster, 1990).

Siegel, Joel G. and Jae K. Shim, *Keys to Starting a Small Business* (New York: Barrons, 1991).

Tetreault, Wilfred F. and Robert W. Clements, *Starting Right in Your New Business* (Reading, MA: Addison-Wesley, 1987).

THE BUSINESS PLAN: A STEP-BY-STEP GUIDE

7

Jeffry A. Timmons

PLANNING AND THE BUSINESS PLAN

The What

Planning is a way of thinking about the future of a venture; that is, of deciding where a firm needs to go and how fast, how to get there, and what to do along the way to reduce the uncertainty and to manage risk and change.

Effective planning is a process of setting goals and deciding how to attain them. Planning occurs in start-up situations, in growing enterprises, and in very large firms.

In some sense, most successful ventures plan. One author writing in the *Harvard Business Review* observed that:

> The smaller companies weathering the current difficult economic times seem to be those following an idea—call it a no-frills, down-to-earth, but clear plan—of how to take advantage of the environment and how to allocate resources.[1]

A business plan is one type of planning document which results from the process of planning. A business plan is a written document that (1) summarizes a business opportunity (i.e., why the opportunity exists and why the management team has what it takes to execute the plan) and (2) defines and articulates how the management team expects to seize and execute the opportunity identified.[2]

A complete business plan usually is of considerable length. In recent years, however—particularly in business based on certain technologies, products, or services, where there is turbulence, greater-than-usual unpredictability, and rapid change—an alternative to a complete full-blown busi-

---

Excerpted and adapted from *New Venture Creation*, 3rd ed., 1990, by Jeffry A. Timmons, Leonard E. Smollen and Alexander L. M. Dingee.

ness plan has become acceptable. This can be called a "dehydrated" business plan. Dehydrated business plans serve most often as trial balloons for prospective investors and are launched before a decision is made to undertake a complete business plan.

In any case, creating a business plan is more a process than simply a product, and the resulting plan is not immutable. By the same token, the business plan for a business is not "the business." A business plan is analogous to a pilot's cross-country flight plan in that it defines the most desired, most timely, and least-hazardous route to a given destination. Yet, innumerable factors, such as unexpected weather and traffic, can significantly alter the course of the actual flight. Similarly, for new companies, it is common for the actual course of the business to diverge from that originally developed in a business plan. For as was said in the first century, B.C., "It is a bad plan that admits of no modification."[3]

The Why

Business plans are used primarily (1) for raising capital and (2) as a means of guiding growth.

The decision whether to plan, and ultimately to write a business plan, then involves the following:

- Whether the venture needs to raise capital, and whether a business plan is valuable for this purpose.
- Whether the planning process itself will be valuable enough in terms of defining and anticipating potential risks, problems, and trade-offs in a venture to justify the time spent.

For ventures seeking to raise venture capital or other equity in today's highly competitive environment, a quality business plan is a must. As William Egan, founding partner of one of the nation's largest and most successful venture capital funds, Burr, Egan & Deleage, put it:

> Ten to fifteen years ago, a high-quality business plan really stood out and gave the entrepreneur a competitive edge in getting our attention. Today, you have to have a high-quality plan as a given—without it you're dead—but since everyone coming to us for money has a highly professional plan, the plan won't give you much of an edge by itself.

As a vehicle for raising capital, a business plan convinces investors that the new venture has identified an opportunity, has the entrepreneurial and management talent to exploit that opportunity, and has a rational, coherent, and believable program for achieving revenue and expense targets on time. If the business plan passes the initial screening, the plan will be given a more detailed evaluation, and it will become a prime measure of the abilities of those involved to define and analyze opportunities and problems and to identify and plan actions to deal with them.

A business plan can be particularly helpful after start-up as a tool to understand and as a means of guiding growth. One can think of developing a business plan as using a flight simulator. The consequences of different strategies and tactics and the human and financial requirements for launching and building the venture can be determined and worked through without the risk and cost of working these out in real time. The learning necessary to start a company can thus be accelerated. As Nolan Bushnell, founder of Atari, responded when asked by a student if he should prepare a business plan:

> That's exactly what you have to do. There is no way around it; you're doing the best thing. Every time you prepare a business plan, you become a better entrepreneur—I really believe that.[4]

And, as the founder and president of one venture that grew to sales of $14 million in seven years put it:

> Once you are in the business, you realize that everyone, including the founders, is learning his or her job. If you have a thoughtful and complete business plan, you have a lot more confidence in your decisions. You have a reference already there to say, "Well I have already run the numbers on inventory, or cost of goods, and this is what will happen."

For example, a business plan can be valuable in areas such as product pricing. The initial strategy of one of the founders of a new venture was to price products below the competition, even though the venture's products were based on a superior product innovation and could compete in a growing market. In the process of writing a business plan, the founders were persuaded, as a result of vigorously arguing about the pricing strategy with their venture investors, to set prices 10 percent above those of the competition. By its second year, the new company enjoyed pretax profits of $850,000, based on about $9 million in sales. Through the detailed analysis of the industry and competition of the marketing section of the business plan, the wisdom of a different pricing strategy became evident.

A business plan also can help in refining strategy and in making difficult decisions. An entrepreneur in Nova Scotia, who built commercial fishing boats, decided to raise his prices by more than 40 percent, based on an outside analysis and a critique of his business plan. Of five original orders, he knew he would lose two orders, but he also knew he would make more profit on the remaining three orders than he did on all five at the old price. His delivery time would be cut in half as well, and the shortened delivery time would lead to additional sales at the higher margins. He also decided to require progress payments. These payments would eliminate the need to raise outside equity capital.

The process also can clarify the venture's financial requirements. For example, an entrepreneur in Kentucky, with a $1 million-plus business erecting coal-loading sites, which was three years old, believed he needed $350,000 in expansion capital. After reflecting on a detailed critique of his presentation of his business plan, he concluded:

> The worst thing I could do right now is put more money into the business. The first thing I should do is get my own backyard more in order. But I will be back in two or three years.

True to his prediction, he returned two and a half years later. His company then approached $3 million in sales and had a business plan for expansion that resulted in a $400,000 debt capital investment without relinquishing any ownership.

The Whether

Philip Thurston of the Harvard Business School identified dimensions that are unique to each venture and management team. Understanding where a venture sits along these dimensions can help it decide whether to plan:[5]

- *Administrative style and ability.*   Whether to plan depends on the ability of the lead entrepreneur or chief executive officer to grasp multiple and interrelated aspects of the business, keep all that is necessary in his or her head, and retrieve it in an orderly fashion. Further, whether to plan depends on the lead entrepreneur's management style.
- *Wishes of the management team.*   Whether (and how) to plan depend on the wishes of the management team. Some management teams want to participate in the planning process, and others do not.
- *Complexity of the business.*   The complexity of a business will determine whether to plan.
- *Strength of competition.*   Strength of the competition is a factor. Some ventures compete in highly competitive environments where there is a need to be lean and tightly disciplined to survive, while others are more insulated and have a larger margin for error.
- *Level of uncertainty.*   Whether to plan depends also on the level of uncertainty the venture faces. Some ventures face a quite volatile, rapidly changing environment and must be prepared for contingencies, while some enter stable, fairly predictable industries where precipitous actions are not warranted.

In addition, ventures have to face different constituencies, both external and internal, including creditors, shareholders, regulators, customers, community groups, employee groups, and the like. The more of these a firm has to contend with and respond to, the greater the potential payoff in some form of organized and disciplined planning.

Among existing firms, especially those backed by venture capital, the harvest issue is especially important. A business plan for an ongoing business can significantly enhance its harvest potential. Such a document can focus and articulate why there is a major opportunity for a prospective buyer in much the same way a business plan does for a venture that is starting up and seeking investors. For firms not backed by professional investors, planning is important, because they do not have such a backer as the prime motivator and a driving force to realize a harvest or easy access to the skills, know-how, and networks of such a backer.

In addition, an existing firm contemplating launching a venture opportunity internally needs to consider a business plan and may already have formal planning processes in place. Take, for instance, one of the founders of a firm that had grown to $20 million in sales in about a dozen years. He used a business plan to present to his partners and to his board a statement of an opportunity for internal expansion—essentially a new business from within.

Other reasons commonly cited for planning are:[6]

- *Working smarter.* Planning helps a management team to work "smarter" (i.e., come up with a "better way" by considering alternatives), rather than simply "harder." Planning enables a management team to understand and clarify the risks and, in turn, to devise ways to manage those risks and reduce them.

- *Future orientation.* Planning necessitates an orientation to the future. Thinking ahead helps a team anticipate and, thus, be more alert for and responsive to problems, opportunities, and changes.

- *Testing ideas.* Planning helps management to develop and then to update strategy by testing the sensibility of its ideas and approaches.

- *Results orientation.* Goal setting also gives a team a "results orientation" (i.e., a concern for accomplishment and progress).[7] Developing and stating a specific goal, which is measurable and phased over time, enables performance to be evaluated.

- *Stress management.* Establishing realistic goals can help in managing and coping with what is by nature a stressful situation.

- *Motivation.* A more subtle consequence of planning is the effect that setting realistic goals has on motivation. Inherent in any goal is some level of effort required to attain it, and this level of effort, once made clear, can be judged in terms of its ease of attainment. Research has shown that individuals pursuing challenging but attainable goals are more motivated to work toward that goal than are individuals pursuing goals that are either too easy or too difficult.

Problems with Planning

Planning is not for everyone. Commonly cited problems, which often result in decisions not to plan, are the following:

- *Currency.* A plan, such as a business plan, can be out of date as soon as, or even before, it is written. For example, in highly volatile and turbulent technologies and rapidly changing market niches, planning tends to be ad hoc and spontaneous and any plans are often obsolete before they get printed.
- *Inflexibility.* It sometimes is undesirable to commit under uncertainty since the future cannot be predicted. Planning requires setting goals, making choices, and setting priorities. Inherent in this process is the possibility that future or yet unknown options, which actually might be more attractive than the one chosen, may be lost or excluded.
- *Inability to plan.* Invariably, an event entirely beyond the control of a management team, such as the Arab oil crisis in the 1970s, may boost or sink its best-laid plans. No planning process can foresee such developments.
- *Time problems.* During the demanding early survival stages of a new company, whose life expectancy at times may be estimated in weeks or months, major allocations of time and effort to planning for next year may not make sense.[8]
- *Sales jeopardy.* A potentially fatal problem for entrepreneurs occurs when planning is substituted for action in getting orders.

While these are usually rationalizations, there may be times when they are valid. An example would be when the window of an attractive opportunity is closing faster than a business plan can be developed.

PITFALLS OF EFFECTIVE PLANNING

What Can Go Wrong

Finally, there are pitfalls in planning. Most important, the process of planning can be carried to extreme. One author warns of the excesses of "planning systems."[9] Excessive detail, analysis, and bureaucratic tendencies toward red tape and "checkups" can detract from the purpose of planning, which needs to be the accomplishment of goals and implementation.

This is one reason why large companies have a difficult time developing new, entrepreneurial business from within. Take, for example, an entrepreneur who headed up a new business venture for a Fortune 500 company. At a conference at the Harvard Business School in early 1989, she described how the "financial overseers" had insisted on 13 very detailed budget reviews, and defenses, during the start-up's first year. The entrepreneurs in attendance, and the author, were astounded at such a mentality and were even more delighted to discover how the competition was approaching the start-up process!

Perhaps there is no greater frustration for entrepreneurs and managers than to experience failure with plans seemingly well prepared and well intended. Not only is it frustrating and consumes precious hours, it is downright demoralizing when a plan does not work initially. The planning process goes awry for some of the following reasons:

- *Wrong emphasis.*   Planning is ineffective if the process itself is overlooked and planning is viewed as an end in itself. If a plan does not seem to work immediately, the lead entrepreneur and his or her team often retreat to the familiar and fall back on an activity-oriented routine or crisis management, which lacks or confuses priorities, has no longer-term purpose, and is not aimed at the attainment of particular objectives.

- *Rigidity.*   Planning fails when the process becomes too rigid and is performed in a lock-step, immutable order. Entrepreneurs need to be very certain that, if their strategies and plans define directions which have irreversible consequences, they are certain they wind up where they want to be and can live with the consequences.

- *Misunderstanding of the function of a business plan.*   Marketability, for example, generally outweighs technical elegance in the success equation, and it usually is necessary to plan to achieve a good fit. Yet some entrepreneurs place more faith, often unwarranted, in a product or invention, especially if it is patented. Readers will recognize the better mousetrap fallacy in this attitude. Even those who understand the value of marketing and business acumen, and who have done a great deal of thinking about how to execute an opportunity, ignore the function of planning in identifying problems, testing the soundness of their ideas internally and with knowledgeable outside sources, and so forth.

- *Misunderstanding of the process of raising capital.*   There is a misconception that a business plan is solely a selling and negotiating tool for raising money. Indeed, more than one entrepreneur has been heard to comment that the plan is "destined for the circular file" once the funds are in the bank. Such a view is wrong for several reasons. First, to prospective partners, investors, or suppliers, such an attitude communicates a shallow understanding of the requirements for creating a successful business. It also can signal to these people a promotional attitude—a search for fast money and a hope for an early sellout—and can create mistrust. In addition, entrepreneurs do not understand that business plans are used, in addition to being the basis of investment decisions, to screen investments. Thus, relying on raising money as an indication that an idea is sound is a cart-before-the-horse approach, which usually results in rejection.

Exhibit 7.1 summarizes some of the ailments of effective planning listed below, which, if not cured, can cause the death of the planning for an organization:

- *Undefined goals.* Admirable missions, such as "improving performance," "pursuing growth," or "increasing business" are not concrete goals, and plans centered around these undefined goals are unlikely to work. Specific, measurable, time-phased, and realistic goals are necessary. New competition, loss of key personnel, overly ambitious timetables, and a host of other uncertainties rear their ugly heads as planning proceeds and as plans are implemented. Goals, therefore, need to be reviewed and revised periodically.

- *Inability to anticipate obstacles.* Excessive optimism and overcommitment can seriously impede efforts to anticipate obstacles. Overcommitment can lead to ignoring reality and pressing ahead on a course that may be unduly risky and costly. Every plan, no matter how carefully prepared, has limitations and built-in conflicts over priorities and resources. And, every firm faces obstacles, planned and unplanned. Effective planners know that planning is not an exercise in identifying the impossible so as to rationalize failure, but rather, so as what is perceived to be impossible can be broken down into small hurdles. Concrete action steps are then established to overcome these. Further, an effective plan contains flexibility to deal with unknown and unexpected problems. Experience obtained during the planning process is used to advantage.

- *Lack of progress milestones and review.* Plans that fail often have no concrete milestones, such as revenue, cost, and cash flow targets, and no progress review dates (or they are allowed to slip by). The rationale usually is expressed by such statements as, "It can wait," "I can remember that," or "I know how I'm doing!" Milestones and planning reviews are necessary to check on progress relative to goals. Further, in the setting of goals and establishment of milestones, interdependencies need to be recognized. For example, goals for sales and for production are related.

EXHIBIT 7.1.   Planning: Its ailments, symptoms, and cures.

Planning	Symptoms	Cure
1. No real goals	Goals are vague, general. Goals not specific, measurable, or time-phased. No subgoals or action steps. Activity oriented, not goal-oriented.	Set specific, time-phased, measurable goals, subgoals, and action steps. Keep the overall aim in mind. Be opportunistic in pursuing goals.
2. Failure to anticipate obstacles	Excessive optimism. No alternative strategies. No conflicts recognized. "Don't worry, I had thought of that." Missed meeting delivery date. Missed lead-time forecasts. Didn't get support when needed. Crises prevail.	Be flexible in planning and anticipating as far as possible obstacles and how to overcome them. Face unanticipated obstacles with confidence—there'll always be some. Ask someone else to brainstorm with you, "What could go wrong or get in our way?" Realism is key.
3. Lack of milestones and progress reviews	"It can wait"; "I can remember that." "I'll know how we're doing when we get there—let's play it by ear." Don't really know how you are doing. Short-term orientation. Can't recall when we last reviewed how we are doing. No recent revisions of plan.	Set specific task milestones and progress review dates; stick to them and revise when needed. Ask each day, "What did I accomplish today toward reaching my goal?" Ask each day, "What have I learned that will help me to make more rapid progress?"
4. Lack of commitment	"I told you it wouldn't work—it wasn't *my* plan!" Procrastination. Focus on routine, daily activities. Failure to meet goals, milestones. Failure to develop specific action steps to meet goals. Lack of priorities. Missed meetings, appointments.	Set goals mutually; utilize *joint* review, negotiation, compromise, and data sharing. Meet periodically, and track progress. Encourage informal discussion with team members, both to test and to renew commitment. Keep team members informed about results obtained. Recognize and reward performance that meets your high standards.
5. Failure to revise goals	Plan never changes, lacks resiliency. Inflexible or stubborn in face of feedback dictating change.	Meet periodically to review goals and progress and to assess the situation.

EXHIBIT 7.1. *(Continued).*

Planning	Symptoms	Cure
	Goals not met or exceeded greatly. Unresponsive to changing situation. Help not sought when needed. Wasted time on unproductive tasks or activities. Activities don't match goal priorities.	Change emphasis and approach as appropriate. Create a climate that is tolerant of bad news and invites constructive critiques and feedback.
6. Failure to learn from experience	Lost sight of goals. Mistake is repeated. Feedback is ignored or denied. Same routine—same crises as previously. Unwillingness to change way of doing things. Not asking: "What do we learn from this experience?"	Set improvement and learning objectives. Use milestones, and reassess periodically. Collaborate more frequently in tracking progress and learning. Document at end of one project/plan lessons, benchmarks, guidelines have emerged. What was learned? Be adaptive, flexible, and responsive to unfolding events. A new venture start-up is full of surprises. Concentrate on producing results, not on reports for their own sake.

While some deviation of progress from goals is normal in start-up situations, the falling behind in revenue targets or cost overruns can result in a firm being more than four to six months behind at the end of the year. In addition, milestones, when they are achieved, provide an important sense of accomplishment and, thus, motivation to succeed further.

- *Lack of commitment.* It is quite easy to obtain only a "lip-service" commitment and not a commitment to and ownership of a plan. Commitment is critical to the success of any plan, because it provides the motivation for critical people to see a plan through to completion. Commitment seems to stem from involving critical people in the process of planning and developing goals from the outset, since this involvement generates their interest, inputs, and, more important, ownership in the plan.

- *Failure to revise goals.* Effective reviews and feedback simply test the velocity, direction, and reality of the plan at any point in time. Failure to reassess and reset goals and revise plans as dictated by the realities that unfold is another reason planning fails. Failure, thus, is programmed into a plan. Progress reviews are wasted if a new situation is not met with a change in emphasis or approach. Failure to learn from current and past experience either because of unwillingness to change or denial of reality is another reason planning fails.

- *Performance expectations.* It is easy to overlook clarity in expectations. Performance expectations need to be made clear and a win/win situation created for critical people.

EXHIBIT 7.2. Do's and don'ts.

DO

DO involve all of the management team in the preparation of the business plan.

DO make the plan logical, comprehensive, and *readable*—and as short as possible.

DO demonstrate commitment to the venture by investing a significant amount of time and some money in preparing the plan.

DO articulate what the critical risks of assumptions are and how and why these are tolerable.

DO disclose and discuss any current or potential problems in the venture.

DO identify several alternative sources of financing.

DO spell out the proposed deal—how much for what ownership share—and how investors will win.

DO be creative in gaining the attention and interest of potential investors.

DO remember that the plan is not the business and that an ounce of "can do" implementation is worth two pounds of planning.

DO accept orders and customers that will generate a positive cash flow, even if it means you have to postpone writing the plan.

DO know your targeted investor group (e.g., venture capitalist, angel, bank, or leasing company) and what they really want and what they dislike, and tailor your plan accordingly.

DO let realistic market and sales projections drive the assumptions underlying the financial spreadsheets, rather than the reverse.

DON'T

DON'T have unnamed, mysterious people on the management team (e.g., a "Mr. G" who is currently a financial vice president with another firm and who will join you later).

DON'T make ambiguous, vague, or unsubstantiated statements, such as estimating sales on the basis of what the team would like to produce.

DON'T describe technical products or manufacturing processes using jargon or in a way that only an expert can understand, because this limits the usefulness of the plan. For example, a venture capitalist will not invest in what he or she does not understand—or what he or she thinks the team does not understand, because it cannot explain these to such a smart person as he or she is.

DON'T spend money on developing fancy brochures, elaborate slide show presentations and other "sizzle"—instead, show the "steak."

DON'T waste time writing a plan when you could be closing sales and collecting cash.

DON'T assume you have a done deal when you have a "handshake" or verbal commitment but no money in the bank. (The deal is done when the check clears!)

Important Do's and Don'ts

Before getting into the details of what needs to be in a business plan, it is worth noting some important general do's and don'ts for preparing such plans. Exhibit 7.2 shows these do's and don'ts. These do's and don'ts have come from the experience of those writing business plans as a result of observations of the reactions of venture capitalists to a great many business plans, as well as from publications dealing with the foibles, pet hates, and preferences of venture capitalists.[10]

A CLOSER LOOK AT THE WHAT

The Relationship between Goals and Actions

Consider a team that is enthusiastic about an idea for a new business and has done a considerable amount of thinking and initial work evaluating the opportunity. Team members believe the business they are considering has excellent market prospects and fits well with the skills, experience, personal goals and values, and aspirations of its lead entrepreneur and the management team. They now need to ask questions about what the most significant risks and problems involved in launching the enterprise are; what its long-term profit prospects are; what its future financing and cash flow requirements will be; what the demands of operating lead times, seasonality, and facility location will be; what the marketing and pricing strategy needs to be; and so forth, so they can take action.

These questions now need to be answered convincingly and the evidence for them shown in writing. The planning and the development of such a business plan is neither quick nor easy. In fact, effective planning is a difficult and demanding process and demands time, discipline, commitment and dedication, and practice. However, it also can be stimulating and fun as innovative solutions and strategies to solve nagging problems are found.

The skills to write a business plan are not necessarily the ones that are needed to make a venture successful (although some of these skills are certainly useful). The best single point of departure for and an anchor during the planning process is the motto on a small plaque in the office of Paul J. Tobin, president of Cellular One, a company that was a pioneer in the cellular car phone business in America. The motto says, "CAN DO," and is an apt one for planning and for making sure that a plan serves the very practical purpose for which it is intended.

Before proceeding, however, it is essential to reiterate that effective planning is goal-oriented, rather than activity-oriented. *It is through effective goal setting that action steps are devised.*

Goals are not dreams, fantasies, or the product of wishful thinking; nor are they mere predictions or guesses about future outcomes. A goal is a decision or choice about future outcomes. Once set, goals should not become static targets. Goal setting is not a task but a process, a way of dealing with the world that is repeated over and over as conditions change.

There are numerous ways of actually going about goal setting and planning. Most of these approaches have in common a balanced emphasis on both the process by which goals are set and the results they seek. Research and practical experience have shown that certain ingredients are common to almost all successful planning efforts:

- Establishment of goals that are:
  - Specific and concrete
  - Measurable
  - Related to time (i.e., specific about what will be accomplished over a certain time period)
  - Realistic and attainable
  - Capable of being modified and adapted
  - Certain to make a significant difference
- Establishment of priorities and identification of conflicts and how to resolve them
- Identification of problems and obstacles
- Specification of necessary tasks and actions steps
- Indication of how results will be measured
- Establishment of progress milestones, especially revenue, expense, and cash targets, deadlines, and dates
- Identification of risks involved and alternatives for coping with possible contingencies
- Identification of outside help and resources that need to be marshalled and controlled
- Periodic review of progress and revision of goals as factors such as the changing competitive situation require

In the process of establishing goals and priorities, a planner needs a sense of perspective. The general wisdom is that 80 percent of a task usually is accomplished using the first 20 percent of the effort. Therefore, one needs to focus first on what will result in 80 percent of the accomplishments. Often, there will not be time to do otherwise.

Who Develops the Business Plan

Consideration often is given to hiring an outside professional to prepare the business plan, so the management team can use its time to obtain financing and start the business.

There are two good reasons why it is not a good idea to hire outside professionals. First, in the process of planning and of writing the business plan, the consequences of different strategies and tactics and the human and financial requirements for launching and building the venture can be examined, before it is too late. For example, one entrepreneur discovered, while preparing his business plan, that the major market for his biomedical product was in nursing homes, rather than in hospital emergency rooms, as he and his physician partner had previously assumed. This realization changed the focus of the entire marketing effort. Had he left the preparation to an outsider, this might not have been discovered, or, at the very least, it is unlikely he would have had the same sense of confidence and commitment to the new strategy.

Further, if a venture intends to use the business plan to raise capital, it is important for the team to do the planning and write the plan itself. Investors attach great importance to the quality of the management team *and* to their complete understanding of the business they are preparing to enter. Thus, investors want to be sure that what they see is what they get— that is, the team's analysis and understanding of the venture opportunity and its commitment to it. They are going to invest in a team and a leader, not in a consultant. Nothing less will do, and anything less is usually obvious.

Segmenting and Integrating Information

In the task of planning and writing a business plan, it is necessary to organize information in a way that it can be managed and that is useful.

An effective way to organize information with the idea of developing a business plan is to segment the information into "sections," such as a section about the target market, a section about the industry, one about competition, one about the financial plan, etc., and then integrate the information into a business plan.

This process works best if sections are discreet and the information within them digestible. Then the order in which sections are developed can vary, and different sections can be developed simultaneously. For example, since the heart and soul of a plan lies in the analysis of the market opportunity, of the competition, and of a resultant competitive strategy that can win, it is a good idea to start with these sections and integrate information along the way. Since the financial and operations aspects of the venture will be driven by the rate of growth and the magnitude and specific substance of the market revenue plans, these can be developed later.

The information is then further integrated into the business plan. For example, the Executive Summary is prepared last.

Establishing Action Steps

The following steps, centered around actions to be taken, outline the process by which a business plan is written.

- *Segmenting information.* An overall plan for the project, by section, needs to be devised and needs to include priorities, who is responsible for each section, the due date of a first draft, and the due date of a final draft.

- *Creating an overall schedule.* A list of specific tasks, their priorities, who is responsible for them, when they will be started, and when they will be completed needs to be made. This list needs to be as specific and detailed as possible. Tasks need to be broken down into the smallest possible components (e.g., a series of phone calls may be necessary before a trip). The list then needs to be examined for conflicts and lack of reality in time estimates. Peers and business associates can be asked to review the list of realism, timing, and priorities.

- *Creating an action calendar.* Tasks on the "do" list then need to be placed on a calendar. When the calendar is complete, the calendar needs again to be examined for conflicts or lack of realism.

- *Doing the work and writing the plan.* The necessary work needs to be done and the plan written. Adjustments need to be made to the "do" list and the calendar, as necessary. As part of this process, it is important to have a plan reviewed by an attorney to make sure that it contains no misleading statements and unnecessary information and caveats, and also reviewed by an objective outsider, such as an entrepreneurially minded executive who has significant profit and loss responsibility, or a venture capitalist who would not be a potential investor. No matter how good the lead entrepreneur and his or her team are in planning, there will be issues that they will overlook and certain aspects of the presentation that are inadequate or less than clear. Few entrepreneurs are good at both planning and communication. A good reviewer also can act as a sounding board in the process of developing alternative solutions to problems and answers to questions investors are likely to ask.

The remainder of this chapter is a sample business plan for the company Rapidrill.

CASE—RAPRIDRILL BUSINESS PLAN

RAPIDRILL CORPORATION*
BUSINESS PLAN

Confidential Plan Number _____

Delivered to _____

BUSINESS PLAN
RAPIDRILL CORPORATION
15 MAIN STREET
NASHVILLE, TENNESSEE
615-365-5749
DECEMBER 10, 19X1

SECURITIES OFFERED:
240,000 SHARES OF COMMON STOCK AT $1 PER SHARE

This business plan has been submitted on a confidential basis solely for the benefit of selected, highly qualified investors in connection with the private placement of the above securities and is not for use by any other persons, nor may it be reproduced. By accepting delivery of this plan, the recipient agrees to return this copy to the Corporation at the address listed above if the recipient does not undertake to invest in the Corporation.

Table of Contents

Summary

1. The Industry, the Company, and the Product
2. The Management Team
3. Market Research and Analysis
4. Marketing Plan
5. Design and Development Plans
6. Manufacturing Plan
7. Schedule
8. Risks
9. Financial Plan
10. Proposed Rapidrill Offering

_____

*The name of the company and other details have been disguised.

Exhibits

- Sales and Earnings Forecasts—Fiscal Years Ended September 30, 19X2–19X6
- Monthly Sales and Earnings Forecasts—Fiscal Year Ended September 30, 19X2
- Quarterly Sales and Earnings Forecasts—Fiscal Years Ended September 30, 19X3–19X4
- Pro Forma Cash Flows—Fiscal Years Ended September 30, 19X2–19X6
- Pro Forma Monthly Cash Flows—Fiscal Year Ended September 30, 19X2
- Pro Forma Quarterly Cash Flows—Fiscal Year Ended September 30, 19X3–19X4
- Pro Forma Balance Sheets—Fiscal Year Ended September 30, 19X1–19X6
- Pro Forma Monthly Balance Sheets—Fiscal Year Ended September 30, 19X2
- Pro Forma Quarterly Balance Sheets—Fiscal Year Ended September 30, 19X3–19X4
- 19X2–19X3 Breakeven Analysis
- Present and Proposed Capitalization

SUMMARY

Rapidrill was formed in April 19X1 and incorporated in the state of Delaware in August 19X1 by a highly knowledgeable and experienced team of five executives in response to what they believed to be an attractive business opportunity created by the following conditions:

1. The market for their product, rotary drills, is substantial ($74 million in 19X0); has demonstrated a 10 percent annual growth for the past six years; and has strong indicators of accelerated future growth.
2. Prices and margins are attractive (earnings after taxes average 9 percent in the industry) and have been firm.
3. The major existing competitive manufacturers have high costs and high fixed investments, in both manufacturing facilities and distribution organizations. They are also producing drills at near capacity.
4. Rapidrill believes it can achieve cost savings over competitors of from 9 percent to 12 percent in total manufacturing and selling expenses.
5. Rapidrill's ability to accomplish its program is significantly related to the know-how and track record of its management team: their past team efforts increased the market share of the present industry leader

from 9 percent to 22 percent of the market in the past five years. The improbability of duplicating this "team" asset by others precludes, for all practical purposes, the effective near-term entry to the market of additional competitors.

As a result of these conditions, Rapidrill believes that it has a unique opportunity to provide superior quality drills at attractive prices, and capture 7.5 percent of the rotary drill market in three years. This market share would produce for Rapidrill forecast sales in 19X4 of $7,585,000 and after-tax earnings of $733,000.

Rapidrill is seeking an equity investment of $240,000 to implement the plans described herein. The common stock sold for the $240,000 investment will represent about 35 percent of Rapidrill's outstanding common stock after the offering is completed.

1. THE INDUSTRY, THE COMPANY, AND THE PRODUCT

The Industry

Virtually all mining and medium-to-large-scale construction activities require the penetration and/or removal of significant amounts of rock. Typical applications are as follows:

- Surface mining, both coal and metals
- Quarrying
- Water-well drilling
- Highway construction
- Pipeline construction
- Foundation excavations
- Mineral explorations
- Gas- and oil-well drilling

In the various mining, quarrying, and construction applications that require removal of rock, "blast holes" are drilled into the rock so that it may be blasted into small pieces to facilitate its removal. Similar, though generally much deeper, penetration is required in the drilling of wells or exploration holes.

Over the past 15 years, the "rotary drill" has emerged as the preeminent tool for rock-drilling requirements in the above applications. Its ease of operation and superior productivity have developed in parallel with the larger capacities of complementary equipment, such as loaders, shovels, trucks, and breakers; and have created a market that has expanded from less than $10 million in 19X3 to $74 million in 19X0.

The principals of Rapidrill have collectively accumulated in excess of 70 years of marketing, engineering, manufacturing, and general management experience with rotary drills and have formed a new company to design and produce rotary drills based on their assessment of conditions in the industry, which they believe create a viable business opportunity favorable to their planned program.

There are 11 manufacturers of rotary drills that presently have a significant share of the market. Only four of these manufacturers produce a line of drills applicable to a broad range of drilling applications and attempt national market coverage. These four manufacturers command about 50 percent of the total market, and all market their drills through equipment distributors (Ingersol-Rand utilizes "company owned" stores.)

The four manufacturers are:

- Indiana Tool, Inc.
- Ingersol-Rand
- Davey
- Joy Manufacturing (Robbins)

They all manufacture a full line of products (gear drives, pumps, etc.) for mining, construction, and industrial markets and share the common characteristic that all gravitated to the manufacture of drills based on their prior experience with the manufacture and packaging of air compressors. This packaging experience coupled with their existing channels of sales to the mining and construction industries created what seemed to be a natural product opportunity.

In the manufacture and packaging of compressors, however, these manufacturers commonly added between 50 and 80 percent of the manufacturing cost content. In a rotary drill, the compressor accounts for less than 10 percent of the total costs and the total value added by the packager is about 25 percent, including the compressor, with the remainder in purchased material. Nevertheless, the manufacture of drills by these companies is accomplished in existing compressor manufacturing facilities with production control systems and overhead structures geared to machine shop operations. These facilities are generally very complex, with high fixed investments, rigidly unionized, and located in high-cost labor areas, all of which leads to rotary drill manufacturing costs that are unnecessarily inflated.

In addition, the product design of rotary drills by these manufacturers has generally been prejudiced by the type and size of compressors in their product line and by their ability to use their own components for mechanical drive systems, instead of basing their designs on the optimum utilization of all available components.

While these manufacturing and design decisions use as a rationale higher facility utilization and increased value added, they, in fact, force rotary drill designs that do not provide the best solution to market application requirements. And the high-cost labor content adds materially to unnecessarily inflated costs.

Rotary drills can be produced more economically in a simple assembly shop operation, located in a low-rent area, and utilizing the most cost-effective components available (there are 27 manufacturers of compressors in the United States alone).

In combination, the above considerations create a situation whereby a product line of rotary drills may be designed that better satisfies market requirements and that can be produced and distributed at costs significantly below those of the present manufacturers. An opportunity exists for the right new venture to get into the rotary drill business with significant competitive advantages.

The Company

The opportunity for a new manufacturer to enter the rotary drill industry was perceived by April 19X1 by a group of five key executives employed by the present industry leader. These executives collectively had more than 70 years of marketing, engineering, manufacturing, and general management experience in the rotary drill business. Their analysis and assessment of conditions in the industry convinced them that there was a viable growth opportunity for a new rotary drill company and that the equity capital requirements for such a new venture were very reasonable (i.e., less than $400,000).

Accordingly, these five executives formed a new company—Rapidrill—to design, manufacture, and sell rotary drills. Rapidrill was formally incorporated in the state of Delaware in August 19X1 and the principals invested $128,000 of their funds in it. Rapidrill plans to produce modern, state-of-the-art rotary drills that will be marketed through independent mining and construction equipment distributors.

The Product

The rotary drill that Rapidrill proposes to make and sell and that is discussed in this plan is a mobile system, either truck- or crawler-mounted, for drilling relatively large holes (generally 6″ to 12″ diameter) in rock formations. The drill is driven at its top by a hydraulic motor. Basically, a rotary drill provides a large downthrust and torque force to a drill stem so that a drill bit or hammer can fragment rock at the bottom of the hole being drilled. In addition, compressed air is provided to remove rock cuttings from the hole during the drilling.

Rather than being a simple manufactured product, the rotary drill is in fact a complex technical system design consisting of hydraulic, pneumatic, electrical, and mechanical components integrated into a complete drill-rig assembly having a typical value of $100,000. It is significant that for *all* present manufacturers the cost of purchased components for assembled drills is from 60 percent to 70 percent of manufacturing costs. It is also pertinent that no present manufacturer has a sufficient market share to enjoy a "most favored" position with the suppliers of such components.

The strip mining, open-pit mining, construction, quarrying, and water-well drilling industries utilize rotary drills in their operations. In the various mining, quarrying, and construction operations, blast holes are drilled into the rock overlying the coal or ore, or into the rock structures to be moved. Blasting this waste rock into small pieces enables its removal. An infinite number of different rock structures are encountered in these operations, and a wide range of hole diameters and hole depths are required. In the last 15 years, the demand for increased productivity has forced a trend toward faster production of larger, deeper holes, which has best been provided by rotary drills.

While the rotary drills used for drilling blast holes are increasing in size and productivity, the water-well drilling contractor must cope with problems of mobility. His rotary drill must have the same fast drilling capability, but it must be small enough in size to travel over the public highways and be set up to drill in small, tight areas—often between buildings.

Product Line

Design studies have been conducted by Rapidrill to determine how to best configure Rapidrill's rotary drills so that they will meet most present drilling requirements and use available components (e.g., trucks, compressors, and diesel engine frames). As a result of these studies, Rapidrill has decided on three basic drill frame sizes:

- D-30K for 6″ diameter and smaller holes
- D-40K for 6″ to 8″ diameter holes
- D-70K for 9″ to 12″ diameter holes

All of these will be hydraulic top-drive drills that are now standard in the drilling industry.

An analysis has also been conducted to determine the suitability of truck- and crawler-mounted versions of each of the above basic drill models for blast hole and well drilling applications in the principal market segments.

EXHIBIT 7.3.   **Percentage of total rock-drilling applications met by Rapidrill's possible product lines (by market segment).**

Market Segment	Rotary Drill Model					
	D-30K		D-40K		D-70K	
	Truck	Crawler	Truck	Crawler	Truck	Crawler
Wells	70%		90%			
Blast hole drilling:						
Coal mining	20%	20%	80%	50%	30%	30%
Quarrying	30	30	30	30	10	5
Construction	10	5	35	5		
Copper mining			20	30	20	50
Iron mining				20		50

Note: Some overlap exists in the applications for each drill size. For example, 90 percent of all water wells drilled provide water for residential use. These wells are generally 6" in diameter, and both the D-30K model and the D-40K model can be used to drill them.

Results of this study are shown in Exhibit 7.3. Examination of these data shows that good application coverage can be obtained with only six basic rotary drill models: a truck-mounted D-30K and D-40K for well drilling; a truck-mounted D-30K and D-40K for blast hole drilling; and a crawler-mounted D-40K and D-70K for blast hole drilling The crawler-mounted version of D-30K and the truck-mounted version of the D-70K provide insufficient market coverage to warrant their design and manufacture by Rapidrill during its early operations. The data in Exhibit 7.3 also indicate that the most desirable order of drill development, to achieve the earliest coverage of the maximum number of market segments would be: first the D-40K, then the D-30K, and last the D-70K.

Exhibit 7.4 shows the selected Rapidrill product lines and the relationships among them. Note the high degree of component commonality that can be achieved in the different versions of the basic drill models. The prices shown are list prices to the end user (distributor prices will be about 25 percent lower). Sufficient detail design and component selection have been accomplished to permit accurate cost estimates to be made and to assure that the 25 percent discount to distributors can be achieved.

2. THE MANAGEMENT TEAM

Rapidrill believes that the most important element supporting the feasibility of its proposed program is the strength and proven ability of its management team. Every key functional position in which rotary drill experience would enhance the performance of the company is filled with an individual unquestionably preeminent in the industry.

EXHIBIT 7.4. Proposed Rapidrill models.

Parameters	Model		
	D-30K	**D-40K**	**D-70K**
Truck-mounted drills			
Well drills:			
Hole diameter (inches)	6	6–8	
Rated depth (feet)	1,000–2,000	1,000–2,000	
Bit pressure (pounds)	30,000	40,000	
Bit RPM	0–200	0–200	
Stem length (feet)	20	25	
Compressor	450 CFM-250 psi	750 CFM-250 psi	
Mounting (truck)	T-800 Ford	Crane Carrier	
Estimated weight			
(pounds)	40,000	56,000	
Selling price	$95,000	$125,000	
Blast hole drills:			
Hole diameter (inches)	6	6–8	
Rated depth (feet)	1,000	1,000	
Bit pressure (pounds)	30,000	40,000	
Bit RPM	0–200	0–200	
Stem length (feet)	20	25	
Compressor	450 CFM-250 psi	750 CFM-100 psi	
		750 CFM-250 psi	
		900 CFM-50 psi	
Mounting (truck)	T-800 Ford	Crane Carrier	
Estimated weight			
(pounds)	40,000	56,000	
Selling price	$90,000	$120,000	
Crawler-mounted drills			
Blast hole:			
Hole diameter (inches)		6–8	9–12
Rated depth (feet)		1,000	1,000
Bit pressure (pounds)		40,000	70,000
Bit RPM		0–200	0–100
Stem length (feet)		25	30–50
Compressor		750 CFM-250 psi	1050 CFM-100 psi
Estimated weight			
(pounds)		60,000	100,000
Selling price		$135,000	$225,000

Perhaps more important than the individual competence of team members is their demonstrated ability to work effectively as a team. Over the last five years, their efforts—and significant effort was required of each of them—increased the market share of their former employer from 9 percent to 22 percent of the total rotary drill market. This 22 percent market share was twice the share of the nearest competitor, and it was accomplished with handicaps in capacity, delivery, and costs at least as great as those of any of their competitors.

Consideration of this performance and review of the qualifications of team members are important in judging the validity of Rapidrill's knowledge of the industry and the feasibility of its proposed marketing, product, and manufacturing plans.

The Team

The following tabulation shows the organization of Rapidrill management and the responsibility of each member prior to association with Rapidrill.

Rapidrill Organization	Former Positions with Indiana Tool, Inc., Machinery Division
S.A. Price, President	Division President
M.F. Einman, VP Marketing	Product Manager, Rotary Drills
F.T. Samuels, VP Engineering	Manager of Engineering
G.A. Miller, VP Finance	Controller
W.D. MacMillan, Manager Manufacturing	Production Superintendent

Qualifications

The following summaries describe the individual qualifications of team members.

Samuel A. Price, President

Mr. Price, age 42, has both BS and MS degrees in engineering from Michigan State University. His experience includes 15 years of increasing responsibilities in engineering and marketing management and over five years of general management responsibilities in the design, manufacture, and sale of equipment for the mining, construction, and utility markets. This experience was accumulated with General Electric, Dresser Industries, and Indiana Tool, Inc.

In 19X3, as general manager of the then new Gas Turbine Division of Dresser Industries, Mr. Price staffed the division (predominantly from outside sources) and supervised the design, fabrication, and installation in customer facilities of over $5 million worth of gas-turbine-powered pipeline booster compressors within 15 months of division start-up. This program was accomplished well within original cost and time objectives.

During the four-year period from 19X5 through 19X0, under his management as president of the Machinery Division of Indiana Tool, Inc., division sales to the mining and construction markets rose from $17 million per year to $32 million per year and were profitable. This represented the most significant sales and profit growth rate of any of Indiana Tool's divisions and substantial market share improvement in all product lines. The rotary drill product lines accounted for $14 million of those 19X0 sales.

Marshal F. Einman, Vice President, Marketing and Sales

Mr. Einman, age 49, attended the Illinois State Teachers College and has prior experience of three years as president of a small privately held company. His 27 years' total experience includes 19 years in marketing and sales of rotary drills with both Hamilton Manufacturing Company and the Machinery Division of Indiana Tool, Inc.

From 19X0 to 19X1, he was product manager for rotary drills, responsible for domestic and foreign sales, sales forecasting, production requirements, product definition, product pricing, advertising, sales training, and definition of product support programs.

Under his marketing management, Indiana Tool's sales of rotary drills rose from $2.5 million in 19X0 to $14.4 million in 19X9. Much of this sales increase was directly attributable to his personal expertise in drill applications work. He has extensively traveled the United States, and, in fact, the entire free world, solving difficult drilling problems and promoting drill sales. Recent foreign trips to Australia, Vietnam, the Philippines, Morocco, Spain, Zambia, Rhodesia, and South Africa attest to the worldwide acceptance of his applications and market knowledge.

Mr. Einman is a member of the American Institute of Mining Engineers.

Frank T. Samuels, Vice President, Engineering

Mr. Samuels, age 45, holds degrees in civil engineering from Michigan State College, mechanical engineering from Worcester Polytechnic Institute, and has done graduate work in mechanical engineering at Illinois Institute of Technology. His 24 years of engineering experience includes high-pressure hydraulic research with Standard Oil Company of Indiana and 20 years of design responsibility for rotary drills commencing in 19X1, when he joined the Hamilton Manufacturing Company as chief engineer. Hamilton Manufacturing, under Mr. Samuels's engineering leadership, pioneered and developed the highly successful hydraulic top-drive rotary drill that has become the standard of the industry.

During this period, and after acquisition of Hamilton Manufacturing by Indiana Tool, Inc., in 19X7, in the capacity of chief engineer for Indiana Tool's Machinery Division, he supervised the engineering of over 1,200 rotary drills, ranging in size and application from 5,000-pound high-speed diamond core drills to 200,000-pound crawler-mounted machines, used to bore 15″ blast holes in taconite on the Mesabi Range. He has become accepted as the technical leader and innovator in the field. In 19X0, he had engineering responsibility for over $32 million worth of mining and construction machinery sales that included $14 million worth of rotary drills.

He is a member of the Society of Automotive Engineers and is a registered professional engineer in Indiana, Pennsylvania, and New York.

George A. Miller, Vice President, Finance, Secretary, Treasurer

Mr. Miller, age 32, has a degree in accounting from Michigan State College and graduate work toward an MBA at Wayne State College.

His initial experience was with Federal-Mogul Corporation, culminating in the position of controller for its Bearings Division plant, where he designed and installed a standard cost system specifically suited for job-shop operations.

In 19X6, he joined the Vare Corporation (now Microdot, $170 million annual sales, NYSE) as group controller of its Plastics Division. Promoted to assistant corporate controller, he assisted in the $37 million loan negotiated for the acquisition of Microdot, Inc., by Vare Corporation.

Mr. Miller joined Indiana Tool, Inc., in 19X9. As division controller of the $32 million-per-year Machinery Division, he revised and modernized the division's accounting and management reporting systems and worked extensively on financial analysis of new product and manufacturing opportunities.

William D. MacMillan, Manager of Manufacturing

Mr. MacMillan, age 45, has 25 years' experience in directing the operation of machining, welding, and assembly plants. Starting in job shops, he joined Hamilton Manufacturing Company in 19X6 as its first employee and assisted in its growth to 100 employees. He was responsible for all manufacturing operations when the company was acquired by Indiana Tool, Inc., in 19X7.

With Indiana Tool's Machinery Division, he was superintendent of rotary drill production until 19X8, when he was made responsible for the production of all Machinery Division products, and in 19X0 accomplished $32 million in shipments. In this capacity he was responsible for directing the scheduling and operations of the rotary drill assembly, portable compressor assembly, and welding and fabricating departments. He initiated many cost reduction programs; most notable was modernizing the welding and fabricating departments and realizing a 30 percent reduction in direct labor cost.

In his total experience, Mr. MacMillan directed the assembly and test of over 1,200 rotary drill rigs, an accumulated experience unmatched in the industry.

EXHIBIT 7.5.   Compensation and ownership of Rapidrill principals.

Principals	Shares Owned	Direct Investment	Annual Salary	Previous Salary	Salary Reduction
S.A. Price	136,000	$ 20,400	$38,000	$62,000*	40%
M.F. Einman	78,000	20,280	25,000	32,000	22
F.T. Samuels	78,000	20,280	25,000	30,000	17
G.A. Miller	42,000	12,600	25,000	27,000	8
W.D. MacMillan	36,000	14,400	18,000	20,000	10
Three district sales managers (each)	27,000	13,500	24,000	32,000	
Investment total		$128,460			

*Does not include stock options for 4,000 shares of Indiana Tool, Inc.

Compensation and Ownership

Exhibit 7.5 lists the ownership, the cash investment, and the previous salary of each of Rapidrill's team members. These data demonstrate the dedication, commitment, and belief of the principals in Rapidrill and their recognition of the relative responsibility and authority of their functional positions.

Future Team Members

In addition to these five principals, three other key personnel are presently committed to Rapidrill's program. These men are district sales managers who collectively account for annual drill sales of $9 million for their present employer and are scheduled to join Rapidrill on March 1, 19X2.

Other functional skills will be required in future operations (purchasing, inventory control, etc.) and will be added when operations volume warrants their addition. However, specific rotary drill experience is not felt to be critical in these functional areas.

Board of Directors

Rapidrill's bylaws call for a board of directors of from four to six members. The present directors are Messrs. Price, Einman, Samuels, and Miller, with two directorships reserved for representation of equity investors.

Supporting Professional Services

Rapidrill is presently represented by Walter I. Bobbin of Taylor, Dolan, and Bobbin of Nashville, Tennessee, as general counsel.

The firm of Tanner, Foster, and Company, CPAs, has been retained as independent auditor.

3. MARKET RESEARCH AND ANALYSIS

Market Description

The rotary drill has enjoyed a steady market growth, with an annual growth rate of 10 percent achieved for the last six years and sales of $74 million in 19X0. This market is shown graphically in Exhibit 7.6, which illustrates the total size of the market, the noncyclic nature of its growth since 19X4, and a projection of sales through 19X5. The 19X6 sales forecast of $114 million is based on the past seven-year trend.

EXHIBIT 7.6.   Market size and trends of rotary drill sales.

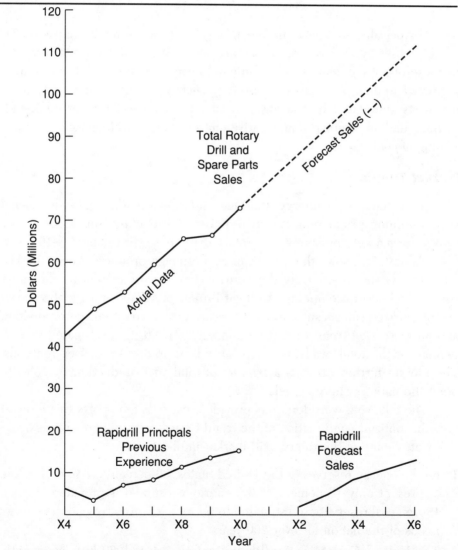

Sources: U.S. Bureau of Mines, Compressed Air and Gas Institute (CAGI), and *Survey of Rotary Drill Manufacturers and Suppliers,* by P.J. Lang.

Market Segmentation

The noncyclic growth performance may be explained principally by the lack of a dominating market segment in the sale of drills. The five principal market segments contributed the following market shares in 19X0:

Market Segment	Market Share
Well drills	35%
Quarrying	18
Coal mining	26
Metal mining	10
Construction	11

Historically, soft performance in any of these segments has been favorably offset by stronger sales to other segments or by favorable response in those other segments to governmental economic stimulus. For example, highway and dam programs increase construction and quarrying sales, housing starts stimulated by the lowering of interest rates increase water-well drilling, and an interest in alternative energy sources stimulates the surface mining of coal.

Market Trends

The projected future energy shortage and the attendant growth in coal surface-mining production, which requires rock drilling, represent a very significant market opportunity for rotary drill sales over the next 5–10 years.

Exhibit 7.7 shows the growth of coal tonnage production over the last 10 years. As shown, virtually the entire growth in production has been accomplished in surface mining. A recent Bureau of Mines forecast, also shown on this curve, projects substantial increases in total coal tonnage production and an increasing trend to surface mining. In 19X6, it is estimated that 57 percent of the total production of coal will be mined by surface methods. The bureau further predicts a *tripling* of total coal production by 19X5 to meet the nation's energy needs.

The following considerations provide a basis that supports this forecast growth, confirms continuation of the trend to surface-mining operations, and delineates some of the rotary drill market implications:

1. Of the energy reserves in the United States, 88 percent are in coal, while at present only 18 percent of the energy consumed is provided by coal. Proven coal reserves are estimated to be sufficient to satisfy all the energy needs of the nation for over 200 years.
2. The Federal Coal Mine Health and Safety Act of 1969 has significantly lowered the productivity of underground coal-mining operations. In the

EXHIBIT 7.7. U.S. coal production.

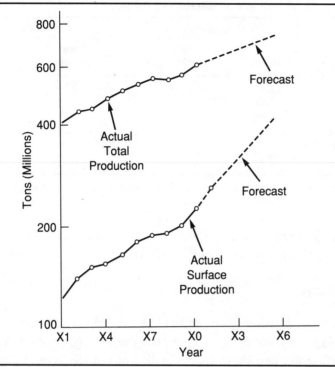

Source: U.S. Bureau of Mines.

1960s, a typical miner produced 15 tons of coal per day; today this figure has dropped to 10 tons, with two thirds of the decline laid to safety legislation.

3. Recent reverses to environmentalist efforts have decimated organized opposition to surface mining.

4. Present pending legislation is directed at regulation, rather than curtailment, of surface-mining activities.

5. Achievement of the above 19X6 forecast coal production would require approximately 4,000 drills to be in operation compared to the present 1,000 working drills.

Exhibit 7.8 shows how market segment sales of rotary drills will change in response to this forecast increase in coal production and illustrates the magnitude of the opportunity that this rapidly growing segment will offer in sales growth.

Rapidrill believes this coal surface-mining market for rotary drills to be an important opportunity for concentration of its initial efforts. Those

EXHIBIT 7.8.   **Market segment comparison (19X0 versus forecast 19X4; total unit sales, number of drills).**

Market Segment	19X0		19X4	
	Sales	**Percent of Market**	**Sales Forecast**	**Percent of Market**
Water well	250	35	329	31
Quarrying	125	18	159	15
Coal mining	175	26	371	35
Metal mining	70	10	95	9
Construction	80	11	106	10
	700		1,060	

Sources: Compressed Air and Gas Institute (CAGI), Bureau of Census, Bureau of Mines, and Drilltech Forecast.

elements, in addition to this projected segment sales growth, that support this decision will be discussed in the following sections of this plan.

Competition

Exhibit 7.9 lists all present competitive manufacturers of rotary drills, indicates the range of their product lines, the market segments in which they actively participate, and their approximate present share of the total rotary drill market.

    As shown, the 11 manufacturers break down into three general categories that are discussed below.

Large-Drill Manufacturer

Bucyrus-Erie (B-E) manufactures and sells only large drills as a complement to its large-shovel and dragline equipment. It presently has the market for large drills to itself and its 60 units per year produce sales of over $14 million. It sells direct, as it sells its shovels, and has made several abortive excursions into other market segments. These attempts to enter the other drill market segments were unsuccessful primarily because of its unfamiliarity with distributor marketing—the predominant method of selling drills in all but the large rotary drill market.

    Gardner-Denver has initiated a program to enter the large-drill market. This program was initiated by recruitment of six of B-E's principal engineering personnel and as yet has produced no significant results. Rapidrill considers this program to be premature and believes that marketing as well as technical know-how will be required in such a program.

    Successful quantity gasification or liquid conversion of coal, estimated to be practicable by the late 1970s (pilot plants are presently operating),

EXHIBIT 7.9. Rotary drill competition.

	Product Line*	Market	19X0 Share of Total $ Market
Large-drill manufacturers:			
Bucyrus-Erie (B-E)	I, L	Coal, metal mining	20%
Broad-line manufacturers:			
Indiana Tool, Inc.	S, M, I	All	22
Ingersol-Rand	S, M	All	11
Davey	S+	All	9
Joy (Robbins)	M, I	All, except water well	7
			49%
Water-well drill manufacturers:			
Gardner-Denver	S, L	Mixed, no iron mining	6
Failing	S	Water well	5
Koehring Speedstar	S	Water well	5
Schramm	S	Water well	5
Sanderson-Cyclone	S	Water well	5
Winter-Weiss	S	Water well	5
			31%
Rapidrill	S, M, I (L in future)	All	
			100%

*Hole Capability   List Price
S = 6" or less $ 60,000–90,000
M = 6–8" $110,000–150,000
I = 6–12" $200,000–250,000
L = 15–17" or larger $350,000 up

Note: Both product line and market classifications for the above-listed manufacturers are limited to products that are competitive and markets where efforts are effective. There are some overlaps of both product and market that are not listed; but these are of limited significance.

will provide a new and large market for low-sulfur western coal. This new application will require "large" drills and will offer a significant new market opportunity for drill sales and penetration of B-E's dominance of the large-drill market.

Broad-Line Manufacturers

Only four present manufacturers offer a product line applicable to a broad range of market segment applications: Indiana Tool, Inc. (the market leader), Ingersol-Rand, Davey, and Joy Manufacturing.

These manufacturers share several common characteristics:

1. All are compressor manufacturers attracted to drills by their use of compressors.
2. All manufacture an extensive line of mining and construction equipment products in addition to rotary drills.

3. All sell through local equipment distributors. (Ingersol-Rand utilizes "company owned" stores for distribution.)

4. All offer relatively modern machines (5- to 14-year-old designs) with good performance and high productivity. This is more important than price in these markets. However, all would benefit in both cost and performance by major update of designs.

The drills of these manufacturers are suitable to applications in all market segments, and as a group they account for 49 percent of all drill sales. Most pertinently, this 49 percent includes virtually all of the coal surface-mining drills: the market segment most likely to enjoy significant near-term sales growth. These manufacturers in general have had difficulty in providing sufficient productive capacity to match sales growth, so that their pricing and discounting have been firm over the last seven years. Recent increases in forecast demands will further exacerbate their capacity problem. Accordingly, Rapidrill believes that a new manufacturer can achieve significant drill sales without the disruption of drill pricing structures and that the market segments served by the broad-line drill manufacturers represent the best opportunity for market entry by a new manufacturer.

These manufacturers share one further common characteristic favorable to a new drill manufacturer—they unanimously have a well-deserved reputation for poor service and product support.

Water-Well Drill Manufacturers

Failing, Koehring Speedstar, Schramm, Sanderson-Cyclone, and Winter-Weiss all manufacture only small drills aimed primarily at the low-price portion of the water-well drill market. In general, they distribute and sell most effectively on a regional basis. Of the well drill manufacturers, only Gardner-Denver attempts national distribution and has a broad range of product lines.

The average drill offered by these manufacturers utilizes mechanical drive systems, reciprocating compressors, and other components consistent with a 30- to 40-year-old technology, and most of these manufacturers would have difficulty in developing a modern rotary drill design. While the obsolete design and generally poor productivity of these machines is apparent to knowledgeable operators, price remains an important consideration in this market and the low-price drills capture 70 percent to 80 percent of water-well drill sales.

Conversion of the market from cable tool drills to high-quality, hydraulic top-drive rotary drills has been pervasive over the last five years and will continue at a steady rate as operators become familiar with the increase in productivity available through their use of hydraulic drills. Rapidrill plans to achieve its share of water-well drill sales in the high-quality end of the market. However, attempts by Rapidrill to accelerate this conversion and capture an early dominating share of the entire market segment could be met by severe price competition in the price-conscious segment of the market.

Exhibit 7.10 presents and compares Rapidrill's primary specifications, list prices, and distributor net prices with those of the competition in each of the three hole-capability ranges. In the case of the 6" or less hole capability, only those competitors that produce high-quality rotary drills and market them nationally are shown and considered. As noted above, Rapidrill does not intend to compete in the low-price, low-quality portion of the well market.

The data in Exhibit 7.10 show that Rapidrill's proposed drill designs have equal or better specifications than those of its competition and are competitively priced with sufficient margins to provide significantly lower distributor net prices, if required.

As noted earlier, the model D-40K rotary drill will be the first product that Rapidrill will produce and market. The design of the D-40K is sufficiently accomplished that reasonably firm detail specifications have been

EXHIBIT 7.10.   Comparison of competing drills.

Manufacturer	Model	Drill Bit Pressure (Pounds)	Air Compressor Vol./Pres.	List Price	Distrib- utor Net
6" or less hole capability:					
Rapidrill	D-30K Truck	30,000	450/250	$ 90,000	$ 68,400
Indiana Tool, Inc.	T-650	30,000	450/150	101,120	85,952
Ingersol-Rand	T-3	30,000	600/125	92,080	78,268
Davey	M-8A-HP	30,000	490/250	92,195	78,366
Gardner-Denver	15W	30,000	640/150	102,855	87,427
6" to 8" hole capability:					
Rapidrill	D-40K Truck	40,000	750/250	120,000	91,200
Indiana Tool, Inc.	T-670	30,000	600/250	120,551	102,468
Ingersol-Rand	T-4	32,000	600/250	120,510	102,433
Rapidrill	D-40K Crawler	40,000	750/250	135,000	102,600
Ingersol-Rand	DM-4	32,000	600/250	139,610	118,668
9" to 12" hole capability:					
Rapidrill	D-70K Crawler	70,000	900/250	225,000	171,000
Bucyrus-Erie (B-E)	45-R	70,000	900/240	246,977	209,930
Robbins (Joy)	RR-12	70,000	875/250	227,962*	206,518

*Includes new D-9 Caterpillar tractor at $85,000 list.

EXHIBIT 7.11. Rotary drills: Detailed comparison of competing products.

	Manufacturer and Model		
	Rapidrill D-40K	Ingersol-Rand T-4	Indiana Tool, Inc. T-670
Hole diameter (inches)	6–8	6–8	6–8
Bit pressure (pounds)	40,000	32,500	30,000
Machine weight (pounds)	56,000	42,000	43,500
Bit speed (RPM range)	0–100	0–10	0–86
	0–150		
	0–195		
Bit torque (pounds per inch)	54,000	50,000	36,000
Compressor type	Screw (domestic)	Vane	Screw (imported)
Air volume and pressure	750 @100	750 @150	600 @250
	750 @250	750 @250	
	900 @ 50		
Engine power	Caterpillar 4-cycle diesel	GM 2-cycle diesel	Caterpillar 4-cycle diesel
Horsepower	325	260	300
Drill stem break-out in mast	Yes	Yes	No
Automatic drill stem loader	Yes	Yes	No
Stem loader inside mast	Yes	No	No
Feed rate (FPM):			
Standard	12	12	5.5
Rapid	62	64	40
Retract	110	100	75
Leveling capacity (inches)	48	48	24
Drill stem threads	Low torque (2 thread/inch)	High torque (4 thread/inch)	High torque (4 thread/inch)
Number of best features	17	6	2

developed for it. Exhibit 7.11 compares a full range of the features of the D-40K with the best of its present competition with 6" to 8" hole capability. As can be seen, the D-40K will have significant superiority in specifications to the machines of either of its competitors and about a 10 percent lower price to the distributor (Exhibit 7.10). Rapidrill is able to achieve this lower price without sacrificing profitability through cost savings in purchased components, manufacturing (see Section 6), and selling expenses (see Section 4).

Estimated Market Share and Sales

Rapidrill's sales forecasts for each of its planned rotary drill models for the next five years are shown in Exhibit 7.12. Sales for truck-mounted D-30K and D-40K drills have been separately estimated for the well-drilling and

EXHIBIT 7.12. Rapidrill Corporation sales forecast (in $000).

	19X2		19X3		19X4		19X5		19X6	
	Units	$	Units	$	Units	$	Units	$	Units	$
Models:										
D-40K truck-mounted (blast hole)	8	$730	16	$1,460	22	$2,006	29	$ 2,645	36	$ 3,283
D-40K truck-mounted (well)			10	950	14	1,330	20	1,900	24	2,280
D-40K crawler-mounted			7	718	8	821	9	923	12	1,231
D-30K truck-mounted (blast hole)			6	410	8	547	9	616	12	821
D-30K truck-mounted (well)			4	289	12	866	20	1,444	24	1,733
D-70K crawler-mounted					6	1,026	9	1,539	12	2,052
Spares		51		383		989		1,813		2,280
Total	8	$781	43	$4,210	70	$7,585	96	$10,880	120	$13,680

blast hole-drilling applications of these units. Sales are estimated to rise from $781,000 for the second half of 19X2 to $13,680,000 in 19X6.

Exhibit 7.13 shows the total rotary drill market for the next five years; Rapidrill's total sales in each year, and the share of the total rotary drill market that the sales represent. Achievement of Rapidrill's sales forecasts would require its share of the market to rise from 2 percent at the end of the first year to 11.9 percent in the fifth year of operation.

The sales and market share forecasts shown in Exhibits 7.12 and 7.13 are believed to be reasonable—if not conservative—and attainable by the Rapidrill team. There are five principal reasons why Rapidrill believes this to be so:

1. While working for their former employer (Indiana Tool, Inc.), Rapidrill's management team increased that company's share of the total rotary drill market from 9 percent to 22 percent in the five-year period from 19X5 to 19X0. Drill sales during that time went from $4 million to $15 million. Rapidrill's management believes that it should be able to duplicate that kind of performance and capture 11.9 percent of the rotary drill market and $13,680,000 of profitable sales in the first five years of Rapidrill's operation.

2. Rapidrill's marketing team will include three distributor representatives who, as district sales managers, collectively produced annual rotary drill sales of $9 million for their previous employer. They should be able to obtain a large portion of this business for Rapidrill.

3. Rapidrill's distributors (see Section 4) will include three that are among the most effective in the industry. Together these three distributors could absorb all of Rapidrill's projected production in its first two or three operating years.

4. Rapidrill's rotary drills will have performance equal to or better than that of competing units and a lower price to the distributor. The superior drill performance will be achieved by upgrading the design of Rapidrill's machines and using the best and most cost-effective components that are

EXHIBIT 7.13. Rapidrill market share forecast (sales in $000).

	19X2 1st year		19X3 2nd year	19X4 3rd year	19X5 4th year	19X6 5th year
	3rd Qtr.	4th Qtr.				
Total market*	$22,000	$23,000	$94,000	$100,500	$108,000	$114,000
Rapidrill share	1.3%	2.1%	4.4%	7.5%	10.1%	12.0%
Rapidrill sales*	$293	$488	$4,210	$7,585	$10,880	$13,680

*Both total market figures and Rapidrill sales include spare parts.

available. Regarding engineering, F. T. Samuels, Rapidrill's vice president of engineering, is recognized as a technical leader in the industry. The selection of components as well as overhead and labor costs (see Section 6) that are less than those of other manufacturers will enable Rapidrill to offer its units to distributors at a price below that of its competition.

5. Rapidrill will offer service, warranty, and application engineering that is superior to that provided by its competition.

4. MARKETING PLAN

Distributor Plan

Rapidrill plans to sell drills through well-established equipment distributors in the mining, construction, and well-drilling industries. Close to 100 percent of all the drills in Rapidrill's proposed model sizes are sold through this channel of sale.

Users, rather than the manufacturers, have created this dominant channel (very favorable to a small independent manufacturer), based on their experience with the present manufacturers' failure to provide service and spare-parts support on a sufficiently localized basis. Distributors, conversely, recognize that their success will ultimately be determined by their ability to support equipment in the field and are continuously searching for more reliable and maintenance-free product lines adequately supported by a manufacturer's service and spare-parts programs.

Sufficient dissatisfaction with the product lines and support programs of present competitive manufacturers exists to create a high probability of success for Rapidrill's efforts to establish an effective distributor network.

It will be important during Rapidrill's introduction to the market to have exceptionally strong, well-established distributors. In order to attract such distributors, Rapidrill plans to offer significantly larger than standard industry discounts during an introductory period. Cost estimates have established sufficient manufacturing margins to provide discounts of 24 percent to 26 percent to distributors, compared to a firm industry standard of 15 percent. Such discounts would provide up to 60 percent greater margin to distributors, that, on a national average, achieve earnings of 2.5 percent on sales.

In order to minimize Rapidrill's working capital requirements during early periods, these larger discounts will be identified with prompt cash payments for drills (i.e., 7 percent discount for 15-day payment). Such strategy will further ensure well-financed dealers and will allow a future rationale for decreases in discounts if higher net prices are competitively available.

Over the last three months, Rapidrill has discussed its proposed drill models with three strong, well-established distributors and has tentative agreements with them for the distribution of Rapidrill's drills. These distributors are:

- Mining Supplies, Inc.
  Gadsen, Alabama
- Pierce Mining Equipment Company
  Cincinnati, Ohio
- Pennsylvania Machinery Company
  Scranton, Pennsylvania

These distributors, in the opinion of Rapidrill's principals, are among the most effective drill distributors in the industry. They adequately cover a large part of the coal-mining market for rotary drills, and they could, by themselves, absorb Rapidrill's total forecast production in its first two or three years.

The sales forecast for the next five years (Exhibit 7.12) projects sales reaching $13,680,000 by 19X6. Support of this sales forecast will require only 2 or 3 additional major distributors and a total network of 12 to 14 distributors to achieve adequate national coverage of the total drill market.

Sales Plan

Rapidrill will sell to and support the direct selling efforts of distributors with a team of distributor representatives. It plans to have at least one distributor representative for every major distributor. Representatives to cover the three above-listed distributors have already committed themselves to join Rapidrill early in 19X2. These three men are experienced rotary drill sales managers who presently are collectively responsible for annual drill sales of over $9 million.

Rapidrill believes that its single-product selling requirements and, in particular, the large "ticket" price of rotary drills offer an additional cost advantage to Rapidrill in comparison to its competitors, which sell several products (rotary drills, compressors, diesel engines) to the same distributor. Rapidrill believes that its selling expenses for rotary drills may be maintained at 9 percent of sales (after a sufficient production base is achieved), compared to the 12 percent to 13 percent common to competitive manufacturers. The simplistic explanation for this reduction is that a $100,000 rotary drill is about as easily sold as a $5,000 compressor or a $500 air tool. Rapidrill plans to achieve about $1 million in sales per distributor representative. The industry average for competitors is from $350,000 to $500,000.

Applications Support

An additional strong influence in rotary drill sales is provided by applications support: The ability to determine for a user the most economic equipment requirements to satisfy his drilling needs. Rapidrill's principals have marketwide recognition and extensively proven records in providing effective applications services directly to users.

Advertising and Promotion

Rapidrill's advertising and promotional efforts will be concentrated in those areas shown by experience to be the most effective. These are primarily the exhibition of equipment at trade association shows, particularly regional "buying" shows where immediate sales may be obtained, and demonstration programs where the productivity of drills can be demonstrated on a user's particular job. Rapidrill will maintain at least one rig in inventory for demonstration purposes at all times and plans to offer additional discount incentives to distributors on demonstrator machines. Demonstrator machines are customarily sold by distributors after 100 to 200 hours of operation at about a $1,500 price markdown.

Warranty and Service

Most of the problems that have earned present manufacturers their poor reputations may be attributed to the multiplicity and complexity of the various product lines (compressors, rotary drills, diesel engines, etc.) they manufacture and to plain poor management attention.

Rapidrill believes that proper attention to service, product support, and a competitive warranty posture will enhance market penetration to a degree that pricing in these productivity-conscious market segments would never accomplish alone. Rapidrill's ability to provide such services and support for its drills is definitely aided by the single-product nature of its planned operations.

An initial step in providing good product support is Rapidrill's recently completed study of inventory stocking requirements. This study identified the minimum parts inventory that is required to have a satisfactory response time to predicted customer demands for spare parts.

5. DESIGN AND DEVELOPMENT PLANS

Rapidrill's planned product line will not require extension of any state-of-the-art technologies. The designs of all competitors are from 5 to 14 years old. The task and the opportunity consist of knowledgeable application of the latest component technology and performance available and an optimum balanced utilization of those components. The result should be significant improvements in product performance at competitive price levels.

Status

The model D-40K series of drills (e.g., truck-mounted well or blast hole and crawler-mounted units) have been selected, for reasons previously discussed, for initial design, development, and market introduction. The development of the D-40K drills will be followed by the design and development of the D-30K truck-mounted well drill and the D-70K crawler-mounted drill, in that order.

It should be emphasized that development and test work on the finished D-40K, D-30K, and D-70K designs should be minimal. The reason for this is that all the components of these drills will be used well within their operating ranges, and testing efforts are principally required to check out control feedback, valve suitability, and other minor design details. After the prototype drills have been tested and their design proven, they will be sold at a slight markdown. This is common practice in the rotary drill industry.

The product design schedule is shown on the master schedule in Section 7.

Parts Grouping

One additional Rapidrill design criterion merits discussion. In the detail design of Rapidrill's product line, "parts grouping" will be utilized. The parts grouping concept defines all optional features, such as compressor size, as a complete and interchangeable group of parts. The parts grouping requirements of the D-40K are shown graphically in Exhibit 7.14. The assembly of different versions of a drill model is facilitated by using interchangeable parts groups. Moreover, decisions made by parts groups (on a forecast, lead-time, and max-min basis) permit maximum production feasibility with minimum inventory and simplified production control requirements.

Future Products

The technology of rock drilling and the history of the rotary drill suggest that evolution of drilling equipment will be continuous. Rapidrill believes that in five to ten years the development of western coal will require "large" drills with higher capacity than that of those presently planned in its product line and that this will present a new, additional (not replacement) market for drills.

Constant desire for improved productivity will eventually create a market for automated operation of drills. Rapidrill plans to be the innovator of such systems and has already discussed a possible joint development program with a hydraulic component manufacturer.

EXHIBIT 7.14. Parts grouping—model D-40K.

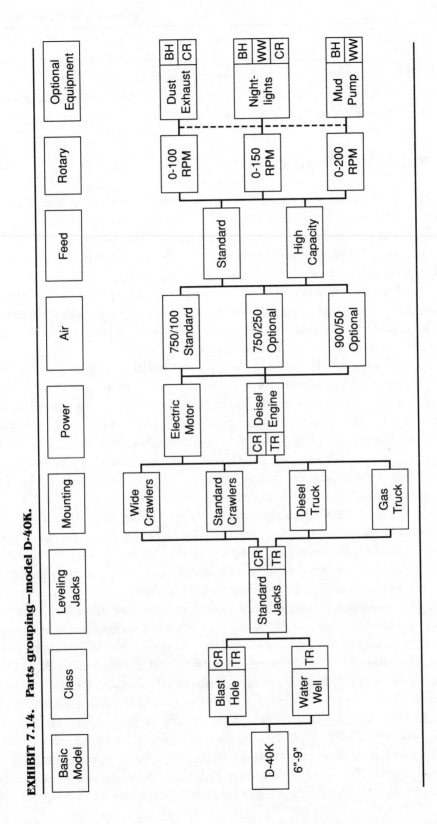

Finally, new methods for mineral exploration and sampling may offer opportunities for innovative drill equipment design. Rapidrill plans to keep abreast of such developments and be an industry leader in the development of any new drill equipment that might be required.

6. MANUFACTURING PLAN

As previously discussed, Rapidrill's rotary drill will be essentially an engineered package with a high content of purchased components. The nature of the manufacturing efforts consists primarily of fabricating welded mounting and mast structures and assembly of all components into a final drill. Other than minor welding and painting of equipment, virtually no high-cost machine tool or other fixed investments are required. Assembly can be accomplished in simple warehouse-type structures with a modest overhead crane capacity. Such structures are available for lease or purchase in virtually every industrial area of the United States.

While most of the value added by the packager consists of this assembly labor, unit production volume is not sufficient to warrant the high fixed cost of a modern assembly line facility (and no present manufacturer has such a facility). Minimizing manufacturing costs makes low hourly labor rates, worker productivity, efficiency, and flexibility paramount considerations. Such characteristics are not typical of the operations of present competitive drill manufacturers whose plants are rigidly unionized and located in highly industrialized, high labor-rate locations.

A study by Rapidrill's principals has been conducted to identify the effects of different plant locations on the manufacturing costs of rotary drills. In its evaluation of alternative plant locations, this study considered: labor rates, labor law, labor availability and attitudes, freight and transportation costs, centers of markets, taxes, travel access, facility costs, utility costs, suitability for professional staff, and other pertinent considerations. It concluded that the manufacturing requirements for Rapidrill's operation would best be met in a southeastern city of modest size, in a state with right-to-work laws. After evaluation of several potential locations and detailed analysis of final candidates, Rapidrill has selected the Nashville, Tennessee, area for its plant location. Nashville is well located with respect to rotary drill markets.

Exhibit 7.15 illustrates some of the results of this evaluation study. It shows the net cost of typical operations in Nashville and compares these to the costs of equivalent operations at the locations of present major drill manufacturers. For the comparisons in Exhibit 7.15, which shows an average cost advantage of close to 3 percent for Rapidrill operations in Nashville, an

EXHIBIT 7.15. Comparison of Rapidrill's operation at Nashville, Tennesee, with major competitors' locations (base = $10 million annual Rapidrill sales to distributors: 86,000 productive hours).

Location	BLS Index	Direct Labor Cost ($/hr.)	Production Hour Cost L and OH	Total Cost L and OH (000)	Freight In and Out (000)	Total Value-added Cost (000)	Nashville Advantage $ (000)	Nashville Advantage Percent Rapidrill Sales
Nashville	74.2	$2.70	$12.45	$1,071	$196	$1,267	Base	Base
Competitors:								
Dallas (G-D)	90.6	3.30	14.70	1,264	191	1,455	$188	2.3%
Franklin, Pa. (ITI)	105.6	3.85	16.70	1,436	150	1,586	319	4.0
Birmingham (Joy)	87.3	3.18	14.25	1,226	157	1,383	116	1.4
West Virginia (I-R)	94.0	3.42	15.26	1,312	139	1,451	184	2.3
Milwaukee (B-E)	104.3	3.79	16.70	1,436	144	1,580	313	3.9
New Jersey (I-R)	98.6	3.59	15.82	1,360	163	1,523	256	3.2
Average							$229	2.8%

Legend:
G-D = Gardner-Denver   B-E = Bucyrus-Erie
ITI = Indiana Tool, Inc.   BLS = Bureau of Labor Statistics
Joy = Joy Manufacturing   L = Labor
I-R = Ingersol-Rand   OH = Factory overhead (rent, heat, light, etc.)

equal number of productive hours and equal labor productivity and efficiency were assumed for all locations.

Improvements in efficiency and productivity are, in fact, of equal importance and represent a higher potential for cost savings than do the lower labor rates themselves. Estimates of improvements of 20 percent to 25 percent in productivity for a well-managed, open-shop fabrication and assembly operation in Nashville are considered conservative. With typical value added of about 16 percent of manufacturing cost for present rotary drill manufacturers, such productivity improvements would result in an additional 3 percent to 4 percent decrease in total manufacturing cost. For subsequent financial analysis these productivity improvements were assumed to be achieved by Rapidrill over a three-year period, utilizing a 90 percent "learning curve" on assembly operations.

Rapidrill's manufacturing operations will also seek further efficiencies through the use of modern production, inventory control, and purchasing systems that will be focused on reducing the costs of buying, storing, and handling the large content of purchased components used in rotary drills. The implementation of these systems will be significantly aided by employing "parts grouping" techniques (see Section 5) in the product line design. Parts grouping will allow flexibility in assembly scheduling and will minimize inventory requirements.

The total result of such manufacturing operations will be minimum capital equipment and inventory investment and manufacturing costs (after sufficient "learning curve" improvement) from 6 percent to 8 percent below those of present competition. This manufacturing cost reduction, together with the anticipated 3 percent to 4 percent reduction in Rapidrill's selling expenses, as compared to those of its competitors, means that Rapidrill's manufacturing and selling costs should be from 9 percent to 12 percent less than those of its competitors. Cost advantages of this order in products with a high purchased content could give Rapidrill a strong competitive advantage.

7. SCHEDULE

Exhibit 7.16 (page 211) shows the master schedule for Rapidrill.

8. RISKS

As with any new venture, there are risks in Rapidrill's plans. Recognition of these risks, evaluation of their severity, and proper contingency planning for their possible occurrences have been considered in Rapidrill's planning.

EXHIBIT 7.16. The master schedule for Rapidrill.

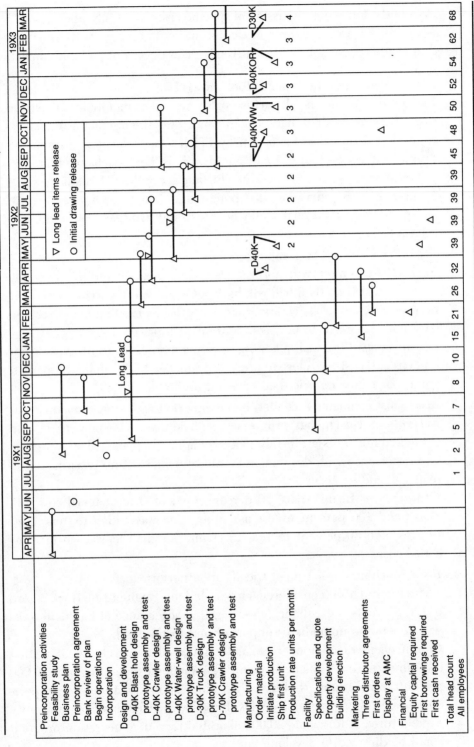

While the following discussion of specific risks is not intended to be all-inclusive, it is felt to cover those of significant possible impact. Risks are *not* listed in order of probability of occurrence or of degree of possible impact.

1. *Risk:* Legal action by Indiana Tool, Inc. (ITI).
   Evaluation: While the departure of its key team members has jeopardized ITI's rotary drill market dominance, it is the opinion of Rapidrill's counsel that no cause for action by ITI has been created. Letters between legal counsel for ITI and Rapidrill have been exchanged, and the prognosis is that the likelihood for further action by ITI is slim.
   Contingency: Rapidrill has had policy guidelines prepared by counsel and plans no actions that could be construed as unfair competition or breach of ITI's legal rights.

2. *Risk:* Price cutting by competitors.
   Evaluation: Market will absorb everyone's capacity for the next few years. At that time Rapidrill will have sufficient volume to be price competitive with any of its competitors. Historically, existing manufacturers have not responded to new competition with price cuts.
   Contingency: Financial planning included generous contingencies in unit costs. If costs are close to present estimates, Rapidrill has immediate ability to reduce its prices and remain profitable.

3. *Risk:* Cost estimates exceeded by engineering and/or manufacturing.
   Evaluation: Design has progressed sufficiently so 60 percent of purchased components are firmly priced. Rapidrill's principals have extensive experience with design and manufacturing start-up phases, so estimates should be accurate.
   Contingency: In financials, 10 percent was added to material cost estimates and 100 percent excess assembly time was added to Year 1 estimates, and 80 percent to Year 2, giving Rapidrill leeway on meeting actual costs.

4. *Risk:* Machine doesn't meet specification performance.
   Evaluation: This is considered a low-risk item. Engineering track record of F.T. Samuels is excellent; however, rapid acceptance of Rapidrill units will depend on immediate support of unit in the field.
   Contingency: In addition to $25,000 allocated to development testing (2.5 times normal), financial planning includes expenditure of $10,000 per unit in field support of first eight units (about five times past experience levels), then progressively less but allowance for significant warranty expenditures. Additional $20,000 allocated for a demonstration program could be directed to development.

5. *Risk:* Sales forecasts not achieved.
   Evaluation: Analysis shows a low breakeven level (less than 50 percent of

Year 2 forecasts), and some fixed costs can be delayed to reduce further the breakeven if sales are falling well below forecasts.

Contingency: Procurements will be committed for lower-level production than forecast but at forecast rate, allowing time for additional procurements within lead time if sales trend to forecast levels or higher.

6. *Risk:* Delays in design and/or manufacturing.

   Evaluation: Delays in design unlikely for first unit since most design work now complete. Delays in either can be minimized to about $20,000 additional cash requirement per month delay. Financial plan shows cash balance of $64,000 for first year-end, allowing, in worst case, a two- to three-month delay.

   Contingency: Watch design and manufacturing schedule closely, and expedite procurements closely. An additional $60,000 borrowing is available to Rapidrill in Year 2 within debt-equity guidelines; so another three-month contingency could be available.

7. *Risk:* Long lead-time procurements encountered.

   Evaluation: Trucks, diesel engines, compressors, and hydraulic components are on order, with satisfactory shipments promised. Rapidrill's early requirements, two per month, can be met with minor disturbance even if vendors have major problems. Vendors have confirmed this.

   Contingency: Closely follow procurements—some purchased components have four- to five-month lead times—and we cannot afford to order backup from other vendors.

8. *Risk:* Economy downturn or fuel shortage affecting sales.

   Evaluation: Energy shortages should enhance the sale of drills to mining markets and accelerate, rather than deter, Rapidrill's growth.

   Contingency: Watch signals closely; trend should be apparent before manufacturing is started.

9. *Risk:* Tight money affecting Rapidrill's ability to obtain the required line of credit.

   Evaluation: Plan has been reviewed by three largest banks in Nashville, which supported financial assumptions regarding borrowing. Money supply has eased somewhat since those commitments.

   Contingency: Secure committed lines of credit in excess of forecast requirements to the limit of reasonable debt-equity ratios.

10. *Risk:* Legislation to curtail strip mining.

    Evaluation: In light of the forecast energy shortage and the fact that 10 percent of the nation's energy presently comes from surface-mined coal, this eventuality is considered small.

    Contingency: Diversion of initial selling efforts to other market segments. Planned sales of first two years could be achieved in several other market segments.

9. FINANCIAL PLAN

Introduction

Using the sales levels and rotary drill prices developed by the marketing forecast, detailed estimates of material, labor, and burden generated by engineering and manufacturing, and estimates of design, development, and general sales and administrative expenses, detailed financial statements were drawn up depicting the forecast results of Rapidrill's operations for the five years from 19X2 to 19X6, inclusive. The following assumptions were used in arriving at the results:

1. All operations are performed in a leased facility in Nashville, Tennessee. Labor rates, shipping costs, lease rates, etc., used are consistent with the area.
2. All projections are in 19X1 dollars.
3. Interest payments are computed at 15 percent on borrowings. Borrowings will be provided by bank lines of credit.
4. Balance sheet assumptions are:
    a. Accounts receivable: 30-day collection through mid-19X5; 45 days thereafter.
    b. Notes receivable: Average 36-month repayment schedule at 10 percent simple interest. Financing by Rapidrill will commence in the fourth quarter of 19X5. Earlier financing to be accomplished utilizing an independent financial institution. Cavanagh Leasing Corporation has expressed interest.
    c. Inventories: Four turns per year.
    d. Accounts payable: 60-day average through 19X5; 36–40 days thereafter.
5. Income taxes include state and federal.
6. Loss for 19X2 carried forward and deducted from 19X2 income in accordance with IRS Code Section 172.
7. Organizational expenses and initial design cost, estimated to be $14,000 and $240,000, respectively, have been expensed.

Pro forma financial statements are presented as Exhibits 7.17 through 7.25, and Exhibit 7.26 is a breakeven chart.

Financial Performance

1. *Sales and Earnings Forecasts* (see Exhibits 7.17 through 7.19): Sales of Rapidrill are projected to increase from $730,000 in 19X2 to $13,680,000 in 19X6. After a projected loss of $229,000 in the first year, after-tax

EXHIBIT 7.17.   Rapidrill Corporation: Sales and earnings forecasts, Fiscal years ended September 30, 19X2–19X6 (000s omitted).

	19X2	19X3	19X4	19X5	19X6
Sales:					
Units	$ 730	$3,827	$6,596	$ 9,067	$11,400
Spares	51	383	989	1,813	2,280
Total sales	781	4,210	7,585	10,880	13,680
Cost of sales:					
Material	434	2,204	3,722	5,269	6,620
Labor	16	98	201	258	323
Burden	98	387	500	589	631
Total cost of sales	548	2,689	4,423	6,116	7,574
Gross Margin	233	1,521	3,162	4,764	6,106
In percent	29.8	36.1	41.7	43.8	44.6
Overhead expenses:					
Selling and marketing	84	430	648	991	1,246
Engineering	77	134	273	425	534
Administration and general	296	483	705	1,103	1,387
Total overhead expenses	457	1,047	1,626	2,519	3,167
Earnings before interest and taxes	(224)	474	1,536	2,245	2,939
Interest expense (income)	5	48	52	(3)	(64)
Earning before federal and state taxes	(229)	426	1,484	2,248	3,003
Federal and state taxes		214	751	1,137	1,519
Net earnings before extraordinary item	(229)	212	733	1,111	1,484
Extraordinary item—reduction in federal income taxes resulting from carryover of prior year's operating losses		114			
Net earnings	$(229)	$ 326	$ 733	$ 1,111	$ 1,484
Percent sales before extraordinary item		5.0	9.7	10.2	10.8
Percent sales after extraordinary item		7.7	9.7	10.2	10.8

profits are expected to increase from $326,000 in 19X3 to $1,484,000 in 19X6 (see Exhibit 7.17). After-tax profit as a percentage of sales is 7.7 percent in the second year of Rapidrill's operation and increases to 10.8 percent in the fifth year. Even if actual sales are one-half of those forecast, Rapidrill will be profitable in its second year of operation (see breakeven chart, Exhibit 7.26, and Exhibit 7.17).

EXHIBIT 7.18. Rapidrill Corporation: Monthly sales and earnings forecasts, Fiscal year ended September 30, 19X2 (000s omitted).

	Oct.	Nov.	Dec.	Jan.	Feb.	Mar.	Apr.	May	June	July	Aug.	Sept.	Total
Sales:													
Units								$92	$182	$92	$182	$182	$730
Spares								6	13	6	13	13	51
Total sales								98	195	98	195	195	781
Cost of sales:													
Material								54	109	54	109	108	434
Labor								2	4	2	4	4	16
Burden								12	24	12	25	25	98
Total cost of sales								68	137	68	138	137	548
Gross margin								30	58	30	57	58	233
In percent								30.6	29.7	30.6	29.2	29.7	29.8
Overhead expenses:													
Selling and marketing						$2	$13	13	13	14	14	15	84
Engineering	$5	$2	$3	$6	$4	7	7	7	8	9	9	10	77
Administration and general	45*	15	14	16	16	17	28	39	29	29	29	29	296
	50	17	17	22	20	26	48	59	50	52	52	54	457
Earnings before interest and taxes	(50)	(17)	(17)	(22)	(20)	(26)	(48)	(20)	8	(22)	5	5	(224)
Interest expense (income)										1	2	2	5
Earnings before federal and state taxes	(50)	(17)	(17)	(22)	(20)	(26)	(48)	(20)	8	(23)	3	3	(229)
Federal and state taxes													
Net earnings	$(50)	$(17)	$(17)	$(22)	$(20)	$(26)	$(48)	$(20)	$8	$(23)	$3	$3	$(229)

* *Note:* Includes expenses during five months prior to incorporation.

EXHIBIT 7.19a. Rapidrill Corporation: Quarterly sales and earnings forecasts, Fiscal year ended September 30, 19X3 (000s omitted).

	19X3				
	1Q	2Q	3Q	4Q	Total
Sales:					
Units.....................	$ 764	$ 874	$1,126	$1,063	$3,827
Spares..................	76	88	113	106	383
Total sales.............	840	962	1,239	1,169	4,210
Cost of sales:					
Material.................	464	516	641	583	2,204
Labor....................	13	20	32	33	98
Burden..................	83	88	113	103	387
Total cost of sales.....	560	624	786	719	2,689
Gross margin..............	280	338	453	450	1,521
In percent...............	33.3	35.1	36.6	38.5	36.1
Overhead expenses:					
Selling and					
marketing..............	97	98	127	108	430
Engineering..............	33	33	33	35	134
Administration					
and general..............	115	117	124	127	483
Total	245	248	284	270	1,047
Earnings before interest					
and taxes..................	35	90	169	180	474
Interest expense (income)...	11	13	13	11	48
Earnings before federal					
and state taxes............	24	77	156	169	426
Federal and state taxes.....	12	39	78	85	214
Net earnings before					
extraordinary item........	12	38	78	84	212
Extraordinary item— reduction in federal income taxes resulting from carryover of prior year's operating losses............	6	21	42	45	114
Net earnings................	$ 18	$ 59	$ 120	$ 129	$ 326
Percent sales before					
extraordinary item........	1.4	4.0	6.3	7.2	5.0
Percent sales after					
extraordinary item........	2.1	6.1	9.7	11.0	7.7

EXHIBIT 7.19b. Rapidrill Corporation: Quarterly sales and earnings forecasts, Fiscal years ended September 30, 19X4 (000s omitted).

	19X4				
	1Q	2Q	3Q	4Q	Total
Sales:					
Units......................	$1,382	$1,657	$2,086	$1,471	$6,596
Spares...................	207	249	313	220	989
Total sales..............	1,589	1,906	2,399	1,691	7,585
Cost of sales:					
Material.................	776	937	1,175	834	3,722
Labor....................	42	51	61	47	201
Burden..................	103	126	152	119	500
Total cost of sales......	921	1,114	1,388	1,000	4,423
Gross margin...............	668	792	1,011	691	3,162
In percent................	42.0	41.6	42.1	40.9	41.7
Overhead expenses:					
Selling and					
marketing..............	136	163	205	144	648
Engineering..............	68	68	69	68	273
Administration					
and general.............	176	177	176	176	705
Total...................	380	408	450	388	1,626
Earnings before interest					
and taxes.................	288	384	561	303	1,536
Interest expense (income)...	13	18	14	7	52
Earnings before federal					
and state taxes............	275	366	547	296	1,484
Federal and state taxes.....	139	185	277	150	751
Net earnings before					
extraordinary item........	136	181	270	146	733
Extraordinary item—					
reduction in federal income					
taxes resulting from					
carryover of prior year's					
operating losses...........					
Net earnings...............	$ 136	$ 181	$ 270	$ 146	$ 733
Percent sales before					
extraordinary item........	8.6	9.5	11.2	8.6	9.7
Percent sales after					
extraordinary item........	8.6	9.5	11.2	8.6	9.7

2. *Cash Flow* (see Exhibits 7.20 through 7.22): The equity capital raised in this offering, together with the investment of the principals and lines of credit of $250,000 in 19X2, $350,000 in 19X3, and $475,000 in 19X4, should be enough to finance Rapidrill's operations. Ideally, a slightly larger line of credit should be sought to increase Rapidrill's cash in the third and fourth quarters of 19X3. Note that the cash flow provided by operations becomes positive in the third year. In the first two years, cash is being used to finance Rapidrill's start-up and working capital. Because bank borrowings are used principally to finance working capital, sales volumes less than forecast will require that less of the line of credit be drawn down.

3. *Balance Sheets* (see Exhibits 7.23 through 7.25): Rapidrill's proposed financial plan provides financial strength and liquidity. The lowest ratio of current assets to current liabilities plus bank loans payable is not projected to be less than about 1:2. And much of Rapidrill's inventory

EXHIBIT 7.20. Rapidrill Corporation: Pro forma cash flows, Fiscal years ended September 30, 19X2–19X6 (000s omitted).

	19X2	19X3	19X4	19X5	19X6
Cash receipts					
Accounts receivable.............	$ 586	$3,824	$7,320	$10,379	$13,330
Notes receivable................					200
Interest				5	64
Total cash receipts...........	586	3,824	7,320	10,384	13,594
Cash disbursements:					
Purchase of materials..........	504	2,178	4,015	5,587	6,698
Manufacturing labor...........	56	224	418	552	617
Manufacturing overhead........	74	183	185	222	225
Warranty expense..............	20	60	100	100	100
Administration, general, selling, and engineering	453	1,044	1,624	2,518	3,166
Equipment.....................	28	12	12	10	10
Federal and state taxes.........		100	751	1,137	1,519
Interest	5	48	52	2	
Total cash disbursements.....	1,140	3,849	7,157	10,128	12,335
Cash provided (drained) by operations.....................	(554)	(25)	163	256	1,259
Investment in long-term notes receivable				163	1,275
Bank borrowing (repayment)......	250	(25)	(150)	(75)	
Sale of common stock	280				
Net increase (decrease) in cash balance	$ (24)	$ (50)	$ 13	$ 18	$ (16)

EXHIBIT 7.21. Rapidrill Corporation: Pro forma monthly cash flows, Fiscal year ended September 30, 19X2 (000s omitted).

	19X2												
	Oct.	Nov.	Dec.	Jan.	Feb.	Mar.	Apr.	May	June	July	Aug.	Sept.	Total
Cash receipts:													
Accounts and notes received									$ 98	$195	$ 98	$195	$ 586
Interest													
Total cash receipts									98	195	98	195	586
Cash disbursements:													
Purchases of materials							$ 52		113	115	113	111	504
Manufacturing labor					$ 1	$ 4	8	$ 8	8	9	9	9	56
Manufacturing overhead					11	13	9	9	9	9	7	7	74
Warranty expense							2	3	4	3	4	4	20
Administration, general, selling, and engineering	$ 44	$ 22	$ 17	$ 22	19	26	48	49	48	55	50	53	453
Equipment	2			1		10	10			5		2	28
Federal and state taxes													
Interest										1	2	2	5
Total cash disbursements	46	22	17	23	31	53	129	69	182	197	185	186	1,140
Cash provided (drained) by operations	(46)	(22)	(17)	(23)	(31)	(53)	(129)	(69)	(84)	(2)	(87)	9	(554)
Investment in long-term notes receivable													
Bank borrowing (repayment)								50	100		100		250
Sale of common stock		40			240								280
Net increase (decrease) in cash balance	$(46)	$ 18	$(17)	$(23)	$209	$ (53)	$(129)	$(19)	$ 16	$ (2)	$ 13	$ 9	$ (24)
Opening cash balance	88*	42	60	43	20	229	176	47	28	44	42	55	
Closing cash balance	42	60	43	20	229	176	47	28	44	42	55	64	

*Initial cash balance from investments of principals made prior to October 1, 19X1. No corporate expenditures prior to October 1, 19X1.

EXHIBIT 7.22. Rapidrill Corporation: Pro forma quarterly cash flows, Fiscal years ended September 30, 19X3–19X4 (000s omitted).

	19X3					19X4				
	1Q	2Q	3Q	4Q	Total	1Q	2Q	3Q	4Q	Total
Cash receipts:										
Accounts and notes received	$719	$890	$1,008	$1,207	$3,824	$1,375	$1,848	$2,052	$2,045	$7,320
Interest										
Total cash receipts	719	890	1,008	1,207	3,824	1,375	1,848	2,052	2,045	7,320
Cash disbursements:										
Purchases of materials	453	531	561	633	2,178	852	1,034	1,028	1,101	4,015
Manufacturing labor	31	45	74	74	224	82	111	112	113	418
Manufacturing overhead	38	52	50	43	183	45	45	48	47	185
Warranty expense	12	14	17	17	60	22	25	26	27	100
Administration, general, selling, and engineering	243	248	283	270	1,044	379	408	449	388	1,624
Equipment	5	3	2	2	12	5	2	5		12
Federal and state taxes	25	25	25	25	100	191	191	191	178	751
Interest	11	13	13	11	48	13	18	14	7	52
Total cash disbursements	818	931	1,025	1,075	3,849	1,589	1,834	1,873	1,861	7,157
Cash provided (drained) by operations	(99)	(41)	(17)	132	(25)	(214)	14	179	184	163
Investment in long-term notes receivable										
Bank borrowing (repayment)	100			(125)	(25)	250		(200)	(200)	(150)
Sale of common stock										
Net increase (decrease) in cash balance	$ 1	$(41)	$(17)	$ 7	$(50)	$ 36	$ 14	$(21)	$(16)	$ 13
Opening cash balance	$ 64	$ 65	$ 24	$ 7		$ 14	$ 50	$ 64	$ 43	
Closing cash balance	65	24	7	14		50	64	43	27	

**EXHIBIT 7.23.   Rapidrill Corporation: Pro forma balance sheets,
Fiscal years ended September 30, 19X1–19X6
(000s omitted).**

	19X1	19X2	19X3	19X4	19X5	19X6
Current assets:						
Cash	$88	$ 64	$ 14	$ 27	$ 45	$ 29
Accounts receivable		195	581	846	1,360	1,710
Notes receivable					150	1,225
Inventory		393	563	824	1,315	1,502
Total current assets		652	1,158	1,697	2,870	4,466
Property, plant, and equipment		28	40	52	62	72
Less: Depreciation		5	13	23	33	43
		23	27	29	29	29
Total assets	$88	$675	$1,185	$1,726	$2,899	$4,495
Current liabilities:						
Accounts payable and accrued expenses		$286	$ 495	$ 453	$ 590	$ 702
Bank loans payable		250	225	75		
Total liabilities		536	720	528	590	702
Equity:						
Capital stock — common 10¢ par value, 720,000 authorized shares	$37	69	69	69	69	69
Paid-in surplus	51	299	299	299	299	299
Retained earnings		(229)	97	830	1,941	3,425
Total equity	88	139	465	1,198	2,309	3,793
Total liablilities and equity	$88	$675	$1,185	$1,726	$2,899	$4,495

consists of standard components and materials that should be readily
salable. After the investment of this offering (assumed to be in February
19X2), Rapidrill's working capital is estimated not to fall below about
$140,000.

Rapidrill's liquidity should hold up reasonably well if sales are somewhat less than forecast. This is because Rapidrill has little invested in
fixed assets and bank borrowings are primarily used for working capital.
If sales fall from forecasts, current assets, current liabilities, and bank borrowings should tend to drop proportionately and the effect of the sales
drop on liquidity or the ratio of current assets to current liabilities plus
bank debt should tend to be small.

EXHIBIT 7.24. Rapidrill Corporation: Pro forma monthly balance sheets, Fiscal year ended September 30, 19X2 (000s omitted).

	Oct.	Nov.	Dec.	Jan.	Feb.	Mar.	Apr.	May	June	July	Aug.	Sept.
Current assets:												
Cash	$40	$18	$43	$20	$229	$176	$47	$28	$44	$42	$55	$64
Accounts receivable								98	195	98	195	195
Notes receivable												
Inventory					13	83	216	283	282	347	337	393
Total current assets	40	18	43	20	242	259	263	409	521	487	587	652
Property, plant, and equipment —												
at cost	2	2	2	3	3	13	23	23	23	28	28	28
Less: Depreciation						1	2	2	3	4	4	5
	2	2	2	3	3	12	21	21	20	24	24	23
Total assets	$42	$20	$45	$23	$245	$271	$284	$430	$541	$511	$611	$675
Current liabilities:												
Accounts payable and accrued expenses	$ 4	$ 1	$ 1	$ 1	$ 3	$ 55	$116	$232	$235	$228	$225	$286
Bank loans payable								50	150	150	250	250
Total liabilities	4	1	1	1	3	55	116	282	385	378	475	536
Equity:												
Capital stock — common 10¢ par value, 720,000 shares authorized	37	45	45	45	69	69	69	69	69	69	69	69
Paid-in surplus	51	83	83	83	299	299	299	299	299	299	299	299
Retained earnings	(50)	(67)	(84)	(106)	(126)	(152)	(200)	(220)	(212)	(235)	(232)	(229)
Total equity	36	19	44	22	242	216	168	148	156	133	136	139
Total liabilities and equity	$42	$20	$45	$23	$245	$271	$284	$430	$541	$511	$611	$675

223

EXHIBIT 7.25. Rapidrill Corporation: Pro forma quarterly balance sheets, Fiscal years ended September 30, 19X3–19X4 (000s omitted).

	19X3				19X4			
	1Q	2Q	3Q	4Q	1Q	2Q	3Q	4Q
Current assets:								
Cash	$ 65	$ 24	$ 7	$ 14	$ 50	$ 64	$ 43	$ 27
Accounts receivable	316	388	619	581	795	853	1,200	846
Notes receivable								
Inventory	439	477	424	563	651	630	538	824
Total current assets	820	889	1,050	1,158	1,496	1,547	1,781	1,697
Property, plant, and equipment —								
at cost	33	36	38	40	45	47	52	52
Less: Depreciation	7	9	11	13	15	18	20	23
	26	27	27	27	30	29	32	29
Total assets	$846	$916	$1,077	$1,185	$1,526	$1,576	$1,813	$1,726
Current liabilities:								
Accounts payable and accrued expenses	$339	$350	$ 391	$ 495	$ 450	$ 319	$ 486	$ 453
Bank loans payable	350	350	350	225	475	475	275	75
Total liabilities	689	700	741	720	925	794	761	528
Equity:								
Capital stock — common 10¢ per value, 720,000 shares authorized	69	69	69	69	69	69	69	69
Paid-in surplus	299	299	299	299	299	299	299	299
Retained earnings	(211)	(152)	(32)	97	233	414	684	830
Total equity	157	216	336	465	601	782	1,052	1,198
Total liabilities and equity	$846	$916	$1,077	$1,185	$1,526	$1,576	$1,813	$1,726

4. *Breakeven Analysis* (see Exhibit 7.26): At its currently proposed sales prices and costs, Rapidrill's breakeven sales are about 19 units and $1,900,000. Rapidrill recognizes that this may be somewhat high. It is also apparent that a 10 percent increase in Rapidrill's prices would lower the breakeven to 12 units and $1,300,000 in sales. Accordingly, Rapidrill will closely watch its competitors' pricing behavior and, if appropriate, consider the possibility of increasing its prices. In any case, if sales volume should drop, it should be possible to lower Rapidrill's fixed cost by cutting back on some of its general and administrative expenses.

Cost Control

Achievement of the financial plan delineated above will depend in significant measure on Rapidrill's ability to control its costs. To do this, Rapidrill's principals will draw on their experience in designing and implementing systems to control the costs of design, development, and manufacturing programs.

Design and development programs will use a job cost reporting system. Each equipment development project will be broken down into subtasks, and labor, overhead, purchased materials, and subcontracting costs will be separately reported for each subtask. Cost reports will be issued every two weeks and the cost and progress to date monitored and compared to budgets.

EXHIBIT 7.26.   Rapidrill Corporation: 19X2–19X3 breakeven analysis.

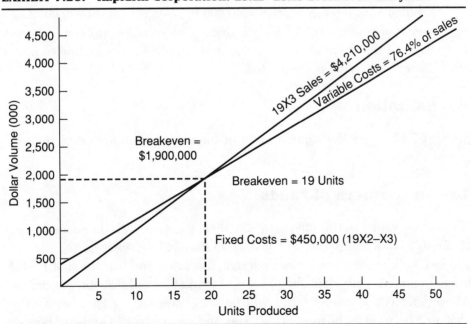

These reports will be monitored by Messrs. Miller, Price, and MacMillan, and weekly meetings will be held to discuss and determine solutions to actual or potential cost problems.

When a drill model (e.g., D–40K) is released for production, a set of standard costs for assembly labor, purchased components, overhead, etc., will be established. Actual costs will be accumulated by subtask and cost category and compared to the standards. Significant differences between actual and standard costs will be evaluated to see if these are due to inefficiencies or are real cost increases. If the former, corrective actions will be identified and taken; if the latter, the standards may need revision. Warranty and field service costs will also be carefully monitored to ensure that Rapidrill's allowance for these is adequate.

Finally, ratio analysis of costs to sale price will be used to identify any cost element that may be deviating significantly from the norms and be cause for concern.

10. PROPOSED RAPIDRILL OFFERING

Financing

Rapidrill Corporation is incorporated in the state of Delaware and currently has 720,000 shares of 10 cents par value common voting stock authorized, with 451,000 shares issued as of November 30, 19X1.

Rapidrill now intends to raise $240,000 through the sale of 240,00 shares of its common voting stock at $1 per share. The common stock sold in this financing will represent about 35 percent of Rapidrill's outstanding common stock after the offering is completed.

Capitalization

Exhibit 7.27 shows the capitalization of Rapidrill before and after the proposed offering.

Use and Sources of Funds

The money raised in this offering ($240,000), together with the money raised ($128,460) earlier from the sale of stock to Rapidrill's principals and key employees, will be used primarily to design, fabricate, and test the first D–40K truck-mounted rotary drill and to set up a marketing and distribution system. These $368,000 of equity funds will be supplemented by bank borrowings that will be used to finance inventories and receivables. The bank borrow-

EXHIBIT 7.27. Rapidrill Corporation—Present and proposed capitalization.

Stockholders	Shares Owned		Percent Ownership Post-Offering	Investment	Cost per Share
	Pre-Offering	Post-Offering			
S. A. Price	135,000	135,000	19.6%	$ 20,400	$0.15
M. F. Einman	78,000	78,000	11.3	20,280	0.26
F. T. Samuels	78,000	78,000	11.3	20,280	0.26
G. A. Miller	42,000	42,000	6.1	12,600	0.30
W. D. MacMillan	36,000	36,000	5.2	14,400	0.40
J. Jones*	27,000	27,000	3.9	13,500	0.50
D. Mead*	27,000	27,000	3.9	13,500	0.50
S. Ross*	27,000	27,000	3.9	13,500	0.50
Investors of this offering		240,000	34.8	240,000	1.00
	450,000	690,000	100.0%	$368,460	

*These are the three distributor representatives mentioned in Section 2.

ings reach maximums of $250,000 in 19X2, $350,000 in 19X3, and $475,000 in 19X4 (see Pro Forma Cash Flows and Balance Sheets). Rapidrill expects to have a $600,000 to $700,000 revolving line of credit with Nashville banks and has obtained preliminary approval of such a line of credit. Final approval will be contingent on raising the $240,000 of this offering.

NOTES TO BALANCE SHEET

Accounts Receivable

Thirty days. Considered to be 100 percent collectible due to financial strength of customers. These customers have demonstrated prompt and consistent payment of invoices in past associations with Rapidrill's principals. The few drills that have been repossessed have repeatedly been sold in the used market for up to 90 percent of their original selling price, thus limiting the loss from an uncollected receivable. Experience of Rapidrill's principals indicates that with proper credit control, industrywide losses are insignificant.

Notes Receivable

Range from 12 to 60 months in duration. Usually secured by the equipment. Loss expectancy extremely low.

Inventory

Approximately 80 percent value in off-the-shelf, standard, stock items easily returnable; therefore, more liquid than custom-specified items.

Accounts Payable

Sixty days, 19X2 through second quarter of 19X3. Vendors have indicated a willingness to work on these terms during Rapidrill's start-up period.

Loans

Currently negotiating with local banks for a $600,000–$700,000 revolving line of credit. Already have had preliminary approvals of loans and now preparing a package to be presented to the credit committees. Final approval contingent on raising $240,000 of this offering.

Retained Earnings

No dividend payments are planned during program.

Rapidrill has 29,000 shares of common stock authorized but unissued. These shares will be used to attract additional management personnel or reserved for future use as stock options to key employees.

FOR FURTHER READING

Baty, Gordon, *Entrepreneurship for the Nineties* (Englewood Cliffs, NJ: Prentice-Hall, 1990).

Bygrave, William D. and Jeffry A. Timmons, *Venture Capital at the Crossroads* (Boston: Harvard Business School Press, 1992).

Cohen, Herb, *You Can Negotiate Anything* (Toronto: Bantam, 1980).

Fisher, Roger and William Ury, *Getting to Yes* (Boston: Houghton-Mifflin, 1981).

Gladstone, William, *Venture Capital Investing* (Englewood Cliffs, NJ: Prentice-Hall, 1988).

Gumpert, David E. and Stanley R. Rich, *Business Plans That Win $* (New York: Harper & Row Publishers, 1985).

Hornaday, J. A. (Ed.), J. A. Timmons, F. Tarpley and K. H. Vesper, *Frontiers of Entrepreneurship Research* (Babson Park, MA: Babson College, 1991).

Kao, John, *Entrepreneurship, Creativity and Organization* (Homewood, IL: Richard D. Irwin, 1989).

Timmons, Jeffry A., *The Entrepreneurial Mind* (Acton, MA: Brick House Publishing, 1989).

———, *New Business Opportunities* (Acton, MA: Brick House Publishing, 1989).

———, *New Venture Creation* 2nd ed. (Homewood, IL: Richard D. Irwin, 1989).

———, *Planning and Financing a New Business* (Acton, MA: Brick House Publishing, 1989).

Weinrauch, Donald J. and Nancy Croft Baker, *The Frugal Marketer* (New York: AMACON, 1989).

Wilson, John W., *The New Venturers* (Reading, MA: Addison-Wesley, 1985).

8 FORECASTS AND BUDGETS

Les Heitger

THE CONCEPT OF BUDGETING

Few accounting terms are used more often in everyday conversation than the term budget or budgeting. Television news people talk of city or state budget problems. The federal government budget deficit grows ever larger. Employees are told that attending a professional conference is, "Just not in the budget this year." A wife tells her husband, "Our spending seems to be out of hand, we need a family budget." Budgeting is mentioned regularly in the news, in our business experiences, and in our personal lives. Unfortunately, budgets do not mean the same thing to everyone. The concept of budgeting is simple enough, but the experience that people have with budgets varies significantly from person to person.

There are many budgeting definitions, but most are similar to the following definition. A budget is a comprehensive, formal plan, expressed in quantitative terms, describing the expected operations of an organization over some future time period. As you can see, the characteristics of a budget are that it deals with a specific entity, covers a specific future time period, and is expressed in quantitative terms.

Virtually all organizations prepare some form of budget. City, state, and federal government organizations, for example, are required by law to prepare budgets. Businesses, although not required by law to prepare budgets, find that they just cannot operate effectively and efficiently without budgets. Even many individuals find that budgets are useful, if not essential, in many aspects of their personal lives. Below is a simple illustration of a budget for a specific activity two people are planning.

A Simple Budget Illustration

Dave and Karen are engaged to be married in five months. They are trying to decide where to go on their honeymoon. Both would like to go to the Hawaiian Islands for two weeks if they can afford the trip. In order to make their decision, Dave and Karen need to determine what the trip would cost and also, how much money they will have available for the trip. In order to estimate the cost of the trip, Dave and Karen must make many decisions about the trip. How many islands should they visit? Where will they stay? How often will they eat in restaurants, and what type will they be? Will they rent a car? What kinds of entertainment and special sight-seeing trips do they want? The more precise Dave and Karen's plans are, the more accurate they can make their cost estimate for the trip. Below is the result of their cost estimates for the trip:

Airfare to/from the islands	$1,500
Inter-island airfares	300
Hotel rooms	1,960
Meals	1,400
Tours and boat trips	350
Car rental	450
Souvenirs	200
Camera film, miscellaneous	200
Budgeted cost for the trip	$6,360

The above cost estimate is a cost budget for the trip. The numbers are based on Dave and Karen's plan to visit three islands and spend a total of two weeks in the Hawaiian Islands. The couple is somewhat surprised by the total cost for the two-week trip. This is not uncommon. Often people find that plans, once converted to detailed cost estimates, are more costly than they at first imagined. A major value of budgeting is its ability to provide a basis for cost comparisons between various alternative plans.

The cost budget presented above is only part of the trip budget. The other part is the revenue budget. In other words, how much money will Dave and Karen have available for the trip and what are the sources of the funds?

Dave and Karen have a total of $9,000 in their savings accounts. In addition, they expect to receive about $1,500 in cash as wedding gifts. Both Dave and Karen have jobs earning a combined total of $3,000 per month. Their total resources are $9,000 of savings, $1,500 of expected wedding gifts, and $15,000 ($3,000 per month times 5 months) of earnings. The total of $26,500, however, is not all available for their honeymoon expenses. Dave and Karen know that virtually all of their earnings over the next five months will be needed to meet their daily living expenses. In addition, they want to have at least $5,000 of savings in their account after they are married. They will need this amount to cover the expenses of setting up their new apartment and to cover any unexpected expenses such as car repairs or medical expenses. Therefore, the revenue budget for the honeymoon trip is as follows:

Savings ($9,000 − $5,000)	$4,000
Expected cash wedding presents	1,500
Earnings during the next five months	0
Budgeted revenue for the trip	$5,500

The budgeted revenues are not large enough to cover the budgeted costs. Dave and Karen must make some decisions about how to eliminate the difference. Perhaps they can change their plans somewhat and reduce the budgeted costs of the trip. Alternatively, they may be able to find some additional revenue for the trip. Of course, they may make some adjustments to both budgets.

In this case, Dave and Karen decided they could use $500 more of their savings for the trip. This increased their total revenue budget to $6,000. On the cost side, they decided to visit only two islands, saving some inter-island airfare. In addition, they found a cheaper round-trip airfare to the islands and cut their food budget somewhat. The revised budgets for the trip were as follows:

Budgeted Costs

Airfare to/from the islands	$1,400
Inter-island airfares	150
Hotel rooms	1,960
Meals	1,290
Tours and boat trips	350
Car rental	450
Souvenirs	200
Camera film, miscellaneous	200
Budgeted cost for the trip	$6,000

Budgeted Revenues

Savings ($9,000 − $4,500)	$4,500
Expected cash wedding presents	1,500
Earnings during the next five months	0
Budgeted revenue for the trip	$6,000

The process of changing budgets to reflect new information and changing plans is called budget revision. In businesses, budget revision occurs as managers from many different functional areas of the business bring together their plans for the upcoming budget period. As management attempts to coordinate the resource needs of many different business activities, it is necessary to make many revisions of individual budgets.

Another important concept illustrated by the simple budget presented above is the entity concept. This concept simply stated says that we must always know precisely what activity or business segment we are dealing with in measuring costs and revenues. The illustration above presents a budget for a trip to Hawaii for Dave and Karen. The costs included in the budget must relate only to the trip to Hawaii. Cost for any other trip, or costs of furnishing a new apartment are not a part of this budget. Similarly, the revenue budget only includes resources available for the trip. Savings required for other items or activities are not included. Likewise, Dave and Karen's earnings are needed for daily living costs and therefore are excluded from the travel budget. The entity concept is essential in the creation of any budget.

FUNCTIONS OF BUDGETING

The two basic functions of budgeting are planning and control. Planning encompasses the entire process of preparing the budget, from the initial ideas through the development of the budget. Planning is the process that most people think of when the term budgeting is mentioned. The majority of the time and effort devoted to budgeting is expended in the planning stage. Careful planning provides the framework for the second function of budgeting.

Control is the comparison of actual results with budgeted data, evaluation of the differences, and taking corrective actions to adjust for differences when necessary. The comparison of budget and actual data can occur only after the period is over and actual accounting data are available. For example, April manufacturing cost data are necessary to compare with the April production budget to measure the difference between plans and actual results for the month of April. The comparison of actual results with budget expectations is called performance reporting. The budget acts as a gauge against which managers compare actual costs and revenues.

Exhibit 8.1 is a budget performance report for manufacturing overhead for the first quarter of 1992. The difference between budgeted cost and actual cost is called a budget variance. Budget variances are reported for each cost so that favorable and unfavorable variances do not net out, thus hiding potential problems.

REASONS FOR BUDGETING

Budgeting is a time-consuming and costly process. Managers and employees are asked to contribute information and time in preparing the budget and in responding to performance reports and other control phase budgeting

EXHIBIT 8.1. Jamestown Corporation manufacturing overhead performance report: First quarter 1992.

Manufacturing Overhead	Budget	Actual	Variance (Favorable) Unfavorable	
Variable costs:				
Indirect materials	$ 13,725	$ 15,225	$ 1,500	U
Indirect labor	27,450	24,500	(2,950)	F
Employee fringe benefits	54,900	67,800	12,900	U
Payroll taxes	13,725	17,100	3,375	U
Utilities	16,470	20,250	3,780	U
Maintenance	10,980	10,650	(330)	F
Total variable costs	$137,250	$155,525	$18,275	U
Fixed costs:				
Supervision	$ 27,000	$ 27,000	$ 0	
Depreciation	36,000	36,000	0	
Maintenance	13,500	14,250	750	U
Property taxes	7,368	7,800	432	U
Insurance	4,500	4,950	450	U
Total fixed costs	$ 88,368	$ 90,000	$ 1,632	U
Total manufacturing overhead costs	$225,618	$245,525	$19,907	U

activities. Is it all worth it? Do firms get their money's worth from their budgeting systems?

The answer to those questions cannot be stated, in general, for all firms. Some firms receive far more value than other firms for the dollars they spend on budgeting. Budgets do, however, provide a wealth of value for many firms that effectively operate their budgeting systems. Below we discuss some of the reasons for investing in formal budgeting systems. In the next section of this chapter we will discuss issues that contribute to effective budgeting.

Budgets offer a variety of benefits to organizations. Some common benefits of budgeting include the following:

1. Requires periodic planning
2. Fosters coordination, cooperation, and communication
3. Forces quantification of proposals
4. Provides a framework for performance evaluation
5. Creates an awareness of business costs
6. Satisfies legal and contractual requirements
7. Orients a firm's activities toward organizational goals

Periodic Planning

Virtually all organizations require some planning to ensure efficient and effective use of scarce resources. Some people are compulsive planners who continuously update plans that have already been made and plan for new activities and functions. At the other extreme are people who do not like to plan at all and, therefore, find little or no time to get involved in the planning process. The budgeting process closes the gap between these two extremes, by creating a formal planning framework that provides specific, uniform periodic deadlines for each phase of the planning process. People who are not attuned to the planning process must still meet budget deadlines. Of course, planning does not guarantee success: People must execute the plans. But budgeting is an important prerequisite to the accomplishment of many activities.

Coordination, Cooperation, and Communication

Planning by individual managers does not ensure an optimum plan for the entire organization. The budgeting process, however, provides a vehicle for the exchange of ideas and objectives among people in the various organizational segments. The budget review process and other budget communication networks should minimize redundant and counterproductive programs by the time the final budget is approved.

Quantification

Because we live in a world of limited resources, virtually all individuals and organizations must ration their resources. The rationing process is easier for some than for others. Each person and each organization must compare the costs and benefits of each potential project or activity and choose those that will result in the most appropriate resource allocations.

Measuring costs and benefits requires some degree of quantification. Profit-oriented firms make dollar measurements for both costs and benefits. This is not always an easy task. For example, the benefits of an advertising campaign are increased sales and a better company image, but it is difficult to estimate precisely the additional sales revenue caused by a particular advertising campaign. It is even more difficult to quantify the improvements in the company image. In not-for-profit organizations, such as government agencies, quantification of benefits can be even more difficult. For example, how does one quantify the benefits of better police protection, more music programs at the city park, or better fire protection, and how should the benefits be evaluated in allocating resources to each activity? Despite the difficulties, resource allocation decisions necessitate some reasonable quantification of the costs and benefits of the various projects under consideration.

Performance Evaluation

Budgets are estimates of future events, and as such they serve as estimates of acceptable performance. Managerial performance in each budgeting entity is appraised by comparing actual performance with budgeted projections. Most managers want to know what is expected of them so that they may monitor their own performance. Budgets help to provide that type of information. Of course, managers can also be evaluated on other criteria, but it is valuable to have some quantifiable measure of performance.

Cost Awareness

Accountants and financial managers are concerned daily about the cost implications of decisions and activities, but many other managers may not be. Production supervisors focus on output, marketing managers on sales, and so forth. It is easy for people to overlook costs and cost-benefit relationships. At budgeting time, however, all managers with budget responsibility must convert their plans for projects and activities into costs and benefits. This cost awareness provides a common ground for communication among the various functional areas of the organization.

Legal and Contractual Requirements

Some organizations are required to budget. Local police departments, for example, cannot ignore budgeting even if it seems too much trouble, and the National Park Service would soon be out of funds if its management decided not to submit a budget this year. Some firms commit themselves to budgeting requirements when signing loan agreements or other operating agreements. For example, a bank may require a firm to submit an annual operating budget and monthly cash budgets, throughout the life of a bank loan.

Goal Orientation

Resources should be allocated to projects and activities in accordance with organizational goals and objectives. Logical as this may sound, it is sometimes difficult to relate general organizational goals to specific projects or activities. Many general goals are not operational—meaning that it is difficult to determine the impact of specific projects on the achievement of the general goals of the organization.

For example, organizational goals may be stated as follows:

1. Earn a satisfactory profit
2. Maintain sufficient funds for liquidity
3. Provide good quality products for customers

The above goals which use terms such as "satisfactory," "sufficient," and "good quality" are not operational goals. The goals stated above may be interpreted differently by each manager. To be effective, goals must be more specific and provide clear direction for managers.

For example, the above goals can be made operational as follows:

1. Provide a minimum return on gross assets invested of 18 percent.
2. Maintain a minimum current ratio of 2:1 and a minimum quick ratio of 1.2:1.
3. Products must receive at least an 80 percent approval rating on customer satisfaction surveys.

EFFECTIVE BUDGETING

We have already noted that almost all organizations and many individuals do some budgeting. In this country huge amounts of time and money are spent on budgeting activities. Unfortunately, everyone does not achieve the same return for the time and money invested in budgeting. There are many reasons why some firms use budgeting more effectively than others. Some of these reasons are discussed below.

1. Budgets should be goal oriented so that they help a firm accomplish its goals and objectives.
2. Budgets must be realistic plans of action, rather than wishful thinking.
3. The control phase of budgeting must be used effectively to provide a framework for evaluating performance and improving activities at the budget planning stage.
4. Participative budgeting should be utilized to instill a sense of cooperation and team play.
5. Budgets should not be used as an excuse for denying appropriate employee resource requests.
6. The budgeting process should be used by management as an excellent vehicle for modifying the behavior of employees to achieve company goals.

Goal Orientation

Virtually all organizations operate with limited resources. Some firms have more resources than others, but no firm seems to have all of the resources it needs to accomplish all of its goals. Consequently, budgets should provide a means by which resources are utilized for projects, activities, and business units, in accordance with the goals and objectives of the organization.

A prerequisite to goal-oriented budgeting is the development of a formal set of operational goals. Some organizations have no formally defined goals, and even those that do often have only general goals for the entire organization. Major operating units may function without written or clearly defined goals or objectives. General organizational goals should be as specific as possible, carefully established, and written. Next, each major unit of the organization should develop more specific operational goals. The process should continue down the organizational structure to the lowest level of budget responsibility. This goal-development process requires management at all levels to resolve difficult issues, but it results in a budgeting framework that is much more likely to be effective. Even individuals need to understand their goals and objectives, as they prepare for their own activities.

Realistic Plan

Budgeting is not wishful thinking; instead it is a process designed to optimize the use of scarce resources, in accordance with the goals of the company or individual in question. Unfortunately, some managers view the planning process as a welcome respite from the daily rigors of dealing with business activities, when projects are not going as well as expected. Some managers view budget planning as an opportunity to dream of a future when business may be better. Any improvement in the current situation must be based on solid executable plans, not just wishful thinking. Many firms have budget plans that call for sales growth, higher profits, and improved market share; but to be effective, such plans must be based on specific executable plans. Such plans must be based on available resources and management talent. If the management of a firm wants to move from one level of operations to another, there must be a clearly defined path between the two points, which the firm is able to travel.

The Control Phase of Budgeting

The first and most time-consuming phase of budgeting is the planning process. The control phase of budgeting, however, may be when firms get the most value from their budgeting activities. Comparing actual results with the budget, adjusting plans when necessary, and evaluating the performance of managers are essential elements of budget control. These steps enable the organization to stay on track, or get back on track if performance has fallen short. Many people, however, find the control phase difficult. When business results are less than expected, it may be painful to evaluate the results. For some it is much easier to look ahead, to a period when things may be better. But, frequently, plans for future success can only be made realistically when management learns from its past mistakes. The control phase of budgeting provides much of that learning process. Firms must be willing to evaluate performance carefully, adjusting plans and performance to stay on track.

Many companies have intricate budget performance reporting systems in place, but the firms achieve little control from their use. In order to provide effective control, a business must use the system as an integral part of the reward system of the company. That is, employees must understand that budget performance reports are a component of their performance evaluation. There should be a relationship between budget performance and rewards, such as pay raises, bonuses, and promotions.

Generally it is easy to determine if a company's budget performance reporting system is working effectively. If discussions with managers yield comments such as, "If we fail to achieve the budget, we just add more to it next period," it is likely that the budget control process is not effective. If, on the other hand, employees state, "If we are over our budget by more than 2 percent, we will be called on the carpet and forced to explain the problem," then one knows the control process is having an effect.

Participative Budgeting

Most behavioral experts believe that individuals work harder to achieve objectives that they have had part in creating. Applied to budgeting, this concept states that employees will strive harder to achieve performance levels defined by budgets, if the employee has had a part in creating the budget. On the other hand, budgets imposed by top-level management may get little support from employees. The concept of building budgets up from the bottom, with input from all employees and managers affected, is called participative budgeting.

Improper Use of Budgets

Sometimes managers use budgets as scapegoats for unpopular decisions. For example, rather than telling a department head that her budget request for three additional employees was not convincing when compared with all of the other budget requests, the vice president says, "The budget just would not allow any new employees this year." In another case, the director of the marketing department requested travel funds to send all of his staff to an overseas education program. The vice president believes the program is a waste of money. Instead of telling the marketing director his opinion, the vice president says, "We would really like to send your staff to the program, but the budget is just too tight this year." Of course, the truth in this situation is that the trip is not a good use of business resources, regardless of the condition of the budget. The marketing director is left with the impression that the real problem is the state of the budget, when in fact his travel proposal was not sound business. Management should be careful not to undermine the budgeting process by assigning to it adverse characteristics. The author recalls a conversation with the chief engineer of a company who was asked his definition of budgeting. He responded, "Budgeting is the formal process whereby my department is denied those things that we want and deserve, to effectively carry on our engineering function within the company."

Behavioral Issues in Budgeting

Many of the internal accounting reports prepared in business are intended to influence managers and employees to behave in a particular way. For example, many manufacturing cost reports are designed to make employees aware of costs, with the intent of controlling costs or keeping costs at some desired or acceptable level. Similarly, reports that compare the performance of one division with the performance of other divisions are used to evaluate the performance of division managers and encourage better results for each division.

Budgets and budget performance reports are among the more useful internal accounting reports used by businesses to influence employee performance in a positive manner. Budget control is based on the concept that managers are held responsible for activities they manage. Performance reports reflect the degree of achievement of plans as embodied in the budget. To minimize adverse behavioral problems, care should be taken to develop and administer budgets appropriately. Budgets should not be used as a hammer to demand unattainable performance from employees. The best safeguard against unrealistic budgets is participative budgeting.

DEVELOPING A BUDGET

The Structure of Budgets

Budgets are useful, and in most cases essential, to the success of virtually all organizations whether they are profit seeking or not-for-profit organizations. The larger and more complex the organization, the more time, energy, and resources that must be used in preparing and using the budget. Regardless of the size or type of organization, most budgets can be divided into two categories: the operating budget and the financial budget. The operating budget consists of plans for all of those activities that make up the normal repetitive operations of the firm. For a manufacturing business, the operating budget includes plans for sales, production, marketing, distribution, administration, and any other activities that the firm carries on in its normal course of business. For a merchandising firm, the operating budget includes plans for sales, merchandise purchases, marketing, distribution, advertising, personnel, administration, and any other normal activities of the merchandising firm. The financial budget includes all of the plans for financing the activities described in the operating budget plus any plans for major new projects such as a new production plant or plant expansions. Both the operating and financial budgets will be described in more detail below.

The Master Budget

The master budget is the total budget package for an organization; it is the end product of the budget preparation process. The master budget consists of all the individual budgets for each part of the organization, combined into one overall budget for the entire organization. The exact composition of the master budget depends somewhat on the type and size of the business. However, all master budgets represent the organization's overall plan for a specific budget period. Exhibit 8.2 lists the common components of a master budget for manufacturing business.

The components of the master budget form the firm's detailed operating plan for the coming year. As noted above, the master budget is divided into the operating budget and the financial budget. The operating budget includes revenues, product costs, operating expenses, and other components of the income statement. The financial budget includes the budgeted balance sheet, cash budget, capital expenditure budget, and other budgets used in financial management. A large part of the financial budget is determined by the operating budget and the beginning balance sheet.

EXHIBIT 8.2.   A manufacturing firm's master budget.

Operating budget
  Sales budget
  Budget of ending inventories
  Production budget
    Materials budget
    Direct labor budget
    Manufacturing overhead budget
  Budgeted cost of goods sold
  Administrative expense budget
  Marketing expense budget
  Budgeted net income from operations
  Budgeted nonoperating items
  Budgeted net income

Financial budget
  Capital expenditure budget
  Cash budget
  Budgeted statement of financial position (balance sheet)
  Budgeted statement of cash flows

Operating Budget Components

Sales Budget

The sales budget or revenue budget is the first budget to be prepared. It is usually the most important budget because so many other budgets are directly related to sales and are therefore derived from the sales budget. Inventory budgets, production budgets, personnel budgets, marketing budgets, administrative budgets, and other budgets areas are all affected significantly by the amount of expected revenue.

Sales budgets are influenced by a wide variety of factors, including general economic conditions, pricing decisions, competitor actions, industry conditions, and marketing programs. For example, the invasion of Kuwait by Iraq in August of 1990 had a negative impact on the American economy, in general, and, in particular, on directly affected industries such as oil. The outbreak of war in January 1991 had an even bigger impact on the economy. Stock prices rose with news of military successes and crude oil prices fell. On the other hand, travel, particularly overseas travel, plummeted, causing a severe recession in travel and travel related industries. Although many managers in the industries most heavily affected were able to predict much of the impact of these events, most had trouble predicting the severity and length of the economic impact. In particular, it was difficult to predict the positive economic impact of the war. Even in complex times, it is essential that firms attempt to make very precise sales budgets.

Often the sales budget starts with individual sales representatives or sales managers predicting sales in their particular areas. The basic sales data are aggregated to arrive at a raw sales forecast that is then modified to reflect many of the variables mentioned previously. The resulting sales budget is expressed in dollars. It must include sufficient detail on product mix and sales patterns to provide the information necessary to determine optimum changes in inventory levels and production quantities.

Budget of Ending Inventories

Inventories comprise a major portion of the current assets of many manufacturing firms. Separate decisions about inventory levels must be made for raw materials, work in process, and finished goods. Raw material scarcities, management's attitude about inventory levels, inventory carrying costs, inventory ordering costs, and other variables may all affect inventory level decisions.

Production Budget

The first step in making a production budget is to determine production quantity. The materials budget, direct labor budget, and manufacturing overhead budget are all derived from the production quantity budget. Together these budgets are called the production budget. Managers incorporate current and expected inventory levels and sales estimates into the materials budget. Monthly materials budgets reflect sales patterns and the time required between ordering and receiving materials.

In the last few years, many manufacturing businesses have implemented just in time (JIT) inventory systems. JIT inventory systems are based on the premise that the only value of inventories is to facilitate efficient manufacturing and to provide finished inventory for sales. With a JIT system, production inventories are delivered or produced only as they are needed for production activities. The implementation of JIT inventory systems requires careful planning, major changes in most firms' production philosophies, and a great emphasis on quality. Although JIT inventory reduces significantly the level of production inventories, it actually increases the amount of planning and budgeting that firms must do for materials inventory.

Budgeted Cost of Goods Sold

For a manufacturing firm, cost of goods sold is the production cost of products that are sold. Consequently, the cost of goods sold budget follows directly from the production budget. The cost of goods sold figure is different from the production budget figure because it is affected by beginning and ending inventories.

Administrative Expense Budget

The expected administrative costs for an organization are presented in the administrative expense budget. The administrative expense budget may contain many fixed costs, some of which may be partly or fully avoidable, if subsequent operations indicate the need for cost cuts. These avoidable costs, sometimes called discretionary fixed costs, include such items as research and development, employee education and training programs, and portions of the personnel budget. Fixed costs that cannot be avoided during the period are called committed fixed costs. Mortgage payments, bond interest payments, and property taxes are classified as committed costs. Variable administrative costs may include some personnel costs, a portion of the utility costs, computer service bureau costs, and supply costs.

Marketing Expense Budget

Sales volume is determined, to some degree, by the marketing effort. Consequently, the marketing expense budget is prepared, at least in part, early in the budgeting process when the sales budget is being prepared. Some marketing costs, such as marketing management salaries and machinery and building depreciation for marketing, do not vary directly with sales volume. Other marketing costs, such as sales commissions and product distribution costs, may vary with the level of sales volume. Marketing costs for some consumer products, such as toothpaste, are very high and, in some cases, may even exceed the cost of producing the product. In such cases, the marketing budget is a very important budget.

Budgeted Income Statement

The budgeted income statement is the combination of all of the preceding budgets. This budget shows the expected revenues and expenses from operations during the budget period. Budgeted income is a key figure in the firm's profit plan and reflects a majority of the firm's commitment of talent, time, and resources for the period.

A firm may have budgeted nonoperating items such as interest on investments or gains or losses on the sale of fixed assets. Usually, they are relatively small, although in large firms, the dollar amounts can be sizable. If nonoperating items are expected, they should be included in the firm's budgeted income statement. Income taxes are levied on actual, not budgeted, net income, but the budget plan should include expected taxes. Therefore, the last figure in the budgeted income statement is budgeted after-tax net income.

The Financial Budget

The financial budget presents the plans for financing the operating activities of the firm. The financial budget is made up of a number of different budgets, each providing essential financial information.

Capital Expenditure Budget

The capital expenditure budget is one of the budget components that makes up the financial budget. Each of the budget components has its own unique contribution to make toward the effective planning and control of business operations. Some budget components, however, are particularly crucial in the effective management of businesses. The cash budget and the capital expenditure budget are two of the most important.

Capital budgeting is the process of identifying, evaluating, planning, and financing major investment projects of an organization. Decisions to expand production facilities, acquire new production machinery, buy a new computer, or remodel the office building are all examples of capital expenditure decisions. Capital budgeting decisions made now, determine to a large degree how successful an organization will be in achieving its goals and objectives in the years ahead. Capital budgeting plays an important role in the long-range success of many organizations because of several characteristics that differentiate it from most other elements of the master budget.

First, most capital budgeting projects require relatively large commitments of resources. Major projects, such as plant expansion or equipment replacement, may involve resource outlays in excess of annual net income. Relatively insignificant purchases are not treated as capital budgeting projects, even if the items purchased have long lives. For example, the purchase of 100 calculators at $15 each, for use in the office, would be treated as a period expense by most firms, even though the calculators may have a useful life of several years.

Second, most capital expenditure decisions are long-term commitments. The projects last more than 1 year, with many extending over 5, 10, or even 20 years. The longer the life of the project, the more difficult it is to predict revenues, expenses, and cost savings. Capital budgeting decisions are long-term policy decisions and should reflect clearly an organization's policies on growth, marketing, industry share, social responsibility, and other goals.

Cash Budget

Of all the components of the master budget, none is more important than the cash budget. Liquidity is of paramount importance to a firm; it is more important than earning a satisfactory profit. Some companies may lose money for many years, but with adequate financing they are able to remain in business until they can become profitable. On the other hand, firms that cannot remain liquid are unable to pay their bills as they come due. In such cases, creditors can, and often do, force firms out of business. Even government and not-for-profit organizations such as churches and charities must eventually pay their bills and other obligations in order to survive.

Meeting cash obligations as they come due is not as simple as it may appear. Profitability and liquidity do not necessarily go hand in hand. Some firms experience their most critical liquidity problems when they go from a break-even position to profitability. At that time, growing receivables, increased inventories, and growing capacity requirements may create cash shortages.

The cash budget is a very useful tool in cash management. Managers estimate all expected cash flows for the budget period. The typical starting point is cash from operations, which is net income adjusted for noncash items, such as depreciation. All nonoperating cash items are also included. Purchase of land and equipment, sales of bonds and common stock, and the acquisition of treasury stock are a few examples of nonoperating items affecting the cash budget. The net income figure for an accounting period usually is very different from the cash flow for the period because of nonoperating cash flow items or changes in working capital.

Often, cash budgets are prepared much more frequently than other budgets. For example, a company may prepare quarterly budgets for all of its operating budget components, such as sales and production, and also for its other financial budget components, such as capital expenditures. For its cash budget, however, the firm prepares weekly budgets, to ensure that it has cash available to meet its obligations each week and that any excess cash is properly invested. In companies with very critical cash problems, even daily cash budgets may be necessary to meet management's information requirements. The frequency of cash budgets depends on management's planning needs and the potential for cash management problems.

Cash budgeting in general has become more and more essential to effectively managing businesses. Tight money and high interest rates make cash budgeting even more important. This author has known a number of small business owners and managers who have been ineffective and sometimes uninterested in budgeting in general, but they have been very good "seat-of-the-pants" cash budgeters. I have seen people prepare pretty effective weekly cash budgets on a paper napkin at lunch or on the edge of a newspaper. Such individuals recognize that cash budgeting often is the difference between being in business and being forced into bankruptcy. The essential issue is not how pretty or professional the cash budget is, but rather how accurately it reflects the expected cash receipts and required disbursements during the budget period.

Cash management is intended to optimize cash balances; this means having enough cash to meet liquidity needs, but not having so much cash that profitability is sacrificed. Excess cash should be invested in earning assets: It should not be allowed to remain idle in the cash account. Cash budgeting is useful in dealing with both types of cash problems.

Budgeted Balance Sheet

The budgeted balance sheet, sometimes called the budgeted statement of financial position, is derived from the budgeted balance sheet at the beginning of the budget period and the expected changes in the account balances, reflected in the operating budget, capital expenditure budget, and cash budget. It is necessary to use a budgeted balance sheet for the beginning of the period because the new budget is prepared before the previous accounting period has ended. When the budgeted balance sheet for the coming accounting period is prepared, there may be several months left in the current accounting period.

The budgeted balance sheet is more than a collection of residual balances resulting from other budget estimates. Undesirable projected balances and account relationships may cause management to change the operating plan. For instance, if a lending institution requires a firm to maintain a certain relationship between current assets and current liabilities, the budget must reflect these requirements. If it does not, the operating plan must be changed until the agreed requirements are met.

Budgeted Statement of Cash Flows

The final element of the master budget package is the statement of cash flows. The increased emphasis by management in recent years on cash and the sources and uses of cash have made this an ever more useful management tool. This statement is usually prepared from data in the budgeted income statement and changes in the estimated balance sheet between the beginning and end of the budget period.

FIXED BUDGETS VERSUS FLEXIBLE BUDGETS

Many organizations operate in an environment where they can predict with great accuracy the volume of business they will experience during the upcoming budget period. In such cases, budgets prepared for a single level of activity are very useful in planning and controlling business activities. Budgets prepared for a single level of activity are called fixed budgets.

Organizations that have trouble predicting the volume of activity they will experience during the budget period often find that a budget prepared for only one level of activity is not very helpful in planning and controlling their business activities. These organizations can operate better with a budget prepared for a range of possible activity levels. This type of budget is called a flexible budget.

Fixed Budgets

A fixed budget, sometimes called a static budget, contains budget data for only one specific volume of activity. Because fixed budgets use only one volume of activity in determining all budgeted data, the fact that some costs are fixed and some costs are variable has no impact on the budgeted figures. The budget data used in preparing the budget for the planning phase are also in budget performance reports during the control phase, regardless of whether the expected volume of activity is actually achieved.

The planning and control framework provided by a budgeting system is an essential element of effective management. In many organizations, fixed budgets are tools that offer managers the ability to plan and control operations and to evaluate performance. If, however, the actual volume of activity achieved by a firm is significantly different from the volume of activity planned in the fixed budget, the fixed budget may be a very poor measure on which to evaluate employees.

Flexible Budgets

A flexible budget, also called a dynamic budget, is prepared for more than one level of activity. For example, a firm may prepare budgets for 10,000, 11,000, and 12,000 units of production. The purpose of preparing budgets for multiple activity levels is to provide managers with information about a range of activity, in case the actual activity volume differs from the expected level. Managers continue to rely heavily on the budget, based on the expected activity level for planning material acquisitions, labor needs, and other resource requirements. But the flexible budget provides additional information, which is useful in modifying plans, if operating data indicate that some other activity level will occur. When performance reports are prepared, actual results are compared with a budget based specifically on the activity level achieved.

Actual activity may differ significantly from budgeted activity because of an unexpected strike, cancellation of a large order, an unexpected new contract, or other factors. In a business that frequently experiences variations in its activity volume, a flexible budget tends to be more useful than a fixed budget. Flexible budgets provide managers with more useful information for planning and a better basis for comparing performance when activity levels fluctuate.

The Profit Plan

The term profit plan is sometimes used to refer to a master budget. Profit plan probably best describes the operating part of the master budget of a profit-oriented firm. However, it can be argued that the entire master budget of profit-oriented firms is the total profit plan for the firm. The operating budget shows details of budgeted net income, but the financial budgets, such as cash and capital expenditure budgets, are also an integral part of the overall profit planning of the firm.

Naturally, the term profit plan is not suitable for public-sector firms. Organizations such as a fire department do not generate a net income. For public-sector organizations, master budget is the more logical term for the total budget package. Because we are concerned with both public- and private-sector organizations, we use master budget predominantly. However, be aware of the term profit plan because it is used occasionally.

THE BUDGET REVIEW PROCESS

The budget plan determines the allocation of resources within the organization. Typically the resources available are less than the demand for the resources. Consequently, there should be some systematic process for evaluating all proposals relating to the budget. The process of systematically evaluating budget proposals is referred to as the budget review process.

In the early planning stages, budget review may not be a formal process. Sometimes, a few people or even a single individual make the budgeting decisions. For example, production line supervisors may determine resource allocations within their department. A plant budget committee may evaluate budget proposals for all production supervisors. The budget proposals for the entire plant usually go to a division budget committee, and the final budget review is made by a budget committee, consisting of the controller and corporate vice presidents.

The budget review process varies among organizations. Even within a single firm, different budget review processes may be used by various segments of the firm, and at various levels of responsibility. However, the basic review process is fairly standard. Exhibit 8.3 illustrates the general flow in the budget review process.

Accountants and financial managers participate in the preparation and implementation of the budget, but all business managers, including marketing managers, production supervisors, purchasing officers, and other nonfinancial managers are interested in developing budgets for their particular part of the business. In addition each functional manager must be able to present and defend his or her budget to higher level management. Defending the budget means convincing the budget review committee that a particular budget proposal should be accepted. For some managers, defending the budget is the single most important activity in their job, because if they fail at this task, even a tremendous management effort cannot obtain desired results.

With the crucial importance of defending the budget, one might conclude that it is an exceedingly difficult process. Not so! Actually the process

EXHIBIT 8.3. Budget review process.

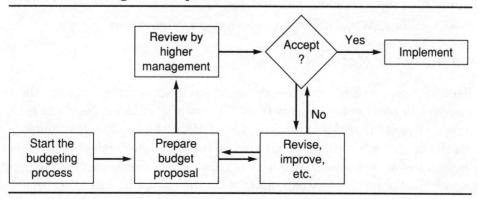

requires a mixture of logic and diligence. There is no precise formula for success, but some general suggestions are:

1. Know your audience
2. Make a professional presentation
3. Quantify the material
4. Avoid surprises
5. Set priorities

Know Your Audience

A large part of the budget presentation strategy may be determined by the nature of the budget review audience, whether it is one person or a group of people. Information that may prove essential to the successful budget approval effort includes:

1. Strategies that have succeeded or failed in the past
2. Pet peeves or special likes of review members
3. A variety of other committee characteristics

Make a Professional Presentation

Not all managers approach the budgeting process with the same level of enthusiasm. By the time budget review arrives, some managers just want it to be over. Such an attitude can easily show during the budget review process. Review committees may interpret such attitudes as disdain for their job and their management function in general. Often the result is unfavorable action on the budget proposals under review.

A professional presentation includes:

- An enthusiastic and polished presentation
- A neat, concise, and understandable budget proposal
- Ample supporting documentation
- A willingness and ability to answer relevant questions

Quantify the Material

Because most resource allocation decisions are in some way affected by their cost-benefit relationships, it is necessary to quantify both the costs and benefits of virtually all budget proposals. Cost estimation is seldom easy, but it is usually far easier than the measurement of probable future benefits. Even in the private sector, benefits are not always easy to measure in terms of the corporate goals of profitability and liquidity. In the not-for-profit sector, benefit measurement is even more difficult. For example, how does one measure the benefits of 20 new park rangers, 10 new police cars, or a decorative fountain in the city park? The quantification process would be different for each of these, and direct comparisons could be inconclusive. Yet, such comparisons may be necessary in arriving at final budget allocations.

It is easy to dismiss the value of quantification when the resulting numbers are hard to compare with other budget proposals, or the numbers are hard to verify. Nevertheless, some quantitative support typically is better than just general statements about the desirability of the budget proposal. If certain budget proposals have benefits that are difficult to quantify directly, various types of statistics might support the projects in an indirect way. For example, if a police department wants to justify 10 new police officers, it might offer supporting statistics on the increase in population in the community, increasing crime rates, or relatively low per-capita police cost. None of the suggested statistics measure direct benefits, but they may be more useful to a budget review committee than some vague statement about the value of more officers. Statistics that are not direct measures of benefits can be used widely in both the public and private sector in support of budget proposals.

Avoid Surprises

Avoid surprises to the review committee as well as surprises to the people presenting the budget. Brand new proposals and information are hard to defend to a budget review committee. Anything startlingly new should be introduced and developed long before the final review process.

Surprises to managers presenting budgets most often occur during the questioning process or when a budget proposal is more detailed than prior budgets. To minimize this problem, budget presentations should be carefully rehearsed in great detail. The rehearsal might include a realistic or even pessimistic mock review committee. This committee should ask pointed and difficult questions. Sometimes knowing the answer to a relatively immaterial question is enough to secure a favorable opinion.

Set Priorities

Few managers receive a totally favorable response to all budget requests. In a world of limited resources, wants exceed available resources: Managers should be prepared for a budget allocation that is somewhat different from the initial request. All proposed budget items are not equally desirable. Some projects and activities are essential; others are highly desirable. Some would be nice, but are really not essential.

Priority systems, established by the managers of each budgeting entity before the review process starts, aid in structuring the budget proposal so that important items are funded first. Setting priorities avoids embarrassing questions and last-minute crises that affect the quality of a professional presentation.

GLOSSARY

Budget: A comprehensive quantitative plan for utilizing the resources of an entity for some specified period of time.

Budget Entity: Any accounting entity, such as a firm, division, department, or project, for which a budget is prepared.

Budget Performance Report: An internal accounting report that shows the difference between actual results and expected performance planned in a budget.

Budget Review Process: The process of evaluating budget proposals and arriving at the master budget.

Budget Variance: The difference between budgeted data and actual results.

Capital Budgeting: The systematic process of identifying and evaluating capital investment projects to arrive at a capital expenditure budget.

Committed Fixed Costs: The fixed costs of providing production facilities and other relatively long-term commitments of resources. Fixed costs that cannot be easily or quickly eliminated.

Control: The concept of monitoring activities and taking action to correct undesirable performance or to ensure that goals and objectives are achieved, often using budgets as a basis for measuring performance.

Discretionary Fixed Cost: Fixed costs that can be eliminated at management's discretion in a relatively short period of time, e.g., some administrative salaries, research and development, and new systems development.

Financial Budget: The set of budgets including capital expenditures budget, cash budget, budgeted balance sheet, and budgeted statement of changes in financial position.

Fixed Budget: A budget prepared for a single expected level of activity. Also called a static budget.

Flexible Budget: A budget prepared for more than one level of activity, covering several levels within the relevant range of activity. Also called a dynamic budget.

Master Budget: The total budget package of an organization, including both the operating and financial budgets. Sometimes referred to as the profit plan.

Operating Budget: The set of budgets for the normal operations of a business, including all activities involved in generating operating income.

Participative Budgeting: The process of preparing the budget using input from managers who are held responsible for budget performance.

Performance Reporting: The comparison of actual results with the expected results embodied in the budget, often resulting in the reporting of variances.

Planning: The process of developing the set of budgets used in achieving organizational goals. A design or scheme for achieving specific goals or objectives.

Profit Plan: A company's total budget used in achieving a desired profit goal. Sometimes the term refers only to the operating budget, and sometimes it is used synonymously with the term master budget.

FOR FURTHER READING

Carruth, Paul J., and Thurrel O. McClendon, "How Supervisors React to Meeting the Budget Pressure," *Management Accounting* (November 1984).

Chandler, John S., and Thomas N. Trone, "Bottom Up Budgeting and Control," *Management Accounting* (February 1982).

Collins, Frank, Paul Munter, and Don W. Finn, "The Budgeting Games People Play," *The Accounting Review* (January 1987).

Geurts, Michael D., and Thomas A. Buchman, "Accounting for Shocks in Forecasts," *Management Accounting* (April 1981).

Leitch, Robert A., John B. Barrack, and Sue H. McKinley, "Controlling Your Cash Resources," *Management Accounting* (October 1980).

Merchant, Kenneth A., "The Design of the Corporate Budgeting System: Influences on Managerial Behavior and Performance," *The Accounting Review* (October 1981).

Merewitz, Leonard, and Stephen H. Sosnick, *The Budget's New Clothes* (Chicago: Markham Publishing Company, 1973).

Trapani, Cosmo S., "Six Critical Areas in the Budgeting Process," *Management Accounting* (November 1982).

Wildavsky, Aaron, *The Politics of the Budgetary Process*, 2nd. ed. (Boston: Little, Brown and Company, Inc., 1974).

MANAGING LONG-TERM INVESTMENTS: FINANCIAL STRUCTURE, COST OF CAPITAL, AND CAPITAL BUDGETING

9

Kenneth S. Most

Len Samuels was the chief financial officer (CFO) of Super Terrific Industries Incorporated. He sat in his corner office on the 99th floor and looked over the corporation's "wish list" for long-term projects. The list was certainly impressive. Included in the many items listed was the following sample of capital spending proposals:

- A new semiconductor plant to be built in Austin, Texas ($1.1 billion)
- Installation of anti-pollution equipment at the Orange, New Jersey plant ($651 million)
- Replacement of the central computer system at head office ($167 million)
- Addition of two executive jets to the existing fleet of corporate aircraft ($49 million)
- Purchase of laptop computers for every member of the sales force ($4 million)
- Installation of a daycare facility at the divisional office in San Diego ($0.3 million)

The wish list added up to $2.4 billion. Available funds were only $1.7 billion So, the first problem was how to cut the capital expenditure proposals down from $2.4 billion to $1.7 billion. How could the projects be put into a prioritized order? Which projects were essential in order to sustain or advance the company's competitive edge? Which projects offered the best "bang for the buck?" Which projects were the most risky and which the most safe? Which projects were best able to attract new financing on desirable terms from the investment community?

These are the kind of vital questions involved in selecting long-term investments. This chapter will address these key issues.

The financial manager is responsible for acquiring funds at the lowest cost, to meet planned requirements, in accordance with the decisions of the board of directors. These financial requirements are specified in two types of budget, the operating budget and the capital budget. Chapter 8 discussed the preparation of the operating budget. This chapter reviews the capital budgeting process. Terms used in capital budgeting are defined and techniques used in making capital budgeting decisions are demonstrated.

THE TIME VALUE OF MONEY

Capital budgeting decisions are long-term decisions, extending over periods that may amount to decades. Because of this, it is essential to take into consideration the time value of money. This concept refers to the fact that a dollar received or paid today has a different value from a dollar received or paid a year ago, or a year from now. Let's consider a simple example. If a firm receives $100 on January 1, 19X0 and deposits it in an interest-bearing account, it will have earned interest of (say) $5 by December 31, 19X0. The value of this $100 received on January 1 is therefore $105 on *December 31.* Similarly, if the firm is owed $100 on January 1, 19X0 and this amount is not paid until December 31, the value of the expected receipt on *January 1* is less than $100, because of the interest foregone during the waiting period. (The calculation of how much less will be demonstrated later in this chapter.)

Money receipts and payments are equated at different points in time by means of the concept of present value. Time is viewed as a line and the action moment is referred to as the present or "time zero." This device permits us to adjust the amount of any cash receipt or payment by the interest factor that must be considered when calculating its value at time zero.

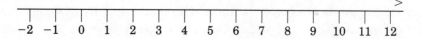

In the above diagram, 0 represents the point at which a firm's action will result in money being received or paid in the future. The intervals may be days, weeks, months, or years: In long-term capital budgeting decisions, it is customary to use years as a time unit. The negative numbers designate periods prior to time zero in which actions may result in receipt or payment of money. For example, a firm that decides to build a new factory may acquire land two years before development starts; the payment for the land involves interest paid or foregone, which is part of the factory's development cost. Similarly, if an airline orders an aircraft from Boeing and pays money in advance of delivery, the interest cost associated with this advance represents a component of the aircraft's cost above it invoice price.

THE CAPITAL BUDGETING DECISION MODEL

The basic equations of capital budgeting are:

$$\text{Finance} = \text{Investment}$$

$$\text{Investment} = \text{Fixed assets} + \text{Working capital}$$

Investment is the allocation of scarce funds to future production (as contrasted with consumption.)[1] Such allocation is only rational if the value of future production is greater than the value of the present resources sacrificed. Return on investment (ROI) is a measure of the excess value, and is conventionally expressed as a percentage ratio. For example, if $100 is invested in an inventory of goods for one year, which are sold for $130 at the end of the year, then the profit of $30 can be expressed as a rate of 30 percent per year.

$$\frac{\$30 \times 100}{\$100} = 30\%$$

This ratio is the ROI.

The funds must be acquired from their owner(s) and this necessitates a payment, which can also be expressed by means of a ratio, called the cost of capital. If the $100 required to buy the inventory is borrowed from a bank that requires a payment of $115 at the end of the year, then the cost of capital as a rate is 15 percent [($115 − $100) × 100/$100].

One capital budgeting decision model is shown in Exhibit 9.1. Investment opportunities are plotted in order of decreasing returns, assuming that a rational investor would seek to maximize profits. Financing costs are plotted on the assumption that the cost of capital increases as the total amount of financing exceeds some specific limit. The model graphs ROI and cost of capital defines the size of the capital on the y axis. The point at which ROI equals cost of capital defines the size of the capital budget I_o because no other amount can be more profitable. Below I_o, profits will be made (returns exceed costs) and above I_o, losses will be incurred (costs exceed returns).

EXHIBIT 9.1.   The capital budgeting decision model.

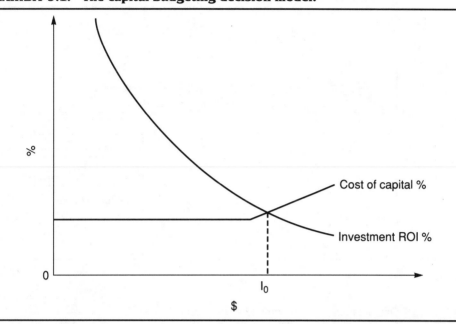

This model may also be used as a screening model, to identify the investment projects that meet a specified criterion (ROI exceeds cost of capital), or as a preference model, to rank projects in ROI order. However, the model has limitations in both of these situations. These limitations will be examined in later examples.

FINANCIAL LEVERAGE

Leverage denotes the use of fixed-income securities, debt, and preferred stock, to increase returns on common stockholders' equity. In this section, illustrations will be restricted to the case of debt. (The case of preferred stock is similar, except that preferred dividends are not tax deductible.)

The use of financial leverage is one of the most important factors underlying financial structure. Equity capital is more costly than debt capital because (a) equity capital providers expect a premium for the higher degree of risk they run and (b) interest on debt is tax deductible, while dividends on equity capital are not. Therefore the after-tax cost of debt is less than that of equity. As a result, a debt-financed firm that is profitable receives a subsidy equal to the tax on the debt interest expense. This is deducted from revenues when calculating taxable income.

If assets producing a given rate of return are financed in part by low-cost debt and in part by high-cost equity, the excess of the return over the

EXHIBIT 9.2. Financial leverage.

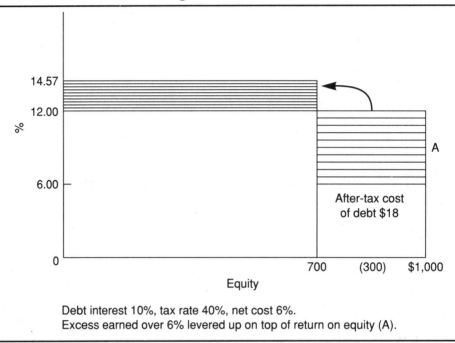

Debt interest 10%, tax rate 40%, net cost 6%.
Excess earned over 6% levered up on top of return on equity (A).

cost of the debt is "levered up" to increase return on common equity. This is depicted in Exhibit 9.2.

This diagram shows a firm that earns a 12 percent (income before interest but after taxes × 100/total assets) of $120 on total assets of $1,000. Assets are financed by common equity (70 percent) and debt (30 percent). The debt pays interest of 10 percent which, at a 40 percent tax rate, represents a 6 percent after-tax cost. The net interest cost is represented by the horizontally shaded area under the 12 percent line. Because the firm earned 12 percent on $300 of debt capital, or $36, and its 6 percent after-tax cost was only $18, the difference is profit for the equity. The diagram shows this $18 (the diagonally shaded area) being levered up over the equity, increasing the ROE from 12 percent to 14.57 percent ($84 + $18 × 100/$700).

If the after-tax interest cost debt is greater than the return on assets the effect is the opposite; this is called "negative leverage." In this case the ROE is reduced by the leverage, not increased. In addition, debt represents a constant threat to the survival of the firm. Should it be unable to pay interest or any part of the principal falling due, the debt holders can sue for recovery, and eventually force the firm into liquidation. For these reasons, many entrepreneurs attempt to keep their financial structure debt-free, and even some large corporations maintain a similar policy.

There are several ways of measuring the leverage factor in a particular financial structure. One common approach is calculating the ratio of return with leverage to return without leverage. In the illustration, this is 14.57/12.00 or 1.21.

FINANCIAL STRUCTURE AND THE COST OF CAPITAL

In financial investment theory, the cost of capital may be defined in terms of maintaining the market value of the firm's securities. These, however, are also affected by many factors outside the control of the firm, such as political events; income tax rates; interest and foreign currency exchange rate movements; and the price of energy, to name just a few. For this reason the financial manager looks inward to the firm's cost structure and balance sheet, rather then outward to the stock and bond markets, to find the cost of capital. Because the cost of capital is prospective (what it will cost to finance the planned investments), estimates have to be made of the future state of the stock and bond markets and other important factors, such as income tax rates.[2]

For this purpose we use the concept of financial structure. Viewed through a firm's financial statements, the basic equation of finance is reflected in the basic equation of accounting: Assets equal liabilities plus owners equity. Financial structure refers to the components of the right-hand side of this equation. In this light, a firm's cost of capital is the necessary expense required to raise and maintain that capital. If a company's capital consists of equity (common and preferred) plus borrowings, both dividends and interest must be considered. In the calculation it must be remembered that interest is tax-deductible and dividends are not. For a profitable company, the cost of debt is the after-tax cost and is found by multiplying the interest rate by $1 - t$ (the tax rate). The following example assumes a steady state.

Example

A corporation has a capital structure consisting of 100,000 shares of common stock, par value and issue price of $5 each, paying a $1 dividend; 5,000 shares of preferred stock, par value and issue price $100, dividend rate 10 percent yearly; $200,000 long-term notes bearing interest of 8 percent yearly, issued at par; and a mortgage loan of $100,000 bearing interest at 13 percent each year. The tax rate is 50 percent. The following calculation shows the weighted average cost of capital.

	Amount	Weight %	Annual Dividend or Interest	Annual After-tax Cost
Common stock	$ 500,000	38.5	$100,000	$100,000
Preferred stock	500,000	38.5	50,000	50,000
Notes payable	200,000	15.4	16,000	8,000
Mortgage loan	100,000	7.6	13,000	6,500
Totals	$1,300,000	100.0	$179,000	$164,500

The after-tax weighted average cost of capital is $164,500/$1,300,000, or 12.65 percent.

Note that the firm's entire financial structure is looked at in calculating cost of capital. Suppose the firm is about to buy a building, and can borrow the full price at an after-tax interest rate of 10 percent. The problem with regarding the cost of capital, for this decision, as 10 percent is that debt can be obtained only if there is an equity margin of security. By borrowing, the firm is using some of its equity, which would otherwise be the support for future borrowings. If the firm is unable to sell debt securities because its ratio of debt to equity is seen as being too high, then acceptance of other projects will necessitate issuance of more equity securities. For this reason, an average cost of capital is used in capital budgeting.

Component Cost

We have stated that the cost of debt capital is found on an after-tax basis. One complication arises when the stated interest rate differs from the effective interest rate, or yield to maturity. In extreme cases, such as zero-coupon bonds, there is no stated interest rate; the firm borrows, say $600,000 now and repays $1,000,000 ten years from now. The difference of $400,000 is tax deductible interest, and the interest rate and tax deductible amounts are found by means of the present value method, explained later in this chapter.

Cost of Stockholders' Equity

Three subcomponents of stockholders's equity have to be considered separately: Retained earnings, common stock, and preferred stock. The cost of retained earnings is the rate of return that stockholders require to remain invested. In principle, this should be known from the stockholders themselves, but a conventional approach is to estimate it from the present value of future expected dividends. In a growth situation this can be found from the equation:

$$K_c = \frac{D}{P} + g$$

where K_c represents cost of capital
         D   is the current dividend
         g   is the expected rate of dividend growth, and
         P   is the price of the firm's common shares

Example

A firm's stock sells for $22.80 per share; it pays a dividend of $1.60, which is expected to grow at the rate of 7 percent. K_c is [($1.60 /$22.80 × 100) + 7 percent], or 14 percent. If the firm earns a return of less than 14 percent, the price of the firm's stock may be expected to fall, all other factors remaining unchanged.

For new issues of common stock it is necessary to deduct issuance costs from the price of a share, P, in the above equation. Thus, assuming that a new issue could be made at the current price of $22.80, which would net $20.00 to the firm, the cost of capital would be [($1.60/$20.00 × 100) + 7 percent] = 15 percent.

Preferred stock is similar to debt, except that preferred dividends are tax-deductible. However, if a corporation holds shares in another corporation, upstream dividends may be shielded from income tax by the recipient, so that preferred stock may be sold to yield a lower rate of dividend than the rate of interest that would have to be paid on the debt.

ALTERNATIVE APPROACHES TO COST OF CAPITAL

There are several practical problems associated with the weighted average cost of capital, the principal one being the impossibility of determining an optimal financial structure. If the existing proportions of debt and equity are suboptimal, and are used, the resulting cost per capital is likewise suboptimal, and there is no way of projecting a financial structure that will be optimal in the light of current and future investments.

Example

On December 31, 19X0, a firm has a financial structure consisting of 50 percent debt (cost 8 percent) and 50 percent equity (cost 16 percent). The weighted average cost of capital is 12 percent. If the ratios had been 25 percent debt and 75 percent equity, the weighted average cost of capital would have been 14 percent. If projects returning, say, 13 percent are accepted and the firm improves its financial structure by paying off debt, these projects will yield less than the cost of capital. The reason is that the lower proportion of debt will raise the average cost of capital.

To avoid such problems, some firms arrive at the screening (or hurdle) rate by a process similar to that resulting from use of the capital asset pricing model (CAPM). In the CAPM approach, the firm starts with the riskless interest rate, either the U.S. Treasury bond or 30-day Treasury bill rate, and adds risk points. Risk points are found by:

1. Estimating the firm's beta coefficient, β. The beta coefficient indicates how volatile the firm's stock price is compared to the stock market as a whole. Betas can be found for specific companies in financial sources such as *The Value Line*.

    If a stock has a beta of 1.0, this means that it fluctuates up and down exactly in line with the stock market as a whole. If the market rises by 9 percent, then this stock also goes up by about 9 percent. If the market drops 15 percent, so does this stock. However, a market with a beta of 1.5 is 1.5 times as volatile as the market, and if the market increases 20 percent then this stock tends to increase 30 percent (1.5 times 20 percent). But if the market declines 18 percent, then this stock is likely to go down by 27 percent (1.5 times 18 percent). Stocks with a beta well in excess of 1.0 are high fliers. On the other hand, some stocks are very stable and have betas below 1.0. If such a stock has a beta of 0.75 then it will go down only about 15 percent when the market drops by 20 percent (0.75 times 20 percent), and it will increase only 9 percent when the market rises by 12 percent.

2. Estimating the rate of return on the stock market as whole, K_m.

3. Estimating the rate of return $K_s = R_f + \beta(K_m - R_f)$. In this equation R_f is the risk-free rate of return. Assume that the risk-free rate (represented by the return on the U.S. Treasury bills) is 8 percent, the market rate of return as whole is 12 percent, and the beta is 1.25. Then the firm's cost of common equity is:

$$8\% + 1.25\ (12\% - 8\%)$$
$$= 8\% + 5\%$$
$$= 13\%$$

With a beta larger than 1.0, the firm is riskier than the market average. Logically, therefore, it has a cost of common equity (13 percent) which is larger than the 12 percent equity cost of the market as a whole. If the firm's beta was not 1.25 but 1.5 instead, then its costs of equity would be 14 percent [$8\% + 1.5\ (12\% - 8\%)$]. Thus, the higher risk, the higher the beta, and the higher the resulting cost of equity.

Another approach is for the firm to identify the risks that it runs and attempt to add an estimate of the rate at which it might be insured against such risks. Such a calculation might appear like this (risks are presented in summary form):

Risk-free rate	8%
Premium for demand risks	8%
Premium for supply risks	6%
Premium for financing risks	2%
Screening (hurdle, cut-off) Rate	24%

Note that this is a pretax rate.

Yet another approach proceeds from the argument that investment risks attach to assets, not liabilities or equity, and should be calculated with this in mind. This necessitates identifying an optimal asset structure, which is made easier because firms in particular industries can be seen to hold different types of assets in similar proportions.

In the following illustration, the firm's asset structure is normal, that is, it does not hold excessive cash balances or significant amounts of idle equipment. The cost represents opportunity cost, that is, the amount that the firm would pay if it did not hold the asset. Cash is assumed to earn 8%, accounts receivable could be factored at 10 percent, inventory could be purchased as it is used at a premium of 30 percent (annualized), and equipment rental has an implicit cost of 20 percent.

Asset	Amount	Rate %	Cost
Cash	$ 1,000	8	$ 80
Receivables	20,000	10	2,000
Inventory	15,000	30	4,500
Equipment	30,000	20	6,000
Totals	$66,000		$12,580

In order to "earn its keep," an investment calling for a similar distribution of assets must earn a minimum of $12,580. The project would break even at about 19 percent ($12,580/$66,000) and this becomes the screening or hurdle rate. Projects with different asset structures could have different screening rates, and the capital budget would then be determined by finding the amount of total investment that produces the highest rate of profit; this is a linear programming problem.

THE INFLATION PROBLEM

Inflation presents many problems in calculating cost of capital and should be explicitly considered in all aspects of ROI evaluation. The impact of inflation is felt in two main aspects of the investment decision. The ROI and present value calculations are based on cash flows that do not reflect the fact that replacement value is rising. Thus, income taxes have a heavier effect on profits than calculations show. The depreciation tax shield, which will be described later in this chapter, is a historical cost adjustment and is not inflation-adjusted. Further, the ranking of projects according to their discounted cash flow returns does not incorporate important data, relevant to the capital budgeting decision in times of inflation. Such ranking doesn't consider whether the inflows and outflows are primarily fixed, and, therefore subject to inflation effects; or whether they are variable, and thus capable of being changed to avoid those effects.

Various simple ways of adjusting the discounted cash-flow model for inflation have been proposed. These include: Using a higher discount rate (cost of capital plus expected rate of inflation); shortening the time period used to calculate present value; and modifying the expected cash inflows and outflows using the expected rate of inflation. None of these is satisfactory, and the methods described in the following pages must be substantially changed in order to give explicit effect to inflation adjustments. The various methods of allowing for inflation in capital budgeting remain the subject of considerable debate at the present time.

RATE OF RETURN ON INVESTMENT (ROI)

An ROI concept is in general use. This ROI is found by dividing some measure of return, notably net income, by some measure of investment, notably total capital employed (total assets minus current liabilities). This ROI concept is sometimes called the accounting rate of return or the unadjusted rate of return. The word unadjusted means that it does not use the compounding process that adjusts returns for the time value of money. The accounting rate of return has usefulness as a ratio for evaluating performance, but is defective as a measure to be used in investment decisions.

Example

Consider the case of a machine that is to be bought for $1,000 and will produce net income of $100 annually for five years. It will then be scrapped without residual value. Assuming straight-line depreciation, the following accounting ROIs can be calculated.

Year	Investment Beginning	Profit before Depreciation	Depreciation	Net Income	ROI on Average Investment
1.	$1,000	$300	$200	$100	11.1% (a)
2.	800	300	200	100	14.3 (b)
3.	600	300	200	100	20.0 (c)

Year	Investment Beginning	Profit before Depreciation	Depreciation	Net Income	ROI on Average Investment	
4.	400	300	200	100	33.3	(d)
5.	200	300	200	100	100.0	(e)

(a) $100/.5(1,000 + 800)
(b) $100/.5(800 + 600)
(c) $100/.5(600 + 400)
(d) $100/.5(400 + 200)
(e) $100/.5(200 +   0)

Which ROI shall we use for the investment decision? Note that this problem becomes infinitely more complex if we (a) admit accelerated or production-based depreciation methods, (b) confront fluctuating profit from year to year, (c) consider the effect of income taxes on each year, and (d) expect to have additional capital expenditure on the machine during its useful life.

One possibility is to use the average return, found by summing the ROIs and dividing by N, the number of periods. In the above example, it becomes 35.7 percent (178.7/5). This indicator is also defective because, like all the others, it ignores the time value of money. Reverse the order of the ROIs and the average stays the same, even though it is intuitively obvious that a series of returns starting with 100 percent in Year 1 and ending with 11.1 percent in Year 5 is preferable to a series of returns in the reverse order, the example, the returns were constant in amount from year to year; consider the following comparison.

Example

Two projects are being considered; both require an investment of $100, which is not recoverable until the end of the project's three-year life. Project 1 produces returns of $60, $50, and $40 over the three-year period; Project 2 produces returns of $40, $50, and $60. The average return for each is 50 percent per annum:

$$\frac{(\$150/3) \times 100}{\$100}$$

Which would you prefer?

In summary, the accounting ROI is not adequate for use in the two main forms of investment decisions, screening and preference. For screening decisions—those that involve determining whether a project meets a specified criterion—the accounting ROI fails to give an unequivocal answer. For preference decisions—selecting from several valid alternatives—the accounting ROI fails to give effect to the time value of money.

USING THE TABLES TO CALCULATE PRESENT VALUES

Before proceeding to a consideration of investment decisions, we will examine the use of Exhibits 9.3 and 9.4.

Example

I own a house that I wish to rent for two years while I am working in another country. Two prospective tenants appear, John Doe and Steve Smith. Doe offers me $1,000 on the signing of the lease and $3,000 at the end of each year. Smith offers me $4,000 at the end of Year 1 and $3,500 at the end of

EXHIBIT 9.3.   The present value of one dollar discounted annually for N years.

Year	1%	2%	3%	4%	5%	6%	7%	8%	9%	10%
1	.990	.980	.971	.962	.952	.943	.935	.926	.917	.909
2	.980	.961	.943	.925	.907	.890	.873	.857	.842	.826
3	.971	.942	.915	.889	.864	.840	.816	.794	.772	.751
4	.961	.924	.888	.855	.823	.792	.763	.735	.708	.683
5	.951	.906	.863	.822	.784	.747	.713	.681	.650	.621
6	.942	.888	.837	.790	.746	.705	.666	.630	.596	.564
7	.933	.871	.813	.760	.711	.665	.623	.583	.547	.513
8	.923	.853	.789	.731	.677	.627	.582	.540	.502	.467
9	.914	.837	.766	.703	.645	.592	.544	.500	.460	.424
10	.905	.820	.744	.676	.614	.558	.508	.463	.422	.386
11	.896	.804	.722	.650	.585	.527	.475	.429	.388	.350
12	.887	.789	.701	.625	.557	.497	.444	.397	.356	.319
13	.879	.773	.681	.601	.530	.469	.415	.368	.326	.290
14	.870	.758	.661	.577	.505	.442	.388	.340	.299	.263
15	.861	.743	.642	.555	.481	.417	.362	.315	.275	.239
16	.853	.726	.623	.534	.458	.394	.339	.292	.252	.218
17	.844	.714	.605	.513	.436	.371	.317	.270	.231	.198
18	.836	.700	.587	.494	.416	.350	.296	.250	.212	.180
19	.828	.686	.570	.475	.396	.331	.277	.232	.194	.164
20	.820	.673	.554	.456	.377	.312	.258	.215	.178	.149
21	.811	.660	.538	.439	.359	.294	.242	.199	.164	.135
22	.803	.647	.522	.422	.342	.278	.226	.184	.150	.123
23	.795	.634	.507	.406	.326	.262	.211	.170	.138	.112
24	.788	.622	.492	.390	.310	.247	.197	.158	.126	.102
25	.780	.610	.478	.375	.295	.233	.184	.146	.116	.092
30	.742	.552	.412	.308	.231	.174	.131	.099	.075	.057
35	.706	.500	.355	.253	.181	.130	.094	.068	.049	.036
40	.672	.453	.307	.208	.142	.097	.067	.046	.032	.022
45	.639	.410	.264	.171	.111	.073	.048	.031	.021	.014
50	.608	.372	.228	.141	.087	.054	.034	.021	.013	.009

Year 2. My time value of money is 10 percent per annum. Which deal do I prefer, assuming that the tennants are equally desirable in other respects?

To find the present value of Doe's offer: The first expected receipt of $1,000 takes place at t_0 and is, therefore, not discounted. This can be expressed as $1,000 multiplied by a factor of 1 (not found in the exhibits). Exhibit 9.3 shows the present value of $1, at different rates of discount, for various periods other than the present. The present value of $3,000 is found by multiplying it by the factor in Exhibit 9.3, in the column headed "10 percent" along the row labeled Year 1. The present value of the receipt is found by multiplying it by the factor under 10 percent at Year 2.

EXHIBIT 9.3. *(Continued).*

Year	11%	12%	13%	14%	15%	16%	17%	18%	19%	20%
1	.901	.893	.885	.877	.870	.862	.855	.847	.840	.833
2	.812	.797	.783	.769	.756	.743	.731	.718	.706	.694
3	.731	.712	.693	.675	.658	.641	.624	.609	.593	.579
4	.659	.636	.613	.592	.572	.552	.534	.516	.499	.482
5	.593	.567	.543	.519	.497	.476	.456	.437	.419	.402
6	.535	.507	.480	.456	.432	.410	.390	.370	.352	.335
7	.482	.452	.425	.400	.376	.354	.333	.314	.296	.279
8	.434	.404	.376	.351	.327	.305	.285	.266	.249	.233
9	.391	.361	.333	.308	.284	.263	.243	.225	.209	.194
10	.352	.322	.295	.270	.247	.227	.208	.191	.176	.162
11	.317	.287	.261	.237	.215	.195	.178	.162	.148	.135
12	.286	.257	.231	.208	.187	.168	.152	.137	.124	.112
13	.258	.229	.204	.182	.163	.145	.130	.116	.104	.093
14	.232	.205	.181	.160	.141	.125	.111	.099	.088	.078
15	.209	.183	.160	.140	.123	.108	.095	.064	.074	.065
16	.188	.163	.141	.123	.107	.093	.081	.071	.062	.054
17	.170	.146	.125	.108	.093	.080	.069	.060	.052	.045
18	.153	.130	.111	.095	.081	.069	.059	.051	.044	.038
19	.138	.116	.093	.083	.070	.060	.051	.043	.037	.031
20	.124	.104	.087	.073	.061	.051	.043	.037	.031	.026
21	.112	.093	.077	.064	.053	.044	.037	.031	.026	.022
22	.101	.083	.068	.056	.046	.038	.032	.026	.022	.018
23	.091	.074	.060	.049	.040	.033	.027	.022	.018	.015
24	.082	.066	.053	.043	.035	.028	.023	.019	.015	.013
25	.074	.059	.047	.038	.030	.024	.020	.016	.013	.010
30	.044	.033	.026	.020	.015	.012	.009	.007	.005	.004
35	.026	.019	.014	.010	.008	.006	.004	.003	.002	.002
40	.015	.011	.008	.005	.004	.003	.002	.001	.001	.001
45	.009	.006	.004	.003	.002	.001	.001	.001	.000	.000
50	.005	.003	.002	.001	.001	.001	.000	.000	.000	.000

Present value of John Doe's offer − $1,000 × 1.000 = $1,000
$$3,000 \times .909 = 2,727$$
$$3,000 \times .826 = 2,478$$
Total $6,205

To find the present value of Steve Smith's offer: The first expected receipt of $4,000 takes place at t_1 and the present value is found by multiplying it by the factor under 10 percent in Year 1. The present value of the re-

EXHIBIT 9.4.   **The present value of an annuity of one dollar discounted annually for N years.**

Year	1%	2%	3%	4%	5%	6%	7%	8%	9%	10%
1	.990	.980	.971	.962	.952	.943	.935	.926	.917	.909
2	1.970	1.942	1.913	1.886	1.859	1.833	1.808	1.783	1.759	1.736
3	2.941	2.884	2.829	2.775	2.723	2.673	2.624	2.577	2.531	2.487
4	3.902	3.808	3.717	3.630	3.546	3.465	3.387	3.312	3.240	3.170
5	4.853	4.713	4.580	4.452	4.329	4.212	4.100	3.993	3.890	3.791
6	5.795	5.601	5.417	5.242	5.076	4.917	4.767	4.623	4.486	4.355
7	6.728	6.472	6.230	6.002	5.786	5.582	5.389	5.206	5.033	4.868
8	7.652	7.326	7.020	6.733	6.463	6.210	5.971	5.747	5.535	5.335
9	8.566	8.162	7.786	7.435	7.108	6.802	6.566	6.247	5.995	5.759
10	9.471	8.983	8.530	8.111	7.722	7.360	7.024	6.710	6.418	6.145
11	10.368	9.787	9.253	8.760	8.306	7.887	7.499	7.139	6.805	6.495
12	11.255	10.575	9.954	9.385	8.863	8.384	7.943	7.536	7.161	6.814
13	12.134	11.348	10.635	9.986	9.394	8.853	8.358	7.904	7.487	7.103
14	13.004	12.106	11.296	10.563	9.899	9.295	8.746	8.244	7.786	7.367
15	13.865	12.849	11.938	11.118	10.380	9.712	9.108	8.560	8.061	7.606
16	14.718	13.578	12.561	11.652	10.838	10.106	9.447	8.851	8.313	7.824
17	15.562	14.292	13.166	12.166	11.274	10.477	9.763	9.122	8.544	8.022
18	16.398	14.992	13.754	12.659	11.690	10.828	10.059	9.372	8.756	8.201
19	17.226	15.679	14.324	13.134	12.085	11.158	10.336	9.604	8.950	8.365
20	18.046	16.352	14.878	13.590	12.462	11.470	10.594	9.818	9.129	8.514
21	18.857	17.011	15.415	14.029	12.821	11.764	10.836	10.017	9.292	8.649
22	19.661	17.658	15.937	14.451	13.163	12.042	11.061	10.201	9.442	8.772
23	20.456	18.292	16.444	14.857	13.489	12.303	11.272	10.371	9.580	8.883
24	21.244	18.914	16.936	15.247	13.799	12.550	11.469	10.529	9.707	8.985
25	22.023	19.524	17.413	15.622	14.094	12.783	11.654	10.675	9.823	9.077
30	25.808	22.397	19.601	17.292	15.373	13.765	12.409	11.258	10.274	9.427
35	29.409	24.999	21.487	18.665	16.374	14.498	12.948	11.655	10.567	9.644
40	32.835	27.356	23.115	19.793	17.159	15.046	13.332	11.925	10.757	9.779
45	36.095	29.490	24.519	20.720	17.774	15.456	13.606	12.108	10.881	9.863
50	39.197	31.424	25.730	21.482	18.256	15.762	13.801	12.234	10.962	9.915

ceipt of $3,500 is found by multiplying it by the factor under 10 percent in Year 2.

$$\text{Present value of Steve Smith's offer} - \$4,000 \times .909 = \$3,636$$
$$- \$3,500 \times .826 = \quad 2,891$$
$$\text{Total} \quad \$6,527$$

Thus, no matter how tempted I may be to receive $1,000 right away from John Doe, the present value of Steve Smith's proposal is $322 higher, and a rational individual would prefer this, given the assumptions of the transactions.

EXHIBIT 9.4. *(Continued).*

Year	11%	12%	13%	14%	15%	16%	17%	18%	19%	20%
1	.901	.893	.885	.877	.870	.862	.855	.847	.840	.833
2	1.713	1.690	1.668	1.647	1.626	1.605	1.585	1.566	1.547	1.528
3	2.444	2.402	2.361	2.322	2.283	2.246	2.210	2.174	2.140	2.106
4	3.102	3.037	2.974	2.914	2.855	2.798	2.743	2.690	2.639	2.589
5	3.696	3.605	3.517	3.433	3.352	3.274	3.199	3.127	3.058	2.991
6	4.231	4.111	3.998	3.889	3.784	3.685	3.589	3.498	3.410	3.326
7	4.712	4.564	4.423	4.288	4.160	4.039	3.922	3.812	3.706	3.605
8	5.146	4.968	4.799	4.639	4.487	4.344	4.207	4.078	3.954	3.837
9	5.537	5.328	5.132	4.946	4.772	4.607	4.451	4.303	4.163	4.031
10	5.889	5.650	5.426	5.216	5.019	4.833	4.659	4.494	4.339	4.192
11	6.207	5.938	5.687	5.453	5.234	5.029	4.836	4.656	4.487	4.327
12	6.492	6.194	5.918	5.660	5.421	5.197	4.988	4.793	4.611	4.439
13	6.750	6.424	6.122	5.842	5.583	5.342	5.118	4.910	4.715	4.533
14	6.982	6.628	6.303	6.002	5.724	5.468	5.229	5.008	4.802	4.611
15	7.191	6.811	6.462	6.142	5.847	5.575	5.324	5.902	4.876	4.675
16	7.379	6.974	6.604	6.265	5.954	5.669	5.405	5.162	4.938	4.730
17	7.549	7.120	6.729	6.373	6.047	5.749	5.475	5.222	4.990	4.775
18	7.702	7.250	6.840	6.467	6.128	5.818	5.534	5.273	5.033	4.812
19	7.839	7.366	6.938	6.550	6.198	5.877	5.585	5.316	5.070	4.843
20	7.963	7.469	7.025	6.623	6.259	5.929	5.628	5.353	5.101	4.870
21	8.075	7.562	7.102	6.687	6.312	5.973	5.665	5.384	5.127	4.891
22	8.176	7.645	7.170	6.743	6.359	6.011	5.696	5.410	5.149	4.909
23	8.266	7.718	7.230	6.792	6.399	6.044	5.723	5.432	5.167	4.925
24	8.348	7.784	7.283	6.835	6.434	6.073	5.747	5.451	5.182	4.937
25	8.422	7.843	7.330	6.873	6.464	6.097	5.766	5.467	5.195	4.948
30	8.694	8.055	7.496	7.003	6.566	6.177	5.829	5.517	5.235	4.979
35	8.855	8.176	7.586	7.070	6.617	6.215	5.858	5.539	5.251	4.992
40	8.951	8.244	7.634	7.105	6.642	6.233	5.871	5.548	5.258	4.997
45	9.008	8.283	7.661	7.123	6.654	6.242	5.877	5.552	5.261	4.999
50	9.042	8.305	7.675	7.133	6.661	6.246	5.880	5.554	5.262	4.999

Note that the $6,205, $6,527, and $322 are not units of money in the form of purchasing power. The amounts in that kind of dollar are $7,000 for John Doe and $7,500 for Steve Smith. The other amounts are present values, representatives of value in terms of money, at the same point in time.

Example

A wealthy aunt would like to help you through school and into your first job. She offers you the choice of two annuities, the Provident Benefit Annuity, you would receive $5,000 at the end of each year for 5 years. Under the Southeastern Mutual Annuity you would receive $6,250 at the end of each year for 4 years. A regular periodic receipt (or payment) is called an annuity, and present values for annuities of $1 are shown in Exhibit 9.4. Your time value of money is 20 percent per annum. Using Exhibit 9.4, under the column 20 percent, for 5 and 4 years, respectively, we calculate that:

Present value of the Provident Benefit proposal: $5,000 × 2.991 = $14,955
Present value of the Southeastern Mutual proposal: $6,250 × 2.589 = $16,181
Advantage to the Southeastern Mutual proposal: $1,226.

Note that if your time value of money had been 10 percent per annum, the advantage would have been smaller:

Present value of the Provident Benefit proposal: $5,000 × 3.791 = $18,955
Present value of the Southeastern Mutual proposal: $6,250 × 3.170 = $19,812
Advantage to the Southeastern Mutual proposal: $857.

The higher the discount rate and/or the longer the waiting period, the smaller the present value. This is simply the mathematical result of assuming that money has a positive time value.

DISCOUNTED FUTURE CASH FLOWS AND NET PRESENT VALUE

If the amount of an investment, the expected future cash flows, and the time value of money are known, the present value of the returns can be found (Exhibit 9.5). This information can be converted into a decision rule: Invest if the present value of the returns is greater than the amount of the investment. The difference between the present value of the returns PV, and the investment, I, is called the net present value (NPV). Thus, the decision rule can be restated as: Invest if NPV is positive.

Example

A firm is contemplating opening a new sales office, expected to produce net cash flows (receipts from sales less out-of-pocket purchase and expense costs)

EXHIBIT 9.5. Diagram showing relationship between present value and future value.

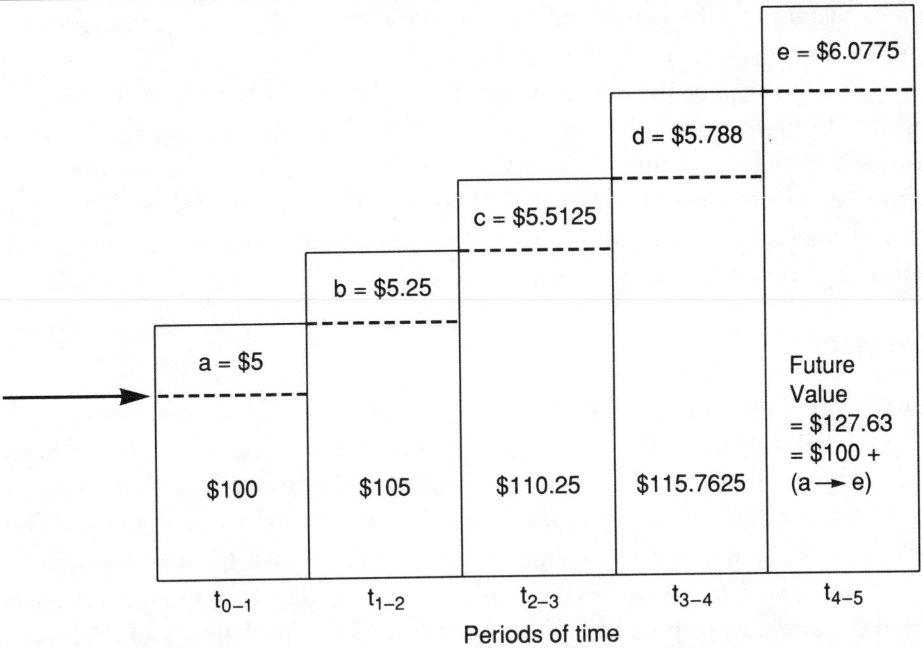

e = $6.0775

d = $5.788

c = $5.5125

b = $5.25

a = $5

Future Value = $127.63 = $100 + (a → e)

| $100 | $105 | $110.25 | $115.7625 | |

t_{0-1} t_{1-2} t_{2-3} t_{3-4} t_{4-5}

Periods of time

of $80,000 per year. It will cost $200,000 to equip this office, which will also require working capital of $300,000. The life of the office is estimated to be 10 years, after which it will be expanded significantly or closed down. The investment cut-off rate (the time value of money) is 15 percent. Ignore income tax for the time being. This problem demonstrates the present value of the investment and the present value of the returns.

	Amount	Time	Factor	PV
Investment at t_0—Equipment	$200,000	0	1	$200,000
—Working capital	300,000	0	1	300,000
Total investment (I)				$500,000
Returns—Annual net cash flows	80,000	1–10	5.019[1]	401,520
—Working capital liquidation	300,000	10	0.247[2]	74,100
Present value of returns (PV)				475,620
Net present value (PV − I)				$ (24,380)

---

[1] From Exhibit 9.4.

[2] From Exhibit 9.3.

It will be seen that although the absolute value of the returns ($1,100,000) exceeds the absolute value of the investment ($500,000), the effect of taking into consideration the time value of money produces the opposite result, for their present values.

In cases such as the above, where the estimates for the future are clearly subject to great uncertainty, a decision of this kind may be approached via sensitivity analysis. A number of scenarios can be analyzed by using different estimates of net cash flows. Probabilities can also be introduced, by asking several managers to state their subjective probability estimates for each of a number of possible results.

Example

To the previous example, three managers are now added: Bob Jones, Bill Coe, and Jim Marks. They are asked to state their beliefs about the potential outcome of opening the new sales office and to attach probabilities to its success. Their natural responses are then converted to percentages. For example, Mr. Jones reports "a one-in-five chance of cash flows of $50,000."

This can be expressed as a 20 percent chance. The three managers each provide estimates of possible net cash flows and the probability of each (see Exhibit 9.6). Each manager's total probabilities must add up to 100 percent, because the opening of the new sales office will surely produce some net cash flow, positive or negative.

EXHIBIT 9.6. Project sensitivity analysis.

Cash Flows	Bob Jones Prob.	Value	Bill Coe Prob.	Value	Jim Marks Prob.	Value
$ 30,000 ×	0.1 =	$ 3,000	0.0	$ 0	0.0	$ 0
50,000 ×	0.2 =	10,000	0.1	5,000	0.0	0
80,000 ×	0.4 =	32,000	0.2	16,000	0.1	8,000
100,000 ×	0.2 =	20,000	0.4	40,000	0.3	30,000
150,000 ×	0.1 =	15,000	0.2	30,000	0.5	75,000
200,000 ×	0.0 =	0	0.1	20,000	0.1	20,000
Expected values		$ 80,000		$111,000		$133,000
Present values at 15% (× 5.019)		$401,520		$557,109		$667,527
Present value of recovery of working capital		74,100		74,100		74,100
Total		$475,620		$631,209		$741,627
Net present values		$ (24,380)		$131,209		$241,627

This series of calculations draws attention to the critical significance of the assumptions about future net cash flow. If the manager Bob Jones is regarded as more reliable, the project will not be accepted; if the other managers, Bill Coe and Jim Marks have better track records as predictors, it probably will. A similar sensitivity analysis may also be undertaken, using different cost of capital (cut off) rates, to see the effect of these assumptions.

To summarize: One capital budgeting decision tool is the calculation of NPV, which can serve to both screen and rank potential investment decisions. To calculate NPV, we must know the time value of money (the cut-off or cost of capital rate), the total cash investment and its timing, and the estimated future net cash flows and their timing. We can then calculate the present value of the investment and the present value of the return. If the sum of the present value of the returns exceed the sum of the present value of the investment outlays, the NPV is positive, and the project should be accepted.

Note that the calculation of NPV is performed entirely with cash flows. There is no place in this decision model for any accounting data other than cash receipts and payments and discounting factors.

INCORPORATION OF INCOME TAX EFFECTS

In the real world, investors must pay income taxes on the profits. The preparation of an investment decision, therefore, involves the calculation of after-tax cash inflows and outflows. This complicates the calculations, and care must be taken in adapting the model for this purpose.

Example

Suppose in the previous example, that the estimated net cash flows are $100,000 per annum for 10 years; the profit from the investment is subject to income tax at the rate of 50 percent; when equipment is purchased for $100,000, other equipment will be sold for $10,000, and the firm will use straight-line depreciation on this equipment over 10 years for book and tax purposes. The net present value is calculated in a slightly expanded format from that used earlier (Exhibit 9.7). If we had used the pretax figures, NPV would have been positive:

$$PV = \$501,900 + \$74,100 = \$576,000; \quad I = 500,000; \quad NPV = \$76,000.$$

This example illustrates the effect of income taxes on investment decisions and explains the businessman's argument that high income taxes are bad for the economy. Many projects that appear viable before the income tax effect is calculated, prove unacceptable on an after-tax basis. This reduces the volume of investment, and with it the amount of employment and the

EXHIBIT 9.7.   Calculating the net present value.

	Amount	Tax Effect	After-tax Amount	Time	Factor @ 15%	Present Value
Investment:						
Sale of old equipment	$(10,000)			0	1.00	$(10,000)
Purchase equipment	100,000		$100,000	0	1.00	100,000
Remodel building	100,000		100,000	0	1.00	100,000
Working capital	300,000		300,000	0	1.00	300,000
I =						$490,000
Returns:						
Annual net cash flow	100,000	50,000[1]	50,000	1–10	5.019	250,950
Depreci. effect	10,000	5,000[2]	5,000	1–10	5.019	25,095
Working capital	300,000	–	300,000	10	0.247	74,100
PV =						$350,145
Net present value (PV − I)						$(139,855)

[1] This is the amount of income tax that would be payable on the incremental annual cash flows if there were no depreciation "tax shield", given the income tax rate of 50%.

[2] Depreciation of $10,000 is an annual tax deduction, giving rise to a tax saving of 50% × $10,000 = $5,000 each year for 10 years.

future income taxes to be collected by the government. Inflation and the accompanying high cost of capital rates aggravate this situation. High income taxation coupled with high inflation are a recipe for economic disaster.

The situation is only partially relieved by the ability of firms to use accelerated depreciation methods for computing taxable income. In the above example, if we had used double-declining balance depreciation of 20 percent, the present value of the depreciation tax shield would have been $4,289 higher.

Year 1	$ 20,000 × 50% × 0.870 =	$ 8,700	(from Exhibit 9.3)
2	16,000 × 50 × 0.756 =	6,048	
3	12,800 × 50 × 0.658 =	4,211	
4	10,240 × 50 × 0.572 =	2,929	
5	8,192 × 50 × 0.497 =	2,036	
6	6,554 × 50 × 0.432 =	1,416	
7[1]	6,554 × 50 × 0.376 =	1,232	

Year	8	6,554 × 50% × 0.327 =	1,072
	9	6,554 × 50 × 0.284 =	931
	10	6,552 × 50 × 0.247 =	809
		$100,000	$29,384

---

[1] Switch to straight-line here.

The project would still have shown a negative NPV of $135,556.

INTERNAL RATE OF RETURN

In the examples at the beginning of this chapter, we assumed that the rate of ROI could be found. In such cases, the investment decision could be stated in the form: Invest in any project with an ROI greater that the cost of capital (or the cut-off rate). The ROI referred to here is known by many names: Discounted cash flow (DCF) rate of return; time adjusted rate of return; true rate of return; internal rate of return, and more. Because it best describes how this ROI is calculated, we shall call it the internal rate of return (IRR).

Example

Consider an investment that produces an after-tax net cash flow of $2,000 annually for 10 years, and costs $10,000. At a discounted rate of 6 percent the present value is $2,000 × 7.36 or $14,720. Discounted at 8 percent, the present value is $13,420 ($2,000 × 6.71). Notice that the higher the discount rate, the lower the present value. Clearly, there must be a discount rate at which the present value of the future cash flows is equal to $10,000, the amount of the investment. That discount rate is called the IRR. In this example it is slightly more than 15 percent: the present value of the cash flows, discounted at 15 percent, is equal to $10,038 ($2,000 × 5.019).

Thus, the IRR is defined as that rate of discount at which the sum of the present values of a series of expected future cash flows is equal to the amount required to produce them. Given a known I = investment and a known R = cash flow, we can solve the IRR equation for i.

$$I = \frac{R_1}{(1 + i)} + \frac{R_2}{(1 + i)^2} + \ldots + \frac{R_n}{(1 + i)^n}$$

With a computer program the IRR is easy to find. Without a computer or programmed calculator, two possible methods can be used. If the future cash flows are unequal in amount, then trial and error is needed. A "high-low" approach will help in finding the internal rate of return, as follows.

Example

An investment of $10,000 will produce the following expected future cash flows:

End of year 1	$7,000
End of year 2	3,000
End of year 3	2,000
End of year 4	1,000

Present Value at 5%	**Present Value at 20%**
$7,000 × 0.952 = $ 6,664	$7,000 × 0.833 = $5,831
3,000 × 0.907 = 2,721	3,000 × 0.694 = 2,082
2,000 × 0.864 = 1,728	2,000 × 0.579 = 1,158
1,000 × 0.823 = 823	1,000 × 0.482 = 482
$11,936	$9,553

The internal rate of return is slightly less than 20 percent. Try 18 percent and 16 percent:

Present Value at 18%	**Present Value at 16%**
$7,000 × 0.847 = $5,928	$7,000 × 0.862 = $ 6,034
3,000 × 0.718 = 2,148	3,000 × 0.743 = 2,229
2,000 × 0.609 = 1,218	2,000 × 0.641 = 1,282
1,000 × 0.516 = 516	1,000 × 0.552 = 552
$9,810	$10,097

The IRR is between 16 and 18 percent, and a better approximation can be found using an interpolation formula.

$$16\% + \frac{97}{97 + 190}(2\%) = 16.7\%$$

If the future cash flows represent an annuity, the payback number can be used. Payback is defined as the period over which net cash flows liquidate the investment and is calculated by the formula:

$$\frac{I}{R}$$

where I equals investment and R equals periodical receipt.

An approximation of the IRR can be found by inspecting the line on Exhibit 9.4, for the life on the project, to obtain the column in which appears a number close to the payback number. Thereafter interpolation will provide the exact IRR.

Example

Consider the investment of $10,000 that produces $2,000 annually for 10 years. The payback number is 5 (10,000/2,000). In row 10 of Exhibit 9.4, the number 5 appears in the column for 15 percent (the factor is actually 5.019). Thus, the IRR must be more than 15 percent but less than 16 percent (factor 4.833). Interpolation then allows the approximate IRR to be determined.

Factors from Exhibit 9.4

15%	5.019	5.019
Payback		5.000
16%	4.833	
Differences	0.186	0.019

$$15\% + \frac{.019}{.186}(1\%) = 15.1\%$$

Payback is sometimes used as an investment decision model. The payback of several possible investments is calculated, and the project with the shortest payback (the lowest payback number) is preferred. This decision model abstracts from ROI and ignores the time value of money for this reason it is not generally recommended for investment decisions, but may be useful for expressing the period over which the investment is expected to be at risk.

IRR AND NPV COMPARED

The IRR would appear to be more useful for capital budgeting decisions than the NPV. In straightforward comparisons between rate of return and cost of capital, the IRR constitutes the rate of return; it can be interpreted as the maximum rate of interest that could be paid for the capital employed over the life of the investment in order to break even. A positive difference between IRR and cost of capital, therefore, means that the investment is profitable. A project that has a positive NPV must have an IRR higher than the cut-off rate.

The IRR is capable of giving clearer indications than the NPV in preference decisions. Consider these cases:

I	NPV	IRR
$20,000	$1,234	15%
10,000	544	30%

Most investors would prefer an investment producing a 30 percent annual return to one producing a 15 percent annual return, yet the first project has a higher NPV than the second. Thus, it would be preferred in a system that ranked projects by NPV.

Further, the IRR can be used for comparisons with other investments, and, thus, fulfill a control function, as well as a planning function.

The two decision models share the same basic assumptions and methods, as the following amoritzation tables demonstrate. In this example, an investment of $1,000 produces net cash flows of $250 annually for five years.

Calculation of net present value at 6%.

Year	Amount at Beginning	Interest for 1 Year at 6%	Principal Plus Interest	Return	Amount at End
1	$1,000	$60	$1,060	$250	$810
2	810	48.6	858.6	250	608.6
3	608.6	36.5	645.1	250	395.1
4	395.1	23.7	418.8	250	168.8
5	168.8	10.1	178.9	250	(71.1)

NPV of the project at 6 percent is $71.10, the excess of returns over principal plus interest.

Calculation of net present value at 7.9%.

Year	Amount at Beginning	Interest for 1 Year at 7.9%	Principal Plus Interest	Return	Amount at End
1	$1,000	$79	$1,079	$250	$829
2	829	65.5	894.5	250	644.5
3	644.5	50.9	695.4	250	445.4
4	445.4	35.2	480.6	250	230.6
5	230.6	18.2	248.8	250	(1.2)

IRR of the project is fractionally above 7.9 percent, approximation being responsible for the small NPV of $1.2. The true IRR would have produced a NPV of 0.

CAPITAL BUDGETING

This chapter is concerned with investment decisions on making capital expenditures. Capital expenditures represent the acquisition of additional or replacement capacity: They provide the firm with equipment and working capital that will permit it to produce more goods or services, or to produce the same amount at a lower total cost. By definition, they have effects on more than one year, and can be viewed as long-term expenditures. Simply stated, a capital investment decision involves incurring a current cost in the expectation of future benefits, extending for more than one year.

There are two theories of financial investment: (1) Each capital expenditure stands on its own. Evaluation of the project involves identification of the source of the capital to be used and explicit inclusion of the cost of capital in the calculation of ROI; (2) The firm has a common fund of capital and does not raise it for specific projects. Thus, there is a cost of capital to the firm as a whole. The decision-making is to calculate ROI before considering cost of capital, so that it may be compared with the latter.

The second of these theories prevails at the present time, perhaps because of the dominant position occupied by very large corporations in our modern economy, and their practice of raising capital by the isssue of shares or bonds for a variety of projects. The methodology of capital budgeting is adaptable to both situations. But why capital *budgeting?*

Example

A firm has a number of capital expenditure projects under review. These projects add up to a total of $1,430,000. In order not to frighten the firm's existing creditors, the chief executive has decided that the maximum amount that can be borrowed at this time is $1,000,000. The company's principal shareholder is at this time opposed to the issue of any amount of additional stock. There is a problem planning which expenditures to make, sometimes referred to as capital rationing. Once the decisions about which projects to include and which to leave out are made, the company can prepare a capital budget. This will show the $1 million to be borrowed and the planned capital expenditures. Additional working capital requirements may be included in the amount allocated to each project, or specified as a separate total.

Assume that the work of calculating ROI has been done. The projects can now be ranked and the decision process can begin (see table, top page 280). Note that the limit resulted in the rejection of projects with ROIs above the cost of capital. The cut-off point may be expressed as a sum of money, as in this example, or as a rate (accept no project with an ROI below 12 percent).

We have outlined in detail two investment decision rules:

1. Invest in a project with a positive net present value; do not invest in a project with a negative net present value.
2. Invest in a project with an internal rate of return greater than the cost of capital; do not invest in a project if the cost of capital is greater than the internal rate of return.

Example of project ranking.

Project Rank No.	Description of Project	Investment Amount	ROI %
1.	New lathes	$ 100,000	30
2.	Conveyor system	200,000	21
3.	Modernize sales offices	400,000	19
4.	Develop new product	300,000	15
	Subtotal	1,000,000 ←— limit	
5.	Replace truck	50,000	14
6.	Research new market	100,000	13
	Subtotal	1,150,000	12 ← cost of capital
7.	New drilling machine	200,000	9
8.	Replace air conditioners	80,000	7
	Total	$1,430,000	

Unfortunately, these two rules do not always produce the identical ranking of projects, as the examples below show. Exhibit 9.8 demonstrates graphically the difference between NPV and IRR.

We could, therefore, rank the projects as follows:

1. Investment $10,000, IRR 49%   NPV of $ 7,370, ranks 4
2. Investment $75,000, IRR 32%   NPV of $107,700, ranks 2
3. Investment $190,000, IRR 21%   NPV of $248,000, ranks 1
4. Investment $50,000, IRR 15%   NPV of $ 22,000, ranks 3.

EXHIBIT 9.8.   The difference between NPV and IRR.

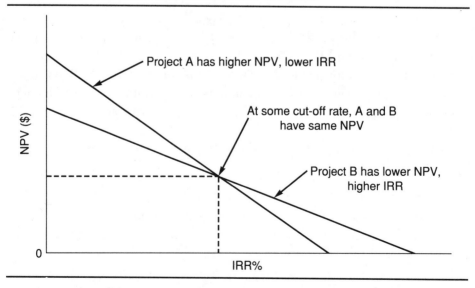

The ranking problem in capital rationing situations is very difficult to handle, and volumes have been written to analyze the possible outcomes. In the literature on finance, the NPV approach, or some adaption of it, is stated to be preferable, because it produces unique mathematical results. The calculation of IRR is complicated not only because of the trial-and-error method by which it is found (a computer or programmed calculator takes care of that), but because in certain situations, multiple IRRs are found. In particular, projects that involve net outflows in any year after t_0 produce multiple IRR percentages that are difficult to interpret.

An additional problem with using the IRR is the concealed reinvestment assumption of the DCF model. This can be seen most easily if we consider projects having lives of unequal length. Suppose that we face two mutually exclusive projects, A and B. A has an IRR of 30 percent over its four-year life; B has an IRR of 20 percent over its five-year life. If we choose A, because of its higher IRR, we are implicitly assuming that we can reinvest the capital portion of the return at the end of each year at an IRR greater than 20 percent.

Unequal project lives can be taken into consideration in capital budgeting problems by making them equal. Two methods allow projects with unequal life spans to be compared. Using the first method, the shortest project life is the time horizon, and projects having longer lives are treated as though they will terminate earlier. This method involves assuming a salvage value at the end of the time horizon.

In the second method, the longest project life is considered the time horizon, and projects having shorter lives are extended to that time horizon by assuming replacement at the earlier termination date. For example, if a three-year lease is being compared with a purchase of a truck having a useful life of six years, the longer period can be used if it is assumed that a new three-year lease is executed at the end of the first lease.

BOOK VALUE OF EQUIPMENT— EXCLUDING TAX EFFECTS

Many investment decisions involve equipment replacement or renovation. We recognize three situations: Emergency, replacement, and improvement. An emergency is a case in which the expenditure is essential if the business is to continue to funtion, such as when a factory building is destroyed by fire. Replacement is the acquisition of a new or used piece of equipment to substitute for a similar or identical piece that will be scrapped or sold for salvage. An improvement is the acquisition of a larger, more productive, or more economical piece of equipment for one that will be scrapped or sold for salvage.

The equipment to be scrapped or sold is referred to as "old equipment;" the replacement or improvement as "new equipment." A capital-budgeting decision is involved in all considerations of substituting new for old equipment. In general, where there are no income tax effects, because the subject is a not-for-profit entity, or a business firm not expected to be liable to pay income tax in the near future, book value of old equipment is irrelevant and should be ignored.

Example

A machine capable of producing net cash flows of $12,000 annually can be replaced with a machine capable of producing net cash flows of $18,000 annually. Both machines have useful lives of five years. The old machine has book value of $12,000 (cost of $20,000, less accumulated depreciation of $8,000), and can be sold for $5,000. The new machine costs $40,000. The firm uses a 12 percent cut-off rate for investment decisions.

The old equipment should be kept because over the five-year period it produces $5,000 more than the new equipment. Note that the advantage to the old equipment becomes more pronounced at any positive discount rate, because the present value of the excess inflows ($6,000 for five years) cannot exceed the present value of the investment ($35,000), that is, $6,000 multiplied by any discount factor (Exhibit 9.4) for five years is still less than $35,000. The result can be demonstrated to be true by preparing comparative operating statements for the five-year period.

	Keep Old Equipment	Buy New Equipment	Difference
Operating income before depreciation	$60,000	$90,000	
Loss on sale of old equipment ($12,000 − $5,000)		(7,000)	
Depreciation on old equipment	(12,000)		
Depreciation on new equipment		(40,000)	
Net operating income	$48,000	$43,000	$5,000

BOOK VALUE OF EQUIPMENT—INCLUDING TAX EFFECTS

To demonstate the effect of income taxes on the computation, assume in the preceding example (a) that income tax will be payable at 40 percent on net income, and (b) tax deductiblity of straight-line depreciation and of the loss on the sale of the old equipment. In this case, although the book value of the old equipment remains irrelevant, the tax effects become relevant, and some of these are found using book value. Using the format recommended for the solution of these capital budgeting problems:

	Amount	Tax Effect	After-Tax Amount	Time	Factor @ 12%	Present Value
Investment						
• Purchase	$40,000		$40,000	0	1.00	$ 40,000
• Salvage old equipment	(5,000)	(2,800)[1]	(7,800)	0	1.00	(7,800)
Net investment						$ 32,200
Returns—						
• Differential net cash flow	6,000	(2,400)[2]	3,600	1–5	3.605[3]	12,978
• Depreciation on new machine	(8,000)	3,200	3,200[4]	1–5	3.605	11,536
• Depreciation on old machine	2,400	960	(960)[5]	1–5	3.605	(3,461)
Present value of returns						21,053
Net present value						$(11,147)

[1]Tax deduction for loss of $7,000 × 40 percent rate in current year.
[2]Tax liability of $6,000 × 40 percent annually.
[3]Factor for $1 at 12 percent for five years, from Exhibit 9.4.
[4]Tax saving equal to 40 percent × straight-line depreciation annually.
[5]Lost tax saving through no longer being able to duduct $2,400 depreciation annually on old equipment ($2,400 × 5 = $12,000; 2,400 × 40 percent = $960).

The effect of taxes in this case is to make the investment even less attractive, in spite of the deductibility of the tax loss on the old equipment.

Note that income tax effects may only be included in the calculations where the investor expects to be in a tax-paying situation. They would not apply to a not-for-profit organization, nor would there be tax effects if the firm had sustained tax losses that could be carried forward to offset taxable income on the new investment.

WORKING CAPITAL AND THE BUSINESS PLAN

The planning requirements of a capital budget include fixed capital, generally referred to as equipment, and working capital. Equipment is found from such sources as priced blueprints, manufacturers's catalogs, and costed specifications. Working capital presents a different kind of measurement problem.

To an accountant, working capital is the excess of current assets over current liabilities. Current assets are those that will be sold, used, or otherwise turned into cash within one year or within the firm's the operating cycle, whichever is longer. Current liabilities are those obligations that must be met from working capital. These are typically liabilities payable within one year. Current assets consist of cash, short-term investments, accounts receivable and other debts owed to the firm, inventories, and prepaid expenses. Current liabilities include accounts payable, accrued expenses (for example, insurance, payroll, and taxes) deferred revenues, and short-term notes payable.

A company's actual working capital usually differs from its working capital requirements, that is, the current assets and liabilities necessarily arising from the firm's operations. Let us call these transaction needs. Current assets will also include precautionary needs and speculative needs. Current liabilities will include additional debts besides those arising from operations.

Precautionary Needs

If demand is likely to fluctuate, a company may have to maintain cash balances in excess of those dictated by operations. For example, suppose that a restaurant usually serves 100 meals on a Saturday night, but is occasionally called upon to cater for a large party on short notice. To do this additional business, it may have to send out for food and drinks, and to hire additional waiters and kitchen staff, both requiring payment in cash. A firm that buys from a major supplier threatened with a strike will stock up on inventory as a necessary business precaution.

Speculative Needs

Sales of some products cannot be expanded through growth; it takes too long, and the risk does not justify the expense. Firms in such industries must be prepared to buy other companies in order to expand, and they accumulate "war chests" for that purpose. The amounts of cash and short-term investments in their balance sheets will include such war chests. A company in the land development business may be offered a property at a very attractive price, which does not fit its construction program, but can be held for resale at a higher price. The property will be included in inventory.

Current Liabilities

Two types of obligation are frequently included in current liabilities, even though they do not arise out of the operations of the firm: Current portion of long term debt and the amount due for purchase of equipment. All or part of a long-term loan will be reclassified as a current liability if it is within one year of repayment, unless refunding has been arranged. And even though the financing for the purchase of equipment may have been obtained from long-term sources (debt or equity), the liability on purchase is classified as a current liability, if payable within one year.

For these reasons, the actual amounts of working capital at any point in time, and the relationship between individual current asset and liability amounts and balance sheet totals, are not the point of departure for calculating working capital requirements. These are derived from the operating budget, a plan for implementing the capacity acquired with the capital budget.

A business plan is a detailed explanation of the assumptions on which the capital budget is based: It reports the research that was carried out to obtain these assumptions and gives a detailed account of how the investment decision based on these assumptions will be executed, and the planned results. A business plan will include sections on:

- Marketing, including credit terms
- Production, including factory layout and product design
- Purchasing, including purchase of equipment
- Personnel
- Financial requirements

It will also give a full set of forecast financial statements for at least the first five years of operations.

The amount of working capital required is found during the preparation of the forecast financial statements, because each of the periods planned will result in a balance sheet, showing the amounts of current assets and current liabilities at the end of the period. For example, if a shoe store is established and plans to sell $1,000,000 of shoes during its first year, the inventory to be carried can be found, if the gross margin and turnover period are known. Suppose that the gross margin is 40 percent of the selling price, and that a shoe store normally turns over its inventory in 90 days. (Inventory turnover is calculated as cost of sales/inventory, and expressed in sales days by dividing this ratio into 365.) The planned sales for the year have a cost of $600,000, and an inventory turnover of 4 (365/90) means that an inventory of $150,000 will be carried at all times during this period. If the same rate of sales is forecast for the first quarter of the second year, then this will be the amount of inventory at the end of the first year.

By the same token, if the marketing plan calls for sales of $85,000 monthly, then the store will need to purchase shoes for $51,000 in order to replenish inventory. If the purchase terms are net 30 days, then the amount owed suppliers at the end of every month will be $51,000, which is the accounts payable component of current liabilities.

The other components are found in the same way. One of the biggest problems is to plan the cash requirement. It seems intuitively advisable to carry a cash balance, and this may well be necessary for the firm as a whole, for precautionary or speculative reasons. In calculating working capital requirements, however, the need to carry cash must be demonstrated in the same way as the other working capital items. If a department store has 50 cash registers, each with a $50 float, then this means that $2,500 of cash must be carried at all times. Cash requirements are located in a part of the operating budget called the cash budget.

CONCLUSION

Capital budget decisions are among the most important decisions made by any business. Upon them rest the firms long-term profitability and, possibly, even its survival. It has been remarked that firms compete principally by means of their investments, which determine the quality of future products, improve production costs, and help achieve operating efficiency. The results of capital budgeting decisions cannot be changed in the short run; they are strategic in focus and sometimes result in permanent long-term investments. Finally, capital budgeting tends to involve large sums of money. For these reasons, capital budgeting decisions are usually made at the top management level, although relatively minor amounts of funds may be allocated by operations management.

The capital budgeting process involves careful long-term planning. Prospective investments must be identified and scarce resources allocated in the most efficient manner possible. Developing an optimal plan for each project ensures the highest probability of an optimal ROI or NPV for the expenditure. These ROIs may be evaluated, using sensitivity analysis, Monte Carlo simulations, and other methods, before projects are prioritized as investments. Risk and inflation must be considered during the process, so that the firm attempts to maximize expected future returns for a given degree of risk. The end result is a capital budget, one of the most essential elements of any firm's overall budget planning.

Although DCF methods of calculating ROI have become widely used since the 1960s, they are not the only way in which investments are evaluated. Two alternatives, frequently used in addition to DCF, are:

1. Calculation of cash flow per share on an annual basis. This calculation indicates the dividends that the company's stock holders may expect to receive during the life of the investment.
2. Preparation of pro forma financial statements to show the effect of the investment on the future earnings per share: Since the advent of the computer, financial simulation has been automated to evaluate a complete series of investments.

A third method of calculating ROI, the unadjusted accounting rate of return, is not recommended.

The importance of the capital budgeting decision cannot be overstated. Many firms calculate, for each proposed investment, the payback number, the unadjusted rate of return, the IRR, and the NPV. They also prepare pro forma income statements and balance sheets to plan five years ahead. Although these calculations may yield conflicting signals, experienced investors and managers can weigh the trade-offs between them, to come up with the best investment decisions possible.

One reason financial managers don't rely exclusively on DCF methods is the inherent difficulty in using these methods to predict future cash flows accurately. Such methods may accurately project cash flows for apartments rented under multi-year leases, or gas wells whose future production is to be delivered under contract at fixed prices. But other business situations make cash flow predictions all but impossible. A pop group that records an album may not sell even one copy; however, it may go platinum. In between these extremes are historical results from previous investments that may prove to be a useful guide to future prospects and proper capital budgeting. DCF methods are best suited for situations in which cash inflows and outflows can be predicted with reasonable assurance, and in which the cost of capital can be estimated in the future. Financial managers with experience know how rare such predictable situations like this are.

GLOSSARY*

Annuity: A regular series of cash receipts or payments, of equal amounts.

Capital Budget: A financial plan for the finance and acquisition of long-term investments.

Cost of Capital: Weighted average after-tax amount of earnings required to maintain the value of the firm's securities.

Cut-off Rate: Minimum rate of return that must be earned by a proposed investment in order to make it acceptable.

Discounted Cash Flow of Return Rate: *see* Internal rate of return.

Discounting: The process of reducing the amounts of a stream of future cash flows to their present value.

Fixed Assets: Equipment.

Hurdle Rate: *see* Cut-off rate.

---

*See also: "Management Accounting Terminology," *Statement on Management Accounting, Number 2,* Montdale, NJ, National Association of Accountants, June 1, 1983.

Internal Rate of Return: That rate of discount which makes the present value of a stream of future net cash flows equal to the amount of the investment that produces them.

Net Present Value: The difference between the amount of an investment and the present value of the future net cash receipts it will produce.

Payback Period: Time it takes to recover an investment.

Present Value: The sum of a stream of future cash receipts discounted at any positive rate of interest (discount).

Rate of Return: The ratio expressing the amount of an investment and the present value of the future net cash receipts it will produce.

Tax Shield: A noncash tax deductible expense, such as depreciation.

Time-Adjusted Rate of Return: *see* Internal rate of return.

Working Capital: Current assets minus current liabilities.

FOR FURTHER READING

Barfield, Jesse T., Cecily A. Raiborn, and Michael A. Dalton, *Cost Accounting* (St. Paul, MN: West Publishing Co., 1991).

Bennett, Robert E., and James A. Hendricks, "Justifying the Acquisition of Automated Equipment," *Management Accounting* (July 1987).

Bierman, Harold, Jr., and Seymour Smidt, *The Capital Budgeting Decision: Economic Analysis of Investment Projects* (New York: Macmillan, 1989).

Brealey, Richard and Stewart C. Meyers, *Principles of Corporate Finance* (New York: McGraw-Hill, 1988).

Brigham, Eugene F. *Financial Management: Theory and Practice* (New York: The Dryden Press, 1982).

Fremgen, James M., "Capital Budgeting Practices: A Survey," *Management Accounting* (May 1973).

Gitman, Lawrence J., and John R. Forrester, "A Survey of Capital Budgeting Techniques Used by Major U.S. Firms," *Financial Management* (Fall 1977).

Harrison, Jan W., *Capital Investment Appraisal* (London: McGraw-Hill, 1973).

Polimeni, Ralph S., Frank J. Fabozzi, Arthur H. Adelberg, and Michael A. Kole, *Cost Accounting* (New York: McGraw-Hill, 1991).

Solomon, Ezra, and John J. Pringle, *An Introduction to Financial Management* (Santa Monica, CA: Goodyear Publishing, 1977).

10 TAXES AND BUSINESS DECISIONS

Richard P. Mandel

It is, of course, not possible to fully describe the federal taxation system in the space of one book chapter. It may not even be realistic to attempt to describe federal taxation in a full volume. After all, a purchaser of the Internal Revenue Code (the "Code") can expect to carry home at least two volumes consisting of more than 6,000 pages, ranging from Section 1 through Section 9,602, if one includes the estate and gift tax and administrative provisions. And this does not even begin to address the myriad of Regulations, Revenue Rulings, Revenue Procedures, Technical Advice Memoranda, private letter rulings, court decisions, and other sources of federal tax law, which have proliferated over the better part of this century.

Fortunately, most people who enroll in a federal tax course during their progression toward an M.B.A. have no intention of becoming professional tax advisers. An effective tax course, therefore, rather than attempting to impart encyclopedic knowledge of the Code, instead presents taxation as another strategic management tool, available to the manager or entrepreneur, in his or her quest to reach goals in a more efficient and cost-effective manner. After completing such a course, the businessperson should always be conscious that failure to consider tax consequences when structuring a transaction may result in needless tax expense.

It is thus the purpose of this chapter to illustrate the necessity of taking taxation into account when structuring most business transactions, and the need to consult tax professionals early in the process, not just when it is time to file the return. This will be attempted by describing various problems and opportunities encountered by a fictitious business owner, as he progresses from early successes, through the acquisition of a related business, to intergenerational succession problems.

289

THE BUSINESS

We first encounter our sample business when it has been turning a reasonable profit for the last few years under the wise stewardship of its founder and sole stockholder, Morris. The success of his wholesale horticultural supply business (Plant Supply, Inc.) has been a source of great satisfaction to Morris, as has the recent entry into the business of his daughter, Lisa. Morris paid Lisa's business school tuition, hoping to groom her to take over the family business, and his investment seems to be paying off as Lisa has become more and more valuable to her father. Morris (rightly or wrongly) does not feel the same way about his only other offspring, his son, Victor, the violinist, who appears to have no interest whatsoever in the business, except for its potential to subsidize his attempts to break into the concert world.

At this time, Morris was about to score another coup: Plant Supply purchased a plastics molding business so it could fabricate its own trays, pots, and other planting containers instead of purchasing such items from others. Morris considered himself fortunate to secure the services of Brad (the plant manager of the molding company) because neither he nor Lisa knew very much about the molding business. He was confident that negotiations then underway would bring Brad aboard with a satisfactory compensation package. Thus, Morris could afford to turn his attention to the pleasant problem of distributing the wealth generated by his successful business.

UNREASONABLE COMPENSATION

Most entrepreneurs long for the day when their most pressing problem is figuring out what to do with all the money their business is generating. Yet this very condition was now occupying Morris's mind. Brad did not present any problems in this context. His compensation package would be dealt with through ongoing negotiations and, of course, he was not family. But Morris was responsible for supporting his wife and two children. Despite what Morris perceived as the unproductive nature of Victor's pursuits, Morris was determined to maintain a standard of living for Victor befitting the son of a captain of industry. Of course, Lisa was also entitled to an affluent lifestyle, but surely she was additionally entitled to extra compensation for her long hours at work.

The simple and natural reaction to this set of circumstances would be to pay Lisa and Morris a reasonable salary for their work, and have the corporation pay the remaining distributable profit (after retaining whatever was necessary for operations) to Morris. Morris could then take care of his wife and Victor as he saw fit. Yet such a natural reaction would ignore serious tax complications.

The distribution to Morris beyond his reasonable salary would likely be characterized by the IRS as a dividend to the corporation's sole stockholder. Since dividends cannot be deducted by the corporation as an expense, both the corporation and Morris would pay tax on these monies (the well-known bugaboo of corporate double taxation). A dollar of profit could easily be reduced to a mere 46 cents of after-tax money in Morris's pocket.

Knowing this, one might argue that the distribution to Morris should be characterized as a year-end bonus. Since compensation is tax deductible to the corporation, the corporate level of taxation would be removed (Exhibit 10.1). Unfortunately, Congress has long since limited the compensation deduction to a "reasonable" amount. The IRS judges the reasonableness of a payment by comparing it to the salaries paid to other employees performing similar services in similar businesses. It also examines whether such amount is paid as regular salary or as a year-end lump sum when profit levels are known. The scooping up by Morris of whatever money was not nailed down at the end of the year would surely come under attack by an IRS auditor. Why not then put Victor on the payroll directly, thus reducing the amount that Morris must take out of the company for his family? Again, such a payment would run afoul of the "reasonableness" standard. If Morris would come under attack despite his significant efforts for the company, imagine attempting to defend payments made to an "employee" who expends no such efforts.

Subchapter S

The solution to the unreasonable compensation problem may lie in a relatively well-known tax strategy known as the subchapter S election. A corporation making this election remains a standard business corporation for all purposes other than taxation (retaining its ability to grant limited liability to its stockholders, for example). The corporation elects to forego taxation at the corporate level and to be taxed as if it were a partnership. This means that a corporation that has elected subchapter S status will escape any taxation on

EXHIBIT 10.1. Double taxation.

$1.00	Earned
− .34	Corporate Tax at 34%
.66	Dividend
− .20	Individual Tax at 31%
.46	Remains

the corporate level, but its stockholders will be taxed on their pro rata share of the corporation's profits, regardless of whether these profits are distributed to them. Under this election, Morris's corporation would pay no corporate tax, but Morris would pay income tax on all the corporation's profits, even those retained for operations.

This election is recommended in a number of circumstances. One example is the corporation which expects to incur losses, at least in its start-up phase. In the absence of a subchapter S election, such losses would simply collect at the corporate level, awaiting a time in the future when they could be "carried forward" to offset future profits (should there ever be any). If the election is made, the losses would pass through to the stockholders in the current year, and might offset other income of these stockholders such as interest, dividends from investments and salaries.

Another such circumstance is when a corporation expects to sell substantially all its assets, sometime in the future, in an acquisition transaction. Since the repeal in 1986 of the so-called General Utilities doctrine, such a corporation would incur a substantial capital gain tax on the growth in the value of its assets from their acquisition to the time of sale, in addition to the capital gain tax, incurred by its stockholders, when the proceeds of such sale are distributed to them. The subchapter S election (if made early enough), again eliminates tax at the corporate level, leaving only the tax on the stockholders.

The circumstance most relevant to Morris is the corporation with too much profit to distribute as reasonable salary and bonuses. Instead of fighting the battle of reasonableness with the IRS, Morris could elect subchapter S status, thus rendering the controversy moot. It will not matter that the amount paid to him is too large to be anything but a nondeductible dividend, because it is no longer necessary to be concerned about the corporation's ability to deduct the expense.

Not all corporations are eligible to elect subchapter S status. However, contrary to common misconception, eligibility has nothing to do with being a "small" business. In simplified form, to qualify for a subchapter S election, the corporation must have 35 or fewer stockholders, holding only one class of stock, all of whom must be individuals who are either U.S. citizens or resident aliens. The corporation cannot have any subsidiaries or be a subsidiary itself. Plant Supply qualifies on all these counts.

Under subchapter S, Morris can pay himself and Lisa a reasonable salary and then take the rest of the money either as salary or dividend without fear of challenge. He can then distribute that additional money between Lisa and Victor, to support their individual lifestyles. Thus, it appears that the effective use of a strategic taxation tool has solved an otherwise costly problem.

Gift Tax

Unfortunately, like most tax strategies, the gift tax may not be cost free. It is always necessary to consider whether the solution of one tax problem may create others, sometimes emanating from taxes other than the income tax. To begin with, Morris needs to be aware that under any strategy he adopts, the gifts of surplus cash he makes to his children may subject him to a federal gift tax. This gift tax supplements the federal estate tax, which imposes a tax on the transfer of assets from one generation to the next. Lifetime gifts to the next generation would, in the absence of a gift tax, frustrate estate tax policy. Fortunately, in order to accommodate the tendency of individuals to make gifts for reasons unrelated to estate planning, the gift tax exempts gifts by a donor of up to $10,000 per year to each of his or her donees. That amount is doubled if the donor's spouse consents to the use of his/her $10,000 allotment to cover the excess. Thus, Morris could distribute up to $20,000 in excess cash each year, to each of his two children, if his wife consented.

In addition, the federal gift/estate tax does not take hold until the combined total of taxable lifetime gifts in excess of the annual exclusion amount plus taxable bequests exceeds $600,000. Thus, Morris can exceed the annual $20,000 amount by quite a bit before the government will get its share.

These rules may suggest an alternate strategy to Morris, under which he may transfer some portion of his stock to each of his children, and then have the corporation distribute dividends to him and to them directly each year. The gift tax would be implicated to the extent of the value of the stock in the year it is given, but, from then on no gifts would be necessary. Such strategy, in fact, describes a fourth circumstance in which the subchapter S election is recommended: when the company wishes to distribute profits to nonemployee stockholders, for whom salary or bonus in any amount would be considered excessive. In such a case, like that of Victor, a company can choose a subchapter S status, a gift to the nonemployee of stock, and a policy of distributing annual dividends from profits, thus avoiding any challenge to a corporate deduction, based on unreasonable compensation.

MAKING THE SUBCHAPTER S ELECTION

Before Morris rushes off to make his election, however, he should be aware of a few additional complications. Congress has historically been aware of the potential for corporations to avoid corporate level taxation on profits and capital gains earned prior to the subchapter S election, but not realized until afterward. Thus, for example, if Morris's corporation has been accounting for its inventory on a last in, first out (LIFO) basis, in an inflationary era (such as virtually any time during the last 50 years), taxable profits have been depressed by the use of higher cost inventory as the basis for calculation. Earlier lower cost inventory has been left on the shelf (from an accounting point of view), waiting for later sales. However, if those later sales will now come during a time when the corporation is avoiding tax under subchapter S, those higher taxable profits will never be taxed at the corporate level. Thus, for the year just preceding the election, the Code requires recalculation of the corporation's profits on a first in, first out (FIFO) inventory basis to capture the amount which was postponed. If Morris has been using the LIFO method, his subchapter S election will carry some cost.

Similarly, if Morris's corporation has been reporting to the IRS on a cash accounting basis, it has been recognizing income only when collected, regardless of when a sale was actually made. The subchapter S election, therefore, affords the possibility that many sales made near the end of the final year of corporate taxation will never be taxed at the corporate level, because these receivables will not be collected until after the election is in effect. As a result, the IRS requires all accounts receivable of a cash basis taxpayer to be taxed as if collected in the last year of corporate taxation, thus adding to the cost of Morris's subchapter S conversion.

Of course, the greatest source of untapped corporate tax potential lies in corporate assets that have appreciated in value, while the corporation was subject to corporate tax, but are not sold by the corporation until after the subchapter S election is in place. In the worst nightmares of the IRS, corporations which are about to sell all their assets in a corporate acquisition, first, elect subchapter S treatment and then immediately sell out, avoiding millions of dollars of tax liability.

Fortunately for the IRS, Congress addressed this problem in 1986, by revamping an older provision of the Code to provide for taxation on the corporate level of all so-called "built-in gain," realized by a converted S corporation within the first 10 years after its conversion. Built-in gain is the untaxed appreciation, which existed at the time of the subchapter S election. It is taxed not only upon a sale of all the corporation's assets, but any time the corporation disposes of an asset it owned, at the time of its election. This makes it advisable to have an appraisal done for all the corporation's assets as of the first day of subchapter S status, so that there is some objective basis for the calculation of built-in gain upon sale somewhere down the line. This appraisal will further deplete Morris's coffers, if he adopts the subchapter S strategy. Despite these complications, it is still likely that Morris will find the subchapter S election to be an attractive solution to his family and compensation problems.

Pass-Through Entity

Consider how a subchapter S corporation might operate were the corporation to experience a period during which it was not so successful. Subchapter S corporations (like partnerships and limited partnerships) are known as "pass-through entities," because they pass through their tax attributes to their owners. This not only operates to pass through profits to the tax returns of the owners (whether or not accompanied by cash), but also results in the pass-through of losses. As discussed earlier, these losses can then be used by the owners to offset income from other sources, rather than having the losses frozen on the corporate level, waiting for future profit.

The Code, not surprisingly, places limits upon the amount of loss which can be passed through to an owner's tax return. In a subchapter S corporation, the amount of loss is limited by a stockholder's basis in his investment in the corporation. Basis includes the amount invested as equity plus any amount the stockholder has advanced to the corporation as loans. As the corporation operates, the basis is raised by the stockholder's pro rata share of any profit made by the corporation and lowered by his pro rata share of loss and any cash distributions received by him.

These rules might turn Morris's traditional financing strategy on its head, the next time he sits down with the corporation's bank loan officer to negotiate an extension of the corporation's financing. In the past, Morris has always attempted to induce the loan officer to lend directly to the corporation. This way Morris hoped to escape personal liability for the loan (although, in the beginning he was forced to give the bank a personal guarantee). In addition, the corporation could pay back the bank directly, getting a tax deduction for the interest. If the loan were made to Morris, he would have to turn the money over to the corporation, and then depend upon the corporation to generate enough profit so it could distribute monies to him to cover his personal debt service. He might try to characterize those distributions to him as repayment of a loan he made to the corporation, but given the amount he had already advanced to the corporation in its earlier years, the IRS would probably object to the debt/equity ratio and recharacterize the payment as a nondeductible dividend, fully taxable to Morris. We have already discussed why Morris would prefer to avoid characterizing the payment as additional compensation: His level of compensation was already at the outer edge of reasonableness.

However, under the subchapter S election, Morris no longer has to be concerned about characterizing cash flow from the corporation to himself, in a manner which would be deductible by the corporation. Moreover, if the loan is made to the corporation, it does not increase Morris's basis in his investment (even if he has given a personal guarantee). This limits his ability to pass losses through to his return. Thus, the subchapter S election may result in the unseemly spectacle of Morris begging his banker to lend the corporation's money directly to him, so that he may in turn advance the money to the corporation and increase his basis.

Passive Losses

No discussion of pass-through entities should proceed without at least touching on what may have been the most creative set of changes made to the Code in the 1986 revision. At that time, an entire industry had arisen to create and market business enterprises whose main purpose was to generate losses to pass through to their wealthy investor/owners. These losses, it was hoped, would normally be generated by depreciation, amortization, and depletion. These would be mere paper losses, incurred while the business itself was breaking even or possibly generating positive cash flow. They would be followed some years in the future by a healthy long-term capital gain. Thus, an investor with high taxable income could be offered short-term pass-through tax losses, with a nice long-term gain waiting in the wings. In those days, long-term capital gain was taxed at only 40 percent of the rate of ordinary income, so the tax was not only deferred, it was substantially reduced. These businesses were known as "tax shelters."

The 1986 Act substantially reduced the effectiveness of the tax shelter, by classifying taxable income and loss into three major categories: active, portfolio, and passive. Active income consists mainly of wages, salaries, and bonuses; portfolio income is mainly income and dividends; while passive income and loss consist of distributions from the so-called "pass-through" entities, such as limited partnerships and subchapter S corporations. In their most simple terms, the passive activity loss rules add to the limits set by the above described basis limitations (and the similar so-called "at-risk rules"), making it impossible to use passive losses to offset active or portfolio income. Thus, tax shelter losses can no longer be used to shelter salaries or investment proceeds; they must wait for the taxpayer's passive activities to generate the anticipated end-of-the-line gains, or be used when the taxpayer disposes of a passive activity at a profit (Exhibit 10.2).

Fortunately for Morris, the passive activity loss rules are unlikely to affect his thinking for at least two reasons. First, the Code defines a passive activity as the conduct of any trade or business "in which the taxpayer does not materially participate." Material participation is further defined in a series of Code sections and Temporary Regulations—which mock the concept of tax simplification, but let Morris off the hook—to include any taxpayer who participates in the business for more than 500 hours per year. Morris is clearly materially participating in his business, despite his status as a stockholder of a subchapter S corporation, and thus, the passive loss rules do not

EXHIBIT 10.2.   Passive activity disposal.

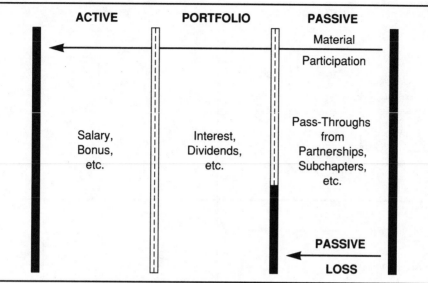

apply to him. The second reason Morris is not concerned is that Morris does not anticipate any losses from this business. It is, historically, very profitable. Therefore, let us depart from this detour into unprofitability and consider Morris's acquisition of the plastics plant.

ACQUISITION

Morris might well believe that the hard part of accomplishing a successful acquisition is locating an appropriate target and integrating it into his existing operation. Yet, once again, he would be well advised to pay some attention to the various tax strategies and results available to him, when structuring the acquisition transaction.

To begin with, Morris has a number of choices available to him in acquiring the target business. Simply put, these choices boil down to a choice among acquiring the stock of the owners of the business, merging the target corporation into Plant Supply, or purchasing the assets and liabilities of the target. The choice of method will depend upon a number of factors, many of which are not tax-related. For example, acquisition by merger will force Plant Supply to acquire all the liabilities of the target, even those of which neither it nor the target may be aware. Acquisition of the stock of the target by Plant Supply will also result in acquisition of all liabilities, but isolates them in a separate corporation, which becomes a subsidiary., (The same result would be achieved by merging the target into a newly formed subsidiary of Plant Supply—the so-called triangular merger). Acquisition of the assets and liabilities normally results only in exposure to the liabilities Morris chooses to acquire and is thus an attractive choice to the acquirer (Exhibit 10.3).

EXHIBIT 10.3.   Acquisition strategies.

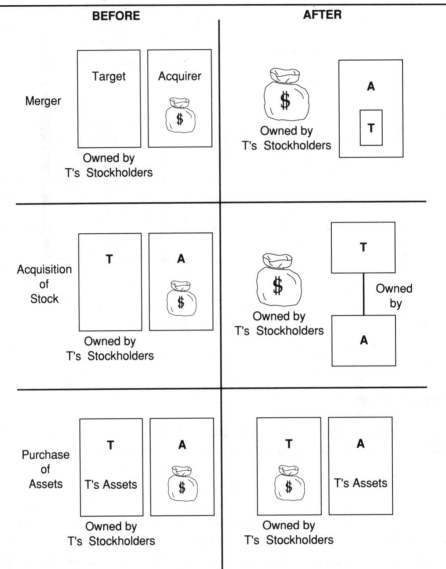

Yet tax factors do normally play a large part in structuring an acquisition. For example, if the target corporation has a history of losses and thus boasts a tax-loss carryforward, Morris may wish to apply such losses to its future profitable operations. This would be impossible if he acquired the assets and liabilities of the target, since the target corporation would still exist after the transaction, keeping its tax characteristics to itself. If the acquirer obtains the stock, or merges the two entities, the acquirer has taken control of the taxable entity itself, thus obtaining its tax characteristics for future use. This result inspired a lively traffic in tax-loss carryforwards in years past, where failed corporations were marketed to profitable corporations seeking tax relief.

Congress has put a damper on such activity in recent years by limiting the use of a tax-loss carryforward, in each of the years following an ownership change of more than 50 percent of a company's stock. The amount of that limit is the product of the value of the business at acquisition (normally its selling price) times a deregulated federal interest rate (approximately 9 percent). This amount of tax-loss carryforward is available each year, until the losses expire (15 years after they were incurred). Since a corporation with significant losses would normally be valued at a relatively low amount, the yearly available loss is likely to be relatively trivial.

Acquisition of the corporation's assets and liabilities eliminates any use by the acquirer of the target's tax-loss carryforward, leaving it available for use by the target's shell. This may be quite useful to the target, because, as discussed earlier, if it has not elected subchapter S status for the last 10 years (or for the full term of its existence, if shorter), it is likely to have incurred a significant gain upon the sale of its assets. This gain would be taxable at the corporate level before the remaining portion of the purchase price could be distributed to the target's shareholders (where it will be taxed again).

The acquirer of assets may have lost any carryforwards otherwise available, but it does not obtain the right to carry the acquired assets on its books at the price paid (rather than the amount carried on the target's books). This is an attractive proposition because the owner of assets used in business may deduct an annual amount, corresponding to the depreciation of those assets, subject only to the requirement that it lower the basis of those assets by an equal amount. The amount of depreciation available corresponds to the purchase price of the asset. This is even more attractive because Congress has adopted available depreciation schedules that normally exceed the rate at which assets actually depreciate. Thus, these assets likely have a low basis in the hands of the target (resulting in even more taxable gain to the target upon sale). If the acquirer were forced to begin its depreciation at the point at which the target left off (as in a merger or purchase of stock), little depreciation would likely result. All things being equal (and especially if the target has enough tax-loss carryforward to absorb any conceivable gain), Morris would likely wish to structure his acquisition as an asset purchase and allocate all the purchase price among the depreciable assets acquired.

This last point is significant because Congress does not recognize all assets as depreciable. Generally speaking, an asset will be depreciable only if it has a demonstrable "useful life." Assets which will last forever, or whose lifetime is not predictable (as with goodwill), are not depreciable, and the price paid for them will not result in future tax deductions. The most obvious example of this type of asset is land. Unlike buildings, land has an unlimited useful life and is not depreciable. This has spawned some very creative theories, including one enterprising individual who purchased a plot of land containing a deep depression, which he intended to use as a garbage dump. The taxpayer allocated a significant amount of his purchase price to the depression and took depreciation deductions as the hole filled up.

Congress has recognized that the above rules give acquirers incentive to allocate most of their purchase price to depreciable assets like buildings and equipment and very little of the price to nondepreciable assets such as land and goodwill. Additional opportunities for this include allocating high prices to acquired inventory, so that it generates little taxable profit when sold. This practice has been limited by recent legislation requiring the acquirer to allocate the purchase price in accordance with the fair market value of the individual assets, applying the rest to the dreaded, nondepreciable goodwill.

Although this recent legislation will limit Morris's options significantly, if he chooses to proceed with an asset purchase, he should not overlook the opportunity to divert some of the purchase price to noncompetition and consulting contracts for the previous owners. Such payments will be deductible by Plant Supply over the life of the agreements and are, therefore, just as useful as depreciation. However, the taxability of such payments to the previous owners cannot be absorbed by the target's tax-loss carryforward. And, the amount of such deductions will be limited by the now familiar "unreasonable compensation" doctrine.

EXECUTIVE COMPENSATION

Brad's compensation package raises a number of interesting tax issues, which may not be readily apparent, but which deserve careful consideration in crafting an offer to him. Any offer of compensation to an executive of his calibre will include, at the very least, a significant salary and bonus package. These will not normally raise any sophisticated tax problems; the corporation will deduct these payments, and Brad will be required to include them in his taxable income. The IRS is not likely to challenge the deductibility of even a very generous salary, since Brad is not a stockholder or family member and, thus, there is little likelihood of an attempt to disguise a dividend.

Business Expenses

However, even in the area of salary, there are opportunities for the use of tax strategies. For example, Brad's duties may include the entertainment of clients or travel to suppliers and other business destinations. It is conceivable that Brad could be expected to fund these activities out of his own pocket, on the theory that such amounts have been figured into his salary. Such a procedure avoids the need for the bookkeeping associated with expense accounts. If his salary reflects these expectations, Brad may not mind declaring the extra amount as taxable income, since he will be entitled to an offsetting deduction for these business expenses.

Unfortunately, however, Brad would be in for an unpleasant surprise under these circumstances. First of all, these expenses may not all be deductible in full. Meals and entertainment expenses are only deductible, if at all, to the extent they are not "lavish and extravagant" and even then, they are deductible only for 80 percent of the amount expended. In addition, Brad's business expenses as an employee are considered "miscellaneous deductions": They are only deductible to the extent that they, and other similarly classified deductions, exceed 2 percent of Brad's adjusted gross income. Thus, if Brad's gross taxable income is $150,000, the first $3,000 of miscellaneous deductions will not be deductible.

Moreover, as itemized deductions, these deductions are valuable only to the extent that they, along with all other itemized deductions available to Brad, exceed the "standard deduction," an amount Congress allows each taxpayer to deduct, if all itemized deductions are foregone. Furthermore, under tax legislation passed in late 1990, itemized deductions that survive the above cuts are further limited for taxpayers whose incomes are over $100,000. The deductibility of Brad's business expenses is, therefore, greatly in doubt.

Knowing all this, Brad would be well advised to request that Morris revise his compensation package. Brad should request a cut in pay by the amount of his anticipated business expenses, along with a commitment that the corporation will reimburse him for such expenses or pay them directly. In that case, Brad will be in the same economic position, since his salary is lowered only by the amount he would have spent anyway. In fact, his economic position is enhanced, since he pays no taxes on the salary he does not receive, as well as escaping from the 80 percent ceiling and 2 percent floor described above.

The corporation pays out no more money this way than it would have if the entire amount were salary. Tax-wise, the corporation is only slightly worse off, since the amount it would have previously deducted as salary can now still be deducted as ordinary and necessary business expenses (with the sole exception of the 80 percent ceiling on meals and entertainment). In fact, were Brad's salary below the Social Security contribution limit (FICA), both Brad and the corporation would be better off, because what was formerly salary (and thus subject to additional 7.65 percent contributions to FICA by both employer and employee) would now be merely expense reimbursements and exempt from FICA.

Before Brad and Morris adopt this strategy, however, they should be aware that in recent years, Congress has turned a sympathetic ear to the frustration the IRS has expressed about expense accounts. Recent legislation has conditioned the exclusion of amounts paid to an employee, as expense reimbursements, upon the submission by the employee to the employer of reliable documentation of such expenses. Brad should get into the habit of keeping a diary of such expenses for tax purposes.

Deferred Compensation

Often, a high-level executive will negotiate a salary and bonus which far exceed his current needs. In such a case, the executive might consider deferring some of that compensation until future years. Brad may feel, for example, that he would be well-advised to provide for a steady income during his retirement years, derived from his earnings while an executive of Plant Supply. He may be concerned that he would simply waste the excess compensation and consider a deferred package as a form of forced savings. Or, he may wish to defer receipt of the excess money to a time (such as retirement) when he believes he will be in a lower tax bracket. This latter consideration was more common when the federal income tax law encompassed a large number of tax brackets and the highest rates were as high as 70 percent. It may not be as prominent a consideration with today's three, comparatively low brackets.

Whatever Brad's reasons for considering a deferral of some of his salary, he should be aware that deferred compensation packages are generally classified as one of two varieties, for federal income tax purposes. The first such category is the qualified deferred compensation plan, such as the pension, profit-sharing, or stock bonus plan. All these plans share a number of characteristics. First and foremost, they afford taxpayers the best of all possible worlds, by granting the employer a deduction for monies contributed to the plan each year, allowing those contributions to be invested and to earn additional monies without the payment of current taxes, and finally, taxing the employee only when he withdraws the funds, as needed in the future. However, in order to qualify for such favorable treatment, these plans must conform to a bewildering array of conditions imposed by both the Code and the Employee Retirement Income Security Act (ERISA). Among these requirements is the necessity to treat all employees of the corporation on a nondiscriminatory basis with respect to the plan, thus rendering qualified plans a poor technique for supplementing a compensation package for a highly paid executive.

The second category is nonqualified plans. These come in as many varieties as there are employees with imaginations, but they all share the same disfavored tax treatment. The employer is entitled to its deduction only when the employee pays tax on the money, and if money is contributed to such a plan, the earnings are taxed currently. Thus, if Morris were to design a plan under which the corporation receives a current deduction for its contributions, Brad will pay tax now on money he will not receive until the future. Since this is the exact opposite of what Brad (and most employees) have in mind, Brad will most likely have to settle for his employer's unfunded promise to pay him the deferred amount in the future.

Assuming Brad is interested in deferring some of his compensation, he and Morris might well devise a plan which gives them as much flexibility as possible. For example, Morris might agree that the day before the end of each pay period, Brad could notify the corporation of the amount of salary, if any, he wished to defer for that period. Any amount thus deferred would be carried on the books of the corporation as a liability to be paid, per their agreement, with interest, after Brad's retirement. Unfortunately, such an arrangement would be frustrated by the "constructive receipt" doctrine. Using this potent weapon, the IRS will impose tax (allowing a corresponding employer deduction) upon any compensation which the employee has earned and might have chosen to receive, regardless of whether he so chooses. The taxpayer may not turn his back upon income otherwise unconditionally available to him.

Taking this theory to its logical conclusion, one might argue that deferred compensation is taxable to the employee because he might have received it if he had simply negotiated a different compensation package. After all, the impetus for deferral in this case comes exclusively from Brad; Morris would have been happy to pay the full amount when earned. But the constructive receipt doctrine does not have that extensive a reach. The IRS can only tax monies the taxpayer was legally entitled to receive, not monies he might have received if he had negotiated differently. In fact, the IRS will even recognize elective deferrals if the taxpayer must make the deferral election sufficiently long before the monies are legally earned. Brad might, therefore, be allowed to choose deferral of a portion of his salary if the choice must be made at least 6 months before the pay period involved.

Frankly, however, if Brad is convinced of the advisability of deferring a portion of his compensation, he is less likely to be concerned about the irrevocability of such election as about ensuring that the money will be available to him when it is eventually due. Thus, a mere unfunded promise to pay in the future may result in years of nightmares over a possible declaration of bankruptcy by his employer. Again, left to their own devices, Brad and Morris might well devise a plan under which Morris contributes the deferred compensation to a trust for Brad's benefit, payable to its beneficiary upon his retirement. Yet such an arrangement would be disastrous to Brad, since the IRS would assess income tax to Brad upon such arrangement, using the much criticized "economic benefit" doctrine. Under this theory, monies irrevocably set aside for Brad grant him an economic benefit (presumably by improving his net worth or otherwise improving his creditworthiness), upon which he must pay tax.

If Brad were aware of this risk, he might choose another method to protect his eventual payout, by requiring the corporation to secure its promise to pay with such devices as a letter of credit or a mortgage or security interest in its assets. All of these devices, however, have been successfully taxed by the IRS under the self-same economic benefit doctrine. Very few devices have survived this attack. However, the personal guarantee of Morris himself (merely another unsecured promise) would not be considered an economic benefit by the IRS.

Another successful strategy is the so-called "rabbi trust," a device first used by a rabbi who feared his deferred compensation might be revoked by a future hostile congregation. This device works similarly to the trust described earlier, except that Brad would not be the only beneficiary of the money contributed. Under the terms of the trust, were the corporation to experience financial reverses, the trust property would be available to the corporation's creditors. Since the monies are thus not irrevocably committed to Brad, the economic benefit doctrine is not invoked. Of course, this device does not protect Brad from the scenario of his nightmares, but it does protect him from a corporate change of heart regarding his eventual payout. From Morris's point of view, he may not object to contributing to a rabbi trust, since he was willing to pay all the money to Brad as salary, but he should be aware that since Brad escapes current taxation, the corporation will not receive a deduction for these expenses until the money is paid out of the trust in the future.

Interest-Free Loans

As a further enticement to agree to work for the new ownership of the plant, Morris might additionally offer to lend Brad a significant amount of money, to be used, for example, to purchase a new home or acquire an investment portfolio. Significant up-front money is often part of an executive compensation package. While this money could be paid as a bonus, Morris might well want some future repayment (perhaps, as a way to encourage Brad to stay in his new position). Brad might wish to avoid the income tax bite on such a bonus so he can retain the full amount of the payment for his preferred use. Morris and Brad might well agree to an interest rate well below the market, or even no interest at all, to further entice Brad to his new position. Economically, this would give Brad free use of the money for a period of time, during which it could earn him additional income with no offsetting expense. In a sense, he would be receiving his salary in advance while not paying any income tax until he earned it. Morris might well formalize the arrangement by reserving a right to offset loan repayments against future salary. The term of the loan might even be accelerated should Brad leave the corporation's employ.

This remarkable arrangement was fairly common until recently. Under current tax law, however, despite the fact that little or no interest passes between Brad and the corporation, the IRS deems full market interest payments to have been made and further deems that said amount is returned to Brad by his employer. Thus, each year, Brad is deemed to have made an interest payment to the corporation, for which he is entitled to no deduction. Then, when the corporation is deemed to have returned the money to him, he realizes additional compensation upon which he must pay tax. The corporation realizes additional interest income, but gets a compensating deduction for additional compensation paid (assuming it is not excessive when added to Brad's other compensation).

Moreover, the IRS has not reserved this treatment for employers and employees only. The same treatment is given to loans between corporations and their shareholders and loans between family members. In the latter situation, although there is no interest deduction for the donee, the deemed return of the interest is a gift and is thus excluded from income. The donor receives interest income, and has no compensating deduction for the return gift. In fact, if the interest amount is large enough, he may have incurred an additional gift tax on the "returned" interest. The amount of income created for the donor is, however, limited to the donee's investment income, except in very large loans. In the corporation/stockholder situation, the lender incurs interest income and has no compensating deduction as its deemed return of the interest is characterized as a dividend. Thus the IRS gets increased tax from both parties (Exhibit 10.4).

All may not be lost in this situation, however. Brad's additional income tax arises from the fact that there is no longer any deduction allowable for interest paid on unsecured personal loans. However, interest remains deductible in limited amounts on loans secured by a mortgage on either of the taxpayer's principal or secondary residence. If Brad grants Plant Supply a mortgage on his home to secure the repayment of his no- or low-interest loan, his deemed payment of market interest will become deductible and may thus offset his additional deemed compensation from the imaginary return of this interest. Before jumping into this transaction, however, Brad will have to consider the limited utility of itemized deductions described earlier.

SHARING THE EQUITY

If Brad is as sophisticated and valuable an executive employee as Morris believes he is, Brad is likely to ask for more than just a compensation pack-

EXHIBIT 10.4. Taxable interest.

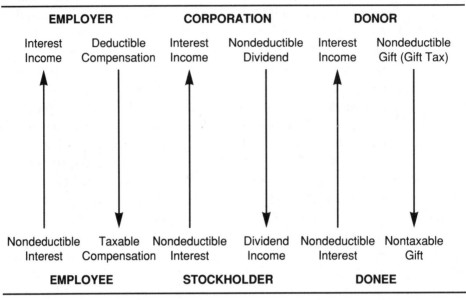

EMPLOYER		CORPORATION		DONOR	
Interest Income	Deductible Compensation	Interest Income	Nondeductible Dividend	Interest Income	Nondeductible Gift (Gift Tax)
Nondeductible Interest	Taxable Compensation	Nondeductible Interest	Dividend Income	Nondeductible Interest	Nontaxable Gift
EMPLOYEE		**STOCKHOLDER**		**DONEE**	

age, deferred or otherwise. Such a prospective employee often demands a "piece of the action" or a share in the equity of the business, so that he may directly share in the growth and success he expects to create. Morris may even welcome such a demand because an equity share (if not so large as to threaten Morris's control) may serve as a form of golden handcuffs, giving Brad additional reason to stay with the company for the long term.

Assuming Morris is receptive to the idea, there are a number of different ways to grant Brad a share of the business. The most direct way would be to grant him shares of the corporation's stock. These could be given to Brad without charge, for a discount from fair market value or for their full value, depending upon the type of incentive Morris wishes to design. In addition, given the privately held nature of Morris's corporation, the shares will probably carry restrictions, designed to keep the shares from ending up in the hands of persons who are not associated with the company. Thus, the corporation will retain the right to repurchase the shares should Brad ever leave the corporation's employ or wish to sell or transfer the shares to a third party. Finally, in order to encourage Brad to stay with the company, the corporation will probably reserve the right to repurchase the shares from Brad at cost should Brad's employment end before a specified time. As an example, *all* the shares (called "restricted stock") would be subject to forfeiture at cost (regardless of their then actual value) should Brad leave before one year, two thirds would be forfeited if he left before two years, and one third if he left before three years. The shares not forfeited (called "vested" shares) would be purchased by the corporation at their full value at the time periods described above.

One step back from restricted stock is the stock option. This is a right granted to the employee to purchase a particular number of shares for a fixed price over a defined period of time. Because the price of the stock does not change, the employee has effectively been given the ability to share in whatever growth the company experiences during the life of the option, without paying for the privilege. If the stock increases in value, the employee will exercise the option near the end of the option term. If the stock value does not grow, the employee will allow the option to expire, having lost nothing. The stock option is a handy device when the employee objects to paying for his piece of the action (after all, he is expecting compensation, not expense), but the employer objects to giving the employee stock whose current value represents growth from the period before the employee's arrival. Again, the exercise price can be more than, equal to or less than the fair market value of the stock at the time of the grant, depending upon the extent of the incentive the employer wishes to give. Also, the exercisability of the option will likely "vest" in stages over time.

Often, however, the founding entrepreneur cannot bring himself to give an employee a current or potential portion of the corporation's stock. Although he has been assured that the block of stock going to the employee is too small to have any effect on his control over the company, the objection may be psychological and impossible to overcome. The founder seeks a device which can grant the employee a growth potential similar to that granted by stock ownership, but without the stock. Such devices are often referred to as phantom stock or stock appreciation rights (SARs). In a phantom stock plan, the employee is promised that he may, at any time during a defined period, so long as he remains employed by the corporation, demand payment equal to the then value of a certain number of shares of the corporation's stock. As the corporation grows, so does the amount available to the employee, just as would be the case if he actually owned some stock. SARs are very similar, except that the amount available to the employee is limited to the growth, if any, that the given number of shares has experienced since the date of grant.

Tax Effects of Phantom Stock and SARs

Having described these devices to Morris and Brad, it is, of course, important to discuss their varying tax impacts upon employer and employee. If Brad has been paying attention, he might immediately object to the phantom stock and SARs as vulnerable to the constructive receipt rule. After all, if he may claim the current value of these devices at any time he chooses, might not the IRS insist that he include each year's growth in his taxable income, as if he had claimed it? Although the corporation's accountants will require that these devices be accounted for in that way on the corporation's financial statements, the IRS has failed in its attempts to require inclusion of these amounts in taxable income, because the monies are not unconditionally available to the taxpayer. In order to receive the money, one must give up any right to continue to share in the growth represented by one's phantom stock or SAR. If the right is not exercisable without cost, the income is not constructively received.

However, there is good reason for Brad to object to phantom stock and SARs from a tax point of view. Unlike stock and stock options, both of which represent a recognized form of intangible capital asset, phantom stock and SARs are really no different from a mere promise by the corporation to pay a bonus based upon a certain formula. Since these devices are not recognized as capital assets, they are not eligible to be taxed as long-term capital gains when redeemed. This difference was quite meaningful when the maximum ordinary income tax rate was 50 percent and the maximum long-term capital gain rate was 20 percent. It is beginning to take on significance again today when the maximum rates have once again diverged to 31 percent and 28 percent, respectively. Most prognosticators, moreover, expect these maximum rates to diverge further in the near future. Thus, Brad may have good reason to reject phantom stock and SARs, and insist upon the real thing.

Taxability of Stock Options

If Morris and Brad resolve their negotiations through the use of stock options, careful tax analysis is again necessary. The Code treats stock options in three different ways, depending upon the circumstances, and some of these circumstances are well within the control of the parties.

If a stock option has a "readily ascertainable value," the IRS will expect the employee to include in his taxable income the difference between the value of the option and the amount paid for it (this amount is normally zero). Measured in that way, the value of an option might be quite small, especially if the exercise price is close or equal to the then fair market value of the underlying stock. After all, the value of a right to buy $10 of stock for $10 is only the speculative value of having that right when the underlying value has increased. That amount is then taxed as ordinary compensation income, and the employer receives a compensating deduction for compensation paid. When the employee exercises the option, the Code imposes no tax, nor does the employer receive any further deduction. Finally, should the employee sell the stock, the difference between the price received and the total of the amounts paid for the option and the stock is included in his income as taxable gain. No deduction is then granted to the employer as the employee's decision to sell his stock is not deemed to be related to the employer's compensation policy.

This taxation scenario is normally quite attractive to the employee, because he is taxed upon a rather small amount at first, escapes tax entirely upon exercise, and then pays tax on the growth at a time when he has realized cash with which to pay the tax, at a lower long-term capital gain rate. Although the employer receives little benefit, it has cost the employer nothing in hard assets, so any benefit would have been a windfall.

Because this tax scenario is seen as very favorable to the employee, the IRS has been loathe to allow it in most cases. Generally, the IRS will not recognize an option as having a "readily ascertainable value" unless the option is traded on a recognized exchange. Short of that, a case has occasionally been made when the underlying stock is publicly traded, such that *its* value is readily ascertainable. But the IRS has drawn the line at options on privately held stock and at all options that are not themselves transferable. Since Morris's corporation is privately held and since he will not tolerate Brad's reserving the right to transfer the option to a third party, there is no chance of Brad's taking advantage of this beneficial tax treatment.

The second tax scenario attaches to stock options which do not have a readily ascertainable value. Since, by definition, one cannot include their value in income on the date of grant (it is unknown), the Code allows the grant to escape taxation. However, upon exercise, the taxpayer must include in income the difference between the then fair market value of the stock purchased and the total paid for the option and stock. When the purchased stock is later sold, the further growth is taxed at the applicable rate for capital gain. The employer receives a compensation deduction at the time of exercise, and no deduction at the time of sale. Although, the employee receives a deferral of taxation from grant to exercise in this scenario, this method of taxation is generally seen as less advantageous to the employee, since a larger amount of income is exposed to ordinary income rates, and this taxation occurs at a time when the taxpayer has still not received any cash from the transaction with which to pay the tax.

Recognizing the harshness of this result, Congress has recently invented a third taxation scenario which attaches to "incentive stock options." The recipient of such an option escapes tax upon grant of the option and again upon exercise. Upon sale of the underlying stock, the employee includes in taxable income the difference between the price received and the total paid for the stock and option, and pays tax upon that amount at long-term capital gain rates. This scenario is extremely attractive to the employee who defers all tax until the last moment and pays at a lower rate. Under this scenario, the employer receives no deduction at all, but since the transaction costs him nothing, that is normally not a major concern.

However, the Code imposes many conditions upon the grant of an incentive stock option. Among these are that the options must be granted pursuant to a written plan, setting forth the maximum number of shares available and the class of employees eligible; only employees are eligible recipients; the options cannot be transferable; no more than $100,000 of underlying stock may be initially exercisable in any one year by any one employee; the exercise price of the options must be the fair market value of the stock upon the date of grant; and the options must expire substantially simultaneously with the termination of the employee's employment. Perhaps most important, the underlying stock may not be sold by the employee prior to the expiration of two years from the option grant date or one year from the exercise date, whichever is later.

This latter requirement has led to what was probably an unexpected consequence. Assume that Plant Supply has granted an incentive stock option to Brad. Assume further that Brad has recently exercised the option, and has plans to sell the stock he received. It may occur to Brad that by waiting a year to resell, he will be risking the vagaries of the market for a tax savings which cannot exceed 3 percent (the difference between the maximum income tax

EXHIBIT 10.5. The effects of timing on value.

		GRANT	EXERCISE	SALE
READILY ASCERTAINABLE VALUE	Employee	Tax on Value	No Tax	Capital Gain
	Employer	Deduction	No Deduction	No Deduction
NO READILY ASCERTAINABLE VALUE	Employee	No Tax	Tax on Spread	Capital Gain
	Employer	No Deduction	Deduction	No Deduction
ISOP	Employee	No Tax	No Tax	Capital Gain
	Employer	No Deduction	No Deduction	No Deduction

rate of 31 percent and the maximum capital gain rate of 28 percent). By selling early, Brad will lose the chance to treat the option as an incentive stock option, but will pay, at worst, only a marginally higher amount at a time when he does have the money to pay it. Furthermore, by disqualifying the options, he will be giving his employer a tax deduction at the time of exercise. An enterprising employee might go so far as to offer to sell early in exchange for a split of the employer's tax savings (Exhibit 10.5).

Tax Impact on Restricted Stock

The taxation of restricted stock is not markedly different from the taxation of nonqualified stock options without a readily ascertainable value. Restricted stock is defined as stock that is subject to a condition that affects its value to the holder and which will lapse upon the happening of an event or the passage of time. Since the value of the stock to the employee is initially speculative, the receipt of the stock is not considered a taxable event. In other words, since Brad may have to forfeit whatever increased value his stock may acquire, if he leaves the employ of the corporation prior to the agreed time, Congress has allowed him not to pay the tax until he knows for certain whether he will be able to retain that value. When the stock is no longer restricted (when it "vests"), the tax is payable. Of course, Congress is not being entirely altruistic in this case; the amount taxed when the stock vests is not the difference between what the employee pays for it and its value when first received by the employee, but the difference between the employee's cost and its value at the vesting data. If the value of the stock has increased, as everyone involved has hoped, the IRS receives a windfall. Of course, the employer receives a compensating deduction at the time of taxation, and further growth between the vesting date and the date of sale is taxed upon sale at appropriate capital gain rates. No deduction is then available to the employer.

Recognizing that allowing the employee to pay a higher tax at a later time is not an unmixed blessing, Congress has provided that an employee who receives restricted stock may, nonetheless, elect to pay ordinary income tax on the difference between its value at grant and the amount paid for it, if the employee files notice of that election within 30 days of the grant date. Thus, the employee can choose for himself which gamble to accept.

This scenario can result in disaster for the unaware employee. Assume that Morris and Brad resolve their differences by allowing Brad to have an equity stake in the corporation, if he is willing to pay for it. Thus, Brad purchases 5 percent of the corporation for its full value on the date he joins the corporation, e.g., $5.00 per share. Since this arrangement still provides incentive in the form of a share of growth, Morris insists that Brad sell

EXHIBIT 10.6.   Restricted stock tax impact.

		GRANT	RESTRICTION REMOVED	SALE
RESTRICTED STOCK	Employee	No Tax	Tax Based on Current Value	Capital Gain
	Employer	No Deduction	Deduction	No Deduction
RESTRICTED STOCK 83(b) ELECTION	Employee	Tax Based on Value Without Restriction	No Tax	Capital Gain
	Employer	Deduction	No Deduction	No Deduction

the stock back to the corporation for $5.00 per share should he leave the corporation before he has been employed for 3 years. Brad correctly believes that since he has bought $5.00 shares for $5.00, he has no taxable income, and reports nothing on his income tax return that year.

Brad has failed to realize that despite his paying full price, he has received restricted stock. As a result, Congress has done him the favor of imposing no tax until the restrictions lapse. Three years from now, when the shares may have tripled in value and have finally vested, Brad will discover to his horror that he must include $10.00 per share in his taxable income for that year. Despite the fact that he had no income to declare in the year of grant, Brad must elect to include that nullity in his taxable income for that year by filing such an election with the IRS within 30 days of his purchase of the stock (Exhibit 10.6).

VACATION HOME

Morris had much reason to congratulate himself on successfully acquiring the plastics molding operation as well as securing the services of Brad, through an effective executive compensation package. In fact, the only real disappointment for Morris was that the closing of the deal was scheduled to take place during the week in which he normally took his annual vacation.

Some years ago, Morris had purchased a country home for use by himself and his wife as a weekend getaway and vacation spot. With the press of business, however, Morris and his wife had been able to use the home only on occasional weekends and for his two-week summer vacation each year. Morris always took the same two weeks for his vacation so he could indulge his love of golf. Each year, during that two weeks, the professional golfers would come to town for their annual tournament. Hotels were always booked far in advance, and Morris felt lucky to be able to walk from his home to the first tee and enjoy his favorite sport, played by some of the world's best.

Some of Morris's friends had suggested that Morris rent his place during the weeks that he and his wife didn't use it. Even if such rentals would not generate much cash during these off-season periods, it might allow Morris to deduct some of the expenses of keeping the home, such as real estate taxes, mortgage payments, maintenance and depreciation. Morris could see the benefit in that, since the latter two expenses were only deductible in a business context, and although taxes and mortgage interest were deductible as personal expenses (assuming, in the case of mortgage interest, that Morris was deducting such payments only with respect to this and his principal residence and no other home), the above mentioned limits on the use of itemized deductions made the usefulness of these deductions questionable.

However, in addition to the inconvenience of renting one's vacation home, Morris had discovered a few unfortunate tax rules which had dissuaded him from following his friends' advice. First of all, the rental of a home is treated by the Code in a fashion similar to the conduct of a business. Thus, Morris would generate deductions only to the extent that his expenses exceeded his rental income. In addition, to the extent he could generate such a loss, the rental of real estate is deemed to be a passive activity under the Code, regardless of how much effort one puts into the process. Thus, in the absence of any relief provision, these losses would be deductible only against other passive income, and would not be usable against salary, bonus or investment income.

Such a relief provision does exist, however, for rental activities in which the taxpayer is "actively" involved. In such a case, the taxpayer may deduct up to $25,000 of losses against active or portfolio income, unless his total income (before any such deduction) exceeds $100,000. The amount of loss which may be used by such taxpayer, free of the passive activity limitations, is then lowered by $1 for every $2 of additional income, disappearing entirely at $150,000. Given his success in business, the usefulness of rental losses, in the absence of passive income, seemed problematic to Morris, at best.

Another tax rule appeared to Morris to limit the usefulness of losses even further. Under the Code, a parcel of real estate falls into one of three categories: personal use, rental use, or mixed use. A personal use property is one which is rented 14 days or less in a year and otherwise used by the taxpayer and his family. No expenses are deductible for such a facility except taxes and mortgage interest. A rental use property is used by the taxpayer and his family for less than 15 days (or 10 percent of the number of rental days) and otherwise offered for rental. All the expenses of such an activity are deductible, subject to the passive loss limitations. A mixed use facility is one which falls within neither of the other two categories.

If Morris were to engage in a serious rental effort of his property, his occasional weekend use, combined with his two-week stay around the golf tournament, would surely result in his home falling into the mixed-use category. This would negatively impact him in two ways. The expenses, which are deductible only for a rental facility (such as maintenance and depreciation), would be deductible only on a pro rata basis for the total number of rental days. Worse yet, the expenses of the rental business would be deductible only to the extent of the income, and not beyond. Expenses which would be deductible anyway (taxes and mortgage interest) are counted first in this calculation and only then are the remaining expenses allowed. The result of all this is that it would be impossible for Morris to generate a deductible loss, even were it possible to use such a loss in the face of the passive loss limitations.

Naturally, therefore, Morris had long since decided not to bother with attempting to rent his country getaway when he was unable to use it. However, the scheduling of the closing this year presents a unique tax opportunity of which he may be unaware. In a rare stroke of fairness, the Code, while denying any deduction of not otherwise deductible expenses in connection with a home rented for 14 days or less, reciprocates by allowing taxpayers to exclude any income should they take advantage of the 14 day rental window. Normally, such an opportunity is of limited utility, but with the tournament coming to town and the hotels full, Morris is in a position to make a killing, by renting his home to a golfer or spectator during this time at inflated rental rates. All that rental income would be entirely tax-free. Just be sure the tenants don't stay beyond 2 weeks.

LIKE-KIND EXCHANGES

Having acquired the desired new business and secured the services of the individual he needed to run it, Morris turned his attention to consolidating his two operations, so that they might function more efficiently. After some time, he realized that the factory building acquired with the plastics business was not contributing to increased efficiency because of its age and, more important, because of its distance from Morris's home office. Morris located a more modern facility near his main location, which could accommodate both operations and allow him to eliminate some amount of duplicative management.

Naturally, Morris put the molding facility on the market and planned to purchase the new facility with the proceeds of the old, plus some additional capital. Such a strategy will result in a tax upon the sale of the older facility, equal to the difference between the sale price and Plant Supply's basis in the building. If Morris purchased the molding company by purchasing its assets, then the capital gain to be taxed here may be minimal, because it would consist only of the growth in value since this purchase, plus any amount depreciated after the acquisition. If, however, Morris acquired the molding company through a merger or purchase of stock, his basis will be the old company's pre-acquisition basis, and the capital gain may be considerable. Either way, it would surely be desirable to avoid taxation on this capital gain.

The Code affords Morris the opportunity to avoid this taxation, if, instead of selling his old facility and buying a new one, he can arrange a trade of the old for the new, so that no cash falls into his hands. Under Section 1031 of the Code, if properties of "like-kind" used in a trade or business are exchanged, no taxable event has occurred. The gain on the disposition of the older facility is merely deferred until the eventual disposition of the newer facility. This is accomplished by calculating the basis in the newer facility, starting with its fair market value on the date of acquisition and subtracting from that amount, the gain not recognized upon the sale of the older facility. That process builds the unrecognized gain into the basis of the newer building, so that it will be recognized (along with any future gain) upon its later sale. There has been considerable confusion and debate over what constitutes like-kind property outside of real estate, but there is no doubt that a trade of real estate used in business for other real estate to be used in business will qualify under Section 1031.

Although undoubtedly attracted by this possibility, Morris would quickly point out that such an exchange would be extremely rare, since it is highly unlikely that he would be able to find a new facility which is worth exactly the same amount as his old facility, and thus any such exchange will have to involve a payment of cash as well as an exchange of buildings. Fortunately, however, Section 1031 recognizes that reality by providing that the exchange is still nontaxable to Morris so long as he does not receive any non-like-kind property (i.e., cash). Such non-like-kind property received is known as "boot," and will include, besides cash, any liability (such as a mortgage debt) assumed by the exchange partner. The facility he is purchasing is more expensive than the one he is selling, so Morris will have to add some cash, not receive it. Thus, the transaction does not involve the receipt of boot and still qualifies for tax deferral. Moreover, even if Morris did receive boot in the transaction, he would only recognize gain to the extent of the boot received, so he might still be in a position to defer a portion of the gain involved. Of course, if he received more boot than the gain in the transaction, he would recognize only the amount of the gain, not the full amount of the boot.

But Morris has an even more compelling, practical objection to this plan. How often will the person who wants to purchase your facility own the exact facility you wish to purchase? Not very often, he would surmise. In point of fact, the proposed buyer of his old facility is totally unrelated to the current owner of the facility Morris wishes to buy. How then can one structure an exchange of the two parcels of real estate? It would seem, therefore, that a taxable sale of the one, followed by a purchase of the other, will be necessary in almost every case.

Practitioners have, however, devised a technique to overcome this problem, known as the "three-corner exchange." In a nutshell, the transaction is structured by having the proposed buyer of Morris's old facility use his purchase money (plus some additional money contributed by Morris) to acquire the facility Morris wants to buy, instead of giving that money to Morris. Having thus acquired the new facility, he then trades it to Morris for Morris's old facility. When the dust settles, everyone is in the same position they would have occupied in the absence of an exchange. The former owner of the new facility has his cash; the proposed buyer of Morris's old facility now owns that facility and has spent only the amount he had proposed to spend; and Morris has traded the old facility plus some cash for the new one. The only party adversely affected is the IRS, which now must wait to tax the gain in Morris's old facility until he sells the new one.

This technique appears so attractive that when practitioners first began to use it, they attempted to employ the technique, even when the seller of the old facility had not yet found a new facility to buy. They merely had the buyer of the old facility place the purchase price in escrow and promise to use it to buy a new facility for the old owner as soon as he picked one out. Congress has since limited the use of these so-called "delayed" like-kind exchanges, by requiring the seller of the old facility to identify the new facility to be purchased within 45 days of the transfer of the old one, and further requiring that the exchange be completed within six months of the first transfer.

DIVIDENDS

Some time after Morris had engineered the acquisition of the molding facility, the hiring of Brad to run it, and the consolidation of his company's operations through the like-kind exchange, Plant Supply was running smoothly and profitably enough for Morris's thoughts to turn to retirement. Morris intended to have a comfortable retirement funded by the fruits of his life-long efforts on behalf of the company, so it was not unreasonable for him to consider funding his retirement through dividends, on what would still be his considerable holdings of the company's stock. Although Brad already held some stock, and Morris expected that Lisa and Victor would hold some at that time, he still expected to have a majority position and thus sufficient control of the board of directors to ensure such distributions.

However, Morris also knew enough about tax law to understand that such distributions would cause considerable havoc from a tax point of view. We have already discussed how characterizing such distributions as salary or bonus would avoid double taxation, but with Morris no longer working for the company, such characterization would be unreasonable. These payments would be deemed dividends on his stock. They would be nondeductible to the corporation (if it were not a subchapter S corporation at the time) and would be fully taxable to him. However, Morris had another idea. He would embark upon a strategy of turning in small amounts of his stock on a regular basis, in exchange for the stock's value. Although not a perfect solution, the distributions to him would no longer be dividends, but payments in redemption of stock. Thus, they would only be taxable to the extent they exceeded his basis in the stock, and even then, only at long-term capital gain rates (not as ordinary income). Best of all, if such redemptions were small enough, he would retain his control over the company for as long as he retained over 50 percent of its outstanding stock.

However, the benefits of this type of plan have attracted the attention of Congress and the IRS over the years. If an individual can draw monies out of a corporation, without affecting the control he asserts through the ownership of his stock, is he really redeeming his stock, or simply engaging in a disguised dividend? Congress has answered this question with a series of Code sections purporting to define a redemption.

Substantially Disproportionate Distributions

Most relevant to Morris is Section 302(b)(2), which provides that a distribution in respect of stock is a redemption (and thus taxable at preferential rates after subtraction of basis), only if it is substantially disproportionate. This is further defined by requiring that the stockholder hold, after the distribution, less than half of the total combined voting power of all classes of stock, and less than 80 percent of the percentage of the company's total stock that he owned prior to the distribution.

Thus, if Morris intended to redeem 5 shares of the company's stock at a time when he owned 85 of the company's outstanding 100 shares, he would be required to report the entire distribution as a dividend. His percentage of ownership would still be 50 percent or more (80 of 95 or 84 percent), which in itself dooms the transaction. In addition, his percentage of ownership will still be 80 percent or more than his percentage before the distribution (dropping from 85 percent to 84 percent or 99 percent).

To qualify, Morris would have to redeem 71 shares, since only that amount would drop his control percentage below 50 percent (14 of 29 or 48 percent). And since his percentage of control would have dropped from 85 percent to 48 percent, he would retain only 56 percent of the percentage he previously had (less than 80 percent).

Yet, even such a draconian sell-off as described above would not be sufficient for the Code. Congress has taken the position that the stock ownership of persons other than oneself must be taken into account in determining one's control of a corporation. Under these so-called "attribution rules," a stockholder is deemed to control stock owned not only by himself, but also by his spouse, children, grandchildren and parents. Furthermore, stock owned by partnerships, estates, trusts, and corporations affiliated with the stockholder may also be attributed to him. Thus, assuming that, Lisa and Victor owned 10 of the remaining 15 shares of stock (with Brad owning the rest), Morris begins with 95 percent of the control and can qualify for a stock redemption only by selling all his shares to the corporation.

Complete Termination of Interest

Carried to its logical conclusion, even a complete redemption would not qualify for favorable tax treatment, since Lisa and Victor's stock would still be attributed to Morris, leaving him in control of 67 percent of the corporation's stock. Fortunately, however, Code Section 302(b)(3) provides for a distribution to be treated as a redemption if the stockholder's interest in the corporation is completely terminated. The attribution rules still apply under this section, but they may be waived if the stockholder files a written agreement with the IRS requesting such a waiver. In such agreement, Morris would be required to divest himself of any relationship with the corporation other than as a creditor and agree not to acquire any interest in the corporation for a period of ten years.

In addition to the two safe harbors described in Sections 302(b)(2) and (3), the Code, in Section 302(b)(1), grants redemption treatment to distributions which are "not essentially equivalent to a dividend." Unlike the above two sections, however the Code does not spell out a mechanical test for this concept, leaving it to the facts and circumstances of the case. Given the obvious purpose of this transaction to transfer corporate assets to a stockholder on favorable terms, it is unlikely that the IRS would recognize any explanation, under this section, other than that of a dividend.

Thus, Morris's plan to turn in his stock and receive a tax-favored distribution for his retirement will not work out as planned, unless he allows the redemption of all his stock, resigns as a director, officer, employee, consultant, etc. and agrees to stay away for a period of ten years. He may, however, accept a promissory note for all or part of the redemption proceeds and thereby become a creditor of the corporation. Worse yet, if Lisa obtained her shares from Morris within the ten years preceding his retirement, even this plan will not work, unless the IRS can be persuaded that her acquisition of the shares was for reasons other than tax avoidance. It may be advisable to be sure she acquires her shares from the corporation rather than from Morris, although one can expect, given the extent of Morris's control over the corporation, that the IRS would fail to appreciate the difference.

Employee Stock Ownership Plans

Although Morris should be relatively happy with the knowledge that he may be able to arrange a complete redemption of his stock to fund his retirement and avoid being taxed as if he had received a dividend, he may still believe that the tax and economic effects of such a redemption are not ideal. Following such a plan to its logical conclusion, the corporation would borrow the money to pay for Morris's stock and be forced to pay a market interest rate (perhaps prime plus two points or more). Its repayments would be deductible only to the extent of the interest. At the same time, Morris would be paying a substantial capital gain tax to the government. Before settling for this result, Morris might well wish to explore ways to increase the corporation's deduction and decrease his own tax liability.

Such a result can be achieved through the use of an Employee Stock Ownership Plan (ESOP), a form of qualified deferred compensation plan as discussed above in the context of Brad's compensation package. Such a plan consists of a trust to which the corporation makes deductible contributions, either of shares of its own stock, or cash to be used to purchase such stock. Contributions are divided among the accounts of the corporation's employees (normally in proportion to their compensation for that year), and distributions are made to the employees at their retirement or earlier separation from the company (if the plan so allows). ESOPs have been seen as a relatively noncontroversial way for American employees to gain more control over their employers, and they have been granted a number of tax advantages not available to other qualified plans, such as pension or profit-sharing plans. One advantage is illustrated by the fact that a corporation can manufacture a deduction out of thin air by issuing new stock to a plan (at no cost to the corporation) and deducting the fair market value of the shares.

A number of attractive tax benefits would flow from Morris's willingness to sell his shares to an ESOP, established by his corporation, rather than to the corporation itself. Yet, before he could appreciate those benefits, Morris would have to be satisfied that some obvious objections would not make such a transaction inadvisable.

To begin with, the ESOP will have to borrow the money from a bank in the same way the corporation would; yet the ESOP has no credit record or assets to pledge as collateral. This is normally overcome, however, by the corporation's giving the bank a secured guarantee of the ESOP's obligation. Thus, the corporation ends up in the same economic position it would have enjoyed under a direct redemption.

Morris might also object to the level of control an ESOP might give to lower level employees of Plant Supply. After all, his intent is to leave the corporation under the control of Lisa and Brad, but qualified plans must be operated on a nondiscriminatory basis. This objection can be addressed in a number of ways. First, the allocation of shares in proportion to compensation, along with standard vesting and forfeiture provisions, will tilt these allocations toward, highly compensated, long-term employees, such as Lisa and Brad. Second, the shares are not allocated to the employees' accounts until they are paid for. While the bank is still being paid, an amount proportional to the remaining balance of the loan would be controlled by the plan trustees (chosen by management). Third, even after shares are allocated to employee accounts, in a closely held company, employees are allowed to vote those shares only on questions which require a two-thirds vote of the stockholders, such as a sale or merger of the corporation. On all other more routine questions (such as election of the board) the trustees still vote the shares. Fourth, upon an employee's retirement and before distribution of his shares, a closely held corporation must offer to buy back the distributed shares at fair market value. As a practical matter, most employees will accept such an offer, rather than moving into retirement with illiquid, closely held company stock.

If Morris accepts these arguments and opts for an ESOP buyout, the following benefits accrue. Rather than being able to deduct only the interest portion of its payments to the bank, the corporation may now contribute the amount of such payment to the plan as a fully deductible contribution to a qualified plan. The plan then forwards it to the bank as a payment of its obligation. Better yet, the Code allows the bank to exclude from its taxable income one half of the interest received from an ESOP loan, if the ESOP owns more than 50 percent of the sponsoring company. Freed of this tax burden, most banks will lower the interest rate charged to the plan by two or more points.

Finally, the Code allows an individual who sells stock of a corporation to

EXHIBIT 10.7. Corporate redemption versus ESOP purchase.

CORPORATE REDEMPTION	ESOP PURCHASE
Only Interest Deductible	Principal and Interest Deductible
Commercial Interest Rate	Lower Rate Due to 50% Interest Exclusion
Capital Gain	Gain Deferred If Proceeds Rolled Over

the corporation's ESOP to defer paying any tax on the proceeds of such sale, if the proceeds are rolled over into purchases of securities. No tax is then paid until the purchased securities are ultimately resold. Thus, if Morris takes the money received from the ESOP and invests it in the stock market, he pays no tax until and unless he sells any of these securities, and then, only on those sold. In fact, if Morris purchases such securities and holds them until his death, his estate will receive a step-up in basis for such securities and thus avoid income tax on the proceeds of his company stock entirely (Exhibit 10.7).

ESTATE PLANNING

Contemplating the complete divorce from the Company, which will be necessary for Morris to achieve his tax-favored retirement, his thoughts may naturally turn to the tax consequences of his remaining employed by the company in some capacity until his death. Morris's lifelong efforts have made him a rather wealthy man, and he knows that the government will be looking to reap a rather large harvest from those efforts upon his death. He would no doubt be rather disheartened to learn that after a $600,000 exemption, the federal government will receive from 37 percent to 55 percent of the excess upon his death. Proper estate planning can double the amount of that grace amount by using the exemptions of both Morris and his wife, but the amount above $1,200,000 appears to be at significant risk.

Redemptions to Pay Death Taxes and Administrative Expenses

Since much of the money to fund this estate tax liability would come from redemption of company stock, if Morris had not previously cashed it in, Morris might well fear the combined effect of dividend treatment and estate taxation. Of course, if Morris's estate turned in all his stock for redemption at death, redemption treatment under Section 302(b)(3) would appear to be available, since death would appear to have cut off Morris's relationship with the company rather convincingly. However, if the effect of Morris's death on the company, or other circumstances, made a wholesale redemption inadvisable or impossible, Morris's estate could be faced with paying both income and estate tax on the full amount of the proceeds.

Fortunately for those faced with this problem, Code Section 303 allows capital gain treatment for a stock redemption, if the proceeds of the redemption do not exceed the amount necessary to pay the estate's taxes and those further expenses, allowable as administrative expenses on the estate's tax return. To qualify for this treatment, the company's stock must equal or exceed 35 percent of the value of the estate's total assets. Since Morris's holdings of company stock will most likely exceed 35 percent of his total assets, if his estate finds itself in this uncomfortable position, it will at least be able to account for this distribution as a stock redemption instead of a dividend. This is much more important than it may be at first appear, and much more important than it would have been were Morris still alive. The effect, of course, is to allow payment at long-term capital gain rates (rather than ordinary income tax rates), for only the amount received in excess of the taxpayer's basis in the stock (rather than the entire amount of the distribution). Given that the death of the taxpayer increases his basis to the value at date of death, the effect of Section 303 is to eliminate all but that amount of gain occurring after death, thus eliminating virtually all income tax on the distribution.

Of course, assuring sufficient liquidity to pay taxes due upon death is one thing; controlling the amount of tax actually due is another. Valuation of a majority interest in a closely held corporation is far from an exact science, and the last thing most entrepreneurs wish is to have their spouses and other heirs engage in a valuation controversy with the IRS after their deaths. As a result, a number of techniques have evolved over the years which may have the effect of lowering the value of the stock to be included in the estate, or, at least, making such value more certain for planning purposes.

Estate Freezes

One technique that attained great popularity before attracting the attention of Congress, during the last decade, is the "estate freeze." In its simplest form, the estate freeze involves a recapitalization of the corporation, through declaration of a stock dividend to all holders of common stock, in the form of a preferred stock issue. The preferred stock is structured with par value, liquidation, and dividend preferences, such that virtually all of the present value of the corporation resides in the preferred stock, upon its issuance. In our case, Morris would arrange this recapitalization while he owns virtually all the common stock. Thus, when the recapitalization is completed, virtually all of the corporation's value would be represented by the preferred stock Morris would then own.

Although the preferences and par value of the preferred stock have absorbed virtually all of the value of the corporation, the nature of the preferred stock is such that its value will not typically increase substantially, no matter how well the corporation may be doing. Although this recapitalization has taken virtually all the value out of the common stock, all increase in value due to future growth will nonetheless reside there.

This presents Morris with the opportunity and mechanism to make gifts of large amounts of the common stock without much gift tax impact. Because the value of the corporation has been absorbed by the preferred stock, Morris will be able to dispose of much of the common stock (to his daughter, for example) without exceeding the $10,000 per donee gift tax exemption ($20,000 if his wife agrees to have the gift count against her annual quota as well). How much of the stock he gives away depends only upon the amount of control he wishes to retain. Most likely he will wish to retain at least a majority interest in the corporation, while he is still actively involved in it. In any case, whatever portion of the common stock he gives away removes that portion of the corporation's future growth from his estate, "freezing" his estate's value at its current level. As growth accumulates in the common stock, it belongs to Lisa without ever having passed through Morris's estate.

The enormous potential for tax avoidance inherent in this technique caused Congress to enact Code Section 2036(c), the "anti-freeze" provision. This provision purported to include in the estate of the donor, any portion of an enterprise given away by the donor, if the portion did not give a measure of control over the enterprise proportionate to its value. This section and the regulations proposed thereunder were both immensely complex and arguably overinclusive. Congress repealed this section shortly after its enactment. Replacing it is a series of Code sections, designed to ensure that the valuation of the common and preferred stock is based upon valid economic realities.

The corporation's post estate freeze common stock, for example, cannot be assigned less than 10 percent of the value of the corporation. Another example of this approach deals with the valuation of the preferred stock on the basis of its dividend preference. In earlier times, the dividend preference was calculated to enhance the value of the preferred stock, but it was commonly understood that the preference would not be paid. Each year, the directors (with the founder's tacit approval) would vote to skip that year's dividend, which in extreme circumstances was not even cumulative. Under the new rules, the preference must be cumulative, and, for all practical purposes, the dividend must be paid. This should not concern Morris, however, since he is already the recipient of a significant cash flow from the corporation and can adjust his compensation to accommodate this new imperative. It may even be a welcome supplement to his retirement income later on. However, Morris would be forced to forego the benefits of subchapter S, since the corporation would now have more than one class of stock.

Preferred Stock Bailouts

The last step in the estate freeze scenario is the redemption of the preferred and common stock held by Morris, upon his eventual death. This ensures that there will be adequate liquid assets to pay the amount of estate tax which is assessed upon his estate, even with the lower valuation achieved. At this point, the wary taxpayer is presented with another trap that he must be careful to avoid.

If a corporation has significant earnings and profits, accumulated during a period of time when it was not treated as a subchapter S corporation, a dividend to its stockholders would not be deductible to the corporation and would be taxable income to its stockholders. If, instead of declaring a cash dividend, the corporation declared a stock dividend and distributed preferred stock, whose value approximated the accumulated earnings and profits of the corporation, the stockholders would then be presented with two alternative opportunities. They could sell the preferred stock to a third party and declare the difference between the sale price and the basis allocated to that stock as capital gain, or they could cause the corporation to redeem the preferred stock, again at capital gain rates. Both options convert ordinary dividend income to capital gain.

This apparent abuse was curbed by the enactment of Section 306 of the Code. This provision, as applied to the scenario just described, puts a "taint" on stock, issued as a dividend on other stock (except for common on common), if the corporation making such distribution has earnings and profits at the time. Upon a sale of the tainted stock to a third party, the proceeds are taxed to the selling stockholder as receipt of a dividend, to the extent of the pro rata earnings and profits existing at the time of the stock's issuance. Thus, Section 306 does not impose a tax at the time of the stock dividend, but recovers tax on the foregone cash dividend at the time of the preferred stock "bailout." If the preferred stock is eventually redeemed by the corporation instead of being sold to a third party, the Code imposes an even more disfavored treatment. It taxes the proceeds as a dividend to the extent of the corporation's earnings and profits at the time of the redemption, not at the time of issuance.

Morris's corporation did not have much in the way of accumulated earnings and profits in its early years, because it distributed most of its earnings in the form of compensation. After the subchapter S election, all earnings and profits were immediately taxed to the stockholders, so Section 306 would not apply. Thus, Morris may not be overly concerned that the eventual redemption of his preferred stock would be taxed as a dividend. Fortunately for him, however, even if some untaxed earnings and profits remain, the Code specifically exempts a redemption from the operation of Section 306, if the redemption acts as a complete termination of the stockholder's interest in the corporation. Thus, the same analysis which freed Morris from dividend treatment upon a redemption, in the absence of an estate freeze, will free him from such treatment after a freeze, if both his preferred and any remaining common are redeemed together.

Buy-Sell Agreements

Having been assured that his stock would not be "tainted," if he were to attempt an estate freeze, Morris would likely be interested in an arrangement requiring the corporation or its stockholders to purchase whatever stock he may still hold at his death. Such an arrangement can be helpful with regard to both of Morris's estate planning goals: setting a value for his stock that would not be challenged by the IRS and assuring sufficient liquidity to pay whatever estate taxes may ultimately be owed.

There are two basic variations of these agreements. Under the most common, Morris would agree with the corporation that it would redeem his shares upon his death, for a price derived from an agreed formula. The second variation would require one or more of the other stockholders of the corporation (e.g., Lisa) to make such a purchase. In both cases, in order for the IRS to respect the valuation placed upon the shares, it will be necessary for Morris to agree that he will not dispose of the shares during his lifetime without first offering them to the other party to his agreement at the formula price. Under such an arrangement, the shares will never be worth more to Morris than the formula price, so it can be argued that whatever higher price the IRS may calculate is irrelevant to him and his estate.

This argument had led some stockholders in the past to agree to formulas that artificially depressed the value of their shares, when the parties succeeding to power in the corporation were also the main beneficiaries of the stockholders' estates. Since any value foregone would end up in the hands of the intended beneficiary anyway, only the tax collector would be hurt. Although the IRS had long challenged this practice, this strategy was put to a formal end at the same time as the repeal of 2036(c), by requiring that the formula used result in a close approximation to fair market value.

Which of the two variations of the buy-sell agreement should Morris choose? If we assume for the moment that Morris owns 80 of the 100 outstanding shares and Lisa and Brad each own 10, a corporate redemption agreement leaves Lisa and Brad each owning half of the 20 outstanding shares remaining. If, however, Morris chooses a cross-purchase agreement with Lisa and Brad, each would purchase 40 of his shares upon his death, leaving them as owners of 50 shares each. Both agreements leave the corporation owned by Lisa and Brad in equal shares, so there does not appear to be any difference between them.

Once again, however, significant differences lie slightly below the surface. To begin with, many such agreements are funded by the purchase of a life insurance policy upon the life of the stockholder involved. If the corporation were to purchase this policy, the premiums would be nondeductible, resulting in additional taxable profit for the corporation. In a subchapter S corporation, such profit would pass through to the stockholders in proportion to their shares of stock in the corporation. In a C corporation, the additional profit would result in additional corporate tax. If, instead, Lisa and Brad bought policies covering their halves of the obligation to Morris's estate, they would be paying the premiums with after-tax dollars. Thus, a redemption agreement will cause Morris to share in the cost of the arrangement, while a cross-purchase agreement puts the entire onus on Lisa and Brad. This can, of course, be rationalized by arguing that they will ultimately reap the benefit of the arrangement by succeeding to the ownership of the corporation. Or, their compensation could be adjusted to cover the additional cost.

If the corporation is not an S corporation, however, there is an additional consideration, which must not be overlooked. Upon Morris's death, the receipt of the insurance proceeds by the beneficiary of the life insurance will be excluded from taxable income. However, a C corporation is also subject to the corporate alternative minimum tax. Simply described, that tax guards against profitable corporations paying little or no tax by "overuse" of certain deductions and tax credits, otherwise available. To calculate the tax, the corporation adds to its otherwise taxable income, certain "tax preferences" and then subtracts from that amount a $40,000 exemption. The result is taxed at 21 percent. If that tax amount exceeds the corporate tax otherwise payable, the higher amount is paid. The result of this is additional tax for those corporations with substantial tax preferences.

Among those tax preferences is a concept known as "adjusted current earnings." This concept adds as a tax preference, three quarters of the difference between the corporation's earnings for financial reporting purposes and the earnings otherwise reportable for tax purposes. A major source of such a difference would be the receipt of nontaxable income. And the receipt of life insurance proceeds is just such an event. Therefore, the receipt of a life insurance payout of sufficient size will ultimately be taxed, at least in part, to a C corporation, while it would be completely tax free to an S corporation or the remaining stockholders.

An additional factor pointing to the stockholder cross-purchase agreement rather than a corporate redemption is the effect this choice would have upon the taxability of a later sale of the corporation after Morris's death. If the corporation were to redeem Morris's stock, Lisa and Brad would each own one half of the corporation through their ownership of ten shares each. If they then sold the company, they would be subject to tax on capital gain measured by the difference between the proceeds of the sale and their original basis in their shares. However, if Lisa and Brad purchased Morris's stock at his death, they would each own one half of the corporation through their ownership of 50 shares each. Upon a later sale of the company, their capital gain will be measured by the difference between the sale proceeds and their original basis in their shares plus the amount paid for Morris's shares. Every dollar paid to Morris lowers the taxable income received upon later sale. In a redemption agreement, these dollars are lost (Exhibit 10.8).

EXHIBIT 10.8.   Corporate redemption versus a cross-purchase agreement.

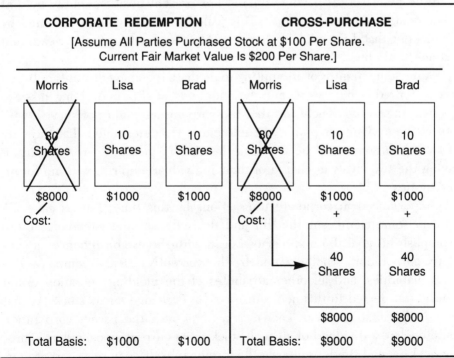

CORPORATE REDEMPTION			CROSS-PURCHASE		
[Assume All Parties Purchased Stock at $100 Per Share. Current Fair Market Value Is $200 Per Share.]					
Morris	Lisa	Brad	Morris	Lisa	Brad
80 Shares	10 Shares	10 Shares	80 Shares	10 Shares	10 Shares
Cost: $8000	$1000	$1000	Cost: $8000	$1000 +	$1000 +
				40 Shares	40 Shares
				$8000	$8000
Total Basis:	$1000	$1000	Total Basis:	$9000	$9000

Pointing in the other direction, however, is the Section 306 taint, if Morris dies after attempting an estate freeze, at a time when the corporation had untaxed accumulated earnings and profits from its existence as a C corporation. Even though Morris contemplates a sale, which would completely terminate his interest in the corporation after his death, a cross-purchase would involve a purchase by a person (Lisa) whose ownership would be attributable to Morris under the attribution rules discussed above. Although such attribution may be waived and a complete termination of interest achieved, for the purpose of removing the 306 taint in a redemption by the corporation, the Code does not allow such a waiver for 306 purposes, when the tainted stock is sold to Lisa. Thus, redemption is indicated after an estate freeze, if a C corporation's earnings and profits existed at the time of the freeze.

SPIN-OFFS AND SPLIT-UPS

Morris's pleasant reverie caused by thoughts of well-funded retirement strategies and clever estate plans was brought to a sudden halt, a mere two years after the acquisition of the molding operation, when it became clear that the internecine jealousies between Brad and Lisa were becoming unmanageable. Ruefully, Morris conceded that it was not unforeseeable that the manager of a significant part of his business would resent the presence of a rival who would be perceived as having attained her present position simply by dint of her relationship to the owner. This jealousy was, of course, inflamed by the thought that Lisa might succeed to Morris's stock upon his death and become Brad's boss.

After some months of attempting to mediate the many disputes between Lisa and Brad, which were merely symptoms of this underlying disease, Morris came to the conclusion that the corporation could not survive with both of them vying for power and influence. He determined that the only workable solution would be to break the two businesses apart once again, leaving the two rivals in charge of their individual empires, with no future binding ties.

Experienced in corporate transactions by this time, Morris gave the problem some significant thought and devised two alternate scenarios to accomplish his goal. Both scenarios began with the establishment of a subsidiary corporation, wholly owned by the currently existing company. The assets, liabilities, and all other attributes of the molding operation would then be transferred to this new subsidiary in exchange for its stock. At that point in the first scenario (known as a "spin-off"), the parent corporation would declare a dividend of all such stock to its current stockholders. Thus, Morris, Lisa, and Brad would own the former subsidiary in the same proportions in which they owned the parent. Morris, as the majority owner of the new corporation, could then give further shares to Brad, enter into a buy-sell agreement with him, or sell him some shares. In any case, upon Morris's death, Brad would succeed to unquestioned leadership in this corporation. Lisa would stay as a minority stockholder, or sell her shares to Morris while he was alive, if she wished. Lisa would gain control of the former parent corporation upon Morris's death.

In the second scenario (known as a "split-off"), after the formation of the subsidiary, Brad would sell his shares of Plant Supply to that parent corporation in exchange for stock, affording him control of the subsidiary. Lisa would remain the only minority stockholder of the parent corporation (Brad's interest having been removed) and would succeed to full ownership upon Morris's death through one of the mechanisms discussed above.

Unfortunately, when Morris brought his ideas to his professional advisers, he was faced with a serious tax objection. In both scenarios, he was told, the IRS would likely take the position that the issuance of the subsidiary's stock to its eventual holder (Morris in the spin-off and Brad in the split-off) was a taxable transaction, characterized as a dividend. After all, this plan could be used as another device to cash out the earnings and profits of a corporation, at favorable rates and terms. Instead of declaring a dividend of these profits, a corporation could spin off assets, with the fair market value of these profits, to a subsidiary. The shares of the subsidiary could then be distributed to its stockholders as a nontaxable stock dividend, and the stockholders could sell these shares and treat their profits as capital gain. The second scenario allows Brad to receive the subsidiary's shares and then make a similar sale of these shares, at favorable rates and terms.

As a result, the Code characterizes the distribution of the subsidiary's shares to the parent's stockholders as a dividend, taxable to the extent of the parent's earnings and profits at the time of the distribution. This would certainly inhibit Morris, if he was the owner of a profitable C corporation. It would be less of a concern if his corporation was operating as an S corporation, although even then, he would have to be concerned about undistributed earnings and profits dating from before the S election.

Recognizing that not all transactions of this type are entered into to disguise the declaration of a dividend, the Code does allow spin-offs and split-offs to take place tax-free, under the limited circumstances described in Section 355. These circumstances track the scenarios concocted by Morris above, but are limited to circumstances in which both the parent and subsidiary will be conducting an active trade or business after the transaction. Moreover, each trade or business must have been conducted for a period exceeding five years prior to the distribution and cannot have been acquired in a taxable transaction during such time. Since Morris's corporation acquired the molding business only two years previously, and such transaction was not tax-free, the benefits of Section 355 are not available now. Short of another solution, it would appear that Morris will have to live with the bickering of Brad and Lisa for another three years.

SALE OF THE CORPORATION

Fortunately for Morris, another solution was not long in coming. Within months of the failure of his proposal to split up the company, Morris was approached by the president of a company in a related field, interested in purchasing Plant Supply. Such a transaction was very intriguing to Morris. He had worked very hard for many years and would not be adverse to an early retirement. A purchase such as this would relieve him of all his concerns over adequate liquidity for his estate and strategies for funding his retirement. He could take care of both Lisa and Victor with the cash he would receive, and both Lisa and Brad would be free to deal with the acquirer, regarding future employment and to collect on their equity.

However, Morris knew better than to get too excited over this prospect before consulting with his tax advisers. And his hesitance turned out to be justified. Unless a deal was appropriately structured, Morris was staring at a significant tax bite, both on the corporate and the stockholder levels.

Morris knew from his experience with the molding plant that a corporate acquisition can be structured in three basic ways: a merger, a sale of stock, and a purchase of assets. In a merger, the target corporation disappears into the acquirer by operation of law, and the former stockholders of the target receive consideration from the acquirer. In the sale of stock, the stockholders sell their shares directly to the acquiring corporation. In a sale of assets, the target sells its assets (and most of its liabilities) to the acquirer, and the proceeds of the sale are then distributed to the target's stockholders, through the liquidation of the target. The major theme of all three of these scenarios involves the acquirer forming a subsidiary corporation to act as the acquirer in the transaction.

In each case, the difference between the proceeds received by the target's stockholders and their basis in the target's stock would be taxable as capital gain. Morris was further informed that this tax at the stockholder level could be avoided, if these transactions qualified under the complex rules that define tax-free reorganizations. In each case, one of the requirements would be that the target stockholders receive stock of the acquirer rather than cash. As the acquirer in this case was closely held, and there was no market for its stock, Morris was determined to insist upon cash. He thus accepted the idea of paying tax on the stockholder level.

Morris was quite surprised, however, to learn that he might also be exposed to corporate tax on the growth in the corporation's assets over its basis in them, if they were deemed to have been sold as a result of the acquisition transaction. For one thing, he had been under the impression that a corporation was exempt from such tax, if it sold its assets as part of the liquidation process. He was disappointed to learn that this exemption was another victim of the repeal of the General Utilities doctrine in 1986. He was further disappointed, when reminded that even subchapter S corporations recognize all "built-in gain" that existed at the time of their subchapter S election, if their assets are sold within ten years after their change of tax status.

As a result of the above, Morris was determined to avoid structuring the sale of his corporation as a sale of its assets and liabilities, in order to avoid any tax on the corporate level. He was already determined not to structure it as a sale of stock by the target stockholders, because he was not entirely sure Brad could be trusted to sell his shares. If he could structure the transaction at the corporate level, he would not need Brad's minority vote to accomplish it. Thus, after intensive negotiations, he was pleased that the acquiring corporation had agreed to structure the acquisition as a merger between Plant Supply and a subsidiary of the acquirer (to be formed for the purpose of the transaction). All stockholders of Plant Supply would receive a cash-down payment and a five year promissory note from the parent acquirer in exchange for their stock.

Yet even this careful preparation and negotiation leaves Morris, Lisa, and Brad in jeopardy of unexpected tax exposure. To begin with, if the transaction remains as negotiated, the IRS will likely take the position that the assets of the target corporation have been sold to the acquirer, thus triggering tax at the corporate level. In addition, the target's stockholders will have to recognize, as proceeds of the sale of their stock, both the cash and the fair market value of the promissory notes, in the year of the transaction, even though they will receive payments on the notes over a period of five years.

Under the General Utilities doctrine, it was necessary for a corporation that was selling substantially all its assets, to adopt a "plan of liquidation" prior to entering into the sale agreement, in order to avoid taxation at the corporate level. The repeal of the doctrine may have left the impression that the adoption of such a liquidation plan is unnecessary, because the sale will be taxed at the corporate level in any event. Yet, the Code still requires such a liquidity plan, if the stockholders wish to recognize notes, received upon the dissolution of the target corporation, on the installment basis. Moreover, the liquidation of the corporation must be completed within twelve months of adoption of the liquidation plan.

Thus, Morris's best efforts may still have led to disaster. Fortunately, a small adjustment to the negotiated transaction can cure most of these problems. Through an example of corporate magic known as the "reverse triangular merger," the newly formed subsidiary of the acquirer may disappear into Morris's target corporation, but the target's stockholders can still be jettisoned for cash, leaving the acquirer as the parent. In such a transaction, the assets of the target have not been sold; they remain owned by the original corporation. Only the target's stockholders have changed. In effect,

EXHIBIT 10.9. A reverse triangular merger.

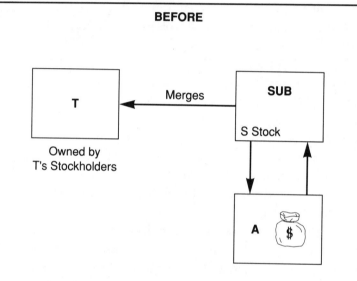

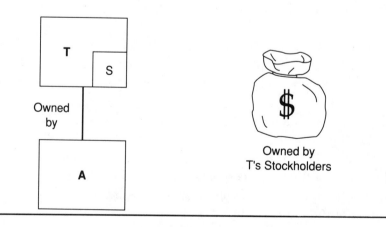

the parties have sold stock without the necessity of getting Brad's approval. Because the assets have not changed hands, there is no tax at the corporate level. In addition, since the target corporation has not liquidated, no plan of liquidation is required, and the target stockholders may elect installment treatment, as if they had sold their shares directly (Exhibit 10.9).

CONCLUSION

Perhaps no taxpayers will encounter quite as many cataclysmic tax decisions, in as short a time, as did Morris and Plant Supply. Yet, Morris's experience serves to illustrate that tax issues lurk in almost every major business decision made by a corporation's management. Many transactions can be structured to avoid unnecessary tax expense, if proper attention is paid to tax implications. To be unaware of these issues is to play the game without knowing the rules.

GLOSSARY

Adjusted Gross Income: The taxpayer's gross taxable income, diminished by certain deductions (mostly relating to the conduct of a business). This concept serves as a basis for calculating the deductibility of certain itemized deductions, such as medical expenses, casualty losses, and miscellaneous employee expenditures.

Alternative Minimum Tax: An alternative method of calculating a taxpayer's income tax liability, which results in higher tax if the taxpayer has made excessive use of certain tax deductions and tax credits.

Attribution Rules: The treatment, for certain purposes, of securities owned by relatives and affiliates of a taxpayer, as if they were owned by the taxpayer.

Basis: The cost to a taxpayer of a capital asset, adjusted upward by later capital investment in it and adjusted downward by various forms of return of capital such as depreciation. Used to calculate the taxpayer's gain or loss upon disposition of the asset.

Boot: Cash or property received in exchange for a capital asset which does not qualify as like-kind property.

Constructive Receipt: A doctrine requiring a taxpayer to pay income tax on income unconditionally available to the taxpayer, even though such income is not yet received.

Economic Benefit: A doctrine requiring a taxpayer to pay income tax on income not yet received, if the eventual receipt of such income has been collateralized in such a way as to confer a present economic benefit on the taxpayer.

Employee Stock Ownership Plan: A form of qualified deferred compensation plan in which the plan's assets are invested almost exclusively in the securities of the sponsoring employer.

General Utilities Doctrine: The doctrine (since repealed) exempting from income taxation at the corporate level, gain from the sale of a corporation's assets, if the sale was done in the context of a corporate liquidation and dissolution.

Like-Kind Exchange: The exemption from taxation of gain from the disposition of a business or investment-use capital asset, if such asset is exchanged for a similar asset.

Pass-Through Entity: A form of business entity, which is not itself subject to income taxation, but which, instead, passes all its taxable income and loss through to its owners' tax returns. Examples include subchapter S corporations and limited partnerships.

Passive Loss: Loss generated from a business activity in which the taxpayer does not materially participate. Such loss normally cannot be used to offset active or portfolio income, such as wages, salaries, bonuses, interest, and dividends.

Qualified Deferred Compensation Plans: Varieties of retirement plans, such as pension plans, profit-sharing plans and employee stock ownership plans, which, due to their having met various stringent requirements, provide employers with deductions for contributions, while deferring employee taxation on such contributions and the earnings therefrom, until funds are withdrawn from the plans.

Subchapter S Corporation: A corporation which, having met various definitional requirements, has elected not to be taxed on the corporate level and to have all its taxable income or loss pass through to its stockholders, in proportion to their stock holdings.

Tax Credit: Taxpayer expenditures, such as certain payments of foreign taxes or child-care expenses, which entitle the taxpayer to dollar-for-dollar reductions in his or her income tax liability. It is different from a tax deduction, which allows only a reduction in the taxpayer's taxable income.

Tax Preference: One of various tax deductions or tax credits which, when employed excessively by a taxpayer, may expose such taxpayer to the alternative minimum tax.

FOR FURTHER READING

Herwitz, David R., *Business Planning*, temporary 2nd ed. (Mineola, NY: The Foundation Press, 1984).

Painter, William H., *Business Planning*, 2nd ed. (St. Paul, MN: West Publishing Co., 1984).

Scholes, Myron S. and Mark A. Wolfson, *Taxes and Business Strategy* (Englewood Cliffs, NJ: Prentice-Hall, 1992).

Sommerfeld, Ray M. and Sally M. Jones, *Federal Taxes and Management Decisions* (Homewood, IL: Richard D. Irwin, Inc., 1991).

11

THE IMPACT OF GLOBALIZATION ON MANAGEMENT AND FINANCIAL REPORTING

Eugene E. Comiskey
Charles W. Mulford

EMERGENCE OF MANAGERIAL AND FINANCIAL REPORTING ISSUES AT SUCCESSIVE STAGES IN THE FIRM'S LIFE CYCLE

Fashionhouse Furniture started as a small Southern retailer of furniture acquired mainly in bordering southeastern states. With a growing level of both competition and affluence in its major market areas, Fashionhouse decided that its future lay in a niche strategy involving specialization in a high quality line of Scandinavian furniture. Its suppliers were mainly located in Denmark, and they followed the practice of billing Fashionhouse in the Danish krone. Title would typically pass to Fashionhouse when the goods were dropped on the dock in Copenhagen. Payment for the goods would normally be required within periods ranging from 30 to 90 days. As its business expanded and prospered, Fashionhouse became convinced that it needed to exercise greater control over its furniture supply. This was accomplished through the purchase if its principal Danish supplier. As this supplier also had a network of retail units in Denmark, the manufacturing operations in Denmark supplied both the local Danish market as well as the U.S. requirements of Fashionhouse.

More recently, Fashionhouse has been searching for ways to increase manufacturing efficiency and to lower product costs. It is contemplating relocation of part of its manufacturing activity to a country with an ample and low-cost supply of labor. However, it has noted that most such countries experience very high levels of inflation. Moreover, Fashionhouse has also become aware that, in some of the countries being considered, business practices are occasionally employed that are a source of concern to Fashionhouse management. In some cases, the practices raise issues that extend beyond simple ethical considerations. Fashionhouse management is still attempting to determine how to evaluate and deal with some of the identified managerial and financial issues associated with this contemplated move.

Each of the new stages in the evolution of the Fashionhouse strategy create new issues that have important implications for both management and financial reporting. The evolution from a strictly domestic operation to one involving the foreign purchase of goods thrusts Fashionhouse into the global marketplace with all of the attendant risks and rewards. The major issues implicit in the Fashionhouse scenario outlined above are identified below: They are discussed and illustrated in the balance of this chapter.

1. Fashionhouse incurs a foreign-currency obligation when it begins to acquire furniture from Danish suppliers. A decrease in the value of the dollar between purchase and payment date increases the dollars required to discharge the Danish krone obligation and results in a foreign currency transaction loss.

   Financial Reporting Issue: How are the foreign currency obligations recorded in the Fashionhouse books, which are maintained in U.S. dollars?

   Management Issue: Are there methods available to avoid the currency risk associated with foreign sourcing and should they be employed?

2. Purchase of the Danish supplier requires that it henceforth be consolidated into the financial statements of Fashionhouse and its U.S. operations.

   Financial Reporting Issues: (a) How are the Danish statements converted from the krone in order to consolidate them with the U.S. dollar statements of Fashionhouse? (b) What differences in accounting practices, if any, exist between Denmark and the U.S. and how will these differences be dealt with?

   Management Issues: (a) Is there currency risk associated with the Danish subsidiary comparable to that described above for foreign purchase transactions? Are there methods available to avoid the currency risk associated with ownership of a foreign subsidiary and should they be employed? (b) How will the financial aspects of the management of the Danish subsidiary be evaluated in view of (1) the availability of two different sets of financial statements, i.e., those expressed in kroner and those in U.S. dollars and (2) the fact that most of its sales are to its U.S. parent, i.e., Fashionhouse?

3. Relocation of manufacturing to a high inflation and low labor-cost country.

   Financial Reporting Issue: How will inflation impact upon the local country financial statements and their usefulness in evaluating the performance of the company and its management?

   Management Issues: (a) Are their special risks associated with location in a highly inflationary country and how can they be managed? (b) What are the restrictions on U.S. business practices related to dealing with the business and government entities in other countries?

For clarification, and to indicate their order in the subsequent discussion, the issues raised above are enumerated again below, without distinction this time, between those that are mainly financial reporting issues and those that are managerial issues:

1. Financial reporting of foreign-currency denominated transactions
2. Risk management alternatives for foreign-currency denominated transactions
3. Translation of the statements of foreign subsidiaries
4. Managing the currency risk of foreign subsidiaries
5. Differences in U.S. and foreign accounting policies
6. Evaluation of the performance of foreign subsidiaries and their management
7. Impact of inflation on the financial performance of foreign subsidiaries
8. U.S. government restrictions on business practices associated with foreign subsidiaries and governments

Financial Reporting of Foreign-Currency Denominated Transactions

When a U.S. company buys from or sells to a foreign firm, a key issue is the currency in which the transaction is to be denominated. In the case of Fashionhouse, its purchases from Danish suppliers were invoiced to Fashionhouse in the Danish krone. This creates the risk of a *foreign currency transaction loss* should the dollar fall in value (or a gain should the dollar increase) between the time that the furniture is dropped on the dock in Copenhagen and the required payment date. That is, the Fashionhouse *dollar* cost for the furniture will be more than the dollar obligation originally recorded. Fashionhouse would be said to have *liability exposure* in the Danish krone. If, instead, Fashionhouse had been invoiced in the U.S. dollar, then it would have no currency risk. Rather, its Danish supplier would bear the currency risk associated with having a claim, in the form of an account receivable, to U.S. dollars. If the dollar were to decrease in value, the Danish supplier would incur a foreign exchange translation loss (or a gain should the dollar increase). A summary of foreign currency gains and losses, by type of exposure, due to exchange rate movements follows.

Type of foreign currency exposure.

Movement of Foreign Currency	Asset	Liability
Appreciates	Gain	Loss
Depreciates	Loss	Gain

To illustrate the computational aspects of the above discussion, and the nature of exchange rates, assume that Fashionhouse recorded a 100,000 krone purchase when the exchange rate for the krone was $.178.[1] That is, it takes 17.8 cents to purchase one krone. The exchange rate is $.182 when the account payable from the purchase is paid.

Dollar amount of obligation at payment date, 100,000 × .182	$18,200
Dollar amount of obligation at purchase date, 100,000 × .178	17,800
Foreign currency transaction loss	$ 400

The dollar depreciated against the krone over a time period when Fashionhouse had an obligation in the krone. As a result, it took $400 more to discharge the obligation than the amount at which it was originally recorded by Fashionhouse.

If the foreign currency losses incurred were significant, it might prove difficult to pass on this increased cost to Fashionhouse customers, and it could cause its furniture to be somewhat less competitive than that offered by other U.S. retailers with domestic suppliers. Fashionhouse might attempt to avoid the currency risk by convincing its Danish suppliers to invoice it in dollars. However, this means that the suppliers would bear the currency risk. Experience indicates that suppliers would expect to be compensated for bearing this risk and would likely charge more for their products.[2] An alternative approach, the use of hedging transactions, is the more common method employed to manage the risk of foreign currency exposure.

RISK MANAGEMENT ALTERNATIVES FOR FOREIGN-CURRENCY DENOMINATED TRANSACTIONS[3]

Hedging is designed to protect the dollar value of a foreign-currency asset position or to hold constant the dollar burden of a foreign-currency liability. At the same time, the volatility of a firm's earnings stream is also reduced.

This is accomplished by maintaining an offsetting position that produces gains when the asset or liability position is incurring losses and vice versa. Such offsetting positions may be created as a result of arrangements involving internal offsetting balances of a firm, created through operational activities, or they may entail specialized external transactions with financial firms or markets.

Hedging with Internal Offsetting Balances

California First Bank (now Union Bank) provides an example of hedging with offsetting balances, created through internal operational activities. In its 1987 Annual Report (p. 20), California First reported that it had incurred a 20 million Swiss franc obligation. The dollar valuation of the obligation (number of dollars required to buy the francs to pay off the debt) increased to $15,494,000 at the end of 1987 from $12,281,000 at the end of 1986. However, the transaction loss that this liability growth produced was offset by a gain on an offsetting, i.e., hedge, transaction. As the 1987 Annual Report disclosed (p. 20): "A transaction has been entered into for the same foreign currency, with a similar term and principal amount which eliminates any significant earnings impact...." California First booked a Swiss franc loan (an asset balance), an operational activity for the Bank, to hedge its liability exposure in the Swiss franc. If the franc appreciates against the dollar, then the asset balance produces a gain that offsets a loss, due to expansion in the dollar valuation of the Swiss franc liability.

Like California First, Federal Express created a debt hedge, denominated in its case in the Japanese yen, through a creative structuring of business transactions with its own customers. Its 1989 Annual Report disclosed (p. 35) that, "To minimize foreign exchange risk on the term loan (payable in yen), the Company has commitments from certain Japanese customers to purchase a minimum level of freight services through 1993." As the yen appreciates, i.e., the dollar devalues against the yen, the dollar burden of the Federal Express yen debt increases, and a transaction loss results. However, this loss is offset by the increased dollar value of the stream of yen receipts from the freight service contracts. If the yen depreciates, a gain on the debt will be offset by losses on the service contracts.[4] A summary of the operation of this hedge is provided below.

Offsetting gains and losses produced by federal express hedge.

Movement of Foreign Currency	Change in Dollar Value of the Loan (Liability)	Change in Dollar Value of the Revenue (Asset)
Appreciates	Increases (loss)	Increases (gain)
Depreciates	Decreases (gain)	Decreases (loss)

California First and Federal Express both employed arrangements with their customers in order to create the above hedges. On occasion, a *natural* hedge will exist due to offsetting balances that result from ordinary business transactions, with no special arrangements being required. For example, Lyle Shipping, a Scottish firm, had borrowings in the U.S. dollar. An increase in the value of the dollar would increase the pounds required to repay Lyle's dollar debt and result in a transaction loss. However, because Lyle's ships were chartered at fixed rates in U.S. dollars, there would be an offsetting increase in the pound value of future lease receipts—a gain.[5] A similar *natural* hedge was generally held to exist for Australian mining companies that produce products priced in U.S. dollars. Should the U.S. dollar depreciate, the exposure to shrinkage in the Australian dollar value of receipts (U.S. dollar asset exposure) was offset by similar shrinkage in the Australian dollar value of U.S. dollar debt (U.S. dollar liability exposure).[6]

Fashionhouse would probably find it difficult to duplicate the hedging techniques used above by California First and Federal Express. Circumstances giving rise to a natural hedge, as in the case of Lyle Shipping, may or may not exist. It might have some capacity to hedge by applying the method of *leading and lagging*. This method involves matching the cash flows associated with foreign currency payables and receivables by speeding up or slowing down their payment or receipt. It is more likely that a specialized external transaction, such as an exchange-traded or privately negotiated hedging instrument would be used to hedge currency risks.

Hedging with Specialized External Transactions

The range of possibilities here include forward contracts to buy or sell currencies in the future at fixed exchange rates, foreign currency swaps, foreign currency futures, options, and options on futures. The forwards, swaps, and over-the-counter options have the advantage of making it possible to tailor the hedge to meet individual requirements in terms of amounts and dates. The exchange-traded futures and options have liquidity and a ready market but a limited number of dates and fixed size. Examples of the use of both classes of instruments, privately negotiated and exchange traded, are discussed below.

Forward Exchange Contracts

AMR Corporation issued $82.4 million of 9.2 percent foreign currency debt in 1982. Through forward exchange contracts, AMR contracted, at a fixed price, to buy the foreign currency required to pay off its foreign currency debt in the future. Initially, $26.2 million of the amount was hedged with a privately-negotiated forward exchange contract. In 1988, the remainder of the debt was hedged. AMR reported in its 1989 Annual Report (p. 51) that "The overall effective interest rate for all the notes during the term of the hedge contracts was 13.5%."

Prior to 1988, when all of the debt became hedged, AMR was still exposed to significant currency risk. AMR's 1987 income statement included $32 million of foreign currency exchange losses; an undisclosed portion of the loss no doubt resulted from the unhedged portion of the 9.2 percent notes. Notice that the effective interest cost increases from 9.2 percent to 13.5 percent as a result of the hedging. This cost increase results from the premium, over the spot value of the foreign currency, that AMR agreed to pay in order to fix the future cost of acquiring the foreign currency to repay the debt.[7] Through fully hedging its foreign-currency debt, AMR incurs a significant increase in overall borrowing cost, i.e., from 9.2 percent to 13.5 percent. However, it also avoids any future transaction losses should the dollar depreciate against the foreign currencies in which its debt is denominated.

Option Contracts

Like AMR, UAL Corporation also had foreign currency debt—in the Japanese yen, and it initially used forward contracts to hedge this exposure. However, during 1988, as its forward contracts expired, UAL switched to exchange-traded currency options. UAL reported (1988 Annual Report, p. 30) that the forward contracts "...were replaced by foreign currency call options. Expiration dates of the foreign currency options range from January 5, 1989 to April 12, 1989. UAL anticipates entering into new hedge arrangements as the previous arrangements expire."

A *call* option gives the holder the right to acquire foreign currency at a fixed price, termed the *strike* price. Should the yen appreciate in value, the option to purchase yen at a fixed price (the call) increases in value. This increase in value would offset, in whole or in part, the loss that results from the increasing number of dollars required to liquidate the yen debt.

If UAL had an asset denominated in yen instead of an obligation, a hedge employing currency options would be established by investing in yen *put* options. Should the yen appreciate in value, the option to sell yen at a fixed price (the put) would decline in value. This decline in value would offset, in whole or in part, the increasing value in dollars of the yen-denominated asset. A summary of the hedging performance of puts and calls with asset and liability exposure follows. Notice that in each case below, offsetting gains and losses result, the essence of a hedge, whether the foreign currency appreciates or depreciates.

Hedging performance of currency options.

Option Position	Movement of Foreign Currency			
	Appreciates		Depreciates	
	Asset Exposure			
	Option	Asset	Option	Asset
Put	Loss	Gain	Gain	Loss
	Liability Exposure			
	Option	Liability	Option	Liability
Call	Gain	Loss	Loss	Gain

Futures Contracts

Southmark Corporation's 1987 Annual Report (p. 40) reported the existence of notes payable denominated in the Swiss franc. Across 1987, the Swiss franc appreciated against the dollar and the dollar valuation of the notes went up sharply. However, Southmark reported (p. 41) that "Southmark uses Swiss franc futures contracts to hedge its exposure to foreign currency fluctuations with respect to its Swiss franc-denominated debt. The gains or losses from this activity are recognized concurrently with, and offset, the gains or losses from fluctuations in the Swiss franc debt liability."

The currency-futures contracts used by Southmark are an exchange-traded instrument (International Monetary Market at the Chicago Mercantile Exchange in the U.S.). The Swiss franc futures contract is for 125,000 francs. A margin deposit is required for each contract, and a roundtrip commission is charged for each contract. A futures contract can either be bought (a long position) or sold (a short position). A gain results if a futures contract is bought and the Swiss franc appreciates. If, initially, a contract is sold, then a loss results from appreciation of the franc. A short position creates a gain if the franc depreciates in value and the position is closed out by buying a contract to cover the short position, at the reduced value of the franc.

Southmark incurs a transaction loss on its Swiss franc notes if the franc appreciates against the dollar. It needs a position in the Swiss franc futures contract that will produce an offsetting gain in the event of appreciation in the franc. Therefore, Southmark would be taking a long position in the franc. If instead of notes payable, Southmark had notes receivable in the Swiss franc, then a short position would be taken in the futures contract. Depreciation of the franc would result in a transaction loss on the note receivable. An offsetting gain would be produced by a short position in the futures market. A falling franc means that the short position can be closed out at a price that is less than the price at which the contract was originally sold, when the short position was established.[8] A summary of hedges of both asset and liability exposure with futures positions is summarized below.

Hedging performance of currency futures.

	Movement of Foreign Currency			
	Appreciates		Depreciates	
	Asset Exposure			
Futures Position	**Futures**	**Asset**	**Futures**	**Asset**
Short	Loss	Gain	Gain	Loss
	Liability Exposure			
	Futures	**Liability**	**Futures**	**Liability**
Long	Gain	Loss	Loss	Gain

Observe above how the hedging positions, long versus short, are determined by whether an asset or liability position exists in the foreign currency. Where a liability position exists, then currency futures are sold; that is, a short position is established. The opposite position, long, is established when a hedge of an asset position is to be established. Consider the short position designed to hedge asset exposure. When the foreign currency appreciates, a gain results because an asset is held in an appreciating currency. The asset is worth more in dollars. However, a loss results on the short position. The short position must be closed out by buying the futures contract. Since the price of the futures contract goes up with the increase in the value of the foreign currency, it costs more to close the short position than the value of the futures contract sale when the hedge was established.

A summary of the appropriate hedging decisions based upon the type of exposure, i.e., asset or liability, and the instrument being used is provided below.

Foreign currency exposure and hedging decisions: Forwards, options, and futures.

Hedging Instrument	Exposure	
	Asset	**Liability**
Forward contract	Sell foreign currency	Buy foreign currency
Option	Buy put options	Buy call options
Future	Sell futures contract	Buy futures contracts

The above information indicates how a number of different instruments can be used to hedge currency risk. However, management must decide whether, and to what extent, to hedge foreign currency. All combinations are observed in practice, from the full hedging of all exposure to leaving all exposure unhedged. Some firms, Southmark was an example, actually create exposure (Southmark invested in futures contracts, long positions, that went beyond their hedging requirements), as a means of taking a position on the movement of exchange rates. The decision to hedge or not will be influenced by the attitude of management toward the risk associated with foreign currency exposure. A highly risk-averse management will be more inclined to hedge all currency-related risk. If hedging is instituted, the choice of instruments will bear on such matters as flexibility and the capacity to tailor the instruments to the hedging needs, liquidity of the instrument, documentation requirements, tax considerations, cost, etc. A more extensive consideration of these issues is beyond the scope of this treatment of transactional exposure and hedging strategies.[9]

TRANSLATION OF THE STATEMENTS OF FOREIGN SUBSIDIARIES

A number of new financial and managerial issues were added to the Fashionhouse agenda when it purchased its former Danish supplier. *Transactional* issues continue to the extent that (1) some of its purchases continue to be made from foreign suppliers and (2) the foreign suppliers continue to invoice Fashionhouse in the foreign currency. Since the Danish company is a wholly-owned subsidiary, the U.S. GAAP requires consolidation. However, the financial statements of the Danish subsidiary are in Danish kroner. This introduces a *translational* issue; the Danish subsidiary's statements must be restated into dollars before its consolidation with Fashionhouse, the parent, can take place. To the extent that the accounting practices used in preparing the subsidiary's statements, i.e., Danish GAAP, differ from those of its parent, i.e., U.S. GAAP, the Danish subsidiary's statements will also need to be restated to conform to the accounting practices of its parent. This latter issue is discussed in a subsequent section of the chapter.

All-Current Translation Procedure

The basic formula used to translate the statements of a foreign subsidiary is quite simple:

Foreign currency balance × exchange rate = translated balance.

In the typical case, under U.S. GAAP, balance sheet and income statement accounts are translated as follows:

1. All assets and liabilities in the balance sheet are translated at the exchange rate at the balance sheet date.

2. Paid-in-capital is translated at the exchange rate existing at the date of the share issue.
3. Income statement accounts are translated at the average exchange rate for the reporting period—unless revenues or expenses are distributed across the reporting period in a distinctly uneven manner.

The above procedure is normally referred to as the *all-current* method. The all-current procedure is illustrated below:

1. Foreign Sub is formed on January 1, 19X1 with an initial funding from a stock issue that netted 1,000 FC (FC = foreign currency units).
2. Selected exchange rates were:

	($ per FC)
At January 1, 19X1	$.58
Average for 19X1	$.62
At December 31, 19X1	$.66

The above rates indicate the amount of U.S. currency required to equal (buy) a single unit of the foreign currency. The increase in the rate across the year means that the dollar has lost value and that the foreign currency has appreciated.

3. The trial balances of Foreign Sub, both in FC and in U.S. dollars, and translated following the all-current rule, are given below. Those accounts that would have debit balances—assets and expenses—are grouped first, and those with credit balances—liabilities, equities, and revenues—are grouped second.

Trial balance in FC and translated US$ at December 31, 19X1.

Accounts	FC	Rate	US$
Cash	200	.66	132
Accounts receivable	100	.66	66
Inventory	300	.66	198
Property and equipment	2,000	.66	1,320
Cost of sales	600	.62	372
SG&A expense	100	.62	62
Tax provision	120	.62	74
Totals	3,420		2,224
Accounts payable	400	.66	264
Notes payable	1,020	.66	673
Common stock	1,000	.58	580
Retained earnings	0		0
Translation adjustment	0		87
Sales	1,000	.62	620
Totals	3,420		2,224

The two collections of account balances must balance. Notice that this is only achieved in the U.S. dollar trial balance through introduction of a translation adjustment account with a balance just sufficient to recreate this equality. Without the addition of the $87 translation adjustment account balance, the total of the *translated* assets and expenses, $2,224, exceeds the total of the *translated* liabilities, equity and sales accounts by $87. The translation adjustment can also be directly calculated as shown below.

Beginning net assets (assets minus liabilities)	FC1,000		
times change in exchange rate from 1/1/X1 to			
12/31/X1 (.66 − .58)		.08	$80
Net income		FC180	
times difference between end			
of year and average exchange rates (.66 − .62)		.04	7
Translation adjustment			$87

The $80 component represents the growth in the beginning net assets due to appreciation in the value of the sub's foreign currency. The $7 component is the additional net assets resulting from the net income for the year due to the translation of the income statement balances at the average rate for the year (.62) and balance sheet amounts at the end of year rate (.66). There is no retained earnings balance in the above trial balance because 19X1 is the first year of operations, and the net income for the year is added to retained earnings through the later process of closing the books.

The translated balance sheet and income statements are presented below. They can be constructed from the translated data above. The translation of the FC data is presented again in these statements to reinforce the nature of the translation process.

Income Statement	FC	Rate	US$
Sales	1,000	.62	620
Less cost of sales	600	.62	372
Gross margin	400		248
Less SG&A	100	.62	62
Pretax profit	300		186
Less tax provision	120	.62	74
Net income	180		112

In the absence of dividends, the retained earnings in the below balance sheet is simply the net income for the year. The translation adjustment of $87 is added to the shareholders's equity of the company. The net assets of Foreign Sub are in a currency that appreciated across the year against the dollar. This growth in net assets is captured in the process of translation and represented, again, by the translation adjustment balance. If, instead, FC had depreciated, then the translation adjustment would reduce shareholders's equity and appear as a deduction above. With the translation completed, the above statements would now be ready for consolidation with their U.S. parent—as long as they had initially been prepared in accordance with U.S. GAAP.

Balance Sheet	FC	Rate	US$
Cash	200	.66	132
Accounts receivable	100	.66	66
Inventory	300	.66	198
Property and equipment	2,000	.66	1,320
Total assets	2,600		1,716
Accounts payable	400	.66	264
Notes payable	1,020	.66	673
Common stock	1,000	.58	580
Translation adjustment			87
Retained earnings	180 (income statement)		112
Total liabilities & equity	2,600		1,716

In addition to the all-current translation procedure illustrated above, an alternative procedure referred to as remeasurement must be employed under certain conditions. Briefly summarized, this alternative procedure is applied when (1) the foreign subsidiary does not conduct its business in the local currency of its country of domicile or (2) the local country is a highly inflationary economy—cumulative inflation of approximately 100 percent over the most recent 3-year period.[10] In both of these cases, the local currency is not considered to be the firm's functional currency. The functional currency is "... the currency of the primary economic environment in which the entity operates ... in which an entity primarily generates and expends cash."[11] There are cases where the functional currency is not the local currency of the country in which the subsidiary operates. For example, The Leslie Fay Company reports in its 1989 Annual Report (p. 18) that its Hong Kong subsidiaries use the U.S. dollar as their functional currency: "The Company's Hong Kong subsidiaries are financed by U.S. dollar advances and all of their sales are to the parent. Accordingly, the functional currency ... is the U.S. dollar ..." In addition to an alternative translation rule, under this approach any translation gain or loss that emerges is included in computing net earnings for the year, and not added or subtracted directly to or from shareholders's equity.[12]

Temporal (Remeasurement) Translation Procedure

The process of remeasurement employs a translation rule that has traditionally been referred to as the temporal method. The method is summarized as follows:

1. All monetary assets (cash, accounts receivable, etc.) and monetary liabilities (accounts payable, accrued liabilities, notes payable, etc.) are translated at the current exchange rate.
2. All nonmonetary assets (inventory, plant and equipment, etc.) and liabilities (deferred income) are translated at historical exchange rates, i.e., rates existing at the transaction date when the asset or liability was recorded.
3. Shareholders's equity is translated just as under the all-current method.
4. Revenues and expenses are generally translated at the average exchange rate for the reporting period. Exceptions are expenses, such as cost of sales and depreciation, which are derived from assets translated at historical rates and, therefore, translated at these historical rates.

The above trial balance, income statement and balance sheet are retranslated to illustrate the impact of this alternative method (Exhibit 11.1). Two new assumptions are necessary: (1) Property and equipment was acquired when the exchange rate was $.58 and depreciation of 60FC was included in SG&A expense and (2) ending inventory was acquired at the average exchange rate of $.62.

Notice how this different translation rule dramatically changes net income. net income was $112 under the all-current method but only $27 under the temporal method. This difference of $85 can be explained as follows:

All-current method net income	$112
Reduction in SG&A, including depreciation, under temporal method (.62 − .60)	.02
Translation loss under temporal method	(87)
Temporal method net income	$ 27

A somewhat intuitive explanation of the *translation loss* is that it results from the change in balance-sheet exposure in going from the all-current to temporal method. In the all-current example all assets are translated using the current rate. Since assets exceed liabilities, the appreciation of the foreign currency resulted in growth (gain) in net assets. This gain of $87 was reported as a direct addition to shareholders's equity. Under the temporal method,

**EXHIBIT 11.1. Financial statements in FC and translated
US$ at December 31, 19X1, Trial balance.**

Accounts	FC	Rate	US$
Cash	200	.66	132
Accounts receivable	100	.66	66
Inventory	300	.62	186
Property and equipment	2,000	.58	1,160
Cost of sales	600	.62	372
SG&A expense	40	.62	25
Depreciation	60	.58	35
Tax provision	120	.62	74
Translation loss			87
Totals	3,420		2,137
Accounts payable	400	.66	264
Notes payable	1,020	.66	673
Common stock	1,000	.58	580
Retained earnings	0		0
Sales	1,000	.62	620
Totals	3,420		2,137

Income Statement	FC	Rate	US$
Sales	1,000	.62	620
Less cost of sales	600	.62	372
Gross margin	400		248
Less: SG&A	40	.62	25
Depreciation	60	.58	35
Translation loss		(above)	87
Pretax profit	300		101
Less tax provision	120	.62	74
Net income	180		27

Balance Sheet	FC	Rate	US$
Cash	200	.66	132
Accounts receivable	100	.66	66
Inventory	300	.62	186
Property & equipment	2,000	.58	1,160
Total assets	2,600		1,544
Accounts payable	400	.66	264
Notes payable	1,020	.66	673
Common stock	1,000	.58	580
Retained earnings	180	(income statement)	27
Total liabilities & equity	2,600		1,544

balance sheet exposure is the net of monetary assets and liabilities, i.e., those balance sheet accounts translated at the ever-changing current rate. None of the other (nonmonetary) balance sheet accounts creates exposure because their dollar value is frozen at fixed, historical exchange rates—for example, $.58 in the case of property and equipment. In the above example, monetary liabilities are well in excess of monetary assets and liability exposure results. Appreciation of the foreign currency increases the dollar valuation of this net liability exposure and produces a translation loss of $87, which is included in computing net income.

Just as with transaction exposure, management must decide whether or not to actively manage translation gains and losses. Central to this decision is whether these translation gains and losses are included in computing net income (temporal method) or reported as direct additions to or deductions from shareholders' equity (all-current method). This matter is discussed next.

MANAGING THE CURRENCY RISK OF FOREIGN SUBSIDIARIES

Many view the currency risk associated with the statements of foreign subsidiaries, *translational exposure,* to be significantly different from that associated with recording foreign denominated transaction balances, i.e., *transactional exposure.* Transactional exposure has the potential to expand or contract the cash flows associated with foreign currency asset and liability balances. However, in the case of translation exposure, there are no identifiable cash inflows or outflows associated with the translational gains or losses that result from application of either the all-current or temporal translation procedures. A recent study of both U.S. and U.K. multinationals by Collier, Davis, Coates and Longden, found that "...it was generally agreed that translation exposure management was a lesser concern" (than transaction exposure management).[13]

The absence of the same cash-flow risk in the case of translation leads some companies not to apply currency risk management methods to translation exposure. For example, in discussing the impact of translating statements of its foreign subsidiaries, Phillips Petroleum noted the following (1989 Annual Report, p. 29): "The company does not hedge these exposures because gains and losses... *do not impact cash flow.* The company hedges, where feasible and appropriate, foreign exposures *which impact cash flow*" (emphasis added).

Others do attempt to manage translation risk to avoid the potential negative impact on (1) earnings, in the case of subsidiaries whose statements are subject to remeasurement, i.e., temporal-method translation, and on (2) shareholders's equity in the case of application of the all-current method. A common view is that hedging activities are more likely to be applied if the temporal method is being used because resultant gains and losses are included in the income statement. The translation exposure of subsidiaries, translated using the all-current method, creates gains and losses that go directly to shareholders's equity; the absence of an impact on earnings makes it less necessary to hedge exposure in this case.

Prior to the issuance of Financial Accounting Standards Board (FASB) *Statement No. 52: Foreign Currency Translation,* all firms were required to use the temporal method and include all translation gains and losses in the computation of net income.[14] As a result, one would expect the hedging of translation exposure to decline after the issuance of Statement No. 52. Available evidence supports this view. For example, Houston and Mueller note, "In particular, firms which must no longer include all translation gains (losses) arising from their foreign operations in their income statements are more likely to have stopped or reduced hedging translation exposure."[15]

Where management decides to hedge *translation* exposure, all of the hedging vehicles discussed for use in hedging *transaction* exposure could also be used. Moreover, where the translation gains or losses are reported in shareholders's equity, the offsetting gains or losses on the hedging instrument are also included in shareholders's equity. For example, the 1990 Annual Report of Quaker Oats Company notes the following (p. 51): "Realized and unrealized gains and losses on foreign currency options, currency swaps, and forward contracts which are effective as net investment (i.e., translation) hedges are recognized in shareholders's equity."

In addition to the use of hedging instruments such as options, forwards, swaps and futures, hedging of translation exposure can involve transactions structured by the firm itself. Recall that California First hedged liability exposure in the Swiss franc by denominating one of its loans, an asset, in the Swiss franc. This technique is also used by some firms in hedging translation exposure. For example, DEKALB Genetics, with subsidiaries in Argentina, reported that "Significant interest expense was incurred in Argentina on a hedge loan . . . In anticipation of continued hyperinflation and significant devaluation of the austral (the Argentine currency), a portion of the austral-

Operation of the DEKALB genetics translation hedge.

Value of the Austral	Austral Receivables (Asset)	Austral Loan (Liability)
Appreciates	Gain	Loss
Depreciates	Loss	Gain

based receivables was hedged . . ." (1990 Annual Report, p. 21). Notice how the hedge was designed to function.

As sometimes happens with the best laid plans, the hedge did not work quite as planned. DEKALB reported that " . . . unexpected Argentine government action resulted in the austral strengthening against the dollar, while at the same time interest rates soared. Interest expense incurred because of this transaction was $4.1 million" (1990 Annual Report, p. 21). Offsetting gains and losses still would result from revaluation of both the asset and liability at the current rate for the austral. However, the cost of achieving the hedge was increased by unexpected movement in interest rates.

Bear in mind that because Argentina is a highly inflationary country per Statement 52, DEKALB's translation exposure is related to the relationship between its monetary assets and liabilities; these are the balances that create currency risk (exposure) because they must be translated at the current rate. If accounts receivable were the major monetary balance on the statements of the Argentine subsidiaries, then appreciation or depreciation of the austral could produce significant translation (remeasurement) gains or losses. These gains or losses would be included in DEKALB's consolidated earnings. Again, protection of earnings from a translation loss on the austral receivables was achieved by the hedge, but at the cost of more interest expense than DEKALB apparently anticipated.

Practice obviously varies with regard to whether or not to hedge either transaction or translation exposure and, if so, how to accomplish such hedging. Practice would seem to suggest the following ordering of management demand for hedging, from high to low:

1. To protect cash flow and earnings, both level and stability
2. To protect earnings, both level and stability
3. To protect shareholders's equity

In continuing to observe hedging motivated by (2) and (3), one should be aware of the significance of earnings and equity amounts without regard to the issue of cash flows. Two examples: 1. Management compensation is frequently based, at least in part, upon reported earnings. 2. Covenants in debt and loan agreements typically call for maintenance of specified amounts of shareholders's equity or ratios of debt to shareholders's equity. The Phillips Petroleum position, presented above, of hedging only where there is an impact on cash flows, is obviously not embraced by all companies. Differences in hedging practices are no doubt explained, in part, by different attitudes towards bearing currency risk, as well as such matters as compensation arrangements and features of debt agreements.

DIFFERENCES IN U.S. AND FOREIGN ACCOUNTING POLICIES

A variety of new financial, accounting, tax, and managerial issues faced Fashionhouse when it acquired its Danish subsidiary. The issues of statement translation and currency risk-management were discussed above. Recall that the requirement to consolidate the Danish subsidiary into the dollar-based statements of Fashionhouse, the parent, necessitates translation. In addition, to the extent that Danish accounting practices differ from those in the U.S., adjustments must be made so that the subsidiary's statements conform to U.S. GAAP.

International GAAP Differences and the IASC

A review of the financial statements of companies located in different countries would reveal many financial reporting examples that are in agreement and many that are in disagreement. In order to address the high level of disagreement found in accounting practices internationally, the International Accounting Standards Committee (IASC) was formed in 1973. The IASC, which was comprised initially of representatives from the leading professional accounting bodies of Australia, Canada, France, Germany, Japan, Mexico, The Netherlands, the United Kingdom and Ireland, and the United States, began working toward the harmonization of accounting standards internationally. Today, the IASC represents accounting bodies from over 70 countries. Each member body has agreed to work towards the compliance of accounting standards in their home countries with the standards issued by the IASC. In fact, a number of countries, such as India, Kuwait, Malaysia, Singapore, and Zimbabwe, either adopt IASC standards as their own generally accepted accounting principles or place heavy reliance on them in developing their own accounting standards. To date, 31 international accounting standards and several exposure drafts have been issued. Recently, the IASC issued a document that identifies major differences in international accounting practices and categorizes them in terms of their being, (a) a required or preferred treatment, (b) an allowed alternative treatment, or (c) an eliminated treatment.[16] The immediate goal of the proposal is to eliminate most of the choices in accounting treatment now available in standards issued by the IASC. The IASC enumerated the expected benefits of this harmonization in financial reporting as follows:[17]

1. Improve the quality of financial reporting
2. Make easier the comparison of the financial position, performance and changes in financial position of enterprises in different countries

3. Reduce the costs borne by multinational enterprises which presently have to comply with different national standards
4. Facilitate the mutual recognition of prospectuses for multinational securities offerings

A subsequent statement has reported responses to this initial document and outlined plans for implementation of some of the initial proposals and additional study for others.[18] The major approach to implementation of the IASC proposals is to incorporate those proposals on which agreement has been reached into revised International Accounting Standards. These standards, now numbering over 30, have been issued on a broad range of financial reporting topics.

Examples of some of the accounting treatments that would be *eliminated* under the IASC proposals follow:

1. Completed contract method for the recognition of revenue on construction contracts
2. Deferral of exchange gains and losses on long-term monetary items
3. Translation of statements of subsidiaries operating in hyperinflationary economies, without first applying price-level adjustments
4. Use of the closing (end of period) exchange rate to translate income statement balances
5. Maintenance of investment properties on the books without depreciation
6. Immediate deduction of goodwill against shareholders's equity

Examples of U.S. and international GAAP differences are provided in the next section along with illustrations of how international firms attempt to mitigate the impact of differences for U.S. statement users.

U.S. and International GAAP Differences

Reviewing the accounting policies of a selection of non-U.S. firms quickly highlights many GAAP differences. Some of the more prominent of these GAAP differences are presented in Exhibit 11.2.

With the continuing globalization of financial markets, international firms have become more sensitive to the analytical burdens that result from foreign/domestic GAAP differences. Further, the U.S. Securities and Exchange Commission requires that some foreign firms file reports that include schedules reconciling earnings under U.S. and foreign GAAP (the F-20 Report). An example of such disclosure is provided below from the PolyGram N.V. 1989 Annual Report (p. 34). As is typical of these disclosures, PolyGram

EXHIBIT 11.2.   Examples of international GAAP differences.

Accounting Policy	Country/Company	GAAP Difference
Software costs	England/Reuters Holdings	Reuters expenses all software costs; some would be capitalized under U.S. GAAP.
Tax accounting	Malaysia/United Malacca Rubber Estates, Berhad	Deferred taxes are not booked where timing differences are deferred indefinitely; deferred taxes are booked on all timing differences under U.S. GAAP.
Investments	Australia/BHP Limited	Equity accounting is not applied to investments in excess of 20% of voting shares; U.S. GAAP requires equity method.
Property	Hong Kong/ Hong Kong Telecommunications	Tangible fixed assets and property may be restated on the basis of appraised values; upward revaluations not permitted under U.S. GAAP.
Sale/leaseback gains	Netherlands/PolyGram	Gains on sale/leaseback transactions are recognized in the year of sale; such gains are deferred and amortized under U.S. GAAP.
Construction interest	Sweden/Pharmacia	Interest related to the construction of assets is expensed; U.S. GAAP requires capitalization and amortization.
Foreign currency gains and losses (on loans to acquire aircraft)	England/British Airways	Foreign exchange gains and losses are deducted from or added to the cost of aircraft; included in income as incurred under U.S. GAAP.
Unrealized foreign currency gains and losses	Germany/Continental Aktiengesellschaft	Losses are deducted from income but gains are not recorded; U.S. GAAP recognizes both in earnings.

provides reconciliations, from Dutch to U.S. GAAP, of both net income and shareholders's equity.

PolyGram commentary on the adjustments in the schedule below indicates the following:

1. Goodwill arising on the purchase of other companies is deducted immediately from shareholders's equity. U.S. GAAP requires that it be amortized over a period not to exceed 40 years. The income adjustment deducts the goodwill amortization that U.S. GAAP requires. The equity

(balance sheet) adjustment reflects addition of the unamortized goodwill back to the balance sheet—both the asset goodwill and shareholders's equity are increased.

2. The catalogue of recorded music is only amortized to the extent that the net present value of the expected income from the label is less than book value. PolyGram bases U.S. GAAP amortization on an expected life of 25 years. The adjustment suggests that U.S. amortization deducts the cost more rapidly than under PolyGram's application of Dutch GAAP.

3. The PolyGram translation procedure for subsidiaries in hyperinfla-tionary countries does not follow U.S. GAAP. PolyGram applies the cur-rent-rate method to the foreign-currency statements and includes any translation adjustment in shareholders's equity; U.S. GAAP calls for ap-plication of the temporal method and includes any translation gain or loss in earnings.

4. PolyGram included the gain on a 1984 sale and leaseback transaction in earnings of that year. U.S. GAAP calls for amortization of the gain into earnings over the term of the lease. The addition to U.S. GAAP-basis earnings reflects the impact of the amortization policy.

The reconciliations from Dutch to U.S. GAAP of 1989 net income and shareholders's equity for PolyGram, N.V. are provided below. Notice that PolyGram's earnings are lower when computed under U.S. GAAP. This is a fairly typical outcome when the results of foreign firms are restated in

Reconciliations from Dutch to U.S. GAAP of 1989 net income and shareholders' equity: PolyGram, N.V. (in millions of Netherlands guilders).

Net income as per consolidated statements of income of the PolyGram Group	333
Adjustments to reported income:	
a. Amortization of goodwill	(5)
b. Amortization of the catalogue of recorded music	(9)
c. Remeasurement of financial statements of entities in hyper-inflationary countries	(29)
d. Sale and leaseback transactions	2
Net income in accordance with U.S. GAAP	292
Shareholders' equity as per consolidated balance sheets of the PolyGram Group	937
Adjustments to reported equity:	
a. Goodwill	362
b. Catalogue of recorded music	(9)
c. Other provisions	(11)
Shareholders' equity in accordance with U.S. GAAP	1,279

accordance with U.S. GAAP, and it has raised questions about a possible negative impact on the international competitiveness of U.S. firms.

GAAP Differences and the Level Playing Field

Some argue that international competitiveness of a country can be impaired if earnings and financial position appear to be weaker under local GAAP versus that of its major competitor countries. That is, the playing field will not be level. As an example, in recent years concern about international GAAP differences have focused on acquisition (of other companies) accounting. A typical acquisition will include the payment of a premium, in some cases involving billions of dollars, for what is collectively termed *goodwill*. This amount consists of the difference between the purchase price and the current value of the net assets acquired, as in the following example:

Purchase price	$1,000
Current fair value of net assets acquired (assets − liabilities)	700
Goodwill	$ 300

It has been a common practice in other countries to deduct immediately, from shareholders's equity, the goodwill recorded in an acquisition. (This is one of the practices that the IASC hopes to see eliminated under its harmonization project discussed earlier.) U.S. GAAP requires that goodwill be amortized through the income statement. Notice in the PolyGram reconciliation above that U.S. GAAP earnings are lowered to adjust for the failure of PolyGram, under Dutch GAAP, to amortize goodwill.

If PolyGram and a U.S. firm were both bidding for the same company, PolyGram would forecast a stronger post-acquisition earnings picture. This results because PolyGram would deduct the goodwill directly from its current balance sheet, i.e., shareholders's equity, whereas the U.S. firm will take the charge through its future income statements. A further negative for a U.S. firm is the fact that the goodwill amortization is not deductible for tax purposes.

It could be argued, the tax issue aside, that the profit differences that result from the disparity in accounting for goodwill are purely cosmetic, and that they should not cause a U.S. bidder to be at a disadvantage in the acquisitions market. That is, the impact of the acquisition on the bidder's future cash flow should be the central issue. Differences in accounting policy should not have a direct impact on future cash flow. However, it should be noted that, cash flow aside, the reported numbers take on a significance in their own right, to the extent they are (1) a factor in determining managerial compensation or (2) are used by lenders to monitor compliance with debt agreements.

More recently, the international competitiveness issue has been raised with respect to a FASB proposal to require companies to apply accrual accounting to what are termed other postretirement benefits, mainly health and life insurance.[19] Some excerpts from a statement to the FASB by the Chief Financial Officer of Chrysler Corporation make the key points:[20]

> ...this higher cost recognition will depress reported profitability, and thereby ultimately discourage capital formation in job-creating enterprises in the U.S. There will be a powerful incentive to move our employment base to Canada, Europe, and Third World countries....
>
> Foreign based companies will not be forced to adopt your new rules—all other things being equal, a European or Japanese company will report a billion dollars more profit doing the same business as Chrysler. In that environment, we will simply be unable to compete fairly for investor capital. Ultimately, I believe you will have added to the trend of foreign ownership of our U.S. industrial base.

One can only hope for the success of the IASC program to increase international harmony in reporting practices, if the arguments concerning the anticompetitive potential of diversity in international GAAP are meritorious.

EVALUATION OF THE PERFORMANCE OF FOREIGN SUBSIDIARIES AND THEIR MANAGEMENT

With the acquisition of its Danish subsidiary, Fashionhouse is faced with the need to report and evaluate the performance of the subsidiary as an economic entity, as well as the performance of the subsidiary's management. The discussion here will focus only on those differences that result from the foreign character of the subsidiary. Aside from this, performance evaluation should be fundamentally the same as for a domestic firm. The fact that, after the translation process, financial statements are available in both the domestic currency—krone in the case of Fashionhouse—and the U.S. dollar is an important difference. Should performance of the subsidiary and its management be judged on the basis of krone or dollar results? Moreover, the earnings performance of the Fashionhouse subsidiary will be affected each year by (1) the movement of the krone against the dollar and (2) prices set (a transfer price) on the goods sold to Fashionhouse in the U.S.

Impact of Exchange Rate Movements on Performance Evaluation

A number of years ago, an issue arose concerning the incentive compensation of the manager of the Dutch subsidiary of a major U.S. heavy equipment manufacturer. A strong profit performance was produced in the European currency but the translated results were a loss (note: translation followed the temporal and not the all-current method). After lengthy consideration by senior management, a decision was made that no incentive compensation was to be awarded. Management held that failure of the Dutch subsidiary to earn a profit in dollars resulted in its making no contribution to the parent, which was striving to maximize the dollar earnings of the consolidated entity. The Dutch manager was not pleased.

A central precept of performance evaluation is that managers should only be held responsible for results that incorporate factors over which they exercise some significant influence. Depending upon the circumstances, this might mean that in judging the performance of a department foreman, the quantity of material used is considered controllable, but not its price. For performance evaluation purposes, the material used would be priced at some prearranged standard and not its actual cost. On the other hand, the vice president of manufacturing might well be held responsible for actual material cost, on the basis that he or she has been assigned responsibility for the price of material used, as well as its quantity. Applied to evaluating the performance of management of the foreign subsidiary, the concept of a *controllable* performance indicator would call for either (1) using the profit results from the foreign currency statements or (2) using the translated dollar earnings after adjustments designed to remove the effects of changes in the value of the dollar, i.e., the price of the dollar. As (1) involves no unique adjustments related to foreign subsidiary status, only (2) will be discussed further.

Consider below the translated income in foreign currency (FC) and the U.S. dollar used in the earlier all-current translation example—now designated Year 1.

Year 1 income statement.

	FC	Rate	US$
Sales	1,000	.62	620
Less cost of sales	600	.62	372
Gross margin	400		248
Less SG&A	100	.62	62
Pretax profit	300		186
Less tax provision	120	.62	74
Net income	180		112

Assume that in the following year, domestic results are as given below and the foreign currency has depreciated to an average rate of $.50 for the year (recall that income statement amounts are translated at the average rate under the all-current method). The new translation would now be as follows:

Year 2 income statement.

	FC	Rate	US$
Sales	1,200	.50	600
Less cost of sales	660	.50	330
Gross margin	540		270
Less SG&A	115	.50	58
Pretax profit	425		212
Less tax provision	128	.50	64
Net income	297		148

Net income in Year 2, in the foreign currency, increased by 65 percent over Year 1. However, the income improvement on a translated dollar basis was less than half this amount, only 32 percent. The impact of the change in exchange rates needs to be removed if the translated income statement is to be used to evaluate performance of the subsidiary's management—on the grounds that management has no control over exchange rates. Net income can be adjusted as follows:

Foreign currency Year 2 net income	FC297
Translate at Year 1 exchange rate	× .62
Year 2 net income at constant exchange rate	$184

The above adjustment holds constant the value of the foreign currency in measuring net income for purposes of performance evaluation. In judging the subsidiary itself as an economic unit, translation at the depreciated value of the foreign currency would remain appropriate. The value of the net income produced is indeed lower because of the currency depreciation in the subsidiary's home country.

There is ample evidence in U.S. annual reports of adjustments to control for the impact of exchange movements on performance. It is standard for the Management's Discussion and Analysis of Operations section, a Securities and Exchange Commission (SEC) requirement, to include commentary on the impact of exchange rate changes on sales and earnings. Two examples follow:

1989 Annual Report of American Brands, Inc. (p. 23)

1989 compared to 1988
Lower exchange rates, primarily for sterling, resulted in a $594.1 million decrease in revenues for 1989 based on the change in average translation rates from 1988 levels.

1988 compared to 1987
Higher exchange rates, primarily for sterling, resulted in a $567.7 million increase in revenues for 1988 based on the change in average translation rates from 1987 levels.

1989 Annual Report of AMP Incorporated (p. 18)

International sales to customers ... increased 13% in local currencies, but only 7% in U.S. dollars ... The exchange value of the U.S. dollar ... obviously is critical to the Company's reported results in U.S. dollars.

The exchange value of the U.S. dollar has some effect upon international margins, increasing or decreasing the cost of imports from other segments. ...

In addition to commentary by management, security analysts often comment on the implications of exchange rate changes for both the diagnosis of past performance and the implications for future performance. The selections below are from the December 21, 1990 issue of *The Value Line Investment Survey;* brief explanatory commentary follows each excerpt.[21]

Coherent, Inc. (p. 136)

The company's gross margin slipped back some two percentage points last year to 40%—as a result of ... 2) the adverse effect of currency rates on products manufactured in Europe for shipment to the United States ...

Explanatory comments: The dollar depreciated against European currencies during 1990. Unless prices in European currencies were lowered, the decline of the dollar increases the cost of these imported goods in dollars as shown in the example below:

End of the year:	1,000 German mark purchase @ $.68 =	$680
Beginning of the year:	1,000 German mark purchase @ $.58 =	580
Cost increase due to dollar depreciation		$100

Dionex Corporation (p. 137)

The weakening of U.S. currency is enhancing this company's revenues. Sales are growing in most international markets, partly due to the strengthening of foreign currencies against the dollar. In the September quarter, currency translation benefits accounted for $1.2 million of Dionex's sales, to say nothing of how much business might have been obtained because of the increased buying power of foreign funds. It should be noted, however, that most of the translation benefit does not flow through to pretax profit, and that Dionex's bottom line would probably have been little different without it.

Explanatory comments: The weakening of the dollar, and strengthening of the foreign currencies, increases sales in dollars in two ways: (a) U.S. goods now become cheaper to foreign customers and (b) translated sales also increase due to increased value of the foreign currencies. The claim that "most of the translation benefit does not flow through to pretax profit" probably is based upon the fact that translation of the foreign income statements at the higher foreign currency values increases expenses as well as revenues.

Fischer & Porter Company (p. 141)

Reported sales increases at Fischer & Porter are not as good as they look. The company does a lot of business through its foreign subsidiaries. Because of the weakness of the dollar, these sales translate into more U.S. currency. In the third quarter, for example, reported corporate sales of $62.2 million would have been about $57 million if exchange rates had been the same as a year earlier. In other words, sales declined about 3% in real terms. The currency gains don't bolster profits because expenses also gain in the translation.

Explanatory comments: (a) The issue of how profits are affected by strengthening foreign currencies is raised in the comments here just as in the Dionex case above. Notice that sales would have declined in the absence of the currency appreciation. This highlights a weakness in sales that might otherwise be masked by the impact of the sales growth due to the exchange rate effects. This decline in real sales is even more troublesome given that, other things being equal, the Fischer & Porter products are cheaper to foreign customers, in view of the appreciation in the value of their currencies. (b) Isolating the impact of exchange rate changes on sales growth helps to identify that growth that is more likely to be sustainable and is not due to currency appreciation, which cannot be counted on to be repeated in subsequent periods. (c) The characterization of the impact of currency gains on profits, i.e., that "The currency gains don't bolster profits..." is a bit of an overstatement. Consider the data below, which assume that sales and expenses in the FC are the same in Years 1 and 2:

FC Results		Year 1		Year 2	
		FX Rate	$ Results	FX Rate	$ Results
Sales	100	$.50	$50	$.60	$60
Expenses	80	$.50	40	$.60	48
Profit	20		$10		$12

Profits do not go up by the amount of the sales increase due to FC appreciation: 100FC ($.60 − $.50) = $10. This is because the translated value of expenses also go up due to the FC appreciation: 80FC × ($.60 − $.50) = $8. However, because sales exceed expenses, profits do increase by the percentage growth in the FC value: (.60 − .50)/.50 = 20 percent.

Nicolet Instrument Corporation (p. 148)

The weak dollar is aiding the income statement, but isn't vital to Nicolet's progress. Sales abroad are made in local currencies, and the equipment is produced in the United States. Thus, revenues and profits have benefited from this year's currency moves, but the benefit will disappear if the dollar strengthens. On the other hand, the sales strength is real because Nicolet has not been passing on benefits in the form of lower prices to foreign customers who are buying more units at the same prices as before.

Explanatory comments: Nicolet's circumstances are an interesting contrast to those of Fischer & Porter. A modified version of the translation example used for Fischer & Porter is used below to expand upon the Value Line commentary on Nicolet:

	FC Results		Year 1		Year 2	
	Year 1	Year 2	FX Rate	$ Results	FX Rate	$ Results
Sales	100	100	$.50	$50	$.60	$60
Expenses	80	67	$.50	40	$.60	40
Profit	20	23		$10		$20

Notice that the expenses, which for simplicity are *all* assumed to be associated with the cost of product imported from the U.S., are reduced due to appreciation of the FC. That is, the same quantity of goods can be purchased for less FC. What was purchased for FC 80 in Year 1 (translated value of $40) could be purchased for FC 67 in Year 2 (translated value of $40 also).

Profits doubled in the above example because the growth in translated sales revenue is not partially offset by growth in the translated value of expenses. Again, this is due to the fact that goods are imported from the U.S. and the appreciated FC reduces their cost.

The above discussion of actual case examples should make it clear that the evaluation of foreign subsidiaries and their management provides an added challenge, due to the many ways in which exchange rate movements can affect financial indicators of performance. Another factor that was implicit in much of the above discussion is the prices charged when goods are transferred between related foreign and domestic firms. This issue of *transfer pricing* is discussed next.

Transfer Pricing and the Multinational Firm

The prices at which goods or services are transferred between related entities, e.g., parents and subsidiaries and divisions of the same firm, are referred to as transfer prices. Transfer prices will be a major factor in determining the profits of the Fashionhouse Danish subsidiary because much of its product is shipped to its U.S. parent. As in the case above, the discussion here will focus on the dimensions of transfer pricing that are influenced by the foreign status of the subsidiary. The general topic of transfer pricing has been the subject of much debate over many years. A general agreement on the setting of transfer prices to both encourage optimal decision making and to facilitate performance evaluation has not, as yet, been reached.

Transfer prices are generally based upon cost, cost plus some markup, or some approximation of market. Firms with international operations typically disclose their method of pricing transfers of goods and services among different taxing jurisdictions—typically countries. Below are some recent examples of international transfer pricing policies.

1. *Market value*

Bausch & Lomb (1989 Annual Report, p. 45)

Inter-area sales to affiliates represent products which are transferred between geographic areas on a basis intended to reflect as nearly as possible the market value of the products.

2. *Cost plus a markup*

The Dow Chemical Company (1989 Annual Report, p. 54)

The Company conducts its worldwide operations through separate geographic area organizations which represent major markets or combinations of related markets. Transfers between areas are valued at cost plus a markup.

3. *Comparable to normal sales*

Western Digital Corporation (1990 Annual Report, p. 33)

Transfers between geographic areas are accounted for at prices comparable to normal sales through outside distributors.

4. *Reasonable profit*

Brown & Sharpe Manufacturing Company (1988 Annual Report, p. 9)

Transfers between geographic areas include a reasonable profit.

The levels at which transfer prices are set is influenced by a wide range of sometimes conflicting objectives. These include maximizing worldwide after-tax profits, maintaining flexibility in the repatriation of profits, encouraging optimal decision making by profit center management, providing profit data that are reliable indicators of managerial performance and entity profitability, building market share and maintaining competitiveness in foreign markets.[22]

Taxes and Transfer Pricing

A major issue surrounding transfer prices in the international arena is how they impact on the total tax burden of parent firms. Each of the above disclosures of transfer pricing policy conveys a sense of inherent reasonableness. The levels of income taxes and tariffs vary considerably across countries. For example the corporate income tax rate is 18 percent in Hong Kong and ranges up to 50 percent and more in such countries as Korea (including its defense surtax), Denmark, India, and Ireland. This opens up the possibility that transfer prices may be set in part to minimize a firm's worldwide tax bill. Establishing the reasonableness of international transfer prices is the principal defense against a charge of transfer price manipulation.

Ignoring other factors bearing on the setting of transfer prices, assume that the objective is to minimize worldwide income taxes. The income tax rate of the parent is 40 percent and that of the foreign subsidiary is 30 percent. Further, the parent is the manufacturer and transfers are made to the foreign subsidiary. The total cost of the product is $100 per unit and it can be sold by the foreign subsidiary at insignificant additional cost for an amount equal to $150. Therefore, the total worldwide profit to be recognized is $50.

While the parent would not have unlimited flexibility in setting the transfer price, the objective of tax minimization would call for recognizing as much of the profit as possible in the earnings of the subsidiary. This is accomplished by setting a relatively low transfer price as illustrated below.

International transfer pricing and tax minimization.

	Low Transfer Price		High Transfer Price	
Parent revenue	$110		$140	
Cost	100		100	
Pretax profit	10		40	
Income tax (40%)	4	$ 4	16	$16
Subsidiary revenue	150		150	
Cost (transfer price)	110		140	
Pretax profit	40		10	
Income tax (30%)	12	12	3	3
Worldwide tax		$16		$19
Composite tax rate		32%		38%
		($16/$50)		($19/$50)

The tax authorities of countries are well aware that multinationals have strong incentives to shift profits into low-rate countries. Recent years have seen governments increasingly willing to challenge tax computations which they believe are based upon the use of unreasonable transfer prices. Therefore, the example above simply shows how total tax payments can be influenced by alternative transfer prices. The degree of flexibility shown above may or may not be available.

Notice, in the above example, that no change in policy would result if the foreign country also had an ad valorem (imposed at a rate percent of value) tariff. Worldwide taxes would still be minimized by a low transfer price because this would also minimize the tariff. However, circumstances would differ if the parent's income tax rate were less than that of the subsidiary. Setting a high transfer price would cause more of the profit to be taxed at the lower income tax rate of the parent. However, this benefit is offset to some extent by the higher tariff in the subsidiary's country. The analysis would need to be extended to include tariffs in the total taxes to be minimized.

Other Influences on Transfer Pricing Policy and Potential Conflicts

Factors other than tax minimization also bear on the establishment of transfer prices. An effort to build market share or to respond to severe price competition might call for low transfer prices. At the same time this could be in conflict with a tax minimization objective, if income tax rates in the country receiving the transferred goods (transferee country) had higher rates than the country from which the transfer was made (transferor country).

Restrictions on the ability to repatriate profits are sometimes circumvented by charging high transfer prices. This effectively involves taking out profits, in the form of payments for goods shipped. There are, of course, some potential offsetting disadvantages to this practice:

1. Charging higher transfer prices will increase ad valorem tariffs.
2. Charging higher transfer prices will lower profits of the transferee firm and potentially present problems in the evaluation of the profit performance of the unit and its management.
3. Charging higher transfer prices might impair the competitive position of the transferee firm.
4. Charging higher transfer prices lowers profits of the transferee firm and could reduce its apparent financial strength in the eyes of lenders and other users of its financial statements.

The above enumeration of factors bearing on the setting of transfer prices is not exhaustive. However, it should be sufficient to highlight the inherent complexity of setting transfer prices. This complexity is magnified as the global reach of multinational firms extends into greater numbers of countries with wide variations in taxes, competitive conditions, business practices, types of governmental control, variability in exchange rates, and rates of inflation. This last factor is discussed next, in terms of its impact on measuring the financial performance of both domestic firms and foreign subsidiaries.

IMPACT OF INFLATION ON THE FINANCIAL PERFORMANCE OF FOREIGN SUBSIDIARIES

As Fashionhouse continued its evolution as a global firm it considered locating manufacturing capacity in countries with low labor costs. However, in many cases, high rates of inflation were linked to low labor costs. Judging performance in highly inflationary environments presents special problems. At some point, financial statements prepared from unadjusted (historical) cost data lose their ability to provide reasonable indicators of either the financial performance or status of firms. Several different approaches have been developed to adjust historical cost financial statements. The principal methods can be classified as involving either (1) general price level or (2) current cost adjustments. These two methods are illustrated below and are contrasted using the historical-cost statement as the baseline. To provide some useful background, commentary on the impact of inflation on financial performance, drawn from selected U.S. annual reports, is presented first.

Management Commentary on the Impact of and Response to Inflation

Management's Discussion and Analysis, a section of the annual report required by the SEC, often includes commentary on the impact of inflation on financial performance. This commentary provides useful insight into both management's assessment of the impact of inflation, as well as any company circumstances or actions taken, which mitigate inflation's negative effects. A series of these comments are presented below, along with explanatory comments where appropriate.

1. *Selling price adjustments and cost efficiencies.*

Campbell Soup Company (1990 Annual Report, p. 17)

The Company attempts to mitigate the effects of inflation on sales and earnings by appropriately increasing selling prices and aggressively pursuing an ongoing cost improvement effort...

2. *Selling price adjustments, cost efficiencies and use of LIFO.*

Brush Wellman, Inc. (1989 Annual Report, p. 29)

New products, process improvements and product pricing policies have generally enabled the Company to offset the impact of inflation. The Company employs the last-in, first-out (LIFO) inventory valuation method to more closely match current costs with revenues.

Explanatory comment: LIFO deducts the cost of the most recently acquired goods in computing earnings. These are the highest costs in a period of inflation; therefore, LIFO results in lower reported earnings. This reduces tax payments on what could be considered illusory profits if some other inventory valuation method such as FIFO were used.

3. *Selling price adjustments, cost efficiencies, use of LIFO, use of accelerated depreciation and depreciation approximating current costs, due to relatively new assets.*

Baldor Electric Company (1989 Annual Report, p. 11)

Cost increases were offset by productivity improvements... and price increases during 1988 and 1989... Most of Baldor's machinery has been acquired in recent years; therefore depreciation expense approximates the effect of current costs. Also, we utilize primarily the LIFO valuation method for inventory which more closely matches current costs with current revenues...

Newport Corporation (1990 Annual Report, p. 16)

Additionally, the Company depreciates its equipment using accelerated depreciation methods which lessen the impact of expensing historical dollars of depreciation when compared to fixed asset replacement cost...

Explanatory comment: Both Baldor's and Newport's depreciation expenses have the same character as LIFO-based production costs—i.e., approximating the current cost of machinery. As with LIFO, depreciation, in this circumstance, avoids profit overstatements that would result if depreciation were mainly comprised of the costs of machinery, acquired years earlier at older, lower costs.

4. *Price escalation provisions.*

Overseas Shipholding Group, Inc. (1989 Annual Report, p. 25)

In some cases, these (cost) increases were offset by... charter escalation provisions.

AMP Incorporated (1989 Annual Report, pp. 20–21)

Gold and plastic resins... are also subject to wide price fluctuations, particularly gold. Sales contracts frequently allow for price adjustments on the gold content of the Company's product.

Management concerns, revealed above, center on avoiding an erosion of profits due to inflation's impact on both costs and revenues. Techniques employed included raising prices on a timely basis, lowering costs through operating efficiencies, and, though less common, achieving some price protection through the use of escalation features in pricing arrangements. Protection from cost inflation of *commodities* is often achieved through the use of the same types of hedging vehicles employed to avoid the cost increases created by exchange rate movements. An example: "Genetics has contractual commitments with seed growers for payments based on Chicago Board of Trade futures prices. These payments are hedged by using Chicago Board of Trade futures and options contracts" (DEKALB Genetics, 1990 Annual Report, p. 29). Public transit systems and airlines also seek cost protection by investing in petroleum futures. Should petroleum prices increase, the gain on futures contracts will offset the increased cost of petroleum products, used by the transit systems and airlines.

The other major concern revealed in the above selections was that profits may be overstated in periods of significant inflation. The most commonly cited solution was use of the LIFO method of inventory valuation. This ensures that the cost of inventory items deducted from revenues approximates their replacement cost. Profit overstatement was also avoided if depreciable assets were relatively new, so that the depreciation expense deducted from revenues was much closer to replacement cost, than if depreciation were comprised mainly of the lower costs of older assets.

The use of LIFO and the reliance upon relatively new depreciable assets to cause expenses to approximate current (replacement) costs suffers from (1) only representing a partial adjustment for the impact of inflation and (2) not being uniformly available or applicable to all firms. That is, some firms may find it disadvantageous from a tax standpoint to use LIFO, and others may not be endowed with mainly new depreciable assets. Price-level adjusted profit calculations are applied uniformly to historical-cost statements, regardless of the accounting policies applied, e.g., LIFO versus FIFO, or the vintage of fixed assets.

Price-Level Adjusted Performance Measurement[23]

Beginning in 1979, certain large U.S. firms were required to provide supplemental information on the impact of inflation on financial performance.[24] The primary new disclosures called for earnings computed on both a constant-dollar and a current-cost basis. The *constant-dollar* method retains historical cost as the basis of financial measurement. However, it does make selected restatements, so that all financial statement balances are presented in units of the same purchasing power, i.e., expressed in the same price index. The *current-cost* method replaces historical-cost balances with current (replacement) costs as the basis for financial statement measurement. An example of disclosure of adjusted profit presentations is provided in the Tiger International 1980 Annual Report (p. 39). Excerpts from the Tiger International presentation are provided below.

Tiger International, Inc. and Subsidiaries' statement of income adjusted for changing prices for the year ended December 31, 1980 (in thousands).

	Historical Financials	Constant Dollar	Current Cost
Revenues	$1,562,270	$1,562,270	$1,562,270
Cost and expenses			
Cost of operations	1,104,672	1,109,324	1,108,673
Selling, general & admin.	139,462	139,462	139,462
Depreciation and amortization	118,332	171,096	151,924
Interest, net	140,929	140,929	140,929
Income tax provision	16,500	16,500	16,500
	$1,519,895	$1,577,311	$1,557,488
Net income	$ 42,375	$ (15,041)	$ 4,782

The major message conveyed by the above schedule is that a significant level of historical-cost profits is almost eliminated, when current-cost adjustments are applied, and that profit actually turns into a loss under the constant-dollar alternative. The investment of purchasing power, represented by the constant-dollar amount of expenses, exceeds that recovered, as represented by Tiger's constant-dollar revenues. Closer study of the above data is necessary to understand the reasons behind these quite different messages.

The revenues in each of the three earnings statements are measured in the average price level for the year. The index used is the *Consumer Price Index for All Urban Consumers*. Tiger's revenues are earned fairly evenly across the year, and therefore, the revenues in the historical (as reported) income statement are already expressed in average prices for the year. Accordingly, the same revenue amount can be used in both the constant-dollar and current-cost statements. The same applies to the amounts for selling, general and administrative; interest, net; and the income tax provision.

Modest adjustments were made to cost of operations in the historical income statement to convert them to constant dollar and current cost, respectively. The constant-dollar adjustment is made by multiplying the historical cost of operations by a ratio of price indices. The index in the numerator is the average price index for the current year, and in the denominator, it is the value of the index, at the date closest to the date on which the expense was incurred. To illustrate, assume that a $1,000 expense was recorded on January 1, 19X1 when the price index was 100; the average price index for 19X1 was 110. Adjustment to constant dollars is:

$$\$1,000 \times (110/100) = \$1,110$$

The same methodology is applied in adjusting historical cost of operations to current cost amounts. The difference is that indices of specific replacement cost, or alternative measures of replacement cost, are used in place of a general price index.

Tiger reported that increases in inventory costs, included in cost of operations, accounted for the adjustments to historical cost of operations. In general, adjustments of historical cost of sales will be small if the LIFO inventory valuation method is used; the LIFO cost flow ensures that cost of sales already approximates current costs. Adjustments will generally be greater where the FIFO or average-cost methods are in use.

Impact of Differences in General and Specific Price Index Movements

The major Tiger cost adjustment was to depreciation and amortization. Depreciation and amortization represent the conversion to expense, of asset balances carried on the balance sheet. In many cases, these balances were recorded years earlier, when the price indices were at far lower values. Notice that the percentage increase in the constant-dollar and current-cost depreciation and amortization, over the historical-cost amount, is 45 percent and 29 percent, respectively. Tiger's disclosures explain the reason for the differences: "Depreciation expense...(is) greater when adjusted for general inflation than when adjusted for changes in specific prices. The difference reflects the Consumer Price Index (general inflation) rising faster than the increase of costs over the last several years of the type of property, plant and equipment used in the Company's various businesses..." (1980 Annual Report, p. 39).

Impact of Monetary Balances on Adjusted Results

In addition to the above two inflation-adjusted income presentations, Tiger provided additional income data because it did not feel that the required disclosures, adjusting mainly depreciation and cost of sales, were adequate. These adjustments, added to the above display, are shown below.

Tiger International, Inc. and Subsidiaries.

	Historical Financials	Constant Dollar	Current Cost
Net income	$42,375	$(15,041)	$ 4,782
Decrease in depreciation and interest expense...from decline in purchasing power of net monetary liabilities		82,195	82,195
Net income adjusted for decrease in depreciation and interest expense	$42,375	$ 67,154	$86,977

Tiger's final adjusted net incomes tell a totally different story than that of the initial display. The new income element results from the impact of changes in the price level, on the purchasing power of monetary assets and liabilities. Tiger explains the impact of price changes on monetary balances as follows (1980 Annual Report, p. 40):

A monetary asset represents money or a claim to receive money without reference to future changes in prices. Similarly a monetary liability represents an obligation to pay a sum of money which is fixed or determinable without reference to changes in future prices. Holding a monetary asset during periods of inflation results in a decline in the value of the asset since the dollar loses purchasing power when it is held. Conversely, holders of monetary liabilities benefit during inflationary periods because less purchasing power is required to satisfy future obligations when they can be paid with less valuable dollars.

Under this reasoning, Tiger earned an unrealized purchasing-power gain because its monetary liabilities exceeded its monetary assets. The impact of both inflation and deflation on purchasing-power gains, under conditions of both monetary assets exceeding monetary liabilities (net asset exposure) and monetary liabilities exceeding monetary assets (net liability exposure), are summarized below.

Purchasing power gains and losses and net monetary position.

	Net Monetary Position	
Price Movement	**Asset**	**Liability**
Inflation	Loss	Gain
Deflation	Gain	Loss

Tiger treats the purchasing power gain as an adjustment to depreciation and interest expense, based upon the following reasoning (1980 Annual Report, p. 40): "Because Tiger finances substantially all of its fixed assets with long-term debt, it effectively hedges against the impact of inflation on depreciation and interest expense." Tiger's liability exposure serves as a hedge because it produces a gain under inflationary conditions, to offset increases in the cost of asset replacement and interest expense, which go hand-in-hand with inflation. The GAAP requirement followed by Tiger, FASB Statement No. 33, did call for computation and disclosure of the purchasing power gain or loss.[25] However, it did not permit its inclusion in income adjusted for changing prices.

The price-level adjusted reporting illustrated above proved to be a very controversial requirement. It proved difficult to document that the data were used by creditors or investors, or that they aided analysis and decision making in any significant way. In 1986, *FASB Statement No. 89: Financial Reporting and Changing Prices*, was issued, which eliminated mandatory disclosure of price-level adjusted data.[26] The statement did, however, encourage continued disclosure on a voluntary basis.

Like the Americans, the British, who debated for years whether to require price-level adjusted data, finally required current-cost data to be provided. Then, in response to much the same pressure as in the U.S., they abandoned the requirement.[27] Disclosure of price-level adjusted data continues to be a requirement in countries that have been subject to high and sustained inflation, e.g., Argentina, Brazil, Chile, and Mexico. However, deciding when and how to adjust financial data for the impact of changing prices remains a contentious and unresolved issue.

U.S. GOVERNMENT RESTRICTIONS
ON BUSINESS PRACTICES ASSOCIATED WITH
FOREIGN SUBSIDIARIES AND GOVERNMENTS[28]

The last issue raised in the opening Fashionhouse scenario dealt with U.S. governmental restrictions on business practices associated with overseas operations. Recall that, in reviewing the possibility of relocation of manufacturing to a high inflation/low labor-cost country, Fashionhouse management became aware of potential ethical or legal issues.

In recent years, the U.S. government became concerned with the practices sometimes followed by U.S. firms, when doing business overseas. Of special concern, were payments to foreign government officials made to obtain business. From hearings over a number of years, which focused on such incidents, a recurring theme emerged: In addition to the fact that such payments did indeed take place, companies were unaware that such payments were being made.

The U.S. Congress addressed the issue of controlling what it saw to be improper activities, by passing the *Foreign Corrupt Practices Act of 1977*. The key features of this law were:

1. The prohibition of bribery of foreign governmental or political officials in order to promote business.
2. The requirement that firms (a) keep accurate and detailed records of the company financial activities and (b) maintain a system of internal accounting controls sufficient to provide reasonable assurance that transactions are properly authorized, recorded, and accounted for.

The above requirements are incorporated as amendments to Section 13(b) of the Securities Exchange Act of 1934, and they apply to all publicly held companies. The recordkeeping and internal control features of the Act were a response to claims that companies had been unaware of bribery payments, because their internal control systems had failed to detect or prevent them.

In a report addressed to the SEC, the National Commission on Fraudulent Financial Reporting, made the following recommendation:

> All public companies should be required by SEC rule to include in their annual reports to stockholders management reports signed by the chief executive officer and the chief accounting officer and/or the chief financial officer. The management report should acknowledge management's responsibilities for the financial statements and internal control, discuss how these responsibilities were fulfilled, and provide management's assessment of the effectiveness of the company's internal controls, (p. 44).[29]

While the SEC has not adopted the Commission's recommendation, many companies have elected to provide voluntarily a report of management's responsibilities.[30] And while the precise title of the report may vary, representative titles include, Report of Management Responsibility for Financial Statements and Internal Control and Financial Reporting Responsibility. Although the precise language of the report differs from company to company, the relevant section from the 1990 Annual Report (p. 19) of General Mills is representative:

> Management has established a system of internal controls that provides reasonable assurance that, in all material respects, assets are maintained and accounted for in accordance with management's authorization, and transactions are recorded accurately on our books. Our internal controls provide for appropriate separation of duties and responsibilities, and there are documented policies regarding utilization of company assets and proper financial reporting. These formally stated and regularly communicated policies demand high ethical conduct from all employees.

The precise meaning of the provisions of the Act continue to evolve. However, in considering expansion into a country, where improper payments may have a long and durable tradition, Fashionhouse must pay special attention to the existence and requirements of the Foreign Corrupt Practices Act.

SUMMARY

The evolution of Fashionhouse from a purely domestic firm to a truly global entity continues to confront it with new and increasingly complex problems of accounting, finance, and management. This chapter has followed Fashionhouse through this evolution and has attempted to help the reader become aware of the problems faced and how they might be addressed. The range of issues addressed is broad and increasingly complex. It has not been possible, nor would it have been appropriate in a volume such as this, to deal with all aspects of every issue raised. The reader should consult the many books and articles cited throughout the chapter for additional background reading.

GLOSSARY

All-Current Method: A method for translating foreign currency financial statements whereby all assets and liabilities are translated at the current (balance sheet date) exchange rate, contributed capital accounts are translated at historical exchange rates (rates in existence when the account balances first arose), and all revenues and expenses are translated at the average exchange rate in existence during the reporting period. Translation differences (foreign-exchange gains and losses) resulting from fluctuating exchange rates are accumulated and reported as a separate component of stockholders's equity.

Constant-Dollar Method: A method of inflation accounting whereby accounts, which are measured according to historical cost accounting principles, are expressed in units of the same purchasing power, i.e., using the same price index.

Current-Cost Method: A method of inflation accounting, which replaces historical cost accounting principles with current (replacement) cost, as the basis for financial statement measurement.

Foreign Corrupt Practices Act of 1977: An act of Congress, which, among other things, explicitly prohibits the bribery of foreign government or political officials and requires firms to keep accurate and detailed records of company financial activities and maintain an adequate system of internal controls.

Foreign Currency Transaction: Any transaction (e.g., the sale or purchase of inventory, the lending or borrowing of money) that creates a balance-sheet account that is denominated in a foreign currency. Examples include foreign-currency denominated receivables and loans, and foreign-currency denominated payables and long-term debt.

Forward Exchange Contract: A privately-negotiated agreement to purchase foreign currency for future receipt or to sell foreign currency for future delivery. The amount of foreign currency, the rate of exchange, and the future date of settlement are established at the time the contract is made.

Futures Contract: An exchange-traded instrument with a preestablished expiration date, whose market value is linked to the relative exchange rates between two currencies. A futures contract can be purchased (a long position), resulting in a gain, if the foreign currency appreciates, or sold (a short position), resulting in a gain, if the foreign currency depreciates.

Hedging: Steps taken to protect the dollar value of a foreign-currency asset or to hold constant the dollar burden of a foreign-currency liability, in the presence of fluctuating exchange rates, by maintaining offsetting foreign-currency positions.

International Accounting Standards Committee (IASC): An organization representing accounting bodies from over 70 countries whose mission is to harmonize accounting standards internationally.

Leading and Lagging: A foreign-currency hedging technique, which involves the matching of cash flows associated with foreign currency payables and receivables, by speeding up or slowing down their payment or receipt.

Monetary Assets and Liabilities: Assets and liabilities which represent a fixed number of monetary units. Monetary assets include cash and accounts receivable; monetary liabilities include accounts and notes payable. During inflationary periods, monetary assets (liabilities) result in purchasing power gains (losses), respectively.

Option Contract: The right, but not the obligation, to purchase foreign currency at a fixed price (a call option), or the right, but not the obligation, to sell foreign currency at a fixed price (a put option).

Temporal (Remeasurement) Translation Procedure: A method for translating foreign currency financial statements, whereby monetary assets and liabilities are translated at the current (balance sheet date) exchange rate, other assets, liabilities, and contributed capital accounts are translated at historical exchange rates (rates in existence when the account balances first arose), cost of goods sold and depreciation expense are translated at the rates in existence when the related inventory or fixed asset was purchased, and revenues and other expenses are translated at the average exchange rate in existence during the reporting period. Translation differences (foreign-exchange gains and losses) resulting from fluctuating exchange rates are reported as a component of net income.

Transfer Pricing: Prices charged when goods or services are transferred between related firms.

Translation of Foreign Currency Financial Statements: The conversion of the financial statements of a foreign entity (typically, a subsidiary) from that entity's local (foreign) currency to the reporting currency (typically, the parent company's currency).

FOR ADDITIONAL READING

General

Arpan, J. and L. Radebaugh, *International Accounting and Multinational Enterprises* (New York: Warren, Gorham & Lamont, 1981).

Beaver, W. and W. Landsman, *Incremental Information Content of Statement 33 Disclosures* (Stamford, CT: FASB, 1983).

Choi, F. and G. Mueller, *An Introduction to Multinational Accounting* (Englewood Cliffs, NJ: Prentice-Hall, Inc., 1978).

Collier, P. Davis, E.J. Coates, and S. Longden, "The Management of Currency Risk: Case Studies of U.S. and U.K. Multinationals," *Accounting and Business Research* (Summer, 1990).

Comiskey, E. and C. Mulford, "Risks of Foreign Currency Transactions: A Guide for Loan Officers," *Commercial Lending Review* (Summer, 1990).

Financial Accounting Standards Board, *Proposed Statement of Financial Accounting Standards: Employers' Accounting for Postretirement Benefits Other Than Pensions* (Stamford, CT: FASB, 1989).

———, *Statement of Financial Accounting Standards Number 8: Accounting for the Translation of Foreign Currency Transactions and Foreign Financial Statements* (Stamford, CT: FASB, 1975).

———, *Statement of Financial Accounting Standards Number 33: Financial Reporting and Changing Prices* (Stamford, CT: FASB, 1979).

———, *Statement of Financial Accounting Standards No. 52: Foreign Currency Translation* (Stamford, CT: FASB, 1981).

———, *Statement of Financial Accounting Standards Number 89: Financial Reporting and Changing Prices* (Stamford, CT: FASB, 1986).

Flicker, S. and D. Bline, "Managing Foreign Currency Exchange Risk," *Journal of Accountancy* (August, 1990).

Frishkoff, P., *Financial Reporting and Changing Prices: A Review of Empirical Research* (Stamford, CT: FASB, 1982).

Holmes, G., ed., "FX Translation—Lyle Shipping's Losses," *Accountancy* (December, 1984).

Houston, C. and G. Mueller, "Foreign Exchange Rate Hedging and SFAS No. 52—Relatives or Strangers?" *Accounting Horizons* (December, 1988).

Institute of Chartered Accountants in England and Wales, Accounting Standards Committee, *Statement of Standard Accounting Practice No. 16: Current Cost Accounting* (London: Institute of Chartered Accountants in England and Wales, 1980).

International Accounting Standards Committee, *Exposure Draft 32: Comparability of Financial Statements* (London: IASC, 1989).

———, *Statement of Intent: Comparability of Financial Statements* (London: IASC, 1990).

Largay, J. and J. Livingstone, *Accounting for Changing Prices: Replacement Cost and General Price Level Adjustments* (Santa Barbara, CA: Wiley/Hamilton, 1976).

Lewent, J. and A. Kearney, "Identifying, Measuring and Hedging Currency Risk at Merck," *Journal of Applied Corporate Finance* (Winter, 1990).

Maloney, P. "Managing Currency Exposure: The Case of Western Mining," *Journal of Applied Corporate Finance* (Winter, 1990).

Miller, Jr., R., *Prepared Remarks to the Financial Accounting Standards Board* (Washington, DC: November 3, 1989).

National Commission on Fraudulent Financial Reporting, *Report of the National Commission on Fraudulent Financial Reporting* (Washington, DC, 1987).

Schiff, J. and C. May, "What Is Internal Control? Who Owns It?" *Management Accounting* (November, 1990).

Skousen, K., *An Introduction to the SEC*, 4th ed. (Cincinnati, OH: South-Western Publishing Company, 1987).

Value Line Publishing, Inc., *The Value Line Investment Survey: Ratings & Reports* (New York: Value Line Publishing, Inc., 1990).

Annual Reports to Shareholders

American Brands, Inc., *Annual Report to Shareholders* (1989).

AMP, Inc., *Annual Report to Shareholders* (1989).

AMR Corporation, *Annual Report to Shareholders* (1989).

Baldor Electric Company, *Annual Report to Shareholders* (1989).

Bausch & Lomb, Inc., *Annual Report to Shareholders* (1989).

Brown & Sharpe Manufacturing Company, *Annual Report to Shareholders* (1988).

Brush Wellman, Inc., *Annual Report to Shareholders* (1989).

California First Bank, *Annual Report to Shareholders* (1987).

Campbell Soup Company, *Annual Report to Shareholders* (1990).

DEKALB Genetics, *Annual Report to Shareholders* (1990).

Dow Chemical Company, *Annual Report to Shareholders* (1989).

Federal Express Corporation, *Annual Report to Shareholders* (1989).

General Mills Inc., *Annual Report to Shareholders* (1990).

Leslie Fay Company, *Annual Report to Shareholders* (1989).

Newport Corporation, *Annual Report to Shareholders* (1990).

Overseas Shipholding Group, Inc., *Annual Report to Shareholders* (1989).

Phillips Petroleum Company, *Annual Report to Shareholders* (1989).

PolyGram, N.V., *Annual Report to Shareholders* (1989).

Quaker Oats Company, *Annual Report to Shareholders* (1990).

Southmark Corporation, *Annual Report to Shareholders* (1987).

Tiger International, Inc., *Annual Report to Shareholders* (1980).

UAL Corporation, *Annual Report to Shareholders* (1989).

Western Digital Corporation, *Annual Report to Shareholders* (1990).

PART THREE

MAKING KEY STRATEGIC DECISIONS

12 GOING PUBLIC

Paul G. Joubert

"Going public" refers to the process of transforming a company from a privately owned, often owner-managed concern to a publicly owned company. The decision to take a company public is usually a complex one, and the actual process of going public can be time-consuming, expensive, and take a substantial amount of key management effort away from the day-to-day operations of the company. To illustrate the decision-making process and what needs to be done to take a company public, we will follow Acme Business Software, a fictional, but not atypical, example of a company deciding to go public and working through the process.

John Hand, founder, CEO, and majority owner of Acme Business Software prepared for a critical meeting with his board of directors. He and the board would hear a presentation by Pam Burns, Acme's CFO, on the pros and cons of taking Acme Business Software public. At their last meeting, the board concluded that going public was the primary alternative source of cash left, to finance Acme's planned expansion overseas and its new product development: They asked Burns to make a presentation at the next meeting. Hand did not know much about the process of going public, but he did realize that the company he had started, just five years ago, would change dramatically if it became a public company.

John Hand was a computer jock during his college days as an engineering student at Massachusetts Institute of Technology. After graduating, he couldn't resist his father's offer to join the family's hearing-aid manufacturing business. Once at work, Hand's fascination with computers lead to his work on and eventual development of a state-of-the-art MRP software for his father's company. Shortly after developing the software, Hand realized he had an excellent piece of software, which he believed could help many small to mid-size manufacturing firms. Hand convinced his father and a few of his father's friends to provide the seed money to produce, market, and sell the MRP software. With seed money and one product, Acme Business Software was born.

After a year in operation, Acme Business Software had a few sales, a lot of potential, and very little cash. To grow and compete in its market, the company needed significant funds for research and development and marketing. One of Hand's initial investors introduced Hand to a venture capital firm, specializing in start-up businesses. After extensive analysis of the management team and due diligence on the technology, the venture capital firm eventually agreed to invest in Acme. Although Hand was happy to get the needed capital, he had to give up 40 percent of his ownership in Acme to the venture capitalists. His deal with the venture capitalists also required that he form a board of directors and that two of the five members be selected by the venture capital firm. With a new board of directors, Hand now had to answer to someone for his business decisions, a hard pill to swallow for this founder, owner, and manager.

With the venture capital money, Acme prospered: Over the next four years, Acme grew to $10 million in sales and was extremely profitable. Hand had assembled a professional management team, at the board's urging, and the company had several new state-of-the-art products in the final design stage, which Hand believed were sure winners. Management and the board were convinced that, with a little luck and lots of hard work, Acme could grow to $50 million in sales over the next five years.

The major problem they now faced was finding the capital to bankroll Acme's overseas expansion and new product introductions. The venture capitalists wanted to spread the risk and were not interested in investing any more money. After four years, the venture capitalists were looking for a way to cash in on their Acme investment. Initial discussions with Acme's bankers also made it clear that the bank would not lend Acme the kind of money it needed, unless Acme received a substantial infusion of equity. As a software company, Acme had few tangible assets to use as collateral for additional bank lines. Acme's board felt that taking Acme public was the most promising alternative, if Acme wanted to take advantage of the tremendous growth opportunities in the software market.

THE DECISION TO GO PUBLIC

The presentation on taking Acme public was the only item on the board's agenda for the meeting. Burns brought a representative from Gold Brothers, a well-known investment bank, to assist her with the presentation. Gold Brothers had extensive experience taking companies public and came highly recommended by the venture capitalists on Acme's board. If Acme did decide to go public, Gold Brothers would certainly want to bid for the opportunity to be the lead underwriter on the public offering.

Burns began the presentation by stating that there were many advantages and disadvantages to taking Acme public, and she thought it would be helpful to put these on the table for discussion. Although the venture capitalists on the board were already well-schooled in public offerings, Hand and the other board members needed a full education.

Burns began by discussing the advantages of going public.

Advantages of Going Public

Access to Permanent, Noninterest-Bearing Capital

If Acme went public, it would be able to raise enough capital to pay for its planned overseas expansion and several new product introductions. She suggested that the Company issue its common stock to the public, in what is termed an initial public offering (IPO). Acme would never have to pay the investors their money back and would reward the investors by paying dividends (if the board decided it was appropriate) and by growing the business under its five-year business plan. The investors would expect to receive their return primarily through stock appreciation and subsequent trading of the stock on the open market. Therefore, as long as Acme remained profitable and the stock appreciated, the investors would be happy.

Access to Subsequent Capital

Once Acme became a public company, raising additional capital would be much easier. As long as the company remained attractive to investors, Acme could finance future projects with new stock offerings or public debt offerings.

The Opportunity for Owners to Cash Out

Taking Acme public would give Hand, the venture capitalists, and the other initial investors a chance to get some of their initial investment out of the business. This could be accomplished by including a secondary offering, selling shares that are already owned by individuals, with the IPO of newly created shares, or by selling stock in the open market, after Acme had gone public. At this point in the meeting, the representative from Gold Brothers pointed out that it was important to decide how much existing stock would be included in the initial offering. He warned that if Hand or others on the senior management team were perceived by the market to be bailing out of their company, potential investors would be turned off, as would Gold Brothers and the other investment bankers who would be involved in the underwriting.

Increased Public Awareness of the Company

As a publicly traded company, Acme would have a much higher profile with the public. Business pages in newspapers across the country would print Acme's quarterly and annual financial results, and Acme and its products would receive increased attention from the business press in general. Hopefully, this additional exposure would lead to new opportunities and new customers. The representative from Gold Brothers discussed the importance of public relations in an IPO and its importance for publicly traded companies in general. He also warned of the various securities laws prohibiting inappropriate release of confidential information before, during, and after an IPO. The laws are extensive and the board agreed that a more expansive discussion was needed before an IPO was undertaken.

Enhanced Credibility with Suppliers, Banks, and Customers

Acme's credibility would also be enhanced in the eyes of its existing suppliers, banks, and customers because of the respect most in the business community give to well capitalized public companies. This could lead to better credit terms with suppliers and banks and to more loyalty from existing customers.

Ability to Attract and Retain Key Management Through Use of Stock and Options

As a public company, Acme could craft creative incentive packages for important managers, using various combinations of cash, stock, and options, to purchase stock in the future, at current stock prices. With a publicly traded stock, managers could evaluate their incentive package and feel comfortable that they could cash in their shares, when and if they so chose. In addition, managers would see a tangible reward from higher stock prices and would feel that they were sharing the fruits of Acme's success. Cashing in the stock of a private company is often difficult, if not impossible, and often leads to disputes as to stock value. Free trading in the company's stock would result in an open-market determination of the company's value.

Others Can Participate in the Company's Success

All levels of employees, in addition to senior management, customers, suppliers, distributors, and others could buy into the company and share the rewards, if the company was successful. This could be an important tool to help Acme get the most out of its employees and vendors.

Equity Allows Access to More and Possibly Cheaper Debt

As the bankers told Acme several weeks ago, if the company had more equity, it could also borrow more. With a stronger equity base, the company's borrowing rate should decrease as well.

Merger or Acquisition Is Easier

Although Acme has no plans to merge or to acquire other companies, the day may arrive when a strategic alliance with another company makes sense. If Acme wanted to acquire another company, Acme could potentially offer the other owners Acme stock, instead of cash. If Acme wanted to merge with another company, a public market would make valuation of the two companies, and the transaction, much easier.

After finishing her discussion of all the advantages of taking Acme public, Burns was quick to point out that there was a long list of disadvantages to be considered, before everyone jumped on the "going public" bandwagon.

Disadvantages of Going Public

The Cost and Time of an IPO

Burns had lived through a public offering at her previous job, so she spoke from personal experience about how difficult and time consuming the public offering process was for senior managers. No one on the senior management team would be spared, and it would be difficult if not impossible for managers to do much of anything else, once the process got rolling. In addition to the time involved, the process would be extremely expensive. Acme would spend 15 to 20 percent of the offering proceeds to pay the underwriters, accountants, printers, and lawyers. There would also be risk that some unforeseen trouble would arise, either in the financial markets or at Acme which would kill the offering after Acme had already spent a lot of money on it.

The Lack of Operating Confidentiality

Going public requires companies to tell all. Information about Acme's markets, margins, salaries, and plans for the future would all be public information. This would mean that Acme's competitors, customers, suppliers, and employees would all have access to information about the inner work ings of the company. The potential problems that could result from this are numerous.

Possible Loss of Management Control

Already, the senior management of Acme only owns 60 percent of the company. A public offering of any size would dilute that holding to possibly 15 percent. The other large stockholders would probably want representation on the board and some input into how Acme should be run.

Possible Loss of Business Flexibility
Due to Required Board Approvals

With an expanded board and public oversight, senior management would have to install expanded systems of controls and approvals. Currently, the board runs very informally and can usually reach agreement rather quickly. It is difficult to imagine a larger, more diverse board, under public oversight, running as effectively.

Pressure on Short-Term Performance

The aspects of going public that would be most frustrating would be emphasis on short-term performance. Like all public companies, Acme would have to report earnings on a quarterly basis. The financial markets, investment bankers, and shareholders would be very unforgiving if Acme had a bad quarter. What makes this particularly frustrating is that, sometimes, lower quarterly earnings result from smart, strategic, long-term investment decisions. No matter how much management fought it, it would find itself managing with an eye toward the next earnings report. Every strategic decision would be framed by its effects on near-term performance and the resulting stock market reaction to that performance. This pressure would make management of Acme a much more difficult task.

Restrictions on Management
as a Result of SEC Regulations

As a public company, Acme would be required to comply with a host of SEC regulations.

The SEC is the principal federal regulatory agency for the securities industry in the United States. Created in 1934 by an act of Congress, it functions as an independent agency, performing a vital and quasi-judicial role in the regulation of securities distribution and exchange. The Securities Act of 1933 originally came under the jurisdiction of the Federal Trade Commission. However, the Securities and Exchange Act of 1934 created the SEC and, subsequently, the administration of the Securities Act of 1933 was transferred to this new agency.

The SEC is governed by presidentially appointed commissioners. They are responsible for administering the following statutes: the Securities Act of 1933; the Securities and Exchange Act of 1934; the Public Utility Holding Company Act of 1935; the Trust Indenture Act of 1939; the Investment Company Act of 1940; and the Investment Advisors Act of 1940.

The Securities Act of 1933 was designed to protect the public from misrepresentation, manipulation, and other fraudulent practices during the purchase and sale of securities. The 1933 Act requires that securities be registered with the agency, prior to their sale to the public. Securities of the U.S. government; state, municipal, and other governmental units; and securities of certain common carriers are exempt from registration.

The objectives of the Securities Act of 1933 are to provide protection for the investor, through the full and fair disclosure of financial and other information, pertinent to new securities being offered and to the business of the issuer. With few exceptions, an issuer of registered securities falling under the 1933 Act is subject to the quarterly and annual reporting requirements of the Securities and Exchange Act of 1934.

The Securities and Exchange Act of 1934, in contrast to the 1933 Act, is concerned with the trading of outstanding (previously issued) securities. Two of its principal objectives are:

1. The dissemination of significant financial and other information related to the trading of securities
2. The regulation of the securities market

The Act also empowers the SEC to regulate the pledging of customers's securities by dealers and the proxy solicitation of stockholders by registered companies.

Other regulations directly affect senior management who qualify as "insiders" according to the SEC. As insiders, they have to be careful not to discuss Acme's affairs with people outside the Company, who could unfairly use the insider information to make money by trading Acme stock. There are also strict rules regulating when and how insiders are able to buy and sell Acme shares as individuals. In other words, the key management team and board of directors cannot trade their stock as freely as other investors.

More Extensive Accounting and Tax Requirements

As a public company, Acme would have a host of new and more stringent reporting requirements. Acme's independent outside accountants would have to issue audit reports, expressing an opinion on whether the financial statements were prepared in accordance with GAAP, and Acme would have to comply with various SEC accounting and reporting requirements. Acme would almost certainly have to improve its accounting systems and beef up its staffing in the accounting area, to be able to meet all the new requirements. This would be expensive and would be an ongoing expense.

Ongoing Costs as a Public Company

In addition to the costs necessary to enhance Acme's accounting capabilities, there would be several other new, ongoing costs that Acme would bear as a public company. First, there would be the cost of issuing all the reports that are required of public companies. Second, the company would have to hire staff to handle shareholder relations. The new shareholders would be owners of Acme and management would have to answer their questions, address their concerns, and keep them informed about what was happening at Acme. Burns cautioned that management might be surprised at the level of attention shareholders would demand. Finally, new shareholders would eventually demand dividends. As a new public company, shareholders would understand that the cash generated probably needed to be reinvested in the business. However, there would come a time when shareholders would expect Acme to start paying dividends, particularly if the shareholders were not seeing a return on their investment through stock appreciation.

Susceptibility to Hostile Takeover

If Acme became a public company, senior management would no longer control 50 percent of the stock and the company would become a potential takeover target. Anyone could decide that the stock was undervalued, or that they could do a better job running the company than current management, and attempt a takeover of the company. If they were successful in accumulating enough shares, the company would become their company, and there would be little that management could do about it. As a private company, the owners only have to sell if they want to sell.

IPOs Are Typically Priced at a 10–15 Percent Discount

Although the underwriters would assure Acme that it was getting a fair price for its new shares in the IPO, it is common knowledge that IPOs are generally priced at a discount, to encourage an upward movement in the stock, in the period after the offering. Basically, this discount on the initial offering represents value being transferred from the initial investors to the investors who purchase the stock in an IPO. Furthermore, the final price of the offering is not set until days before the public offering. Thus there would be no guarantee that Acme would get the price per share that its underwriters initially estimated, in their proposals to be the lead underwriter.

Burns finished her presentation on the advantages and disadvantages of taking Acme public and opened the meeting to discussion. The representative from Gold Brothers spoke up, and, not surprisingly, stated that he thought Acme was an excellent candidate to take public and believed that

Acme would command a good price from the market. He concluded by stating that if Acme went public, at the price level he thought was attainable, the venture capitalists would have an opportunity to get an excellent return on their investment in Acme. He noted that John Hand would end up a very wealthy man, and the other senior managers who owned shares in the company would receive a very large payoff for all of their hard work.

After the investment banker was done speaking, Hand looked around the room. He knew that the venture capitalists on the board wanted an exit vehicle from Acme and were strongly in favor of taking the company public. He also knew that the other senior managers on the board would like the "large payoff" that the representative from Gold Brothers spoke of, but that they would ultimately follow Hand's lead in the boardroom. He was very reluctant to take Acme public. He was nervous about the loss of control, the many operating changes that would become necessary, and the fact that Acme would become a very different company from the one he had spent his entire adult life building. However, he recognized that Acme was ready to enter a new stage and badly needed the additional capital. If Acme did not go public, its growth would slow and its long-term viability would be in doubt. Furthermore, Hand liked the potential of becoming a rich man. When all of the factors were considered, Hand felt he had no choice but to support taking Acme public.

As Hand expected, the rest of the board agreed with his conclusion. The board's final act at this meeting was to instruct Burns to come to a special board meeting in four weeks, to explain the details of the process of going public to the board. In addition, Burns was charged with soliciting bids from several investment banks for the position of the lead underwriter of Acme's public offering. The board would evaluate the proposals and choose a lead underwriter at the next meeting.

CHOOSING A LEAD UNDERWRITER

Four weeks later, Burns came to the board with proposals from four investment banks. On Burns's recommendation, the board decided to evaluate the proposals using six criteria:

1. The investment bank's valuation of Acme's worth and its recommended offering price
2. The investment bank's reputation and experience with similar IPOs
3. The investment bank's experience in the software industry
4. The investment bank's distribution network and its ability to sell Acme's shares

5. The investment bank's record of postoffering support: its ability to avoid a post-offering fall in Acme's stock price

6. The type of underwriting the bank was offering: best efforts, best efforts—all or none, or firm commitment

The board evaluated each proposal using the criteria listed above. The board initially eliminated a proposal from a regional investment bank because of the board's desire to use a bank with the ability to sell Acme nationwide. Acme sold software throughout the country, and the board believed that a national distribution effort would make the offering more successful.

The board eliminated a second proposal because of the type of underwriting the investment bank was offering. Acme's board wanted a firm-commitment underwriting agreement, which means that the investment bank agrees to buy all of the shares being offered, and the investment bank assumes the risk of not being able to sell the shares. Much of this risk is minimized by the bank, in this case, because of its preselling effort and its ability to adjust the offering price just before the offering becomes effective. The rejected proposal suggested a best efforts underwriting agreement, in which the investment bank agrees to make a best effort to sell as many shares as possible, but does not commit to purchasing any shares. The third type of agreement, best efforts—all or none—means that the offering is cancelled if all shares are not sold.

The two remaining proposals were from large, national investment banks with extensive public offering experience and experience in the software industry. Not surprisingly, the valuations of the two banks were very similar. The board actually chose the bank with the slightly lower valuation—Gold Brothers—based on Burns's recommendation and the positive report from the venture capitalists who had dealt with the investment bank on previous offerings. The board was impressed with the representative who had attended the earlier meeting and felt very comfortable with its choice of lead underwriter.

With a lead underwriter now chosen, the next step for the board was to assemble the rest of the underwriting team. Burns explained that the underwriting team is usually made up of the lead underwriter, the underwriter's counsel, the company's counsel, an independent accountant, and a financial printer. Each member of the team has a critical role. The lead underwriter is ultimately responsible for selling the stock to the public. The lead underwriter generally chooses the underwriter's counsel, who drafts the underwriting agreements for the underwriter. The company's counsel advises the company on the steps it must take to abide by all SEC rules and regulations. The independent accountant issues an audit opinion on the financial statements, which must be filed with the SEC, and a comfort letter to the underwriter (see Appendix 1). The contents of the comfort letter are negotiated with the company's management: The letter comments generally on the financial statements, their compliance with SEC regulations, and the changes in the company's financial position since the last audit. The financial printer prints all the various financial statements: It must be large enough to handle large, last-minute jobs and be familiar with SEC requirements.

Burns had the name of a financial printer recommended by Gold Brothers, and Acme already had corporate counsel and a "big six" independent accountant, Coopers & Lybrand. The lead underwriter would choose its own counsel: Then the team would be complete. The board suggested that the underwriting team meet the next week with Hand and Burns to review the steps Acme needs to take and initiate the offering process. As they were leaving the meeting, Hand asked Burns to set up a meeting with Acme's counsel so that the counsel could brief him and Burns on the SEC's rules and regulations.

THE SEC

Acme's counsel began the briefing meeting with Hand and Burns by explaining that there are two primary laws that guide public companies: the Securities Act of 1933 and the Securities Exchange Act of 1934.

The Securities Act of 1933 requires new issues of public securities to be registered with the SEC prior to issuance. The Act outlines the registration process, specifies exempt securities and exempt transactions, and outlines antifraud provisions, which apply to all securities, whether exempt or not. The focus of this act is the protection of the public from fraudulent activity during the process of issuing new securities.

The Securities Exchange Act of 1934 established the SEC and focuses on regulation of public companies after they have gone public. The act details who must register and report to the SEC on an ongoing basis. Basically, any company with publicly traded stock and assets of over $1 million must register and report. Typically, these companies must file 10-Qs (quarterly financial reports), 10-Ks (annual reports with financial statements audited by a qualified independent public accounting firm), and 8-Ks (reports of certain material events, filed within 15 days of the event). Although there are many different provisions in the act, the lawyer pointed out that the most important provisions for Acme's senior management are the rules regarding insiders and short-swing profits. These provisions define officers, directors, and large shareholders as "insiders." Insiders must report their initial holdings to the SEC and report any changes by amending their initial report. Insiders are prevented from making short-term profits on the purchase and sale of company stock within a six-month period. The provision preventing short-swing profits states that no one may use inside information to make short-term profits in the stock market. Therefore, senior management has a responsibility to keep inside information inside the company.

THE PROCESS OF GOING PUBLIC

The underwriting team gathers together, several days later, to discuss the process and develop a timetable for going public. The representative from Gold Brothers took the lead in outlining the process to the other participants.

The first step in the process is preparing the initial registration statement. The registration statement is the primary document that is filed with the SEC during the process of going public. The document in this first step is called an initial statement because the SEC will review and comment on this statement. It is probable that the company will make changes to the statement after the SEC review.

There are several different types of registration statements. The appropriate form to use depends on the size of the public offering and whether any of the industry-specific forms are required. Acme will use the S-1 form, the basic form for large public offerings (see Appendix 2).

The registration statement consists of two parts: The first part usually doubles as the prospectus. It contains information about the company, financial statements, management's discussion and analysis of the business, information about the intended use of the offering proceeds, potential risks faced by the company, as well as a host of other information and documents. The second part of the registration statement contains more technical information, which will be available to the public through the SEC, but is usually not widely distributed.

The preparation of the initial registration statement for Acme's public offering will be particularly demanding on two fronts: writing the analysis of the business and presenting its financial results and activities over the past five years. Even though the senior management at Acme is very knowledgable about its business, writing the analysis of the business is usually a very time-consuming and difficult task. The primary reason this task is so difficult is the dual nature of the registration statement. On the one hand, the SEC requires that the statement contain an accurate description of the risks that Acme faces and a discussion of everything that could go wrong. On the other hand, this part of the registration statement is going to be used by investors to evaluate whether Acme is a good investment. Therefore, the discussion of all that can go wrong with Acme's business has to serve also as a selling document. Constructing an effective selling document is critical to the success of the offering, and management needs to spend a lot of time making sure it is perfect. The lawyers will be active in the development of the document, to ensure compliance with applicable laws and to minimize potential litigation related to inadequate disclosure.

The second big task is obtaining audited financial statements for the last three years and presenting the results of operations for five years. Acme has had its financial statements reviewed by its independent public accountants for the last four years. But there is a big difference between a review of financial statements and an audit of those same statements, in compliance with SEC rules and regulations. The objectives of an audit are to obtain and evaluate evidence to corroborate management's assertions regarding its financial statements, and to express an opinion on the financial statements, taken as a whole. A review does not include evaluation of corroborating information and does not provide a basis for expressing an opinion. An audit provides reasonable assurance that the financial statements fairly present the company's financial position and the results of operations, while a review offers a much lower degree of assurance. Due to Acme's excellent financial record-keeping and the accountant's familiarity with Acme's financial statements, the underwriting team decides to have Acme's audit conducted at the same time that the financial information is put into the format required by the SEC for the registration document.

The representative from Gold Brothers thought that the initial registration statement could be done within six to eight weeks. This would require a herculean effort, but Gold Brothers felt it was important to get this process moving as quickly as possible because the market was performing well and was very receptive to software IPOs. The market could change at any time, so Acme needed to put the offering on a fast track to take advantage of current positive conditions.

When the initial registration statement is filed with the SEC, the SEC will review it, focusing on whether Acme has followed all the rules, or has omitted or misstated any material facts, and will determine whether a full and complete disclosure was made. The SEC review can take up to two months. Once the SEC completes their review, they will document their findings in a letter of comment. In all likelihood, Acme will change the registration statement to address any comments or suggestions noted by the SEC. During this review period, it is critical that corporate counsel keep in touch with the SEC. If there are major problems with the registration statement, the SEC will let Acme know during the review process, so that management can begin work on resolving the issues.

During this review period, sometimes called the "cooling off" period, management and the investment bankers will begin to market the offering. Gold Brothers will begin to distribute the preliminary prospectus, known in the trade as a "red herring" (because of the bright red letters in the cover, stating that it is preliminary), to potential investors and possible participants in the underwriting syndicate. This document is basically the same document as the initial registration statement filed for review with the SEC. The underwriting syndicate is a group of investment bankers from other firms who agree to sell a certain portion of the offering to their clients. During this cooling off period, the red herring is the only written material used to market the offering.

After distributing the preliminary prospectus, Acme's senior management and representatives from Gold Brothers will travel around the country for approximately two weeks, making presentations to investors and underwriters about the offering and Acme Business Software. This trip is called a "road show" and is very time-consuming. Several of Acme's senior managers should be present at all of these meetings.

While distributing the red herring and doing the road show, the lawyers will be filing the various forms required by the different states before securities can be sold in that state. These various state requirements are called the "Blue Sky Laws" and must be compiled for each state within which Acme plans to offer stock. Acme has chosen to market the stock nationally, so meeting all the blue sky requirements will take a lot of work.

Toward the end of the cooling off period, a due diligence meeting will be held, where all parties will gather and go over Acme's business statements to make sure that Acme has made a full disclosure and has not omitted anything that could be considered material by the SEC.

The cooling off period ends when the company receives the SEC comments on the initial registration statement. If the SEC notes some deficiencies in the registration statement, or if some aspect of Acme's business has changed, in the period since it filed the statement originally, the registration statement will be amended.

Once Acme addresses the SEC's comments, Acme will agree to the final offering price for the stock and sign an underwriting agreement with the underwriter. Usually this is done the day before the issue is effective, so that the underwriter can adjust the price to the market conditions that exist at the time of issuance. Once the price is established and the final underwriting agreement is signed, a final amendment to the registration statement will be filed.

At this point, the registration statement will automatically become effective in 20 days. However, the SEC can accelerate the effective date of the registration statement to the date of the final amendment. The SEC will generally grant an acceleration, unless a company has not responded properly to the issues the SEC identified during its review. The accelerated effective date is very important to ensure that the price set reflects current market conditions. A lot can change in the market in twenty days.

As soon as the SEC gives its approval, selling starts. Seven days later, the closing takes place. The accountant will give the underwriters a comfort letter as part of the due diligence process, and the company will exchange cash for shares. Except for some postoffering support work by Gold Brothers, the process of going public will be complete, and Acme will begin its life as a public company.

FIVE YEARS LATER: A LOOK BACK

Five years later, John Hand looked back on the IPO process and analyzed what had made the Acme IPO a success and what had happened at Acme in the five years since the public offering. Hand remembered that the three months from the beginning of the IPO process to the actual closing were the worst three months he had spent at Acme to that point. Instead of doing what he enjoyed, running his own software company, Hand had spent virtually all of his time doing what he hated, dealing with investment bankers, lawyers, and accountants. Ultimately, however, the effort had paid off and the public offering had been a tremendous success. Acme did not get as much per share as it had expected, but Hand knew that this was typical of IPOs.

On reflection, Hand thought that there were two major groups of factors that had led to the success of Acme's public offering. The first group of factors were characteristics of Acme as a company.

Acme Was Well-Established with a Competitive Product Line

Although Hand knew very little about the financial markets before going through the IPO process, he soon realized that it would be difficult to fool the markets. Looking back, Hand concluded that if Acme had not been a well-established company with a successful and promising product line, it would never have been able to go public.

Acme Had a Record of Profitable Performance

Acme's record of profitable performance over the several years immediately prior to the IPO had been just as important as a strong product line. During the selling process, Hand noted, investors had looked very closely at Acme's profitability over the last four to six quarters to see if there had been any bad quarters or indications of weakness. Hand believed that if Acme had experienced one or two losing quarters in the year or two prior to the offering, the offering would not have been as successful.

Acme Had a Strong Management Team

Investors were ultimately investing in Acme's future performance, not its track record of past success. Hand believed that Acme's strong and experienced management team gave investors confidence that Acme could continue to succeed in the future, even if times got tougher for the software industry.

Acme's Senior Management Was Not Bailing Out

In addition to seeing a strong management team in place, investors want to make sure the team is sticking around and not just cashing out. Hand had wanted to sell a significant block of shares in the offering. Gold Brothers had advised against it, arguing that if investors thought Hand might be leaving, the offering would suffer. Hand had taken their advice and held off selling shares until almost a year after the offering was complete. The other senior managers with stock had also refrained from selling their shares, and Hand believed that this had been an important factor in the offering's success.

Acme Had a Need for Long-Term Capital

Acme had a clear, demonstrable need for more capital. Without additional capital, Acme would not have been able to introduce several new products or expand overseas. Investors looked very closely at Acme's plans for the offering proceeds. Hand concluded that if Acme had not clearly needed capital, the offering would not have been successful.

Acme Had the Potential for Long-Term Growth

Investors bought Acme's stock because they believed that Acme could continue to grow for a long time. Investors counted on a return from stock appreciation. Most investors knew that Acme would not pay any dividends in the near future. Investors also knew that the only way the stock would appreciate was if Acme continued to grow and remain profitable for several years.

In addition to the positive influence of Acme's characteristics on the IPO, Hand also felt that there had been some other important factors in Acme's success: Factors which had little to do with Acme itself, and over which Acme had little control or influence.

Acme Was in a "Hot" Industry

In the mid Eighties, software companies were very attractive to investors and Acme was able to capitalize on this through its public offering. Although there were IPOs by companies in a wide variety of industries during the year Acme went public, the fact that Acme was a successful software company helped create the tremendous demand for Acme stock by investors. What's "hot" can change quickly, so an entrepreneur needs a lot of luck to hit it just right.

The Market Conditions Were Receptive to IPOs

Acme went public at a time when the market was very receptive to IPOs, but that is not always the case. The sixties and the eighties (up until the 1987 crash) were generally known as good times for IPOs, but the seventies were considered very difficult years for public offerings. However, positive conditions do not last for entire decades. Market conditions can change dramatically overnight, and today's very attractive public offering can be tomorrow's cancelled IPO. The combination of market factors and company characteristics were just right to result in a successful IPO for Acme.

LIFE AS A PUBLIC COMPANY

Hand thought about the five years after the IPO with very mixed feelings. On the positive side, Acme Business Software had used the capital wisely and watched its business soar. Several of the new products had been successful, and the company had built an international reputation. The original investors were extremely pleased. They had seen Acme's stock price rise steadily for the first couple of years after the offering. Hand had reason to be most pleased of all. By following his investment banker's advice and not selling a large part of his stock holdings in the IPO, Hand had benefited from the company's success. He had seen the value of his holdings grow tremendously, as the stock price climbed after the offering: He was wealthy beyond his wildest dreams.

Despite all the positive aspects of going public, Hand also saw a negative side. Like many other successful entrepreneurs, Hand had been unprepared for the role of running a public company. Prior to going public, Hand had felt that he really had a hand in every phase of business. He had been active in new product development, he had played an important role in selling Acme's products to some of its larger customers, and he had been able to meet regularly with his senior managers to help them solve their problems. He had created a smoothly functioning team, and he was their captain.

After taking Acme public, Hand noticed that his role changed very quickly. The most difficult change for Hand was responding to all of the new constituents. Wall Street analysts and brokers always seemed to be on the phone looking for information. Shareholders called at all times and reporters nosed around, looking for good stories. Acme was forced to hire a company spokesperson to handle press inquiries and prepare regular press releases, as well as several new employees to deal with shareholder relations. In addition, the newly expanded board of directors took a much more active role in the affairs of the company. Hand felt as if there were always someone looking over his shoulder. He was constantly explaining and justifying his decisions. To make matters worse, all of his decisions began to be framed by their effect on short-term earnings. The discussions inevitably turned to what the decision would do to the quarterly earnings number.

Hand found that he had little time for new product development, and dealt with customers principally when they had a major complaint. He became increasingly disenchanted with his role as CEO of Acme. After two years of watching Acme's sales and profits grow along with his unhappiness, Hand suggested to the board of directors that maybe it was time to consider bringing in a new CEO. The board reluctantly agreed and created a new position for Hand in which he would oversee new product development.

The new position kept Hand happy for a little while. He was happy to be working with computers and other engineers, rather than with Wall Street analysts and institutional investors. But after a time, he realized that what he enjoyed doing the most was running his own company. He loved putting everything he had into his company, and he loved the thrill of living or dying with the company's success. He yearned for the early days of Acme Business Software and wished that there was some way he could turn Acme back into the company it had been before it went public.

Hand realized that this could never happen and so, almost five years after taking Acme public, John Hand left the company he had founded and began making plans to start a new software company. Ironically, because of the success of the IPO and the value of Acme stock, this time Hand would not have to worry about attracting venture capitalists or investment bankers to finance his new company. At least, not for a few years.

GLOSSARY

Blue Sky Laws: State laws regulating securities, coordinated with federal laws, many of which provide for licensing brokers and dealers and registration of new securities.

Comfort Letter (Letter for Underwriters):   Communication from the independent auditor to the underwriter, at the time of registration of the securities, which includes information about the auditor's role, auditor's independence, compliance of the financial statements with the Securities Acts, and any changes in the financial statements, subsequent to those included in the registration statement.

Dilution: Relative loss or weakening of equity position.

Independent Auditors (Accountants):   An outside public accountant, having no financial stake or other interest in the person or company on whose financial statements a professional opinion is to be rendered.

Insiders: A corporate director, officer, or owner of more than 10 percent of a registered security whose position allows access to information on the security before the information is available to the other stockholders.

Investment Banker: An organization that buys bond or stock issues in their entirety from the issuing corporation.

Offering Proceeds: Proceeds from the initial public offering and sale of securities of a company.

Prospectus: A document issued for the purpose of describing a new security issue.

Red Herring: An announcement describing a proposed issue of securities. Called a "Red Herring" because of the disclaimer emblazoned in red on the document.

Registration Statement: A formal statement filed with the SEC by a company, containing financial information and other information for buyers of a proposed security issue.

SEC: Securities and Exchange Commission.

Short-Swing Profits: Profits realized by insiders who take advantage of inside information for personal gain.

10-K, 10-Q, 8-K: Principal periodic reports filed by most companies registered under the Securities Acts.

FOR FURTHER READING

Arkebauer, James B., and Ronald M. Schultz, *Cashing Out: The Entrepreneur's Guide to Going Public* (New York: HarperBusiness, 1991).

Dobbin, Muriel, *Going Public* (New York: Carol Publishing Group, 1991).

Malone, Michael S., *Going Public: MIPS Computer and the Entrepreneurial Dream* (New York: HarperCollins, 1991).

Roberts, Holme, and Harold A. S. Bloomenthal, *Going Public Handbook*, 1991 ed. (New York: Clark Boardman, 1991).

Weiss, Martin, *Going Public* (New York: Tab Books, 1990).

Wood, Ira, *Going Public* (Zoland Books, 1991).

APPENDIX 1

Comfort Letter

(Letters for Underwriters)

The following items are covered in a typical comfort letter.

1. A statement regarding the independence of the accountants.
2. An opinion regarding whether the audited financial statements and schedules included in the registration statement comply in form, in all material respects, with the applicable accounting requirements of the Act and the related published rules and regulations.
3. Negative assurance with respect to whether the unaudited condensed interim financial statements included in the registration statement: (a) Comply in form, in all material respects, with the applicable accounting requirements of the Act and the related published rules and regulations; (b) Are in conformity with GAPP, applied on a basis substantially consistent with that of the audited financial statements included in the registration statement.
4. Negative assurance with respect to whether, during a specified period following the date of the latest financial statements in the registration statement and prospectus, there has been any change in capital stock, long-term debt, or any decrease in other specified financial statement items.

Source: AICPA Professional Standards by Commerce Clearing House, 1982.

Example of a Comfort Letter

June 30, 19X6

[Addresse]

Dear Sirs:

We have audited the consolidated balance sheets of the Blank Company, Inc. (the company) and subsidiaries as of December 31, 19X5 and 19X4 and the consolidated statements of income, retained earnings, and cash flows for each of the three years in the period ended December 31, 19X5 and the related schedules all included in the registration statement (no. 2-00000) on Form S-1 filed by the company under the Securities Act of 1933 (the Act); our reports with respect thereto are also included in that registration statement. The registration statement, as amended on June 23, 19X6, is herein referred to as the registration statement.*

In connection with the registration statement—

1. We are independent certified public accountants with respect to The Blank Company, Inc., within the meaning of the Act and the applicable published rules and regulations thereunder.

2. In our opinion [include the phrase "except as disclosed in the registration statement," if applicable], the consolidated financial statements and schedules audited by us and included in the registration statement comply in form in all material respects with the applicable accounting requirements of the Act and the related published rules and regulations.

3. We have not audited any financial statements of the company as of any date or for any period subsequent to December 31, 19X5; although we have conducted an audit for the year ended December 31, 19X5, the purpose (and therefore the scope) of the audit was to enable to us to express our opinion on the consolidated financial statements as of December 31, 19X5, and for the year then ended, but not on the financial statements for any interim period within that year. Therefore, we are unable to and do not express any opinion on the unaudited consolidated condensed statements balance sheet as of March 31, 19X6, and unaudited consolidated condensed statements of income, retained earnings, and cash flows for the three-month periods ended March 31, 19X6, and 19X5, included in the registration statement, or on the financial position, results or operations, or cash flows as of any date or for any period subsequent for December 31, 19X5.

4. For purposes of this letter we have read the 19X6 minutes of meetings of the stockholders, the board of directors, and [include other appropriate committees, if any] of the company and its subsidiaries as set forth in the minute books at June 25, 19X6, officials of the company having advised us that the minutes of all such meetings through the date were set forth therein; and we have carried out other procedures to June 25, 19X6 (our work did not extend to the period from June 26, 19X6, to June 30, 19X6, inclusive), as follows:

a. With respect to the three-month periods ended March 31, 19X6 and 19X5, we have—

(i) Read the unaudited consolidated condensed balance sheet as of March 31, 19X6, and unaudited consolidated condensed statements of income, retained earnings, and cash flows for the three-month periods ended March 31, 19X6 and 19X5, included in the registration statement; and

(ii) Made inquiries of certain officials of the company who have responsibility for financial and accounting matters regarding (1) whether the unaudited consolidated condensed financial statements referred to in a(i) comply in form in all material respects with the applicable accounting requirements of the Act and the related published rules and regulations and (2) whether those unaudited consolidated condensed financial statements are in conformity with generally accepted accounting principles applied on a basis substantially consistent with that of the audited consolidated financial statements included in the registration statement.

b. With respect to the period from April 1, 19X6, to May 31, 19X6, we have —

(i) Read the unaudited consolidated financial statements of the company and subsidiaries for April and May of both 19X5 and 19X6 furnished us by the company, officials of the company having advised us that no such financial statements as of any date or for any period subsequent to May 31, 19X6, were available; and

(ii) Made inquiries of certain officials of the company who have responsibility for financial and accounting matters regarding whether the unaudited financial statements referred to in b(i) are stated on a basis substantially consistent with that of the audited financial statements included in the registration statement.

The foregoing procedures do not constitute an audit conducted in accordance with generally accepted auditing standards. Also, they would not necessarily reveal matters of significance with respect to the comments in the following paragraph. Accordingly, we make no representations regarding the sufficiency of the foregoing procedures for your purposes.

5. Nothing came to our attention as a result of the foregoing procedures, however, that caused us to believe that—

a. (i) The unaudited consolidated condensed financial statements described in 4a(i), included in the registration statement, do not comply in form in all material respects with the applicable accounting requirements and (ii) the unaudited consolidated condensed financial statements are not in conformity with generally accepted accounting principles applied on a basis substantially consistent with that of the audited consolidated financial statements; or

b. (i) At May 31, 19X6, there was any change in the capital stock or long-term debt of the company and subsidiaries consolidated or any decreases in consolidated net current assets or net assets as compared with amounts shown in the March 31, 19X6, unaudited consolidated condensed balance sheet included in the registration statement or (ii) for the period from April 1, 19X6, to May 31, 19X6 there were any decreases, as compared with the corresponding period in the preceding year, in consolidated net sales or in the total or per-share amounts of income before extraordinary items or of net income, except in all instances for changes or decreases that the registration statement discloses have occurred or may occur.

6. As mentioned in 4b, company officials have advised us that no consolidated financial statements as of any date or for any period subsequent to May 31, 19X6, are available; accordingly, the procedures carried out by us with respect to changes in financial statement items after May 31, 19X6, have, of necessity, been even more limited than those with respect to the periods referred to in 4. We have made inquiries of certain company officials who have responsibility for financial and accounting matters regarding whether (a) there was any change at June 25, 19X6, in the capital stock or long-term debt of the

company and subsidiaries consolidated or any decreases in consolidated net current assets or net assets as compared with amounts shown on the March 31, 19X6, unaudited consolidated condensed balance sheet included in the registration statement or (b) for the period from April 1, 19X6, to June 25, 19X6, there were any decreases, as compared with the corresponding period in the preceding year, in consolidated net sales or in the total share or per-share amounts of income before extraordinary items or of net income. On the basis of these inquiries and our reading of the minutes as described in 4, nothing came to our attention that caused us to believe that there was any such change or decrease, except in all instances for changes or decreases that the registration statement discloses have occurred or may occur.

7. This letter is solely for the information of the addresses and to assist the underwriters in conducting and documenting their investigation of the affairs of the company in connection with the offering of the securities covered by the registration statement, and it is not to be used, circulated, quoted, or otherwise referred to within or without the underwriting group for any other purpose, including but not limited to the registration, purchase, or sale of securities, nor is it to be filed with or referred to in whole or in part in the registration statement or any other document, except that reference may be made to it in the underwriting agreement or in any list of closing documents pertaining to the offering of the securities covered by the registration statement.

---

*As described in paragraph 18, the accountants may refer in the introductory paragraphs to the fact that they have issued reports on other financial information. For example, if the accountants refer to the fact that a review of interim financial information had been performed, an additional introductory paragraph, such as the following, may be added.

Also, we have made a review of the unaudited consolidated condensed financial statements for the three-month periods ended March 31, 19X6 and 19X5, as indicated in our report dated May 15, 19X6, which is included [incorporated by reference] in the registration statement.

Source: Reprinted, by permission, from *Professional Standards*, Copyright ©1991 by American Institute of Certified Public Accountants, Inc.

APPENDIX 2

Registration Statement Form

UNITED STATES
SECURITIES AND EXCHANGE COMMISSION
Washington, D.C. 20549

OMB APPROVAL
OMB Number: 3235-0065
Expires: May 31, 1994
Estimated average burden
hours per response . 1258.00

FORM S-1

REGISTRATION STATEMENT UNDER THE SECURITIES ACT OF 1933

_____
(Exact name of registrant as specified in its charter)

_____
(State or other jurisdiction of incorporation or organization)

_____
(Primary Standard Industrial Classification Code Number)

_____
(I.R.S. Employer Identification Number)

_____
(Address, including zip code, and telephone number,
including area code, of registrant's principal executive offices)

_____
(Name, address, including zip code, and telephone number,
including area code, of agent for service)

_____
(Approximate date of commencement of proposed sale to the public)

If any of the securities being registered on this Form are to be offered on a delayed or continuous basis pursuant to Rule 415 under the Securities Act of 1933 check the following box: ☐

Calculation of Registration Fee

Title of Each Class of Securities to be Registered	Amount to be Registered	Proposed Maximum Offering Price Per Unit	Proposed Maximum Aggregate Offering Price	Amount of Registration Fee

SEC 870 (8/91) 1 of 5

GENERAL INSTRUCTIONS

I.   Eligibility Requirements for Use of Form S-1

This Form shall be used for the registration under the Securities Act of 1933 ("Securities Act") of securities of all registrants for which no other form is authorized or prescribed, except that this Form shall not be used for securities of foreign governments or political subdivisions thereof.

II.   Application of General Rules and Regulations

    A.   Attention is directed to the General Rules and Regulations under the Securities Act, particularly those comprising Regulation C (17 CFR 230.400 to 230.494) thereunder. That Regulation contains general requirements regarding the preparation and filing of the registration statement.

    B.   Attention is directed to Regulation S-K (17 CFR Part 229) for the requirements applicable to the content of the non-financial statement portions of registration statements under the Securities Act. Where this Form directs the registrant to furnish information required by Regulation S-K and the item of Regulation S-K so provides, information need only be furnished to the extent appropriate.

III.   Exchange Offers

If any of the securities being registered are to be offered in exchange for securities of any other issuer, the prospectus shall also include the information which would be required by Item 11 if the securities of such other issuer were registered on this Form. There shall also be included the information concerning such securities of such other issuer which would be called for by Item 9 if such securities were being registered. In connection with this instruction, reference is made to Rule 409.

PART 1—INFORMATION REQUIRED IN PROSPECTUS

Item 1.   Forepart of the Registration Statement and Outside Front Cover Page of Prospectus.

    Set forth in the forepart of the registration statement and on the outside front cover page of the prospectus the information required by Item 501 of Regulation S-K (§229.501 of this chapter).

Item 2.   Inside Front and Outside Back Cover Pages of Prospectus.

    Set forth on the inside front cover page of the prospectus or, where permitted, on the outside back cover page, the information required by Item 502 of Regulation S-K (§229.502 of this chapter).

Item 3.   Summary Information, Risk Factors and Ratio of Earnings to Fixed Charges.

    Furnish the information required by Item 503 of Regulation S-K (§229.503 of this chapter).

Item 4.   Use of Proceeds.

    Furnish the information required by Item 504 of Regulation S-K (§229.504 of this chapter).

Item 5.   Determination of Offering Price.

    Furnish the information required by Item 505 of Regulation S-K (§229.505 of this chapter).

Item 6.   Dilution.

    Furnish the information required by Item 506 of Regulation S-K (§229.506 of this chapter).

Item 7.   Selling Security Holders.

    Furnish the information required by Item 507 of Regulation S-K (§229.507 of this chapter).

Item 8.   Plan of Distribution.

Furnish the information required by Item 508 of Regulation S-K (§229.508 of this chapter).

Item 9.   Description of Securities to be Registered.

Furnish the information required by Item 202 of Regulation S-K (§229.202 of this chapter).

Item 10.   Interests of Named Experts and Counsel.

Furnish the information required by Item 509 of Regulation S-K (§229.509 of this chapter).

Item 11.   Information with Respect to the Registrant.

Furnish the following information with respect to the registrant:

(a) Information required by Item 101 of Regulation S-K (§229.101 of this chapter), description of business;

(b) Information required by Item 102 of Regulation S-K (§229.102 of this chapter), description of property;

(c) Information required by Item 103 of Regulation S-K (§229.103 of this chapter), legal proceedings;

(d) Where common equity securities are being offered, information required by Item 201 of Regulation S-K (§229.201 of this chapter), market price of and dividends on the registrant's common equity and related stockholder matters;

(e) Financial statements meeting the requirements of Regulation S-X (17 CFR Part 210) (Schedules required under Regulation S-X shall be filed as "Financial Statement Schedules" pursuant to Item 15, Exhibits and Financial Statement Schedules, of this Form), as well as any financial information required by Rule 3-05 and Article 11 of Regulation S-X;

(f) Information required by Item 301 of Regulation S-K (§229.301 of this chapter), selected financial data;

(g) Information required by Item 302 of Regulation S-K (§229.302 of this chapter), supplementary financial information;

(h) Information required by Item 303 of Regulation S-K (§229.303 of this chapter), management's discussion and analysis of financial condition and results of operations;

(i) Information required by Item 304 of Regulation S-K (§229.304 of this chapter), changes in and disagreements with accountants on accounting and financial disclosure;

(j) Information required by Item 401 of Regulation S-K (§229.401 of this chapter), directors and executive officers;

(k) Information required by Item 402 of Regulation S-K (§229.402 of this chapter), executive compensation;

(l) Information required by Item 403 of Regulation S-K (§229.403 of this chapter), security ownership of certain beneficial owners and management; and

(m) Information required by Item 404 of Regulation S-K (§229.404 of this chapter), certain relationships and related transactions.

Item 12.   Disclosure of Commission Position on Indemnification for Securities Act Liabilities.

Furnish the information required by Item 510 of Regulation S-K (§229.510 of this chapter).

PART II—INFORMATION NOT REQUIRED IN PROSPECTUS

Item 13. Other Expenses of Issuance and Distribution.

Furnish the information required by Item 511 of Regulation S-K (§229.511 of this chapter).

Item 14. Indemnification of Directors and Officers.

Furnish the information required by Item 702 of Regulation S-K (§229.702 of this chapter).

Item 15. Recent Sales of Unregistered Securities.

Furnish the information required by Item 701 of Regulation S-K (§229.701 of this chapter).

Item 16. Exhibits and Financial Statement Schedules.

(a) Subject to the rules regarding incorporation by reference, furnish the exhibits as required by Item 601 of Regulation S-K (§229.601 of this chapter).

(b) Furnish the financial statement schedules required by Regulation S-X (17 CFR Part 210) and Item 11(e) of this Form. These schedules shall be lettered or numbered in the manner described for exhibits in paragraph (a).

Item 17. Undertakings.

Furnish the undertakings required by Item 512 of Regulation S-K (§229.512 of this chapter).

SIGNATURES

Pursuant to the requirements of the Securities Act of 1933, the registrant has duly caused this registration statement to be signed on its behalf by the undersigned, thereunto duly authorized in the City of _____,

State of _____, on_____, 19_____.

_____
(Registrant)

_____
By (Signature and Title)

Pursuant to the requirements of the Securities Act of 1933, this registration statement has been signed by the following persons in the capacities and on the dates indicated.

_____
(Signature)

_____
(Title)

_____
(Date)

407

Instructions.

1. The registration statement shall be signed by the registrant, its principal executive officer or officers, its principal financial officer, its controller or principal accounting officer and by at least a majority of the board of directors or persons performing similar functions. If the registrant is a foreign person, the registration statement shall also be signed by its authorized representative in the United States. Where the registrant is a limited partnership, the registration statement shall be signed by a majority of the board of directors of any corporate general partner signing the registration statement.

2. The name of each person who signs the registration statement shall be typed or printed beneath his signature. Any person who occupies more than one of the specified positions shall indicate each capacity in which he signs the registration statement. Attention is directed to Rule 402 concerning manual signatures and to Item 601 of Regulation S-K concerning signatures pursuant to powers of attorney.

INSTRUCTIONS AS TO SUMMARY PROSPECTUSES

1. A summary prospectus used pursuant to Rule 431 (§230.431 of this chapter), shall at the time of its use contain such of the information specified below as is then included in the registration statement. All other information and documents contained in the registration statement may be omitted.

   (a) As to Item 1, the aggregate offering price to the public, the aggregate underwriting discounts and commissions and the offering price per unit to the public;

   (b) As to Item 4, a brief statement of the principal purposes for which the proceeds are to be used;

   (c) As to Item 7, a statement as to the amount of the offering, if any, to be made for the account of security holders;

   (d) As to Item 8, the name of the managing underwriter or underwriters and a brief statement as to the nature of the underwriter's obligation to take the securities; if any securities to be registered are to be offered otherwise than through underwriters, a brief statement as to the manner of distribution; and, if securities are to be offered otherwise than for cash, a brief statement as to the general purposes of the distribution, the basis upon which the securities are to be offered, the amount of compensation and other expenses of distribution, and by whom they are to be borne;

   (e) As to Item 9, a brief statement as to dividend rights, voting rights, conversion rights, interest, maturity;

   (f) As to Item 11, a brief statement of the general character of the business done and intended to be done, the selected financial data (Item 301 of Regulation S-K (§229.301 of this chapter)) and a brief statement of the nature and present status of any material pending legal proceedings; and

   (g) A tabular presentation of notes payable, long term debt, deferred credits, minority interests, if material, and the equity section of the latest balance sheet filed, as may be appropriate.

2. The summary prospectus shall not contain a summary or condensation of any other required financial information except as provided above.

3. Where securities being registered are to be offered in exchange for securities of any other issuer, the summary prospectus also shall contain that information as to Items 9 and 11 specified in paragraphs (e) and (f) above which would be required if the securities of such other issuer were registered on this Form.

4. The Commission may, upon the request of the registrant, and where consistent with the protection of investors, permit the omission of any of the information herein required or the furnishing in substitution therefor of appropriate information of comparable character. The Commission may also require the inclusion of other information in addition to, or in substitution for, the information herein required in any case where such information is necessary or appropriate for the protection of investors.

SEC 870 (8/91) 5 of 5

408

MERGERS AND ACQUISITIONS: STRATEGIES FOR GROWTH

13

William W. Alberts

The subject of this chapter is growth by acquisition, the strategy of entering new product markets by purchasing the common stock or assets of a business or businesses already operating in these markets. The aim of the chapter is to outline answers to six major questions that face a typical industrial company about to undertake such a strategy:

1. What should be the rationale for our acquisition strategy?
2. What are the principal acquisition options open to us, both directional (the different kinds of markets we should consider entering) and structural (the different ways we can effect a purchase)?
3. What test must any acquisition pass to be profitable for us?
4. What are the conditions of profitable growth by acquisition (the determinants of whether a purchase in fact will pass the profitability test)?
5. Based on these profitability conditions, which criteria should be used to target acquisition candidates?
6. What must we do to ensure that the profitability potential of an acquisition is fully realized, once it is made?

The company currently is organized into three business units called Red, Green, and Blue in internal planning documents. Each operates in a distinct product market. The company itself, General Products (GP), is a publicly owned corporation whose common shares trade on a stock exchange. One third of its assets are financed with long-term debt. Its percentage cost of equity capital (the minimum rate of return that is acceptable to its owners) has been averaging about 13 percent: This represents the sum of the risk-free rate of interest (as measured by the long-term U.S. Treasury bond rate) and a risk premium, appropriate for the company.

ACQUISITION OBJECTIVE AND GOAL(S)

When a company undertakes growth by acquisition, it ordinarily has at least one *immediate* reason, or motive, and an *ultimate* one for doing so. The immediate reason for an acquisition is called a goal of the undertaking, and the ultimate reason is called its objective.

Almost always, a goal is formulated when a perception surfaces in management's mind that the company has or will have a "problem" or "deficiency" that can be remedied by diversification in general (defined in this chapter simply as an increase in the number of businesses a company operates), and diversification by acquisition, in particular. Different companies have different problems that they want to solve by diversifying through growth and, thus, cite different goals for the strategy. Exhibit 13.1 shows the eight goals (and the problems that give rise to them) that seem to be cited most frequently.

The first two goals share the perception that the company's overall growth target cannot be achieved by internal growth alone; external, or diversifying, growth also is needed. The next four goals share the perception that a particular business in the company's portfolio faces a competitive threat, and that this threat can be neutralized by the right acquisition. In the case of the third goal, this means acquiring a business in a position to use the

EXHIBIT 13.1. Alternative goals of growth by acquisition.

- Goals that trigger CLASSIC diversification
  1. Countering a significant decrease in the company's overall earnings growth. ("All our major product markets are mature and a couple face decline.")
  2. Countering the effect on the company's earnings of an absolute decline in one of its major businesses. ("Our commodity chemical company is dead and we have to replace it.")
- Goals that trigger DEFENSIVE diversification
  3. Putting excess capacity to work. ("We've got three facilities operating only part time and that's hurting our cost position badly.")
  4. Coping with a vertical competitive threat. ("Rivals are buying up the companies that supply components to our industry, and we're afraid that if we don't get one ourself, we may face control problems.")
  5. Protecting a competitive position. ("A Japanese company has beachheaded a market segment adjacent to ours, and we're afraid that if we don't get in there and cause it some trouble, we may come under attack ourself.")
  6. Correcting inadequacies in the company's technology base. ("We need to buy somebody who can educate us in laser printing technology.")
- Goals that trigger OPPORTUNISTIC diversification
  7. Moving up in the *Fortune* size rankings. ("We want to double our present size in five years.")
  8. Putting accumulated cash holdings to work. ("We've got $5 billion and want to invest it.")

excess capacity; for the fourth goal, it means acquiring an upstream business; for the fifth goal, it means acquiring a business whose product complements or substitutes for the company's product; and for the sixth goal, it means acquiring a business which is a potential or actual supplier of technology or a product incorporating that technology. The only commonality of the last two goals is that they are neither classic nor defensive in nature.

Because GP is a typical company, we can assume that at least one of the goals in the exhibit will motivate each of its own planned acquisitions. We can also assume that GP's objective in growing by acquisition is to increase its profitability, and that the company measures profitability by the magnitude of the cash flows it can generate for its owners over time, or equivalently, by the magnitude of the discounted present value—the "market value"—of these flows.

By implication, for any acquisition to meet the company's objective, it must cause this market value to be greater than it would be in the absence of the acquisition. The acquisition will fail to meet the company's objective, if it causes the company's market value to be *less* than it otherwise would be. Will a "value-creating" acquisition also achieve the company's goal or goals? Ordinarily, yes. But there is no guarantee that the converse holds. The prospect that an acquisition will solve the problem or problems that triggered it, tells the company nothing about the prospect that the acquisition also will be profitable, and thus create value. Whether an acquisition is profitable depends not on why it is done, but on how it is done.

Many acquisition specialists would argue that the seventh goal cited in Exhibit 13.1 is a dubious one; management should not use shareholder capital to finance an advance in the Fortune 500 rankings. If an acquisition is triggered by this goal and works to destroy value, the point obviously is well-taken. But if the acquisition works not to destroy, but to create value, management can argue that it doesn't really matter what the immediate motive was. A similar line of argument can be articulated about the eighth goal. If management faces a choice between distributing its cash holdings to shareholders or investing them unprofitably, it should distribute the holdings. But if the choice is between distributing the holdings and investing them in a profitable acquisition, shareholders will probably want management to go with the second option.

Finally, it should be noted that there are at least some companies for whom growth by acquisition is *not* triggered by one of the classic or defensive goals. Rather, these companies want simply to exploit value-creating acquisition opportunities which they have spotted. For them, the immediate and the ultimate reasons for undertaking the acquisitions are the same; their goal is to achieve their value-creation objective.

ACQUISITION OPTIONS: DIRECTIONAL AND STRUCTURAL

GP begins the development of an acquisition strategy by working out for itself, first, the directions in which it can look for candidates, and then the means by which it can best structure the acquisition. We shall assume that GP already has decided that it doesn't want to undertake "megadiversification": the acquisition of large, multibusiness companies and, as a result, the *simultaneous* entry into a number of new markets. Instead, it wants to enter new markets one at a time and, accordingly, plans to acquire only single-business companies (or divisions of companies).

In recent years the number of reported acquisitions has been running between 3,000 and 4,000 a year. Most appear to have been single-business acquisitions. Price per transaction (*including* megaacquisitions) has averaged about $50 million.

Directional Options

As Exhibit 13.2 shows, GP can undertake entry into two broad groupings of markets, those that are related in some way to the markets which Red, Green, and Blue now serve, and those that have no relation to any of the company's served markets. Some managers use the term diversification, not as a synonym for entry into new markets in general, but as a synonym for entry into unrelated markets.

There are six classes of markets that can be described as related to Red's market or markets:

1. *Regional Market Extensions.*   These are markets for Red's product outside the geographical region in which Red now operates. An example would be an entry into the Mexican market for the product.
2. *Technology Market Extensions.*   These are markets for products, based on the core technology Red uses in its current product. If Red produces aluminum siding for buildings, an example would be the market for aluminum boats. If Red produces engine valves, an example would be the market for engine carburetors.
3. *Markets for Substitute Products.*   These are markets for products that use different technologies to meet the needs of Red's current customers. If Red produces minicomputers, an example would be the market for workstations. If Red produces glass milk containers, an example would be the market for plastic milk containers.
4. *Markets for Complementary Products.*   These are markets for products that Red's customers view as complementary to Red's product. If Red

EXHIBIT 13.2.   The company's directional options for diversifying growth.

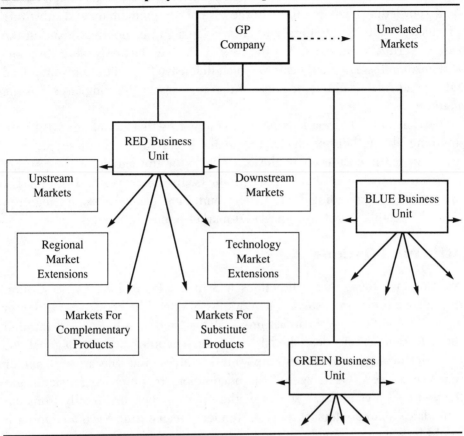

produces lawnmowers, an example would be the market for lawn fertilizer. If Red produces personal computers, an example would be the market for printers.

5. *Upstream Markets.*   These are markets for products that Red now buys (supplies, parts, components). If Red produces personal computers, an example would be the market for disc drives. If Red publishes a newspaper, an example would be the market for newsprint.

6. *Downstream Markets.*   These are markets in which Red's product is now sold. If Red produces lawnmowers, an example would be the retail lawnmower market. If Red produces wool yarn and sells it to sweater manufacturers, an example would be the sweater market.

What these markets (and the markets that similarly surround Green and Blue) all have in common, from GP's perspective, is that there are key managers in the company who know at least something about them. In the case of regional extensions, it is the product itself (and knowledge about competitors); in the case of technology extensions, it is the technology itself (and knowledge of competitors); in the case of complementary and substitute products, it is the customers (and knowledge about competitors); and in the case of vertical extensions, it is the new rivals (who formerly were suppliers and customers). The markets into which defensive diversification would lead GP are all related in one or more of these senses to the company's existing markets.

What unrelated markets have in common is that no one in GP knows anything about their products, the technologies in which these products are rooted, the customers of these products, or the nature of competition between companies that sell these products. In short, every related market opportunity surrounding Red, Green, and Blue passes to some degree a "knowledgeability" test. No unrelated market opportunity does.

Structural Options

Not only are there many directions in which GP can look for acquisition candidates, there are also various ways it can effect the actual acquisition of a specific candidate. We can assume that the candidate has passed through the selection screen, described later in this chapter, and that negotiations with the management group empowered to make the sale are well under way. Conceivably, GP triggered the negotiations by purchasing a significant fraction of the candidate's shares in the open market, or directly from the candidate's shareholders (through a "tender" mechanism). Such an approach would be unusual, though. In the last two or three decades, negotiations for all but a small minority of acquisitions (and these were megaacquisitions) have begun with a face-to-face meeting between a candidate's managers and the managers who want to acquire it.

Exhibit 13.3 shows the three alternative legal means by which GP can effect the acquisition: statutory merger, affiliation, and asset purchase. If GP chooses the first or third option, it will add the acquiree's current and fixed assets to the left side of the balance sheet; if it chooses the second option, it will add its holdings of the acquiree's common shares to the left side of its balance sheet.

Note that the terminology in this exhibit is not universally used. Some people define the term "merger" generically (as a synonym for "acquisition," as that term is used here). Others define the term "acquisition" narrowly as a synonym for affiliation and asset purchase. When investment bankers say "We do mergers and acquisitions" or "We do M&A work," they are saying that they help effect mergers, affiliations, and asset purchases.

If the acquiree is a nonaffiliate of another company (and thus has no common shares of its own), GP will purchase its assets. If the acquiree *does* have

EXHIBIT 13.3. Growth by acquisition: Structural options.

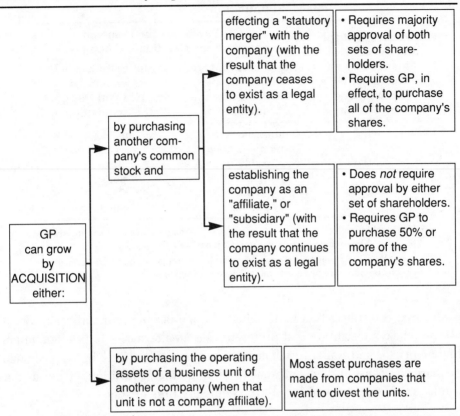

its own shares, GP will find it administratively much simpler (and therefore less expensive) to purchase these shares, unless the acquiree has significant liabilities of a questionable nature that would have to be taken off its balance sheet. But will GP merge with the acquiree or set it up as an affiliate? That depends on how GP will take joint account of seven related considerations: (1) the percentage of the acquiree's shares that GP wants to purchase (100 percent or between 50 and 100 percent); (2) the percentage of this purchase that GP wants to finance by an exchange of shares (100 percent, between 50 and 100 percent, or less than 50 percent); (3) the tax implications, shown in Exhibit 13.4, of each of these three financing options for each structural option; (4) the tax option that the acquiree prefers; (5) the weight that GP thinks should be given to this preference; (6) the weight that GP thinks should be given to *its own* tax preference; and (7) the ease or difficulty of securing shareholder approval of the merger option.

Assuming that, as is usually the case, the purchase price per share of the acquiree exceeds the tax basis of typical shareholders (that is, exceeds the average price paid originally by these shareholders), the acquiree will

EXHIBIT 13.4. The tax implications of alternative structural-financing options.

Percentage of the Purchase Price Financed by an Exchange of GP's Common and Preferred Shares	If GP Purchases the Common Shares of the Candidate Company	
	and Effects a Meger with It, the IRS Will Designate the Acquisition a:	and Establishes It as an Affiliate, the IRS Will Designate the Acquisition a:
100%	Nontaxable "type A" reorganization	Nontaxable "type B" reorganization
50 – 100%	Nontaxable "type A" reorganization	Taxable purchase
< 50%	Taxable purchase	Taxable purchase

- Nontaxable: selling company shareholders pay no gains tax on the difference between the purchase price and the "tax basis" of their shares.
- Taxable: selling company shareholders *do* pay a gains tax on the difference between the purchase price and the tax basis of their shares.

prefer that the transaction be designated a nontaxable reorganization. So, if GP puts heavy weight on that preference (as an alternative to paying a much higher price), and wants to finance the acquisition entirely by an exchange of shares (because it does not want to leverage the acquisition, or because it thinks its shares are overpriced), the company presumably:

- Will opt for the affiliation route if it wants to limit its dollar investment in the candidate, or if it views the task of obtaining shareholder approval as onerous, and
- Will opt for the merger route if it wants to purchase all the candidate's shares and does not see the shareholder approval requirement as a problem.

If GP puts heavy weight on the acquiree's preference for nontaxable status and wants to finance up to 50 percent of the acquisition with cash (borrowed or on hand), presumably it will choose the merger option. If GP does not put heavy weight on the acquiree's preference for nontaxable status and does not want to finance the acquisition by an exchange of shares (because it wants to leverage the acquisition significantly, or because it thinks its shares are underpriced), GP will choose between a merger and affiliation, based on the importance it places on obtaining shareholder appeal, and on whether it wants to purchase less than 100 percent of the acquiree.

Finally, suppose the prospective purchase price is considerably greater than the acquiree's book value. Then, if the acquisition was designated a taxable purchase, GP would be able to reduce its tax bills over time, by writing off the part of the purchase price allocated to the acquiree's depreciable assets. This consideration will increase GP's inclination to finance and structure the acquisition in such a way as to achieve purchase status. However, this inclination may have to be balanced against an inclination to satisfy the acquiree's desire for reorganization status, and, perhaps, an inclination to finance the acquisition by an exchange of shares.

If GP does not finance the acquisition by an exchange of shares, it will be required under GAAP to both: (a) add to its balance sheet, not the book value of the candidate's assets. but the price paid for them; and (b) amortize over 40 years or less, any difference between the latter and the former. Even if the premium over book value paid for the acquiree—usually called goodwill—is large, meeting this amortization requirement will have no affect on the new unit's postacquisition cash flows over time; "amortization of goodwill" is a noncash charge. Accordingly, accounting considerations should play no significant role in GP's determination of which structural option to choose.

CANDIDATE SCREENING: THE PROFITABILITY TEST

Targeting candidates for acquisition is a two-stage process. First, screen for candidates that look as though they *might* be profitable. Then, screen the survivors for those that look as though they *will* be profitable. Both screens depend on having a specific test, or criterion, for distinguishing between profitable and unprofitable acquisitions. What should this test be?

The Positive NPV Test

Because GP's objective in growing by acquisition is to increase its overall market value, it should specify a profitable acquisition as one that is worth more to GP than it costs. Put more precisely, the test requires that the market value to GP of the new business, M, must exceed the increment of the equity capital, or equity cost, EC, that GP would have to invest in order to take control of the business. Because GP is likely to speak of the difference between M and EC as the NPV of the investment, a profitable investment also can be characterized as one that has a positive NPV.

In general, M, for any candidate, will equal the discounted value of the equity cash flows, ECF, it would generate each year as a business unit of GP. For any particular year, ECF is simply another way to designate the dividend which the unit would distribute to GP. Accordingly, it will equal the difference between the unit's earnings, E, and the fraction of these earnings, r, that is retained and used to finance additions to the unit's fixed and current assets.

The Test Specified More Elaborately for a Zero-Growth Candidate

If the unit's earnings are not expected to grow over time, no investment will take place, r will be zero each year, and earnings will be fully distributed. In this case, M can be determined with the simple equation

$$M = \frac{E}{k_e}$$

where E designates the unit's uniform annual earnings, and k_e is the percentage cost of equity capital for the unit. For example, if k_e equalled 13 percent (GP's own k_e), and if GP would have to invest \$40 million in equity capital to acquire the unit, the profitability of this investment would depend on the size of the units earnings stream:

Scenario	EC	E	M	NPV	Evaluation
1	\$40m	\$7.8m	\$60m	\$20m	profitable
2	40	6.5	50	10	profitable
3	40	5.2	40	0	normally profitable
4	40	3.9	30	−10	unprofitable
5	40	2.6	20	−20	unprofitable

The Test Specified More Elaborately for a Growing Candidate

If the new unit's earnings are expected to grow over time, then almost certainly its assets will grow too. Thus, some mix of new equity funds and debt (borrowed) funds will have to be raised each year to finance this asset growth. Since the equity funds will come from earnings retention, r will be some positive magnitude each year. Whether it is large or small will depend on whether the asset additions are large or small, and on whether GP will finance the additions with a small amount or a large amount of debt funds.

With earnings being partly retained each year, M must be determined with the more complicated equation:

$$M = \frac{E_1[1 - r_1]}{(1 + k_e)} + \frac{E_2[1 - r_2]}{(1 + k_e)^2} + \frac{E_3[1 - r_3]}{(1 + k_e)^3} + \frac{E_4[1 - r_4]}{(1 + k_e)^4}$$
$$+ \frac{E_5[1 - r_5]}{(1 + k_e)^5} + \frac{TM_6}{(1 + k_e)^5}$$

In this equation the planning period equals 5 years; E_3, for example, represents a forecast of the earnings the new unit would generate in Year 3, and r_3 represents a forecast of the fraction of E_3 that would be reinvested; $E_3[1 - r_3]$, therefore, represents a forecast of ECF in Year 3; and TM_6 represents a forecast of the unit's "terminal" market value at the beginning of Year 6 (and end of Year 5). The latter is the best estimate of what the unit would be worth (and thus could be sold for), at that time, and would depend on what ECF stream the unit could be expected to generate after Year 5.

How would GP actually use this equation to calculate M for a particular candidate? It first must study:

- The economics of the candidate's market (especially its future growth and the intensity of price competition)
- The candidate's probable competitive strategy as a unit of GP (especially, the extent to which its product will be differentiated)
- The historical financial statements of both the candidate and the candidate's major rivals

Then GP must forecast, in the light of these studies, the most likely magnitudes, for each year over the planning period, of the new units:

- Sales growth (given its sales in the current year)
- Ratio, or margin, of pretax operating earnings to sales
- Net fixed asset turnover (ratio of sales to net fixed assets)
- Current asset turnover (ratio of current assets to sales)
- Percentage of asset additions that will be financed with debt
- Percentage cost of this debt
- Effective tax rate

The debt ratio would reflect GP's opinion of the appropriate debt policy for the unit. In addition, GP must decide how much of the unit's present long-term debt it will assume.

Next, GP must deduce from these forecasts (and a forecast of future interest charges on its assumed debt) the new unit's pro forma financial statements for the period: sales, pretax operating earnings, operating earnings, earnings, debt (assumed plus new), equity (the initial EC plus new equity investments in the form of earnings retention), and ECF. For purposes of understanding more fully the prospective profitability performance of the new unit, GP also ought to calculate the unit's ROE for each of the 5 years. For Year 3, for example, ROE would equal the ratio of E_3 to the equity capital on the pro forma balance sheets, as of the beginning of Year 3.

Finally, GP must estimate the TM as of the end of the planning period, TM_6. This would require, essentially, forecasting the new unit's earnings for Year 6, E_6, and then multiplying this forecast by the best estimate possible of the appropriate "price earnings" or "value-earnings" ratio for the unit, at that point in time. Assuming k_e continues to equal 13 percent, this ratio will be given by the equation:

$$\frac{TM_6}{E_6} = \left[1 - \frac{g}{\Delta ROE}\right] \div .13 - g,$$

where g is the unit's prospective long-run earnings growth rate, ΔROE is the unit's prospective long-run incremental ROE (the average annual rate of return on *new* equity investments beyond Year 5), and the ratio of g to ΔROE will give the unit's prospective long-run retention ratio.

So if, for example, g is forecasted to be 2 percent and ΔROE is forecasted to equal k_e plus 1 point, the value-earnings multiple will be:

$$\left[1 - \frac{.02}{.14}\right] \div [.13 - .02] = 7.8$$

But if g is forecasted to equal 6 percent and ΔROE is forecasted to equal k_e plus 3 points, the multiple will be:

$$\left[1 - \frac{.06}{.16}\right] \div [.13 - .06] = 8.9$$

What are the long-term growth rate and ΔROE likely to be for a candidate unit that GP thinks may be promising? If the unit's product market will *not* slip from maturity to decline, g presumably will run somewhere between zero and the average rate at which nominal GNP is expected to grow: The exact location depends on just how mature the market will be. The ΔROE probably cannot exceed k_e by more than two or three percentage points, unless barriers to market entry are unusually high and durable; the best bet for most markets is that the "spread" between ΔROE and k_e will be about one percentage point. Note that the closer to zero this long-term spread is, the less sensitive the value-earnings multiple will be to the magnitude of g.

To illustrate the actual evaluation of the candidate, after all the forecasts have been made, we can suppose that GP determines for the candidate that

- The present discounted value of the unit's ECF stream over the planning period equals $30 million.
- The present discounted value of TM_6 equals $90 million.

Thus, if the initial EC of the candidate equalled $140 million, GP would conclude that

$$NPV = \$30m + \$90m - \$140m = -\$20m$$

Therefore, the acquisition is prospectively unprofitable; the price is too high, given the margins, turnovers, and growth rates being forecasted. But if EC equalled $100m, GP would conclude instead that

$$NPV = \$30m + \$90m - \$100m = \$20m$$

In this case, the acquisition is prospectively profitable.

Complications in Applying the Test

In applying the positive NPV test to any particular acquisition opportunity, GP's biggest problem is producing realistic forecasts. But that is not the company's only problem. It will have to judge the riskiness of the new unit and the extent to which the unit should be financially leveraged. If the unit holds cash or the acquisition offers the prospect of synergistic benefits, account must be taken of this element (or these elements, if both prevail).

Risk and the Percentage of Equity Capital, k_e

For an average large company and the average business unit of this company, k_e is given by the equation

$$k_e = k_T + MRP,$$

where k_T is the long-term U.S. Treasury bond rate, and MRP is the market, or average, risk premium. In the early part of 1991, the former was running at about 8.5 percent. Over the last decade, the latter appears to have averaged about 4.5 percent. For companies and business units in general, k_e is given by the equation

$$k_e = k_T + B[MRP], \quad B \gtrless 1,$$

where B (beta) should be thought of as a multiplier that tells the company or unit whether its own risk premium is greater or less than average, and if so, by how much. For most large companies and most business units of these companies, B is somewhere between 0.7 and 1.3. Whether B, and thus k_e, for a particular company or unit, is small or large relative to the average depends primarily on whether the variability of margins over time (business risk) is small or large, and on whether the percentage of assets financed with long-term debt (financial risk) is small or large.

Financial Leverage

What percentage of the new unit's assets should be financed with long-term debt? There are two principles GP can use to answer this question.

The first is that as this percentage increases (and the ratio of pretax operating earnings to interest payments—the coverage ratio—decreases), the negative impact on earnings each year is dominated by the decrease in equity capital that GP has to invest initially, and over time. As a consequence, the average ROE (calculated against an initial base of EC) generated by the acquisition also increases with the use of leverage, subject to two critical conditions. The first is that the product of the unit's asset turnover and operating earnings margin must *exceed* consistently the aftertax cost of debt funds. The asset turnover, in the first year of the new unit's life, is defined as the ratio of sales to the sum of EC and all of the candidate's debt that GP assumes. The second condition is that all the debt GP chooses to use in financing the new unit will be long-term, and therefore permanent (in the sense that each debt instrument will be replaced at maturity with a comparable instrument). If these conditions do not hold, leverage will *not* magnify the new unit's ROE's *consistently* over time.

The second principle is that although financial risk, and therefore k_e, increases as the average permanent coverage ratio decreases, the ROE increases faster, at least until this ratio reaches some threshhold level. Unfortunately, for most companies, it is unclear precisely what this threshhold is: 4.0, 3.0, 2.0, or some other magnitude. There is reason to believe, however, that taking the coverage ratio down to 3.0, and perhaps even 2.5, would add only about three percentage points to k_e, and that this increment ordinarily would be significantly less than the concomitant increment in ROE (assuming the two magnification conditions are being met).

What do these two guidelines tell us about the profitability of "leveraged buyouts," acquisitions financed with a very large fraction of debt? (In some cases—for example, the Safeway and R.J. Reynolds acquisitions by Kravis, Kohlberg, and Roberts (KKR)—the debt is so large that, initially, the coverage ratio is *less than* 1.0.) By themselves, the guidelines do not actually tell us very much. The reason is that, with few exceptions, companies that leverage acquirees heavily undertake as soon as possible to reduce debt-to-asset ratios significantly. Returning to the R.J. Reynolds example, KKR, by early 1991, already had replaced about one third of the $25 billion in debt that it had put on the company's balance sheet, at the time of the acquisition, two years earlier. So, for leveraged buyouts in general, if *long-run* leverage ratios are not very different from the leverage ratios that characterize acquisitions in general, the *relative* profitability of leveraged buyouts will depend on other factors. The two most important are the relative prices paid for them (do these buyouts command higher premiums?) and the relative effectiveness with which they are managed, subsequent to the deals (do these buyouts show greater improvement in margins and turnovers?).

Cash

If the candidate holds, say, $15 million in nonoperating "cash" (funds that are not needed to facilitate transactions and that, accordingly, are invested in some type of securities), GP can account for the $15 million in its evaluation, in one of two ways. It can treat the cash as an inflow and add it to M, or it can treat the cash as a discount from the price and subtract it from EC. Some companies, in calculating an acquisition NPV, do both, but that is double counting. It also would be double counting to add the cash to M *and* include interest returns on the cash, to the forecasted ECF stream.

Synergy

GP's acquisition of a particular candidate might work because of the combination's ability to generate synergistic benefits for the new unit ("synergy-out"), for the company ("synergy-in"), or for both. Synergy-out benefits could take the form of an increase in demand for the new unit's product (because GP's brand is put on the product) or a decrease in the unit's production costs (because GP makes excess capacity available to the unit), or both. Synergy-in benefits could take the form of an increase in demand for, say, Red's product (because the *new unit's* brand is put on the product) or a decrease in GP's costs (because the unit brings a tax-loss carry-forward with it), or both.

If the positive NPV test is applied along the lines described earlier, the impact of synergy-out benefits would be included in the forecasts GP makes of the new unit's sales, pretax operating earnings margins, and asset turnovers. The impact of synergy-in benefits would not be included in these forecasts. They would have to be factored into the NPV calculation as add-ons.

CANDIDATE SCREENING: PROFITABILITY CONDITIONS

Suppose GP has identified both a target market and a company, Brown, operating in this market that is for sale at some price. What are the conditions that must be met for the acquisition of Brown to be profitable? It is easier to deal with this question if we first look at the conditions necessary for entering the market profitably, by start-up (that is, by constructing the plant and assembling the people and equipment required, to conduct operations in the market at the desired scale).

Conditions of Profitable Growth by Start-up

GP would assess the profitability of a start-up, the same general way it would assess the profitability of an acquisition: by comparing the M of the resulting new business unit with the initial EC of the undertaking. For M to be greater than EC, there are three major conditions that must be met.

First, the target market must represent a good "fit" for GP. Fit is a shorthand term for the idea that the new market is related to one or more of GP's existing markets, at least to some significant degree. Without a good fit—without knowledge of either the market's customers, its major incumbent rivals, its technology, or some combination of the three—GP would soon find itself at a disadvantage in the market. With a good fit, GP at least stands a chance of being able to compete effectively. Fit alone is not sufficient for a good competitive position, but it is a necessary component.

Second, the economics of the market must be good. This means that there is little excess capacity in the market (and that price competition therefore is not intense), that warfare in the promotion arena is not too expensive, that barriers to entry by newcomers are on the high side, and that the market will not slide from maturity to decline. In such a market, there is a strong presumption that incumbent rivals are generating ROEs that, on average, exceed k_e significantly.

Third, the unit must stand not just a chance, but a good chance, of being able to compete effectively in the market. This is equivalent to saying that although advantage barriers around the market are high, the unit, unlike other prospective entrants, can surmount them by the development of offering and cost advantages that neutralize or dominate the advantage of incumbents.

For any particular start-up that meets the fit test, the relationship between M and EC will depend on the combined impact of the market economics that GP expects to see, and the competitive position that it expects to attain. If the market economics and competitive position are strong, M will be greater than EC; if the market economics and competitive position are weak, M will be less than EC.

The Conditions of Profitable Growth by Acquisition

Entry by acquisition is not likely to be profitable unless it meets the fit test. If GP doesn't know very much about the market in which Brown operates, the odds are stacked against success.

Let M(M) be Brown's *actual* preacquisition market value, M(SA) be GP's opinion of Brown's stand-alone market value (its value as an independent company), and M be, again, GP's opinion of Brown's market value as one of its own business units. In addition, note that Brown's present owners almost certainly will not accept less than M(M) for their shares. Finally, assume for the time being that GP does not think that Brown is underpriced on a stand-alone basis, that GP will not have to pay a premium over M(M) for Brown, and that GP will keep Brown's stand-alone ratio unchanged (and by implication will not finance any part of the price of Brown with debt). Together, these temporary assumptions tell us that

$$M(M) = M(SA) = EC$$

It follows that the equity cost of Brown's common stock will reflect fully the economics of the market and Brown's stand-alone competitive position in that market. For example, suppose that Brown's book equity equals $100 million and that because the market economics and competitive position are both weak, the ratio of M(M) to book is 0.7. Then we would see

$$M(M) = \$70m$$
$$M(SA) = \$70m$$
$$EC = \$70m$$

If instead, market economics and competitive position both are strong, with the result that the ratio of M(M) to book is 1.4, we would see

$$M(M) = \$140m$$
$$M(SA) = \$140m$$
$$EC = \$140m$$

The more Brown is worth as an independent company (the "better" a company it is), the more it will cost.

It also follows that for the acquisition to be profitable, M must be greater than M(M); Brown must be worth more to GP than it is worth as an independent company, to Brown's present owners. Regardless of what drives M(M) and M(SA), there must be some benefit or set of benefits from acquiring Brown, which are not reflected in M(SA). Brown must represent to GP one or more types of a "value bargain." Under our current assumptions, there are four such types:

1. *"Turnaround" Bargain.* The prospect exists that GP can create value (that is, add an increment to M), by improving Brown's management performance.
2. *"Expansion" Bargain.* The prospect exists that GP can create value by undertaking profitable investments in new related businesses, which Brown could have undertaken itself, but didn't.
3. *"Synergy" Bargain.* The prospect exists that GP can create value by combining one or more of its own units with Brown in a way that generates favorable side effects on demand or cost in Brown, GP, or both.
4. *"Restructure" Bargain.* The prospect exists that GP can create value by selling or "divesting" Brown units for an equity price greater than their current contributions to M(SA).

In short, subject to one caveat, the Brown acquisition will be profitable if, for any combination of these four reasons, GP can increase Brown's ECF stream (defined broadly to include the net equity proceeds from any divestiture GP might make of a Brown operation) relative to what the stream would be on a stand-alone basis. The caveat? Before GP can elevate Brown's ECF stream, it must be able to replicate the stand-alone stream. The base from which it improves Brown's financial performance must be the base it acquires. Here is where the "fit" condition specifically enters the picture. GP cannot in fact achieve this replication, unless it starts from a competitive position that is at least as good as Brown's stand-alone position. To do this it must be knowledgeable about Brown's market. The less this knowledgeability, the weaker the chance that Brown is a potential value bargain.

But won't Brown bring that knowledge with it? After all, GP would be acquiring more than Brown's assets and customer base; it also would be taking on board the people that *now* manage Brown. Judging from case materials reported primarily in the business press, GP, at best, would have a year or two after acquiring Brown before the current top management group leaves and has to be replaced by managers from GP's own cadre. If Brown is a turnaround bargain, GP would have to supply new managers immediately; the same may be true if Brown is a threshhold bargain.

Are there any other reasons Brown might represent a value bargain to GP? If we introduce the possibility that M(M) is *less* than M(SA), and that GP would be able to decrease Brown's interest coverage ratio, there are two. Subject, again, to our fit caveat, Brown could be either or both of these bargain types:

1. *"Underpricing" Bargain.* The prospect exists that GP will experience value creation if the market currently undervalues Brown, but at some point can be expected to revise upward its forecast of Brown's stand-alone ECF stream.
2. *"Leverage" Bargain.* The prospect exists that GP can create value by increasing the degree to which Brown is leveraged with long-term debt.

What are the clues that tell GP it may face a turnaround, expansion, synergy, restructure, underpricing or leverage bargain? How can GP persuade itself that these clues really do signal the potential for value creation?

Exhibit 13.5 answers these questions in a stylized way for each of the six types of bargains. Note that some of the clues in Column 2 probably can be picked up from publicly available financial statements (ROE, relative use of leverage, relative margins, relative asset turnovers, relative growth), while some cannot (excess capacity, offering position relative to positions of comparable offerings in other regions, complementarity and brandability of the offering, business profitability and value, percentage cost of equity capital). Note, too, that none of the cases in Column 3 can be made routinely. GP must put work into them before it can say with confidence that Brown is a potential value bargain.

EXHIBIT 13.5. Targeting value bargains.

Bargain Types	Targeting Criteria: Clues — Establishing Potential	Targeting Criteria: Establishing Realizability
Turnaround	Brown is an underperformer relative to incumbent rivals; its margin, asset turn, and growth levels all fall below theirs.	GP must make a case that it can fix the problem by reducing costs, improving the offering, and pricing for return instead of volume.
Expansion	Brown's regional offering has features and characteristics that beat the features and characteristics of similar offerings in other regions.	GP must make a case that it has the resources (management and financial) to take Brown's offering national.
Synergy	Brown has excess capacity that can be used in a GP operation; further, Brown's offering complements one of GP's product lines and may be able to take GP's stronger brand.	GP must make a case that Brown's capacity can be put to work *efficiently,* that the Brown offering is indeed brandable, and that branding will build demand, relative to what it otherwise would be.
Restructure	One of Brown's units is unprofitable, and is therefore contributing negatively to Brown's value, M(SA); it would be very difficult to turn around.	GP must make a case that it can divest the unit for equity proceeds considerably greater than the unit's contribution to M(SA).
Underpricing	Brown's ROE is running above the company's cost of equity capital but its market-to-book ratio is significantly less than 1.0.	GP must make a case that this ROE is sustainable *and* that the stock market eventually will pick this up, even if Brown eventually becomes part of GP.
Leverage	Brown uses significantly less leverage (has a higher coverage ratio) than incumbent rivals.	GP must make a case that matching the interest coverage ratios of rivals would not increase Brown's cost of equity capital very much.

The Premium Problem

History indicates that contrary to what we have been assuming, GP will not just have to pay more than M(M) for Brown, it will have to pay significantly more. For 172 acquisitions (many of which were large), undertaken over the period 1976–1986, premiums over M(M) ranged up to 120 percent and averaged about 60 percent; the range quartiles ran as follows:

First quartile : 38%

Third quartile : 81%

The prospect of having to pay a premium for Brown means that for the acquisition to be profitable, Brown must be not just a value bargain, but a value bargain of sufficient magnitude to permit both "recapture" of the premium and generation of GP's minimum acceptable level of value creation. For example, suppose that the latter is 15 percent, that M(M) equals $100 million, and (to keep matters from getting too complicated) that Brown is not a leverage bargain. Then GP would have to turn Brown into a business unit worth

- $145m, if it pays a below-average 30 percent premium ($145m equals $100m times the sum of 1.30 and .15)

- $175m, if it pays an average 60 percent premium ($100m times the sum of 1.60 and .15)

- $205m, if it pays an above-average 90 percent premium ($100m times the sum of 1.90 and .15)

How should GP deal with this problem? To begin with, it must acknowledge to itself that fully recapturing a typical premium (to get 15 percent value creation) is a very challenging task. If, on a stand-alone basis, Brown is growing at the GNP rate and generating an ROE of 14 percent (calculated against an initial base of Brown's present book equity), GP, in order to turn Brown into a $175 million unit, would have to push its book-based ROE up *permanently* to the 19 percent level (unless it can add permanently a point or two of growth). This would be difficult to do in most U.S. industrial markets. Competition ordinarily is simply too fierce to allow *sustainable* increases in ROE of this magnitude. Put another way, GP must realize that unless the Brown acquisition is very unusual, it cannot expect to make a value-creating investment, unless it can keep the premium under a level, significantly below the average.

But how can GP achieve, in practice, this appealing goal of premium limitation? If Brown has hired an investment banker, it will have heard a number of times that "every acquiree gets a large premium and so should you." If GP also has hired a banker, it will have heard, first, that "a large premium is the going price for doing a deal," and then, that "there is no need to worry: As long as there's no dilution you're all right."

There are two general approaches GP can take to the problem of premium limitation. Both presuppose that the company and its candidate will use outside help (for dealing with legal, valuation, and strategic issues), only on a time-based or fixed-fee basis. Taking advice from people who charge a fee geared to the acquisition price is a questionable idea.

The first approach is rooted in the principle that openness is the best policy in growth by acquisition. If GP applied the principle to Brown (let's say, that Brown appears to be a combination expansion, synergy, and leverage bargain), it would show its complete post acquisition value creation plan—its analysis of all Brown's opportunities for value creation—to Brown's managers (who GP probably wants to stay on). Then it would offer to split the sum of value increments on some mutually agreeable basis: perhaps 50:50, or perhaps 60 percent for the company and 40 percent for Brown's current shareholders. Assuming the latter, if GP can add 30 percent to the value of Brown, Brown would get a premium of 12 percent. If GP can add 40 percent to the value of Brown, the premium would equal 16 percent.

An obvious possibility here, though, is that Brown will take issue with the company's analysis: "If you exploit properly the expansion bargain opportunities we represent, Brown's value could be increased 60 percent; our premium ought to be 24 percent." In the event this is said, GP should switch to the second approach. In general, suggest that Brown share the upside risk. In particular, respond to Brown's contention with one of these two proposals: (1) Instead of cash, take our common stock in exchange for your common stock. If the price of our stock does not yet reflect the 40 percent value increment we foresee, you will get a part of the capital gain when the price does reflect that increment, or if you are right, when the price does reflect the value increment you foresee. If the price of our stock *already* reflects the 40 percent value increment and you are right about the 60 percent value increment, you will get part of the capital gain, when the market comes to accept your view. (2) We'll set the deal up as an earn-out. You'll get a 16 percent premium today plus 40 percent of all equity cash flows that Brown generates over the next five years, in excess of those we have projected.

The Implementation Problem

There is one final condition of profitable growth by acquisition. Not only must GP make a case that the investment in Brown will generate good pro formas, it must make these projected statements come true. GP must see to it that Brown's potential for value-creation is realized.

How successful GP's realization effort turns out to be will depend on GP's ability to develop and execute effectively, the strategy called for by the nature of the acquisition. If Brown is a potential turnaround bargain, GP actually must improve its product, reduce its costs, and revise its pricing. If Brown is an expansion bargain, GP actually must carry out profitable start-up entries into the regional markets, where its studies indicate that Brown's offering would be a significant advantage. If Brown is a synergy bargain, GP actually must employ the unit's excess capacity in a way that reduces the company's consolidated average costs, and actually must brand and subsequently promote Brown's offering in a way that builds demand for it.

It was stressed earlier that for GP to have this ability, the company must be knowledgeable about Brown's markets. It also must be stressed that this knowledgeability cannot be brought to bear on the task, unless GP can integrate Brown into the GP management structure. Brown's management "model" must be made compatible with GP's model; Brown soon must come to embrace the same profitability objective that GP does, *measure* profitability in the same way, evaluating strategic alternatives in the same way, set and monitor the achievement of performance targets in the same way, and "incentivize" executive compensation in the same way.

Companies who come up short in their integration efforts sometimes are said to have trouble "digesting" acquirees. Currently, for example, Bridgestone is reported to be having a digestion problem with its Firestone acquisition, and Daimler is reported to be having a similar problem with several large acquisitions it made in the second half of the last decade. In the U.S., indigestion problems are thought to be one of the major reasons for the large fraction—some estimate it at 50 percent—of acquisitions that have ended up as divestitures.

GROWTH BY ACQUISITION: GOOD IDEA, OR NOT SO GOOD?

Should companies undertake to diversify themselves by acquiring other companies? Is growth by acquisition likely to be a profitable strategy? It would be easier to answer these questions if we first could develop full postpurchase profitability audits of all the acquisitions made over the last 20 years. But that is not in the cards. On the one hand, we do not have the comprehensive financial data that is necessary for producing audits of the acquired units themselves; acquiring companies with few exceptions do not publish separate earnings statements and balance sheets for their acquirees. On the other hand, while we do have a lot of financial data on the *acquiring* companies (including the postacquisition behavior of their stock prices), these data do not tell us very much about how profitable the acquisitions turned out to be; if General Electric's ROE and stock price both increased over the two or three years after the company's acquisition of RCA, was that because or in spite of the acquisition?

Nonetheless, we do have some data about postacquisitions: A record of acquisitions that subsequently were divested, a record of premiums paid for acquirees, and a body of brief reports on selected acquisition outcomes, which various acquirors have given to the business press, security analysts, and consultants. And judging from both these data and our knowledge of ROE levels, in most product market groups, there can be little doubt that profitability results have been quite mixed for companies pursuing a strategy of growth by acquisition.

It is not clear exactly what the average outcome has been (although a good guess is that the typical acquisition has been at least somewhat unprofitable). It is clear, though, that the range of outcomes has distributed around this average, whatever its magnitude has been. Those on the lower end of the distribution have done poorly (they have been significantly unprofitable and some have been spectacularly unprofitable), and those on the upper end have done much better (most, and perhaps all, have been profitable and some have been very profitable). Herein lies the moral for companies contemplating growth by acquisition: The moral has two parts.

First, the strategy should be undertaken with a keen awareness of how difficult it is to implement profitably. The road to success is strewn with landmines: Picking the wrong product market in which to look for a candidate; picking the right product market, but the wrong candidate; picking the right candidate, but paying the wrong price for it; or paying the right price for the right candidate, but executing the wrong program for realizing the potential of the acquisition. It is because of these landmines that so many acquisitions have been, and undoubtedly will continue to be, value-destroying.

Second, the strategy also should be undertaken with a keen awareness that the landmines can be dodged. Growth by acquisition has been profitable, when companies carrying it out have avoided all the critical mistakes that companies in the lower end of the distribution make. In short, the question is not whether growth by acquisition can be profitable. It can. The question is what guidelines should be followed in order to raise the odds to a high level that it *will be* profitable.

GLOSSARY

Acquisition: Taking control of a business owned by another company (or division of another company), by purchasing either the assets or from 51 percent to 100 percent of the common stock of the company (or division).

Affiliation: An acquisition of from 51 percent to 100 percent of another company's (or division's) common stock, following which the acquiree is established as an affiliate, or subsidiary, of the acquiror and continues to exist as a legal entity.

Asset Purchase: An acquisition of the assets used in the business of another company (or division), after which an offer usually is made to hire most, or all, of the business's employees.

Net Present Value: For a proposed acquisition, the difference between: (a) the present discounted value of the equity cash flows (earnings less investment) that the acquiree is expected to generate over time; and (b) the present cost in equity capital of the acquiree.

Premium: The difference between the price paid or asked for a public company's common stock and the price at which the stock was selling prior to the actual or prospective acquiror's decision to purchase a controlling interest in this stock.

Profitability: For a proposed acquisition, the NPV of an equity investment in the acquiree; where a profitable acquisition is one with a positive NPV, and the degree of profitability varies directly with the magnitude of the NPV.

Statutory Merger: An acquisition of from 51 percent to 100 percent of another company's (or division's) common stock, following which the acquired unit (the acquiree) is fused into the acquiring company (the acquiror) and ceases to exist as a legal entity.

Value Bargain: An acquiree whose market value to the acquiror is greater than the acquiree's standalone (preacquisition) market value.

Value Creation: A sustainable increase in an acquiror's market value relative to what the value would have been in the absence of the acquisition.

FOR FURTHER READING

Alberts, William W., "The Profitability of Growth by Merger," in William W. Alberts and Joel E. Segall, eds., *The Corporate Merger* (Chicago, IL: University of Chicago Press, 1974).

Alberts, William W., "Can Typical Acquisition Premiums Be Recaptured?" *Sloan Management Review* (January 1992).

Brealey, Richard A., and Stewart C. Myers, *Principles of Corporate Finance,* Third Edition (New York: McGraw Hill, 1988).

Fortier, Diana, "Hostile Takeovers and the Market for Corporate Control," *Economic Perspectives* (Chicago, IL: Federal Reserve Bank of Chicago, January/February 1989).

Haspeslagh, Phillipe, and David B. Jemison, *Managing Acquisitions: Creating Value Through Corporate Renewal* (New York: Free Press, 1991).

Porter, Michael, "From Competitive Advantage to Corporate Strategy," *Harvard Business Review* (May-June 1987).

Rappaport, Alfred, *Creating Shareholder Value* (Chicago, IL: Free Press, 1986).

Salter, Malcolm S., and Wolf A. Weinhold, *Diversification Through Acquisition* (Chicago, IL: Free Press, 1979).

Weston, J. Fred, Kwang S. Chung, Susan E. Hoag, *Mergers, Restructuring, and Corporate Control* (Englewood Cliffs, NJ: Prentice-Hall, 1990).

14 CORPORATE GOVERNANCE: THE BOARD OF DIRECTORS

Charles A. Anderson and Robert H. Anthony

This chapter describes the nature and function of the board of directors, which has the ultimate responsibility for the governance of a corporation. It describes the board's activities in normal meetings, in strategy meetings, and in special situations. It also describes the work of three especially important board committees: the compensation committee, the audit committee, and the finance committee.[1]

The description focuses on the approximately 15,000 corporations that are subject to regulations of the SEC, but most of the description is also relevant to the boards of smaller corporations.

WHY HAVE A BOARD OF DIRECTORS?

Every corporation is required by law to have a board of directors. Its legal function is to govern the affairs of the corporation. However, in a small corporation whose chief executive officer (CEO) is also the controlling shareholder, the CEO actually governs, and the Board acts primarily as an advisor.

When a corporation grows to a size where it needs outside capital, it may go public by selling shares of stock (as explained in Chapter 12), and the board then represents the interests of these shareholders. The shareholders, who are the owners of the corporation, have a say in the way their company is run. They expect to receive regular, reliable reports on the company's operations. If the company is profitable, they expect to receive dividends. If the company has problems, the owners need to know about them, so that they can take remedial action, if necessary.

A corporation may have many shareholders, however. American Telephone & Telegraph Corporation has 2.6 million shareholders, and companies listed on the New York Stock Exchange must have at least 2,200 shareholders. Individual shareholders obviously are too numerous to govern the company directly; moreover, most of them are engaged in their own pursuits and will not give much, if any, time to governance. They therefore elect people to act for them: The board of directors.

SIZE AND COMPOSITION OF THE BOARD

A 1989 survey of large corporations found that the typical size of the board was 14, compared with 16 in the early 1980s.[2] Some boards, especially those in banks, are much larger. Large boards must delegate much of their work to an executive committee.

Most of the members of a typical board are "outside directors"; that is, they are not employees of the corporation. At one time, most board members were "inside directors," and in a few boards, this is still the case. The trend toward outside directors results from the fact that shareholders believe it is in their best interests for the board to have a significant degree of independence from the company's management. After all, the board is responsible for selecting, appraising, and compensating management; if the board and management are the same people, the board can hardly perform its governance role in an objective manner.

The principal sources of outside board members are CEOs and senior officers of other corporations (but not competitors). Other outsiders are lawyers, bankers, physicians (on health care boards), scientists and engineers (on high technology boards), retired government officials, and academics. A few people are professional board members; that is, their full-time occupation is serving on boards. The number of female and minority board members has increased substantially in recent years. The CEO and, perhaps, one or two senior members of management are typically members of the board.

Board members are compensated. In 80 percent of the large companies surveyed in 1989, there was an annual retainer of at least $20,000, plus a fee for each board or committee meeting attended. Two thirds of the boards had retirement plans (compared with only one-fifth in 1983).

Board members are elected at the annual meeting of shareholders. The shareholders almost always elect a slate proposed by the incumbent board; so, as a practical matter, the board is self-perpetuating. The process of selecting candidates for filling board vacancies is an important board function. It is becoming increasingly common to have staggered terms, that is, to elect one third of the board each year, for a three-year term. This practice is intended to discourage corporate raiders from seeking to obtain control of the company.

RELATION TO THE CEO

The board of directors "directs" and the CEO "executes" the board's directions, but these terms are not an accurate description of the roles of these two parties. In the majority of companies, the chief executive officer is also chairman of the board of directors, and is the principal architect of policies, as well as being responsible for their execution. The CEO is indeed the "chief."

The board selects the CEO. Having selected what it believes to be the best available person for the job, the board wants to give the CEO its full support. To do less would inhibit the CEO from doing the job that the board expects. The CEO is accountable to the board and is subject to termination if the board decides that his or her performance is unsatisfactory.

The appropriate relationship is one of trust. The board must believe beyond any question that the CEO is completely trustworthy, will provide the board with all the information it wants and needs, will withhold nothing, and will not slant arguments to support a preconceived position. Conversely, the CEO must believe that he or she has the full support of the board.

Appraising the CEO

A major responsibility of the board is to appraise the CEO. If performance is below expectations, there are two possible explanations: (1) The CEO is to blame; (2) extraneous influences are responsible. In most cases, both factors are involved, and the directors have the extraordinarily difficult job of judging their relative importance. If they conclude that the CEO has made an incorrect decision, they may suggest a different course of action. More likely, however, they will say nothing and mentally file the incident away, for future reference, in evaluating the CEO. The Business Roundtable, a group of CEOs of leading companies, succinctly described the directors' role vis-a-vis the CEO as "challenging, yet supportive and positive."

Thus, an important function of board meetings, of conversations, and even of social occasions, is to give the directors a basis for continuously appraising the CEO. Directors usually cannot make constructive suggestions on the details of current operations. Occasionally, they may call the CEO's attention to a certain matter. Primarily, however, they listen carefully to what the CEO says and do their best to judge whether things are going satisfactorily and, if they are not, decide where the responsibility lies.

The directors want the CEO to be frank and to give an accurate analysis of the company's status and prospects; concealing bad news is one of the worst sins a CEO can commit. Nevertheless, human nature is such that directors cannot expect the CEO to be completely objective. Incipient problems may go away, and making them known, even in the relative privacy of the boardroom, may cause unnecessary alarm. Directors are therefore on the alert for indications of significant problems that may lie ahead. In many of the well publicized bankruptcies of public companies, the directors were significantly responsible; they did not identify or act on the problem soon enough.

Louis B. Cabot, former chairman of the board of Cabot Corporation, had a frustrating experience with the ill-fated Penn Central corporation, one of the largest bankruptcies that had occurred up to that time. He joined the Penn Central board about a year before the company collapsed. From the outset, he was disturbed by management's unwillingness to furnish the information about performance that he felt he needed. A few months after joining the board, he wrote the CEO a letter that contains a succinct description of the director's role:

> I believe directors should not be the managers of a business, but they should ensure the excellence of its management's performance. To do this, they have to measure that performance against agreed-upon yardsticks.

The Next CEO

It is impossible to tell beforehand whether or not an executive will make a good CEO. The best indicator is how well a candidate performs. In most instances, therefore, the board looks to senior executives with proven track records as candidates for the CEO position. And one of the most important jobs that a board assigns to a CEO is to develop a succession plan for the company's senior managers. The purpose of such a plan is to identify potential CEO candidates, provide them with opportunities for growth, and groom them for higher level positions. The board participates actively in this process, by meeting with the CEO (usually once a year) in a meeting devoted largely to reviewing the senior management. Typical questions asked are: How is a key executive performing? What is his or her potential? Who are potential successors for the CEO—now and in the future?

At Carborundum Company, for example, when William Wendel was chairman, such a meeting was referred to as the "truck meeting" because Bill always started with the question: "Suppose I am run over by a truck tomorrow; what will you do?" At Carborundum, two and sometimes three persons were identified as potential CEOs. As time went on, individuals were added to or eliminated from the list, and their relative ranking changed. When this process works properly, an agreed upon CEO candidate is available in an emergency, as well as having a CEO in place to take over from a retiring CEO, in a normal succession.

When boards fail to deal effectively with succession, it is often necessary to go outside the company for a new CEO. This increases the risk and is usually a symptom that the board has not paid sufficient attention to this important responsibility. Under most circumstances, the chances for a successful succession are much higher when the CEO position is filled by a proven executive from within the organization.

NORMAL BOARD MEETINGS

Most boards meet eight, nine, or ten times a year. Some meet only quarterly, and a few meet monthly. The typical meeting lasts two or three hours, but may go considerably longer if contentious issues arise.

Premeeting Material

Prior to the meeting, board members are sent an agenda and a packet of material on topics to be discussed at the meeting. This "homework" usually requires several hours, and prior to the meeting, directors may query the CEO on matters that require clarification.

Current Situation and Outlook

The first substantive topic on the agenda usually is a discussion of current information about the company and its outlook. The CEO leads this discussion, perhaps delegating part of it to another senior officer. Much of the information is financial, that is, condensed income statements for each division, or for groups of division and key balance sheet items, such as inventory, receivables, and corporate expenses. There are three formats for presenting this financial information:

1. Comparison of management's current estimate of performance for the whole year with budgeted performance for the year: How do we now estimate that the company is going to perform for the whole year? This is the most important type of information. However, it is also the most sensitive, and many companies do not circulate it prior to the meeting.
2. Comparison of actual performance for the current period and for the year-to-date with budgeted performance for these periods. Because the actual numbers are firm, they provide a more objective basis for analysis than the current estimate for the year.
3. Comparison of actual performance with performance for the same periods last year. A carefully prepared budget incorporates changes in the business and the economy that have occurred since the prior year. It

is, therefore, a more meaningful basis for comparison than last year's numbers. If, however, the budgeted amounts, particularly the estimate of revenue, are highly uncertain, the numbers for last year provide a firmer foundation for a comparison.

Variances between actual and budgeted performance are discussed. Are unfavorable variances temporary? If not, what steps will be taken to eliminate them or, if they result from unforeseen outside forces, what adjustments in the company's operations will be made?

By reviewing the company's financial performance and raising questions or making suggestions to management, directors form judgements, regarding the company's affairs. In short, they are brought up to date. Moreover, preparing and presenting to the board a report on the company's performance is an important discipline for management.

Other Actions

Next, a number of proposed actions are submitted for board approval. Many of these recommendations come to the full board from committees, which have discussed the topics in meetings, held prior to the board meeting; these are described in a later section of this chapter. Questions may be raised about these recommendations, but these are usually requests for clarification. Board members rely on committee members to explore these matters thoroughly; there is not enough time to do so in the full board meeting. Unless new information surfaces, these recommendations are usually approved.

Then the board covers a number of routine items, each of which is listed on the agenda. These may be requests for approval for capital projects, approval of signature authority for various banking connections, approval of exceptions to pension plans, and approval of certain types of contracts. Except for large capital projects, these items are usually referred to as boiler plate. In most cases, they come to the board because state law, the corporate bylaws, or written policy requires board action. They are approved with little discussion, sometimes en masse, despite the fact that the minutes may state for each of them: "After a full discussion, a motion to adopt the recommendation was duly made and seconded, and the motion was approved."

Education

A division manager assisted by senior associates may make a presentation about the activities of the division. This is an educational experience for the directors. (Some board meetings may be held at company plants or other facilities; this also is a valuable educational device.)

The meeting itself, and the informal activities that usually are associated with it, are also educational. The directors have an opportunity to appraise company officials and their own colleagues. Judgments about these individuals may be invaluable, if the board is at some time required to deal with a crisis situation.

Setting Standards

Partly through written policy statements, but primarily through their attitudes, directors communicate to management, the standards that they believe should govern the organization's actions. There are two general types of standards, which might be labeled economic standards and ethical standards, although neither term is precisely correct.

With respect to economic standards, the directors communicate the overall goals that they believe the company can and should attain: they outline the relative importance of sales growth, earnings per share, and ROI, and the specific numbers that they believe are attainable. They indicate the relative importance of short-run versus long-run performance. In the final analysis, the board generally relies on management's recommendations, but the enthusiasm, or lack of enthusiasm, with which they support a given recommendation conveys important information to management.

Ethical standards are nebulous. The written policy statements are always impeccably virtuous, but the actual expectations of the directors are indicated by the way they react to specific ethical problems. How does the company deal with its women and minority employees? What happens to an employee who has a drinking problem? Does the company have a policy concerning support for the communities in which it has operations? These and many other issues have ethical implications, and the manner in which the board reacts to them, establishes the real policy, regardless of what is in the written statement.

It is easy to rely on counsel's answer to the question: Must we report this unpleasant development to the SEC? The answer depends on the legal interpretation of the regulations. It is much more difficult for the directors to agree, and to convey to management, that a certain course of action, although perhaps within the letter of the law, should not be tolerated. Currently, directors of many companies must wrestle with the policy concerning operations in South Africa. Although it is perfectly legal to be there, does a company's presence do more harm than good?

STRATEGY

A company should have a set of strategies that are well thought out, clear, and well understood by the organization. Strategies include the industry in which the company has decided to operate, its product lines within this industry, the price and quality position of these products, the targeted customers and markets (local, regional, national, international), its distribution channels (direct sales, dealers, distributors), marketing policies (advertising, sales promotion), manufacturing policies (in-house production, plant locations, outside sourcing), and financial policies (mix of debt and equity financing, retained earnings).

The board usually does not have the knowledge necessary to initiate a strategy or to choose among alternative strategies. It must rely on management to take the initiative, make the necessary analyses, and bring its recommendations to the board. What the board can and should do is described by Kenneth R. Andrews in *The Concept of Corporate Strategy*.[3] Andrews writes, as a summary:

> A responsible and effective board should require of its management a unique and durable corporate strategy, review it periodically for its validity, use it as the reference point for all other board decisions, and share with management the risks associated with its adoption.

While it is unrealistic to expect directors to formulate strategies, they should satisfy themselves that management has a sound process for developing them. The strategy is probably acceptable if:

- It is based on careful analysis by people who are in the best position to evaluate it, rather than on an inspiration accepted without study.
- The reasoning seems sensible.
- Directors are not aware of any significant information that has been omitted from the analysis.
- The results expected from the strategy are clearly set forth, so that actual accomplishment can be compared with them.

Strategy Meetings

As a basis for considering strategic plans, many companies arrange a meeting at which directors, together with senior managers, spend one, two, or three days discussing where the company should be headed. In order to minimize distractions and to provide an opportunity for informal discussion and reflection, these meetings are often held at a retreat, distant from the corporate offices. Because of the time required, these strategy meetings are usually held about once every two years.

The primary purpose of a strategy meeting is to explain the strategies and the foundations on which they are based. The explanations themselves provide useful information to the directors. The quality of the rationale for the strategies is an indication of the competence of senior management and of the managers of the divisions concerned. Thus, the strategies provide additional insight about the CEO's abilities and about the abilities of participants who may be candidates for CEO.

Having adopted a corporate strategy, it is important that management adhere to it. Management brings many matters to the board for decision and approval that may impact a company's strategy. Major capital expenditure proposals, acquisitions, divestitures, and financing proposals, are just a few of these. The board makes sure that these proposals are consistent with the adopted strategy. If they are not, the company may drift off course and into serious trouble.

DEALING WITH MAJOR CRISES

In addition to the regular activities described above, boards occasionally must deal with crises. These usually arise unexpectedly and require special board meetings. We describe two of these: firing the CEO and dealing with takeover attempts.

Firing the CEO

There are times when a board must act to replace its CEO. A major criticism of some boards is that they fail to take timely action, when it becomes clear that the CEO should be replaced. Although there may be considerable justification for such criticism, one should recognize that it is much easier for an outside observer to be critical, than it is to actually be a director faced with this decision.

The decision to replace a CEO is subjective and usually emotional. Sometimes there are compelling reasons for taking action—for example, when the CEO has become an alcoholic and has seriously embarrassed the company, or when his or her corporate performance has dramatically deteriorated. In most instances, however, the justification is not so clear. Earnings may not have kept pace with those of industry leaders, because the board discouraged management from assuming additional debt, which would have enabled the company to expand. Or, perhaps, a major acquisition, which the board supported, did not work out. In such instances, it is not obvious whether the primary blame belongs with the CEO.

There are, however, several important signals that can alert a board to potential trouble, when it is evaluating the CEO's capabilities:

- Loss of confidence in the CEO. If a significant number of directors have lost confidence in, or no longer trust, the CEO, he should be replaced.
- Steady deterioration in corporate results. In most instances, this means that earnings seriously lag industry norms for a number of years, without

a defensible explanation. This problem is usually accompanied by the consistent failure to meet projections. The board must act before it is too late.

- Organizational instability. A CEO who consistently has problems in retaining qualified senior executives probably should be replaced.

It is one thing for board members to begin to doubt the CEO's capabilities, but it is quite another thing for them to muster the courage and consensus needed to take action. The CEO and the outside directors have usually worked together for some time and are good, if not close, friends. For the CEO, dismissal is a catastrophic event. It is, therefore, understandable that directors have great difficulty in bringing themselves to take an action that will probably destroy the career of a business associate.

Replacing the CEO precipitates a crisis, not only for the board, but for the entire organization. Furthermore, when it happens, the board must be prepared to announce a successor and to deal with the problems inherent in the transfer of executive authority. Such action puts a major burden on the outside directors. Yet this is their responsibility to the shareholders and to the other constituencies of the corporation.

Unfriendly Takeover Attempts

Another type of crisis event is the hostile or unfriendly takeover attempt. The board of the target company is in a highly stressful situation. Decisions vital to the company's future—even its continued existence—must be made, in circumstances in which emotions are high, vested interests are at stake, and advice is often conflicting. The business press reports daily the dramatic developments of offers and counteroffers, tactics and strategies, as each side in the struggle seeks to gain an advantage. The increase in takeover attempts in recent years has resulted in a preoccupation, on the part of both boards and managements, in seeking ways to avoid attack or to prepare a defense. These efforts are both time-consuming and expensive, and while they may be necessary, they certainly are not productive.

One of the problems in takeover situations is that the board, as the representative of the shareholders, may have different interests from those of management. In most unfriendly takeovers that are successful, the senior management of the target company becomes unemployed. A common accusation, therefore, is that in resisting a takeover, management is simply trying to entrench itself, even though the deal would result in a handsome gain for the shareholders. Directors in these situations must exercise great care to make certain that their decisions are in the shareholders's interest. This is not always easy to determine. What is the intrinsic value of the corporation?

What is the real value of the "junk bonds" being offered to the sharehold-ers? What consideration, if any, should the directors give to the interests of other parties, such as employees, communities, and customers, who could be affected by a change in ownership and a possible breakup of the company? Obviously, these are complex issues for the board.

Although legally the directors are responsible *only* for protecting the interests of the shareholders, conscientious directors do consider the inter-ests of these other parties. In doing so, they run the risk of a lawsuit, alleging that they have not discharged their legal duty.

Directors encounter special problems when the company's management attempts to acquire control through a leveraged buyout. The largest such transaction to date was the 1988 buyout at RJR Nabisco.[4] In that situation, F. Ross Johnson, president and CEO, and several of his senior executives, made an offer to the board to buy the company for $75 per share (at that time the stock was selling in the forties). On the surface this looked like a good deal. The board, however, mindful of its obligation to the shareholders, sought to get the highest price possible. A special committee of outside board members was selected to "auction" the company to the highest bidder. After several offers and counteroffers from a number of parties, and much negotiation, the board agreed to sell the company to Kohlberg Kravis Roberts & Co., and investment banking firm specializing in takeovers, for $109 per share, or a total of $24.9 billion.

One can speculate as to whether or not Mr. Johnson was acting properly as a director and CEO of the company. He was hired to lead and manage the company, not to enrich himself by buying the company. He and his associates had available more information than anyone else as to the company's true value. Even though they offered $75 per share, while the stock market was valuing the company at much less, was it proper for him to try to buy the company, and was his offer fair to the shareholders? The board had to wrestle with these complicated, emotional issues.

In an unfriendly takeover attempt, the directors of the target company must rely on legal advice. Takeovers inevitably give rise to lawsuits. The board also must have expert advice from one or more investment banks. The board must make decisions as to the value of their company and the true value of offers to acquire it.

In practice, when a hostile takeover is initiated, the company's lawyers, investment bankers, accountants and other advisors, together with the board and management, became involved in a hectic struggle that can last for weeks or months. It is a 24-hour day, 7-day week, effort; nearly everything else stops, as there is intense preoccupation on survival or striking the best possible deal. When the episode is over, everyone involved will know that they have experienced a crisis.

Boards can take steps to prepare for an unfriendly takeover attempt. Lawyers can advise on an almost endless series of defensive tactics, such as staggered terms for directors, a variety of "poison pills," and "golden parachutes." Boards are briefed and kept informed on the tactics that might be employed on both sides in a takeover battle. Arrangements are made in advance with lawyers, investment banks, proxy solicitors, and other advisors with whom the board can work, in the event that there is a surprise takeover attempt.

In the final analysis, the board itself plays the key role in dealing with a takeover attempt. This type of crisis is the ultimate test of a board's capability and durability.

DELEGATION OF BOARD WORK

Much of the work of the board is done in committees. They meet prior to the board meeting, hear reports, and prepare summaries and recommendations for full board action. In the board meetings, there is not time for the thorough discussion that takes place in committees. In this section, we describe the activities of the three committees that deal with finance and accounting matters: the compensation committee, audit committee, and finance committee.

COMPENSATION COMMITTEE

The board determines compensation of the CEO and the other principal corporate officers. In many boards, a compensation committee, composed of outside board members, analyzes what the compensation should be and makes its recommendations to the full board.

CEO Compensation

When the board sets the CEO's compensation, it is also establishing a compensation standard for managers throughout the company. Their compensation is integrally related to the CEO's, and this is, therefore, the single most important compensation decision the board must make.

In most instances, this decision is not an easy one. A CEO is typically ambitious and competitive, and compensation is his or her report card. Since compensation of all CEOs of public companies are disclosed in proxy statements, each is able to see just where he or she stands in relation to others. Virtually every CEO would like to stand higher on that list. Thus, the compensation committee deals with a sensitive issue, affecting the corporation's most important person.

The compensation committee considers three principal factors in deciding on compensation. The CEO's compensation should: (1) be related to performance, (2) be competitive, and (3) provide motivation.

Performance

The CEO's compensation should be related to performance. Superior performance should be rewarded with high compensation, while poor performance, if not warranting dismissal, should at least result in minimal compensation. Nevertheless, there is justification to the claim that in some companies, top-executive compensation just keeps going up and up, without regard to performance. The problem is complex. In theory, the CEO should be rewarded for increasing the shareowners' wealth over the long term. Although this is a splendid generalization, the criterion is hard to measure, especially on a year-to-year basis.

Despite the difficulties, most compensation committees do make an effort to relate the CEO's compensation to the company's performance. They arrive at a collective, albeit subjective, judgment as how to well the company has done during the preceding year, as a basis for deciding on an appropriate raise (if any). In addition, most companies have long-term incentive arrangements, such as stock options or performance share plans, that are designed to relate the CEO's compensation to the company's performance over time. These plans, however, are far from perfect, and compensation committees constantly struggle to find new arrangements or formulas in an effort to relate compensation more closely to performance.

Competitive Range

Compensation committees look at where the CEO's compensation stands relative to the competition. What are other companies paying? They can be sure that their CEO has this information, and that if the CEO believes the compensation is not competitive or fair, he or she will become dissatisfied.

There are many sources for salary information. They include proxy statements from similar organizations, as well as published surveys. Some consulting organizations specialize in executive compensation; they can provide data as well as advice on these matters. In the end, however, and with all of the information at hand, the committee makes its judgment, as to where in the competitive spectrum they want the CEO's compensation to fall.

Motivation

The third element that compensation committees consider is: How can we structure a compensation package that motivates the CEO to do what the board expects? If the company has a plan to move aggressively and take unusual risks in the near term, with the possibility of significant long-term payoff, the committee can structure a compensation plan for the CEO that will reward that kind of behavior. For example, it might give the CEO a multiyear contract, to provide assurance of employment during the high-risk phase, together with a long-term stock option plan. At the other extreme, a mature company might be interested in moderate growth but secure dividends. In this instance, the compensation committee might structure a plan weighted heavily toward a fixed salary, reviewed annually, with only modest incentive features.

There are a wide variety of compensation arrangements, each of which provides some type of motivation: base salary reviewed annually; base salary plus annual discretionary bonus; base salary with bonus based on a formula; stock option plans; performance share plans; and multiyear incentive plans. Benefits play an important part in CEO compensation arrangements, retirement programs in particular. Each plan has its own motivational features, and the compensation committee attempts to structure a plan that provides the kind of motivation for the CEO that the board wishes to generate.

Compensation Reviews

In addition to setting the CEO's compensation, the committee also determines compensation for the other senior executives, that is, corporate officers and others whose salary is above a given level. The review process usually takes place at a meeting of the compensation committee, with the CEO and the compensation and personnel policy staff officer.

At the review meeting, the CEO, with the assistance of the staff officer, presents the committee with a recommendation for each executive in the group. The compensation history of each executive is made available, and the CEO gives reasons for each recommendation. There is usually some discussion about a few of the recommendations, and a few changes may be made. For the most part, however, the committee accepts the CEO's recommendations. Nevertheless, the review process is important. It enables the compensation committee to assure itself that the CEO is following sensible guidelines and consistent policies and is not playing favorites. It is also good discipline for the CEO to have to justify his recommendations to the committee.

Board Remuneration

Another function of the compensation committee is to recommend the compensation arrangements for the board itself. This is a delicate matter, since the board is disbursing company funds (actually shareholder funds) to itself.

Directors' compensation is disclosed on the annual proxy statement. Most companies would like to see their directors "respectably" compensated, and while compensation usually is not the compelling reason for holding a directorship, directors want to feel that they are being compensated on a competitive basis. On the other hand, most directors want to feel confident that their compensation is not excessive, and that they could never be exposed to criticism for improperly compensating themselves.

To help reach a balanced level of compensation, a good deal of survey information is available on corporate practices, with respect to board retainer fees, board meeting fees, compensation for committee chairs, and so on. The committee evaluates this information from similar corporations and then decides the appropriate level of compensation for its own board. This recommendation is then made to the full board.

AUDIT COMMITTEE

The audit committee is responsible for making certain that the company's published financial statements are fairly presented, that they are in conformance with GAAP, and that the company's internal control system is effective. The audit committee also deals with important cases of alleged misconduct on the part of employees, including violations of the company's code of ethics. It also ratifies the selection of the company's external auditor.

Until 1960, only a few boards had audit committees. Currently, all companies listed on major stock exchanges are required to have audit committees, and most other corporations have them also.

Responsibility

Although the full board can delegate certain functions to the audit committee, this delegation does not relieve an individual board member from his or her responsibility for governance. In its 1967 decision in the BarChris case, the federal court emphasized this fact:

> Section 11 [of the Securities Act of 1933] imposes liability in the first instance upon a director, no matter how new he is.... He is presumed to know his responsibility when he became a director. He can escape liability only by using that reasonable care to investigate the facts which a prudent man would employ in the management of his own property.[5]

Directors have directors's and officers's (D&O) insurance, but this is only a partial protection against loss from suits claiming that they acted improperly. Recent decisions suggest that the courts are increasingly willing to examine directors's decisions. For example, in a 1985 decision the Delaware supreme court stated that the directors of Trans Union Corp. acted too hastily and without sufficient information in approving the sale of the company to another group; the directors settled out of court for $23.5 million, of which only $10 million was covered by D&O insurance.

A study of the experience of nearly 2,000 companies, conducted by the Wyatt company, found that 300 of these companies had filed claims under their D&O policies. Forty percent of these claims resulted from actions initiated by shareholders, with "misleading representation" being the most prominent allegation. Payments were made in 39 percent of the cases, at an average cost (including both claims cost and legal defense fees) of $1.3 million.

Audit committee members walk a tightrope. On the one hand, as directors, they want to support the CEO—the person whom the board itself selected. On the other hand, they have a clear responsibility to uncover and act on management inadequacies. If they do not do so, they, along with the other board members, are subject to criticism at the very least, and at worst they may go to jail. Their task is neither easy nor pleasant.

Published Financial Statements

Obviously, the audit committee does not directly conduct audits; it relies on two other groups to do this. One is the outside auditor, a firm of certified public accountants. All listed companies (that is, companies whose securities are listed on stock exchanges) are required to have their financial statements examined by an outside auditor, and most other corporations do so in order to satisfy the requirements of banks and other lenders. The other group is the company's internal audit staff, a group of employees whose head reports to a senior officer, usually the CEO or CFO.

Selection of Auditors

Ordinarily, management recommends that the current auditing firm be appointed for another year and that a proposed audit scope and fee schedule be adopted. After some questioning, the audit committee usually recommends that the board approve the selection. Subsequently, the recommendation is submitted to the shareholders in the annual meeting. Occasionally, the audit committee gives more than routine consideration to this topic.

There may be advantages in changing auditors, even when the relationships between the audit firm and the company have been satisfactory for a period of years. One reason for doing this is that the possibility of the board seeking bids from other firms may cause the current firm to think carefully about its proposed fees. However, the public may perceive a change in outside auditors as evidence that the superseded firm would not go along with a practice that the company wanted; in fact, the SEC requires that if a new auditing firm is appointed, the reason for making the change be reported on Form 8-K. Also, a new firm's initial task of learning about the company requires management time; this is a reason why management may be reluctant to recommend a change.

Public accounting firms often perform various types of consulting engagements for the company: developing new accounting and control systems, analyzing proposed pension plans, and analyzing proposed acquisitions. The compensation for this work may exceed the compensation for audit work.

The Audit Opinion

In its opinion letter, the public accounting firm emphasizes the fact that management, not the auditor, is responsible for the financial statements. Most companies receive a "clean opinion," in which the auditor states that the financial statements "present fairly, in all material respects" the financial status and performance of the company in accordance with GAAP. If the auditing firm cannot make this statement, it gives a "qualified opinion," or it states that it is unable to give any opinion. In these circumstances, the stock exchange immediately suspends trading in the company's stock. Note that the auditor's statement does not say that the financial statements are 100 percent accurate, or whether different numbers would have been even more fair. The audit committee's task is to decide whether the directors should concur with the outside auditor's opinion (or, occasionally, to resolve differences if the auditors are unwilling to give a clean opinion on the numbers that management proposes).

Management has some latitude in deciding on the amounts to be reported, especially the amount of earnings. Since managers are human beings, it is reasonable to expect them to lean in the direction of reporting performance in a favorable light. The examples of this tendency are discussed below: smoothing of earnings, reporting unfavorable developments, and the "big bath."

Smoothing Earnings

There is a widespread belief (not necessarily supported by the facts) that ideal performance is a steady growth in earnings, certainly from year to year, and desirably from quarter to quarter. Within the latitude permitted by GAAP, therefore, management may desire to smooth reported earnings—to move income from what otherwise would be a highly profitable period to a less profitable period. The principal techniques for doing this are to vary the adjustments for inventory amounts, for bad debts, and for returns, allowances, and warranties.

The audit committee therefore pays considerable attention to the calculations of these adjustments and allowances and to the accounts receivable, inventory, and accrued liability amounts that result from them. Changes in the reserve percentages from one year to the next are suspect. Within limits, the audit committee tolerates a certain amount of smoothing; indeed, it may not be aware that smoothing has occurred. Outside these limits, however, the committee is obligated to make sure that the reserves and accrual calculations are reasonable.

Not all attempts to smooth earnings are improper. For example, there are documented stories of managers who personally worked around the clock at year end, loading goods into United Parcel Service containers for shipment. This enabled them to count the value of the goods in the containers as revenue in the year that was about to end. Counting as revenue goods that actually were shipped is legitimate. By contrast, certain division managers at H.J. Heinz counted millions of dollars's worth of items as revenues, even though the goods had not been shipped. This practice is wrong; when it was uncovered, there was unfavorable publicity, an SEC investigation, and punishment.[6]

Reporting Unfavorable Developments

The SEC requires that a report, Form 8-K, be filed promptly, whenever an unusual, material event that affects the financial statements becomes known. The principal concern is with the bottom line, the amount of reported earnings. Management, understandably, may be inclined not to report events that might (but also might not) have an unfavorable impact on earnings. Such potentially material events include the probable bankruptcy of an important customer; an important inventory shortage; a reported cash shortage that might (or might not) turn out to be a bookkeeping error; a possibly defective product that could lead to huge returns or to product liability suites; possible safety or environmental violations; an allegation of misdeeds by a corporate officer; the departure of a senior manager; a lawsuit that might (or might not) be well-founded. It is human nature to hope that borderline situations will not actually have a material impact on the company's earnings.

Furthermore, publicizing some of these situations may harm the company unnecessarily. Disclosure of a significant legal filing against the company is necessary; disclosure of the amount that the company thinks it might lose in such litigation, in a report that the plaintiff can read, would be foolish. Both management and the audit committee have difficulty deciding which items should be reported on a Form 8-K report or its equivalent.

The audit committee should be kept fully informed about all events that might eventually require filing a Form 8-K. One might think that the CEO would welcome the opportunity to inform the board of these events, because this would shift the responsibility for disclosure to the board. Nevertheless, managers, like most human beings, prefer not to talk about bad news, if there are reasonable grounds for waiting awhile.

Occasionally, a manager may attempt to "cook the books," that is, to produce favorable accounting results by making entries that are not in accordance with GAAP. The Stirling Homex case is a prominent example; management reported sales revenues for 10,000 of its modular homes, even though 9,100 of these homes were still in inventory.[7] The audit committee must rely on the auditors (or occasionally on a whistle blower) to detect these situations.

The Big Bath

A new management may "take a big bath"; that is, it may write off or write down assets in the year in which it takes over, thereby reducing the amount of costs that remain to be charged off in future periods. This increases the reported earnings in the periods for which the new management is responsible. Because the situation that led to the replacement of the former CEO may justify some such charge-offs, and because the directors don't want to disagree with the new CEO during the honeymoon period, this tactic is sometimes tolerated. If the inflated earnings lead to extraordinarily high bonuses in future years, the board may come to regret its failure to act.

Audit Committee Activities

In probing for the possible existence of any of the situations described above, the audit committee takes two approaches. First, it asks probing questions of management: Why has the inventory-reserve percentage or the receivables-reserve percentage changed? What is the rationale for a large write-off of assets?

Second, and much more important, the committee asks similar questions of the outside auditors. The audit committee usually meets privately with the outside auditors and tells them, in effect: "If you have any doubts about the numbers, or if you have any reason to believe that management has withheld material information, let us know. If you don't inform us, the facts will almost certainly come to light later on. When they do, you will be fired."

A more polite way of probing is to ask questions such as the following:

- Is there anything more you should tell us?
- What were your largest areas of concern?
- What were the most important matters, if any, on which you and management differed?

- Did the accounting treatment of certain events differ from general practice in the industry? If so, what was the rationale for the difference?
- How do you rate the professional competence of the finance and accounting staff?

Usually, these questions are raised orally. Because the auditors know from past experience what to expect, they come prepared to answer them. Some audit committees state their questions in writing.

Although cases of inadequate disclosure make headlines, they occur in only a tiny fraction of one percent of all listed companies. Most such incidents reflect poorly on the work of the board of directors and its audit committee. Increasingly, the courts penalize such boards for their laxness. Directors ponder this fact: When serious misdeeds surface, the CEO often leaves the company, but the directors must stay with the ship and endure public criticism and the blot on their professional reputations. Their lives will be much more pleasant in the long run of they act promptly.

Quarterly Reports

In addition to the annual financial statements, the SEC requires companies to file a quarterly summary of key financial data on Form 10-Q. Because the timing of the release of this report usually does not coincide with an audit committee meeting, the audit committee ordinarily does not review it. Instead, it asks the CEO to inform the chairman of the committee, if there is an unusual situation that affects the quarterly numbers. The chairman then decides either to permit the report to be published as proposed, or, if the topic seems sufficiently important, to have the committee meet in a telephone conference call to discuss it.

Internal Control

In addition to its opinion on the financial statements, the outside auditing firm writes a management letter. This letter lists possible weaknesses in the company's control system that have come to the auditor's attention, together with recommendations for correcting the situation. In the boiler plate preceding this list, the auditor disclaims responsibility for a complete analysis of the system; the listed items are only those that the auditing firm happened to notice. Internal auditors also write reports on the subject.

Audit committees follow up on these reports by asking management to respond to the criticisms. If management disagrees with the recommended course of action, its rationale is considered and either accepted or rejected. If action is decided, the committee keeps the item on its agenda until it is satisfied that the matter has been resolved.

If an especially serious problem is uncovered, the committee may engage its public accounting firm, or another firm, to make a special study. If the problem involves ethical or legal improprieties, an outside law firm may be engaged. As soon as such problems are identified, they must be reported promptly to the SEC on Form 8-K, if they are material.

The audit committee has a difficult problem with internal audit reports. In the course of a year, even a moderately sized staff may write one hundred or more reports. Many of them are too trivial to warrant the committee's attention. (One of us participated in an audit committee meeting of a multibillion dollar company, in which 15 minutes was spent discussing a recommendation for an improvement in data processing, which was expected to save $24,000 annually.) Drawing a line between important reports and trivial ones is difficult, however. A rule of thumb, such as "Tell us about the dozen most important matters," may be used, but it does not allow for the possibility that the thirteenth matter may also warrant committee attention.

In its private meeting with the head of internal audit, the audit committee assures itself that the CEO has given the internal audit staff complete freedom to do its work. The committee also makes it clear that the head of internal audit has direct access to the audit committee chairman, if a situation that may warrant immediate board attention is uncovered. The internal auditor normally would report the matter in question to his superior first, but his primary obligation is to the audit committee. The committee, in turn, should guarantee, as well as it can, that the internal auditor will be fully protected against possible retaliation.

Internal Audit Organization

The committee also considers the adequacy of the internal audit organization. Is it large enough? Does it have the proper level of competence? (For example, does at least one member know how to audit computer systems?) In many companies, the internal audit organization is a training ground, where promising accountants are groomed for comptrollership. The audit committee may find it useful to get acquainted with the internal audit staff, as a basis for judging future candidates for the controller organization.

When campaigns to reduce overhead are undertaken, the internal audit staff may be cut more than is healthy for the organization. The committee questions such cuts and asks the outside auditing firm for its opinion as to the desirability of such cuts. Because internal auditors do much of the verifying that otherwise would be done by external auditors, and at a lower cost per hour, external auditors may not have an unbiased view of the proper size of the internal audit organization.

Treadway Commission

In 1985, the five largest accounting professional organizations created the National Commission on Fraudulent Financial Reporting (usually called the Treadway Commission, after James C. Treadway, Jr., its chairman). The Commission reported in October 1987, and made a number of recommendations for improving financial reporting in companies, for strengthening the role of outside auditors, for changes in regulations of the SEC and other bodies, and for better accounting education. It stressed the importance of the audit committee, but, even more important, it emphasized the role of the CEO in creating an atmosphere that would not tolerate fraudulent financial reporting.

Responding to these recommendations, the American Institute of Certified Public Accountants, which sets standards for auditing by public accounting firms, adopted stricter standards for these firms; and the Institute of Internal Auditors, which performs a similar function for internal auditors, also strengthened its standards. In 1990 a bill was introduced in Congress that would require public accounting firms to accept responsibility for detecting all material instances of fraudulent reporting. In the opinion of many business leaders, this would result in a doubling or tripling of audit fees, an increase that was not warranted by the relatively small number of additional situations that would be uncovered. Pressure for passage of this bill was strengthened by the obvious failure of auditors to discover inadequacies in the financial statements of savings & loan associations. As of 1991, this bill had not been enacted.

FINANCE COMMITTEE

The board is responsible to the shareholders for monitoring the corporation's financial health and for assuring that its financial viability is maintained. The finance committee makes recommendations on these matters. (Nevertheless, as pointed out in the preceding section, the full board cannot escape its ultimate responsibility for making sound decisions on these and other matters.)

The committee's agenda includes analyses of proposed capital and operating budgets, regular reviews of the company's financial performance as reported on the income statement, and its financial condition as reported on the balance sheet. It also reviews the estimated financial requirements over the next several years and decides how these requirements will be met. It recommends the amount of quarterly dividends. The finance committee (or a separate pension committee) reviews pension fund matters and also those of the fund for paying health care and other postemployment benefits; it reviews the policies that determine the annual contribution to the funds and the performance of the firm or firms that invest these funds.

This section describes aspects of these matters that are dealt with at the board of directors level. In some companies, the functions described here are divided among three committees—a budget committee, a finance committee, and a pension committee—and the names may be different. Our purpose is to describe what the committee or committees do, regardless of their titles.

Analysis of Financial Policies

Financial policies are recommended by management. Tools of analysis are increasingly sophisticated. Management, not finance committee, is responsible for using these tools to evaluate risk and return. These tools help to quantify risk, but they are not a substitute for a definite policy on risk. An attitude toward risk is a personal matter, and the finance committee should recognize it as such. Each CEO has a personal attitude toward risk, and so does each individual director.

The committee's responsibility is to probe management's rationale for its policies and thereby assure itself that management has thought them through and that the policies are within acceptable limits.

Dividend Declaration

A financial policy that is specifically a matter for board decision is the declaration of dividends. Dividends are paid only if the company declares them; this declaration usually is made quarterly.

Some companies regularly distribute a large fraction of earnings, while others retain a large fraction within the corporation. Although generous dividends may be fine for the shareholder in the short run, they can deprive the corporation of resources that are needed for growth, thereby penalizing the shareholder in the long run. Conversely, if a large fraction of earnings is retained, shareholders may be deprived of the opportunity to make profitable alternative investments. Thus, the finance committee must weigh the interest of the corporation against the interest of individual shareholders.

Some boards take a simplistic approach to dividends: "Always pay out X percent of earnings," or "Increase dividends each year, no matter what." Either statement has merit as a guide, but neither is more than a guide. In some industries, a certain payout ratio is regarded as normal, and a company that departs substantially from industry practice may lose favor with investors. There is good evidence that a record of increasing dividends over time, or at least a record of stable dividends, is well regarded by investors. By contrast, an erratic dividend pattern is generally undesirable; it creates uncertainty for investors.

Dividend policy warrants careful analysis. The principal factors that the board considers are:

- What are the company's financial needs? These needs depend on how fast the company wants to grow and how capable it is for growing. Or, as is the case with some companies, what is needed to preserve the company during a period of adversity?

- How does the company want to finance its requirements for funds? It can meet its needs by retaining earnings, by issuing debt, by issuing equity, or some combination. Each source of funds has its own cost and its own degree of risk.

- What return does the company expect to earn on shareholder equity, and what degree of risk is it willing to assume in order to achieve this objective? The trade-off between risk and return will determine the appropriate type of financing and thus influence the extent to which earnings should be retained or paid out in dividends.

These are complex questions. Moreover, the factors involved in arriving at answers to them interact with one another. Hewlett-Packard is a useful example. When the company was organized in 1939, the founders decided to finance growth by reinvesting earnings. They thought that earnings would generate adequate funds to finance growth, and they believed that retaining earnings was the best investment the shareholders could make. Contributing to this decision was the fact that the company was originally a "garage-in-the-backyard" start-up, with no reputation, so the company would have had to pay dearly for outside financing, of either debt or equity. This key decision established a dividend policy that continues today. Hewlett-Packard's growth has been financed from retained earnings, it has never issued stock to the public, and it has only nominal debt. For many years, the company paid no dividends at all, and in 1989 its payout was only about 10 percent of earnings. In 1989, the market value of Hewlett-Packard stock was $10 billion.

AT&T is a successful company with quite different dividend and financing policies. It has a long, unbroken record of stable dividends, which are a relatively high percentage of earnings, ranging from 50 to 90 percent. Even in the depression in the 1930s, the company maintained its regular dividends, although these dividends exceeded earnings in some periods. AT&T gained the reputation of being a "widows' and orphans'" stock; that is, its dividends were dependable, through thick and thin.

These two examples indicate the extent to which dividend policy depends on an individual company's circumstances and needs. They also highlight the relationships between dividend policy, the company's need for financing, and the methods that it selects in order to meet its financial requirements.

Pension Funds

The finance committee considers two aspects of pension fund policy: The amount required to be added to the fund and the investment of the fund.

Size of the Pension Fund

Most corporate pension plans are defined-benifit plans. In deciding on the size of the fund required to make benefit payments to retirees, directors tend to rely heavily on the the opinion of an actuary. Given facts about the size and demographic characteristics of the covered employees, facts about the provisions of the plan, and assumptions about the ROI of the fund and about probable wage and salary increases over time, an actuary can calculate the size of the pension fund that is currently needed to meet those requirements. (With available software, the company can make the same calculations.)

However, there is no way of measuring the reasonableness of two key assumptions: the future ROI and the future wage and salary payments, on which the pensions are based. Since the actuarial calculations are no more valid than the accuracy of these assumptions, the calculations should not be taken as gospel. Both of these variables are roughly related to the future rate of inflation, and the spread between the two should remain roughly constant, that is, when one variable changes by one percentage point.

Pension Fund Investments

The most conservative practice is to invest the pension fund in annuities or in bonds whose maturities match the anticipated pension payments. Such a policy is said to "lock in" the ability to make payments. For employees who have already retired, this is so. It is not necessarily so, however, for employees who are currently working. If their compensation increases at a faster rate than is assumed in the actuarial calculations, or if the plan itself is sweetened, the fixed return will turn out to be inadequate. Under a defined-benefit plan, there is no sure way of guaranteeing that the cash will be available when it is needed. In any event, with such a conservative policy, the company gives up the opportunity of earning what is usually a greater return from an investment in equities.

Most companies hire one or more banks or investment firms to manage their pension fund. Voluminous data are available on the past performance of such managers. The catch is, however, that an excellent past record is no guarantee of excellent future performance. Any firm is a collection of individuals. Investment performance is partly a function of the individual doing the investing, and the fund's record may change when that individual leaves or loses his skill. For many years, when it was managed by Peter Lynch, the Magellan Fund was the most successful of all mutual funds; but after Mr. Lynch left, its performance was below the average of all stocks. Performance is also partly a matter of luck.

Some companies divide the pension fund among several managers, periodically compare their performance, and replace the one with the poorest record. This may spread the risk somewhat, but it does not guarantee optimum performance; luck and the individual who manages the fund continue to be dominant factors. Although judging performance is difficult, some managers are better than others. The finance committee watches performance carefully and is cautious about making changes based primarily on short-run performance; it will do so promptly when it is convinced that a better manager has been identified.

The finance committee also decides the broad investment policies: How much should be in equities, how much in fixed income securities, how much in real property, how much in new ventures, how much in overseas securities, and the maximum percentage to be placed in a single company or industry.

Beginning in 1993, companies will also be required to provide for the costs of health care and other benefits of employees who have not yet retired. The problems of estimating these costs are similar to those facing pension fund managers, but with the additional complication that health care costs continue to increase at an unpredictable rate.

SUMMARY

In doing its job, the board accepts certain responsibilities. It should:

- Actively support the CEO, both within the organization and to outside parties, as long as his or her performance is judged to be generally satisfactory.
- Discuss proposed major changes in the company's strategy and direction, major financing proposals, and other crucial issues, usually as proposed by the CEO.
- Formulate major policies regarding ethical or public responsibility matters and convey to the organization the fact that the board expects adherence to these policies. Assure that violations of these policies are not tolerated.
- Ensure, to the extent feasible, that the CEO has identified a successor and is grooming that person for the job.

- Require that the CEO explain the rationale behind operating budgets, major capital expenditures, acquisitions, divestments, dividends, personnel matters, and similar important plans. Accept these proposals if they are consistent with the company's strategy and if the explanation is reasonable. Otherwise, require additional information.

- Analyze reports on the company's performance, raise questions to highlight areas of possible concern, and suggest possible actions to improve performance, but always with the understanding that the CEO, not the board, is responsible for performance.

- Assure that financial information furnished to shareholders and other outside parties fairly presents the financial performance and status of the company. Assure that internal controls are satisfactory.

- Replace the CEO promptly if it concludes that his or her performance is, and will continue to be, unsatisfactory.

- Participate actively in decisions to elect or reelect directors.

- Decide on policies relating to compensation of senior management, including bonuses, incentives, and perquisites. Determine the compensation of the CEO. Review recommendations of the CEO and ratify compensation of other executives.

GLOSSARY

Audit Committee: A committee of the board of directors that is responsible for assuring that the financial statements are fairly presented, that the internal control system is effective, and that allegations of misconduct or other irregularities are investigated promptly. The SEC requires that audit committee members be outside directors.

Auditor: A person or group that examines the validity of financial information and also, in many companies, recommends ways of improving performance. An external auditor is an outside firm of certified public accountants. This firm gives an audit opinion, stating either that the financial statements are fairly presented in accordance with GAAP principles (a clean opinion), or the reasons why they are not (a qualified opinion). An internal auditor is a company employee.

Board of Directors: The body that is responsible to shareholders and other outside parties for the overall goverance of a corporation.

Budget: A financial plan showing the planned revenues, expenses, and resulting earnings, usually for one year, together with a planned balance sheet and cash flow statement.

Business Unit: An organization that is responsible for both the production and the marketing of a product or a family of related products; it is also called a division or profit center.

Chairman: A person who presides over the board of directors. Increasingly called chair or chairperson to avoid gender implications.

Chief Executive Officer (CEO):   A person who is responsible to the board of directors for the management of an organization; often combined with another title, such as president and CEO.

Compensation Committee: A committee that recommends to the full board the compensation of the CEO and other principal executives. Usually, its members are outside directors.

Corporation: An organization that is a legal entity with rights, privileges, and responsibilities that are separate from those of its owners, that is, its shareholders.

Director: A member of the board of directors.

Dividend: A payment made to shareholders at a stated amount per share, usually quarterly, and usually in cash.

Earnings: The difference between the revenues and the expenses for an accounting period. Also called net income.

Executive Committee: A committee of the board of directors that is empowered to act between board meetings, and that brings to the board proposals that are not within the jurisdiction of other committees.

Finance Committee: A committee of the board of directors that is responsible to the shareholders for monitoring the corporation's financial health and for assuring that its financial viability is maintained.

Headquarters: The CEO and the control, finance, legal, personnel, and other staff units. Usually these persons work in the same building or building complex. Also refers to the headquarters of a business unit.

Inside Director: A director who is also an employee of the company.

Manager: The leader of a group of individuals who work together to accomplish part of the organization's goals. These individuals are subordinates. A manager does not personally do the work; he or she ensures that the work gets done by others.

Management: A loosely defined term for all the managers of a company or a subdivision of a company. Senior managers are the managers at the top of the organizational hierarchy. Division managers are all the managers in a division.

Outside Director: A director who is not an officer or employee of the corporation on whose board he or she sits. An outside director is not usually a principal shareholder.

Pension: A promise to make regular payments to an employee after he or she has retired. The pension may be an amount fixed by the corporation (a defined-benefit plan); or it may be an amount that depends on the amount contributed to the pension fund by the employee, by the company, or by both (a defined-contribution plan.)

Securities and Exchange Commission (SEC):   A U.S. government body, with a large staff, which regulates the conduct of about 11,000 of the largest corporations and the exchanges in which securities are traded (stock exchanges), so as to protect investors from fraud and misleading financial information.

Senior Management: A loosely defined term for the CEO executive officer and his or her principal subordinates.

Shareholders: The owners of a corporation, as evidenced by their ownership of shares of the corporation's stock; also known as stockholders.

Standard: A measure of desired performance. It may be a budget amount, a standard cost, or a nonquantitative statement of desired ethical performance.

Strategy: A broad course of action that the board of directors and CEO have adopted, as the best way of attaining the organization's goals.

Takeover: Acquisition of one company by another, or an attempt to do so. The company that is potentially being acquired is the target company. In an unfriendly or hostile takeover attempt, the target company resists the efforts of the acquiring company.

Variance: The difference between an actual amount and some other amount. The actual amount is the company's or manager's performance. The other amount may be a budget, the amount for the same period in the preceding period, the amount for another organization, or the average amount of other organizations.

FOR FURTHER READING

Anderson, Charles A. and Robert N. Anthony, *The New Corporate Directors* (New York: John Wiley, 1986).

Burrough, Bryan and John Halyar, *Barbarians at the Gate: The Fall of RJR Nabisco* (New York: Harper & Row, 1990).

Donaldson, Gordon and Jay W. Lorsch, *Decision Making at the Top* (New York: Basic Books, 1983).

Ivancevich, John M., James H. Donnelly, and James L. Gibson, *Management: Principles and Functions*, 4th ed. (Homewood, IL: BPI/Irwin, 1989).

Kotter John P., *The General Managers* (New York: The Free Press, 1982).

Lorsch, Jay W., *Pawns or Potentates: The Reality of America's Corporate Boards* (Boston: Harvard Business School Press, 1989).

Mace, Myles L., *Directors: Myth and Reality* (Boston: Division of Research, Harvard Business School, 1971).

Newman, William H., E. Kirby Warren, and Andrew R. McGill, *The Process of Management: Strategy, Actions, Results*, 6th ed. (Englewood Cliffs, NJ: Prentice-Hall, 1987).

Stoner, James A.F. and R. Edward Freeman, *Management*, 4th ed. (Englewood Cliffs, NJ: Prentice-Hall, 1989).

Vance, Stanley C., *Corporate Leadership, Boards, Directors, and Strategy* (New York: McGraw-Hill, 1983).

Vancil, Richard F., *Passing the Baton: Managing the Process of CEO Succession* (Boston: Harvard Business School Press, 1987).

Worthy, James C. and Robert P. Neuschel, *Emerging Issuance in Corporate Governance* (Evanston, IL: Northwestern University Press, 1983).

15 BANKRUPTCY

Ronald J. Sutter and
Grant W. Newton

THE SCENE IS SET

Even as a teenager, David Brown knew that one day he would own a professional basketball team. While other kids were practicing free throws, David would rush home from school, flip through his collection of basketball cards, and choose twelve stars to play for his imaginary team.

Those memories seemed a bit distant as he rode the elevator to the executive suite of the North American Basketball League (NABL). His dream seemingly crushed, David, now 38, was going to tell the commissioner of the league that his team, the Hartford Crabs, could not pay its bills. David, who had realized his dream three years earlier, when he purchased the Hartford Crabs for $75 million, needed financial help.

Just where David went wrong, he wasn't sure. Maybe he had overestimated his ability to pay the debt service on the $35 million he had borrowed to buy the team. Had he overlooked the fact that he was buying into a highly competitive market? In nearby Boston, another NABL team had a seeming monopoly in the region.

That team drew hordes of fans to its cavernous arena and tapped the wealthiest local cable television stations for fat broadcast right fees. His team, which had never been a winner, was often relegated to the back of the newspapers's sports sections.

The Crabs had no cable television contract and attendance at its games was likely to remain at its current level. Later, David would find out that even this projection was overly optimistic.

The Crabs's other two revenue streams, a share of the league's national television contract and team-licensing pie, had risen only modestly in three years.

On the other side of the ledger, the Crabs's biggest expense was payroll. The year he had bought the team, payroll had accounted for 55 percent of his expenses. A year later, that number had climbed to 70 percent; it went to 80 percent during the 1990-1991 season. There were serious cost overruns when general and administrative expenses were added to the mix.

Unlike most other owners, David had nowhere to turn for help. There were no car dealerships or family money that he could use to subsidize his team. David had no choice but to file for bankruptcy.

Is Bankruptcy the End?

Does bankruptcy mean a business has irrevocably failed? Are there any alternatives? When and how does a company file a bankruptcy petition? Is there any chance of recovery? These are just a few of the terrifying questions raised, when bankruptcy looms as an imminent occurrence in a troubled company.

Such feelings are certainly justified considering the history of bankruptcy: debtors suffered physical punishment and imprisonment until early bankruptcy laws were reformed. In the United States, this reform started in 1787. Even today, we hear tales of woe from those exposed to our bankruptcy system.

After listening to one debtor complain about the injustice over the handling of his second bankruptcy proceeding, a chief bankruptcy judge stated very eloquently that debtors generally come before the bankruptcy court system with very high, and often unrealistic expectations. They often blame everyone else, when these expectations are not reached, while at the same time overlooking their own failures, which brought them before the bankruptcy court.

Unrealistically high expectations are not limited to debtors. Creditors, too, fall into this frame of mind. This is especially so for the victims of fraudulent schemes, which are perpetuated on the uninformed and vulnerable. Here, the creditors expect the bankruptcy system to completely recover their lost investments.

Bad publicity, high cost, prolonged and stressful periods of time, restraints imposed by the bankruptcy system, and the need for professionals and turnaround specialists are all viewed negatively.

So what about some positives? What of the opportunity for a fresh start, continued employment of personnel, a learning experience, and a partial or complete reorganization? These positives may be achieved if the right ingredients exist.

Early recognition of the problem or problems and their causes are essential to any successful reorganization of a troubled business. It gives one time to consult with professionals (attorneys, CPAs, and bankers) who can provide for adequate planning or opportunities for:

- Selection of alternatives to a bankruptcy petition, such as out-of-court workouts
- Selection of the most advantageous time to file the bankruptcy petition
- Minimization of taxes for both pre- and postpetition periods
- Determination of the causes of the business problems and a plan for their elimination
- Development of a reorganization plan for consideration shortly after, or in some cases even before, a bankruptcy petition is filed

A reorganization plan is in itself a good faith gesture to the court and creditors. It indicates that the petition was well thought out and was not used as just another delaying tactic, as is the case with many bankruptcy petitions.

All too often, the troubled business seeks specialized professional consultation only hours before a major asset is to be lost, through foreclosure. Cash flow problems may have existed over an extended period of time, without any real acknowledgement of the problems; even though default notices have been received on unpaid loans or leases. Such last-minute bankruptcy petitions are almost doomed to failure before they start.

Did David react quickly enough? Probably. David hired an attorney, specializing in professional sports team management, to review his operation. The attorney soon discovered that David was somewhat lacking in managerial skills. Among other things, David didn't recognize the leverage he had over the city, when he began lease negotiations for the arena. David could have asked for and gotten, a percentage of the parking and concessions, or at least bid down the $10,000 per game rental fee.

David, who served as the team's general manager, had also been wildly inconsistent in negotiating contracts with his players. One minute, he was giving an untested rookie a $1 million signing bonus. The next, he was stonewalling a veteran starting guard over a $100,000 clause in the player's contract.

The attorney picked up on these inadequacies right away. He had seen it numerous other times, when teams were pushed to the brink of bankruptcy and called on him for help.

Preparation: Become Informed

Bankruptcy services are complex, and this chapter can serve only as an introduction: It should not be used as a substitute for complete authoritative research of legal and financial issues. If this chapter heightens your interest in the subject of bankruptcy the next steps are to:

1. Obtain and study thoroughly texts on the accounting and tax considerations in reorganization and bankruptcy proceedings (see suggestions for further reading at the end of the book).

2. Take seminars on accounting, tax, and legal aspects of reorganization and bankruptcy proceedings. Seminars are available through your state CPA Society, the American Institute of CPAs, the Association of Insolvency Accountants, the Practicing Law Institute, the American Bar Association, and many universities.

3. Take other seminars related to litigation support services and special-report writing.

Copies of the Bankruptcy Code and Rules are also essential tools of the trade. Like most laws, the Bankruptcy Code is often amended, thus requiring your *continued* education. This chapter will deal principally with issues related to Chapter 7 (liquidation) and Chapter 11 (reorganization) of the Bankruptcy Code (Title 11 of the United States Code).

WHERE TO START

The greatest service to a troubled business is to prevent its failure. Accordingly, the best time to help is when problems first begin to develop. Action, if taken early enough, can avoid the need to file a bankruptcy petition.

David's troubles might not have mushroomed, if he had hired an experienced executive from another team, when he purchased the Crabs. At the very least, he would have obtained knowledge of how other teams in the NABL handled management issues. David might also have hired a marketing executive; someone to provide his team with a new image. That executive could have probed the weaknesses of the Crabs's competitor in Boston and helped the Crabs generate revenue at the gate and interest from the media.

Now, David was faced with a much more costly option. A bankruptcy proceeding, which must at all times weigh the interests of the debtor, its creditors, and other involved parties, is very expensive, and it takes considerable time to sort out the facts and determine the appropriate action. Far too often, a business facing severe financial problems will attempt to cure its ills by cutting back on the very experts that it needs: the specialized professionals who can determine the underlying cause of the financial difficulty and develop a plan of action, which will allow the company to recover, without filing a bankruptcy petition. The old saying, "An ounce of prevention is worth a pound of cure" also holds true for a troubled business.

A professional, diagnosing David's team and helping him avoid financial ruin, would attempt to gather information about the organization, its operating results, its financial position, competition, industry trends, and analysis ratios. The word "attempt" is used because some or much information about a troubled business may not be available. Lack of this data may be related to the causes of the business problem. What is unavailable will also be instructive. The following is the information that should be put together:

1. Samples of operating management financial reports
2. Detailed financial reports for at least the last five years
3. A completed internal control questionnaire
4. Industry operating ratios and statistics
5. The structure (both legal and operational) of the business and its operations, including: (a) organizational charts, (b) operating locations, and (c) a brief description of all its business operations (production, marketing, customer service)
6. A list of the major assets of the business and a determination of their liquidation and market values, indicating whether or not the assets are pledged as collateral for debts
7. A description of the parts of the business that are responsible for most of the historical profits or losses and cash flow
8. An aging of the receivables *and* payables
9. The terms of all leases, loans, and contracts payable
10. The status of deposits for taxes with the IRS and state taxing authorities

The next step is to analyze the information obtained. Plotting trends and ratios is generally the first analytical process, and one that very often provides early fruitful results. These ratios should then be compared with industry statistics.

Often management simply does not know what negative changes have taken place. Often their *only* financial reports are the classic, summarized balance sheet, profit and loss statements, and income tax returns they receive from their bookkeeper or accountant. These are *not* adequate to manage most businesses. Detailed aging reports of receivables could have saved many businesses if they had been available and properly used.

The major cause of business failures is inadequate management, evidenced by a lack of profits and inadequate sales. Experience has shown that a significant portion of the blame for lack of profits and inadequate sales rests with management.

David's experience is typical of many business failures. Consider the following pattern: A business is started by a person who is technically competent in a particular area, but has very little, if any, capital or management experience. The business prospers, but as it grows, it fails to grow in management depth. The owner/manager is very self-confident, based upon his or her earlier success, and will not believe that the company will be unable to grow without additional specialized management in the areas of marketing, production, accounting, and finance.

Receivables and payables climb. A bank loan is obtained but, as time goes on, that is not enough. High risk transactions are entered into for the appearance of success. Accounting records and procedures are neglected. Excessive salaries and questionable "perks" (generally personal expenses) continue, no matter what projects must be pushed aside. The owner/manager is typically an eternal optimist who believes that a big new contract or "a deal" will come in very soon and will cure everything. His or her philosophy is: "when up a tree, branch out." New facilities and equipment are obtained. Questionable "deals" are recorded, and doubtful receivables are carried without reserves. Payroll taxes go unpaid, and the bank loan goes into default. The business is then forced to file a bankruptcy petition at the very last minute. Of course, the debtor will claim that "it's all the fault of the bank or a supplier because they would not increase the amount of a loan and extend the repayment terms."

Studies have found that approximately 50 percent of business failures generally occur in the enterprise's first 5 years of operation, with the retail and services industries leading the way. (Source: *Business Failure Record*, New York: Dun & Bradstreet, Inc., 1988.)

Aside from inadequate management, many other factors can contribute to a business failure. There is often a combination of factors, including:

- Credit extension policies
- Aging of notes and accounts receivable
- Collection policies and efforts
- Competition
- Inadequate sales
- Improper pricing
- Collection policies and efforts
- Excessive expenses
- Excessive debt often resulting from an LBO
- Insufficient working capital
- Insufficient equity capital in relation to debt and the size and composition of assets
- Purchasing policies
- Policy concerning payment of debt

- Overinvestment in fixed assets or inventories (i.e., obsolete, excessive, utilization)
- Operational inefficiencies
- Marketing and distribution methods and policies
- Inadequate cash management
- Over expansion
- Excessive discounting

Many of these factors can be determined by simple ratio and trending techniques. Use of a good graphics program will greatly enhance these analytical methods. The use of percentages to indicate relationships is also useful.

The art of predicting a business failure or bankruptcy has been addressed by scholars for some time now. Edward I. Altman and others utilized selected key financial ratios to develop a bankruptcy probability index. If properly utilized, such methods can prove very useful for the early detection of a business that is headed for trouble.

The importance of good business plans (see chapter 7) and forecasts (see chapter 8) cannot be overlooked. When prepared with diligence, and used as a comparison to actual achievements, the variances between budgeted and actual financial results can provide a signal for astute managers, allowing them to head off a problem before it gets out of control (see chapter 5).

BANKRUPTCY: AN OVERVIEW
FROM BEGINNING TO END

Alternatives for the Troubled Business

The debtor's first alternatives are to locate new financing, merge with another company, or find some other basic solution to its situation, in order to avoid the necessity of discussing its problems with representatives of its creditor body. David Brown wants desperately to avoid going to the bank and admitting that he has a problem. Fortunately, he may not have to take that step. By approaching the league and the city, two entities that can least afford the Crabs's demise, David is hoping he can get financial assistance to relieve his problems. Other companies may not have these kind of options. The debtor may be required to seek a remedy from creditors, either informally (out of court) or with the help of judicial proceedings.

Out-of-Court Settlements

The informal settlement is an out-of-court agreement that usually consists of an extension of time (stretch-out), a pro rata cash payment for full settlement of claims (composition), an issue of stock for debt, or some combination of these options. The debtor, through counsel or a local credit association, calls an informal meeting of the creditors for the purpose of discussing its financial problems. In many cases, the credit association makes a significant contribution to the out-of-court settlement by arranging a meeting of creditors, providing advice, serving as secretary for the creditors's committee, and serving as a disbursing agent, under an informal arrangement with creditors.

A credit association is composed of credit managers of various businesses in a given region. Its functions are to provide credit and other business information to member companies concerning their debtors, to help make commercial credit collections, to support legislation favorable to business creditors, and to provide courses in credit management for members of the credit community.

At the creditors's meeting the debtor will describe the causes of failure, discuss the value of assets (especially those unpledged) and its unsecured liabilities, and answer any questions the creditors may ask. The main objective of the meeting is to convince the creditors that they will receive more if the business is allowed to operate than if it is forced to liquidate, and that all parties will be better off if a settlement can be worked out.

In other cases the debtor may elect to meet with each of the largest creditors individually, before a meeting of all creditors is arranged.

Creditors's Committee

To make it easier for the debtor to work with the creditors, a committee of creditors is often appointed during the initial meeting of the debtor and its creditors, providing, of course, that the case is judged to warrant some cooperation by the creditors. It should be realized that the creditors are often as interested in working out a settlement as is the debtor. The debtor's job, running the business while under the limited monitoring of the creditors's committee, can be made easier if the creditors selected are those most friendly to the debtor.

Duties of the Committee

The creditors's committee, where appointed, serves as the bargaining agent for the creditors, monitors the operation of the debtor during the development of a plan, and solicits acceptance of a plan once it has been approved by the committee. Generally, the creditors's committee will meet as soon as it has been appointed, for the purpose of selecting a presiding officer and counsel. The committee may also engage an independent accountant to review, audit, or analyze the books and records of the debtor, as well as its proposed reorganization plan and related forecasts or projections.

At the completion of the financial analysis, the creditors's committee will meet to discuss the results. If the study reveals that the creditors are dealing with something less than a completely forthright and honest debtor, the amount of settlement that will be acceptable to the creditors will be increased significantly. It becomes very difficult for a debtor to avoid a bankruptcy court proceeding under these conditions. On the other hand, if the debtor is honest and demonstrates the ability to reverse the unprofitable operating trend and reestablish the business, some type of plan may eventually be approved.

Plan of Settlement

There is no set pattern for the form that a plan of settlement proposed by the debtor must take. It may call for 100-percent payment over an extended period of time; payments on a pro rata basis, in cash, for full settlement of creditors's claims; satisfaction of debt obligations with stock; or some combination of these options. A carefully developed forecast of operations, based on realistic assumptions—developed by the debtor with the aid of its accountant—can help creditors determine if the debtor can perform under the terms of the plan and operate successfully in the future.

Generally for creditors to accept a plan, the amount they will receive must be at least equal to the dividend they would receive if the estate were liquidated. This dividend, expressed as a percent of the amount owed, is equal to the sum of forced-sale values of all assets, including accounts receivable, cash, and prepaid items; less the cost of asset liquidations, priority claims, secured claims, and expenses of administration; divided by the total amount of unsecured claims.

This valuation process is illustrated in Exhibits 15.1 and 15.2. In this case, the general unsecured creditor must decide to take a small 16 percent return through a plan of reorganization.

In bankruptcy, a key issue is how to distribute the assets (which are usually few) to the creditors (who are usually many). Exhibit 15.1 is an analysis of the liquidation values of all of the assets of the Hartford Crabs. The total book value of the assets is $927,000, but the estimated liquidation value amounts to only $760,800, which is $166,200 less than book value. Of the $760,800 estimated liquidation value, upledged assets amount to only $41,300 (leaving $719,500 for the pledged assets).

A secured creditor has first call against the particular asset that has been pledged against that creditor's claim. The claims of the secured creditors total $666,600 out of the estimated $719,500 liquidation value of the pledged assets, which results in an overall surplus of $52,900 ($719,500 less $666,600) on secured claims, as shown in Exhibit 15.1.

The fact that there is an overall surplus does not mean that each and every secured creditor can be paid in full, from the proceeds of the asset

EXHIBIT 15.1. Hartford Crabs, Inc., Analysis of free and pledged assets, December 31, 1993.

	Book Value	Estimated Liquidation Value	Other Creditors	Last National Bank	Supplier A	NABL	Finance Company A	Finance Company B	Unencumbered Assets
			Assets Pledged as Collateral to Creditors						
Cash in banks	$ 13,800	$ 13,800		$ 5,500					$ 8,300
Accounts receivable	327,500	205,000		205,000					
Allowances for bad debts	(32,000)								
Inventories:									
Stationery and supplies	19,000	7,500			15,000				7,500
Promotional materials	34,000	20,000							5,000
Uniforms and shoes	17,000	4,000		4,000					
Souvenirs & programs	47,000	22,500		22,500					
Prepaid expenses	7,500	4,500							4,500
Other assets	8,500	8,500	$ 8,500						
Franchise fee	288,500	380,000				$380,000			
Scoreboard & equipment	102,500	58,000					$ 25,000	33,000	
Automobiles	58,700	21,000						21,000	
Leasehold improvements	52,000								
Depreciation & amortization	(113,000)								
Notes receivable	75,000	15,000							15,000
Interest receivable	15,000								
Trademark	6,000	1,000							1,000
Total assets	$927,000	$760,800	$ 8,500	$ 237,000	$15,000	$380,000	$ 25,000	$ 54,000	$ 41,300
Less total assets		927,000							
(Loss) on liquidation		(166,200)							
Collateralized debts									
Principal balance			$ 11,500	$ 250,000	$13,000	$258,400	$ 24,500	$ 73,000	
Accrued interest				5,200	400	25,500	900	4,200	
Total collateralized debts			$ 11,500	$ 255,200	$13,400	$283,900	$ 25,400	$ 77,200	
Collateral excess (shortage)			$ (3,000)	$ (18,200)	$ 1,600	$ 96,100	$ (400)	$(23,200)	

Summary

	Total	Partially Secured	Fully Secured
	$630,400	$359,000	$271,400
	36,200	10,300	25,900
	$666,600	$369,300	$297,300
	$ 52,900	$ (44,800)	$ (97,700)

EXHIBIT 15.2. Hartford Crabs, Inc., Statement of affairs as of December 31, 1993.

Assets	Net Book Values	Estimated Liquidation Values	Gain/(Loss) Upon Liquidation	Estimated Assets Available for Unsecured Creditors
1. Assets pledged to fully secured creditors:				
Inventories	$ 15,000	$ 15,000	$ –0–	
Franchise	247,500	380,000	132,500	
Total		395,000		
Less fully secured debts (contra)		297,300		
Excess available for unsecured creditors		$ 97,700		$ 97,700
2. Assets pledged to partially secured creditors:				
Cash	5,500	5,500	–0–	
Accounts receivable	295,500	205,000	(90,500)	
Inventories	64,000	26,500	(37,500)	
Other assets	8,500	8,500	–0–	
Scoreboard	71,500	58,000	(13,500)	
Autos	26,700	21,000	(5,700)	
Total deducted (contra)		$324,500		
3. Assets unencumbered:				
Cash	8,300	$ 8,300	–0–	8,300
Inventories	38,000	12,500	(25,500)	12,500
Prepaid expenses recoverable	7,500	4,500	(3,000)	4,500
Notes and interest receivable	90,000	15,000	(75,000)	15,000
Trademark	6,000	1,000	(5,000)	1,000
Leasehold improvements	43,000	–0–	(43,000)	–0–
Total		$ 41,300		139,000
Less debts having priority(contra)				107,500
4. Assets estimated to be available for unsecured creditors (approximately 16¢/$)				31,500
5. Estimated deficiency to unsecured creditors				169,300
6. Estimated gain/(loss) upon liquidation of assets(deducted contra)			$(166,200)	
Totals	$927,000			$200,800

EXHIBIT 15.2. *(Continued).*

Liabilities and (Deficiency) in Net Assets	Net Book Values	Amounts Unsecured
7. Liabilities fully secured:		
NABL	$283,900	$283,900
Payable to suppliers	13,400	13,400
Total deducted (contra)		$297,300
8. Liabilities partially secured:		
Payable to bank on line of credit	255,200	$255,200
Payable to finance companies	102,600	102,600
Payable to other creditors	11,500	11,500
Total		$369,300
Less assets pledged (contra)		324,500
Amount unsecured		$ 44,800	$ 44,800
9. Liabilities with priorities:		
Estimated liquidation and other administrative costs	85,000	$ 85,000
Wages payable	10,000	10,000
Payroll taxes payable	12,500	12,500
Total deducted (contra)		$107,500
10. Unsecured liabilities:		
Trade payables	121,000		121,000
Loans from shareholder	35,000		35,000
11. Total liabilities	$930,100		$200,800
12. Stockholders' (deficiency):		
Common stock issued	1,000	1,000
Accumulated (deficiency) at December 31, 1987	(4,100)	(4,100)
Estimated loss upon liquidation (contra)		(166,200)
Total stockholders (deficiency)	(3,100)	$(169,300)
Totals	$927,000		$200,800

pledged to that creditor. For example, Last National Bank has a deficiency of $18,200 on its claim, and Finance Company A has a shortage of $400. On the other hand, the NABL has a surplus of $96,100. Secured creditors who have deficiencies will be treated in the same manner as unsecured creditors, with respect to the amount of their deficiencies. For secured creditors with surpluses, the amount of the surplus is added to the pool available for distribution to unsecured creditors.

Who gets what is shown in Exhibit 15.2. First, consider the left side of the exhibit, starting with Section 1. Section 1 consists of assets pledged to secured creditors who have surpluses. These are (from Exhibit 15.1) the inventory of promotional materials, $15,000, pledged to Supplier A, and the $380,000 value of the franchise, which has been pledged to the NABL. As reflected in Section 7, the total amount owed to these secured creditors is $297,300. After paying these two secured creditors in full, the amount of

$97,700 is left over as surplus, which becomes available for unsecured claims, as shown in Section 1 of Exhibit 15.2.

Section 2 of Exhibit 15.2 shows assets pledged to creditors with deficiencies. These assets are estimated to have a total liquidation value of $324,500, while as shown in Section 8, the related claims total $369,300. The resulting total deficit, reflected in Section 8, is $44,800.

Section 3 shows unpledged assets, estimated at a total value of $41,300. To this is added the surplus of $97,700 from Section 1, for a total of $139,000. This $139,000 will be used to pay unsecured claims that have priority under the laws of bankruptcy, as shown in Section 9; these total $107,500. These claims are mainly fees and expenses to be incurred by the trustee in order to liquidate the assets and pay out the proceeds to the creditors. Once these priority unsecured claims of $107,500 have been paid, there will be $31,500 left (reflected in Section 4) to cover all remaining unsecured creditors.

The remaining unsecured claims consist of two components: one is the $44,800 total deficit on the secured creditors's claims (see Section 8). The second component is unsecured claims of $121,000 and $35,000, as shown in Section 10. The total of the unsecured claims is $200,800, as reflected in Section 11.

Therefore, there are estimated funds of $31,500 available to pay claims of $200,800. These will be shared equally and the resulting payout to unsecured creditors will be about 16 cents on the dollar ($31,500/$200,800 = 0.16) as Section 4 shows. The remaining unpaid 84 cents on the dollar is a loss to the unsecured creditors, as reflected in Section 5, and it totals $169,300.

Finally, last in line are the shareholders. Since there was insufficient money to fully pay the creditors, there are no funds left for the shareholders. They are wiped out; Section 12 shows their sad tale.

It is worth summarizing the order of payment in bankruptcy which is as follows:

1. Secured creditors, from the proceeds of the specific assets collaterized to respective creditors. A surplus on a secured creditor's claim leaves funds which will be used to pay the next category of creditor. A deficit on any secured claim acquires the status of an unsecured creditor.
2. Unsecured claims that have priorities, such as the costs of liquidating the assets and making the distribution of funds.
3. Unsecured creditors without priorities.
4. Stockholders.

Advantages and Disadvantages

Summarized below are a few of the reasons why the informal settlement is used in today's environment.

1. The out-of-court settlement is less disruptive to a business that continues operations.
2. The debtor can receive considerable benefits from the advice of a committee, especially if some of the committee members have substantial business experience, preferably, but not necessarily, in the same line of business.
3. The informal settlement avoids invoking the provisions of the Bankruptcy Code and, as a result, more businesslike solutions can be adopted, without as much negative publicity as is associated with a formal bankruptcy.
4. Frustrations and delays are minimized because problems can be resolved properly and informally without the need for court hearings.
5. An agreement can usually be reached much faster, informally, than in court proceedings.
6. The costs of administration are usually less in an out-of-court settlement than in a formal reorganization.

The weaknesses of informal (sometimes called composition) settlements are as follows:

1. A successful plan of settlement requires the approval of substantially all creditors, and it may be difficult to persuade certain creditors to accept a settlement that calls for payment of less than 100 cents on the dollar.
2. The assets of the debtor are subject to attack while a settlement is pending. (The debtor can, of course, point out to the creditor that if legal action is taken, a petition in bankruptcy court will have to be filed.)
3. The informal composition settlement does not provide a method to resolve individual disputes between the debtor and specific creditors.
4. Executory contracts, especially leases, may be difficult to avoid.
5. Certain tax law provisions make it more advantageous to file a bankruptcy court petition.
6. Priority debts owed to the United States under Rev. Stat. section 3466 must be paid in full, before other creditors can be paid.

Assignment for Benefit of Creditors

A remedy available to a debtor in serious financial difficulties, under some state laws, is an assignment for the benefit of creditors. In this instance, the debtor voluntarily transfers title to its assets to an assignee, who then liquidates them and distributes the proceeds among the creditors. An assignment for the benefit of creditors is an extreme remedy because it results in the cessation of the business. This informal liquidation device (court-supervised in many states) requires the consent of all creditors, or at least their agreement to refrain from taking separate action. The appointment of a custodian over the assets of the debtor gives creditors the right to file an involuntary bankruptcy petition.

Bankruptcy Code Protection

Bankruptcy court proceedings are generally the last resort for the debtor whose financial condition has deteriorated, to the point, where it is impossible to acquire additional funds. When the debtor finally agrees that bankruptcy court proceedings are necessary, the liquidation value of the assets often represents only a small fraction of the debtor's total liabilities. If the business is liquidated, the creditors get only a small percentage of their claims. The debtor is discharged from its debts and is free to start over; however, the business is lost and so are all of its assets.

Normally liquidation proceedings result in large losses to the debtor, to the creditor, and also to the business community in general. Chapter 7 of the Bankruptcy Code covers the proceedings related to liquidation. Another alternative under the Bankruptcy Code is to seek some type of relief, so that the debtor will have enough time to work out agreements with creditors, and with the help of the Bankruptcy court, will be able to continue operations. Chapters 11, 12, and 13 of the Bankruptcy Code provide for this type of operation, referred to generally as "reorganization" cases.

A summary of bankruptcy law is given in Exhibit 15.3. This law is very comprehensive and covers liquidation (Chapter 7 of the bankruptcy code), reorganization (the famous "Chapter 11"), and compromise with creditors for individuals with regular income (Chapter 13 of the code).

Chapters 1, 3, and 5 apply to all proceedings under the code, except Chapter 9, to which only specified sections of Chapters 1, 3, and 5 apply. A case commenced under the Bankruptcy Code (Chapters 7, 9, 11, 12, or 13) is referred to as a "Title 11" case.

EXHIBIT 15.3. The bankruptcy law.

The bankruptcy law is contained in Title 11 of the U.S. Code. The code is divided into eight chapters:

    Chapter 1: General provisions
    Chapter 3: Case administration
    Chapter 5: Creditors, the debtor, and the estate
    Chapter 7: Liquidation
    Chapter 9: Adjustment of debts of a municipality
    Chapter 11: Reorganization
    Chapter 12: Adjustment of debts of a family farmer with regular income
    Chapter 13: Adjustment of debts of an individual with regular income

Included within the general provisions of Chapter 1 are the "definitions" used in the Bankruptcy Code. If you are to be involved in a bankruptcy proceeding, be sure to read, if nothing else, the relatively few pages devoted to these definitions. They contain a wealth of information upon which the balance of the Code rests.

Bankruptcy Courts

The Bankruptcy Reform Act of 1978 established a bankruptcy court in each judicial district, with jurisdiction to decide almost any matter related to bankruptcy. This jurisdiction included not only the traditional "case matters," such as objections to discharge or claims, but also affirmative actions against third parties, such as for the recovery of preferential transfers or fraudulent transfer actions.

The Bankruptcy Amendments and Federal Judgeship Act of 1984 provides that the bankruptcy judge may hear and decide all cases and all "core proceedings" arising in a case, referred to the bankruptcy court by the district court. Generally, "core proceedings" include such matters as the administration of the estate, operation of the business during reorganization, allowance of claims, objections to discharge, and confirmation of plans.

The Office of the U.S. Trustee

Within each federal judicial district, except for those in Alabama and North Carolina, there is an appointed U.S. Trustee. The Office of the U.S. Trustee is an agency operated under the U.S. Attorney General, U.S. Department of Justice.

The purpose of this office is to establish, maintain, and supervise a panel of private trustees, serve as trustee if need be, and supervise the administration of all cases under Chapters 7, 11, 12, and 13 of the Bankruptcy Code.

Such duties include monitoring applications for employment of professionals, their compensation applications, monitoring and appointing trustees, examiners, creditor, and equity holder committees, monitoring reorganization plans and disclosure statements, setting guidelines and reporting requirements (i.e., operating reports) for operating businesses during the bankruptcy proceedings and, in general, monitoring the progress of each case.

Cooperation by a debtor with the U.S. Trustee is essential to the smooth administration of the bankruptcy proceedings. For most purposes, the U.S. Trustee becomes a party-in-interest in each case pending. As such, it may on its own accord, file motions and make appearances before the bankruptcy court.

Chapter Selection

The Bankruptcy Code consists of 5 Chapters, under which a petition can be filed. An *individual* may file under Chapters 7, 11, 12, or 13. (Chapter 12 deals with the special case of family farmers and is not covered in this chapter.) A *partnership or corporation* may file under Chapters 7, 11, or 12. A *municipality* files under Chapter 9. In the following sections, the general provisions for Chapters 7, 11, and 13 are discussed.

Chapter 7—Liquidation

Chapter 7 is concerned with the liquidation of a debtor in financial trouble and contains provisions for the appointment of a trustee, liquidation of the business and its assets, distribution of the estate to the creditors, and discharge of the debtor from liability.

The person filing voluntarily need not be insolvent in either the bankruptcy or equity sense; the essential requirement is that the petitioner have debts. As soon as the order for relief has been entered, the U.S. Trustee will appoint a disinterested person, from a panel of private trustees, to serve as the interim trustee. If a person was serving as trustee, in an involuntary case, prior to the order for relief, he may also be appointed as interim trustee.

Unless the creditors at a meeting, called under section 341(a), elect a trustee, the interim trustee appointed by the office of the U.S. Trustee will continue as the trustee.

The trustee may, with court approval, operate the business for a short time period, if this is necessary to increase the amount that is available to creditors. After the property of the estate has been reduced to money, and the secured claims have been satisfied to the extent allowed, the property of the estate shall be distributed to the holders of claims in a specified order. Unless a claim has been subordinated under the provisions of section 510, section 726(a) provides that the balance is distributed in the following order:

1. To the holders of priority claims, as set forth in section 507
2. To the holders of general unsecured claims who filed timely proof of claim, and those who filed late because of lack of notice or knowledge of the case
3. To the holders of general unsecured claims, filed late
4. In payment of an allowed secured or unsecured claim, not compensation for actual pecuniary losses, for fines, penalties, forfeitures, or damages suffered by the claim holder
5. In payment of interest on the above claims, at the legal rate, from the date of filing the petition
6. Any balance to the debtor

Section 726(b) provides for claims within a particular classification to be paid on a pro rata basis, when there are not enough funds to satisfy all of the claims of a particular classification in full. There is one exception to this policy. If there are not enough funds to pay all administrative expenses, and part of the administrative expenses related to a Chapter 11, 12, or 13 case, prior to conversion to Chapter 7, then those administrative expenses incurred in Chapter 7, after conversion, will be paid first. Thus, accountants's fees in a Chapter 11 case, unpaid at the time of conversion, might not be paid in full, if there are insufficient funds for all Chapter 7 administrative expenses.

After the assets have been liquidated and the proceeds distributed in proper order, the trustee will make a final report and file a final account of the administration of the estate with the court. At this time the trustee will be discharged from further responsibility, and the case is concluded.

Chapter 11—Reorganization

The purpose of Chapter 11 is to provide the debtor with court protection, allow the debtor (or trustee) to continue the operations of the business while a plan is being developed, and minimize the substantial economic losses associated with liquidations. Chapter 11 is designed to allow the debtor to use different procedures, depending on the nature of the debtor's problems and the needs of the creditors. Agreements under this chapter can affect unsecured creditors, secured creditors, and equity holders. A voluntary or involuntary petition can be filed under Chapter 11.

Upon the filing of the *involuntary* petition, the court may, on request of an interested party, appoint a trustee. The appointment is not mandatory and the debtor may, in fact, continue to operate the business as if a bankruptcy petition had not been filed, except that certain transactions may be avoided under the Bankruptcy Code. If the creditors prove the allegations set forth in the involuntary petition, an order for relief is entered, and the case will then proceed in a manner identical to a voluntary case.

The Bankruptcy Code provides that a creditors's committee will be appointed in a Chapter 11 case. Chapter 11 proceedings will determine if the business (or some part of the business) is worth saving, and whether it will be able to operate profitably in the near future. If it is determined that it is not worth saving, then the business should be liquidated without incurring further losses. The current bankruptcy law allows that if it is determined that the business should be liquidated, the debtor may propose a plan that would provide for the orderly liquidation of the business, without conversion of the proceedings to Chapter 7.

In Chapter 11, the debtor, through its own management team, will continue to operate the business, unless a party-in-interest requests that the court appoint a trustee, on certain specified grounds. Appointment of a trustee is the exception, not the rule. It is not necessary, as it was under prior law, for an order to be granted to allow the debtor to continue to operate the business. A party cannot solicit the acceptance or rejection of a plan, from creditors and stockholders affected by the plan, unless they are given a written disclosure statement containing adequate information, as approved by the court. Section 1125(b) of the Bankruptcy Code requires that this disclosure statement be provided prior to, or at the time of, the solicitation. The disclosure statement must be approved by the court, after notice and hearing, as containing adequate information. See section "S" for a more detailed discussion of the disclosure statement.

In cases where the debtor is allowed to operate the business, as debtor-in-possession, the debtor has 120 days after the order for relief, to file a plan, and 180 days after the order for relief, to obtain acceptance, before others can file a plan. This is sometimes referred to as the "plan exclusivity period." These time periods may be extended by the court. After the creditors and the equity holders have approved the plan, the court will hold a hearing to confirm the plan, and the debts not provided for in the plan will be discharged.

Only a very small percentage of petitions, filed by businesses under Chapter 11, result in a successful reorganization. Most are either liquidated in Chapter 11, converted to Chapter 7 where a trustee is appointed to liquidate the estate, or dismissed outright from the protection provided by the bankruptcy system.

Chapter 13—Adjustment of Debts of an Individual with Regular Income

The objective of Chapter 13 is to provide individuals (employees as well as proprietors) with regular income, with some alternative other than liquidation, when they experience financial trouble. Chapter 13 allows the individual, with court supervision, to work out a plan which can provide for full or partial payment of debts over an extended period of time. This concept is similar to a Chapter 11 reorganization, but on a less formalized and more practical scale.

Section 109(e) of the Bankruptcy Code provides that only an individual with regular income who owes, at the time the petition is filed, noncontingent, liquidated, unsecured debts of less than $100,000, and noncontingent, liquidated, secured debts of less than $350,000, can file a petition under Chapter 13. The definition of regular income requires that individuals filing the petition have sufficient, stable and reliable income to enable them to make payments under the Chapter 13 plan. The limit on amount of indebtedness will prevent some wage earners from filing a petition. The purpose of this limitation is to allow some small sole proprietors to file under this chapter—because the filing of a Chapter 11 petition might be too cumbersome for them—but to still require the larger individually owned businesses to use Chapter 11.

Commencement of Case

A *voluntary* case is commenced by the filing of a bankruptcy petition under the appropriate chapter, selected by the debtor. The filing of a voluntary petition constitutes an order for relief, resulting in the debtor and the debtor's property being under the supervision of the court.

An *involuntary* petition can also be filed by creditors with aggregate unsecured claims of at least $5,000 and can be initiated only under Chapter 7 or 11. If there are 12 or more creditors with unsecured claims, at least 3 creditors must sign the petition, and if the number of unsecured creditors is less than 12, a single creditor can force the debtor into bankruptcy. Only one of two requirements must be satisfied, in order for the creditors to force the debtor into bankruptcy:

1. The debtor generally fails to pay debts that are not disputed, as they become due.
2. Within 120 days prior to the petition, a custodian was appointed, or a custodian took possession of substantially all of the debtor's property.

To discourage creditors from filing petitions that are unwarranted, section 303(i) provides that the court may require the petitioners to cover the debtor's costs and reasonable attorney's fees; compensate for any damages, resulting from the trustee (if appointed) taking possession of debtor's property; and, if filed in bad faith, compensate for any damages caused by the filing, including punitive damages.

Automatic Stay

Section 362 of the Bankruptcy Code provides that the filing of a petition results in an automatic stay of the actions of creditors. As a result of the stay, no party, with minor exceptions, including unsecured creditors and creditors having a security or adverse interest in the debtor's property, can take any action that will interfere with the debtor or its property, regardless of where the property is located, until the stay is modified or removed. The debtor or the trustee is permitted to use, sell, or lease property (other than cash collateral), in an ordinary course of business, without notice or hearing, providing the business has been authorized to operate in a Chapter 7, 11,

12, or 13 proceeding and that the court has not restricted the powers of the debtor or trustee, in the order authorizing operation of the business.

The stay of an act against the property of the estate continues, unless modified, until the property is no longer the property of the estate. The stay of any other act continues until the case is closed or dismissed, or the debtor is granted or denied a discharge. The earliest occurrence of one of these events terminates the stay. The automatic stay provision does not operate as a stay against the commencement or continuation of a criminal action or proceeding against the debtor, the enforcement of governmental police or regulatory powers, or certain other actions.

Section 362(d) provides that for relief of the stay to be granted, it is necessary for a party to institute action with the Bankruptcy Court, requesting such relief. The court may grant relief, after notice and hearing, by terminating, annulling, modifying, or conditioning the stay. The court may grant relief for cause, including the lack of adequate protection of a secured creditor's interest. With respect to an act against property, relief may be granted under Chapter 11, if the debtor does not have an equity in the property, and the property is not necessary for an effective reorganization.

Filing Schedules and the Statement of Affairs

"Schedules" are a prescribed form for the listing of the assets and liabilities of the debtor, required by section 521. The assets, according to the schedule requirements, are reported at their "market value," including a brief description of the asset and its location; however, the court may accept "book values." Each individual liability is reported in defined classifications:

1. Creditors having priority (as defined by statute)
2. Creditors holding security
3. Creditors having unsecured claims without priority

In the case of secured claims, the related collateral and its market value is reported. The status of the claim is also reported and has a very important impact upon the proceeding. If a claim is reported by the debtor as "disputed," the creditor will be required to file a "proof of claim" in the proceeding. If it is not disputed, the claim is deemed to be filed for the amount shown, on behalf of the creditor, by means of the schedules filed by the debtor. Claims may also be listed as contingent, unmatured, or unliquidated.

The Statement of Financial Affairs (not to be confused with the accountant's use of the same term) is a prescribed series of questions concerning the debtor, its business, and its financial records. The statement contains information regarding the operations and actions of the debtor within the last year or so.

Schedules and the Statement of Financial Affairs are filed with the bankruptcy court at the time the petition is filed, or shortly thereafter, and are filed under penalty of perjury. The accountant for the debtor often assists in the preparation of these reports, which also serve as the basis for inquiry by creditors, a trustee, and other parties-in-interest.

Employment of Professionals

In proceedings before the bankruptcy court, all professionals must, upon application to the court, obtain an order authorizing their engagement under section 327. This order should be obtained prior to commencing services. If for some reason, work must start before obtaining such an order, it must be obtained relatively soon (within a few weeks) thereafter, and the application should explain the reason for the delay and request retroactive treatment.

Obtaining authority from the court is required for any engagement, where the bankruptcy estate will be requested to pay for such services. Without this authority, request for compensation is subject to rejection, even though the services were performed.

Engagements which must have authority from the court (excluding services as a trustee or examiner, where the order of appointment suffices) include all professional services, including those of an accountant, attorney or expert witness for the debtor, trustee, or official creditors's committee. If a professional is engaged by a creditor or other parties-in-interest, and the creditor or interested party has agreed to pay for these services, no application to the court is required. However, if reimbursement will be sought from the bankruptcy estate, an application is necessary. The application to the court must provide disclosure of all relationships, which the professional now has, or had, with the debtor or any other parties involved.

Under section 330, fees for services may be paid only after a very detailed application is made, and upon a noticed hearing before the court. The professional should work closely with the appropriate attorneys, in the preparation and filing of the fee application. Generally, the fee application is far more detailed than those in other areas of professional practice. It should include a specific description of the service performed, the date it was performed, and the time and charges involved. This is detailed for each individual working on the engagement. Descriptive and detailed time records are essential. Fee applications are subject to challenge by the court and all parties-in-interest to the case, and the court may not always award compensation for the full amount requested. All compensation must be reasonable and for actual and necessary services rendered. Lack of adequate time records may be a basis to reduce or deny compensation.

Debtor-in-Possession

When the management of a Chapter 11 debtor continues to control and operate the business (as opposed to its takeover by a trustee), it is referred to as the debtor-in-possession. As such, under section 1107, its management has a *fiduciary responsibility*, which must be exercised with utmost care. The debtor-in-possession must place the best interest of the estate above the best interest of management, directors, and shareholders. To view the bankruptcy estate as an entity separate from the interest of equity holders becomes very difficult, when management and ownership are the same. In fact, the strong willed owner manager is often unable to recognize this distinction and act in the required fiduciary capacity.

Many actions of a debtor-in-possession (like those of a trustee) require prior approval of the court. Such actions include the approval of wages to key management personnel; the hiring of professionals; the obtaining of additional capital by way of loans; the issue of new equity certificates; the pledging of assets; and the sale of assets (other than goods normally held for sale). The advice of counsel should be obtained in all such cases.

Creditor and Equity Security Holder Committees

In Chapter 11, a committee of unsecured creditors is appointed by the U.S. Trustee, as soon as is practical, after an order for relief is entered. Other creditor or equity security holder committees may also be appointed by the U.S. Trustee, when authorized by the court, though this usually occurs only in larger cases. The committees generally consist of the seven largest parties, in each class, who are willing to serve. Under section 1103, the committees are the "watch dogs" over the activities of the debtor, and will be the primary negotiating bodies with the debtor, for the formulation of a reorganization plan. The members of these committees must exercise care that they act in a fiduciary capacity, for the benefit of all members in their class, and not solely in their individual best interest. The official committees may apply to the court for authority to engage professional assistance. This is another opportunity for an accountant, knowledgeable of bankruptcy proceedings, to provide a unique service.

Surprisingly, the appointed committees are often completely inactive. An active committee can provide a great benefit to the debtor, when a good working relationship exists. This relationship becomes very important when seeking the acceptance of a proposed plan of reorganization. Without the committees's support, acceptance of a reorganization plan will be extremely difficult. Open, truthful, and complete communication between the debtor and the committees is generally the best policy.

The creditor and equity security holder committees also need to be active in protecting their own interests. These committees must see that adequate controls are in place, to assure that the asset base of the debtor is not dissipated.

Trustee and Examiner

Under section 1104, the bankruptcy court may, after giving notice and conducting a hearing, order the U.S. Trustee to appoint a trustee for cause, including fraud, dishonesty, incompetence, or gross mismanagement of the affairs of the debtor by current management. This appointment may occur before or after the commencement of the case, if such appointment is in the interest of creditors, any equity security holders, and other interests of the estate.

If the court does not order the appointment of a trustee, upon request of a party-in-interest and after notice and hearing, the court may order the U.S. Trustee to appoint an examiner, to conduct an appropriate investigation of the debtor. The examiner will investigate any allegations of fraud, dishonesty, incompetence, misconduct, mismanagement, or irregularity in the management of the affairs of the debtor, on the part of the debtor's current or former management and will report on the investigation. An examiner may be appointed upon request, if the court determines such appointment to be in the best interests of creditors, equity security holders, or other interests of the bankruptcy estate, or if the unsecured liabilities of the debtor exceed $5,000,000.

When a trustee is appointed, he or she becomes the chief executive of the business with all the associated powers. However, like a debtor-in-possession, the trustee must file operating reports and seek the approval of the court, for the sale of assets not used in the ordinary course of business. Additionally, according to section 1106, the trustee has all the duties of a debtor-in-possession *and* investigates:

> "... the acts, conduct assets, liabilities, and financial condition of the debtor, the operation of the debtors's business and the desirability of the continuance of such business, and any other matter relevant to the case or to the formulation of a plan [of reorganization] ... "

The trustee then prepares a report of his or her investigation of the affairs of the debtor and of its current and past management.

An examiner's duties are generally limited to conducting an investigation and preparing a report on the investigation. However, the court has the power to limit or expand upon the duties of an examiner. The expansion of the duties of an examiner is becoming a more frequent tool of the court.

The selection of a trustee or examiner may be made from a panel of trustees, maintained by the U.S. Trustee, who devote most or all of their time to such matters, or to parties who possess a particular expertise in business and financial management: Attorneys and CPAs often fill this role.

A trustee is compensated based upon a percentage of monies disbursed. The percentage is set by section 326 (15 percent on the first $1,000 or less, 6 percent on the next $2,000 and 3 percent on an amount in excess of $3,000). The court may award less than the percentage formula. The compensation of a trustee depends largely upon the facts of a particular case, and the trustee's ability to make the case as successful as possible.

The compensation of an examiner is handled in the same manner as other professionals, generally on an hourly rate.

Filing Operating Reports

Operating reports are filed monthly with the court and the U.S. Trustee, to reflect the financial activities of the operating bankruptcy estate. These reports show the cash receipts, cash disbursements, and cash position in detail, as well as other financial information, prepared in the format prescribed by the U.S. Trustee.

The operating reports are extremely important because they act as the key source of information between the debtor and the court and the court-appointed committees. The purpose of the reports is to provide the parties-in-interest with current financial information, concerning the results of operations of the debtor and its financial position. Often, it is information included (or intentionally excluded) from the operating report, which, in part, forms the basis for the appointment of a trustee or examiner.

The preparation of monthly operating reports is another service that can be provided by CPAs: It is often the area in which CPAs obtain their first exposure to bankruptcy practice.

Liquidation Versus Reorganization

Should the debtor liquidate or attempt a reorganization? If that question has not been thoroughly analyzed and answered before the filing of a petition for relief, it will become the first major question addressed, after the filing of a Chapter 11 petition.

As previously discussed, the assets of the debtor may be reported at their market value in the schedule of assets and liabilities filed with the court at the beginning of the case. In general, these reported market values are on the high side due to the optimism of a debtor, in hope of reorganization.

The valuation of the business as a going concern should be carefully evaluated, with regard to the possibilities of selling the business as a whole, or selling only part of its operating divisions or assets. It is entirely possible that a portion of the business is highly saleable, at the same time that another portion would require liquidation. An open and imaginative mind will produce the best solution.

On the other side of the value range, is the liquidation value. At what value will the assets be realized, upon sale in an orderly liquidation, net of selling expenses? The unsecured and secured creditors will compare the liquidation return, with the amount that may possibly be received under the proposed reorganization plan, and with the likelihood of the debtor's success under the plan. Based on this analysis, the creditors will decide whether to advocate liquidation or to support the proposed reorganization plan.

Proofs of Claims or Interests

A proof of claim is filed by a creditor. A proof of interest is filed by an equity security holder of the corporation, or a general or limited partner, in the case of a partnership. A properly filed claim, under section 502, is deemed allowed, unless a party-in-interest files an objection. If any party objects to a claim, a court hearing is held, after notice, to determine the allowable amount.

If the debtor listed the creditor's claim or equity security holders's interest in the filed schedules (in a Chapter 11 case), as undisputed and in an amount and classification (i.e., secured versus unsecured) which that party agrees is correct, this is considered prima facie evidence of the validity and amount of such claim or interest, and the creditor or equity security holder shall not be required to file a proof of claim or interest. This illustrates the care that must be taken when the debtor prepares the schedules. Still, every creditor should protect its own interest and, in most cases, file a proof of claim. In a Chapter 7 case, it is mandatory that creditors file a proof of claim. Claims may be disallowed only for specific reasons set forth in the Bankruptcy Code.

Remember that a creditor filling a collateralized claim may have two classes of claim:

1. A secured claim, to the extent of the related equity (based upon value) in the collateral
2. An unsecured claim, for the balance of the total claimed amount

The administration of claims and interests is another significant task, which is undertaken by a bankruptcy estate. Depending upon the number of claims and interests involved, such tasks can be significant, and the use of a computer is essential. Such tasks may include:

1. Investigation of all or some claims and interests
2. Comparison of proofs of claims and interests filed, to the books and records of the debtor and to the schedules filed
3. Elimination of duplicate proofs of claims and interests
4. Classifications, such as secured versus unsecured, different equity security interests, reorganization plan classes, or other descriptive categories
5. Calculation of the results of voting for the acceptance or rejection of a reorganization plan
6. Determination of amounts allowed, allowable or disallowed
7. Determination of amounts to be paid or securities (i.e., stock of a corporation) issued, in accordance with a reorganization plan
8. Maintenance of the claim and interests register and the master mailing list

In actual practice, duplicate proof of claims and interest and multiple classifications of a single proof of claim are common. Materiality and the extent and nature of investigation are matters that must be thoroughly explored with the debtor or trustee and the case attorney, before undertaking such tasks and before developing a database. Revisions at a later time are costly.

Information from these services will be used to assist in the development of a reorganization plan and to assess its feasibility. Additionally, the information collected and summarized from the claim analysis, for use in the objection to certain proofs of claim or interests, may be used by the accountant in testimony as an expert witness.

Conversion or Dismissal of Bankruptcy Petition

When a case is converted from one chapter to another, section 348(a) provides that the conversion constitutes an order for relief, under the chapter to which converted; the date of filing of the petition, the commencement of the case, and the original order for relief do not change. The conversion from one chapter to another terminates the services of any trustee or examiner who is serving, at the time of conversion.

Relief from Stay

A creditor may make a motion under section 362(d), for relief from the automatic stay, discussed earlier. After proper notice and hearing, the court will either grant relief from the stay, or deny the relief requested. Such hearings can become very controversial, with each side calling various expert witnesses to support its cause.

Consider the following example: A creditor holds a first-mortgage debt of $100,000 on real property, owned by the debtor, having a value, determined by the creditor, of $75,000. The creditor will seek relief from the stay on foreclosure on the property, by claiming that the debtor has no equity in the property, that the property is not essential to the reorganization of the debtor, or that reorganization is not possible or feasible.

The debtor may argue that the value of the property exceeds the $75,000 value, assigned by the creditor. What value did the debtor assign to this asset, on the schedules filed with the court? It may be difficult to argue that the asset is worth over $100,000, if the value listed on the schedules is $75,000. Once again we see the significance of the determination of value in a bankruptcy case.

Assurance that the asset will not diminish in value is another consideration, which must be addressed. Often the collateral for a loan is the inventory and accounts receivable of the debtor. The value of these receivables may be in a constant state of change, due to continued business operations. The cash generated from the sale of items in inventory, or the collection of accounts receivable, is referred to as "cash collateral." The collateral of the creditor must be protected, and its use is subject to challenge by a "relief from stay" motion, before the court. The use of cash collateral and the related adequate protection consideration is a very complicated issue; it is often a key issue in a Chapter 11 reorganization proceeding.

Classification and Priorities of Claims and Interests

Classification

Claims and interests are classified, in accordance with section 1122, by their nature, and all claims and interests, placed into a particular class (a common group), must be substantially similar. Generally, such classifications are determined by the legal description of the claim or interest. As an example, preferred stockholders and common stockholders have different rights and, therefore, their claims require separate classifications. Creditors holding claims collateralized by different property will generally be classified separately, as will general unsecured trade creditors.

Priorities

Claims and interests are assigned a priority; this leaves their legal, equitable, and contractual rights unaltered, with certain exceptions. Generally speaking, the priority status takes the following order.

1. Collateralized claims, to the extent that they are secured, but only against the property that is collateral for that claim
2. "Priority" claims, as defined (see below)
3. Unsecured claims, including undersecured claims
4. Equity interests

Section 507 in the Bankruptcy Code creates a special category of allowed expenses and claims, which have "priority" in the following order:

1. Administrative expenses and costs of preserving the bankruptcy estate, including compensation for services rendered to the estate, after the commencement of the bankruptcy proceeding
2. Unsecured claims arising after the filing of an involuntary case, but before the entry of an order for relief
3. Wages earned by an individual, written 90 days prior to the filing of the bankruptcy petition, but only to the extent of $2,000 per individual
4. Unsecured claims for contributions to an employee benefit plan, in connection with services rendered within 180 days prior to the filing of the bankruptcy petition, but only to the extent of $2,000, multiplied by the number of employees so covered, less:
   a. The aggregate amount paid under (3) above, and
   b. The aggregate amount paid by the bankruptcy estate, on behalf of the employees, to any other benefit plan
5. Certain unsecured claims of farmers and fishermen, but only to the extent of $2,000 for each individual
6. Certain unsecured claims of individuals arising from the deposit of money, for the purchase, lease, or rental of property, or the purchase of services that were not delivered or provided, but only to the extent of $900 for each individual
7. The unsecured claims of government units, but only for:
   a. A tax, measured by income or gross receipts, for a taxable year ending on the date or prior to the filing of the bankruptcy petition, and for which a return (if required) was last due (including extensions of time for filing), within three years prior to the filing of the bankruptcy petition
   b. A property tax, assessed prior to the filing of the bankruptcy petitions, which was last due, without penalty, within one year prior to the filing of the bankruptcy petition
   c. A tax, collected or withheld, in whatever capacity
   d. An employment tax on wages or other forms of compensation, earned from the debtor prior to the filing of the bankruptcy petition (whether or not actually paid), for which a return was last due

(including extensions of time for filing), within three years prior to the filing of the bankruptcy petition

e. An excise tax, relating to a transaction occurring prior to the filing of the bankruptcy petition, for which a return was last due (including extensions of time for filing), within three years prior to the filing of the bankruptcy petition

f. Custom duties on merchandise imported within one year prior to the filing of the bankruptcy petition

g. A penalty, related to claims specified above as priority claims, and as compensation for actual pecuniary loss

h. Unsecured claims, allowed to the Federal Deposit Insurance Corporation, the R.T.C., the Director of the Office of Thrift Supervision, the Comptroller of the Currency, or the Board of Governors of the Federal Reserve System, to maintain the capital of an insured depository institution

Subordination

The court, under the authority of section 510(c), may, after notice and hearing, subordinate a claim or interest. Such subordination, under principles of equity, is generally seen to apply to circumstances where the claimant, generally an "insider," is found guilty of inequitable conduct.

Preferences and Fraudulent Transfers

The detection and assertion of preferences and fraudulent transfers may require a determination of the point in time, when the debtor became insolvent, and performance of a liquidation analysis of the debtor. A trustee may avoid such transactions, by bringing an action before the court.

The transfer of property of the debtor can be voided, as a preference, under section 547, if it was:

1. For the benefit of a creditor
2. For, or on account of, an antecedent debt, owed by the debtor before such transfer was made
3. Made at a time when the debtor was insolvent
4. Made on or within 90 days preceding the filing date of the bankruptcy petition (such time is extended to one year if that creditor, at the time of the transaction, was considered to be an insider)
5. A transaction that enabled the creditor to receive more than it would have received, if: the case had been in a Chapter 7 liquidation; the transfer had not been made; or the creditor had been paid under other provisions of the Bankruptcy Code (i.e., under the reorganization plan)

There are exceptions to a preference transfer including:

1. Contemporaneous exchange for new value
2. A transfer made in the ordinary course of business of the debtor, according to ordinary business terms
3. The creation of a security interest in property, acquired for new value

An action brought to recover a preference is one that in most cases boggles the mind of the preference recipient. Take the case of Mr. A, an innocent party who unknowingly invested in a fraudulent Ponzi scheme, who within 90 days of the bankruptcy petition, got back his principal and a significant return. Given that the bankruptcy estate is grossly insolvent and that other equally innocent but unpaid investors would receive significantly less, or nothing, shouldn't Mr. A be required to return to the estate, the funds he received, and participate in a pro-rata equitable distribution to all creditors? Generally speaking, this is the intent of the law, but just try to explain this, as a trustee, to a very upset Mr. A, when he is presented with this dilemma.

The transfer of an interest of the debtor, in property, or any obligation incurred by the debtor, made or incurred within one year (the one year period may be extended, depending upon applicable state law), before the filing of the bankruptcy petition, may be avoided by the trustee, as a fraudulent transfer under section 548, if the debtor:

1. Made such transfer, or incurred such obligation, with actual intent to hinder, delay, or defraud a creditor; or,
2. Received less than fair value; and (a) was or became insolvent as result of such transaction; (b) was left with an unreasonably small amount of capital; (c) intended or believed that it would not be able to pay the debts incurred as they matured.

The preference and fraudulent transfer avoidance provisions are very controversial and powerful tools, to a trustee or debtor-in-possession, especially in cases where the debtor acted in a fraudulent manner. A keen eye must be used when evaluating transactions of the debtor, and especially so, for those involving insiders, including those involved in leveraged buyout transactions.

Dischargeable Debts

The extend to which a debt is discharged depends on whether the debtor is an individual or corporation, the chapter under which the petition is filed, and the nature and priority of the debt.

Individual Debtors

Section 523 lists several debts that are excepted from a discharge of an individual debtor. These debts are exempted from discharge, in a filing under Chapters 7, 11, and 12; but Chapter 13 has special provisions. Among the items listed, are taxes with priority under section 507(a), incurred by false pretenses, false representations, or actual fraud, including issuance of false financial statements; debts which were not scheduled in time to permit timely action by the creditors to protect their rights, unless they had notice or knowledge of the proceedings; and alimony, maintenance, or support obligations.

Chapter 7 Cases

Only an individual debtor can obtain a discharge in a Chapter 7 case. A partnership or a corporation may not obtain a discharge in a Chapter 7 case. Further, a corporation or partnership, liquidating under a plan adopted in a Chapter 11 case, would not obtain a discharge. Because a corporation effectively goes out of business, as a result of the liquidation, it might appear that the actual granting of a discharge is unimportant. A corporation, however, does not have to go out of existence, and shareholders have kept these corporate shells alive, so that they could be reactivated at a later date, for tax reasons, or to avoid the costs of creating another corporation. A debtor will be reluctant to use these corporate shells, under the current bankruptcy law, because any assets owned by the corporation are subject to attachment by creditors, for prebankruptcy debts.

Chapter 11 Cases

Section 1141(d) provides that in a Chapter 11 case—except to the extent that debt repayment has been agreed to in the plan—confirmation of the plan, discharges the debtor from any debt that arose before the confirmation of the plan. This discharge takes place whether or not the proof of claim was filed or deemed filed, and whether or not such claim is allowed under section 502, or the holder of such claim has accepted the plan. Individuals may not discharge a debt that is of the type listed in section 523. This provision makes it very important for creditors to review thoroughly any proposed Chapter 11 reorganization plans.

Plan of Reorganization

A plan of reorganization is the blueprint that delineates how creditors and equity security holders will be satisfied, under Chapter 11 of the Bankruptcy Code. It is not necessary that all creditors and equity security holders be completely satisfied, in a plan, because there may simply not be sufficient assets or earning power available to do so.

Provisions

Section 1123 promulgates certain provisions, which are mandatory for all Chapter 11 plans. A plan must designate classes for all claims and interests; specify those classes that are not impaired; specify the treatment of all classes which are impaired; provide for the same treatment for each claim or interest in a particular class (unless a particular party agrees to a less favorable treatment); and provide adequate means to implement the provisions of the plan. In addition, if the debtor, or its successor, is a corporation, the plan must provide a provision prohibiting the issuance of nonvoting equity securities and provide other provisions, regarding the seniority of different equity security classes.

Other provisions *may* be included in a plan, such as to impair or leave unimpaired any class of claims or interests; provide for the assumption, rejection, or assignment of executory contracts or unexpired leases; settle, adjust, retain, and enforce any claim or interest belonging to the debtor; provide for the sale of all, or substantially all, the assets of the debtor; and distribute the resulting proceeds to holders of claims and interests of the debtor.

Impaired Claims and Interests

Section 1124 states that claims and interests are impaired if the legal, equitable, and contractual rights of the holder of such claims or interests are altered, any defaults are not cured, and damages are not compensated for by the debtor. The debtor may provide for the payment in cash, equal to the allowed amount of the claim or interest, at the effective date of the plan. In this case, such claim or interest will not then be considered impaired.

To make a reorganization plan work, claims and interests may have to be impaired, but the impact of this leads to another significant consideration, which is discussed later in this chapter.

Development of the Reorganization Plan

A reorganization plan is created with a sequence of steps, starting with its development and ending with its implementation. Aside from the various technical provisions mandated by the Bankruptcy Code, the key issue is feasibility. Will the plan, if effected, really work? This question is addressed formally by the court, at the confirmation hearing. Some practitioners will go out of their way to avoid the feasibility issue, until the confirmation hearing (which is at the end of the sequence of steps taken). If the issue is properly addressed in the early development of a plan, much time, cost, and frustration can be avoided later. Feasibility should be the first major issue studied in the development of a reorganization plan, and the issue should be openly addressed in the disclosure statement and the plan approval hearings.

With this in mind, the plan development begins by addressing some very basic questions:

- Where have we (the debtor) been?
- Where are we now?
- How did we get here?
- What do we have to work with?
- Where do we want to go?
- How do we get there?

Each question must be addressed from several viewpoints; economic (financial), marketing and managerial. Each viewpoint is dependent upon the other. The greatest product is of little value, if it cannot be economically produced and marketed, this in turn, cannot be accomplished without competent management. These questions can only be answered after the debtor has developed a complete business plan. Cash and income projections for at least the next five years should be included in the business plan.

Once it has been determined that there are some aspects of the debtor's operation that can in fact be profitable, the structure of the reorganized entity must be considered. For the plan to be feasible, the debtor must be able to make the debt payments, required under the plan. To determine the structure (amount of debt and amount of stockholders's equity) of the reorganized entity, the reorganization value of the entity must be determined. This value is often determined by discounting the future cash flows, which have been projected in the business plan.

For example, if it is determined that the reorganization value of the surviving business is $10.5 million, a plan that provides for the issuance of $10 million in new debt, in settlement of prepetition claims, will most likely not be feasible.

Various alternative plans may be considered, based on factors considered in developing the business plan and assumptions made regarding the structure of the reorganized debtor. Each of these alternatives should be analyzed, by showing the pro forma effect on the current balance sheet, in conjunction with the appropriate cash flow forecast over the subsequent life of the plan (the time it takes to complete all terms of the proposed plan). Financial forecasts must also be considered for the time between the current balance sheet date and the expected effective date of the plan (the date when the plan goes into effect following its confirmation by the court).

After considering the various alternatives, a plan is proposed. Such decisions must be a team effort, between the debtor or trustee and its attorneys and accountants, and hopefully, between the debtor and the creditor and equity security holder committees.

Disclosure Statement

A disclosure statement is a report, which is presented, together with the proposed reorganization plan, to the creditors and equity security holders when their vote is requested on the acceptance or rejection of the proposed plan. It is similar to a prospectus, in its nature and intended use. The Bankruptcy Code Does not specify in detail the required content of the disclosure statement, leaving this to the judicial discretion of the court. The Bankruptcy Code in section 1125 does, however, define "adequate information" as

> "...information of a kind, and in sufficient detail, as far as is reasonably practical in light of the nature and history of the debtor and the condition of the debtors's books and records, that would enable a hypothetical reasonable investor typical of holders of claims or interests of the relevant class to make an informed judgment about the plan...."

The issues that should be included in a disclosure statement will vary, depending on the specific case. Inclusion of all of the following matters should be given serious consideration:

1. Opinions, disclaimers, assumptions and risks, concerning the content of the financial statements, including forecasts and projections (here lies a special reporting issue for an accountant)
2. A brief description of the debtor and a history of its past and current business activities
3. A description of the proposed management team, with individual profiles and current and proposed compensation
4. A summary of the proposed reorganization plan, including a description of the classes of creditors and equity security holders, and the treatment the plan affords each class
5. Disclosure of related parties, affiliates, and major equity security holders, under terms of the proposed plan, and a description of any transactions with such parties
6. A liquidation analysis
7. Special risk factors
8. Income tax issues
9. Financial information including: historical operating results for pre- *and* postpetition periods; current financial position; cash flow forecast for the plan life; pro forma effect of the plan and the forecast

10. A statement indicating how the plan will be accomplished

11. A brief description of pending legal proceedings

12. A valuation of the specific assets and the surviving business as a going concern

13. Marketing plans

14. Major postpetition events and transactions, including information concerning the appointment of and reports from the trustee, examiner, and official creditor or equity security holder committees

15. Terms of new debt or security instruments issued, or to be issued, under terms of the plan

The disclosure statement must be approved, after a noticed hearing, by the court, before its release. The accountant's presence may be required, as an expert witness, on matters concerning the content of the disclosure statement and its adequacy.

Acceptance or Rejection of the Plan

After the disclosure statement has been approved by the court, the statement, the plan, and an approved ballot are sent to each holder of a claim or interest. This is the formal solicitation for approval of the plan, in accordance with section 1126 of the Bankruptcy Code. Prior and unauthorized solicitation activities can result in severe consequences. Promises, representations, and terms of treatment, which are not included in the approved plan and disclosure statement, are improper and not authorized; the plan and the disclosure document should include a statement of this fact.

Each holder of a claim or interest is entitled to vote for the acceptance or rejection of a proposed plan of reorganization. However, a class of claims or interests that is not impaired is presumed to have accepted the plan and its formal solicitation and vote is not required. A class of creditor claims has accepted a plan, if claims representing at least two thirds of the value of the claims and more than one half of the number of allowed claims vote to accept the plan. A class of interests has accepted a plan, if claims representing at least two thirds of the value of allowed interests vote to accept the plan.

A very important element of the acceptance or rejection of a plan is that the required vote computations are based upon the total claims or interests, by each class that actually cast votes (as opposed to the entirety of the amount and number of allowed claims or interests making up a defined class).

The Bankruptcy Court fixes the time within which the voting takes place. Generally, this is done in conjunction with the approval of the form of the ballot and related procedures.

Confirmation of the Plan

Following the voting process for a proposed plan of reorganization, the proponent of the plan will seek its confirmation by the court. Certain requirements must be met before the bankruptcy court will confirm a plan. The section 1129 requirements are:

1. The plan complies with the applicable provision of the Bankruptcy Code (Title 11, United States Code).
2. The proponent of the plan complies with the applicable provisions of the Bankruptcy Code.
3. The plan has been proposed in good faith and not by any means that is forbidden by law.
4. Payments made, or to be made, in connection with the case or the plan are reasonable and have been approved by the court, or are subject to such approval.
5. The plan makes disclosure of management or proposed management, insiders, and affiliates.
6. Approval of government regulatory bodies, concerning rate changes.
7. The plan, for each impaired class of claims and interests, has been accepted or will receive or retain under the plan, value (as of the effective date of the plan) that is not less than the amount such holders would receive or retain, if the debtor were liquidated under Chapter 7 of the Bankruptcy Code. This is sometimes known as the best interest test.
8. Each class of claims or interests has accepted the plan (or, if not impaired, is deemed to have accepted the plan).
9. The plan provides for the treatment of priority claims.
10. Acceptance by at least one class of impaired claims, other than a class held by insiders.
11. The plan will not likely be followed by liquidation or the need for further reorganization of the debtor (or its successor), not provided for in the plan. This is known as the feasibility test.
12. All fees payable under section 1930 of the Bankruptcy Code have been paid or provided for.

Notwithstanding requirement number 8, the court may, under certain circumstances and upon request by the plan proponent, confirm the plan, if the plan does not discriminate unfairly, and if the plan is fair and equitable, with respect to an impaired class of claims or interests who rejected the plan. This is known as the "cram-down" provision. Section 1129(b) specifies tests for determining if a plan is fair and equitable.

Postconfirmation Activities

Following the confirmation of a reorganization plan by the court, the plan must be implemented. The date on which the plan is implemented is known as the effective date of the plan. Upon completion of the plan implementation, in accordance with its terms, the plan is referred to as consummated, and the case is considered closed.

GLOSSARY

Adequate Protection: Holders of secured claims, lessors, co-owners, conditional vendors, consignors, and so forth, are entitled to adequate protection of their interest in the property, when such holders request relief from the automatic stay. Adequate protection is also required, before the debtor or trustee can see, sell, or lease certain kinds of collateral, or before a lien that is prior to or equal to the creditor's lien can be granted.

Administrative Expenses: The actual, necessary costs of preserving the estate, including wages, salaries, and commissions for services rendered after the commencement of the case, are considered administrative expenses. Compensation awarded a professional person, including accountants and attorneys, for postpetition services, is an expense of administration.

Automatic Stay: A petition, filed under the Bankruptcy Code, which automatically stays virtually all actions of creditors to collect prepetition debts. As a result of the stay, no party, with minor exceptions, having a security or adverse interest in the debtor's property, can take any action that will interfere with the debtor or the debtor's property, regardless of where the property is located or who has possession, until the stay is modified or removed.

Bankruptcy: The proceedings initiated voluntarily by a financially troubled debtor, or involuntarily by creditors when the debtor is generally not paying debts as they become due, and involving the filing of a petition in a federal court under the Bankruptcy Code.

Bankruptcy Code: A federal statute, enacted October 1, 1979, as Title 11 of the United States Code, by the Bankruptcy Reform Act of 1978, which is applicable to all cases filed on or after its enactment and which provides the basis for the federal bankruptcy system in effect today.

Bankruptcy Court: The United States Bankruptcy Court of trial jurisdiction, that is, a unit of the district court. Responsible for all cases filed under Chapters 7, 11, 12, and 13 of the Bankruptcy Code.

Cash Collateral: Cash collateral is cash, negotiable instruments, documents of title, securities, deposit accounts, or other cash equivalents, where the estate and someone else have an interest in the property. Also included would be the proceeds of noncash collateral, such as inventory and accounts receivable, if converted to proceeds of the type defined as cash collateral, provided the proceeds are subject to the prepetition security interests.

Chapter 7 Proceeding: A liquidation, voluntarily or involuntarily initiated under the provisions of the Bankruptcy Code on or after October 1, 1979, which provides for an orderly liquidation of the business or debtor's estate.

Chapter 11 Proceeding: A reorganization action, either voluntary or involuntary, initiated under the provisions of the Bankruptcy Code, on or after October 1, 1979 that provides for a reorganization of the debt structure of the business and allows the business to continue operations.

Chapter 12 Proceeding: A reorganization, voluntarily initiated, under the provisions of the Bankruptcy Code, for family farmers with regular income.

Chapter 13 Proceeding: A voluntary action, initiated under the provisions of the Bankruptcy Code, on or after October 1, 1979 that provides for the settlement of debts of individuals with regular income. Some small individually owned businesses may also file a petition under Chapter 13.

Claim: Section 101(4) of the Bankruptcy Code defines claim as (A) right to payment, whether or not such right is reduced to judgment, liquidated, unliquidated, fixed, contingent, matured, unmatured, disputed, undisputed, legal, secured, or unsecured, or (B) right to an equitable remedy for breach of performance, if such breach gives rise to a right to payment, whether or not such right to an equitable remedy is reduced to judgment, fixed, contingent, matured, unmatured, disputed, undisputed, secured, or unsecured.

Confirmation: An official approval by the court of a plan of reorganization, under Chapter 11 proceedings that makes the plan binding upon the debtor and creditors. Before a plan is confirmed, it must satisfy eleven requirements in section 1129(a) of the Bankruptcy Code. Plans may also be confirmed in Chapters 12 and 13. The requirements for confirmation differ in some respects from the confirmation requirements under Chapter 11.

Cram-Down: For a plan to be confirmed, a class of claims or interests must either accept the plan or not be impaired. However, the Bankruptcy Code allows the court, under certain conditions, to confirm a plan, even though an impaired class has not accepted the plan. The plan must not discriminate unfairly, and must be fair and equitable, with respect to each class of claims or interests impaired under the plan that has not accepted it. The Bankruptcy Code states conditions for secured claims, unsecured claims, and stockholder interests that would be included by the fair and equitable requirement. It should be noted that, because the word "includes" is used, the meaning of "fair and equitable" is not restricted to these conditions.

Creditors' Committee: In a Chapter 11 case, a committee of creditors holding unsecured claims shall be appointed as soon as practicable after the order for relief is granted. The U.S. Trustee has the responsibility for appointing the committee without any authorization from the court. The committee will ordinarily consist of the seven largest creditors willing to serve or, if a committee was organized before the order for relief, such committee may continue, provided it was fairly chosen and is representative of the different kinds of claims to be presented.

Debtor-in-Possession: Refers to a debtor in a Chapter 11 case, unless a trustee has been appointed. The debtor will remain in possession of its assets in a Chapter 11 case, unless a trustee is appointed.

Equity Security: A share in a corporation (whether or not transferable or denominated stock) or similar security; interest of a limited partner in a limited partnership; or warrant or right (other than a right to convert) to purchase, sell, or subscribe to a share or interest.

Estate: The commencement of a case under the Bankruptcy Code creates an estate comprised of the property of the debtor.

Examiner: An official appointed by the Bankruptcy Court in a Chapter 11 reorganization, if no trustee is serving, to conduct an investigation of the debtor, including an investigation of any allegations of fraud, dishonesty, incompetence, misconduct, mismanagement, or irregularity in the management of the affairs of the debtor by current or former management of the debtor, if (1) such appointment is in the interests of creditors, any equity security holders, and other interests of the estate, or (2) the debtor's fixed, liquidated, unsecured debts, other than debts for goods, services, or taxes, or owing to an insider, exceed $5 million.

Executory Contract: A contract in which something other than payment itself must be performed, wholly or in part, to complete the original agreement. Unexpired leases or purchase commitments are examples of executory contracts, typically found in cases under the Bankruptcy Code.

Exempt Assets: Property of an estate that by federal or state laws is not liable for any debt of the debtor that arose before the commencement of the case. The debtor may maintain possession of exempt assets.

Fraudulent Transfer: A transfer of an interest or an obligation incurred by the debtor, within one year prior to the date the petition was filed, with the intent to hinder, delay, or defraud creditors, or whereby the debtor received less than fair equivalent value and the debtor (1) was insolved before or became insolvent as the result of such transfer, (2) was left with unreasonably small business capital, or (3) intended to incur debts beyond the ability to pay such debts as they matured. Fraudulent transfers may be voided. Certain transfers considered fraudulent under state law may be avoided, even if the transfer occurred more than one year before the petition was filed.

Impairment of Claims: In determining which classes of claims or stockholders's interest must approve the plan, it is first necessary to determine if the class is impaired. A class of claims or interest is impaired under the plan, unless the plan provides for the following: (1) Leaves unaltered, the legal, equitable, and contractual right of a class, (2) Cures defaults that led to acceleration of debts or equity interest, (3) Pays in cash the full amount of the claim or, in the case of equity interest, the greater of the fixed liquidation preference or redemption price.

Insider: Includes director, officer, person in control, relative of management, partner, affiliate, and managing agent of a firm.

Insolvency: In the equity sense, the inability of the debtor to pay obligations as they mature. In the bankruptcy sense, a condition where the liabilities of the debtor exceed the fair valuation of its assets.

Involuntary Petition: A petition filed under Chapters 7 or 11, by creditors forcing the debtor into bankruptcy court.

Order for Relief: An order, whether by decree or by position of law in a case with the Bankruptcy Code (filed on after October 1, 1979), granting relief to (or against) the debtor. In a voluntary case, the entry of the order for relief is the filing of the petition. The court must enter the order or relief in an involuntary case, if the petition is uncontested or if the court determines that (1) the debtor is generally not paying debts as they become due, or (2) within 120 days before the petition was filed, a custodian was appointed for substantially all of the debtor's property.

Petition: A document filed in a court of bankruptcy, initiating proceedings under the Bankruptcy Code.

Plan: An agreement that, when confirmed by the bankruptcy court, provides for the rehabilitation or liquidation of the debtor in a bankruptcy case under Chapters 11, 12, or 13. The plan may affect secured creditors and stockholders as well as unsecured creditors's interests.

Preference: A transfer of property on account of a past debt within ninety days (one year for insiders) prior to filing the petition, while the debtor is insolvent, to a creditor who receives more than would be received if the debtor's estate were liquidated under Chapter 7. The Bankruptcy Code provides exceptions for certain transactions, which are substantially contemporaneous or in the ordinary course of business.

Priority Claim: A claim or expense that is paid after secured claims and before unsecured claims are satisfied, in accordance with statutory categories. The discharge is a privilege and the bankruptcy laws provide exceptions to discharge, in whole or in part, for certain wrongdoing, such as concealment of assets, or certain types of debts, such as alimony. Under the Bankruptcy Code (cases filed after October 1, 1979), a corporation which liquidates all (or substantially all) of its assets is ineligible for a discharge.

Proof of Claim: The Bankruptcy Code permits a creditor or indenture trustee to file a proof of claim and an equity holder to file a proof of interest. The filing of the proof is not mandatory in a Chapter 11 case, and the debtor may obtain a discharge for debts that were listed on the schedules filed with the court, even though a proof of claim is not filed. The debtor or trustee has the power to file a claim on behalf of the creditor, if the creditor did not file a timely claim. Thus, for debts that are nondischargeable, the debtor may file a proof of claim to cause the creditor to receive some payment from the estate and avoid having to pay all of the debt, after the bankruptcy proceedings are over.

Reorganization: Proceedings under Chapter 11 of the Bankruptcy Code (cases filed on or after October 1, 1979), where a debtor attempts to reach an agreement with creditors, secured and unsecured, and continue in business.

Schedules: The detailed lists of debts and assets that the debtor is required to file with a petition in bankruptcy court, or shortly thereafter.

Secured Claim: A claim against a debtor that is secured by collateral, which may be used to satisfy the debt in the event the debtor defaults. Under the Bankruptcy Code, a creditor's claim is secured only to the extent of the value of the collateral, unless the creditor selects, in a Chapter 11 proceeding [section 1111(b)(2)], to have the entire debt considered secured.

Statement of Affairs: A report filed with a petition under Chapter 11 and consisting of answers to twenty-one questions concerning the debtor's past operations. Also used to refer to a statement of a debtor's financial condition, as of a certain date, based on the assumption that the business will be liquidated. The statement consists of an analysis of the debtor's financial position and the status of the creditors with respect to the debtor's assets.

Trustee: The Bankruptcy Code refers to four categories of trustees—U.S. Trustee, interim trustee, trustee under a Chapter 7, 11, 12, and 13 case and standing trustee. *U.S. Trustee*—A trustee appointed by the Attorney General in 21 regions to establish, maintain, and supervise a panel of private trustees who are eligible and available to serve as trustees in a case under Chapters 7, 11, 12, or 13. The U.S. Trustee is responsible for the administrative aspects of the bankruptcy case. Among other duties, the U.S. Trustee approves fee applications, appoints trustees and committees, and reviews operating statements. *Interim Trustee*—As soon as the order for relief has been entered in a Chapter 7 case, the court will appoint a disinterested person, from a panel of private trustees, to serve as the interim trustee. *Chapter 7 Trustee*—At a meeting of creditors called under section 341, a trustee may be elected if an election is requested by at least 20 percent in amount of qualifying claims. The interim trustee will continue to serve, if a trustee is not elected. *Chapter 11 Trustee*—The Bankruptcy Code provides in Chapter 11 cases that a trustee can be appointed in certain situations, based on the facts of the case and not related to the size of the company or the amount of unsecured debt outstanding. The trustee is appointed only at the request of a party-in-interest, after a notice and hearing. *Chapter 12 or 13 case*—The U.S. Trustee may appoint an individual trustee to a Chapter 12 or 13 case, where a standing trustee has not been appointed. *Standing Trustee*—In districts where warranted, the U.S. Trustee may appoint one or more individuals to serve as standing trustees, for cases filed under Chapter 12 or 13. In addition to most of the duties of a trustee in a Chapter 7 or 11 case, the standing trustee collects payments under the plan and distributes them to the creditors. A percentage fee, based on payments under the plan, will be collected by the standing trustee to cover trustee's costs.

Undersecured Claim: A secured claim, where the value of the collateral is less than the amount of the claim.

Unsecured Claim: A claim that is not secured by any collateral. In the case of an undersecured creditor, the excess of the secured claim over the value of the collateral.

FOR FURTHER READING

Altman, Edward J., *Corporate Financial Distress: A Complete Guide to Predicting, Avoiding, and Dealing with Bankruptcy* (New York: John Wiley & Sons, 1983).

Collier Bankruptcy Code and Rules, Parts 1 and 2 (New York: Matthew Bender & Co., 1988).

Dykeman, Francis C., *Forensic Accounting—The Accountant as Expert Witness* (New York: John Wiley & Sons, 1982).

Frank, Peter B., Michael J. Wagner, and L.W. Roman, eds., *Litigation Services Handbook, The Role of the Accountant as Expert Witness* (New York: John Wiley & Sons, 1990).

Myers, Leo O., *Debtor–Creditor Relations—Manual and Forms* (New York: McGraw-Hill Book Co., 1986).

Newton, Grant W., *Bankruptcy and Insolvency Accounting Practice and Procedures*, 2 vols. including forms and exhibits, 4th ed. (New York: John Wiley & Sons, 1989).

Newton, Grant W. and Gilbert D. Bloom, *Bankruptcy and Insolvency Taxation* (New York: John Wiley & Sons, 1990).

Pratt, Shannon, *Valuing Small Businesses and Professional Practices* (Homewood, IL: Dow Jones Irwin, 1986).

Sulmeyer, Irving, D. M. Lynn, et al., *Collier Handbook for Trustees and Debtors in Possession* (New York: Matthew Bender & Co., 1987).

Wagner, Michael S. and Peter B. Frank, *Litigation Services MAS Technical Consulting Practice Aid #7* (American Institute of CPAs, 1986).

Chapter Notes

Chapter 4: Using the Computer in Finance and Accounting

1. Peter Keen and Michael Morton, *Decision Support Systems: An Organizational Perspective* (Reading, MA: Addison-Wesley, 1978).

2. These formulas are simplified for illustrative purposes. A more rigorous model would include, for example, the effect of a change in liabilities on expected profits via a corresponding change in interest cost.

3. Jessica Keywes, "AI in the Big Six," *AI Expert* (May 1990), pp. 37–42.

4. Robert A. Marose, "A Financial Neural–Network Application," *AI Expert* (May 1990), pp. 50–53.

5. Clyde W. Holsapple, Kar Yan Tam, and Andrew B. Whinston, "Adapting Expert System Technology to Financial Management," *Financial Management* (Autumn 1988), pp. 12–22.

6. Stephen A. Moscove, Mark G. Simkin, and Nancy A. Bagranoff, *Accounting Information Systems: Concepts and Practice for Effective Decision Making*, 4th ed. (New York: John Wiley & Sons, 1990), p. 639.

7. Carl E. Keller, Jr., David Yen, Glenn L. Helms, and P. S. Warnock, "What Can Expert Systems Be Doing in Accounting?" *Financial and Accounting Systems* (Summer 1990), pp. 11–20.

Chapter 5: Budgetary Control Analysis

1. National Association of Accountants, *Standard Costs and Variance Analysis*, (New York: NAA, 1974), p. 9.

2. Whyte, W. F., ed. *Money and Motivation: An Analysis of Incentives in Industry* (New York: Harper & Row, 1955).

Chapter 7: The Business Plan

1. Philip Thurston, "Should Smaller Companies Make Formal Plans?" *Harvard Business Review* (September–October 1983), p. 184.

2. See an article by J. A. Timmons, "A Business Plan Is More Than a Financing Device," *Harvard Business Review* (March–April 1980).

3. Publilius Syrus.

4. Taken from comments of Nolan Bushnell, founder of Atari, Pizza Time Theaters, and a venture capital firm, made at a seminar during his induction in 1983 into the Babson College Academy of Distinguished Entrepreneurs.

5. Thurston, "Should Smaller Companies Make Formal Plans?" pp. 162–88.

6. Ibid., pp. 162–88.

7. Peter R. Drucker, *Managing for Results* (New York: Harper & Row, 1964).

8. For a discussion of some approaches to this dilemma, see George A. Steiner, "Approaches to Long Range Planning for Small Business," *California Management Review* (Fall 1967), pp. 3–16.

9. Thurston, "Should Smaller Companies Make Formal Plans?" pp. 162–88.

10. See, for example, Charles P. Waite, "The Presentation and Other Key Elements," in *Pratt's Guide to Venture Capital Sources*, 13th ed. (Needham, MA: Venture Economics, 1989), pp. 36–38.

Chapter 9: Managing Long-Term Investments

1. Financial investment is a special case, where a payment is made in order to acquire future cash receipts. Financial investment theory relies on certain additional propositions.

2. For example, the timing of stock issues is critical. If the stock market is down, firms try not to sell their stock. They hold off until stock prices rise.

Chapter 11: The Impact of Globalization on Management and Financial Reporting

1. Foreign currency exchange rates can be quoted in either a direct or an indirect fashion. When quoted directly, the foreign currency exchange rate is expressed in terms of the reporting currency. Quoting the exchange rate for the krone as $.178 is a direct quote, indicating the number of dollars (the reporting currency) per krone. An indirect quotation for this example would be K 5.618, (or 1 /.178), indicating the number of krone per dollar.

2. A U.S. electronics company recently attempted to eliminate currency risk by having its Japanese supplier provide invoices in the U.S. dollar. The Japanese supplier agreed to do this and introduced a new higher schedule of prices. The U.S. company deemed the increases to be so high that it decided to continue to be invoiced in the Japanese yen and to manage the resultant currency risk.

3. Each of the actual case examples discussed in this section are treated in more detail, including income tax and cash-flow issues, in Comiskey and Mulford, "Risks of Foreign Currency Transactions: A Guide for Loan Officers," *Commercial Lending Review* (Summer, 1990), pp. 44–60.

4. The accounting treatment to insure that the offsetting gains and losses are included in the income statements at the same time is a bit technical. In its 1989 Annual Report, p. 36, Federal Express reports that "...exchange rate gains and losses on the term loan are deferred and amortized over the remaining life of the loan as an adjustment to the related hedge (service) revenue."

5. This example is discussed in B. Holmes, ed., "FX Translation—Lyle Shipping's Losses," *Accountancy* (December, 1984), p. 50. Lyle has an *economic* hedge of its dollar exposure but not an *accounting* hedge. Lyle's risk is controlled, in whole or in part, by the offsetting dollar flows. However, under conventional accounting practices, the gain or loss on the dollar liability is recognized in the periods in which the exchange rates change. Offsetting gains or losses are not recorded in the same periods because the future dollar charter inflows have yet to be earned and are not reflected as an asset on Lyle's books until they are actually collected.

6. See Maloney, "Managing Currency Exposure: The Case of Western Mining," *Journal of Applied Corporate Finance* (Winter, 1990), pp. 29–34 for an analysis of the effectiveness of this natural hedge during the eighties.

7. The forward price of a foreign currency can also be at a discount to the spot price. This premium or discount relationship is determined mainly by the relative level of interest rate in the countries representing, respectively, the foreign and domestic currency.

8. Southmark's 1987 Annual Report, p. 41, reported that "Southmark also invested in additional Swiss franc futures contracts on which it recognized a gain of $16.2 million." These contracts did not serve to hedge Swiss franc debt. Rather, they represented a means of taking a position on the likely movement of the franc. Because the franc appreciated, Southmark made a gain. If the franc had depreciated, then a loss would have resulted. It is common to refer to these nonhedge positions as speculations.

9. See Lewent and Kearney, "Identifying, Measuring and Hedging Currency Risk at Merck." *Journal of Applied Corporate Finance* (Winter, 1990), pp. 19–28.

10. For further detail on all matters related to foreign currency transaction and translation, consult Financial Accounting Standards Board, *Statement of Financial Accounting Standards No. 52: Foreign Currency Translation,* (December, 1981).

11. Ibid., paragraph 39.

12. *Statement of Financial Accounting Standards No. 52: Foreign Currency Translation* refers to this alternative procedure as remeasurement as opposed to translation. However, in the vast majority of cases the remeasurement is from the foreign currency to the U.S. dollar. Therefore, remeasurement produces statements in the U.S. dollar that are ready to be consolidated with the statements of their U.S. parent. Remeasurement is tantamount to translation.

13. The paper is entitled, "The Management of Currency Risk: Case Studies of US and UK Multinationals," and was published in *Accounting and Business Research* (Summer, 1990), p. 208.

14. The relevant accounting standard at the time was, *Statement of Financial Accounting Standards Number 8: Accounting for the Translation of Foreign Currency Transactions and Foreign Financial Statements* (October, 1975).

15. Houston and Mueller, "Foreign Exchange Rate Hedging and SFAS No. 52—Relatives or Strangers?" *Accounting Horizons* (December, 1988), p. 57.

16. International Accounting Standards Committee, *Exposure Draft 32: Comparability of Financial Statements* (January 11, 1989).

17. Ibid., paragraph 6.

18. International Accounting Standards Committee, *Statement of Intent: Comparability of Financial Statements*, (July, 1990).

19. Financial Accounting Standards Board, *Proposed Statement of Financial Accounting Standards: Employers' Accounting for Postretirement Benefits Other Than Pensions* (February, 1989).

20. From a statement made by R. S. Miller, Jr., Executive Vice President and Chief Financial Officer of Chrysler Corporation, to the Financial Accounting Standards Board, Washington, D.C., November 3, 1989, p. 3.

21. *The Value Line Investment Survey: Ratings & Reports* (New York: Value Line Publishing, Inc., 1990).

22. The following two references were of great assistance in preparing this discussion of transfer pricing: Choi and Mueller, *An Introduction to Multinational Accounting* (Englewood Cliffs, NJ: Prentice-Hall, Inc., 1978), esp. chapter 9; and Arpan and Radebaugh, *International Accounting and Multinational Enterprises* (New York: Warren, Gorham & Lamont, 1981), esp., Chapter 10.

23. *Accounting for Changing Prices: Replacement Cost and General Price Level Adjustments,* (Santa Barbara, CA: Wiley/Hamilton, 1976) by Largay and Livingstone was helpful in preparing this section.

24. The standard requiring supplemental inflation information was *Statement of Financial Accounting Standards Number 33: Financial Reporting and Changing Prices* (Stamford, CT: FASB, 1979).

25. Ibid.

26. *Statement of Financial Accounting Standards No. 89: Financial Reporting and Changing Prices* (Stamford, Conn.: FASB, 1986).

27. Institute of Chartered Accountants in England and Wales, Accounting Standards Committee, *Statement of Standard Accounting Practice No. 16: Current Cost Accounting* (London: Institute of Chartered Accountants in England and Wales, 1980).

28. For further background on this topic see: Skousen, *An Introduction to the SEC*, 4th ed., (Cincinnati: South-Western Publishing Company, 1987), pp. 32–35.

29. *Report of the National Commission on Fraudulent Financial Reporting* (Washington, DC, 1987).

30. In an article entitled, "What is Internal Control? Who Owns It?" published in *Management Accounting*, Schiff and May report the results of a Deloitte & Touche survey, which indicates that almost 60 percent of companies with an excess of $500 million in sales include a management report in their annual reports.

Chapter 14: Corporate Governance

1. For a more complete discussion of the topics in the chapter, with many case examples, see Charles A. Anderson and Robert N. Anthony, *The New Corporate Directors* (New York: John Wiley & Sons, 1986).

2. Quantitative data in this section are taken from a survey by Spencer Stuart, an executive search firm, as reported in National Association of Accountants, *Controllers Update* (February 1990), p.2.

3. Kenneth R. Andrews, *The Concept of Corporate Strategy* (Homewood, IL: Dow-Jones Irwin, 1980).

4. Bryan Burrough and John Helyar, *Barbarians at the Gate: The Fall of RJR Nabisco* (New York: Harper & Row, 1990).

5. *Escott* v. *BarChris Construction Corp.*, 283 F. Supp. 643 (S.D.N.Y. 1968).

6. *Wall Street Journal*, issues of March 18, 1980 (p. 7), April 23, 1980 (p. 38), and May 19, 1980 (p. 10).

7. SEC 1975 Release 34–115.4.

About the Authors

William W. Alberts is a professor of business economics and finance at the Graduate School of Business Administration of the University of Washington in Seattle. His teaching and research are concentrated in the areas of industrial economics (including competitive analysis), business strategy (including product pricing analysis), and diversification strategy (including acquisition analysis). In the last few years, he has published papers on the profitability of growth by acquisition, the recapture of acquisition premiums, the profitability of businesses operating in oligopolistic markets, the experience curve doctrine, ROE "drivers" in commercial banks, the profitability of U.S. commercial banks over the last decade, and the nature of value based investment planning. Professor Alberts is also a principal and cofounder of Marakon Associates, a management consulting company with offices in Stamford, CT; London, Melbourne, and San Francisco. The company has pioneered in the development of value-based management and its application to the tasks of formulating and implementing business and diversification strategies.

Charles A. Anderson's career includes academic and business experience. He has been a faculty member of both the Harvard Business School and the Stanford Business School. He was the president, chief executive officer, and a director of Walker Manufacturing Co., J.I. Case, and the Stanford Research Institute. He has served on a number of corporate boards of directors, including NCR Corp., Owens-Corning Fiberglas Corp., Boise-Cascade Corp., and the Eaton Company.

Robert N. Anthony is Ross Graham Walker Professor of Management Control, Emeritus, at Harvard Business School. He has been a director and chairman of the audit committee of Carborundum Company and Warnaco, Inc. He has been a director of several smaller organizations and a trustee (including chairman of the board) of Colby College, and of Dartmouth-Hitchcock Medical Center. He is the author or coauthor of some 20 books and 100 articles on management subjects, especially management control; his books and articles have been translated into 12 languages. He is a past president of the American Accounting Association.

Eugene E. Comiskey received his Ph.D. from Michigan State University and his professional qualifications include both certified public accountant (C.P.A.) and certified management accountant (C.M.A.). Professor Comiskey taught for 15 years at the Krannert Graduate School of Management at Purdue University and also as a visiting faculty member at the University of California, Berkeley. While at Purdue, he twice received the Salgo Noren Foundation Award, as the most outstanding professor in the Graduate Management Program. Since arriving at Georgia Tech in 1980, he has six times been recognized as Professor of the Year by the graduate students in management. Professor Comiskey has published over 50 papers in a wide range of professional and scholarly journals. His current research interests center on earnings forecasts, the relationship between accounting and market-based risk measures, the role of financial data in credit decisions, and international financial reporting practices. Professor Comiskey served for two years in the elective position of director of research for the American Accounting Association.

Michael L. Fetters is a certified public accountant and earned M.B.A. and Ph.D. degrees from the University of Wisconsin-Madison. He is the chairperson of the Accounting and Law Division at Babson College. He previously worked for Arthur Andersen & Co. and currently consults with a variety of businesses, in the area of financial statement analysis. He has published numerous articles in accounting and management journals.

Brian Forst is assistant professor of management science at The George Washington School of Business and Public Management. He received his bachelor of science degree in statistics and his M.B.A. from the University of California at Los Angeles and studied managerial economics in the Ph.D. program at Cornell University. Professor Forst has also been a fellow at Cornell University and is the author of *Power in Numbers: How To Manage for Profit* (John Wiley & Sons, 1987).

Les Heitger is a professor of accounting at the Indiana University Graduate School of Business in Bloomington, Indiana. He received his B.S.B.A. from the Ohio State University, his M.S.B.A. from the University of Denver, and his Ph.D. from Michigan State University. Professor Heitger has written six textbooks and numerous articles for academic and professional journals. He is a certified public accountant who worked for the Denver office of Arthur Young & Company. Dr. Heitger has consulted with over 50 companies on cost/managerial accounting systems and has extensive experience in developing effective planning and control systems. He has also served as an expert witness on financial matters in numerous litigations.

Paul G. Joubert, in additon to his client service responsibilities, is partner-in-charge of the Middlemarket Business Services Group at Cooper & Lybrand's Boston office. He manages a staff of over 150 professionals who provide a full range of auditing, tax, and business advisory services to companies throughout New England. Major services, in addition to reporting on financial statements and tax advice, include business and financial information systems, business strategy, productivity improvements, cash management programs, employee benefit plans, and merger and acquisition assistance. Mr. Joubert joined Coopers & Lybrand in 1971, after graduating from Northeastern University with a degree in finance and accounting. He was admitted to the partnership in 1981 and subsequently served a two-year term as staff director for Coopers & Lybrand's vice chairman of domestic operations. Mr. Joubert has worked extensively with both start-up and mature companies, especially in the manufacturing, high technology, telecommunications, and financial services industries. He has substantial experience in SEC reporting, mergers and acquisitions, and international operations.

William C. Lawler, did his undergraduate work at the University of Connecticut and his Ph.D. studies at the University of Massachusetts. He is currently associate professor of accounting and curriculum coordinator for the M.B.A. program at Babson College. His research and teaching interests focus on financial planning models and the impact of new production technologies on cost information systems. Dr. Lawler has consulted with a number of companies on the design and use of cost information systems for management decision support, in place of traditional external financial reporting.

John Leslie Livingstone has been a consultant on business strategy and finance for many leading corporations, as well as for federal government agencies, including the U.S. Treasury, SEC, and HHS. He was a principal in a well-known international management consulting firm with offices in Boston, Chicago, Dallas, San Francisco, Washington D.C., London, Paris, Rome, Frankfurt, Madrid, Hong Kong, Tokyo, and Buenos Aires. Before that, he was a senior partner in the "Big Six" international accounting firm of Coopers & Lybrand. He is a C.P.A. with M.B.A. and Ph.D. degrees from Stanford University. Dr. Livingstone is an adjunct professor at Babson College, and has previously held endowed professorships at the University of Southern California, Georgia Institute of Technology, and Ohio State University. He has published 10 books, and more than 50 articles in professional periodicals, plus many chapters in authoritative handbooks.

Richard P. Mandel is an associate professor of law at Babson College, where he teaches a variety of courses in business law and taxation. He is also a partner in the law firm Bowditch and Dewey, of Worcester and Framingham, Massachusetts, where he specializes in the representation of small businesses and their executives. Mr. Mandell has written a number of articles regarding the representation of small businesses. He holds an A.B. from Cornell University and a J.D. from Harvard Law School.

Kenneth S. Most has been a professor in the School of Accounting, College of Business Administration, Florida International University, since 1975. He has also taught at other universities in the United States, Europe, and Asia. He received his L.L.B. from the University of London, and his M.A. (accounting) and Ph.D. (economic theory) from the University of Florida. He is a chartered accountant, England & Wales (F.C.A) and a certified public accountant (C.P.A.) in Texas. Dr. Most was in practice as a public accountant and management consultant for 17 years, before becoming an educator. He is the author of 20 books and over 200 articles.

Charles W. Mulford received his doctorate in accounting, with a support area in finance, from the Florida State University in Tallahassee. His is professionally qualified as a certified public accountant (C.P.A.) in Florida and Georgia. In 1983, he joined the faculty of the School of Management at Georgia Institute of Technology. At Georgia Tech, he is a KPMG Peat Marwick Faculty Fellow and associate professor of accounting. In 1985, 1989, 1990, and 1991, he was recognized as the Core Professor of the Year by the graduate students in management. Prior to joining Georgia Tech faculty, Dr. Mulford practiced public accounting with the firm of Coopers & Lybrand. He was an audit senior in the firm's Miami office. Professor Mulford has published numerous papers in scholarly, as well as professional accounting, and finance journals. His research interests center on the effects of accounting standards on investment and credit decision making, earnings forecasts, and relationship between accounting-based and market-based measures of risk, and international accounting and reporting practices. Professor Mulford is a member of the American Institute of C.P.A.s and the American Accounting Association.

Grant W. Newton, C.M.A., C.P.A., Ph.D., is professor of accounting at Pepperdine University, Malibu, California. Grant is the author of *Bankruptcy and Insolvency Accounting: Practice and Procedure*, 4th edition and coauthor with Gilbert D. Bloom of *Bankruptcy and Insolvency Taxation*, published by John Wiley and Sons. His articles have appeared in *Journal of Accountancy, Management Accounting, Practical Accountant, C.P.A. Journal, Commercial Law Journal*, and other professional periodicals. Grant was a member of the AICPA's Task Force on Financial Reporting by Entities in Reorganization Under the Bankruptcy Code that resulted in the issuance of the Statement of Position 90-7. Grant received his Ph.D. degree from New York University and his masters from the University of Alabama. He is currently a member of the board of directors and vice president of the Association of Insolvency Accountants and is a council member of INSOL International.

Ronald J. Sutter, C.P.A., is a litigation services partner of Steres, Alpert & Carne, a San Diego, California C.P.A. firm. He has written and lectured on matters related to the C.P.A.'s role in bankruptcy and insolvency proceedings and has served in various related professional capacities, including that of an expert witness and court-appointed trustee and examiner. He is a member of the board of directors of the Association of Insolvency Accountants and serves on the State Litigation Services Committee on the California Society of C.P.A.s.

Jeffry A. Timmons is nationally and internationally recognized for his work in entrepreneurship, new ventures, and venture capital. In 1989 he became the first to hold a joint appointment at the Harvard Business School, as the first MBA Class of 1954 Professor of New Ventures, and Babson College, as the first Frederic C. Hamilton Professor of Free Enterprise Development. He has authored or coauthored 10 books, including *Venture Capital at the Crossroad* (Harvard Business School Press, 1992) and *New Venture Creation*, 3rd ed, (Irwin, 1990), and over 100 articles and papers, including six articles in *Harvard Business Review* on these topics. He is cofounder and director of several companies, including Boston Communications Group, owners of cellular and telecommunications related ventures, and he is an advisor to BCI Advisors, a $285 million growth capital fund, and to Ernst & Young's national Entrepreneurial Services Group in the U.S. and U.K. He was the first outside director of Cellular One in Boston and is an investor, director, and advisor to several emerging companies. He also serves as an advisor to the Ewing Marion Kaffman Foundation. He is a graduate of Colgate University, where he now serves as a trustee, and he received his M.B.A. and doctorate from Harvard Business School.

Michael F. van Breda teaches at Southern Methodist University, where he was chairman of the Accounting Department from 1987–1991. His courses have included cost and managerial accounting at the graduate level. He obtained his Ph.D. in accounting from Stanford University and was previously on the faculty of M.I.T. He is the author of numerous scholarly publications, one of which won the Lybrand silver medal for its contribution to managerial accounting. He is the coauthor (with Eldon S. Hendriksen) of the 5th edition of *Accounting Theory* (Richard D. Irwin, 1991). In addition, he has consulted for a number of major corporations.

Index

Accounting policies, differences in
    U.S. and foreign, 353–358.
    See also GAAP; International
    Accounting Standards
    Committee
Accounting system modules, 91–92
  accounts payable, 91
  accounts receivable, 91
  fixed assets, 92
  general ledger, 91
  inventory, 92
  job costing, 92
  payroll, 91–92
Accounting systems:
  in large corporations, 93–95
  in small corporations, 95–96
Acquisitions, 297–300, 330, 409–432
  candidate screening, 417–430
    NPV test, 417–423
    profitability conditions, 423–430
    value bargains, 425–430
  directional options, 412–414
  growth by, 430–431
  objectives and goals, 410–411
  structural options, 330, 414–417
  tax-loss carryforward, 298–300

Activity-based cost systems (ABCSs),
    78–82
  steps in the design of, 80–81
Adjusted current earnings, 326–327
Affiliation, 416
All-current translation procedure, 344
Annuity, 287
Artificial intelligence, *see* Expert
    systems

Balance sheet development, 7–10, 16
  assets, 8, 10, 16
  liabilities, 8, 10, 16
  owner's equity, 8, 10, 16
Banana Computer Corporation, 46
Bankruptcy, 463–468
  advantages and disadvantages,
    474–475
  alternatives, 468
  assignment, 475–476
  automatic stay, 481–482
  Bankruptcy Code, 465
  Bankruptcy Reform Act of 1978,
    477
  chapter selection, 476, 478–481

Bankruptcy (*continued*)
  claims and interests, 487–488,
    489–491
  commencement of case, 481
  contributing factors, 467–468
  conversion or dismissal of petition,
    488
  creditor and equity security holder
    committees, 484–485
  debtor-in-possession, 484
  dischargeable debts, 492–493
  disclosure statement, 496–497
  early recognition of, 464
  employment of professionals,
    483
  examiner, 485–486
  filing schedules and statement of
    affairs, 482–483
  fraudulent transfers, preferences,
    491–492
  informal settlement, 468–476
  information needed, 466
  liquidation *vs.* reorganization, 486,
    487
  office of the U.S. trustee, 477
  operating reports, filing of, 486
  out-of-court settlements, 468
    advantages and disadvantages,
      474–475
  proofs of claims or interests,
    487–488
  preparation, 464–465
  relief from stay, 488–489
  reorganization, plan of, 493
    acceptance or rejection of, 497
    confirmation of, 498
    postconfirmation activities, 499
  trustee, 485–486
Bankruptcy Code, 465, 476–477
  chapter selection, 476, 478–481
  protection, 476–477
Bankruptcy Courts, 477
Board of directors:
  audit committee, 447–454
  CEO, responsibilities of and
    desirable qualities in, 433,
    435–437
  compensation committee, 444–447

dealing with crises, 441–444
  firing the CEO, 441–442
  unfriendly takeover attempts,
    442–444
finance committee, 454–458
meetings, 437–439
purpose of, 433
relation to CEO, 435–437, 441
remuneration, 446–447
responsibilities of, 458–459
setting standards, 439
size and composition of, 434
strategy and strategy meetings,
  439–441
Break-even analysis, 33–40
  break-even formula, 38
Budgetary control, 105–112,
  123–124
  activity indices, 111
  defining standards, 106–107
  collecting standards,
    117–119
    engineering studies, 117
    motivation, 118–119
    past data, 119
    time and motion studies,
      117–118
  market effects, 111
  price indices, 109–111
  types of standards, 107
Budgeting, 230
  benefits of, 234–237
    coordination, 235
    cost awareness, 236
    goal orientation, 236–237
    legal requirements, 236
    performance evaluation, 236
    periodic planning, 235
    quantification, 235
  effective, 237–239
    behavioral issues, 240
    control phase, 238–239
    goal orientation, 237–238
    participative, 239
    realistic plan, 238
  functions of, 233
  improper use of, 239–240
  reasons for, 233–237

Budgets:
  components, 242–244
    administrative expense, 243
    cost of goods sold, 243
    ending inventories, 242
    income statement, 244
    marketing expense, 243–244
    production, 242–243
    sales, 242
  developing, 240–247
  financial, 244–247
    balance sheet, 246
    capital expenditure, 244–245
    cash, 245
    statement of cash flows, 247
  fixed, 247
  flexible, 248
  illustration, 231–233
  profit plan, 248
  review process, 248–252
  static vs. flexible, 108–111
  variable costs, 112–117
Built-in gain, 294
Business plans, 166–171
  choosing a developer, 179
  dehydrated business plan, 167
  sample plan, 181–228
  steps in writing, 180
  and working capital, 283–286

Call option, 341
Capital asset pricing model (CAPM),
    262
Capital, cost of, 254, 259–260,
    261–263
Capital budgeting, 254–257,
    278–281, 283–287
  basic equations of, 256
  capital expenditures, 278–279
Cash assessment, 17–22
  capital structure, 17
  cash flow, as related to, 17
  solvency, 17
Cash flows:
  future, 270–273
  statement of, 4–6, 16
    versus income statement, 7

C Corporation, 161, 326
Chief Executive Officer (CEO),
    433–437, 441–442, 444–446
Comfort letter, 400–403
Compensation:
  CEO, 444–446
  deferred, 302–304
  executive, 300–302
  interest-free loans, 304–305
  reviews, 446
  sharing equity, 305–313
  unreasonable, 290–291, 293
Computer, use in finance and
    accounting, 84–90
  hardware, 85–86
  information systems, 86–90
  software, 86
    manufacturing resource planning
      (MRPII), 93
    material requirements planning
      (MRP), 93
Constructive receipt doctrine, 303
Contribution, 28–29, 36–39, 43
Corporate redemption, 310, 312,
    317–328
Corporation, 131, 161. See also Board
    of directors
  acquisition options, 330, 332
  continuity of life, 138
  control, 142–147
  directors, 144–147
    business judgment of,
      145–147
  formation, 133–135
  General Utilities Doctrine, 331
  liability, 149–151
  officers, 147
  operation out of state, 135–136
  recognition as a legal entity, 137
  sale of, 330–333
  stockholders, 142–144
  taxation, 155
  transferability of interest, 140
Cost accounting systems, 79, 80
  fixed cost, 122–123
  government, 121
  variable cost, 121–122
Cost behavior, 29–33

Cost of capital, 254, 259–260,
    261–263
  alternative approaches to,
    261–263
Cost estimation, 46–57
  eyeball technique, 48–50
  high-low method, 48
  regression analysis, 50–55
    beyond regression, 53–55
    interpretation of, 52–53
Cost leverage, 41. *See also* Economies
    of scale
Cost-Profit-Volume (CPV) analysis,
    28–36
  long-run approach, 39
  short-run approach, 39
Costs, fixed, 32–33
Cost-versus-price model, 81
Cross-purchase agreement, 327–328
Cut-off rate, 287

Debt capital *vs.* equity capital,
    257–258
Dehydrated business plan, 167
Disclosure statement, 496–497
Dividends, 316–321
  disproportionate distributions,
    317–318
  Employee Stock Ownership Plans,
    319–321
  termination of interest, 318–319
Dumping, 44–45

Earnings per share (EPS), 26
Economic benefit doctrine, 303–304
Economies of scale, 40–42
Electronic data processing (EDP)
    system, 70
Employee Stock Ownership Plan
    (ESOP), 319–321
Equipment, book value of, 281–283
  excluding tax effects, 281–282
  including tax effects, 282–283
Equity capital *vs.* debt capital,
    257–258
Equity, sharing of, 305–312
  incentive stock options, 309–310

  phantom stock, 307–308
  restricted stock, 306–307, 311–312
  stock appreciation rights (SARs),
    307–308
  stock option, 307, 308
Estate planning, 321
  buy-sell agreements, 325–328
  cross-purchase agreement,
    327–328
  freeze, 322–324
  preferred stock bailout, 324–325
  stock redemptions, 322
  tax liability, 322–323
Executive compensation, taxation and,
    300–305
  business expenses, 300–302
  deferred compensation, 302–304
  interest-free loans, 304–305
Expert systems, 100–101

Federal taxation system, *see* Taxation
Financial investment, theories of, 279
Financial leverage, 23, 257–259,
    421–422
  "levered up," 258
  negative leverage, 258
Financial reporting issues, 335–338
Financial statements:
  balance sheet, 7–10, 16
  cash flow, 4–6, 16
  checklist for, 16
  income, 7–10, 16
  pro forma, 10–15, 84
  projections, 11–15
Financial structure, 254, 259–261
Fixed-cost budgets, 119–121
Fixed costs, 32–37, 119–121
Forecasts, *see* Budgets
Foreign Corrupt Practices Act of 1977,
    373–374
Foreign currency:
  exposure, 338
  transaction loss, 337–338
Foreign-currency-denominated
    transactions, 335–338
  financial reporting of, 337–338
  risk management alternatives for,
    338–344

Foreign subsidiaries, 344–347. *See
    also* Foreign Corrupt Practices
    Act of 1977
  and their management, 358–366
  functional currency, 347
  impact of exchange rate movements
    on, 358–363
  impact of inflation on, 366–372
  managing the currency risk of,
    350–353
  transfer pricing, influences on, 366
  transfer pricing and multinational
    firm, 363–364
  transfer pricing and taxes, 364–365
  translation of the statements of,
    344–350
    all-current translation method,
      344–347
    temporal (remeasurement)
      translation procedure, 347, 348
    U.S. government restrictions on,
      373–374
Forward exchange contracts, 340–341
Functional currency, 347
Futures contracts, 342–344

GAAP (Generally Accepted
    Accounting Practices),
    international differences,
  and the IASC, 353–354
  and the level playing field,
    357–358
  and the United States, 354–357
General Utilities Doctrine, 331
Gift tax, 293
Goal setting, 178
Going public:
  advantages of, 383–385
  aspects of, 397–398
  choosing a lead underwriter,
    389–391
  disadvantages of, 385–389
  process of, 392–395
  registration statement form,
    404–408
  SEC and, 391–392
Goodwill, 357

Hedging, 338–344
  with internal offsetting balances,
    339–340
  management priorities in, 352
  with specialized external
    transactions, 340
Hurdle rate, 287

Incentive stock options, 309–310
Income statement development,
    7–10, 16
  versus cash-flow statement, 7
Income tax effects, 273–275
Inflation, 263–264
  impact on foreign subsidiaries,
    366–372
Information systems, 86
  decision support (DSS), 87–88
  executive (EIS), 88–90
  management (MIS), 87
  transaction processing (TPIS),
    87
Interest-free loans, 304–305
Internal rate of return (IRR),
    275–277, 281
  calculation of, 275
  and NPV, compared, 277–278,
    280
International Accounting
    Standards Committee (IASC),
    353–354
Inventory methods:
  FIFO (first in, first out), 294, 369,
    370
  JIT (just in time), 243
  LIFO (last in, first out), 294,
    368–369, 370

Leading and lagging, 340
Lead underwriter, choosing one,
    390–391
Leveraged buyouts, 421–422
Liability exposure in foreign currency,
    337–338
Like-kind exchanges, 314–316
  three-corner exchanges, 316

Limited partnerships, 131
  continuity of life, 138–139
  control, 147–148
  formation, 135
  operation out of state, 135–136
  recognition as a legal entity, 137
  taxation, 158–160
  transferability of interest, 140
Liquidation, 486–487

Managerial reporting issues,
    335–338
Massachusetts business trust, 160
Mergers and acquisitions,
    409–432. *See also*
    Acquisitions
Monetary asset, 371–372

Negative leverage, 258
Net present value (NPV), 270–273
  and IRR, compared, 277–278, 280
  test, applying the positive, 417–423

Option contracts, 341

Partnerships, 130, 161
  continuity of life, 138
  control, 141–142
  formation, 133
  liability, 149
  out-of-state operation, 135
  recognition as a legal entity,
    136–137
  taxation, 154–155
  transferability of interest,
    139
Payback, 276–277
Pass-through entities, 295–296
Pension funds, 457–458
Period costs, *see* Fixed costs
Phantom stock, 307–308
Planning, 166–170
  do's and don'ts, 176–177
  pitfalls in, 171–177
  problems with, 171

reasons for, 170–171
  relationship between goals and
    actions, 177–178
  segmenting and integrating
    information, 179–180
Predatory pricing, 43–45. *See also*
    Dumping
  testing for, 43–44
Premium limitation, 427–428
Present values, 270–272
  using tables to calculate,
    266–270
Price discrimination, 39
Price/Earnings (P/E) ratio, 26
Price index movements, 370–371
Price-level adjusted
    performance measurement,
    369–370
  constant-dollar method, 369–370
  current-cost method, 369–370
Process-map analysis, 67–72
Product design and procurement,
    67–71
Professional corporation, 131,
    156–157
Profitability assessment, 23
Profitable growth, conditions of,
    423–427
Pro forma statements, 10–15, 84, 97
Project sensitivity analysis, 272
Proprietorship, *see* Sole
    proprietorship
Publicly owned, transforming from
    privately owned, *see* Going
    public
Put option, 341

Rabbi trust, 304
Recharacterization, 158–160
Relevant range, 32
Remeasurement, 347, 348–350
Reorganization, 486–487, 493–499
Restricted stock, 306–307,
    311–312
Return on assets (ROA), 23–26
Return on investment (ROI),
    256–257, 264–265,
    286–287

Return on owner's equity (ROE), 23–26
Reverse triangular merger, 332

SEC (Securities Exchange Commission), 386–387, 391–392
Securities Act of 1933, 387, 391
Securities and Exchange Act of 1934, 387, 391
Shut-down point, 45
Smiling Feline, Ltd., 60–78
Sole proprietorship, 130, 161
  continuity of life, 137–138
  control, 140–141
  formation, 132
  liability, 148
  out-of-state operation, 135
  recognition as a legal entity, 136
  taxation, 152–154
  transferability of interest, 139
Spin-offs and split-ups, 328–330
Spreadsheets, 96–100
Stock appreciation rights (SARs), 308–311
Stockholder's equity, 260–261
  retained earnings, calculation of, 260–261
Stock options, 307–308
Subchapter S Corporation, 131, 161, 291–292, 326
  election, 293–297
  passive losses, 296–297
  pass-through entity, 295–296, 326
  taxation of, 157–158
System analysis, 94–95

Takeover attempts, unfriendly, 442–444
Taxation:
  acquisition and, 298–299
  active income/loss, 296
  built-in gain, 294
  corporations, 155–156
  dividends and, 316–321

  double, 291
  estate planning, 321–328
  executive compensation, 300–305
  federal system, 289
  gift tax, 293
  like-kind exchanges, 314–316
  limited partnerships, 158–160
  partnerships, 154–155
  passive income/loss, 296
  pass-through entities, 295–296
  portfolio income/loss, 296
  professional corporations, 156–157
  sole proprietorship, 152–154
  spin-offs and split-ups, 328–330
  subchapter S corporations, 157–158, 292, 294
  vacation home, 312–314
Tax-loss carryforward, 299
Tax shelters, 296
Temporal translation procedure, 348–350
Three-corner exchange, 316
Time value of money, 255–256
Transactional exposure, 350–352
Transaction risk, 350
Transfer pricing:
  and multinational firms, 363–364
  and taxes, 364–366
  other influences on, 366
Translational exposure, 350–352
Translation loss, 348–350
Translation risk, 350–352
Turnkey systems, 96

Uniform Partnership Act, 131, 139, 141
U.S. International Trade Commission (ITC), 45

Vacation home, taxation and, 312–314
  mixed use, 314
  personal use, 314
  rental use, 314
Value bargains, 425–428

Variable costs budget, 112
    labor indices, 115–116
    material indices, 115
    variable overhead indices, 116

Working capital, 283–286
    current assets and
        liabilities, 283–284,
        284–285

Special Offer

available to
Portable MBA
readers

...*Turn page for details* 🖝

Business $19.95

"Straight from second-year business school courses, the book is full of up-to-date financial and managerial information that will help transform your company from start-up to blue-chip."

—Entrepreneur

"Practical, useful, and accessible. Of immense use to everyone in both business and nonprofit organizations, from the smallest start-up, to the largest corporation."

—Eliza G. C. Collins
Center for Executive Education, former
Senior Editor, *Harvard Business Review*

Here's a complete step-by-step course in "executive number-crunching" for busy managers and professionals who don't have time for a formal MBA program. Written by a team of top business school professors, this book acquaints you with the financial and accounting concepts, strategies, tools, and techniques used at today's leading corporations. And, thanks to its practical, real-world approach and jargon-free language, readers with no prior background in finance and accounting quickly learn how to:

- Read and interpret financial statements
- Develop and use sophisticated cost-analysis tools
- Perform financial forecasting and budgeting
- Create sound business plans
- Use proven strategies for minimizing business income tax
- Master the pros and cons of going public
- Evaluate and act on mergers and acquisitions
- Manage foreign exchange risk exposure
- And much more

Read *The Portable MBA in Finance and Accounting* and learn how to use sophisticated financial and accounting tools to manage your enterprise more efficiently.

JOHN LESLIE LIVINGSTONE, PhD, CPA, directs his own consulting firm, headquartered in West Palm Beach, Florida. He was a senior partner at Coopers & Lybrand and is a principal with the MAC group. His academic positions have included the Arthur Young Distinguished Professor, Ohio State University; Chairman of Accounting, Babson College; and the Fuller E. Callaway Chair, Georgia Institute of Technology.

> ***Get the expertise without the expense from a***
> Jeffrey A. Timmons, Harvard Business School • W
> of Washington • Eugene E. Comiskey and Charle
> tute of Technology • William C. Lawler, Babson C
> University • Robert Anthony, Harvard Busines
> teachers

John Wiley & Sons, Inc.
Professional, Reference and Trade Group
605 Third Avenue, New York, N.Y. 10158-0012
New York • Chichester • Brisbane • Toronto • Singapore

ISBN 0-471-11983-0

51995

9 780471 119838